Musica mechanica organoedi.

Musical mechanics for the organist.

by
Jacob Adlung

edited for publication by
Johann Lorenz Albrecht

with commentary by
Johann Friedrich Agricola

English translation by
Quentin Faulkner

PART 2

Zea E-Books
Lincoln, Nebraska
2011

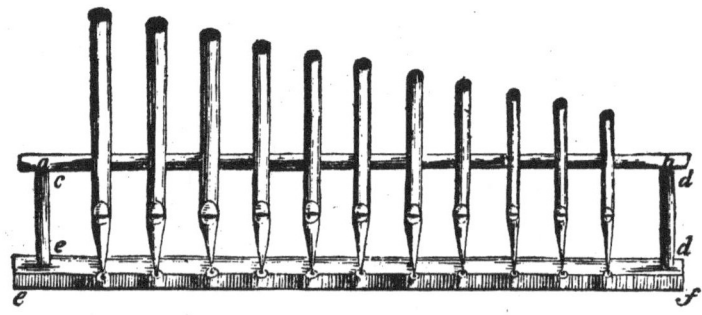

ISBN 978-1-60962-014-1 [Part 2 of 3]

English translation, notes, etc. copyright © 2011 Quentin Faulkner.

Design, layout, and composition, based on the 1768 edition, by Paul Royster.
Set in IM Fell DW Pica typeface, developed and furnished by Igino Marini.

The Fell Types
www.iginomarini.com

Zea E-Books are published by the University of Nebraska–Lincoln Libraries.
http://digitalcommons.unl.edu/zea/

Musica mechanica organoedi • *Musical mechanics for the organist*

Contents

PART 2

Part 2 includes all of "Volume Two" of the 1768 Berlin edition, except the Index.

Dedication to Count Benjamin Christoph von Grasshof [by J. L. Albrecht]	n.p.
Foreword [by J. L. Albrecht, but including Adlung's 11-page account of his life "word for word"]	I–XX
Chapter 11. Concerning the Cost of an Organ	3–10
Chapter 12. Concerning the Exterior Decoration of an Organ	11–21
Chapter 13. Concerning the Merits and Faults of an Organ that have not yet been mentioned	22–48
Chapter 14. Concerning Organ Temperament	48–59
Chapter 15. Concerning Tuning Organs	60–64
Chapter 16. Concerning the Delivery and Examination of Organs	65–79
Chapter 17. Concerning the Windgauge and other Mechanical Tools of [Use to] an Organist	79–81
Chapter 18. Concerning the Maintenance and Repair of Organs	82–92
Chapter 19. Concerning the History of Organs	92–95
Chapter 20. Concerning other Instruments in general that an Organist needs to be familiar with, and in particular Positivs	95–100
Chapter 21. Concerning Regals of all Types	100–102
Chapter 22. Concerning the Harpsichord, Clavicytherium, Spinet, Instrument, Arpichord and Cembal d'Amour	102–126
Chapter 23. Concerning the Violdigambenwerk, Claviergamba, Geigenwerk and Hurdy-gurdy	126–129
Chapter 24. Concerning the *Organon Portatili*, the Water Organ and Hanfling's Claviatur, as well as the Xylorganum	129–132
Chapter 25. Concerning Lute Harpsichords and Carillons	133–143
Chapter 26. Concerning the Clavichord and the Pedal-clavier	143–162
Chapter 27. Concerning other Instruments, and the Tuning of Stringed [Keyboard] Instruments	162–165
Chapter 28. A Discourse on certain Curious Matters here pertinent	165–182

All pages are German-English facing 2-page spreads.
There are two pages numbered 71 and two pages numbered 72 in this volume.
Total of 414 pages.

MUSICA MECHANICA ORGANOEDI.

Das ist:
Gründlicher Unterricht

von
der Struktur, Gebrauch und Erhaltung, ꝛc.
der Orgeln, Clavicymbel, Clavichordien
und
anderer Instrumente,

in so fern einem Organisten von solchen Sachen etwas zu wissen nöthig ist.
Vorgestellet von
M. Jakob Adlung,

weil. der Churfürstl. Maynzischen Akademie nützlicher Wissenschaften in Erfurt ordentlichem Mitgliede,
des evangelischen Rathsgymnasii ordentl. Lehrer, wie auch Organisten an der evangelischen
Raths = und Predigerkirche daselbst.

Aus der hinterlassenen Handschrift des sel. Hrn. Verfassers in Ordnung gebracht,
mit einigen Anmerkungen und einer
Vorrede
in welcher,
theils von dem Leben und gelehrten Bemühungen des Hrn. Adlung überhaupt,
theils von der Ausgabe dieses Werks insbesondere, ausführliche Nachricht
ertheilet wird, versehen und zum Druck befördert
von
M. Johann Lorenz Albrecht,

kaiserl. gekrönten Dichter, Collegen der vierten Classe am Gymnasio, wie auch Cantor und Musikdirektor
bey der oberstädtischen Hauptkirche, Beatä Mariä Virginis, zu Mühlhausen in Thüringen,
und der hochlöbl. deutschen Gesellschaft zu Altdorf Ehrenmitgliede.

Nebst vielen Figuren.

Zweyter Band.

Berlin,
gedruckt und verlegt von Friedrich Wilhelm Birnstiel, königl. privil. Buchdrucker,
1768.

MUSICAL MECHANICS
FOR THE ORGANIST

that is

Fundamental Instruction

concerning

the structure, use, and maintenance, etc.

of Organs, Harpsichords, Clavichords

and

other Instruments

to the degree that it is necessary for an organist to know something about such things.
Set forth by

Jakob Adlung, M.A.

formerly a regular member of the Mainz Electoral Academy of Practical Sciences at Erfurt, regular instructor in the Protestant Municipal Gymnasium, as well as organist of
the Protestant Municipal Predigerkirche there.

Put into order from the manuscript left by the late author,

provided with a number of notes and a

Foreword

in which

a detailed report will be conveyed, in part concerning Mr. Adlung's life
and scholarly efforts in general, and in part concerning the publication
of this work in particular, and conveyed into print

by

Johann Lorenz Albrecht, M.A.

Imperial Poet-Laureate, Colleague of the Fourth Class at the Gymnasium, as well as Cantor and Director of Music of the Principal Church of the Blessed Virgin Mary in the upper town at Mühlhausen in
Thuringia, and Honorary Member of the eminent German Society at Altdorf.

Together with many figures.

Volume Two

Berlin,
printed and published by Friedrich Wilhelm Birnstiel, Printer by appointment
to his Royal Majesty,
1768.

Dem
Hochwohlgebohrnen und Hochgelahrten Herrn,
Herrn
**Benjamin Christoph
von Graßhof,**
Comiti Palatino Cæsareo
Ihro Hochfürstlichen Durchlaucht zu Schwarzburg-
Sondershausen hochbetrautem wirklichem Geheimden Rathe,
wie auch
der Kaiserlichen freyen und des Heil. Römischen Reichs Stadt
Mühlhausen
hochverdientem regierenden Bürgermeister, Syndico
und Canzeleydirectori

Meinem gnädigen hochgebietenden Herrn
und
Hochgeneigten Patron.

To the
most Noble and Learned Lord,

Benjamin Christoph von Grasshof,

Imperial Count of the Palatinate

and most trusted Privy Councillor to his Serene Highness
the Duke of Schwarzburg-Sondershausen,

as well as

Honored reigning Mayor, Trustee and Director of the Chancellery
of the Imperial Free City of the Holy Roman Empire

Mühlhausen

To my gracious sovereign Lord
and
Most Benevolent Patron.

Hochwohlgebohrner, Hochgelahrter,
Insonders
Hochgeehrtester Herr Geheimder Rath,
Gnädiger Patron!

Ew. Hochwohlgebohrnen Excellenz verehrungswürdigen Namen einem solchen Buche, welches, wie das gegenwärtige, durchaus von solchen Sachen handelt, die in die Musik einen großen Einfluß haben, in tiefster Unterthänigkeit vorzusetzen, dürfte vielleicht von manchem als ein verwägenes Unterfangen angesehen werden. Ich selbst würde mir dergleichen Vorwurf machen, wenn ich nicht vollkommen überzeugt wäre, daß Ew. Hochwohlgebohrne Excellenz nicht nur ein großer Patron dererjenigen zu nennen, welche die Musik, als ihr Amt, zu treiben verpflichtet sind, sondern daß Hochdieselben auch in den musikalischen Wissenschaften selbst solche Einsichten besitzen, die man an einem klugen Regenten und hocherfahrnen Staatsmanne höchst bewundern muß.

Most Excellent, Most Learned
 and indeed
Most Honorable Lord Privy Councillor,
 Gracious Patron!

To place in deepest humility Your Most Noble Excellency's honorable name at the head of a book such as this one, that is entirely concerned with those things that have a great influence in music, might perhaps be viewed by some as a rash act. I would reproach myself for the same reason, if I were not perfectly confident in naming your noble Excellency not only a great patron of those who are obliged to practice music as their calling, but also one who possesses a degree of insight into musical knowledge that one cannot help but admire most heartily in a wise ruler and highly experienced statesman.

Sollte ich jedoch um die Ursache befraget werden, welche mich auf die Gedanken gebracht, dergleichen zu unternehmen, zumal da ich mich nicht einmal einen Verfasser, sondern nur einen Herausgeber des gegenwärtigen Buchs nennen kann; so werden Ew. Hochwohlgebohrne Excellenz mir hochgütigst erlauben, unterthänigst zu versichern, daß ich verschiedene Ursachen meines kühnen Unterfangens angeben könnte, welche, wo sie dasselbe nicht rechtfertigen, doch wenigstens solches entschuldigen könnten. Ich will aber unter allem nur nachfolgendes erwähnen, um Hochdenenselben mit Anführung eines mehrern nicht misfällig zu werden.

Es haben nämlich Ew. Hochwohlgebohrne Excellenz seit der Zeit, da ich das Amt eines Cantors und Musikdirektors bey hiesiger Oberstädtischen Hauptkirche B. M. V., nebst dem öffentlichen Schulamte, bekleidet, so viel Gnadenblicke auf meine geringe Person huldreichst herabfallen lassen, und meine wenigen Bemühungen, die ich, nach Erforderung meines zwiefachen Amtes, bis daher unter göttlichem Beystande unternommen, nicht nur hochgeneigt gebilliget, sondern auch mit Hochdero vielvermögenden Beyhülfe unterstützt, daß ich jederzeit, Trotz allen Widerwärtigkeiten! meine angewiesene Arbeit mit innigsten Freuden verrichten können. Ziehe ich nun noch hierbey in Betrachtung, wieviel mir, bey Gelegenheit der ohnlängst edirten geistlichen Kantaten, durch Hochdero gnädige Fürsprache, an unverdienten Wohlthaten zugeflossen; so werde ich billig schaamroth, daß ich noch nicht im Stande gewesen, Ew. Hochwohlgebohrnen Excellenz für alles dieses, und für noch viel andere besondere hohe Gnadenbezeigungen, ein, obwol unvollkommenes, Denkmaal meiner innigsten Dankbegierde zu stiften.

Sie

Were anyone to question me, however, about the cause that engendered in me the idea to undertake this work, especially since I can in no way call myself the author, but only the editor of the present book, I trust that your most noble Excellency will most graciously allow me humbly to assure you, that I am able to cite various reasons for my rash undertaking that, while they cannot justify it, will at least be able to excuse it. Among them all, however, I will mention only the following, so as to avoid displeasing your Excellency by advancing more of them.

Ever since the time that I assumed the office of Cantor and Director of Music here at St. Mary's Church* together with the office of public schoolmaster, Your Noble Excellency has most kindly bestowed such gracious attention upon my unworthy person, and has not only most benevolently permitted but also assisted with Your most influential support my paltry efforts that I have undertaken up to now with God's help after fulfilling my two-fold office, so that I have been able to accomplish the work I have undertaken, in spite of manifold adversities(!), with sincere joy at all times. If I then take into consideration how much unearned favor has accrued to me through Your Excellency's gracious intercession upon the occasion of the recently published sacred cantatas,† then I must simply blush with shame that I have not yet been in a position to create some tangible memorial, albeit imperfect, of my most sincere thankfulness for all this, and for yet many other particular manifestations of your great favor.

* "... bey hiesiger Oberstädtischen Hauptkirche B.V.M.," (here at the Principal Church of the Blessed Virgin Mary in the Upper City). This church is the other major church in Mühlhausen in addition to the Blasiuskirche, where J.S. Bach was organist from 1707-8.

† Albrecht wrote both the text and music of a yearly cycle of cantatas; the texts were published in 1764.

Sie erlauben mir demnach, Hochwohlgebohrner Herr Geheimder Rath! vermittelst dieser unterthänigsten Zuschrift, Ihnen die getreuesten Regungen meines dankvollen Herzens öffentlich bekannt machen zu dürfen, um dadurch einigermaaßen zu bezeugen, daß ich bey verspürter hohen Zuneigung, und bey denen daher auf mich geflossenen großen Wohlthaten, nicht unempfindlich gewesen; obschon diesen meinen Empfindungen, wegen mangelnder Gelegenheit, der Ausbruch bis hieher versaget worden.

Zwar weis ich sehr wohl, daß die hohen Eigenschaften, und die ausgebreiteten Verdienste, welche Ew. Hochwohlgebohrne Excellenz vor vielen Augen zum Wunder machen, und welche auch hohe Fürstliche Personen zu verehren wissen, durch meine unvollkommenen Züge keinen Zuwachs erhalten können: denn die Verdienste eines Graßhofs nach Würden zu schildern und zu erheben, muß ich einer geschicktern Feder, als die meinige ist, überlassen. Dem ohngeachtet aber läßt mich das ungezweifelte Vertrauen, das ich zu Ew. Hochwohlgebohrnen Excellenz hege, zuversichtlich hoffen, daß ich von der Gefahr, durch die ehrfurchtsvolle Zuschrift dieses Buchs Hochdero unschätzbare Zuneigung zu verliehren, gänzlich betreyet bleiben werde.

In dieser angenehmen Hoffnung gestärkt, setze ich nun meinem Vorhaben Schranken, und füge nur noch den Wunsch bey, daß die unerschöpfliche Quelle der ewigen Vorsicht ihre Ströme alles göttlichen Segens mit unaufhörlicher Wonne auf Ew. Hochwohlgebohrne Excellenz und Hochdero vornehmes Hochadeliches Haus reichlich ergiessen wolle, auf daß Hochdero aller Verehrung würdiger Name und berühmtes Geschlecht bis auf die spätesten Welt-

Accordingly permit me, most noble Lord Privy Councillor, by means of this most humble dedication, to make known to all the most sincere feelings of my grateful heart toward You, and thereby to prove in some measure that I have not been insensitive to the noble affection and to the great favors poured out upon me, although these sentiments of mine have been denied expression until now, due to a lack of opportunity.

Indeed I know very well that my imperfect scratchings will in no way increase the noble attributes and the extensive merits that make Your noble Excellency the wonder of many; for worthily to depict and to exalt the merits of a Grasshof must be left to a more skilled pen than that of mine. In spite of this, however, the unalloyed trust that I place in Your Noble Excellency, allows me confidently to trust that I may be entirely spared from the danger of losing Your inestimable affection due to the respectful dedication of this book.

Strengthened in this pleasant hope, I will now restrain myself from further flights, and append only the wish that the inexhaustible spring of eternal providence may pour out in copious streams every divine blessing with ceaseless bliss upon Your Noble Excellency and Your distinguished noble house, so that Your name, worthy of all honor, and your famed family may blossom and flourish until the end of time. Not only all of Mühlhausen will concur with my wish,

Weltjahre blühen und wachsen möge.   Nicht allein ganz Mühlhausen, sondern auch alle, welche die erhabenen Tugenden des Graßhofischen Hauses, und besonders die nie genug zu preisende Wachsamkeit Ew. Hochwohlgebohrnen Excellenz für das Wohl unserer Stadt und Landes, zu kennen und zu verehren das Glück haben, werden meinem Wunsche beypflichten: ich aber werde es für den größten Theil meiner zeitlichen Glückseligkeit halten, wenn ich Lebenslang die Gnade haben kann, mich mit tiefster Ehrfurcht und Unterthänigkeit zu nennen

Hochwohlgebohrner, Hochgelahrter,
Insonders
Hochgeehrtester Herr Geheimder Rath,
Gnädiger Patron!

Ew. Hochwohlgebohrnen Excellenz

unterthänig gehorsamster
Diener
M. Johann Lorenz Albrecht.

but also all those who have the good fortune to acknowlege and to revere the exalted virtues of the house of Grasshof, and in particular the vigilance, impossible to praise adequately, of Your Noble Excellency for the well-being of our city and land. For my part, however, I will consider it the chiefest portion of my earthly joy, if I am permitted the grace to name You for the rest of my life, in the most profound respect and humility

Most excellent, most learned
and indeed
Most honorable Lord Privy Councillor,
Gracious Patron!

Your Noble Excellency's

respectful, obedient
Servant
Johann Lorenz Albrecht, M.A.*

* b. 1732, d. 1773. Writer, composer, Cantor and Music Director at the Marienkirche in Mühlhausen. Albrecht, like Adlung, held an M.A. in philosophy. Beyond his qualifications and his love for church music, it is not known why Adlung's heirs turned to him to prepare the *Musica mechanica organœdi* for print, or why he accepted such an arduous task. Nor is it known why the publisher, Birnstiel in Berlin, lacked confidence in Albrecht's work to the extent that he submitted the volumes to Johann Friedrich Agricola for further inspection. The reason may lie in Albrecht's relative youthfulness (he was only 36 years old when the volumes were published in 1768), or in Agricola's greater stature as Royal Prussian Court Composer and Birnstiel's long acquaintance with him (see the Translator's note †, Foreword, p. XIX below).

Vorrede.

Indem ich dem Publico die Musicam mechanicam Organoedi des sel. Herrn Professoris, M. Jakob Adlung, in öffentlichem Drucke überreiche; so habe ich mir vorgesetzt, dem Hochgeehrtesten Leser in gegenwärtiger Vorrede von dreyen Stücken eine ausführliche Nachricht zu geben. Nämlich

I. Von dem rühmlich geführten Leben und den gelehrten Bemühungen des sel. Herrn Verfassers;

II. Von der Beschaffenheit des Manuscripts, aus welchem dieses Werk ans Licht gestellet worden;

III. Von dem, was ich bey der Ausgabe desselben geleistet habe.

Foreword

In that I am submitting to the public in print the *Musica mechanica Organoedi* of the late Professor Jakob Adlung, I have determined to give the most honorable reader a detailed report in the present Foreword of three sections, namely:

I. Concerning the praiseworthy life and the scholarly efforts of the late author;

II. Concerning the nature of the manuscript from which this work has been published;

III. Concerning that which I have contributed to the edition.

* *

Was das I. betrift; so glaube ich den Verdiensten des sel. Herrn Prof. Adlung, mit welchen sich Derselbe um die schönen Wissenschaften überhaupt, und um die Tonkunst besonders verdient gemacht, diese Pflicht schuldig zu seyn, daß man seinen wohlverdienten Ruhm auch auf die Nachwelt fortpflanze, und sein Gedächtniß solchergestalt verewige. Ich halte mich um so viel mehr dazu verbunden, weil ich durch die nachgelassene Frau Witwe in den Stand gesetzt worden, dem Hochgeehrtesten Leser mit einem vollständigen Lebenslaufe des sel. Herrn Verfassers allhier zu dienen. Es hat zwar schon Hr. Walther im musikalischen Lexico, S. 9. etwas weniges davon eingeschaltet, und ich selbst habe das Leben dieses verdienten Mannes, nach seinem eigenen kurzen Entwurfe, in den zweyten Band der kritischen Briefe über die Tonkunst, S. 451. u. f. einrücken lassen: dem ohngeachtet aber glaube ich, man werde es nicht als eine überflüßige oder gar unnütze Sache ansehen, gedachten Lebenslauf hier noch einmal, wiewol nach einem vollständigern Entwurfe, anzutreffen. Sollte eins und anderes darinnen manchem Leser unerheblich scheinen, der lege mir die Schuld nicht bey, sondern erlaube mir, dieses zu meiner Entschuldigung zu sagen, daß ich, da mir der Lebenslauf des sel. Herrn Professors zur Bekanntmachung ausgeliefert worden, nicht zugleich das Recht erhalten, damit nach eigener Willkühr zu verfahren, sondern alles so mitzutheilen, wie es der sel. Adlung selbst aufgesetzt. Es lautet aber der eigenhändige Aufsatz von Wort zu Wort also:

„Meine Lebensumstände theilen sich von sich selbst in zwey Theile, nämlich in das

1) Was mir von Gott und Menschen Gutes wiederfahren; und

2) Wie und worinne ich andern hinwiederum gedienet habe.

Das erste anlangend; so zähle ich unter die göttlichen Gnadengaben meine ehrliche Geburt, welche geschahe Anno 1699. den 14ten Januar, in einem Erfurtischen Dorfe, Bindersleben genannt. Mein Vater war der dasige Schuldiener und Orga-

As regards number I., I believe the services of the late Professor Adlung, by which he has made special contributions to the *belles-lettres* in general and to music in particular, make it my obligation to transmit his well-deserved fame to posterity, and in this way to perpetuate his memory. I consider myself all the more bound to do this, because his widow has placed me in a position to provide the honorable reader with a complete biography of the late author. To be sure, Mr. Walther has inserted a bit of it in his *Musikalisches Lexicon*, p. 9,* and I have had the life of this deserving man, according to his own short sketch, entered in the second volume of the *Kritische Briefe über die Tonkunst*, p. 451f.† In spite of this, however, I do not believe than anyone would consider it superfluous or even unprofitable once again to encounter here the said biography, albeit in a more complete form. If one thing or another in it should appear to many readers to be insignificant, let them not blame me, but allow me to say in my defense that I did not gain the right, just because the biography of the late Professor was delivered to me to publish, to proceed arbitrarily, but rather to communicate everything just as the late Adlung himself drew it up. His own essay, then, reads word for word thus:

"The circumstances of my life may inherently be divided into two parts, i.e.

1) the good things that have befallen me from God and men; and

2) how and wherein I have been of service to others in return.

As regards the first, I count among the gracious gifts of God my honorable‡ birth, that took place on the 14th of January in the year 1699, in a village called Bindersleben, belonging to Erfurt. My father, Mr. David Adlung, was

---

* Johann Gottfried Walther (1684-1748), *Musikalisches Lexicon* (Leipzig: Wolffgang Deer, 1732; facsimile reprint: Kassel & Basel: Bärenreiter, 1953). The entry on Adlung reads:
 Adelung (Jacob) was born on January 14, 1699 at Bindersleben, a village located an hour away from Erfurt, where his father David Adelung, who died in 1722, was schoolteacher. From 1711-1713 he attended the St.-Andreas School in Erfurt, and from 1713-1721 the Municipal *Gymnasium*. Thereupon he attended the university located there for 2 years, but then attended the University of Jena from 1723-1727. After he had received his masters degree, he wrote as Praeses [i.e., Head of his class] a debate, *de Obligationis veræ natura ac usu* (Concerning the true Obligation of nature and use—[this title differs from the one recorded on p. X below in the Musica mechanica organœdi]). He then returned to Erfurt, succeeding Mr. Buttstedt as organist in the Predigerkirche there in January 1728. He has almost completed a work, *Von den gesamten Theilen der Clavier=Kunst* (Concerning All Aspects of the Keyboard Art), and intends eventually to have it published.

† Friedrich Wilhelm Marpurg (1718-1795). *Kritische Briefe über die Tonkunst*. Berlin: 1760-64, pp. 451-455. Dated December 4, 1762, and entitled "The Biography of Jacob Adlung, M.A. (sketched by himself, and communicated to the Society by Mr. Albrecht, M.A.). Like the lengthier biography in the *Musica mechanica organœdi*, Vol. II, this biography is cast in the first person; it appears to be an abstract of the former.

‡ i.e., legitimate

Vorrede.

Organist, Herr David Adlung. Meine Mutter war Dorothea Elisabetha, gebohrne Meuerin, aus Tondorf. Der Name Jakob, ein Untertreter, ist mir jederzeit vergnügt und bedenklich, auch lehrreich gewesen.

Ich kann mich meiner erstern Jahre wenig besinnen: man hat mir aber gesagt, daß eine Fähigkeit des Verstandes sich sogleich anfangs spüren lassen. So lange als ich denken kann, habe ich eine ziemliche Fertigkeit, auf Dorfmanier zu singen, gehabt, welches ich mehrentheils abgehöret, und meinem Vater wenig Mühe gemacht. So viel daneben in der Schule zu erlernen war, wurde nicht unterlassen, und in andern Dingen bin ich meinen Eltern an die Hand gegangen mit läuten und andern Haushaltungsverrichtungen, so viel meine Kräfte zureichen wollten: denn ich war der Stärksten keiner. Daher liessen sich meine Eltern in die Gedanken kommen, mich zum Studiren zu halten, ohne zu wissen, mit was für Hülfsmitteln, weil der Kinder etliche waren. Anfänglich informirte mich der nunmehro sel. Hr. M. Lüpke, Pfarrer daselbst, nachher Diaconus Regularium in Erfurt. Meiner Mutter leibliche Schwester hatte sich an Herrn Ernst Raben verheurathet, der vorher Cantor und Kirchner zu St. Thomä, nachher aber zu St. Andreä, war. Dieser beredete meinen Vater, mich zu ihm in die Stadt und in sein Haus zu bringen, um auf dem Chore zu singen, und in die Andreasschule zu gehen. An dieser Schule war vorgedachter Herr Cantor Rabe Quartus. Man brachte mich in dessen Classe, und setzte mich unten an. Dieß geschahe nach dem Osterexamen Anno 1711. Noch in selbigem Jahre auf Michaelis rückte ich in tertiam classem. Anno 1712. auf dem Osterexamen fand mich der damalige Herr Pastor, M. Tromsdorf, so weit gekommen zu seyn, daß er den Ausspruch that: *dignus est, qui transferatur ad secundam;* (er ist würdig, in Secunde zu kommen;) welches auch geschahe. Auf Michaelis in eben dem Jahre kam ich in Primam Classem. Auf Ostern 1713. machte ich meine Exercitia ohne merkliche grammatikalische Fehler; auch hatte mich der damalige Herr Conrector an der St. Andreasschule, M. Dreyse, in der Rechenkunst sehr weit gebracht. Im Singen war mir Herr Rabe sehr scharf: und da derselbe weg nach Magdeburg gieng; so kam Herr Cantor Adlung an seine Stelle, welcher mich eine Zeit lang in seinem Hause behielt.

Meine Erhaltung war mit vieler Mühe verknüpft. Ich mußte allezeit über den dritten Tag nach Bindersleben wandern; oder meine Eltern mußten etwas schicken. Doch wurde zu einigen Freytischen Anstalt gemacht. Ich habe

Foreword

the schoolteacher and organist there. My mother was Dorothea Elisabetha, née Meuer,* from Tondorf. The name Jakob, "one who prevails",† has at all times been a source of pleasure and reflection, as well as instruction for me.

    I can recall little of my early years: people have told me that from the very beginning it was evident that I had an able mind. As long as I can remember, I have had considerable skill in singing in a rustic sort of way anything that I have heard several times, and I cost my father little trouble [i.e. in musical training]. In addition, that which was to be learned in school was not neglected,‡ and I gave my parents a helping hand in other things as well, such as ringing [the church bells] and household chores, insofar as my strength would permit, for I was by no means one of the strongest.§ Thereupon my parents hit upon the idea to send me off to study, without having any idea of how to support it, since there were several other children. In the beginning the now deceased Mr. Lüpke, M.A., the Pastor there (later Deacon of the Reglerkirche in Erfurt), taught me. My mother's natural sister had married Mr. Ernst Rabe, who was previously Cantor and sacristan at St. Thomas but later at St. Andreas [both in Erfurt]. This man persuaded my father to bring me into the city to live at his house, in order to sing in the choir¶ and go to the St. Andreas School. In this school the abovementioned Cantor Rabe was the teacher of the fourth [i.e., the lowest] class. I entered his class at the the bottom after the Easter‖ examinations in the year 1711. Already at [the Feast of] St. Michael's** in the same year I moved into the third class. At the Easter†† examination in the year 1712 the Pastor at that time, Mr. Tromsdorf, M.A., found that I had progressed far enough that he declared: *dignus est, qui transferatur ad secundam* (he is worthy to pass into the second [class]); and that is what happened. At St. Michael's‡‡ in the very same year I entered the first class. At Easter 1713§§ I passed my examinations without any evident grammatical mistakes. During this time the then Co-rector at the St. Andreas School, Mr. Dreyse, M.A., had brought me quite far in arithmetic. Mr. Rabe was quite rigorous in singing [instruction], and after he moved to Magdeburg there came Cantor Adlung in his place, who kept me in his house for a while.

    My support entailed a good deal of trouble. Every third day I had to walk to Bindersleben, or my parents had to send something [i.e., food]. Arrangements were made, however, for a number of free meals. I was shown much love

---

* "Meuerin;" the suffix "in" is almost surely a feminine ending, but it is just possible that the name is actually "Meuerin."

† "Untertreter;" modern dictionaries of proper names list the meaning of the name "Jacob" as "supplanter".

‡ The biography that Albrecht submitted to Marpurg's *Kritische Briefe über die Tonkunst* is more specific: " My parents diligently continued to keep me at my school work; ... " (p. 451).

§ The biography in Marpurg, *ibid.*, reads, " ... because I was not one of the strongest, and was thus not well suited to household chores."

¶ "auf dem Chore," i.e., in the choir that sang from the loft.

‖ April 5, 1711.

** September 29, 1711.

†† March 27, 1712.

‡‡ September 29, 1712.

§§ April 16.

von vielen christlichen Herzen viele Liebe genossen, welchen es wohlgehe in Ewigkeit. Als ich nach der Zeit meine Diskantstimme verlohr; so verschwanden auch diese Freytische mehrentheils, und meine Eltern mußten wieder zutragen, bis ich durch des Herrn M. Lüpkens Fürspruch bey dem Herrn Rathsmeister Reichardt zum Informator aufgenommen wurde, und nebst dem Quartier die völlige Unterhaltung bekam. Er war damals nur Organist; ist aber nachdem unter die Rathsglieder gezählt worden, daß er jetzo Rathsmeister ist. Er hatte zu der Zeit einen einzigen Sohn, Hrn. Christoph Reichardt, jetzo auch Rathsmeister. Es sorgeten also meine Eltern nun für nichts mehr, als für Wäsche und Kleider.

Anno 1713. auf Ostern wurde ich ins Gymnasium promovirt, und von dem Herrn D. und Rectore Hogel inscribirt: er war aber alt, und der Herr D. Herrmann Nicolaus Stieler wurde ihm zu eben der Zeit substituiret. Die Musik trieb ich fort, und lernte etwas auf der Violine; hernach nahm ich Lectionen auf dem Claviere bey dem Bruder des Herrn Cantoris Adlung, (welcher mich auch auf den Pauken informirte) um dasjenige weiter fortzusetzen, was ich bey meinem Vater erlernet hatte: und nachdem ich auch eine Zeitlang das Clavierspielen bey Herr Arnolden fortgesetzt hatte; so gieng ich auch wöchentlich ein paarmal nach Marbach zu dem Schulmeister, Herrn Hufeld, bis ich nachgehends von dem Herrn Rathsmeister Reichardt, da ich zu ihm gezogen war, vollends so weit gebracht wurde, als es die Mode der Information damals erforderte. Die Studia trieb ich mit allem Fleiße, und brachte es so weit darinnen, daß ich Anno 1714. auf Ostern in Secundam, und Anno 1715. auf Michaelis in Primam versetzt wurde. Bis Ostern 1721. blieb ich daselbst sitzen, weil ich meine Studentenjahre ohne Geld nicht antreten wollte, und zu dem Amte eines Adiuncti und Præfecti nicht bald gelangen konnte, weil es an guten und geschickten Leuten nicht fehlete. Als ich endlich auch solchen Aemtern vorgestanden, und das Chorgeld fleißig gesammlet hatte, ließ ich mich promoviren, und hielt eine lateinische Abschiedsrede vom Concilio zu Costnitz und Johann Hussen: setzte sie aber meinem Vater zu Gefallen ins Deutsche. Ich kann nicht läugnen, daß in den Gymnasiastischen Jahren mich an meinem Fleiße zuweilen die Schulmeistersgedanken gehindert: ich habe sie aber überwunden, bis nach dem, da ich wenige Zeit ein Studiosus gewesen, mein Vater verstorben, und mir der Zufluß zu verschwinden schien, die Bindersleber mich verlangten, da ich mich überreden ließ, Ja zu sagen. Weil es mich aber hernach gereuete; so gefiel es mir desto besser, daß die Herren Assessores Ministerii, welche mich wohl kenneten, den

Abge=

from many Christian hearts—may they be rewarded in eternity. When in the course of time my voice changed,* these free meals also disappeared for the most part, and my parents once again had to provide, until through the intercession of Mr. Lüpke, Mayor (Rathsmeister†) Reichardt‡ hired me as an Instructor, giving me my full keep as well as lodging. At that time he was only the Organist, but since then he has been elected a member of the City Council, and now he is Head of the Council. At the time he had only one son, Mr. Christoph Reichardt§, who is also now Head of the Council. Thus my parents had to provide for nothing other than my wash¶ and my clothing.

At Easter in the year 1713 I graduated to the Gymnasium,‖ and was enrolled by the Rector, Dr. Hogel. He was old, however, and right at that time Dr. Herrmann Nicolaus Stieler became his substitute. I continued to pursue music, and learned to play the violin a bit. From Cantor Adlung's brother (who also taught me to play the kettledrums) I subsequently took keyboard lessons, in order to continue what my father had taught me. After I had also taken [lessons in] keyboard performance for a while under Mr. Arnold, I then went several times a week to Marbach to the schoolmaster, Mr. Hufeld, until I moved into the home of Rathsmeister Reichardt, who subsequently brought me as far as the type of teaching at that time required. I pursued industriously my [academic] studies, and progressed in them to the point that I graduated into the second class at Easter in the year 1714,** and into the first class at St. Michael's†† in the year 1715. I remained there until Easter 1721,‡‡ because I did not wish to enter upon my student years [at the university] without any money, and could not succeed to the office of an Assistant (Adjuncti) or Prefect (Praefecti§§) right away, since there was no lack of fine and skillful people. When I finally succeeded to these offices, and had industriously accumulated my choir money,¶¶ I sought to gain a degree, and delivered a farewell address in Latin on the Council at Costnitz‖‖ and John Hus, translating it into German to please my father. I cannot deny that during my years in Gymnasium thoughts of becoming a schoolmaster*** hindered my diligence, but I prevailed over them until, after I had been a student [in the university] for a short time, my father died and my support appeared to be at an end. The [authorities at] Bindersleben asked me if I could be persuaded to answer "yes."††† Because I felt badly about it afterwards, it pleased me all the more that the [Erfurt] church authorities, who knew me well, answered the delegation [from Bindersleben], "We can put

---

* Thus Adlung could no longer sing in the choir.

† more precisely translated, "Head of the City Council"; the usual German word for "mayor" is "Bürgermeister."

‡ Probably Christian Reichard, one of the patrons to whom Adlung dedicated his *Anleitung zu der musikalischen Gelahrtheit*.

§ Son of Christian Reichard. During his university studies at Jena, Adlung served as his private tutor, and subsequently included him among the patrons to whom he dedicated his *Anleitung zu der musikalischen Gelahrtheit*.

¶ "Wäsche;" this may mean his underclothing, or it may mean his laundry.

‖ according to the biographical notice in Walther's *Lexicon*, the *Gymnasium Senatorium*, the *Rathsgymnasium*, where Adlung subsequently taught from 1741 until his death in 1762.

** April 1.

†† September 29.

‡‡ April 13.

§§ A student entrusted with non-academic duties, such as directing the choir.

¶¶ i.e., money paid for involvement with the choir.

‖‖ sic; what Adlung must mean, though, is "Constance"; cf. Chap. 11, note 13.

*** and thus not aspiring to go on to the university.

††† i.e., to return and take his father's post.

Vorrede.

Abgeordneten zur Antwort gaben: Wir können den Menschen besser brauchen. Denn was nur damals hier in Erfurt gelesen wurde, das zu meinem Vorhaben schien zu gehören, das frequentirte ich.

1) Die **Philosophie** hörte ich bey dem Herrn M. Motschmann, über die sämmtliche Buddeische Philosophie; übte mich auch im Disputiren anderthalb Jahr lang.

2) Die **Logik** hörte ich bey Herrn M. Sinnhold, nachherigem Diacono Regularium, und Prof. Orat Gymnas. Senat.

3) Die **Moralphilosophie** bey Herrn M. Weingärtner, welcher nachher Pastor Regularium wurde.

4) Das **Recht der Natur** über den Buddeum laß der Herr Prof. Stenger.

5) Den **Stilum latinum** suchte ich zu verbessern bey dem Herrn D. Stieler.

6) Die **Geographie**, besonders über Deutschland, hörte ich bey ebendemselben.

7) Das **Hebräische** über D. Danzens Grammatik lernte ich unter der Anführung des Herrn D. Schütt.

8) Die **Hebräische Accentuation** suchte ich unter der Anführung des Herrn Prof. Heuser zu erlernen.

9) Ein **Collegium Hermenevticæ sacræ** hörte ich bey dem damaligen Seniore, Herrn D Joch.

10) Die **Kirchenhistorie Neues Testaments** hörte ich bey ebendemselben.

11) Eine **Einleitung** dazu würde publice gelesen.

Alle vorher genannte Collegia wurden mir frey gelesen. Als ich es fast zwey Jahre hier angetrieben, und von der Reichardtischen Familie viel Liebe genossen; so fügte es sich, daß ich mit etlichen Jenaischen Professoribus in Bekanntschaft kam. Denn der Herr Prof. Lehmann besuchte, wegen der Verwandschaft, das Reichardtische Haus in Begleitung des Herrn Prof. Wiedeburgs. Sie liebten mich zugleich wegen der Musik, weil der Herr Prof. Lehmann selbst das Clavier spielete. Sie ermahneten mich, nach Jena zu ziehen: und weil ich keine Mittel wußte, versprachen sie mir alle mögliche Hülfe; auch eine Stelle im Convictorio. Ich gieng also

1723

the man to better use." At that time I was attending anything that was being taught here in Erfurt that appeared to suit my purposes.

1) I attended lectures in Philosophy given by Mr. Motschmann, M.A., covering the entire book on philosophy by Buddeus;* I also practiced debating for one and a half years.

2) I attended lectures in Logic given by Mr. Sinnhold, M.A., subsequently Deacon of the Reglerkirche and Professor of Rhetoric at the [Erfurt] Municipal Gymnasium.

3) Moral Philosophy given by Mr. Weingärtner, M.A., who subsequently became Pastor of the Reglerkirche.

4.) Natural Law from the book by Buddeus,† given by Prof. Stenger.

5) My Latin style I sought to improve under Dr. Stieler.

6) Geography lectures, especially of Germany, given by the same man.

7) I studied Hebrew from Dr. Danz's Grammar‡ under the guidance of Dr. Schütt.

8) I sought to master Hebrew Accentuation under the guidance of Prof. Heuser.

9) I attended lectures on Sacred Hermeneutics given by the then Senior Professor, Dr. Joch.

10) I attended lectures on Ecclesiastical History of the New Testament given by the same man.

11) An Introduction to this subject§ was delivered publicly.

All of the classes named above I attended without charge.¶ After I had pursued my studies here almost two years, and had been shown much love by the Reichardt family, it came to pass that I made the acquaintance of certain professors from [the University of] Jena. Prof. Lehmann came to visit the Reichardt household, because he was related to them, in the company of Prof. Wiedeburg. They were immediately drawn to me because of my musical ability, since Prof. Lehmann himself played keyboard.‖ They urged me to move to Jena, and since I did not have the means to do it, they promised me all the help possible, as well as a position at the boarding school.** Thus I went there

---

* *Elementa philosophiae instrumentalis*, Halle, 1703. Buddeus (Johann Franz Budde, 1667-1729) was one of the earliest exponents of a transitional theology from Lutheran orthodoxy to Pietism and toward Enlightenment ideas. His theology developed the ideas of John Locke; revelation could not contain anything that contradicted the natural, reasonable knowledge of God.

† *Historia juris naturalis*, Halle, n.d.

‡ Danz, Dn., ... *Exercitatio critico-litteraria*. Freistadii, Litteris alethinis excusa, A.R.G.H., 1708. Sectio II. Grammaticas ut & Lexico Ebraea ...

§ i.e., no. 10.

¶ It is not clear why Adlung was granted this privilege. Perhaps fees were waived because of his aptitude as a student (as they were later in Jena; see p. IX below), or it may have been due to his connection with Mayor Reichardt.

‖ In his *Anleitung*, p. 114, Adlung states that Lehmann " ... played keyboard so well that he even sought the post of organist here (in Erfurt) at the Reglerkirche, before he received his masters degree; luckily for him, he did not get the post."

** "Convictorio"—apparently an establishment that provided students with meals.

1723. auf Ostern dahin, weil doch in Erfurt nicht alles zu erlernen war. Dem Herrn Rathsmeister Reichardt versprach ich nach zwey Jahren wieder zu kommen. Aber der Mensch denkt; Gott lenkt. In dem Lehmannischen Hause nahm ich mein Quartier: und weil der Lector conuictorii, Herr M. Grosch, als ein Erfurter, mir, als einem Landsmanne, gewogen war, ich auch ein Jahr zuvor mich unter die Expectanten hatte lassen einschreiben; so währte es etwann ein halb Jahr, bis ich als ein Glied des Convictorii aufgenommen wurde. Durch Compagnien habe ich nie etwas verschwendet, und doch war ich so bekannt, und hatte so viel gute Freunde, als einer. Eine besondere Gabe Gottes war die dauerhafte Gesundheit: denn nicht nur von meinem andern Jahre an, bis an die Studentenjahre, sondern auch durch alle Studentenjahre, bis 1742, habe ich von keiner besondern Krankheit gewußt; auch nicht einmal die Masern und Blattern haben mich incommodiret. Ich habe aber in Jena theils durch gute Ordnung, theils durch gute Motiones meine Gesundheit erhalten. Meine Hefte oder Bücher steckte ich zu mir und gieng aufs Feld, bald da, bald dorthin; hütete mich aber allezeit vor den Wirthshäusern. Die Collegia habe ich nicht versäumet, weil ich stets gedacht, es käme zu der Zeit etwas, so zu wissen nöthig wäre, zumal da ich von vielem Schreiben kein Freund war, auch die Sachen besser faßte, wenn discurrirt, als wenn dictirt wurde. Ich konnte aber doch den Discurs, wenn es Gedächtnißsachen waren, complet nachschreiben. Daher kam es, daß ich durch Gottes Beystand in der Musik, Philosophie, Philologie und Theologie viel vor mich brachte, und ich würde in den fünftehalb Jahren (so lange blieb ich in Jena) noch mehr haben thun können, wenn ich mich nicht mit informiren hätte fortbringen müssen: denn anfangs hielt ich etliche Clavierstunden; und nach drittehalb Jahren, als ich mich noch nicht nach Erfurt sehnte, kam der junge Herr Reichardt zu mir nach Jena, welchen ich täglich etliche Stunden in Sprachen und Claviere unterrichten mußte. Was nun

a) Die Musik betrift; so bekam ich von Herr Bachen, Organisten in Jena, zuweilen die Erlaubniß, mich auf der Orgel zu üben. Ich ließ mir auch nach und nach eine ziemliche Anzahl musikalische theoretische Bücher vom Herrn Reichardt aus Erfurt, wie auch vom Herrn Walther aus Weimar bringen, las und excerpirte solche. Der Trieb hierzu war sehr stark, ohnerachtet ich nicht wußte, wozu mir solches helfen würde, weil die Besoldungen der Erfurtischen Organisten mir niemals anstunden, ohne die zun Predigern. Aber Herr Buttstedt daselbst schien mir noch ein vester Mann zu seyn; ja es schien auch dereinst an mich nicht kommen

at Eastertime, 1723,* since not everything could be learned in Erfurt. I promised Mayor Reichardt to return after two years. But man proposes and God disposes. I took my lodging in the Lehmann house, and because the Lector of the boarding school, Mr. Grosch, M.A., was well inclined to me as a fellow Erfurter, and let me enroll a year early on the waiting list, it took about half a year to be accepted as a member of the boarding school. I never squandered anything in revelry, and was nevertheless as popular and had as many good friends as those who did. My strong constitution was a particular gift of God; not only from my second year of life up to my student years, but also throughout all my student years until 1742, I never knew any particular illness. Not even measles or smallpox inconvenienced me. At Jena I maintained my health, in part by a well-ordered lifestyle, in part by good exercise. I would pick up my notes or books and go into the fields, sometimes here, sometimes there; I always stayed clear of the inns. I did not miss classes, because I always thought there would come a time when what was taught would be worth knowing, especially since I was not fond of a lot of writing and also comprehended matters better when they were discussed than when they were read. Nevertheless I could copy down the entire discourse if it were a subject that required memorizing. Thus it came about that I accomplished a great deal, with God's help, in music, philosophy, philology and theology, and I would have been able to do even more in the four and a half years I stayed in Jena if I had not had to support myself by teaching. In the beginning I taught various keyboard lessons, and after the two and a half years, when I was no longer homesick for Erfurt, there came to me in Jena the young Mr. Reichardt, whom I had to instruct several hours daily in languages and keyboard. Now, as regards

    a) music: from time to time I received from Mr. Bach,† organist in Jena, permission to practice on the organ. In the course of time I also ordered a goodly number of musical theoretical books from Mr. Reichardt in Erfurt as well as from Mr. [Johann Gottfried] Walther in Weimar, read them and took notes on them. My urge to do this was very strong, despite the fact that I had no idea what good it would do me, since the salaries of the Erfurt organists, aside from that of the Predigerkirche, would never have suited me. But [the organist] there, Mr. Buttstedt,‡ appeared to me to be still hale and

* Easter Sunday 1723 was March 28.

† Johann Nikolaus Bach [1669-1753], a cousin of J.S. Bach. He became organist at the Stadtkirche in 1694, adding to it the position of organist at the Kollegienkirche, the university church, in 1719.

‡ Johann Heinrich Buttstedt, b. 1666 in Bindersleben (the same village in which Adlung was born), d. 1727; a student and eventual successor of Johann Pachelbel at the Predigerkirche. Adlung succeeded him as organist of the Predigerkirche.

zu können, welches dennoch so wunderbar geschehen ist. Ich schrieb auch in Jena etliche theoretische musikalische Werke, doch heimlich, daß es mein Patron, Herr Prof. Lehmann, nicht merkte.

b) In der **Philosophie** hörte ich 1) den Cursum über Buddei Philosophie, beym Herrn Prof Lehmann, weil dessen eigene noch nicht gedruckt war.

2) Ein **Logicum** über Lehmanns deutsche Logik.

3) Die **Moralphilosophie** über dessen deutsche Moral.

4) Das **Recht der Natur** über Pufendorfs Buch de officio hominis & ciuis, auch das Jus naturae controuersum bey ebendemselben.

5) Die **Prudentiam politicam** über desselben deutsches Werkchen, bey ihm selbst.

6) Die **Physik** hörte ich zuweilen bey Hambergern und Teichmeyern, sonderlich aber bey Wucherern. Uiber desselben lateinische Elementa wurden Disputationes publicæ gehalten, wobey ich auch ein Mitglied war.

7) Als unter dem Vorsitz des Herrn Prof. Lehmanns über Pufendorfs Buch de officio hominis & ciuis disputirt wurde, habe ich publice auch ein paar mal einen Respondenten abgegeben.

8) Den **Cursum mathematicum** hörte ich bey dem Herrn Prof. Wiedeburg, über dessen lateinisches Werk; wobey meine Fertigkeit im Rechnen, so ich mit aus der Schule gebracht, mir ungemein dienete, alles zu begreifen, was andern nicht möglich war.

9) Die **Antiquitates romanas** über den Nieupoort hörte ich bey Hrn. Prof. Walch.

10) Ein **Informatorium**, oder von Auferziehung der Kinder, bey Hrn. M. Christ.

11) Ein

hearty; indeed there seemed no way that one day things would turn out for me as they nevertheless have in so miraculous a way. In Jena I also wrote a number of musical theoretical works, but in secret, so that my patron, Prof. Lehmann, would not notice it.

b) In philosophy I attended 1) the course [of lectures] on the philosophy of Buddeus,* [given] by Prof. Lehmann, because his own [book on the subject] was not yet printed.

2) Lectures on Logic from Lehmann's German book on logic.

3) Moral philosophy from Lehmann's German book on morals.†

4) Natural law from Pufendorf's book *De officio hominis & civis*,‡ as well as natural law refuted, [given] by the same man.§

5) Political prudence from Pufendorf's little work in German, given by the same man.¶

6) I attended lectures in physics for a time given by Hamberger and Teichmeyer, but in particular those by Wucherer.‖ Public debates were held upon his Latin Elementa, in which I also took part.

7) When debates were held over Pufendorf's book *De officio hominis & civis*** with Prof. Lehmann as chair, I delivered a response publicly several times.

8) I attended the course of lectures in mathematics given by Prof. Wiedeburg, taught from his Latin work;†† in this my skill in arithmetic that I had gained in school served me uncommonly well in comprehending everything, which was not possible for others.

9) I attended the lectures on Roman antiquities given by Prof. Walch on Nieupoort's book.‡‡

10) I attended an Informatorium, concerning the education of children, given by Mr. Christ, M.A.

---

* See v. II, p. V, footnote *.

† Lehmann, Johann Jacob (1683-1740), *Neueste und nützlichste art, die sogennante morale oder die natürlich verbesserung des willens gründlich zu erlernen* ... Jena, Meyers witwe, 1715.

‡ Samuel, Freiherr von Pufendorf (1632-1694), *De officio hominis et civis ... illustrati a Io. Iacobo Lehmanno*. Jenae: ... Bielckius, 1721.

§ i.e., Lehmann.

¶ Ibid.

‖ Johann Friedrich Wucherer (1682-1737).

** See note ‡ above.

†† Wiedeburg, Johann Bernhard (1687-1766), *Institutiones mathematicae in usum auditorium conscriptae*. Brunsvigae: L. Schröderi, 1718.

‡‡ Nieupoort, Willem Hendrik (fl. c.1712), *Rituum, qui olim apud Romanos obtinuerunt...* Bassani [Vicenza, Italy]: ex Typographia Remondiniana, 1703.

11) Ein **Parentatorium** beym Hrn. Prof. Walch.

c) In **Philologicis**, oder Sprachen.

1) Das **Fundamentale græcum**, über die Hallische griechische Grammatik, beym Hrn. Adjunct. Kromayer, der hernach als Professor gestorben.

2) Ein **Practicum** über **Luciani Dialogos**, bey ebendemselben.

3) Das **Fundamentale hebraicum** über den Danz, beym Hrn. Prof. Ruß. O wie glücklich war ich für andern, daß ich einen guten Anfang mit von Erfurt gebracht!

4) Die **Accentuation**, nebst dem Chaldäischen und Syrischen, bey ebendemselben.

5) Ein **Practicum** über den Propheten Jesaiam, bey eben demselben; wie auch

6) über die 12 kleinen Propheten. Beyde Versionen habe ich nachgeschrieben.

7) Ueber den **Interpretem Danzii** hörte ich bey dem Hrn. Adjunct. Hofmann.

d) In **Theologicis** hörte ich

1) **Theologiam Theticam** bey dem Herrn D. Buddeo, über sein groß Werk, so erst neu gedruckt wurde.

2) Die **Theologiam polemicam**, bey ebendemselben.

3) Die **Theologiam moralem**, bey ebendemselben, über sein lateinisches Werk.

4) Die **Historiam ecclesiasticam Noui Testamenti**, bey ebendemselben, über Pfaffens Compendium. Diese habe ich vollkommen nachgeschrieben.

5) Die **Historiam recentissimam**, bey eben demselben, wöchentlich 2 Stunden.

6) Ein **Exegeticum** über das Evangelium Johannis, bey ebendemselben.

7) Die **Harmoniam Euangelistarum**, bey dem Herrn Adjunct. Hofmann.

8) Ein **Collegium Catecheticum**, bey dem damaligen M. Joh. Jakob Rambach, nachmaligem Doct. Theol. Prof. und Superint. prim. zu Giessen.

11) a Parentatorium under Prof. Walch.

c) In philology, or languages

1) The fundamentals of Greek, from the book on Greek grammar from Halle* given by Adjunct [Prof.] Kromeyer, who afterwards died as a [full] professor.

2) A practicum on the Dialogues of Lucian, given by the same man.

3) The fundamentals of Hebrew, from the book by Danz,† given by Prof. Russ. O what an advantage I had over the others because I had brought a good grounding with me from Erfurt!

4) [Hebrew] Accentuation, together with Chaldean and Syrian, given by the same man.

5) A practicum on the Prophet Isaiah, by the same man, as well as

6) one on the 12 Minor Prophets. I copied down both of them.‡

7) I attended lectures on the interpretation of Danz§ by Adjunct [Prof.] Hofmann.

d) In theology I attended

1) Thetic theology under Dr. Buddeus, from his major work¶ that had just been published.

2) Polemic theology given by the same man.

3) Moral theology, by the same man, from his Latin work.‖

4) The ecclesiastical history of the New Testament, by the same man, from Pfaff's** Compendium. This I copied down in its entirety.

5) Modern history, by the same man, for two hours per week.

6) An exegesis of the Gospel of John, by the same man.

7) Lectures on the harmony of the Gospels, by Adjunct [Prof.] Hofmann.

8) A Catechetical class, under the then Mr. Joh. Jakob Rambach, M.A., subsequently Doctor and Professor of Theology and Primary Superintendent at Giessen.

---

* "über die Hallische griechische Grammatik:" published at Halle? used at Halle (at the university)? written by a scholar named Halle?

† See v. II, p. V, footnote ‡.

‡ i.e., both practica, numbers 5) and 6).

§ See v. II, p. V, footnote ‡.

¶ Buddeus, Johann Franz, *Theses theologicae de atheismo et superstitione...* Jena: Bielckius, 1717.

‖ Buddeus, *Institutiones theologiae moralis...* Leipzig: Fritsch, 1711.

** Christoph Matthäus Pfaff (1686-1760).

Vorrede.

Weil auch damals der Herr Past. Brumhardt in Wenigen-Jena großen Zulauf hatte wegen der erbaulichen und gelehrten Predigten; so war ich auch oft dabey, und schrieb nach. Kein einziges Collegium von alle den vorhin genannten habe ich bezahlen dürfen, weil mein Fleiß und meine gute Aufführung mir alle Professores gewogen machte, und sie wohl sahen, daß es an mir wohl angewendet wäre. Endlich wurde ich in Jena Magister, welches mir auch niemals im Traume vorgekommen war. Es mußte sich aber wunderlich schicken. Die Herren Professores aus Erfurt, sonderlich der sel. Herr Prof. Heuser, schrieben etliche lateinische Briefe an mich, um dahin zu kommen und Magister zu werden. Weil ich aber kein Geld übrig hatte, über dieses auch der Magistertitel von Erfurt mir mehr hinderlich zu seyn schien, noch allerhand zu lernen; so schlug ich es beständig ab, ob man gleich für 14. Thaler mir es antrug; ja, um durch Reisen mich nicht zu versäumen, ein Thema mir überschicken wollte, um es, anstatt eines Examinis, zu elaboriren. Aber 1726. im November war ich bey meinen Freunden, und mein Bruder kam dahin mit einem Compliment vom Herrn Prof. Lehmann, nebst der Ordre, sogleich zurück nach Jena zu kehren, ich müßte Magister werden, und noch denselbigen Tag das Memorial machen. Mir war es wie ein Traum; doch gieng ich mit, und erfuhr, daß der Herr Prof. Teichmeyer, als Brabeuta, müßte aus der philosophischen Facultät in die medicinische rücken. Nun ist in Jena der Gebrauch, daß 20. Magistri zugleich creirt werden; 18 davon bezahlen, deren jeder kaum unter 60. Thaler wegkömmt: 2 aber bezahlen nur 12. Thaler für den Schmauß, nebst andern Kleinigkeiten. Er hatte nur 10. Magistrandos gesammlet, wollte aber doch die Freude haben, einen Actum zu halten: daher kam ich in Vorschlag, unter denen zu seyn, die Gratuiti hießen, und nicht so viel, als die andern zahlen mußten. Auf mein Memorial folgte gleich das Jawort, und es kam auf das Examen an, welches ein jeder in seinem Hause aus seiner Profeßion mit mir vornahm; als z. E. Wiedeburg aus der Mathesi; Lehmann aus der Moral; Wucherer aus der Physik, u. s. w. Endlich kam es auf das Examen rigorosum an, welches in Gegenwart der Facultät durch Adjunctos vorgenommen wurde. Ueber mich kam Hr. Adjunct. Kromayer. Als der Actus 1726. den 28. November vorgieng, war niemand von dem Magistrandis zugegen, als Herr M. Gnäge, und Herr M. Trautmann, welches wol der andere Gratuitus seyn mochte. Es werden zwo Reden von den neuen Magistris gehalten, die sie aber nicht selbst machen dürfen, sondern die Herren Professores machen solche für 2 Thaler. Die meinige war die Danksagungsrede, welche Hr. Prof. Walch

*** in

Foreword

In addition, because Pastor Brumhardt in Wenigen-Jena was at that time enjoying great popularity due to his edifying and learned sermons, I often attended and copied them down. I was not required to pay for a single one of the classes enumerated above, since all the professors were well-disposed toward me because of my diligence and my good conduct, and they saw that their favor indeed bore fruit in me. Finally I was granted a masters degree in Jena, something I never dreamed would happen. It came about in such a remarkable way. The Professors [at the University] in Erfurt, in particular the late Prof. Heuser, wrote me a number of letters in Latin, [inviting me] to come there and be granted a masters degree. Because, however, I had no extra money, and furthermore [accepting] the masters degree from Erfurt seemed to me to be a hindrance to learning even more,* I persistently refused it, even though they offered it to me for only 14 Thalers;† indeed, to save me from wasting time traveling, they would send me a theme to elaborate upon, in place of an examination. In November of 1726, however, I was visiting my friends,‡ and my brother came there with a greeting from Prof. Lehmann, together with a summons to return immediately to Jena; I was to be awarded a masters degree, and yet that very same day I should enter my petition for it. It was like a dream to me, yet I went along and learned that Prof. Teichmeyer, as referee, had to be transferred from the philosophical to the medical faculty. Now there is a custom at Jena that 20 masters degrees must be conferred at one time; 18 of those must pay, each of which can hardly get away for under 60 Thaler. Two, however, must pay only 12 Thaler for the banquet together with other negligible amounts. He [i.e., Prof. Teichmeyer] had gathered only 10 masters candidates, yet he nevertheless wanted to have the pleasure of holding a formal celebration. Thus my name was suggested to be among those who are called Gratuiti,§ and do not have to pay as much as the others. Immediately after my petition came the assent, and then came the examination, which each [professor] conducted with me in his discipline in his own house; e.g., Wiedeburg in mathematics, Lehmann in ethics, Wucherer in physics, etc. Finally there came the comprehensive examination, which was conducted by the adjunct professors in the presence of the faculty. I was assigned to Adjunct Professor Kromayer. When the ceremony took place on the 28th of November 1726, none of the masters candidates [beside me] was present except Mr. Gnüge, M.A., and Mr. Trautmann, M.A. (who indeed may have been the other Gratuitus). The new masters are to deliver two orations, which however they need not write themselves; the professors write them for 2 Thalers. That of mine was the thanksgiving ad-

* Accepting a masters degree from Erfurt would de facto have terminated Adlung's pursuit of a masters degree at the University of Jena.

† Compare this amount with the figure of 60 Thalers that Adlung states below as the fee required for a masters degree from Jena.

‡ in Erfurt? in Bindersleben?

§ i.e., who receive the degree gratis.

in lateinischen Versen hätte machen müssen. Durch Fürspruch des Herrn Prof. Lehmanns aber erhielt ich die Erlaubniß, meine Verse selbst zu machen *). Hierbey ist zu merken, daß wir nicht zu Magistris, sondern zu Doctoribus Philosophiä gemacht werden, und setzen auch den rothen Doctorhut auf. Der Herr Harz und der damalige Monsieur Reichardt beehrten mich mit einem Carmine. Nun schien ich fast an Jena gebunden zu seyn: und damit ich mir das Recht Collegia zu lesen und anzuschlagen erwerben möchte; so mußte ich mich Anno 1727. resolviren, pro loco zu disputiren, ohne welches in Jena nicht erlaubt ist, Collegia zu lesen. Ich wählte auf Anrathen des Herrn Prof. Lehmanns eine moralische Materie, de obligationis vi & natura. Die Gewohnheit erforderte, daß die Disputation von demjenigen Professore censiret werden mußte, in dessen Profeßion dieselbe läuft; also war mein Censor, Herr Prof. Lehmann. Ich hieng einige mathematische Corollaria an, welche Herr Prof. Wiedeburg censiren mußte. Es gieng bey dieser Disputation nicht allzuscharf her, wie es sonst pflegt, wenn pro loco einer disputirt, welchen die andern Adjuncti und Magistri suchen zu prostituiren, um neben sich keinen empor zu lassen. Die Ursach war diese: Anno 1727. den 1. October war diese Disputation angestellt, und kurz zuvor erfuhr ich, daß die Frau Rathsmeisterin Reichardtin sehr krank, und der Herr Rathsmeister Reichardt seines Herrn Sohnes benöthiget wäre. Ich wurde scharf angestrenget, zurück nach Erfurt zu kehren, bis die Frau Rathsmeisterin wieder genesen wäre; alsdann sollte ich mit meinem Untergebenen eine Zeit lang auf Reisen gehen, und hernach, nach Gefallen, wieder nach Jena. Dieß wurde bekannt, und jeder Jenenser glaubte nicht Ursach zu haben, sich vor mir zu fürchten. Es kam auch die Erfurtische Fuhre noch denselbigen Abend wirklich an, uns abzuholen. Wir fuhren glücklich nach Erfurt, mit gesunden Gliedern und frölichem Gewissen. In Erfurt zeigten sich wieder unzählige Spuren der göttlichen Fürsehung, und ich hatte wieder auf der Reglerorgel meine Freyheit, und man machte aus meinem Spielen etwas. Die Information mit Hr. Reichardten trieb ich täglich 3 bis 4 Stunden fort. Aber anstatt der gehoften Besserung, starb die Frau Rathsmeisterin, und meine Rückkehr nach Jena ward zu Wasser. Gleich darauf gegen Advent starb der Organist bey der Predigerkirche, Herr Buttstedt. Bey der Wiederbesetzung dieser Stelle kam ich, nebst des Herrn Buttstedts ältestem Sohne, und einem Fremden, Herr Völkner, mit in Vorschlag. Ich hatte 1) den Vortheil, daß ich die Theile der Clavierkunst druck-

---

*) Es wurde darinne de Laudibus Ienae gehandelt.

dress, which Prof. Walch was supposed to have written in Latin verses. But upon the recommendation of Prof. Lehmann I received permission to write my verses myself*).* At this point it should be mentioned that we were granted not masters degrees, but Ph.D.'s,† and were invested with red doctoral caps. Mr. Harz and the then Mr. Reichardt‡ honored me with a poem. Now it almost seemed that I was bound to Jena. In order that I might acquire the right to teach classes and to post notices about them, I had to agree in 1727 to debate for the position, without which one is not allowed to lecture at Jena. On the advice of Prof. Lehmann I chose a subject in ethics, de obligationis vi & naturae [Concerning the Obligation of Force and Nature]. Custom demanded that the debate had to be judged by the professor in whose discipline it fell; thus my critic was Prof. Lehmann. I appended several mathematical corollaries that Prof. Wiedeburg had to judge. This debate was not so lively as was usual when one debates pro Loco whom the other Adjuncts and Masters seek to denigrate to prevent him from rising to their rank.§ The reason for this was as follows: this debate was scheduled for October 1st, 1727, and shortly before it I learned that Mrs. Reichardt, wife of the Mayor [at Erfurt] was very ill, and that Mr. Reichardt had need of his son. I was strongly pressured to return to Erfurt until Mrs. Reichardt was again well; then I was to go traveling a while with my charge,¶ and thereafter return to Jena when I wished. This became known, and no one‖ in Jena believed that he had any reason to be afraid of me. Indeed, the coach arrived that very night** from Erfurt to pick us up. With sound bodies and cheerful consciences we travelled merrily to Erfurt. In Erfurt once again there were revealed countless evidences of divine protection; I once again took my ease upon the organ at the Reglerkirche, and people complimented me on my playing. I continued to instruct Mr. Reichardt for 3-4 hours every day. But instead of the hoped-for recovery, Mrs. Reichardt died, and my return to Jena came to naught. Immediately thereafter, toward Advent, the organist of the Predigerkirche, Mr. Buttstedt, died.†† My name was proposed as a candidate for the position, together with Mr. Buttstedt's eldest son and a stranger, Mr. Völkner. 1) I had an advantage, since I had the parts of my *Art of the Keyboard*‡‡

*) they were on the subject de Laudibus Jenae (Concerning the Praises of Jena)

* Thus sparing Adlung the fee of 2 Thalers.

† This seems highly irregular, but the German text is unambiguous.

‡ Apparently the young man from Erfurt whom Adlung was tutoring, and who later bore the title *Rathsmeister* or Head of the City Council at Erfurt.

§ and thus creating competition for students?

¶ the junior Mr. Reichardt, whom Adlung was tutoring.
‖ i.e., no Adjunct.
** i.e., the night following the debate.

†† December 1, 1727.

‡‡ "Clavierkunst:" apparently the musical theoretical work Adlung mentions on p. XIII below as having completed while in Jena.

druckfertig entworfen hatte, welche ich zum Herrn D. Heitmann brachte, der ein guter Kenner des Claviers war, um ihm, wegen der musikalischen Theorie, besser bekannt zu werden. Diesem hatte die Inspection aufgetragen, die Proben anzuhören, und seine Gedanken drüber zu sagen. 2) Hatte ich meine gedruckte Disputation unter die Herren vertheilet, worauf sie auch etwas sahen, weil ich auch in andern Dingen brauchbar zu seyn schien. 3) Meine Probe lief besser ab, als der andern Competenten ihre. Ich erhielt also die Vocation. Mit was für Treue und Fleiß ich seint der Zeit der Kirche gedienet, werden andere besser sagen, als es mir zu sagen anstehet. Nur war ich mit meiner alten Orgel immer nicht zufrieden; ich konnte es aber nicht zu einer Aenderung bringen, bis 1740 etwas resolvirt wurde: denn da fieng man an, die Orgel zu mahlen, und auch innerlich eine so starke Reformation unter meiner Aufsicht vorzunehmen, daß ich sie nun unter die besten Orgeln hier zähle: und dieses halte ich für ein großes Glück für mich; wie ich denn von der Zeit an viel munterer und im Spielen geschickter worden bin, zumal da mir fast die Gedanken vergangen waren, bey dem Studiren zu bleiben. Denn ins Predigtamt wollte ich nicht, weil ich es in den Jenaischen Dörfern etlichemal versucht, ob mein Körper zum Predigen taugte, aber ich konnte nie recht ausdauern. In den Erfurtischen Schulen giebts zwar gute Dienste, aber wenig Besoldungen; also beschloß ich bey mir, Organist zu bleiben, und daneben zu informiren, welches letztere mir auch so von statten gegangen, daß ich zweifele, ob in so wenig Jahren jemand jemals so viel Leute informirt, auch selbige so weit gebracht, als ich, durch Gottes Gnade und Fleiß; indem ich von Anno 1728 bis 1762 im Clavierspielen 218, und in Sprachen 284 Personen informiret habe, ohne die, welche mir entfallen sind. Und ob mir schon die Stunden theurer bezahlet wurden, als andern; so liefen doch die mehresten mir zu. Aus eben der Absicht, nicht weiter zu studiren geschahe es, daß ich anfieng Claviere zu machen, und in der Schreinerey mich zu üben; wie ich denn 16. Stücke verfertiget habe, welche alle verkauft sind, bis auf eins, welches ich noch besitze. Allein 1736. vergieng mir der Appetit, da den 21sten October im großen Erfurter Brande das Werkzeug sogar verlohren gieng, mit allem Vorrathe von rarem Holze, daß ich, alles Suchens ungeachtet, gar nichts von Eisen wieder finden können. Ich resolvirte mich nämlich im gedachten Jahre ein Haus zu kaufen, und zog auf St. Johann ein. Ich war kaum ein Vierteljahr darinnen gewesen, so entstund in der Flasche des Sonntags frühe ein Feuer bey einem heftigen Windsturme. Es war sehr weit von mir, also eilten wir nicht mit ausräumen. Als es aber endlich

ready for print, which I brought to Dr. Heitmann, who was a true connoisseur of the keyboard, in order better to acquaint him with my knowledge of music theory. The church superintendency had charged him to listen to the trials and to pronounce his opinions about them. 2) I had distributed printed [copies of] my debate* among the gentlemen,† which they paid attention to, since I appeared to be of use in other ways as well. 3) My trial went better than those of the other competitors. Thus I was called to the position. Others can better say (than is fitting for me to say) how much faithfulness and diligence I have shown since that time in serving the church. I was never satisfied with the old organ I played, yet I could never convince anyone to make changes until the matter was resolved in 1740. At that time they began to paint the organ [case], and also to undertake such a thorough rebuilding of the [organ's] interior under my supervision, that I now count it one of the best organs here [in Erfurt]; this I consider one of my great joys. From that time on I have become much more lively and skillful in playing, especially since I gave up almost entirely the idea of sticking with my studies. For I did not want to become a preacher, since I had given that a try several times in the villages surrounding Jena, to see if I were strong enough for preaching, but I never had enough stamina to do it right. There are indeed good positions available in the Erfurt schools, but they are poorly paid. Thus I resolved to remain an organist, and to teach on the side; the latter has progressed to the point that I doubt anyone has ever taught so many people in so few years, and has brought them so far, as I have, through diligence and God's grace. From the year 1728 until 1762 I have instructed 218 persons in keyboard playing and 284 in languages, excluding those whom I may have forgotten about. And even though my fees were higher than others, yet the majority came to me. Having purposed not to pursue my [academic] studies any longer, I decided to begin to build keyboard instruments and to develop my skill at cabinetry. I have constructed 16 instruments, all of which are sold with the exception of one that I still own. But in 1736 I lost my enthusiasm,‡ since my tools were completely destroyed on the 21st of October in the great fire at Erfurt, together with my entire supply of rare wood, so that I could not even find a single piece of iron.§ In the abovementioned year I resolved to buy a house, and moved to St. Johann.¶ I had hardly been there for three months when a fire arose during a strong windstorm in the [house or inn] "At the Bottle" early Sunday morning. It was a good distance from me, and so we did not hurry to

* i.e., the debate *pro Loco* in Jena.
† presumably the church superintendents.
‡ literally "appetite;" i.e., to build further instruments.
§ i.e., the fire burned so hot that it even melted metal, so that Adlung could not even find a remnant of a tool.
¶ the "Johannis-Viertel", one of the four traditional divisions or "quarters" of the city of Erfurt, the others being "Andreas", "Viti" and "Mariae".

XII **Vorrede.**

lich überhand nahm, und wir Ernst brauchen wollten; so flog ein Klumpen Feuer auf meiner Nachbarin Schindeldach. Ehe man es sich also versahe, gieng die ganze Gasse auf beyden Seiten an. Mein Haus brannte den ganzen Tag und Nacht. Hier giengen meine Musikalien, Bücher und andere Meublen, fast gänzlich verlohren; was nicht verbrannte, wurde gestohlen: denn es war die Confusion zu groß, weil die ganze Stadt in Gefahr stund. Ich mußte nachgehends wieder von vorn anfangen, und nicht allein mein Haus wieder bauen, sondern auch die Bibliothek und andre Meublen anschaffen.

Ich habe viel verdient durch philologische, mathematische und philosophische Collegia. Ich hatte in Erfurt niemals angeschlagen, und doch wollte die Facultät sauer sehen, und mir mit der Inhibition drohen. Aber 1740. schlugen sich die Herren Studenten nur um destomehr zusammen, an der Zahl sechszehn. Ich hätte mich endlich damals mit der Facultät abgefunden, und mich nostrificiren lassen; aber sie spanneten die Seyten zu hoch, da sie 12. Thaler verlangten, und den öffentlichen Anschlag nicht erlauben wollten, bis ich wirklich eine Disputation pro Loco gehalten hätte. Es war aber so kurz vor Ostern anhängig gemacht, daß es mit der Disputation nicht angehen konnte. Auf Ostern 1741. suchte ich noch einmal an, und erhielt endlich die Nostrification für 6. Thaler. Die Disputation verfertigte ich, übergab sie der Censur des Decani, und versprach, solche zu halten, wenn sich ein Respondens fände; welches aber noch nicht geschehen können. Weil man sich hier in Erfurt auf die Einnahme von den Studiosis nicht verlassen kann; so hatte ich längst gewünscht, meine wenigen Studia in einem gewissen Amte zum Dienste des Nächsten anzuwenden, zumal da ich noch nicht vergessen, daß meine Patroni in Jena es mir sehr übel genommen, daß ich mein Hauptwerk verlassen, und ein Organist geworden. Als derowegen Herr Prof. Heuser 1739. vom Schlage gerührt worden, und die Gedanken hatte, sich jemanden wegen des Gymnasii substituiren zu lassen, ließ ich mich von vornehmen Gönnern bereden, mich bey ihm zu melden. Er schien ganz willig dazu; aber nachher verband er sich mit Hr. Lochmann, welcher hernach bis 1741. Diaconus Regularium gewesen. Die Herren Rathssenieres, welche zugleich mir entgegen waren, schützten vor, daß mein Organistenamt zur Professur sich nicht reime: Gleichwol wollte ich dieses nicht niederlegen, weil es mehr einträgt, als die Professur. Sie hatten aber, daß ich es nur gestehe, auch keine große Ursach, auf mich zu regardiren, weil ich damals weder heimlich noch öffentlich

Collegia

evacuate. But when it had finally gotten out of hand and we had occasion to be concerned, a flaming brand blew onto my neighbor's wooden shingled roof. In the twinkling of an eye both sides of the alley went up [in flames]. My house burned the entire day and night. My music, books and other furniture were almost entirely destroyed. What was not burned up was stolen, for there was too much confusion,* since the entire city stood in danger. Subsequently I had to begin all over, and not only rebuild my house, but also procure a library and other furniture.

I have earned a good deal by giving philological, mathematical and philosophical seminars. I had never posted notice in Erfurt, and yet the faculty† chose to regard me in a surly manner and threaten me with interdiction.‡ But all the more students flocked to me in 1740, sixteen all told. By that time I had finally come to terms with the faculty, and gotten myself approved to teach in Erfurt; but they went too far by demanding 12 Thaler and not wanting to allow me to post notice publicly until I had actually held a debate for the position. The proceedings were instituted so close to Easter, however, that the debate could not be arranged. I applied once again at Easter 1741,§ and finally received approval to teach for 6 Thaler. I completed the debate, turned it over to the Dean for evaluation, and promised to hold it if a Respondent could be found; but this has not yet come to pass. Because one cannot depend upon the income from students here in Erfurt, I had long wanted to serve my fellow citizens by gaining a secure position from which to make use of my few [university] studies, especially since I was ever mindful that my patrons in Jena thought very ill of me that I had abandoned my primary work and become an organist. When therefore Prof. Heuser suffered a stroke in 1739 and was minded for the good of the Gymnasium to procure a substitute to teach for him, I let my distinguished patrons¶ talk me into applying to do it. He appeared quite willing, but then entered into a partnership with Mr. Lochmann, who has subsequently been Deacon of the Reglerkirche since 1741. The city councillors, who were likewise opposed to me, made pretense that my position as organist was not compatible with that of a professor. I did not want to resign the former, however, because it brought in more [money] than the professoriate. I must confess, however, that they had no great reason to take note of me, since at that time I had conducted

* to prevent the looting.

† of the University of Erfurt.

‡ Apparently Adlung had already been teaching unobtrusively for some time before this happened.

§ Easter Sunday that year was April 2.

¶ perhaps the men to whom the *Anleitung zu der musikalischen Gelahrtheit* is dedicated: Elias Friedrich Heitmann, Christian Reichard[t] and his son Christoph Reichard[t].

Collegia gelesen, auch weder disputirt, noch durch Schriften mich bekannt gemacht hatte. Zwar hatte ich in Musicis schon in Jena geschrieben

1) Eine vollständige Anweisung zum Generalbasse, so mir mit verbrannt, und was ich nachdem aufs neue aufgesetzt, ist was weniges dagegen.

2) Eine Anweisung zur italienischen Tabulatur, so ebenfalls mit verbrannt.

3) Eine Anweisung zur Fantasie und zu den Fugen, so auch mit fort.

4) Eine Musicam Mechanicam Organoedi, so noch vorhanden *); und noch verschiedene andere Sachen.

Dieß alles aber war mir mehr nachtheilig, als beförderlich, weil man nicht glaubt, daß ein starker Musikus könne ein starker Gelehrter seyn. Ich hatte auch ein Werk von der lateinischen Sprache druckfertig gemacht; aber auch dieses verbrannte, ehe es bekannt wurde. Es hieß: Parallelismus latinæ linguæ. Nachher aber machte das Lesen und Anschlagen und der Ruf von dem Zulaufe in meine Sprach- und andere Stunden mich nach und nach bekannter. Als Herr M. Loßen zum Diaconat an die Predigerkirche berufen wurde, schrieb ich unter dem Titel: Faber fortunæ, eine lateinische Epistel. Nun war derselbe schon vorher berufen zur Professur des Gymnasii, aber als Diaconus zun Predigern nahm er das Amt nicht an, als der Herr Professor Döring sein Amt niederlegte. Ich ließ mich wieder bereden mit anzuhalten, und der Vorwandt wegen des Organistendienstes fiel weg: aber doch wurde Hr. Prof. Beßler mir vorgezogen, und ich bekam 1741. auf Ostern den Beruf in der Hoffnung. Nun dachte jedermann, ich hätte so lange Zeit, bis von den alten Herren Professoren einer abgienge: aber Gott verhängete kaum nach einem Vierteljahre über den jüngsten unter allen, nämlich Herrn Prof. Lochmann, eine hitzige Krankheit, daß er vor den Erndtenferien starb, zu meinem großen Leidwesen, weil wir gute Freunde waren. Ich bekam sogleich den Beruf an dessen Stelle, und wurde 1741. den 28ten August introducirt, und hielt dabey memoriter eine lateinische Rede de otio litterario.

Ich hatte vor der neuen Akademie nützlicher Wissenschaften allhier sieben musikalische Fragen lateinisch und hernach teutsch beantwortet, unter dem Titel: Musikalisches Siebengestirn, welche zur Untersuchung nach Maynz geschickt worden.

---

*) Dieß ist das Werk, welches hier dem geehrtesten Publico im Drucke überreichet wird.

neither private nor public instruction, nor debated, nor gained recognition as an author. To be sure, I had already written [several treatises] on music in Jena:

1. A *vollständige Anweisung zum Generalbasse* (*Complete Instruction in Figured Bass*), that was destroyed in the fire; what I have subsequently written anew is a trifle by comparison.

2. An *Anweisung zur italienischen Tabulatur* (*Instruction in Italian Tabulature*), likewise burned.

3. An *Anweisung zur Fantasie und zu den Fugen* (*Instruction in Free Improvisation and in Fugues*), also destroyed.

4. A *Musica Mechanica Organoedi* (*Mechanics of Music for the Organist*), still extant *); and various other things as well.

All of this was a greater disadvantage than an advantage to me, however, since no one believed that a competent musician could be a competent scholar. I had also gotten a work on the Latin language ready for print, but it likewise burned before it was published. It was called *Parallelismus latinae linguae* (*Parallelism in the Latin Language*). Subsequently, however, my lecturing and my posting notice, and the word about the popularity of my instruction in languages as well as other subjects, gradually made me better known. When Mr. Lozzen, M.A., was called to be Deacon of the Predigerkirche, I wrote a Latin letter with the title *Faber fortunae* (*The Shaper of Fortune*). This man had already been called earlier to the professoriate at the Gymnasium but, being a Deacon at the Predigerkirche, he did not accept the office when Prof. Döring resigned. I was again urged to apply, and the objection about my holding the position of organist was dropped, but Prof. Besler was given the job over me, and at Easter 1741 I received *the hoped-for call*. Now everyone thought that I would have to wait a long time until one of the older professors passed away; but barely three months later God inflicted a fever upon the youngest of all, namely Prof. Lochmann, so that he died before the fall holidays*—to my great regret, since we were good friends. Immediately I was called in his place, and was installed on the 28th of August, 1741; on that occasion I delivered from memory a Latin oration, *de otio litterario* (*Concerning literary pursuits*).

In the presence of the New Academy of Practical Sciences here I had propounded answers to seven musical questions, first in Latin and thereafter in German, under the title, *Musikalisches Siebengestirn*†, which was sent to Mainz

* These were in July and August.

† a rhetorical title, roughly *The Sevenfold Musical Constellation*.

*) This is the work that is here furnished in print to the honorable public. [Agricola]

worden. Hierauf wurde mir schon X. cal. Ian. 1755. ein gedrucktes Diploma zugeschickt, und ich für ein ordentliches Mitglied angenommen; wie ich denn nachgehends den Sommer über in des Herrn von Linkarts Hause oft der Conferenz beywohnen müssen; da ich auch nicht wenig Artikel ausgearbeitet, welche der gelehrten Zeitung einverleibet worden, sonderlich mathematische und musikalische."

Bis hierher gehet die von dem sel. Herrn Professor eigenhändig aufgesetzte Lebensbeschreibung. Ich füge derselben nur noch 2 Stücke kürzlich bey:

1) Daß sich der Herr Verfasser im Jahre 1732. mit der damaligen Jungfer Beata Elisabetha Ritterin, einer Tochter des Herrn Bürgermeister Ritters in Großwannsleben bey Magdeburg, verheyrathet, und als fast eilf Jahre dieses vergnügten Ehestandes verstrichen, mit einer jungen Tochter gesegnet und erfreuet worden, welche einzige Mademoiselle Tochter, mit Namen Sophia Elisabetha, nebst der Frau Wittwe, annoch am Leben ist, und, als ein tugendhaftes und in verschiedenen schönen Wissenschaften wohl geübtes Frauenzimmer, der Unterweisung ihres sel. Herrn Papas viel Ehre macht.

2) Daß Derselbe im Jahre 1762. am 5ten Julii, an einer auszehrenden Krankheit, im 63sten Jahre seines ruhmvollen Alters verstorben.

Man wird übrigens aus vorstehender Lebensbeschreibung gar leicht wahrnehmen können, wie sauer sichs der sel. Herr Professor Adlung in seinem Leben werden lassen, etwas rechtschaffenes zu erlernen, um sich in den Stand zu setzen, Gott und dem Nächsten hinwiederum nützliche Dienste leisten zu können. Hier sehen sich diejenigen kräftig widerlegt, welche in den irrigen Gedanken stehen, als könne keine andere gründliche Gelehrsamkeit bey der Erlernung und Ausübung der Musik statt finden: denn der sel. Adlung besaß nicht nur eine tiefe Einsicht in die philologischen, philosophischen, mathematischen und theologischen Wissenschaften, und eine gründliche

to be examined. Thereafter a printed diploma was sent to me on December 21, 1754, and I was accepted as a regular member.* During the entire summer following I had to attend the meetings at Mr. von Linkart's house, since I had completed quite a few articles, especially about mathematics and music, that were incorporated into the [Academy's] learned journal.

This is the extent of the late Professor's biography as he himself wrote it. To it I will append only two brief items:

1) In the year 1732 the author was married to the maiden Beata Elisabetha Ritter, a daughter of the Mayor of Grosswannsleben near Magdeburg. After almost eleven years of happy marriage, they were blessed and gladdened by [the birth of] a young daughter. This only daughter, named Sophia Elisabetha, is still alive, together with the widow; as a virtuous little lady, well versed in various *belles-lettres*, she is a great credit to her late papa's teaching.

2) On the 5th of July, 1762, in the 63rd year of his praiseworthy life, the author died of a consumptive disease.

It is easy to perceive from the above biography just how arduous it was for the late Professor Adlung to gain a thorough education in his life, in order to put himself in a position to be able to provide useful service in turn to God and his neighbor. [His life] furnishes a powerful contradiction to those who hold the erroneous idea that the learning and practice of music excludes any other well-grounded learning; for the late Adlung possessed not only profound insight into philology, philosophy, mathematics and theology, and a thorough knowledge of the languages pertaining to them, but he was also exceptionally able in musical theory

* of the Mainz Electoral Academy of Practical Sciences at Erfurt, as the title page of each volume of *Musica mechanica organœdi* states. Erfurt had a longstanding connection with Mainz; it belonged to the territory of the Archbishop of Mainz, and the two churches on its *Domhügel* (cathedral hill) were a Roman Catholic stronghold in staunchly Lutheran Thuringia.

Vorrede.

liche Erkänntniß der dazu gehörigen Sprachen; sondern auch in der musikalischen Theorie und Praxi war seine Stärke ausnehmend groß; wie davon seine hinterlassenen Schriften ein sattsames Zeugniß geben. Man wird hoffentlich der Sache nicht zu viel thun, wenn man Ihn denenjenigen gelehrten und berühmten Männern an die Seite setzt, welche Er in seiner Anleitung zu der musikalischen Gelahrtheit, S. 112.-117. als solche Männer anführt, die, nebst andern gründlich erlernten Wissenschaften, auch in der Musik keine Fremdlinge gewesen, und deren Gelehrsamkeit durch die Musik im geringsten nicht gehindert worden ist. Es ist nur zu bedauren, daß nicht alle von dem sel. Manne verfertigte Schriften dem Publico haben können bekannt gemacht werden, sondern (wie aus dem vorigen zu ersehen) einige beträchtliche Werke, durch den im Jahre 1736. in Erfurt entstandenen großen Brand, im Manuscripte gänzlich verlohren gegangen sind. Was für Schriften von Ihm selbst ans Licht gestellet worden, ist zwar aus dem vorherstehenden Lebenslaufe zu ersehen: da aber daselbst ein Paar davon übergangen worden; so will ich hier die sämmtlichen Adlungischen Schriften der Zeitordnung nach anzeigen, wie sie nach und nach im Drucke erschienen sind, um dasjenige nachzuholen, was man etwann dort vermißt.

*) Von Ihm selbst sind edirt worden

1) Epistola grat. lat. ad Reichardum. 1736. 1 Bogen.
2) Venus sub sole. 1740. 3 Bogen.
3) Faber Fortunæ. 1741. 1 Bogen.

„In eben diesem 1741sten Jahre schrieb Er auch bey Gelegenheit „der Nostrification in Erfurt eine mathematische Disputation, welche „de quibusdam affectionibus quadratorum, cuborum, bi-„quadratorum &c. handelte; sie ist aber, so viel ich weis, nicht ge-„druckt worden.

4) Anlei=

and practice, as the writings he left behind bear ample witness. It would appear to be no exaggeration to place him in the company of those learned and renowned men whom he cites in his *Anleitung zu der musikalischen Gelahrtheit*, pp. 112-117, as men who, besides possessing a thorough mastery of other sciences, are also no strangers to music, and whose erudition is not in the least hindered by [their knowledge of] music. It is only to be regretted that not all of the writings the late author completed could be made known to the public, but rather (as stated above) the manuscripts of several substantial works were completely lost in the great fire that broke out in Erfurt in the year 1736. The above biography reveals those writings that he himself published, but since he has omitted several of them in it, I will list here Adlung's complete writings* according to the order in which they appeared in print, in order to make up for those that one may have missed in the the biography.

* not including a number of musical compositions.

α)† Writings published by Adlung himself:

1) *Epistola grat. lat. ad Reichardum* (*A Latin Epistle in gratitude to Reichardt*). 1736. 1 signature.
2) *Venus sub sole* (*Venus under the sun*). 1740. 3 signatures.
3) *Faber Fortunae* (*The Shaper of Fortune*).‡ 1741. 1 signature.

"Likewise in the year 1741 he wrote a mathematical disputation upon the occasion of his certification in Erfurt, that treated "certain attributes of the second, third and fourth powers, etc." ("de quibusdam affectionibus quadratorum, cuborum, biquadratorum &c."); to the best of my knowledge, however, it was not printed."§

† The greek letters used from this point on do not appear to be additions by Agricola, but are an organizing device used by Albrecht.

‡ See p. XIII above.

§ It is unclear why Albrecht encloses this passage in quotation marks. It is not taken from either of the biographies (Walther or Marpurg) Albrecht mentions on p. 2 above.

4) **Anleitung zu der muſikaliſchen Gelahrtheit.** Mit einer Vorrede des Herrn Kapellmeiſters, **Johann Ernſt Bach.** Erfurt, 1758. 2 Alphab. 9 Bogen in 8vo; nebſt 8 Kupfertabellen.

ß) Nach des Herrn Verfaſſers Tode ſind noch folgende zwo Schriften von mir ans Licht geſtellet worden.

5) Muſica Mechanica Organoedi, und
6) **Muſikaliſches Siebengeſtirn.**

Beyde haben im Anfange dieſes 1768ſten Jahres die Preſſe verlaſſen, und ſind in dem **Birnſtielſchen Verlage in Berlin** zu haben.

Aus allen Schriften leuchtet Fleiß, Einſicht, Deutlichkeit und Ordnung hervor, und zeugen von einem Manne, der ſeine Sachen vorher gehörig überdacht, ehe er die Feder ergriffen, um ſolche niederzuſchreiben.

Ich habe nun II. dem Hochgeehrteſten Leſer von der **Beſchaffenheit des Manuscripts** Nachricht zu geben, aus welchem dieß gegenwärtige Werk ans Licht geſtellet worden.

Es iſt das Manuſcript dieſes Werks eine Frucht eines vieljährigen Fleißes, ſintemal daſſelbige bereits im Jahre 1726. zu ſchreiben angefangen worden, da der Herr Verfaſſer noch in Jena ſich aufhielt; welches daher klar iſt, weil auf dem Titelblate deſſelben die Worte geſchrieben ſtehen: Ienæ 1726. inceptum in aedibus Lehmannianis. Bey der erſten Ausfertigung war das Werk im Manuscripte an der Seitenzahl bis auf 820. ſehr klar geſchriebene Quartſeiten angewachſen. Dieſe Seitenzahl iſt zwar in folgenden Zeiten mit keinem Zuſatze vermehret worden, ſondern immer die vorige geblieben: aber in manchem Kapitel hatte der ſel. Herr Verfaſſer von Jahr zu Jahr ſo viel dazu geſchrieben, daß auf dem Rande herum und zwiſchen dem ordentlichen Texte mehr ſtand, als es der Raum einer Quartſeite zuweilen verſtattete.

Ich

4) *Anleitung zu der musikalischen Gelahrtheit* (*An Introduction to Musical Knowledge*). With a Foreword by Kapellmeister Johann Ernst Bach. Erfurt, 1758. 2 Alphabets [plus] 9 signatures in octavo; together with 8 engraved plates.

β) After the author's death I have published the following two writings in addition:

5) *Musica Mechanica Organoedi* (*Musical Mechanics for the Organist*), and

6) *Musikalisches Siebengestirn* (*The Sevenfold Musical Constellation*)

Both of them have left the press at the beginning of this year, 1768, and may be had from the publisher Birnstiel in Berlin.

From all of these writings shine forth diligence, insight, clarity and order; they bear witness to a man who has appropriately pondered his subject before taking pen in hand to put it into writing.

II. Now I must provide to the honorable reader a report on the nature of the manuscript from which this present work has been published.

The manuscript of this work is the fruit of many years' diligence, inasmuch as it had already begun to be written in the year 1726, while the author was still living in Jena. What makes this clear is that the title page bears the inscription: *Ienae 1726 inceptum in aedibus Lehmannianis* [begun in 1726 at Jena in Lehmann's house]. The first draft of the work grew to be a manuscript of 820 very clearly written quarto pages. There was indeed no subsequent increase in the number of pages; it remained the same. Yet as the years went by, the late author had written so much additional material in many a chapter that at times there was more in the margin and between the regular text than the space available on a quarto page would permit.

Vorrede. XVII

Ich finde, daß der Herr Verfasser auf alles, was sich im Gebiete der Tonkunst zugetragen, aufmerksam gewesen ist, und dasjenige, was er entweder in Büchern hier und da zerstreut angetroffen, oder ihm aus eigener Erfahrung nach und nach bekannt worden, fleißig in sein Manuscript eingetragen, und durch gewisse Zeichen angedeutet hat, wo es in dem Texte seine Stelle haben sollte. Wo eine Sache in der von ihm selbst edirten Anleitung zu der musikalischen Gelahrtheit schon war berührt, oder völlig abgehandelt worden, da hat er nur entweder auf dem Rande, oder auch (wenn der Rand schon vollgeschrieben gewesen) oft zwischen den Textzeilen, in jene verwiesen; manchmal aber auch eine Sache nochmals hier vorgetragen, ob sie gleich in kaum gedachter Anleitung fast mit gleichlautenden Worten zu lesen ist. Diesen letzten Umstand wird man hin und wieder beym Durchlesen bemerken, wenn man sich die Mühe nehmen will, ein und anderes Kapitel der Anleitung mit gegenwärtiger Arbeit zu vergleichen. Es hat aber dieses nicht anders seyn können, weil, wie der Augenschein lehret, einige Kapitel in der Anleitung aus dieser Musica mechanica Organoedi genommen worden, und also blos als ein Auszug aus derselben anzusehen sind. Was Wunder demnach, daß auch die Worte in beyden Büchern an manchen Oertern gleichlautend befunden werden. Ein billig denkender Leser wird diesen Umstand dem sel. Herrn Verfasser gern zu gute halten, und durch die Vorstellung, daß jedes Buch von beyden ein Buch für sich sey, bestens entschuldigen.

Was ich endlich III. bey der Ausgabe dieses Werks geleistet, bestehet in folgenden dreyen Stücken.

1) Habe ich aus dem Manuscripte des Herrn Verfassers ein ganz neues Manuscript zum Drucke verfertiget, in welchem ich alles dasjenige in gehörige Ordnung gebracht, was in der mir von den Adlungischen Erben ausgehändigten Handschrift bald auf dem Rande, bald zwischen den Zeilen

I have found that the author has taken note of everything that pertains to the discipline of music, and has diligently entered into his manuscript those things that he has either encountered scattered hither and yon in books, or has gradually become aware of through his own experience. These he has provided with specific signs that indicate where they belong in the text. If he has already touched upon a matter in the *Anleitung zu der musikalischen Gelahrtheit* that he published, or has covered it thoroughly, then he has simply referred to it in the margin or often (if the margin was already covered with writing) between the lines of the text [in the manuscript]. Sometimes, though, he has also repeated the treatment of a matter, although it may be read in almost identical words in the abovementioned *Anleitung*. One will note this to be the case here and there in reading through [the work], if one wishes to take the trouble to compare this or that chapter of the *Anleitung* with the present work. This could hardly have been otherwise, however, since several chapters of the *Anleitung** were taken from this *Musica mechanica organoedi*, as may clearly be seen, and are thus to be considered simply as excerpts from it. It is no wonder, then, that the words are found to be identical in both books. After a bit of reflection, the reader will consider this situation to the credit of the late author, and gladly excuse it upon realizing that each of the two books is a book in itself.

III. Finally, my part in editing this work may be comprised under the following three headings.

1) from the author's manuscript I have prepared an entirely new printer's manuscript, in which I have arranged in proper order everything that was found, at times in the margin, at times between the lines, and even at times on separate sheets, in the manu-

* Chapters 6-10.

des Textes, bald aber auch auf besondern Blättern geschrieben stand. Dabey habe ich mich äusserst gehütet, daß ich in der Schreibart und im Ausdrucke des Herrn Verfassers nichts geändert, sondern alles so gelassen, wie ich es gefunden. Daß ich aber in diesem Werke die mir gewöhnliche und geläufige Orthographie durchaus beyzubehalten gesucht, wird hoffentlich niemanden zum Anstoße gereichen: denn bey diesem Ablungischen Manuscripte, in welches so viele Jahre ein= und nachgetragen worden, war es schwer, eine gleichförmige Rechtschreibung, so, wie sie der sel. Herr Verfasser etwan möchte im Sinne gehabt haben, zu beobachten: theils weil alle Blätter mit häufigen Abbreviaturen angefüllet waren, theils, weil der Hr. Verfasser selbst auch da, wo sein Manuscript deutlich geschrieben war, nicht immer einerley Regeln der Rechtschreibung vor Augen gehabt hat. Vielleicht werden manche Leser wünschen, ein und andere Stelle dieser musikalischen Mechanik den Sachen nach bestimmter, und der Schreibart nach fließender abgefaßt zu sehen; und ich kann nicht in Abrede seyn, daß dieser Wunsch bey mir selbst unter währender Ausfertigung sich öfters geäußert, so daß ich einmal auf die Gedanken kam, alles, was für den heutigen Geschmack nicht fließend genug schien, anders einzukleiden: allein die Vorstellung, daß ich mir, als ein bloßer Herausgeber, dergleichen Recht wol nicht anmassen dürfe, ohne dazu besondere Erlaubniß zu haben, hat mich davon abgehalten. Wer auch über dieses den Herrn Verfasser aus seiner Anleitung hat kennen lernen, der wird gewiß nicht Ursache haben, sich über dessen Schreibart zu beschweren, sondern überall finden, daß er die Worte den Sachen so anzupassen gewußt, daß man damit sehr wohl zufrieden seyn kann.

2) Sind hin und wieder einige Anmerkungen von mir unter den Text gesetzt worden, um einen und andern Umstand mehr zu erläutern, und dann und wann Anweisung zu geben, wo man von einer vorkommen=

den

script delivered to me by Adlung's heirs. In doing this I have taken great pains not to alter anything in the author's writing style or expression, but to leave everything exactly as I found it. I hope that it will cause no one offense, however, that I have sought to maintain throughout this work the spelling that is usual and familiar to me. It was difficult to observe a uniform spelling practice, such as Adlung might have had in mind, in a manuscript that had been added to over so many years, in part because every page was filled with frequent abbreviations, in part because the author did not always have in mind uniform spelling rules, even where his manuscript was clearly written. Perhaps many readers might have wished to see here or there in this *Musical Mechanics* a matter more precisely worded or more elegantly written, and I cannot deny that I myself often expressed that wish during the process of copying [the work]. At one point I even had the idea of recasting everything that did not seem fluent enough for today's taste; the only thing that kept me from it was the realization that as a mere editor I did not dare to presume that right without special permission. Furthermore, anyone who has become acquainted with the author through his *Anleitung* will certainly have no cause to complain about his writing style, but will find that he has everywhere fitted the words to his subjects so skillfully as to provide complete satisfaction.

2) Here and there I have placed a number of notes of my own underneath the text, to explain this or that detail more fully, and to provide instruction now and then as to where one may find further

Vorrede.

den Materie mehr nachzulesen finden könne; auch ist in denselbigen bisweilen etwas berichtiget worden, wenn ich nämlich fand, daß der Herr Verfasser unsichern Nachrichten getrauet hatte. Wo ich etwann eine gegenseitige Meynung in den Anmerkungen geäußert, da habe ich solche also vorgetragen, daß derjenigen Hochachtung, welche ich für den sel. Herrn Auctor habe, mit keiner Sylbe zu nahe getreten worden. Die Anmerkungen habe ich mit Vorsatz nicht gehäuft, sondern mich in allem so kurz gefasset, als es hat möglich seyn wollen. Sie sind durch das ganze Buch mit Zahlen 1. 2. 3. u. s. w. bezeichnet, und werden dem Hochgeehrtesten Leser zu unpartheyischer Prüfung überlassen.

3) Ist diesem Werke nebst gegenwärtiger Vorrede auch ein nützliches Register von mir beygefüget worden, damit man, indem man etwas von dieser oder jener Sache aufsuchen will, dasselbige durch Hülfe desselbigen sogleich finden könne. Zu dem Ende habe ich dem Register alle mögliche Vollkommenheit zu verschaffen gesucht, damit der Hochgeehrteste Leser nichts drinnen vermissen, sondern alle Hauptsachen, Wörter und Namen finden möge.

So weit gehen meine eigene Bemühungen bey diesem Werke.

Hiernächst kann ich unangezeigt nicht lassen, daß der berühmte Königl. Preußische Hofcomponist, Herr Johann Friedrich Agricola in Berlin, auf des Herrn Verlegers ergebenstes Ansuchen, sich so gefällig erwiesen, diesem Werke theils durch verschiedene Anmerkungen, theils durch beträchtliche Zusätze, noch eine mehrere Vollkommenheit zu verschaffen. Die Besitzer dieses Werks haben dabey sehr viel gewonnen, und es ist kein Zweifel, es werden dieselben dem Herrn Hofcomponisten Agricola für seine Bemühung den verbindlichsten Dank abzustatten nicht ermangeln. Was mich anlanget;

so

information about the matter being discussed. In these notes I have also occasionally corrected something, when I discovered that the author had depended upon dubious information. Where I have occasionally expressed a conflicting opinion in the notes, I have done so in order that not a single syllable [of mine] may transgress upon that great respect in which I hold the author. I have purposely refrained from the proliferation of notes; rather I have been as brief as the matter would permit. Throughout the entire book [the notes] are marked with the numbers 1, 2, 3, etc.. I commend them to the honorable reader's impartial scrutiny.

3) In addition to this foreword, I have also added to this work a useful index, so that with its help one may be able to find immediately this or that subject as desired. To that end I have attempted to make the index as complete as possible, so that the honorable reader will find nothing lacking in it, but may be able to find all the main subjects, words and names.

This is the extent of my efforts on behalf of this work.

Next, I cannot let it pass unnoted that the renowned Royal Prussian Court Composer, Mr. Johann Friedrich Agricola* in Berlin, in response to the publisher's† sincere request, was kind enough to furnish this work a greater degree of completeness, in part through various notes and in part through considerable additional material. Those who own this work have thereby gained a great deal, and without doubt they will not fail to render to Court Composer Agricola their most courteous thanks for his efforts. For my part, I do not hesitate to express to him publicly my heartiest thanks

---

* Agricola (1720-1774) was a student of J.S. Bach from 1738-41, during the time he was a student at the University of Leipzig. Thereafter he moved to Berlin, working with J.J. Quantz and C.P.E. Bach. In 1751 Frederick the Great named him Royal Prussian Court Composer. The notes he added to the *Musica mechanica organœdi* confirm him as a faithful disciple of his teacher.

† The publisher, Friedrich Wilhelm Birnstiel, had a longstanding connection with the students and admirers of J.S. Bach in Berlin. It was he who first published Bach's chorale settings, under the title *Vierstimmige Choralgesänge*, in two volumes: a volume of 100 published in 1765 (ed. F.W. Marpurg and C.P.E. Bach), and a second volume of 100 in 1769 (ed. by J.F. Agricola). Agricola must have been working on the second volume at the same time J.L. Albrecht submitted Adlung's work for publication; it seems likely that Birnstiel requested Agricola's editorial assistance with the *Musica mechanica organoedi*.

so habe ich keinen Anstand nehmen wollen, Demselben für den mir bey diesem Werke geleisteten Beystand mein dankgeflißenstes Herz öffentlich an den Tag zu legen, und Ihn aller möglichsten Gegendienste auf das getreueste zu versichern.

Hierbey muß ich noch erinnern, daß dasjenige, was der Herr Agricola hinzugethan, von dem meinigen entweder durch vorgesetzte (**) oder durch kleine griechische Buchstaben unterschieden sey.

Denen zu Gefallen, welche geschmeidige Bände lieben, hat der Herr Verleger die bequeme Einrichtung gemacht, und dieß Werk in zwey Theile getheilet, damit es ein jeder Besitzer nach Belieben in einen, oder zween Bände könne einbinden lassen.

Ich empfehle dieß Adlungische Werk der geneigten Beurtheilung vernünftiger Kenner; mit dem angefügten Wunsche, daß meine daran gewandte Arbeit nicht ohne Nutzen seyn möge.

Mühlhausen,
im Monat Januar
1 7 6 8.

M. Johann Lorenz Albrecht.

MUSICA

for the assistance he has afforded me in this work, and to assure him most sincerely of all possible service in return.

Here I must also mention, that whatever Mr. Agricola has added may be distinguished from my [notes] either by (**) preceding it or by lower-case Greek letters.

To accommodate those who prefer flexible volumes,* the publisher has devised its convenient layout, and divided this work into two sections, so that each owner may have it bound into one or two volumes, as he wishes.

I commend this work of Adlung to the gracious judgment of enlightened connoiseurs, together with the wish that the labor I have expended upon it may not have been in vain.

* i.e., less thick and cumbersome, more convenient. Most publishers at this time did not provide books already bound, but rather the unbound sheets in signatures. Birnstiel could easily have arranged to have the sheets bound as the customer wished; the copies of the *Mmo* known to survive, however, are in two volumes bound as one.

Mühlhausen,
in the month of January
1 7 6 8.

Johann Lorenz Albrecht, M.A.

MVSICA MECHANICA ORGANOEDI.

Zweyter Band.

MUSICA MECHANICA ORGANOEDI

Volume Two

Das XI. Kapitel.

Von den Unkoſten bey einer Orgel.

Inhalt:

§. 316. Der Preis der Orgeln iſt ungewiß. §. 317. Weil die Materialien nicht allezeit einerley Preis haben §. 318. Eine Orgel hat mehr Materialien als die andere. §. 319. Sonderlich gilt dies bey den Regiſtern. §. 320. Dabey muß man die Proportion treffen. §. 321. auch dabey auf die Intonation regardiren. §. 322. auch ob der Orgelmacher Zeit dazu hat oder nicht. §. 323. Nach anderer Orgeln Preiſe kann man ſich nicht allezeit richten, wenn man nicht weis, ob, und wie die Koſt gerechnet worden. §. 324. Curiöſe Vergleichung der Naumburgiſchen und Jenaiſchen Orgel. §. 325. Was die Schwarzburgiſche gekoſtet hat. §. 326. Imgl. die Büſeleber. §. 327. Das Schnitzwerk. Man ſoll einem guten Arbeiter lieber etwas mehr geben.

§. 316.

Unter allen Kapiteln iſt dies wol das ungewiſſeſte. Den Preis einer Orgel und ihrer Theile zu beſtimmen, iſt meiner Seits eine Verwegenheit; weil es kaum Orgelmachern eintrift: viel weniger mir. Wer es demnach nicht leſen will, oder nicht für nöthig erachtet, der ſchlage es vorbey. Es ſoll auch deswegen kurz werden, und will ich nur einige Dinge anbringen, was für die, welche eine Orgel verdüngen ſollen, dienet. Es ſey aber ferne von mir, daß ich rechtſchaffener Orgelmacher Arbeit taxiren ſollte. Es wird auch keiner ſo einfältig ſeyn, und ſeinen Handel blos darnach einrichten wollen: ſondern ich will nur einiges Nachdenken erwecken, daß man ſehe, es ſey keine ſo leichte Sache, eine Orgel zu bauen.

Chapter XI.

Concerning the Cost of an Organ

Contents:

§.316. The cost of organs varies. §.317. Because the materials are not always the same price. §.318. One organ contains more materials than another. §.319. This is especially true with regard to the stops. §.320. The proportion* must be taken into account. §.321. And the voicing must also be considered. §.322. Also whether the organbuilder has time for it or not. §.323. The prices of other organs cannot always serve as guides, unless the way of calculating their cost is known. §.324. An interesting comparison between the organs at Naumburg and Jena. §.325. What the organ at Schwarzburg cost. §.326. Likewise the one at Büseleben. §.327. The carving. It is preferable to pay a good worker somewhat more.

* i.e., the alloy of the metal.

§. 316.

This is indeed the most indefinite of all the chapters. It would be audacious of me to specify the price of an organ and its components, since organbuilders seldom get it right, much less I. Accordingly, anyone who does not wish to read it, or considers it unnecessary, should turn past it. For that reason it should also be brief; I wish only to bring forward several matters that will serve those who are preparing to contract for an organ. Far be it from me to set a price on the work of upstanding organbuilders. Nor should anyone be so naïve as to conduct his dealings exclusively according to [my suggestions]. Rather I only want to arouse reflection, leading to the realization that building an organ is no easy matter.

Kap. XI. Von den Unkosten bey einer Orgel.

§. 317.

Man hört zuweilen eine Orgel taxiren; man spricht: sie habe so und so viel gekostet; will man nun dergleichen setzen lassen, und erwägt nicht alle Umstände der erstern: so wird man betrogen. Denn es sind verschiedene Dinge, die den Preis der Orgeln ändern. Zum Exempel: die Materialien sind nicht immer in einerley Werth; Holz, Bley, Zinn, Meßing, Drat, Elfenbein, Leder, rc. werden einmal so bezahlt, das anderemal wieder anders. Wer will nun den Orgelmacher zwingen, ein Werk vor eben das Geld, als das andere zu machen, wenn die Materialien theurer, als damals, bezahlt werden müssen? Oder wie kann der Orgelmacher mit gutem Gewissen so viel fordern, wenn die Materialien wohlfeiler sind, als bey der andern? Ferner sind die Materialien nicht allezeit in einerley Güte, daher auch ihr Preis steiget und fällt.

§. 318.

Ein Orgelmacher macht zierlichere und accuratere Arbeit, als ein anderer; folglich so kann man auch von dem einen nicht verlangen, für gleiches Geld gleich große Orgeln zu bauen. Zu einer Orgel werden mehr oder weniger Materialien erfordert; wie kann denn der Preis einerley seyn? Es wird etwann auf einem Dorfe in eine schmale Kirche ein Werk gesetzt, welches die und die Stimmen hat; man hat es enge in einander setzen müssen wegen Mangel des Raums. Es soll aber in der Stadt in einer breiten Kirche ein Werk mit eben denselben Stimmen gebauet werden, da man die Orgel so viel als möglich ausbreiten muß, um den Staat zu formiren; sollte wol dieses für eben das Geld geschehen können? Nimmermehr: denn es gehöret weit mehr Holz, Leder, rc. dazu, als zu der engen Dorforgel.

§. 319.

Die Register sind auch nicht von einerley Materie; also ist auch ihr Werth nicht einerley. Eine zinnerne Pfeife kostet freylich mehr, als eine bleyerne von gleicher Größe: weil ein Centner Bley (nach Beschaffenheit der Zeiten) über 4 Rthlr. nicht kömmt; da das Zinn wol mit 10 Rthlr. bezahlet werden muß. Und obwol das Zinn hingegen leichter wiegt, daß man mehr Pfeifen aus einem Centner machen kann, als aus dem Bley; so trägt es doch so viel nicht aus, das nicht eine zinnerne Pfeife, der Materie wegen, höher kommen sollte. Nicht allein aber dies, sondern man hat auch zu rechnen, daß die Arbeit bey zinnernen Pfeifen gar sehr schwerer und saurer ist, als bey dem Bley. Das Zinn zu hobeln ist gar eine harte Arbeit; aber das Bley wird mit leichter Mühe gehobelt. Auch ist ein Register in der Orgel höher oder geringer legirt, als in der andern; das ist, es ist unter das Zinn mehr oder weniger Bley gemischt, folglich wird so wol wegen der Materie als auch wegen der Arbeit der Preis müssen ungleich werden; denn je weniger Bley dazu kömmt, desto schwerer ist das Metall zu arbeiten.

§. 320.

Chap. XI. Concerning the Cost of an Organ

§. 317.

One hears at times the price of an organ stated; someone says that it has cost this or that much. In determining a price for a similar [organ], one would be misled unless one considers all the factors surround the former's [price]. For there are various things that alter the price of an organ. For example: the materials are not always of the same worth; wood, lead, tin, brass, wire, ivory, leather, etc., are sometimes one price, sometimes another. Who would want to force the organbuilder to build one instrument for exactly the same [amount of] money as another, when the materials must be bought at higher prices than they formerly were? Or how can the organbuilder with a clear conscience demand as much, if the materials are cheaper [for one organ] than for another? Furthermore, the materials are not always of the same quality, and thus their price rises and falls.

§. 318.

One organbuilder does more elegant and accurate work than another. Consequently one cannot demand that they build organs of equal size for the same price. A [given] organ will require more or less materials; how then can prices be identical? Perhaps a small village church will have an organ with such and such stops that have had to be crammed together because space is lacking. On the other hand, a spacious city church is to be provided with an instrument with the same number of stops; here the organ must be spread out as much as possible, for the sake of appearance. Should it cost the same [amount] of money? Of course not! It will require far more wood, leather, etc. that did the cramped village organ.

§.319

Since the stops are not of the same material, their value is therefore not the same. A tin pipe obviously costs more than a lead one of the same size, since a hundred-weight of lead (according to the prevailing economic conditions) will not cost more than 4 Reichsthaler, while [the same amount] of tin will cost 10 Reichsthaler. And even though, on the other hand, tin weighs less, so that more pipes can be made out of a hundred-weight than from lead, nevertheless the difference is not so great as to bring the cost of a tin pipe down to that of a lead one (speaking in terms of material). What is more, one must also consider that working with tin pipes is much more difficult and troublesome than working with lead. Planing tin is very hard work, while planing lead is less trouble. Furthermore, one stop in an organ may have a greater or lesser alloy than another, that is, more or less lead is mixed in with the tin. Consequently prices have to be different both because of the material as well as the work, since the less lead that is used, the harder the metal is to work with.

§. 320.

Es mögte auch einer meynen, Principal 4′ im Gesichte müsse nicht höher kommen, als Oktave 4′ inwendig, posito, daß sie einerley Materie haben, und auch einerley Größe; aber das kann abermal nicht seyn: denn eine Pfeife im Gesichte muß viel netter gearbeitet und gehobelt werden, als sie inwendig sind: die Labia müssen sauberer werden; ja, was das meiste ist, die Füsse müssen nach dem Staat und nach juster Proportion gemacht werden, viel größer als inwendig es nöthig ist: folglich kostet es mehr Metall und Arbeit, also muß es auch theurer kommen. So hat man zu raisonniren von andern, die im Gesicht stehen, oder inwendig. Also muß ein Violon 16′ im Gesichte mehr kosten, als inwendig, ob schon die Materie zuweilen einerley ist.

§. 321.

Es sind auch viel Register, die zwar nicht so viel Materie brauchen, als ein anders, und doch theurer kommen wegen der Intonation, die bey manchen gar schwer ist, und dem Orgelmacher viel Arbeit macht. Also kann man keinem verdenken, wenn er bey dem Violon, Violdigamba, Quintatön 16′ ꝛc. wegen der Intonation mehr fordert, als deren Größe und Materie es scheint zu verstatten.

§. 322.

Auch geht die Rechnung nicht an, daß ich wollte sagen, z. Er. Principal 8′ kostet so viel, 16′ ist noch eins so groß, folglich kostet selbiges noch einmal so viel. Da betrügt man sich sehr. Denn wenn Principal 16′ in einer Weite wäre mit 8′, so wäre es schon noch eins so groß, und kostete schon noch eins so viel Metall, ohne was bey dem Fuße wieder abgehet. Nun ist es aber auch viel weiter, als 8′; also gehört auch vielmehr Metall dazu, als noch einmal so viel, wie §. 243. schon erinnert worden. Hingegen wird die Arbeit in etlichen verdoppelt, als Hobeln, Löthen, ꝛc.; aber im Aufschnitt und Intoniren hat der Orgelmacher nur einfache Arbeit. Das alles muß man rechnen. So ist es auch mit allen Stimmen. Daraus sieht man also, was für Umstände bey der Bestimmung des Werths theils eines ganzen Orgelwerks, theils einzelner Stimmen, zu beobachten. Hierzu kömmt noch dieses, daß der Orgelmacher zuweilen zu Hause bleiben und bauen darf; zuweilen aber darf er dieses nicht thun. Dies letztere thut ihm in der Kundschaft schaden: denn wenn in seiner Abwesenheit etwas zu verdienen kömmt, so ist er drum. Ein anderer bekömmt Zeit zu bauen, so lange er will, und kann alles nach seiner Commodität machen, und was er dazwischen verdienet, ist auch seine: dahingegen ein andermal die Sache getrieben wird. Da wird auch das Pretium verändert. Item, man hört den Preis einer Orgel nennen; aber man weis nicht, ob die Orgelbauer dabey die Kost bekommen, oder nicht, oder, ob Kostgeld dabey sey gegeben worden, oder nicht? Wie kann man sich denn in Bauung einer andern Orgel darnach richten?

Chap. XI. Concerning the Cost of an Organ

§.320.

One might also think that a Principal 4′ in the façade should not cost any more than an Oktave 4′ inside the case, given that they are of the same material and size. Once again this does not hold true, for façade pipes must be far more neatly wrought and planed than ones inside. The lips must be finer, and most of all, for the sake of appearance the feet must be made in proper proportion, much larger than is necessary inside the case. This requires more metal and more work, consequently it has to be more expensive. This is how to evaluate the difference between other [pipes] that stand in the façade and those inside the case. A Violon 16′ in the façade must therefore cost more than one inside, even though the material is sometimes identical.

§.321.

There are also many stops that do not require as much material as others, to be sure, but nevertheless cost more because of their voicing, which in many cases is exceedingly difficult and causes the organbuilder a great deal of work. Therefore no one should be blamed for demanding more for a Violon, Violdigamba, Quintatön 16′, etc., on account of its voicing, than its size and material would seem to permit.

§.322.

Calculating [the cost] also does not work by saying, e.g., that since an 8′ Principal costs so much and a 16′ is twice as large, consequently the latter ought to cost twice as much—this would be totally in error. For if a 16′ Principal were the same width as an 8′, it would indeed be twice as large and would indeed require twice as much metal, discounting the difference in the feet. But it is in fact much wider than an 8′, and thus requires much more than twice as much metal, as has already been mentioned in §.243. On the other hand, in some ways the work would [only] be double, such as in planing, soldering, etc.—but in the cut-up and the voicing the organbuilder would have quite a simple task. All of this must be taken into account. This is the way it is with all the stops. From this may be seen what sort of things have to be considered in part in determining the worth of an entire organ, and in part of single stops. Consider furthermore that the organbuilder may sometimes remain at home to do the building, while at other times this is impossible. His absence from home costs him business; for if any service work arises during his absence, he is out of it. Another [builder] might be given unlimited time to build, and can arrange everything at his convenience; whatever he earns in the meantime is his business. Other times a builder might be pressured to finish. That also affects the price. Likewise one hears an organ's price specified, but does not know whether or not the organbuilder has gotten his board in addition, or whether he has been given an allowance for his board. How is it possible to build another organ using this as a guide?

Kap. XI. Von den Unkosten bey einer Orgel.

§. 323.

So weis man auch zuweilen nicht, ob dem Orgelmacher die Materialien dazu sind gegeben worden. Da nun alles dieses zu regardiren ist; so bleibts dabey, daß es nicht wohl zu bestimmen, was der eigentliche Preis einer Orgel, oder jedes Theils derselben, sey. Von den Orgelmachern selbst könnte man zwar in diesen Stücken vieles erfahren: aber sie sagen die Wahrheit nicht so leicht. Ich will also nur die Kosten etlicher Orgeln hersetzen, deren Dispositionen ich im vorhergehenden 10ten Kapitel eingeschaltet. Ich kann aber nicht allezeit melden, ob diese oder jene Umstände dabey sind, weil ich sie nicht weis. Auch kann ich nicht sagen, ob die Orgelmacher bey deren Setzung die alte Orgel daran bekommen; als welches noch ein Punkt ist, der den Preis der Orgeln verschiedentlich macht. Hernach will ich etliche Stimmen und deren Pretium hinzeichnen, so viel ich nemlich ungefehr gehöret; aber die Legirung ist abermal dabey nicht angemerkt. Es ist also nur eine Nachricht præter propter.

Bey der Orgel zu Gera §. 301. hatte Trost (**) jedes Registers Gewicht be-

(**) Trost hat diese Orgel nicht gebauet, sondern Fink aus Saalfeld. Es muß also dieses wol ein Schreibfehler seyn.

nennet, und endlich die Materie determinirt, die ihm zu reichen. Ich will es hersetzen, nicht als wenn ich glaubte, daß nicht zuweilen etwas zuviel sollte gesetzt seyn; sondern daß der Leser einigermaaßen wisse, was zu den Stimmen gehöre. Principal 8′, 14löthig, hält 184 Pfund. Quintatön 16′, 343 Pfund Metall. Violdigamba 8′, 160 Pf. Bordun 8′, 130 Pf. Vox humana, wie sie §. 301. beschrieben, hat ohne das Blech 140 Pf. Metall. Gemshorn 8′, 165 Pf. Rohrflöt 4′, 48 Pf. Oktave 4′, 68 Pf. Gemsquinte 6′, 70 Pf. Cylinderquint 3′, 28 Pf. Sesquialter 1½′, 25 Pf. Superoktave 2′, 28 Pf. Mixtur 6 fach 2′, 82 Pfund. Principal 4′, 11löthig Zinn, 65 Pf. Nachthorn 4′, 46 Pf. Flöte douce 4′, 38 Pf. Metall. Gemshorn 4′, 60 Pf. Italienische Quinte 3′, 34 Pfund. Gemsquinte 1½′, 28 Pf. Oktave 2′, 28 Pf. Sesquialter aus 2′, 18 Pfund. Mixtur 2′, 4fach, 60 Pf. Quintatön 8′, 68 Pf. Principal 2′, 20 Pf. 14löthig. Gedackt 8′, 64 Pfund. Nachthorn 4′, 36 Pf. Dolcan 4′, 38 Pfund. Oktave 1′, 18 Pf. Quinte 1½′, 20 Pf. Mixtur 3fach, 1′, 28 Pf. Principal 16′, 14löthig Zinn, 588 Pfund. Das Facit jeder Materie kann man selbst machen, wobey zu wissen, daß das Bley nach Mollen gerechnet wird. Hingegen Wißmuth, Meßingen- und Eisendrat, wie auch Meßingenblech wird Pfundweise, und Weißblech Tafelnweise gerechnet. Weißgahre Kalb- und Hammelfelle rechnet man zu Decher; ein Decher hat 10 Stücke oder Felle. Lohgahres Rindleder geht nach Pfunden. Leim kauft man Steinweise. Ein Stein hat 21 Pfund. Hausenblasen in den Leim kauft man ebenfalls Pfundweise. Ueber dies braucht man Eichenholz; reine andere Bretter; noch ander Holz; Unschlitt zum Löthen; Wachs; gerissene Pferdadern zu den Bälgen, welche Pfundweise bezahlt werden; Buchsbaum oder Elfenbein, oder was man sonst für Materie zu den Claviertasten nehmen will; Pfundleder; rothen Bolus;

Kolo-

Chap. XI. Concerning the Cost of an Organ

§.323.

Sometimes it is also not known whether the organbuilder has been given building materials. Since all of this has to be considered, then I repeat that it is not good to specify [here] what the actual price of an organ or any component of an organ should be. Organbuilders themselves could teach us a great deal in these matters, but they are not always so quick to tell the truth. Thus I will merely state the prices of certain organs whose stoplists I have included in Chapter 10 above. I cannot always report, though, whether this or that condition is present, since I do not know. I also cannot say whether the organbuilder has been given the old organ as part of the bargain; this is another point that alters the price of an organ. Afterwards I will indicate certain stops and their prices roughly to the degree I have heard about them. The alloy, though, is not noted with them. Thus this is only an provisional report.

In the organ at Gera, §.301, Trost(**) has stated each stop's weight, and then

(**)Trost did not build this organ, but rather Fink[e] from Saalfeld. This must be a slip of the pen. [Agricola]

specified the materials to be given him. I will record this so that the reader may know to some degree what goes into each stop—not that I do not believe that his amounts are at times exaggerated. Principal 8′ 14-part* [tin] contains 184 pounds; Quintatön 16′, 343 pounds of metal; Violdigamba 8′, 160 lbs.; Bordun 8′, 130 lbs.; Vox humana, as described in §.301, contains 140 lbs. of metal, without the sheet iron; Gemshorn 8′, 165 lbs.; Rohrflöte 4′, 48 lbs.; Oktave 4′, 68 lbs.; Gemsquinte 6′, 70 lbs.; Cylinderquint 3′, 28 lbs.; Sesquialter 1 3/5, 25 lbs.; Superoktave 2′, 28 lbs.; Mixture 6 ranks 2′, 82 lbs.; Principal 4′, 11-part tin, 65 lbs.; Nachthorn 4′, 46 lbs.; Flöte douce 4′, 38 lbs. of metal; Gemshorn 4′, 60 lbs.; Italienische Quinte 3′, 34 lbs.; Gemsquinte 1½, 28 lbs.; Oktave 2′, 28 lbs.; Sesquialter from 2′,† 18 lbs.; Mixture 2′, 4 ranks, 60 lbs.; Quintatön 8′, 68 lbs.; Principal 2′, 14-part [tin], 20 lbs.; Gedackt 8′, 64 lbs.; Nachthorn 4′, 36 lbs.; Dolcan 4′, 38 pounds; Oktave 1, 18lbs.; Quinte 1½, 20 lbs.; Mixture 3 ranks, 1′, 28 lbs.; Principal 16′, 14-part tin, 588 pounds. The reader may figure the total amount of each material for himself, keeping in mind that lead is figured in pigs.‡ On the other hand, bismuth, brass and iron wire, and sheet brass are figured by the pound, and tin-plated sheet iron by the sheet. Tanned white calfskin and sheepskin are figured by bales; one bale has 10 pieces or skins. Tanned cow-leather comes by the pound. Glue is bought by the stone; one stone contains 21 pounds. Isinglass in the glue is likewise bought by the pound. In addition one must have oak, other clean lumber, as well as other wood; tallow for soldering; wax; stripped horse-veins for the bellows (these are bought by the pound); boxwood or ivory, or whatever kind of material the keys are to be made of; heavy leather; Armenian bole;§ resin; spirits; vinegar; not to mention

* "14löthig;" see §. 87.

† i.e., Terz 1 3/5 ′; see §.197.

‡ "Mollen" (=Mulden).

§ See §. 38.

Kap. XI. Von den Unkosten bey einer Orgel. 7

Kolophonien; Brandtewein; Eßig; ohne was das Eisenwerk macht. NB. Man muß beym Zinn und Bley allezeit den 10ten Theil darüber nehmen, als sonst eine Stimme angeschlagen wird; denn an 10 Pfund wird allezeit eins im Gusse abgehen. Man braucht auch Brennholz, Licht und Kohlen.

Werkmeister erzählt in der Orgelprobe Kap. 26. S. 65. daß er, um von dem Gewichte unterrichtet zu werden, aus einem alten Orgelwerke das Pfeifwerk gekauft, und habe, nachdem solches gewogen worden, befunden, daß das zinnerne Principal 8′, von C, D, E, F, Fis, G, Gis, bis $\bar{c}$, 165 Pfund gewogen, andere aber 200, und noch andere 220 Pfund. (Nachdem nämlich das Zinn pur ist, oder nicht: oder nachdem viel Bley dabey; oder nachdem es im Arbeiten dünne ausgeschunden wird.) Das Principal 4′, nach eben den vorigen clavibus 60 Pfund, andere haben 85 Pf. Gedackte von ziemlich gutem Metalle 8′, 127 Pf.; (hierbey hätte Werkmeister das Loth anzeigen sollen) andere haben 120, und noch andere 140 Pf. Quintatön 16′, 260 Pf. und; andere 271. Quintatön 8′, 116 Pfund; andere 125. Oktave 4′, 49 Pf., andere 54. Quinte 3′, 22 Pfund; andere 25 Pf. Oktave 2′, 15 Pfund; andere 18. Gedackt 4′, 72 Pfund; andere 76. Mixtur 5 fach, die größte Pfeife 1′, 60 Pf. 4 fach, die größte Pfeife 2′, kann 90 haben. Oktave 1′, 10 Pfund. Mixtur 3 fach, 1′, 32 Pfund. Man merke noch, daß auch die verschiedene Mensur eine Varietät in der Materie zuwege bringen kann. [61]

§. 324.

Die Naumburgische Wenceslaiorgel, wie sie im 10ten Kapitel der Disposition nach eingeschaltet worden, (**) soll 10000 Rthlr. gekostet haben: etliche aber geben

(**) Es ist wol zu merken, daß hier von der alten Orgel in dieser Kirche die Rede ist. Die ist aber vom Herrn Zacharias Hildebrand ganz umgeschmolzen, und eine sehr schöne an ihre Stelle gesetzt worden, deren Disposition oben auch beygebracht ist.

nur 8000 an. Beydes ist genug. Zwar sind wichtige Stimmen darinnen, als 2 mal Principal 16′; Mixtur 10 fach, ꝛc. Aber wenn man es gegen 2500 Rthlr. hält, so viel nämlich die Jenaische Stadtorgel gekostet, und betrachtet die Orgeln unter sich; so ist entweder jene zu theuer bezahlt worden, oder diese ist halb geschenkt. Wir wollen sie gegen einander halten, und erstlich sehen, was für Stimmen beyden gemein sind, hernach was die Naumburgische voraus hat, und ob der Ueberrest so viel austrägt. [62] Beyden gemein sind: Untersatz 32′, Posaune 16′; Tremulant, Koppelpedal, Trompete 8′, im Pedal; it. 8′ im Manual; Oktave 8′ im Pedal; Oktave 4′ im Pedal;

[61] Die Bälge sind ebenfalls hier nicht zu vergessen, als welche auch eine theure Sache sind. Weis man nun nicht genau, wie viel, oder wie groß, solche gemacht worden; so betrügt man sich in der Rechnung, wenn man sich beym Bau eines neuen Orgelwerks auf ein anders in Absicht auf den Preis der Bälge, berufen will.

[62] Diese Vergleichung hat der Hr. Verfasser in seiner Anleitung zu der musikalischen Gelartheit S. 530. Anmerk. h) dem geehrtesten Leser vorzulegen versprochen. Hier erfüllet er nun sein gethanes Versprechen.

Chap. XI. Concerning the Cost of an Organ

the parts made of iron. N.B. There must always be a tenth more tin and lead than is estimated for a stop, for one pound in ten is always lost in casting. One must also have firewood, lighting and coal.

In his *Orgelprobe*, Chapter 26, p. 65, Werkmeister relates that, in order to become informed about weights, he bought the pipes from an old organ, and discovered upon weighing them that an 8′ Principal of tin, from C, D, E, F, F#, G, G# up to c‴, weighed 165 pounds, while others weighed 200 pounds and still others 220 pounds (that is, according to whether the tin is pure or not; or according to how much lead in mixed with it; or according to how thin it has been cut. A 4′ Principal with the same notes weighed 60 pounds, while others weighed 85 pounds. Gedackts of quite fine quality metal weighed 127 pounds (Werkmeister should have indicated in addition the alloy), while others weighed 120 lbs. and still others 140 lbs. A 16′ Quintatön, 260-271 pounds; 8′ Quintatön, 116-125 lbs; 4′ Oktave, 49-54 lbs; 3′ Quinte, 22-25 lbs; 2′ Oktave, 15-18 lbs; 4′ Gedackt, 72-76 lbs; 5-rank Mixture (the largest pipe being 1′), 60 lbs; 4-rank [Mixture] (the largest pipe being 2′), around 90 lbs; 1′ Oktave, 10 pounds; 3-rank Mixture 1′, 32 pounds. Note in addition that variations in scale can cause variety in the [amount of] material.[61]

§.324.

The organ at St. Wenceslaus Church in Naumburg, whose stoplist has been included in Chapter 10,(**) is said to have cost 10,000 Reichstaler—others indicate

(**) Note that here Adlung is speaking about the old organ in this church. It has been completely melted down, however, by Mr. Zacharias Hildebrand, and replaced by a very beautiful [new organ], whose stoplist has also been included [in Chapter 10] above. [Agricola]

only 8,000. Either amount will suffice. To be sure, there are some heavy stops in it, such as two 16′ Principals, a 10-rank Mixture, etc. But if one compares this amount to 2,500 Reichsthaler, which is what the organ at the Jena Stadtkirche cost, considering the actual organs themselves, then either the former was too expensive, or the latter underpriced. Let us compare them with each other, first to see what stops they have in common, and then what the one at Naumburg has above [the one at Jena], and whether the extra was worth it.[62] They have in common: Untersatz 32′; Posaune 16′; Tremulant; pedal coupler; Trompete 8′, both in the pedal and in the manual; Oktave

61) The bellows must also not be forgotten here, since they are also an expensive item. If one does not know precisely how many there are to be made or how large they are to be, then one can be misled in figuring, if one depends on the price of a given set of bellows to determine that of the ones in the new organ. [Albrecht]

62) On p. 530, note h, of his *Anleitung zu der musikalischen Gelahrtheit*, the author promised to submit this comparison to his honored readers. Here he fulfills his stated promise. [Albrecht]

Pedal; **Waldflöte** 2'; **Stern**; **Principal** 8' im Manual, ist zu Jena zweymal, dort einmal, aber bey **Principal** 16' ist **Oktave** 8', die mag dem gleich gehen; **Oktave** 4' im Manual 2 mal; **Principal** 4'; **Quinte** 3' 2 mal (zu Naumburg 3 mal.) **Rauschpfeife**; **Oktave** 2', 3 mal; **Mixtur** ist daselbst 10fach, zu Jena 6 fach; **Quintatön** 16'; **Violdigamba** 8'; **Gemshorn** 8'; **Quintatön** 8', **Mixtur** 4 fach; **Gedackt** 2 mal, 4' und 8. Was hat denn die Naumburger Orgel voraus? Antwort: Viel; doch die Jenaische auch etliches, und wollen wir sehen, ob wir können einiges dran geben. **Principal** 16' ist dort einmal mehr. Hingegen haben wir zu Jena den **Violon** 16', der wenig nachgiebt, und ist er auch von Metall; wäre also hier in der Güte des Metalls ein Unterschied, welches doch soviel nicht austrägt. Sagt man: der **Violon** geht nur in 2 Oktaven; Antwort: die andern beyden Oktaven machen nicht viel, weil die Pfeifen klein und nur 4' bis 1' sind; doch will ich davor rechnen die **Oktave** 4', welche zu Jena in der Sesquialter ist, da ihre Sesquialter dieselbe nicht mit in sich hält. Dafür ist zu Jena die **Rohrflöte** 8', o von o geht auf. Sie haben den **Fagott** 16'; im Jena ist **Subbaß** 16' dagegen: und glaube ich nicht, daß der Fagott durchs ganze Manual gehe. So brauche ich weiter nichts gut zu thun. Sie haben die **Quinte** 3' einmal mehr, als in Jena. Dafür will ich in Jena eine **Quinte** 3' von der Sesquialter nehmen; so geht es gleich auf. Ihre **Mixtur** ist 10fach, die Jenaische 6fach: allein diese ist 4füßig, jene aber 2füßig, wird also fast mit einander aufgehen. Oder wenn ich freygebig bin, mag ein **Cymbel** 3 fach dafür gerechnet werden. Die dritte Mixtur ist bey ihnen auch 4fach, dafür wollen wir das **Rohrnasat**, und die andere **Cymbel** 3 fach rechnen. Sie haben in Naumburg **Flöte douce** 8'; dahingegen in Jena **Grobgedackt** 8' mehr gezählt wird, als dort. Sie haben die **Waldflöte** einmal mehr; dafür will ich eine **Flöte douce** 4' rechnen. Sie haben **Hohlflöte** 8'; ich will in Jena die **Quinte** 6' und noch eine 1½' dafür rechnen. Sie haben **Quintatön** 8'; dafür will ich eine **Oktave** 4' rechnen aus einer Sesquialter: die sind von einerley Werth. Sie haben drey **Sesquialtern**: aber es sind nichts, als **Terzen** über **Oktave** 2'. Dafür kann ich rechnen diese 2 Terzen von den jenaischen zwoen Sesquialtern, und die **Sifflöte**. Sie haben **Bombard** 8'; dafür ist in Jena **Bordun** 16' im Manual. Ich sehe nichts mehr als 2 **Schallmeyen** 4' und noch ein **Schnarrwerk**, dessen Namen ich nicht weis. Ich besinne mich aber, daß in Jena noch nicht gerechnet worden der **Flötenbaß** 4' im Pedal; eine **Quinte** 3' bey der andern Sesquialter; **Cornetbaß** 2' und die Ventile. Nun ist nichts mehr übrig. Und gleichwol sehe ich fast keinen Vorzug der Naumburgischen Orgel, vor der Jenaischen, es müßte denn derselbe im Gebäude stecken. Doch beliebe man zu überlegen: in Jena sind elfenbeinerne Claviertasten, in Naumburg hölzerne. In Jena ist die Orgel bequem in einander gebauet, in Naumburg aber ist ein Rückpositiv, welches was garstiges ist. 63) Die Jenaische ist vorn mit eichenen Brettern bekleidet; die

Naum-

---

63) Mit diesem Ausdruck dürfte wol nicht jedermann zufrieden seyn. (**)

(**) Viele dürften wol gar sagen, ein gut gebautes Rückpositiv wäre was schönes.

8 Chap. XI. Concerning the Cost of an Organ

8′ and 4′ in the pedal; Waldflöte 2′; [Zimbel]stern; manual 8′ Principal occurs twice at Jena, and only once at Naumburg, but there is an Oktave 8′ with the Principal 16′, and these we may consider identical; Oktave 4′ twice in the manual; Principal 4′; Quinte 3′ twice (three times at Naumburg); Rauschpfeife; Oktave 2′ three times; the Mixture at Naumburg is 10 ranks, that at Jena 6 ranks; Quintatön 16′; Violdigamba 8′; Gemshorn 8′; Quintatön 8′; Mixture 4 ranks; Gedackts at 4′ and 8′, twice. What does the organ at Naumburg have in addition? A great deal—but the organ at Jena has a number of things as well. Let us see if we can indicate some of them. At Naumburg there is another 16′ Principal. On the other hand, Jena has a Violon 16′, which is hardly inferior, and is also of metal; thus the only difference would be in the quality of the metal, and this does not amount to much. It might be said that the Violon has only a two-octave compass; but the other two octaves do not amount to much, because the pipes are small, from 4′ to 1′. But in their place I shall count the Oktave 4′, which is in the Sesquialter at Jena, while Naumburg's Sesquialter does not include it. In its place at Jena is the 8′ Rohrflöte, and the score stands tied. Naumburg has a 16′ Fagott; Jena has a 16′ Subbass instead, and I doubt that the Fagott goes through the entire manual compass. Thus I consider them equivalent. Naumburg has one more Quinte 3′ than Jena; in its stead I will take a 3′ Quinte from the Sesquialter—the score is still tied. Naumburg's Mixture is 10 ranks, while Jena's is 6; but the former begins at 2′, the latter at 4′—thus they are almost equivalent. Or, to be generous, a 3-rank Cymbal could be counted in its stead. The third Mixture at Naumburg is also 4 ranks; for it we may count the Rohrnasat and the other 3-rank Cymbal. Naumburg has a Flöte douce 8′; on the other hand, the Grobgedackt 8′ at Jena counts for more. Naumburg has one more Waldflöte; for it I will count a Flöte douce 4′. Naumburg has an 8′ Hohlflöte; for it I will count Jena's Quinte 6′ together with another 1½′. Naumburg has an 8′ Quintatön; for it I will count an Oktave 4′ from a Sesquialtera, since they are of the same value. Naumburg has three Sesquialteras, but they are nothing but thirds above the 2′ Oktave [i.e., 1 3/5′]. For them I can count the 2 Terzes from the Jena Sesquialteras together with the Sifflöte 1′. Naumburg has an 8′ Bombard; for that there is a manual Bordun 16′ at Jena. I do not see anything else [at Naumburg] except two 4′ Schalmeis and one other reed whose name I do not know.* I recall, however, that the pedal Flötenbass 4′ at Jena has not yet been counted, and also a Quinte 3′ in the second Sesquialtera, a Cornetbass 2′ and the ventils.† That accounts for everything. I must say that I see nothing superior in the Naumburg organ, unless it be the case. Yet consider, if you please: Jena has ivory keys, while Naumburg has wooden ones. In Jena the organ is conveniently built into one case, while Naumburg has a Rückpositiv, a detestable thing.⁶³⁾ **⁾ The front of the organ at Jena is covered with oak boards, while the one at Naumburg is not. The former [organ] is constructed

* See the stoplist for the organ at St. Wenceslas, Naumburg, Pedal, No. 10, in Chapter 10.

† It is curious that Adlung includes the ventils among the stops, but he is obviously trying to make the organ at Jena look as superior as possible to the one at Naumburg.

---

63) Not everyone would be content with this assertion. [Albrecht]

(**) Many would go so far as to say that a well-built Rückpositiv is a beautiful thing. [Agricola]

Naumburgische aber nicht. Jene ist in allen Stücken beständiger und besser gemachet, daher bey großer Dürrung kein besonderer Fehler daran zu spüren, dahingegen diese bey heißem Wetter fast nicht zu brauchen war, und ordinair nach Pfingsten nicht viel taugte, weil der Wind aller Orten ausgieng. In Naumburg waren nur 4 Bälge, |2 ins Manual und 2 ins Pedal, welche alle wenig nutzten, und mit Papier verklebt waren, auch keinen Wind hielten, sondern liefen als wenn sie tolle wären. Zu Jena sind 9 Bälge, davon einer bessere Dienste thut, als dort alle viere. Was den Klang betrift; so klingt die Jenaische Orgel sehr anmuthig, und dabey frisch: hingegen war der Klang der Naumburgischen matt und hölzern: denn sie hatte keine Cymbeln und eigentlich sogenannte Sesquialtern, welche das Leben der Orgeln sind. Ihre 10fache Mixtur machte die Schärfe allein nicht aus. Vielleicht schlugen viel Pfeifen davon nicht an. Kurz: mir hat die Orgel in Jena allezeit besser gefallen, als die in Naumburg, ob sie wol kaum den dritten Theil so theuer ist. Und setzte ich sie auf 5000 Rthlr. an; so ist der Abschlag von 10000 gar zu groß. Der Contrabaß 32′ in Jena hat auch noch 16′ offen bey sich.

§. 325.

Die Reglerorgel in Erfurt kostet 600 Rthlr. doch haben sie eine alte daran gegeben, wie auch die Kost. Die obgemeldete Augustinerorgel daselbst kostet, soviel ich weis, 1000 Rthlr. Die Schwarzburgische Orgel §. 314. kostete 400 Rthlr., wie sie oben erzählet worden; der Orgelmacher bekam aber folgende Materialien dazu: 8 Centner Zinn; 8 Centner Bley; 25 Pfund meßingen Drat und Blech; 1 Centner Leim; 6 Pfund Wißmuth; 5 Pfund Hausenblasen; 4 Kannen *Spiritus vini* unter den Leim; 18 Decher Leder. (Ein Decher ist 10 Stück oder Felle.) 6 Pfund Elfenbein; 8 Cymbeln; 30 Bohlen von Eichen zu den drey Windladen; 1 Schock dergleichen Holz zu den Registerzügen und Ausspündung der Laden; 2 Schock Bretter von Kienbaum zum Gehäuse; 1 Schock Fichtenbretter zu den Abstrakten und Wellen; 30 Bohlen von Kienbaum zu den Balgplatten; 2 Schock Kienbaumbretter zu Pfeifen und Windröhren; 2 Klaftern Holz zum Plattengießen. In Summa alles was noch an Eisenwerk und andern Sachen nöthig war. Dies habe ich beygesetzt, daß, wenn man die Materialien schaffen soll, man einigermaßen wisse, was für Zeug dazu gehöret. Hierbey kann man dasjenige nochmals überlegen, was kurz vorher §. 323. aus Werkmeisters Orgelprobe angeführet worden.

§. 326.

Die Herbstleber Orgel kostet 1100 Rthlr, ohne die alte, welche vor 37 Rthlr. 12 Gr. gerechnet ward. Die Büseleber Orgel, deren Disposition §. 286. zu finden, hat Hr. Schröter aus Erfurt gemacht, da im Contrakt diese Dinge auf folgende Art angeschlagen waren. Z. E. Clavierlade von Eichenholz, darauf stehen sollen die obbenannten Stimmen, für 30 Rthlr. Die andere weis ich nicht. Das Gehäuse und Simswerk kostet 56 Rthlr. Die 2 Claviere von Elfenb..., Pedal und Angehänge 32 Rthlr.

better and more durably in every way, so that no particular fault may be detected in it in a prolonged dry spell; in contrast, the latter [organ] became* almost unusable in hot [dry] weather, and was ordinarily of no use after Pentecost, since the wind leaked out everywhere. In Naumburg there were only 4 bellows, 2 for the manuals and 2 for the pedal; but all of them were of little use; they were patched over with paper, but still did not hold any wind even though they ran like crazy. At Jena there are 9 bellows, any one of which gives better service than all four put together at Naumburg. As far as tone is concerned, the organ at Jena sounds quite pleasant, and brisk as well. In contrast, the tone of the organ at Naumburg was dull and wooden, since it had no Cymbels and true Sesquialteras, that are the life of an organ. Its 10-rank Mixture alone was not enough to provide brilliance; perhaps many of its pipes did not speak. In short, I have always found the organ at Jena more pleasing than that at Naumburg., even though it was barely a third as expensive. Even if I were to give its cost at 5,000 Reichsthaler, the difference between [that sum and] 10,000 is far too great. Oh, yes—the Contrabass 32′ at Jena also has an open 16′ [that plays] with it.

* Now Adlung is speaking of the old organ at Naumburg as a thing of the past.

§. 325.

The organ of the Reglerkirche in Erfurt† cost 600 Reichstaler, but they gave the old organ in trade, as well as supplying room and board [for the organbuilder]. The organ at the Augustinerkirche cited above‡ cost, to the best of my knowledge, 1,000 Reichsthaler. The organ at Schwarzburg, §. 314, cost 400 Rthlr., as has been reported above. However, the organbuilder received in addition the following materials: 8 hundred-weights of tin; 8 hundred-weights of lead; 25 pounds of brass wire and sheet iron; 1 hundred-weight of glue; 6 pounds of bismuth; 5 pounds of isinglass; 4 containers of alcohol mixed with the glue; 18 bales of leather (one bale has 10 pieces or skins); 6 pounds of ivory; 8 little bells; 30 oak planks for the three windchests; 30 pieces of the same [kind of] wood for the drawknobs and for sponselling the chests; 60 pieces of scots-pine lumber for the case; 30 pieces of spruce lumber for the trackers and rollers; 30 scots-pine planks for the bellows-plates; 60 pieces of scots-pine lumber for the pipes and the wind conduits; 2 cords of [fire]wood for casting the sheets [of pipe metal]; in sum, everything necessary for the metal parts and other components. I have included this so that, if one wishes to procure the materials, one may know in some measure what sorts of things are needed. In this regard one might once again ponder what was quoted just above in §.323, from Werkmeister's *Orgelprobe*.

† See the stoplist of this organ in Chapter 10.

‡ See the stoplist of this organ in Chapter 10.

§. 326.

The organ at Herbstleben§ cost 1,100 Rthlr., not including the old organ, which was appraised at 37 Rthlr., 12 Gr[oschen]. The organ at Büseleben, whose stoplist may be found in §. 286,¶ was built by Mr. Schröter of Erfurt, so that these things were agreed upon in the contract in the following way: e.g., "manual chest of oak, upon which are to stand the stops named above, for 30 Rthlr." I do not know about the other [organ‖]. The case and molding cost 56 Rthlr; the two keyboards of ivory, the pedal and [its] action 32

§ See Chapter 10 for this stoplist.

¶ See Chapter 10 for this stoplist.

‖ i.e., the one at Herbstleben, mentioned above.

32 Rthlr. Drey Bälge, jeder 10 Schuhe lang und 5 breit; it. Registratur, Leder, Eßig, Eisen; Druckschrauben, Roßadern, vor 60 Rthlr. Principalbaß 8' im Gesicht, von gutem Zinn, vor 30 Rthlr; weil er nur durch 2 Oktaven geht. Principal 8' im Gesicht, gut Zinn dazu, vor 18 Rthlr. Dito 2' ins Gesicht, 12 Rthlr. Grobgedackt 8', vor 18 Rthlr. Quintatön 8', à 18 Rthlr. Violdigamba 8', 30 Rthlr. Quinte 3', vor 16 Rthlr. Oktave 2' von Metall, vor 10 Rthlr. Mixtur 4fach, vor 25 Rthlr. Cymbel 3fach, vor 10 Rthlr. Stillgedackt 8', vor 16 Rthlr. Nachthorn 1', vor 15 Rthlr. Spitzflöte 4', vor 15 Rthlr. Sesquialtera 3fach, vor 25 Rthlr. Scharp 3fach, vor 18 Rthlr. Quinte 1½', vor 6 Rthlr. Waldflöte 2', vor 8 Rthlr. Posaunbaß 16', von Holz, vor 25 Rthlr. Subbaß 16', von Holz, vor 16 Rthlr. Ich will sagen, daß sie doch wol auf sechstehalb hundert Rthlr. gekommen, ohne die Kost. Ob dies auch allezeit dafür werde gezahlet werden, weis ich nicht.

Von andern Stimmen weis ich wenig specielles, was sie kosten. Das Principal 8', ins Gesicht, wenn es im Manuale ist, mögte etwan auf 40 bis 46 Rthlr. kommen. Die Quintatön 16' wird fast gleiches Werthes seyn. Stern, etwan von 6 Glocken, ungefehr 3 Rthlr. Tremulant à 2 Rthlr. Der Violon ist an einem Orte vor 50 Rthlr. gemacht worden von gutem Metall ins Gesicht; er wird aber zuweilen höher bezahlt. Daß aber so große Stimmen viel kosten, ist kein Wunder. Es gehört gar viel Metall dazu. Prätorius l. c. führet an, daß zu Costnitz die größte Pfeife 24' lang sey, (sie geht nur ins F) und halte 3 Centner im Gewicht. Man hat nicht zu sehen blos auf das Anwachsen der Länge und Weite der Pfeife, sondern in großem Pfeifwerk werden auch die Blätter stärker. So sagt er auch Tom. II. P. IV. p. 162. Das zu Ulm die größte Pfeife 315 Ulmer Maaß Wein (das sind 157½ Stübchen, oder 8 Eimer oder 4 Ohmen) halte. Solche Pfeifen kosten was.

§. 327.

Was zum Gebäude selbst gehört, nebst der Tischlerarbeit, muß der Orgelmacher, besorgen. Aber das Schnitzwerk läßt die Kirche apart machen durch die Bildhauer; welches aber auch eine theure Sache ist. Das Mahlen und Vergolden gehört auch nicht für die Orgelmacher. Mehr fällt mir itzt nicht ein; ich will also nur soviel noch rathen: wenn man einen Orgelmacher haben kann, von dem man gewiß weis, daß er gute Arbeit macht, und auch sonst treu und aufrichtig ist; so nehme man ihn, ob auch gleich ein anderer für weniger Geld eben solche Stimmen verfertigen wollte, von dessen Accuratesse wir uns so viel nicht versprechen können.

Im vorigen 10ten Kapitel ist bey manchen Orgeldispositionen angemerkt, wie hoch dies und jenes Werk zu stehen gekommen. Das kann man dabey nachlesen, um sich einigermaaßen bey Erbauung eines neuen Werks darnach richten zu können. Es wird auch nicht ohne Nutzen seyn, wenn man bey Renovirung eines alten Orgelwerks dasjenige in Ueberlegung nimmt, was ich von neuen Werken beygebracht habe.

Rthlr.; three bellows, each 10 feet long and 5 wide, as well as the stop apparatus, leather, vinegar, iron, screws, and horse veins, for 60 Rthlr.; Principalbass 8′ in the façade, of fine tin, for 30 Rthlr., since it only goes through two octaves; Principal 8′* in the façade of fine tin for 18 Rthlr.; the same at 2′ in the façade, 12 Rthlr.; Grobgedackt 8′ for 18 Rthlr.; Quintatön 8′ for 18 Rthlr.; Violdigamba 8′, 30 Rthlr.; Quinte 3′ for 16 Rthlr.; Oktave 2′ of pipe metal for 10 Rthlr.; Mixtur 4 ranks for 25 Rthlr.; Cymbel 3 ranks for 10 Rthlr.; Stillgedackt 8′ for 16 Rthlr.; Nachthorn 4′ for 15 Rthlr.; Spitzflöte 4′ for 15 Rthlr.; Sesquialtera 3 ranks for 25 Rthlr.; Scharp 3 ranks for 18 Rthlr.; Quinte 1½′ for 6 Rthlr.; Waldflöte 2′ for 8 Rthlr.; Posaunbass 16′ of wood for 25 Rthlr.; Subbass 16′ of wood for 16 Rthlr. I would say that all this would amount to 650 Rthlr.,† without board. Whether these would be always be the prices, I cannot say.

I know little in particular as to what other stops cost. A manual 8′ Principal in the façade might cost, say, between 40 and 46 Rthlr. A 16′ Quintatön would be almost the same amount; a [Zimbel]stern, say with 6 bells, about 3 Rthlr.; a Tremulant, 2 Rthlr.. At one place a Violon [16′?] in the façade of good metal was built for 50 Rthlr., but sometimes [such a stop] will cost more. It is, however, no wonder that such large stops cost a lot—they require a great deal of metal. Praetorius, *l.c.*,‡ indicates that at Costnitz§ the largest pipe is 24′ tall (it only goes down to F) and weighs 3 hundredweights. One must consider not only the increase in the pipes' length and width, but also that the metal sheets must be thicker for large pipes. He also says in Vol. II, Part IV, p. 162, that the largest pipe at Ulm holds 315 *Ulmer Maass* of wine (that is 157½ *Stübchen*, or 8 *Eimer* or 4 *Ohmen*.¶ Pipes like that cost a pretty penny.

§. 327.

The organbuilder must see to whatever pertains to the case itself, as well as to the cabinetry. But the church should have the woodcarving done separately by a sculptor; this is also an expensive item. Painting and gilding are also not part of the organbuilder's work. Nothing else occurs to me at the moment, but I would advise the following: if you can find an organbuilder, the quality of whose work is assured, and who is also honest and upright, you should choose him, even though another (whose exactitude we set no great store by) might be willing to build certain stops for less money.

In Chapter 10 above I have noted in connection with many stoplists how much this or that instrument has ended up costing. You may consult these as guidelines for the approximate cost of building a new organ. It would also be worthwhile when rebuilding old organs to take into consideration the things I have imparted concerning new instruments.

---

* Both the stoplist in as well as the price stated below suggest that Adlung means 4′ instead of 8′.

† This amount does not agree with that stated in the stoplist, 550 Rthlr.

‡ *Syntagma musicum*, Vol 2, p. 162; but there is no prior citation of Praetorius in this chapter.

§ Praetorius is referring to Constance, since he lists Hans Buch[n]er as a former organist there; cf. Vol. II, Foreword (above), p. IV.

¶ An *Ohm* is about 35 modern gallons or 168 liters; thus the pipe would have held about 140 gallons or 672 liters.

Das XII. Capitel.
Vom äusserlichen Zierrath einer Orgel.

Inhalt:

§. 328. Der Endzweck des Kapitels. §. 329. Gegen welche Plagam die Orgel zu setzen? §. 330. Hoch oder niedrig? §. 331. Die Orgel muß Licht haben. §. 332. Ob das Abendlicht durchfallen solle? §. 333. Man soll die Orgel ausbreiten. §. 334. Die größten metällenen Pfeifen kommen heraus. §. 335. Man theilt das Pfeifwerk in Felder und Thürme. It. was die Eurythmie sey? §. 336. Was die Symmetrie erfodere? §. 337. Von blinden Feldern. §. 338. Von hölzernen Pfeifen auswendig. §. 339. Das Pfeifwerk sey von aussen sauber. §. 340. Vom Simswerke. §. 341. Vom Schnitzwerke. §. 342. Von Engeln, Sonnen u. s. w. §. 343 Gitter über den Feldern. §. 344. Elfenbeinene Claviere und Rückpositiv. §. 345. Von den Registerknöpfen. §. 346. Verwahrung der Orgel oben, hinten und auf beyden Seiten.

§. 328.

In diesem Kapitel wird nicht auf das Gehör, sondern blos auf das Gesicht gesehen. Denn wie man in unsern Kirchen nicht nur auf nöthige Dinge reflectirt, sondern auch den Staat oder äusserliches Ansehen observirt, so weit es mit der Andacht bestehen kann: so wird auch dieses beym Orgelbau sonderlich beobachtet. Und gewiß, wenn eine Orgel recht angelegt wird, so ist es eine besondere Zierde des Gotteshauses. Wir wollen einige Principia aus der Architektur und Optik beybringen, nach welchen eine Orgel aufzuführen, in sofern es das äusserliche Ansehen befördern soll. Denn die andern Principia überlassen wir den Zimmerleuten und Tischlern, welche sie gleichfalls wissen.

§. 329.

Nach den principiis opticis fragt es sich: Wohin ein Werk zu setzen? Gegen Morgen, Abend, Mittag oder Mitternacht? in die Höhe oder Tiefe? Das erste anlangend, so werden unsere Kirchen ordentlich länger von Abend gegen Morgen, als sie breit sind von Mittag gegen Mitternacht. Gegen Morgen wird ordentlich der große Altar gebauet, weil die alten Christen, und auch wir an vielen Orten den Gottesdienst mehr früh als des Abends verrichten, wobey die Prediger vor dem Altare singen und lesen müssen, folglich des Lichts, das von Morgen ihnen besser zufällt am meisten benöthiget sind. Nun ist nach der Optik gerade gegen über ein solch groß Werk am bequemsten aufzuführen, das ist, gegen Abend. Das will die Eurythmie haben, welche ist, wenn die Theile eines Gebäudes so angelegt werden, daß auf jeder Seite ein Stück dem andern Stücke respondiret, und je eine Seite gleiche Stücke mit der andern habe; doch verkehrt, daß, was auf einer Seite dem äusserlichen Prospekte nach auf der Linken gestanden, solches auf der andern Seite nach der Rechten zu stehe; die einzelnen Stücke werden

Chapter XII.
Concerning the Exterior Decoration of an Organ

Contents:

§.328. The purpose of this chapter. §.329. On which axis* to place the organ. §.330. High or low? §.331. The organ must receive light. §.332. Whether the evening [sun]light should shine through [from behind the organ.] §.333. The organ should be spread out. §.334. The largest metal pipes should be set in the façade. §.335. The [façade] pipes are divided into flats and towers; the meaning of "Eurythmy." §.336. The requirements of symmetry. §.337. Concerning blind flats. §.338. Concerning wooden pipes in the façade. §.339. The façade pipes must be neat. §.340. Concerning cornices. §.341. Concerning [wood]carving. §.342. Concerning angels, suns, etc. §.343. Pipeshades above the flats. §.344. Ivory keyboards; the Rückpositiv. §.345. Concerning the stopknobs. §.346. Securing the organ on top, behind, and on both sides.

* "Gegen welche *Plagam*;" Adlung also uses the Latin term *plaga* in Chap. 28, p. 166. For him, it seems to mean "hindrance" or "obstacle"; thus the literal translation of this phrase would be "Toward which obstacle," i.e., toward which wall of the church.

§. 328.

In this chapter we will be considering not sound, but exclusively appearance. For our churches do not reflect merely what is necessary, but also take into account display or outward appearance, insofar as it can be reconciled with devotion, and this is observed especially in the building of an organ. To be sure, if an organ is properly constructed, then it is a particular ornament to a place of worship. We shall put forward several principles from architecture and optics according to which an organ should be erected, insofar as they promote [a good] outward appearance. Other principles we shall leave to carpenters and cabinetmakers, since they are also well acquainted with them.

§. 329.

One might ask: According to the principles of optics, where is the best place to position an instrument—in the east, the west, the south or the north? high or low? Concerning the first [question], the length of our churches from west to east is normally greater than their width from south to north. The high altar is usually erected at the east end, since the early Christians (and also we, in many places) conduct our worship more in the morning than in the evening. In doing this, preachers must chant and read in front of the altar, and consequently are most in need of light that falls upon them chiefly from the east.† Visually speaking, then, it is most convenient to erect such a large instrument at the opposite end, that is, at the west end. This is called for by eurythmy,‡ which means that the components of a structure are so arranged that one half has exactly the same components as another, but reversed; i.e., whatever is placed in one half of the façade appears mirrored in the other half; a solitary component is placed

† Adlung presumes the traditional orientation of Christian church buildings, with the main entrance at the west end, opposite the chancel with altar and pulpit at the east end. The early church fathers offer a number of theological explanations for this orientation, but never the practical reason that Adlung assigns to it.

‡ Adlung writes "die Eurythmie".

The English word "eurythmy" means "harmonious proportion", but Adlung's definition makes it clear that he means here the more specific word "symmetry". He introduces the word "die Symmetrie" in §.336, however, with yet another meaning; therefore I have retained the English "eurythmy" for Adlung's "die Eurythmie."

werden in die Mitte gebracht. Da nun nur solche zwey Gebäude in der Kirche sind; so setzt man das andere billig gegen Abend, wenn das eine gegen Morgen steht. Es kömmt dazu, daß man alsdann die ganze Orgel nach der Breite in völligem Staate in der ganzen Kirche, wenigstens an den meisten Orten sehen kann; da hingegen, wo ein Werk an die Mittags = oder Mitternachtsseite gebauet wird, es nur diejenigen sehen, die gegen über stehen: die aber weiter gegen Morgen und Abend gestellet sind, sehen es nur von der Seite, da es gar nicht wohl in die Augen fällt; oder sie sehen wol gar nichts davon: da sonst, wenn die Orgel gegen Abend oder Morgen stehet, alle in der Kirchen sich befindende Personen sie von vornen anschauen können. Man findet sie zuweilen gegen Morgen; doch wollte ich lieber, sie stünde dem Altare gegen über, daß man den Priester sehen könne, als welches man vielmals bedarf. Doch werden sie auch heut zu Tage nicht mehr also gebauet. Die alten haben ihre Orgelwerke oft auf der Seite der Kirche angebracht; aber das ist itzo auch ganz abgekommen.

§. 330.

Fragt man weiter: Ob die Orgel hoch oder niedrig stehen soll? so dient zur Antwort: Nach unserer Verfassung sind die Weiberstühle meistens unten, und die Männerstühle oben; so gehört auch wol die Orgel oben hin. Doch habe ich sie auch ganz unten angetroffen, welches man aber itzo nicht mehr thut. Man muß hierbey billig überlegen, daß es am bequemsten sey, wenn die Sänger und Instrumentalmusici um oder vor der Orgel stehen, daß sie in besserer Harmonie bleiben; daher ich für rathsam erachte, wenn die Orgel auf dem Singchor aufstehet. Es wird aber das Singchor nicht bequem unten angelegt, weil den Sängern das Singen unter den Leuten sauer wird: eben wie eine Kanzel deswegen in der Höhe stehet, daß dem Prediger das Reden nicht so sauer werde, und doch alle ihn besser verstehen können. Folglich muß das Chor, und also mit demselben die Orgel in der Höhe angeleget werden. Wie hoch aber das Chor stehen solle, ist aus der Größe der Orgel zu bestimmen. Ueber das Singchor pflegt man keine Emporkirche aufzuführen, daher man den Platz zum Singchor erwählt, der am höchsten ist; doch muß man so tief herunterrücken, daß die Orgel auch in der Höhe Raum genug bekomme, und man nicht die großen Pfeifen inwendig anbringen, sie kröpfen, oder gar weglassen müsse, als welches das Ansehen der Orgel verdirbt. Z. Er. die Jenaische Stadtorgel hätte wenigstens noch etliche Fuß sollen Raum haben in der Höhe; denn solchergestallt hätte nicht nur Principal 8′ im Oberwerke können herausgesetzt werden, wie es itzo ist, sondern auch im Unterwerke Principal 4′ welches inwendig stehet, und Oktave 2′ ist dafür heraus gesetzt. Das mittlere Principal steht zwar haussen, doch sind die größten Pfeifen davon inwendig, wo man so große Füße nicht nöthig hat. Auch hätte Violon 16′ noch heraus gebracht werden können, da hingegen im Pedale Principal 16′ allein da stehet. Was hätte das für ein Ansehen gemacht? — Man hätte ja nur das Singchor um etliche Schuhe senken dürfen. Gesetzt, es würde itzo keine große Orgel irgendwo gebauet; so wollte ich doch rathen, dem Singchore eine überflüßige Breite

zu

in the middle. Since there are only two such structures in the church,* it is naturally to place one of them at the west end if the other stands at the east end. Moreover, then the entire breadth of the organ in its full splendor is visible throughout the entire church. On the other hand, if an instrument is built either on the south or north side, only those standing opposite it can see it. Those who are located further east and west of it have only a side view of it that does not strike the eye at all well, or indeed is not even visible. Yet if the organ stands at the west or the east end, everyone in the church can have a direct view of it. Occasionally one finds [organs] located at the east end,† but I would prefer that they stood opposite the altar, so that [the organist] can see the priest, something that is often-times required. But nowadays organs are no longer placed there. Our forefathers often erected their organs on the side of the church, but this [practice] has also been entirely abandoned.

*i.e., the altar (with its customary elaborate reredos) and the organ.

† a reference to the German Lutheran practice, already begun in the 16th century, of vertically aligning the altar, pulpit and organ at the east end of a church. A famous example of this is the Frauenkirche at Dresden. See Chap. 28, p.168, note.

§. 330.

Furthermore, if anyone should ask whether the organ ought to be placed high or low, the answer is: according to our system the pews for women are usually lower‡ and those for men are higher.§ Thus the organ should by right be located higher up. Yet I have also encountered them right on the floor, a practice that is no longer followed. In this regard one must merely keep in mind that it is most convenient for the singers and instrumentalists to stand around or in front of the organ, so that they can better maintain their harmony.¶ Therefore I consider it advisable that the organ stand where the choir sings. It is not convenient, however, to place the choir on the floor level, since singers sound harsh in the midst the congregation. For the same reason the pulpit is elevated, so that the preacher's voice does not sound so harsh, and yet everyone can understand him better. Consequently the choir together with the organ must be located up high. Just how elevated the choir should be is to be determined by the size of the organ. It is not usual to erect a balcony above the choir area; thus the place chosen for the choir is the tallest in the church, yet the choir must be kept low enough to leave sufficient height for the organ without mounting the largest pipes inside the case, mitering them or omitting them altogether—such [compromises] spoil the appearance of the organ. For example, the organ in the Jena Stadtkirche should have had at least a few more feet of height; had that been the case, then not only could the Oberwerk Principal 8′ have been placed in the façade (as is now there), but also the Unterwerk Principal 4′; that stop is inside the case and the Oktave 2′ stands in the façade in its place. To be sure, the Mittelwerk Principal [8′] is displayed, but its largest pipes are inside the case, where such large feet are not required. The Violon 16′ could also have been placed in the façade, whereas only the Pedal Principal 16′ is [now] there. What a [splendid] appearance that would have made—if only the choir could have been lowered several feet. Even though a given locale may not be building a large organ at the present time, I would still recommend that the choir area be given some extra width, as well as some extra height, as if a large

‡ i.e., on the floor in the nave.
§ i.e., in the balconies.

¶ This expression is vague; it may refer to ensemble, or harmony, or to both.

zu geben, auch eine überflüßige Höhe, als wollte man noch so ein groß Werk dahin setzen. Denn es kann vielleicht ein dergleichen Bau von unsern Nachkommen vorgenommen werden: und man bauet eher wieder eine neue Orgel, als eine Kirche. Ist aber die Kirche an sich enge; so ist es wol ein Fehler, der nicht zu ändern ist, doch sind die Kirchen selten so enge, daß man die Orgelbreite gar nicht haben könnte, wenn man alles nur recht macht.

§. 331.

Ferner hat man seine Gedanken auf das Licht zu richten. Es muß das ganze Chor, sonderlich aber der Organist, viel Licht haben. Ein Musikus kann die Stimme so nahe legen, als er will: aber ein Organist muß sie legen, wie es das Pulpet leidet; er hat auch die Ziffern bey der Abspielung eines Generalbasses zu erkennen, daher darf man ja das Licht nicht verbauen, sondern man muß es in gehöriger Menge auf das Clavier, Pulpet, ja auf die ganze Orgel fallen lassen, nicht nur der Musik wegen, sondern damit auch das Orgelwerk besser und glänzender in die Augen falle. Es fragt sich nun: Soll das Licht von der Seiten, oder von vornen, oder von hinten zu herauf fallen? Antw. Wenn die Kirche lang ist, wird zwar einiges Licht von den Morgenfenstern hinkommen, aber ein sehr schwaches; und über dies sitzt der Organist zwischen der Orgel und den Morgenfenstern, (ich rede itzt blos von den gegen Abend gebaueten Orgeln) und hält die mehresten Strahlen zurück; die Abendfenster sind hinter der Orgel, und sind nöthig, daß man in der Orgel sehen könne: aber diese Strahlen fallen nicht auf das Clavier; daher zu beyden Seiten Fenster seyn, oder gemacht werden müssen, da das Licht drauf fällt: doch soweit vornen, daß von allen Punkten des Fensters gerade Linien nach dem Claviere und Pulpet gehen: denn die Strahlen gehen in geraden Linien.

§. 332.

Es fragt sich hierbey: Ob es rathsam, einen Ort in der Orgel öfnen zu lassen, dadurch das Licht von der Abendseite in die Kirche falle und dahin etwan die Pauken zu stehen kommen könnten? Antwort: So war anfänglich die Erfurtische evangelische Augustinerorgel gebauet, da auf beyden Seiten das Pfeifwerk des Pedals war, oben das Positiv, in der Mitte auf beyden Seiten das Hauptmanual, zwischen welchen zwey Theilen es offen war, daß da die Pauken sollten geschlagen werden. Auf beyden Enden der Orgel waren auch solche kleine Chöre, darauf die Trompeter stehen sollten. Durch die mittlere Oefnung fiel das Licht durch, von dem hintern Fenster, durch die andern Chöre aber nicht. Allein wer dies hat angegeben, der hat seine Unwissenheit in der Optik dadurch an den Tag gelegt. Denn es ist bekannt, daß radii reflexi, oder zurückprallende Strahlen nicht so helle sind, als radii directi, oder die von dem hellen Sonnenkörper gerade nach eben dem Objekt gehen. Z. Er. der Mond, wenn er ganz helle, oder voll ist, ist zuweilen dem Ansehen nach größer als die Sonne, weil er so nahe ist; doch macht er unsere Erde so helle nicht, als die Sonne:

Chap. XII. Concerning the Exterior Decoration of an Organ 13

instrument were going to be placed there. For perhaps our descendents might undertake such a building project [i.e., a larger organ], and it would be preferable to build only a new organ rather than a [new] church. If the church is already narrow, then this is a fault that cannot be corrected; but churches are seldom so narrow that they cannot accommodate the breadth of an organ, provided that everything is arranged properly.

§. 331.

Furthermore, it is necessary to give some thought to [adequate] lighting. The entire choir, and in particular the organist, must have a great deal of light. An [ensemble] musician can set his score as near as he likes, but an organist must place it as the music-rack permits. He also must be able to read the figures while realizing figured bass. Thus light must certainly not be blocked, but must fall in appropriate quantity on the keyboard, the music-rack—indeed, upon the entire organ—not only for the sake of the music, but so that the organ may strike the eye more clearly and radiantly. One might ask, "Should the light shine down from the side, from the front, or from behind?" My answer would be: if the church is long, some light will indeed enter from the east windows, but it will be very weak; moreover, the organist sits between the organ and the east windows (here I am speaking exclusively of organs build at the west end), and blocks most of the rays. The west windows are behind the organ, and are necessary in order to see inside the organ,* but rays [from these windows] do not fall on the keyboard. Therefore there must be windows on both sides, or they must be be built, so that light falls upon [the keyboards], but [they must be] far enough forward so that from any point in a window a straight line may proceed to the keyboard and music-rack, since rays travel in straight lines.

* i.e., when one opens the rear panels of the case, either for tuning or repairs.

§. 332.

In this regard one might ask whether it is advisable to leave open a section of the organ [case], through which light may enter the church from the west and thus perhaps fall upon the tympani?† In answer: the organ in the Protestant Augustinerkirche at Erfurt was originally built in this way. The pedal pipes were placed on both sides, the Positiv was above, and the main manual was in the middle on both sides; between the two sections of the latter there was an opening in which it was intended that the drums were to be played. At either end of the organ there were also small galleries for the trumpeters to stand on. Light streamed in through the opening in the middle, from the window behind it, but did not fall upon the other galleries. The person who specified this [arrangement] thereby revealed his ignorance of optics. For it is well known that *radii reflexi*, or reflected rays are not as bright as direct rays, those that proceed directly from the sun and strike an object. For example, the moon when it is at its brightest, or full, sometimes appears to be larger than the sun, because it is so near, yet it does not make the earth as bright as the sun does; on the contrary, even when the thickest clouds

† Adlung seems to be posing this question in order to comment on the specific situation at the Augustinerkirche in Erfurt, which he then proceeds to describe. The practice of mounting drums more or less permanently on a gallery rail near the organ, however, was quite common in Thuringia during and after Adlung's lifetime. A set of antique kettledrums is still to be seen mounted on a gallery rail at the side of the organ at the Predigerkirche in Erfurt.

hingegen, wenn auch die dicksten Wolken vor der Sonne stehen, machen ihre Strahlen doch alles weit heller, als der Mond beym hellesten Himmel. Warum? Antw. Weil die Strahlen der Sonne von der Sonne ausgehen, und ohne an einen dichten Körper anzustoßen, gerade zu uns kommen. (Denn die refraktio bleibt wol richtig, welche aber das Licht so sehr nicht schwächt, als die reflexio.) Die Strahlen, die vom Monde zu uns kommen, sind nur reflexi, weil sie von der Sonne auf den Mond, und von dar wieder zurückprallend zu uns kommen. Wenn nun dies richtig ist; so merke man, daß, wenn wir die Orgel und ihre Pfeifen unten in der Kirche sehen wollen; so muß durch die Fenster das Licht drauf fallen, und von den Pfeifen wieder zurückprallen und zu unsern Augen kommen. Also ists ein lumen reflexum, und geringer oder schwächer, als das Licht, welches durch das Abendfenster gerade zu unsern Augen kömmt. Wie es nun in der Optik heißt: lumen maius officit minori, d. i. wo ein groß Licht zugegen, da sieht man das Kleinere nicht; also folgt, daß man bey hellem Tage, wenn die Sonne hat durch die mittlere Oefnung geschienen, die Orgel nicht hat sehen können, so wenig, als uns der Mondschein bey Tage einige sensible Empfindung in unserm Gesichte machen kann. Und so ist auch die Sache allda gewesen; daher man das Ding andern, und es verbauen müssen. Es ist deswegen das dritte Clavier dahinein gesetzt worden, an welches man sonst wol nicht würde gedacht haben. O ihr Herren Baumeister! lernt doch aus der Mathesi ein wenig mehr, als eure Architektur.

§. 333.

Ferner dient auch zum äusserlichen Staat, daß eine Orgel so weit es möglich ausgebreitet werde, nicht nur gegen die rechte und linke Hand, sondern auch in die Höhe, so viel nämlich die Höhe und Weite der Kirche verstattet. Desto eher ist dieses zu recommendiren, weil auch dadurch effektuiret wird, daß man bequem zu allen Theilen der Orgel kommen, und wo was mangelhaft wird, alles bessern und stimmen kann. Wenn man auch von Abend gegen Morgen die Stimmen ausbreiten kann, ist es sehr gut: wenigstens soll man um die Windlade herumkommen können.

§. 334.

Es muß aber in das Gebäude auch etwas kommen; daher man es mit Pfeifen anfüllt. Dabey merke man, daß man des Staats wegen die größten metallenen Stimmen ins Gesicht heraus setzt, welches also die Principale sind. Denn hölzerne Pfeifen machen keinen Staat. Wollte einer sagen: die Laden wären so breit nicht, als ich das Gebäude der Breite nach, erforderte; der merke, daß es nicht nöthig: weil man diese äussere Stimmen ohne dies selten, oder in großen Werken nie auf die Lade setzt, sondern man setzt sie in das Gesimse, welches hohl wird, und darein der Wind von der Lade geleitet wird. Zu jeder Pfeife ist eine besondere Röhre; da können ja die Pfeifen so weit abstehen, als man will, und durch solche Röhren können sie allezeit aus der Lade Wind haben. Es kömmt dazu, daß auch von einer Lade die Stimmen nicht durch das

veil the sun, its rays still make everything far brighter than the moon in the clearest sky. Why? Because the sun's rays proceed directly from the sun, and come directly to us without striking any solid object (to be sure, there is a certain amount of refraction, but that does not weaken light as much as reflection). The rays that come to us from the moon are only reflected, since they proceed from the sun to the moon, and thence are reflected to us. If this be the case, let us note that, if we want to view the organ and its pipes from below in the church, then light must fall upon them through the windows, be reflected from the pipes, and enter our eyes. It is thus reflected light, and scanter or weaker than the light that enters our eyes directly from the west window. As optics informs us: *lumen maius officit minori*,* i.e., when confronted by a greater light, one cannot see a lesser one. Thus it follows that in broad daylight, with the sun shining through the opening in the middle, one would not be able see the organ any better than one can see the moon during the daytime. This was indeed the case at [the Augustinerkirche], and thus the thing had to be changed, and [the opening] blocked up. That is why the third manual was installed there, something that otherwise would never have been considered. O ye architects! Learn a bit of science beyond what you need for your architecture.†

* "A greater light prevails over a lesser one."

† Adlung expands on this matter in Chap. 28, pp. 171-2.

§. 333.

Furthermore, it is helpful to the outward appearance of an organ to spread it out as much as possible, not only horizontally but vertically as well, as much as the height and width of the church permits. This is all the more advisable, since it makes it easy to get to all the parts of the organ to tune it and to repair anything that is defective. It is also a very good thing to leave space between the ranks from front to back; one ought at least to be able to get around on the windchest.

§. 334.

But something needs to be put inside the structure as well, and thus it is filled with pipes. In this regard, take note that the largest metal ranks, that is, the principals, are placed in the façade for the sake of display; wooden pipes do not appear imposing. If anyone should say that the chests are not as broad as I required the width of the case to be,‡ note that this is not necessary, since these façade ranks are seldom (or, in large instruments, never) placed on the chest anyway. They are placed on the case rail, which is hollowed out,§ and the wind from the chest is channeled into it. There is a separate tube [leading] to each pipe, and thus the pipes can stand as far apart as desired, and yet always be supplied with wind from the chest. In addition, the ranks on one chest do not have to be spread out across the entire case; rather, one chest may lie next to another.

‡ i.e., in §.333 above.

§ i.e., a hole is bored into it under the pipe.

Kap. XII. Vom äusserlichen Zierrath einer Orgel. 15

das ganze Gehäuse ausgebreitet werden müssen, sondern es kann eine Lade neben der andern stehen. Entweder hat das Pedal eine große metallene Stimme, oder es hat keine. Hat es keine, und es ist nur 1 Clavier; so muß man dieses freylich ausbreiten so gut man kann: hat es 2 Claviere; so können die Laden neben einander stehen, doch so, daß eine Lade ganz bleibe in der Mitten, die andere aber werde getheilet auf beyde Seiten, so, daß sie eine einschliessen. Ist ein Pedal da; so kann dessen größte Stimme entweder in die Mitte kommen, und die eine Manuallade wird auf beyde Seiten vertheilt; die andere kömmt über beyde in die Höhe, oder mitten in die Brust. Oder die Laden werden über einander gesetzt, und die Pedalstimmen werden auf beyde Seiten vertheilt.

§. 335.

Diese Pfeifen werden in gewisse Felder getheilet. Ein Feld nennet man eine Reihe Pfeifen, welche in einer geraden Linie nach einander stehen, und durch hölzerne Unterschiede von den andern abgesondert sind. Man macht auch Thürme, da eine gewisse Anzahl Pfeifen in einen halben Zirkel, oder in eine Spitze und Dreyeck eingeschlossen werden. Wie nun in allen Stücken die Eurythmie zu beobachten ist, also ist es bey diesem Stücke besonders nöthig. Wie es gegen die linke Hand aussieht, also muß es auch gegen die rechte geordnet werden. Wenn ein Thurm zirkelrund am weitesten gegen die rechte Hand stehet, so muß auch am weitesten gegen die linke Hand dergleichen stehen: wäre nächst auf einer Seite ein conus, oder Dreyeck, oder ein Feld; so muß es auch auf der andern Seite folgen, und zwar so accurat, daß auch die Pfeifen auf beyden Seiten, so viel möglich, einander gleich werden. Daher pflegt man die claues von einander zu reissen, daß, wenn zur rechten Hand c̄ kommt, zur linken cis gesetzet wird, weil es in der Größe einander in eben dem Register am gleichsten kömmt. Und so wechselt es beständig durch und durch. In Feldern und Thürmen, jeden für sich betrachtet, wird eben eine Seite gegen die andere also curythmicè angeordnet, daß unter denen, die zu dem Thurm gehören, die größte in die Mitte, die andere zur Rechten, die dritte zur Linken desselben Thurms, die vierte zur Rechten u. s. w. gestellet werden. 64) Die Felder werden aber zuweilen anders geordnet, das sie so stehen:

ꝛc. immer kleiner. Auf der andern Seite der Orgel wird eben ein solches gemacht. Der Eurythmie wegen werden auch blinde Felder Pfeifen eingesetzt, s. §. 337. Hier merke ich auch an, daß man wol zuweilen ganze Stimmen zum Schein ins Gesicht gesetzt. So ist zum Er. zu Schöningen im Schlosse, teste Prætorio, die kleine Trompet oder Posaune zum vördersten Principale zum Augenscheine hingesetzt, damit dieses dem Oberwerke respondire: die Pfeifen sind aber blind und an deren Statt stehet eine Bärpfeife 8'. §. 336.

64) Zur Eurythmie dienet auch, wenn etliche Principalpfeifen zum Theil verdoppelt werden, daß z. B. C auf beyden Seiten stehe, D auch ꝛc. Prätorius hat diesen Umstand bey Beschreibung der zu Sondershausen S. 197. angemerkt, allwo im Principalbasse 16' C D und E doppelt stehen. Wollte einer vielleicht sagen, man müßte solchergestalt der Eurythmie wegen all

Chap. XII. Concerning the Exterior Decoration of an Organ 15

Sometimes the pedal has one large metal rank, other times it has none. If it has none, and [the organ] has only one manual, one must simply spread the pipes out as best one can. If [the organ] has two keyboards, then the chests may stand next to each other, yet one manual should be directly in the middle, while the other is divided on both sides of it, enclosing the first. If there is a pedal, then its largest rank may be placed in the middle, with one manual chest divided on either side of it and the other either above both on top, or in the middle as a Brustwerk. Alternatively the chests may be placed one over the other, and the pedal ranks divided on both sides.

§. 335.

The pipes are divided into separate flats. "Flat" is the name given to a series of pipes arranged one after another in a straight line, separated from other [sections of the façade] by wooden dividers. There are also towers, in which a certain number of pipes are enclosed in a half circle or in a triangular-shaped point. Eurythmy is to be observed in all elements [of the organ], but it is particularly necessary with these.* The right side must be designed to appear exactly the same as the left. If there is a circular tower on the far right, then the same thing must stand on the far left; if the next [section] on the first side were a wedge† or triangle, or a flat, then the same thing must appear on the other side, indeed so precisely that even the pipes on both sides must be identical to each other, insofar as possible. Thus it is customary to separate notes from each other, so that if c′ stands on the right side, then c# stands on the left, since it is closest in size to the first [pipe] in that rank. This alternation is carried out consistently throughout [the entire façade]. Both halves of each flat and tower are also arranged symmetrically, so that among the pipes belonging to a tower the largest is placed in the middle, the second to the right, the third to the left, the fourth to the right, etc.⁶⁴⁾ Flats, though, are sometimes arranged differently, so that they stand thus, [with pipes becoming] smaller and smaller:

The same sort [of flat] is constructed on the other side of the organ. Blind flats‡ are [sometimes] also inserted, for the sake of eurythmy; see §. 337. Let me also note here that even whole ranks are sometimes placed in the façade for [the sake of] appearance. This is the way it is, e.g., in the Palace at Schöningen, according to Praetorius,§ where the little Trompet or Posaune is placed in view as the furthest forward of the *Principalia*¶ [in the Rückpositiv] so that it corresponds to the Oberwerk; the pipes, however, are mute, and in their place stands an 8′ Bärpfeife.

64) Eurythmy is also promoted if some of the principal pipes [i.e., ranks] are partially doubled, so that, e.g., there is a C on both sides, also a D, etc.. Praetorius had noted this circumstance in describing the [organ] at Sondershausen, [*Syntagma musicum*, Vol. II,] p. 197, where C, D and E are found doubled in the Principalbass 16′. If anyone should say that all [the pipes] should then be doubled

---

* i.e., with flats and towers.

† "*conus:*" in Vol. I, p. 53, Adlung defines the term *conus* as "cone", but here he is apparently using the word as the equivalent of "triangle".

‡ i.e., flats made up of non-speaking pipes.

§ *Syntagma musicum*, vol. II, p.190.

¶ The term *Principalia* signifies ranks standing in front of the case of each of the manual divisions. This is perhaps the most striking visual characteristic of Gottfried Fritzsche's earlier work in middle Germany.

Kap. XII. Vom äusserlichen Zierrath einer Orgel.

§. 336.

Wenn in allen Stücken die Eurythmie beobachtet wird; so läßt es gut, es mögen Thürme oder Felder gesetzt und angebracht werden: doch wenn man die Felder, Dreyecke und runde Thürme unter einander mischt; so läßt es noch besser. Wir dürfen aber auch die Symmetrie nicht vergessen. Dadurch verstehet man, wenn die Höhe und Breite eines Stückes gegen einander eine solche Proportion haben, daß es den Augen gefällt. Also wissen wir, daß ein Fenster welches so breit als lang, oder noch breiter als hoch ist, uns gar nicht gefallen will, sondern wenn die Höhe ohngefähr noch halb so groß ist, als die Breite, da sie sich zu der Höhe verhält wie 3 gegen 2, oder wie die Diapente zu der Diapason; da gefällt es uns: oder wenn eins gegen das andere noch einmal so lang ist, d. i. wie 2 gegen 1; so gehet es auch noch mit. Warum es unsern Augen nicht gefalle, wenn die Proportion anders ist, als wie hier angezeiget worden, können wir nicht sagen. Genug ists, daß, wo die Proportion der Länge gegen die Breite nicht wenigstens ist wie 3 gegen 2, es uns nicht gefällt. Darnach müssen wir uns richten, und die Felder nicht so groß machen. In großen 8füßigen Stimmen können in der untern Oktave 5 Pfeifen genug seyn. Sind die Pfeifen kleiner; so macht man deren mehr in ein Feld.

§. 337.

Wenn das Pedal 16′ im Gesichte hat; so gefällt es mir am besten, wenn die Thürme oder Felder mit den größten Pfeifen die Extremitäten der Seiten einnehmen. Die Manualstimmen können gesetzt werden nach der Symmetrie und Eurythmie, wohin man will. Ist die Höhe oder die Breite des Gebäudes so beschaffen, daß die ordentlichen vördersten Stimmen den Raum nicht alle ausfüllen; so bringe man blinde Felder hin. s. §. 135. Das kann am bequemsten geschehen zwischen den Manualladen, oder wo ein leerer Platz ist. Man kann ja so viel Metall daran wenden und blinde Pfeifen machen, welche, weil sie nicht klingen, auch weiter keiner Arbeit, Kerns, Intonation rc. benöthiget sind. So war z. Ex. bey den Thomanern in Erfurt §. 300. nicht Raum, daß das Rückpositiv wäre auf die Seite, oder über oder unter das Hauptwerk gebracht worden; deswegen Herr Volkland, das Hauptwerk desto mehr auszubreiten, gleich so viel blinde Pfeifen angebracht, als klingende im Gesichte stehen: das Rückpositiv aber stehet hinten. Will man die Pfeifen alle klingend haben, und zugleich den äusserlichen Staat einer Orgel vergrößern; so setzte man von Oktavenstimmen etwas zugleich ins Gesicht. So steht z. Ex. in Alach nebst dem Principal 8′ die Oktave 4′ völlig mit im Gesichte, und nimmt theils ganze Thürme ein, theils ist sie mit dem

Prin-

doppelt setzen, wenn anders die Thürme und Felder einer Orgel einander sollten gleich werden, dem dienet zur Antwort, daß solches nicht nöthig sey: wo aber dergleichen Verdoppelung angebracht worden, da dient sie 1) zur Verstärkung des Klanges, als welcher in der Tiefe schwächer ist, als in der Mitte. 2) So ist auch der Abschlag der Pfeifen, in Ansehung ihrer Größe, in der Tiefe weit merklicher und sichtbarer, als in der Höhe: denn in der Tiefe fällt es ganze Schuhe und Ellen ab; welches aber oben ganz anders ist.

Chap. XII. Concerning the Exterior Decoration of an Organ

§. 336.

It is fine to build either towers or flats, as long as eurythmy is observed in all elements; it is even better, however, if flats, wedges, and round towers are mixed together with each other. We must also not forget symmetry, though, by which is meant that the height and width of an object are in a proportion to each other such as will please the eyes. Thus we know that a window that is as wide as it is high, or even wider than high, cannot hope to please us, but rather if the height is approximately time and a half the width, i.e., the height to the width is in the ratio 3:2, or as the fifth to the octave,* then it pleases us; or if [the height] is twice as long as [the width], i.e., as 2:1, this also satisfies us. We cannot say why it does not please our eyes if the proportion is different than indicated here. Suffice it to say that we are not pleased whenever the proportion of the length to the width is not at least as 3:2. We must guide ourselves accordingly, and not make the flats too wide. 5 pipes may be enough in the lowest octave of large 8′ ranks. If the pipes are smaller, then more of them may be included in a flat.

§. 337.

If there is a 16′ pedal rank in the façade, I find it most pleasing if the towers or flats with the largest pipes occupy the extremities on both sides. The manual ranks [in the façade] may be placed wherever desired, according to symmetry and eurythmy. If the height or the width of a [façade] structure is so constituted that the ranks usually employed in the façade do not fill up the whole space, then blind flats may be included; see §.135.† That can happen most conveniently between the manual chests, or wherever there is a vacant place.‡ A certain amount of metal can be given over to the purpose of making dummy pipes that do not need any [painstaking] labor, languids, voicing, etc., since they do not sound. For example, at the Thomaskirche in Erfurt (§.300) there was not enough space for the Rückpositiv to be placed above, under, or to the side of the Hauptwerk; thus [the builder] Mr. Volkland, in order to spread out the Hauptwerk even further, introduced just as many dummy pipes in the façade as sounding ones; the Rückpositiv stands behind [the Hauptwerk]. If one wishes all the pipes to be sounding ones, and still at the same time to increase the outward splendor of an organ, then one may set some pipes of the octave ranks in the façade as well. Thus, e.g., at Alach the entire Oktave 4′ stands in the façade, as well as the Principal 8′, in part occupying entire

> for the sake of eurythmy, if the towers and flats of an organ are to be identical to each other, the answer is that this is not necessary; but where this sort of doubling is employed, it serves 1) to reinforce the sound, which is weaker in the bass than in the mid-range, [and] 2) to mitigate the decrease in pipe-length, which is far more noticeable and visible in the bass than in the treble; in the bass the decrease is by whole feet or [even] yards, but this is not the case in the treble. [Albrecht]

---

* Here Adlung is expressing a vestige of the notion of the neo-Platonic, neo-Pythagorean doctrine of cosmic harmony, by this late date almost passé everywhere but in Germany, according to which musical consonances are held to be the perfect ratios, to which all other proportions in the universe must conform if they are to be perfect and pleasing.

† This should read "§.335."

‡ i.e., wherever there is no chest directly behind the façade. This comment is yet another indication that Adlung views the case as a decorative screen, independent of the organ's internal structure.

Principal 8′ vermischt, und die Führungen kommen von dem Stocke zu jeder Pfeife besonders. Doch ist die Incommodität dabey, daß, wenn man hernach die Stöcke abschrauben will, man alle solche Führungen abreissen muß.

§. 338.

Das ist auch die Ursach, warum in manchen Orgeln, da keine große metallenen Stimmen sind, hölzerne Pfeifen heraus gesetzt werden, so groß als man sie hat; doch werden die nördersten Ecken abgestoßen, daß sie von vornen rund scheinen. Auch werden sie mit konischen Füßen gemacht, und mit solchen labiis, daß sie wie metallene aussehen, wenn man sie verstaniolt. So habe ich in etlichen Orgeln den Subbaß 16′ auf beyden Seiten angebracht gefunden, dadurch die Orgel noch eins so groß scheint, als vorhin; von weitem merkt man auch nicht, daß es Holz ist.

§. 339.

Damit ein Werk destomehr ausgebreitet werde, muß man die Pfeifen nicht gar zu enge zusammen bringen in den Feldern und Thürmen, sonderlich darf man den Zirkeln der runden Thürmen keinen so kleinen diametrum geben, sondern sie etwas breit anbringen. Das aussenstehende Pfeifwerk muß sonderlich glatt gehobelt und polirt seyn, daß es wie Silber aussehe. Das wissen die Orgelmacher schon zu machen: davon auch Kap. 28. etwas gedacht werden soll. Die labia werden künstlicher gemacht, als inwendig; man macht größere Füße an die Pfeifen, deren labia hernach in einer geraden Linie durch das Feld gehen, oder einen halben Zirkel vorstellen, oder einen Triangel: oder man wechselt hierinnen ab, doch daß alles mit dem passe, was gegen über steht auf der andern Seite, nach den Gesetzen der Eurythmie.

Manche suchen auch darinnen eine Schönheit, wenn man die Pfeifen im Gesichte vergoldet. Heutiges Tages ist es nicht stark Mode. Aber in alten Orgeln findet es sich oft. So sind z. Er. in der Erfurter Andreasorgel etliche Pfeifen des äussern Principals vergoldet und gemahlet. Zu Dresden im Schlosse war eine ganz übergoldete Trompete 8′, auch ein Regal 8′ ganz vergoldet. Zu Schöningen im Schlosse ist eine ganz vergoldete Posaune. (s. von allen diesen Prätor. l. c.) Wenn die ganze Orgel gemahlt ist, sonderlich wenn sie mehr Gold an sich hat, möchte es noch passiren. Sonst gestehe ich, daß mir wenigstens diese Mahlerey nicht gefällt. Will man es aber thun; so muß man auch hierin die Eurythmie nicht vergessen, daß nämlich die einander entgegenstehende Thürme auch hierin einander gleich sind. Man nimmt dazu etwan die größte Pfeife des Thurms wenn er konisch gesetzt ist; auch wol die zwey Nachbarn, der mittlern größern Pfeifen.

340.

Das Gehäuse muß mit starken Gesimswerke gemacht werden, welches über jedem Felde angebracht werden muß: entweder in einer geraden Linie, oder in der Gestalt eines halben Zirkels, oder coni, nachdem das darunter stehende Pfeifenfeld gesetzt werden soll. Man thut mit solchen Gesimsen besser, als wenn man noch so viel Kleinigkeiten daran machte,

Chap. XII. Concerning the Exterior Decoration of an Organ

towers, in part mixed in with the Principal 8′; ducts proceed from the toe-boards to each individual pipe. There is, however, an inconvenience connected with this, in that, if one wants to unscrew the toe-boards at some later time, one must disconnect all the ducts.

§. 338.

That* is also the reason why, if there are no large stops of metal, wooden pipes, the largest ones available, are placed out in front in many organs. Here, however, the forward edges are planed off, so that from the front they appear to be rounded. They are also made with conical feet, and with lips that are covered with tin foil to look like metal. Thus in some organs I have found the Subbass 16′ erected on both sides; in this way the organ appears to be twice as large as before; one does not notice from a distance that they are wooden.

* i.e., the desire to spread out the façade for a splendid display.

§. 339.

In order that an instrument may be all the more spread out, the pipes must not be set too close together in the flats and towers; in particular one must not make the circles of the round towers with such small diameters, but build them quite amply. The façade pipes must be planed especially smooth and must be polished, so that they appear like silver. Organbuilders know how to do this; more will also be said about it in Chapter 28.† The lips [of façade pipes] are made more artfully than [those] inside. The [façade] pipes are given longer feet, and consequently their lips proceed in a straight line across the flat, or form an arc, or a triangle; or these forms are employed alternately, but so that everything on one side corresponds to that which stands on the opposite side, according to the laws of eurythmy.

† p. 182.

Many people also find it beautiful if the façade pipes are gilded. Nowadays this is not the height of fashion. However, it is encountered often in old organs. Thus, e.g., in the organ of the Andreaskirche at Erfurt some of the façade principal pipes are gilded and painted. In the Palace at Dresden there was a Trompete 8′ as well as a Regal 8′, both entirely gilded.‡ In the Palace at Schöningen there is a Posaune that is completely gilded (for all of the above, see Praetorius, l.c.§ If the entire organ is painted, and especially if it has a lot of gold on it, this might fit. Otherwise I must confess that at least this [sort of] painting does not please me. If someone insists on having it, however, then in doing it eurythmy must also not be forgotten, so that the towers that mirror each other are likewise in this respect identical. The largest pipe of a tower might perhaps be chosen for this [sort of treatment] if it is [the foremost pipe] in a wedge setting; perhaps its two neighbors as well, the middle-sized pipes.¶

‡ This is incorrect; in the stoplist (Syntagma musicum, p. 187) Prætorius lists "Trompete gilded 8′, Regal gilded 4′, Krümhorn gilded 8′."

§ Syntagma musicum, Vol. II, pp. 187 and 190.

¶ i.e., presuming that there are five pipes in a tower.

§. 340.

The case must be made with strong cornices built above each flat, either in a straight line, or in the form of an arc or a wedge, according to how the pipe-flat under it is shaped. It is better to use such cornices than to add all sorts of trivia, such as scrolls,

machte, als Schnecken, Federn, Bilderchen, Mahlereyen u. s. w. Jene geben speciem firmitudinis, d. i. sie geben eine Dauerhaftigkeit zu erkennen. Nun wissen wir aus der Architektur, daß, wenn etwas speciem firmitudinis hat, es besser anzusehen sey, als wo vielerley Grips Graps untereinander zu schauen ist. Wenn man vornen Tannenholz nimmt, oder wovon man sonst gemeine Bretter schneidet; so kann man schon zufrieden seyn: wo man aber im Gesichte Eichenholz haben kann; so ist es desto besser, und wenn dasselbe dunkelbraun gebeitzt wird, steht es fast feiner, als wenn man viel Gemahltes anbringen wollte, weil durch vielerley Pinselarbeit species firmitudinis verdorben wird. Das Schnitzwerk aber bleibt weiß, und wird selbiges von Lindenholz gemacht.

§. 341.

Etliche pflegen sehr viel Schnitzwerk anzubringen, als z. Ex. Flammen, Rosen, musikalische Instrumente, Statüen, ꝛc. Das kostet viel Geld und oft wird hierin excedirt, daß die Gesimse verdeckt werden, und species firmitudinis nicht mehr bleibt. Genug ist, wenn zwischen die Füße der Pfeifen Flammen oder Pyramiden angebracht werden, damit man nicht durchsehen könne, weil sonst die hölzernen oder andere Pfeifen gesehen würden, die keinen Staat machen. Auf beyden Seiten bringt man schmale Flügel an, von Schnitzwerk, nicht aber solche, damit man die ganze Orgel bey etlichen alten Werken zuzumachen pflegte, sondern bloß zum Staat: denn von jenen sehe ich keinen Nutzen, auch ist dazu selten Raum vorhanden. Zwischen den Feldern kann etwas angebracht werden; auch oben auf der Krone. [65]

§. 342.

Wenn man Statüen, Engel und dergleichen anbringt; so können sie entweder müßig seyn, oder man giebt ihnen was zu thun, da man sie inwendig mit Pfeifen versieht, und durch Röhren den Wind hinauf kommen läßt, daß sie sich zuweilen können hören lassen. So können auch Sonnen, Stern, Schnecken u. d. gl. von metallenen Pfeifen, entweder blind, oder klingend, angebracht werden; doch so, daß dasjenige, was man nur einfach macht, in die Mitte komme: was aber auf die Seite soll, muß doppelt gemacht werden, daß nach der Eurythmie alles auf beyden Seiten vollkommen gleich sey. Z. Ex. in der Görlitzer Orgel sind viel Sonnen, wie man aus Boxbergs Beschreibung derselbigen Orgeln und dem dabey befindlichen Kupferstiche sehen kann, weswegen sie auch die Sonnenorgel genennet wird. Die kleinern Sonnen daselbst geben viel claues zur großen Mixtur; wie die doppelten Sonnen. Die große Schnecke giebt den obersten clavem im Pedale an, nämlich d; die Engel haben alle ihre

---

[65] Von dem äusserlichen Prospekte und Zierrathe der Orgeln kann man nachsehen, was Johann Jacob Schübler in Kupferstich vorgestellet hat. Mir sind davon 10 Theile in Folioformat bekannt, deren jeder ohngefehr 6 Kupfer in sich fasset: er hat aber weiter nichts dabey erinnert, sondern läßt es bey den bloßen Rissen bewenden.

plumes, cartouches, painting, etc. [The cornices] lend it a *species firmitudinis*,* i.e., they endue it with a sense of durability. We know from architecture that whenever anything has some *species firmitudinis* it looks better than where there is a hodgepodge of elements. It is satisfactory to use fir for the front [of the case], or whatever is being used for common lumber, but if it is possible to have oak for the façade, then that is all the better. If it is [simply] stained dark brown, it looks almost finer than if a lot of painting is put on it, since the *species firmitudinis* is spoiled by a lot of brushwork. The woodcarving however stays unfinished, and is executed in lindenwood.

* Latin "semblance of solidity" or "semblance of stability."

§. 341.

Some follow the practice of affixing a great deal of woodcarving, such as, e.g., flames, roses, musical instruments, statues, etc. These cost a lot of money and are often overdone, so that the cornices are covered and the *species firmitudinis* is lost. It is enough to add flames or pyramids between the feet of the pipes, so that no one can see into [the case], since otherwise the wooden or other pipes would be seen, and these do not make a good appearance. Narrow carved wings are attached on both sides [of the case], but not the sort that used to shut up the entire instrument,† like some old organs, but rather only for the sake of display. I see no use for [such doors], and moreover there is seldom enough room available for them. Some [sort of ornament] may be added between the flats, as well as on the crown at the top.⁶⁵⁾

† i.e., doors.

§. 342.

If statues, angels and the like are added, they may either be at leisure, or they may be given something to do by providing pipes inside them and conducting wind up to them through tubes so that at times they may be heard to sound. Suns, stars, scrolls and such, made of metal pipes, may likewise be added, either dummy or sounding. Yet any single arrangement must be placed in the middle, but whatever is to be on one side must be made double, so that according to eurythmy everything on both sides is perfectly identical. For example, in the Görlitz organ there are many suns, as can be seen from Boxberg's description of that organ and the copper engraving that accompanies it; this is why it is called the "sun organ."‡ In it, the smaller suns as well as the double suns provide many of the notes of the large mixture. The large scroll provides the highest

‡ See Boxberg, p.[18].

---

65) Concerning the exterior façade and the decoration of organs, one may consult the copper engravings produced by Johann Jacob Schübler.§ I am familiar with 10 series of these in folio format, each comprised of approximately 6 engravings. He has written nothing additional [to accompany the plates], but been content to provide merely the engravings. [Albrecht]

§ Johann Jakob Schübler, *Sechs nach dem wahren Ursprung eingerichtete neu-inventirte Hauß- und Kirchen-Orgeln*. [Nürnberg]: Jeremias Wolffs Kunsthändlers seel. Erben [ca. 1724-30]. There are many editions of Schübler's engravings, but only 6 depict organs.

Kap. XII. Vom äusserlichen Zierrath einer Orgel. 19

ihre Töne, (**) Auch sind Kinder da, von welchen jedes aus seiner im Munde ha-

(**) Alle diese Herrlichkeiten sollen mit der Zeit sehr wandelbar geworden seyn. Es ist also nicht rathsam, dergleichen Possen irgendwo noch nachzuahmen.

benden Posaune 8 Töne angiebt. Zu Colberg in der heil. Geistes Kirche ist ein fliegender Adler. Was der sonderliche Stern zu St. Gertrud in Hamburg für Staat mache, ist eben Kapitel 7. §. 133. zu lesen. Bey der Magdeburgischen Domorgel merken die Domküster in der Beschreibung dieser Domkirche: „Daß sie über die „Maaße schön und kunstreich mit vielen Bildern in Mannes Größe gezieret, schön „vergoldet und herrlich gemahlet sey; unter welchen am Oberwerke, zwischen den dreyen „Thürmen, König David mit der Harfe und König Salomo stehen, welche die Köpfe „hin und her drehen. Ueber dem König David stehet ein Engel mit einer Laute, und „über dem König Salomon einer mit einem Citrinchen, welche sich umdrehen: über sol„chen etliche Trompeter, welche ihre Trompeten ansetzen und auch wieder abziehen; und „über solchen allen ein schwarzer Adler, welcher sich in die Höhe hebet. Auf dem Rück„positive stehet in der Mitten ein Engel mit einem Buche und Stabe, welcher den Takt „führet; vor dessen Füßen stehet ein vergoldeter Hahn, welcher, nachdem der Organist „ausgespielet, (wenn man will) die Flügel schläget und krähet. Etwas herunter auf „solchem Rückpositive stehen 2 Engel mit Zinken, welche sich umdrehen, und unter „solchen 2 mit Posaunen, welche selbige aus und einziehen; nebst andern Bildern mehr „mit unterschiedlichen musikalischen Instrumenten". (**)

(**) Welche Kindereyen! Sollen diese die Andacht befördern?

§. 343.

Weil die Felder und Thürme nicht alle Pfeifen gleich lang haben, daß sie bis an ihre Gesimse reichen; so wird die übrige Oefnung auf beyden Seiten mit Gittern oder Schnitzwerk verbauet, daß man nicht so durchsehen könne.

§. 344.

Die Claviere von Elfenbein und Ebenholz geben eine besondere Zierde. Die Vorsetzbretter zwischen jedem Claviere können fournirer seyn. Das Schnitzwerk wird von etlichen vergoldet; und hat die Orgel im Stift Severi in Erfurt 300 Rthlr. zu mahlen und zu vergolden gekostet; die im Dom daselbst 400 Rthlr., wie ich berichtet worden. Daß das Rückpositiv den Prospekt der Orgel verderbe, ist oben schon gemeldet, und widerrathe ich es nochmals. (**)

(**) Diese Meynung muß man endlich einmal dem Hrn. Adlung zu gute halten. Sonst wäre es sehr leicht seinen ganzen Haß gegen die Rückpositive mit guten Gründen zu widerlegen.

§. 345.

Wenn die Registerknöpfe recht angebracht werden; so giebt es auch ein fein Ansehen. Ich rathe deswegen, daß man sie fein breit mache, ob speciem firmitudinis; daß sie von feinem braunen Holze sind; daß man sie mit den Namen der Stimmen versehe,

C 2

Chap. XII. Concerning the Exterior Decoration of an Organ 19

pedal note, i.e., d; each of the angels has a note^(**) There are also [figures of] putti on

(**) All of these splendid decorations are said to have become very undependable with the passing of time. It is therefore not advisable to imitate such follies anywhere else. [Agricola]

it, each one of which produces eight notes from the trumpet held in its mouth.* In the Heilig-Geisteskirche at Colberg there is a flying eagle. A report is given in Chapter 7, §.133, about the splendid effect provided by the remarkable Cymbelstern at St. Gertrud in Hamburg. Concerning the cathedral organ at Magdeburg, the Sacristans report in their description of the Cathedral "that it is extraordinarily beautifully and artistically adorned with many life-sized paintings,† beautifully gilded and magnificently painted; among these, King David with his harp and King Solomon stand between the three Oberwerk towers, and their heads turn to and fro. Above King David there stands an angel with a lute, and above King Solomon one with a small cittern; both of these [figures] revolve. Above these are several trumpeters that lift their trumpets to and from their mouths, and above all these there is a black eagle that is lofting itself on high. On top of the Rückpositiv an angel stands in the middle with a book and a staff, keeping the beat. At his feet there stands a gilded cock that, after the organist has finished playing (if desired), beats his wings and crows. A little lower on the Rückpositiv stand 2 revolving angels with cornetts, and under these there are 2 with trombones, that draw the slides in and out. In addition there are other pictures with various musical instruments."^(**)

(**) What nonsense! Are these things supposed to promote devotion? [Agricola]

* Boxberg, [pp. 5-6] writes: "The two small angels that sit above the Brust-Positiv in front of the central Hauptwerk pipe-flat are put to especially good use. Each one of them has a trumpet in its mouth, and produces from that single pipe eight completely clear and distinct notes of the Hautbois 8' that stands in the Brust[-Positiv], i.e., from great C to tenor e."

† "Bildern;" but what may be meant is "sculptures."

§. 343.

Since not all the pipes in the flats and towers are of equal length to reach up to the cornices, the remaining openings on both sides are covered up with lattice-work or woodcarving [i.e., pipe-shades], so that no one can see into [the case].

§. 344.

Keyboards made of ivory and ebony are especially handsome. The thumper boards between each keyboard may be veneered. Some [builders] gild the woodcarving; the organ at the Collegiate Church of St. Severus in Erfurt cost 300 Reichsthaler to paint and to gild. The organ in Erfurt Cathedral cost 400 Reichsthaler [to paint and gild], as I have been told. It has already been mentioned above that a Rückpositiv spoils the appearance of an organ, and once again I advise against it.^(**)

(**) Once and for all, we must ascribe this opinion to Mr. Adlung. But it would be very easy to refute with good reasons his whole loathing for the Rückpositiv. [Agricola]

§. 345.

It also lends [an organ] a neat appearance if the stop-knobs are arranged properly. For that reason I would advise that they be made good and large, for the sake of *species firmitudinis*. [I would also advise] that they be made of good dark wood, and that they

20   Kap. XII. Vom äusserlichen Zierrath einer Orgel.

welches geschieht, wenn man Metall hinein gießt, und die Namen eingräbt, wie es zu Jena ist. Das Hauptwerk aber ist, daß sie commode geordnet werden, theils, daß man die Register eines Claviers fein beysammen finde, theils, daß sie wohl zu ziehen sind, und der Organist dabey stille sitzen könne. Daher mache man zu jedem Claviere eine Reihe, doch auf beyden Seiten, und zu dem Pedale desgleichen: aber nicht in die Breite, (wie in der alten Orgel zu Naumburg zu St. Wenceslai war) daß der Organist aufstehen müsse, wenn er ziehen will, sondern aufwärts, daß man sie sitzend alle erreichen könne. Es muß aber die Eurythmie abermal beobachtet werden, daß so viel Stimmen zur Rechten in der nächsten Reihe beym Claviere stehen, als deren auch zur Linken in der innersten Reihe befindlich sind. So müssen auch die mittlern gleich seyn, und die 2 äussersten desgleichen. Die manubria aber, die einander in den Reihen gleich gemacht werden, müssen einander auch recht parallel stehen. Wenn etwan ein Clavier zu viel Stimmen hat, daß die Reihen zu groß, die andern zu klein werden; so kann man etliche davon in die benachbarte Reihe bringen. Und weil im Pedale so viel Stimmen nicht sind; so kann man den Tremulanten, Koppel, Ventile, Pauken, ꝛc. dazu nehmen, welche ohne dies der ganzen Orgel gemein sind; so auch den Stern, Vogelgesang, Guckuck. Obgleich diese nicht viel nutzen, so befördern sie doch die Eurythmie. (**)

    (**) Die Eurythmie kann doch erreicht werden, ohne daß man nöthig hat, um eines Registerknopfs willen, solche Tändeleyen in eine Orgel zu setzen.

Ja wenn die Zahl der Stimmen just einzutheilen ungeschickt ist; so thue man blinde manubria dazu. So habe ich z. Ex. oben §. 149. eins angeführt mit einem Fuchsschwanze, it. §. 170. das Noli me tangere in der Orgel zu St. Gertrud in Hamburg. Hat jedes Clavier zu wenig Stimmen; so kann man weniger Reihen machen. Wo Rückpositive, Brustwerke, ꝛc. sind; so bringe man die manubria zusammen vorne hin bey die andern, weil es verdrüßlich ist, hinter dem Rücken die Register zu ziehen. (**)   Nun

    (**) Das ist sehr wahr.

will ich die Naumburgischen hersetzen, wie sie angebracht sind, und hernach die Jenaischen. Man urtheile alsdann selbst, welches von beyden besser in die Augen falle.

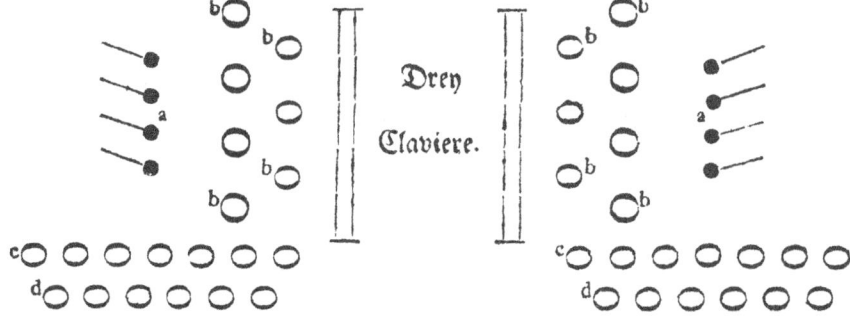

c c sind die 2 Reihen zum Hauptmanuale, welche so weit weggehen, daß der Organist nicht kann stille sitzen wenn er sie ziehen will.   d d sind zum Rückpositive.   b b b b gehören

20   Chap. XII.   Concerning the Exterior Decoration of an Organ

be provided with the stop names by pouring metal into [their faces] and engraving the names on them, as it is at Jena. The main concern, however, is that they be arranged conveniently, in part so that the stops of each division are neatly grouped together, and in part so that they are easy to [reach and] pull with the organist remaining quietly seated while he does it. Therefore a [separate] row should be made for each keyboard, but on both sides, and the same for the pedal—not horizontal rows, however (as there were in the old organ at St. Wenceslaus in Naumburg), that forced the organist to stand up to draw them, but vertical ones, so that all [the stopknobs] can be reached from a sitting position. Once again, however, eurythmy must be observed, so that there are just as many stops in the row just to the right of the keyboards as there are just to the left. The [rows in the] middle must also be identical, and likewise the two outer [rows]. The stopknobs, which are made identical [to each other] within the rows, must also stand exactly parallel to each other.* If one division should perchance have too many stops, so that its row is too long and the others too short, then some of these [stops] may be transferred to a neighboring row. And since there are not as many stops in the pedal, the tremulants, couplers, ventils, kettledrums, etc., may be added to them, since they are common to the whole organ anyway; the same goes for the Cymbelstern, Birdsong and Cuckoo. Even though these stops are of little use, they nevertheless promote eurythmy.(**)

* i.e., the knobs must be parallel horizontally as well as vertically.

(**) Eurythmy can be achieved, though, without necessarily putting such trifles into an organ, just for the sake of [an equal number of] stopknobs. [Agricola]

Indeed, if the the number of stops is not suited to being divided equally, false stopknobs may be added. I have cited one example in §.149 above, a Fox-tail; also in §.170, the *Noli me tangere* in the organ at St. Gertrud in Hamburg. If there are too few stops in each division, then there can be fewer rows. In the case of Rückpositivs and Brustwerks, etc., the stopknobs should be grouped together with the others, since it is annoying to draw the stops behind one's back(**) Now I will set down the arrangement at Naumburg,†

† i.e., the organ by Thayssner at the Wenzelskirche, before the rebuild by Hildebrand; see §.310.

(**) This is very true. [Agricola]

and afterwards the one at Jena.‡ One may judge for oneself which of them is more pleasing to the eye.

‡ see §.302.

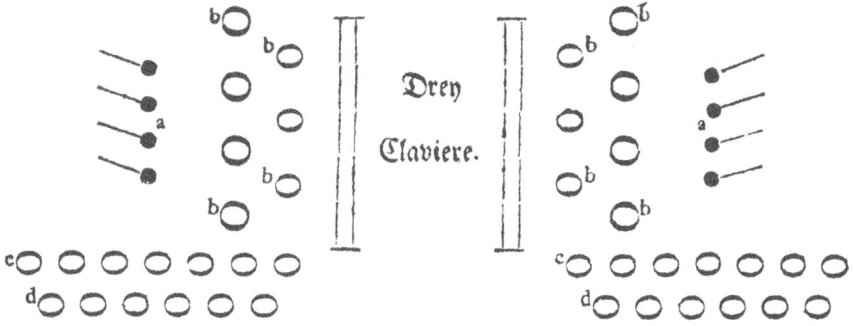

c c are the 2 rows [of stops] for the main manual, that extend so far out that the organist cannot remain seated if he wants to draw them. dd are those for the Rückpositiv. bbbb

Kap. XII. Vom äusserlichen Zierrath einer Orgel. 21

hören ins Pedal, oder sind gemein. a a sind oben an der Brust, und sind von Eisen gemacht, und der Organist muß aufstehen wenn er sie ziehen will, weil er sie sitzend nicht errreichen kann. In Jena sind sie auf folgende Art geordnet:

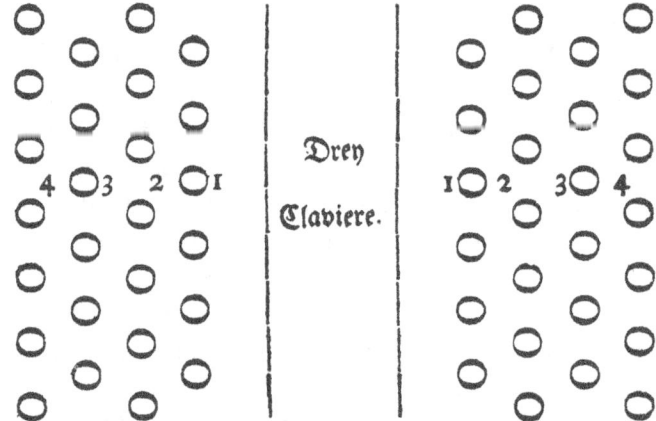

Es darf sich der Organist nicht regen, wenn er sie alle ziehen will. 1.1. Gehören alle zum Hauptmanual. 2.2. zum Mittelwerk, sammt noch einem von 3. 3.3. ist das unterste Clavier, wobey noch 3 Pedalstimmen sind. 4.4. sind die Pedal- und gemeine Register.

§. 346.

Endlich stehet auch nicht fein, wenn die Register allzuweit müssen heraus gezogen werden. Drey oder vier Zoll ist am besten. Noch schlimmer stehts, wenn sie krumm stehen, indem sie heraus gezogen sind. Und so viel ist mir für diesmal eingefallen von der äusserlichen Zierde eines Werks. Wäre es etwan so gebauet, daß man es von der Seite und von hinten zu sehen könnte; so muß es wenigstens mit saubern Brettern bekleidet werden, daß es bedeckt sey. Oben darauf, wenn es nicht bis an den Kirchhimmel reicht, kann ein stark Tuch gespannet werden um den Staub und andere Unreinigkeiten einigermaaßen von den Pfeifen abzuhalten. Es kann auch an dessen Statt ein brettern Dach darüber geleget werden, daß nicht ein Ziegel des Daches durchschlage, und dem Pfeifwerke schade, wie in der Erfurter Reglerorgel vor etlichen Jahren geschahe; da der Westnordwind ein ganz Feld von den Thurmziegeln durch das Kirchdach in die Orgel stürzte. Sind die Bälge irgendswo, daß sie können gesehen werden; so soll man sie decori caussa auch mit Brettern verschlagen. Doch genung davon. Wer nachdenkt, kann bisweilen noch was bessers finden.

Chap. XII. Concerning the Exterior Decoration of an Organ 21

belong to the pedal, or they are general stops. aa are up top next to the Brust[werk], and are made of iron; the organist must stand up if he wants to draw them, since he cannot reach them while seated. In Jena [the stop-knobs] are arranged in the following way:

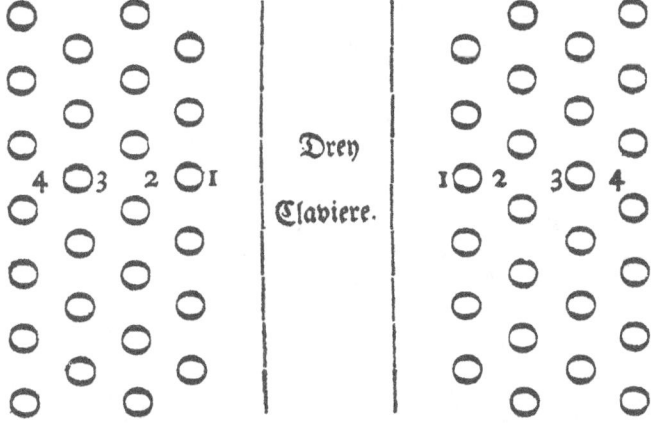

The organist need not bestir himself to draw any of them. 1.1. all belong to the main manual, 2.2. to the Mittelwerk (together with one from row 3), 3.3. to the lowest keyboard (along with 3 pedal stops), and 4.4. to the pedal and the general stops.

§. 346.

Finally, it is not good if the stops have to be drawn out so far. Three or four inches is best. It is even worse if they are crooked when they are drawn out. This is all that comes to my mind at this time about the exterior decoration of an instrument. If [an organ] were going to be built to be visible from the side or the back, then it must at least be faced with neat boards, so that it is covered. On the top, should it not reach to the ceiling of the church, a heavy cloth can be stretched [over it] to prevent to some degree dust and other dirt from getting into the pipes. In place of this, a wooden top may be laid over it, to keep a roof tile from breaking through and damaging the pipes, as happened to the organ in the Reglerkirche at Erfurt several years ago. There a northwest wind caused an entire section of the tower tiles to crash through the church roof into the organ. If the bellows are any place where they can be seen, they should also be screened off with boards, for the sake of decorum. But enough of this. Anyone who thinks it over can eventually find a way to improve [a situation].

Das XIII. Kapitel.
Von den Vollkommenheiten und Fehlern einer Orgel, welche noch nicht berühret worden.

Inhalt:

§. 346. Eintheilung des Kapitels. §. 347. Die Orgel soll weit seyn; Thüren und Schnitzwerk haben. §. 348. Von den Clavieren. § 349. welche ihre rechte Größe haben müssen. §. 350. Sie sollen nicht zu tief fallen. §. 351. Kurze Oktave, Subsemitonia, ꝛc. §. 352. Die Stifte und Lage der Palmulen. §. 353. Vom Pedale. §. 354. Die Federn und numerus der Palmulen. §. 355. Die Registerknöpfe. §. 356. Die Springlade. §. 357. eine andere Art derselben. §. 358. Von der Schleiflade. §. 359. Deren Spünde, ꝛc. §. 360. Die Parallelen und Dämme. §. 361. Eine zieht die andere nach sich. §. 362. Spanische Reuter. §. 363. Der Windkasten. §. 364. Die Ventile. §. 365. Die Federn und Stifte, ꝛc §. 366. Spünde und Beutel. §. 367. Windführungen. §. 368. Abstrakten. §. 369. Wellenbretter. §. 370. Die Bälge. §. 371. 372. 373. Von Gegengewichten. §. 374. Balgventil. §. 375. Noch einige Dinge von Bälgen. §. 376. Rasseln der Bälge innerlich. §. 377. 378. Calcaturclavis. §. 379. Balghaus. §. 380. Kanäle §. 381. ihre Ventile. §. 382. Polirung der Pfeifen. §. 383. Der Salpeter frißt sie. §. 384. andere Fehler. § 385. Loth derselben. §. 386. Saudlöcher, Filpen, Intonation, ꝛc § 387. Eine soll nicht stärker klingen als die andere. §. 388. Wenn bey 2 Pfeifen sich die 3te hören läßt. §. 389 Von den Schnarrwerken.

§. 346.

Dieses Kapitel ist wichtig, und etwas weitläuftig, und soll hierinne noch berühret werden, was an den Orgeln zu loben oder zu tadeln ist. Es wird nach dem vorigen und nach diesem Kapitel der Contrakt aufgerichtet, auch die Orgel probiret, daher davon gehandelt werden muß, ehe von jenem etwas gedacht wird. Bey diesem Kapitel ist Werkmeisters Orgelprobe am meisten zu gebrauchen, nebst dessen Organo grüningensi rediuiuo, und Boxbergs Beschreibung der Görlitzer Orgel. Wir wollen die Ordnung behalten, die wir oben gehabt haben, so, daß wir erstlich die Vollkommenheiten und Fehler des Gehäuses betrachten; hernach der Windlade; hernach des andern Eingeweides, das Pfeifwerk ausgenommen; dann der Bälge und Windführungen; des Pfeifwerks u. s. w. Was aber in vorigen Kapiteln da gewesen ist, will ich nicht wiederhohlen, sondern darauf verweisen.

§. 347.

Was erstlich das Gehäuse anlangt; so kann man die Fehler leicht sehen, wenn man nur das Gegentheil nimmt von dem, was Kap. 12. vorgebracht worden. Ein Hauptfehler ist, wenn man die Orgeln allzuenge bauet; auch sollen keine Rückpositive hinter den Rücken kommen. Es ist gar wohl gethan, und gar nöthig, daß man etliche Thüren in die Orgel bringe, daß man von vornen und hinten zu allen Theilen der Orgel kommen,

Chapter XIII.
Concerning the Merits and Faults of an Organ
that have not yet been mentioned.

Contents:

§. 346. Organization of the chapter. §. 347. The organ [case] should be broad; it should have [entry] doors and wood-carving. §. 348. Concerning the keyboards. §. 349. They must be of the proper size. §. 350. The keyfall should not be too deep. §. 351. Short octaves, subsemitones, etc. §. 352. The pins and the position of the keys. §. 353. Concerning the pedal. §. 354. The springs and the number of keys. §. 355. The stop-knobs. §. 356. The spring chest. §. 357. Another type of the same. §. 358. Concerning the slider chest. §. 359. Its sponsels, etc. §. 360. The sliders and spacers. §. 361. One [stop] may draw another with it. §. 362. Bleed grooves. §. 363. The pallet box. §. 364. The pallets. §. 365. The springs and pins, etc. §. 366. Bung boards and pouches. §. 367. Wind ducts. §. 368. Trackers. §. 369. Rollerboards. §. 370. The bellows. §. 371, 372, 373. Concerning counter-weights. §. 374. The bellows-valve. §. 375. Several additional points concerning bellows. §. 376. Rattling inside the bellows. §. 377, 378. The bellows pole. §. 379. The bellows chamber. §. 380. Wind ducts. §. 381. Their valves. §. 382. Polishing the pipes.* §. 383. Salpeter eats them away. §. 384. Other faults [in pipes]. §. 385. Soldering [the pipes]. §. 386. Sand holes, poor intonation, voicing, etc. §. 387. One [pipe] should not sound louder than another. §. 388. If a third pipe is heard when two pipes are sounding. §. 389. Concerning the reeds. [§. 390. Concerning wooden pipes; doubled stops.]

* §. 382 treats pipe alloys, not polishing. Adlung does, however, discuss polishing façade pipes in Chapter 28, p. 182.

§. 346.†

This chapter is important, and rather lengthy; in it I will touch upon what is to be praised or censured in organs. A contract may be drawn up and an organ examined according to this and the previous chapter; therefore these things‡ must be treated before those [matters§] are even considered. The main [books] to use in conjunction with this chapter are Werkmeister's *Orgelprobe*, together with his *Organum gruningense redivivum*, and Boxberg's description of the Görlitz organ.¶ We will adhere to the organization that we established above, by first considering the merits and faults of the case, then the windchest, next the other internal parts (with the exception of the pipes), then the bellows and wind ducts, the pipes, etc. I will not repeat what I have said in previous chapters, however, but only refer to it.

† The last paragraph of Chapter XII is also numbered §. 346.

‡ i.e., an organ's merits and faults.

§ i.e., contract and examination.

¶ Christian Ludwig Boxberg, *Ausführliche Beschreibung Der Grossen Neuen Orgel . . . zu Görlitz*. Görlitz: 1704.

§. 347.

First, as regards the case: one can easily perceive its faults by considering the opposite of what has been stated in Chapter 12. It is a major fault to build organs too cramped; moreover there should be no Rückpositiv behind one's back. It is very good, indeed necessary, to provide a number of doors into the organ, so that all the parts of the organ are accessible, both from the front and from the back, and also so that light

Kap. XIII. Von den Vollkommenheiten u. Fehlern einer Orgel. 23

men, und auch das Licht durchfallen könne, wenn man in der Orgel etwas zu thun hat. Es soll auch das Schnitzwerk nicht nach schon vollendeter Stimmung angebracht werden; denn es verstimmen sich die Orgeln einigermaßen dadurch, weil man nicht allezeit behutsam damit umgehet. Die obere Decke ist gleichfalls vor der Stimmung aufzulegen.

§. 348.

Bey den Clavieren ist etliches zu erinnern. Wenn zu den diatonischen clavibus soll Burbaum genommen werden, so nehmen betrügliche Orgelmacher Maßilienholz, oder Pfaffenmütze, wie wir es hier zu Lande nennen. Das muß einer wohl zu unterscheiden wissen, weil diese Holzarten einander ziemlich gleichen. Auch gehen im Elfenbein Betrügereyen vor, daß man Elfenbein mou dafür bekömmt. Die chromatischen Claves sind ordentlich schwarz. ⁶⁶) Wollte man sie färben, würden sie bald wieder weiß werden, wenn die Farbe sich abgespielet; daher sie eine Platte von Ebenholz bekommen. Aber wer nicht genau Acht hat, der wird auch darinne betrogen, weil ich weis, das zuweilen nur etliche palmulae auf solche Art fournirt worden, andere aber nicht.

§. 349.

Ein großer Fehler ist auch, wenn die Claviere nicht die ordentliche Länge haben; sondern wenn auf einer Orgel eine Oktave so groß ist, muß man, auf der die Finger weiter aussperren, oder auf einer andern sie zusammen ziehen. Man kann daher nicht gewiß spielen, bis man solcher Orgel erst gewohnt ist. Man behalte die ordinär gebrauchte Größe; und ob mancher wol denken möchte, es wäre gut und commoder, wenn man sie kleiner machte; so schicken sich doch nicht alle Finger darein. (**) Derowegen ists am besten, daß man sie also mache, daß auch starke Finger darauf spielen können. Sind sie gar zu breit gemacht; so wird uns das Spielen so sauer, und viel Spieler, absonderlich junge Scholaren, können die Oktave nicht erreichen. Auch ist ein Fehler, wenn eine palmula breiter ist, als die andere. Imgleichen, wenn sie so große Lucken oder Raum zwischen sich haben, daher sie sich im Spielen zur Rechten und zur Linken begeben, wackeln, und auch ein unleidliches Klappern verursachen.

(**) Daß ein Taste eines Claviers so lang und so breit seyn müsse als der andere seiner Art, versteht sich von sich selbst. Welcher vernünftige Orgelbauer würde auch wol das Gegentheil davon mit Fleiß machen; und welcher vernünftige Examinant würde wol dergleichen Stümperey passiren lassen? Was aber der Hr. Adlung hier von Manchem sagt, der die Claviere kürzer haben möchte, ist nicht so gar wohl überdacht, wenn er ihm deswegen unrecht giebt. Allerdings ist es gut, wenn die Claviere so kurz als möglich sind. Denn wenn deren drey oder vier sind, so kann der Spielende, wenn die Claviere kurz sind, mit viel mehr Bequemlichkeit von einem auf das andere kommen. Er kann gerade sitzen bleiben, wenn er auch auf dem vierten oder gar fünften Claviere spielen will. Da er hingegen Rückenschmerzen bekommen muß, wenn er
auf

⁶⁶) Heut zu Tage pflegt man es meistentheils umzukehren, und die diatonischen Tasten schwarz zu fourniren, und im Gegentheil die chromatischen mit einer elfenbeinernen Platte zu belegen.

can enter if there is something to be done in the organ. Furthermore, the woodcarving should not be affixed after the tuning is completed; doing this puts the organ out of tune to some degree, since it is not always done carefully. The top covering* should likewise be put on before tuning.

* see Chap. XII, §. 346.

§. 348.

There are a number of things to keep in mind in connection with the keyboards. If boxwood is chosen for the diatonic keys, deceitful organbuilders will use "Maßilienholz" or "Pfaffenmütze,"† as we call it in these parts. One must indeed be able to distinguish between the two, since these types of wood closely resemble each other. Ivory is also subject to deceit, by substituting "Elfenbein mou‡" for it. The chromatic keys are ordinarily black.[66] If they are painted, then they soon become white§ again when the paint wears off; thus they are veneered with ebony wafers. But anyone who does not pay careful attention will be deceived here as well, since I am aware that sometimes only some keys are veneered in this way, while others are not.

† The wood of the tree also known as "Spindelbaum" or "Pfaffenkäppel;" *Evonymus europaea* or some other variety of the genus *Evonymus*. The wood is similar to boxwood.

‡ Literally "weak ivory;" evidently an inferior variety of ivory or an ivory substitute.

§ i.e, natural wood color.

§. 349.

It is also a major fault if the keyboards are not made the normal width.¶ For if [the span of] an octave is of different sizes in different organs, then one must spread the fingers further on one and contract them on another. Thus it is impossible to play with precision without first becoming accustomed to the particular organ. The customary [key] size should be maintained, even though some might think it would be better and more comfortable to make them smaller—but not all fingers are suited to fit [smaller keys](**) For that reason it is best to make them so that stubby fingers can also play on them. Playing becomes very onerous if they are made altogether too wide, and many players, especially younger students, cannot reach an octave. It is also a fault if one key is wider than another; likewise if they have large gaps or spaces between them, since they shift right and left, wobble, and make an intolerable racket when being played.

¶ "Länge"—but the context makes it clear that Adlung is speaking here about the width of the keys (i.e., the total "length" of the keyboard), not about key length.

(**) It goes without saying that every key on a keyboard should be of a length and width equal to the others of its type. What sensible organbuilder would deliberately do the opposite, and what sensible examiner would let such shoddy work pass? But Mr. Adlung's criticism here of many who would like to have shorter keys is not very well thought through. Indeed, it it a good thing for the keys to be as short as possible, for if there are three or four manuals with short keys, the player can much more comfortably shift from one to another. He can remain seated in an upright position, even when playing on the fourth or even the fifth manual. In contrast, he will get a backache from playing even on

[66] Nowadays this practice is usually reversed, and the diatonic keys are veneered black, while on the other hand the chromatic ones are overlaid with an ivory wafer. [Albrecht]

auf manchen Orgeln, mit langen Clavieren, nur auf dem dritten Claviere, von unten an zu rechnen, irgend lange spielen will. Wer einer richtigen Fingersetzung gewohnt ist, wird wissen, daß er keinen Finger in Spielen gerade ausstrecken muß. Wozu braucht er denn die so langen Claviere? Was die Breite der Tasten betrift, so weis man, daß absonderlich in der Mark die Tasten schmäler als anderwärts gemacht werden, und doch ist noch kein Mensch mit den Fingern zwischen den Semitonen stecken geblieben. Sind denn in Thüringen Riesen? Jener Organist der sehr breite Schuhe trug, hatte das Pedal seiner Orgel, auf dem er ohnedem nicht viel spielen konnte, so weit aus einander legen lassen, daß jeder anderer, der auf diesem Pedale mehreres als den vom kleinen Finger der linken Hand schon angegebenen Baßton hätte spielen wollen, sich leicht einen Bruch hätte zuwege bringen können. Die Franzosen machen, und zwar mit großem Rechte, sogar ihre Flügeltasten kürzer als in Deutschland: und doch hat sich noch niemand darüber beklagt. Die Semitone müssen überhaupt oben etwas schmäler als unten seyn. So verlangte sie der seel. Kapellm. Bach, welcher auch aus oben angeführten Ursachen, die kurzen Tasten auf Orgeln liebte. Man muß dem Hrn. Adlung, in Betrachtung seiner andern nicht geringen Verdienste, diese seine Meynungen, in diesem Puncte, zu gute halten; ob man gleich nicht verbunden ist sie nachzusprechen, oder gar zur Regel anzunehmen

Es ist auch ein großer Fehler, wenn in manchen neuen Orgeln, absonderlich in denen mit 3 Clavieren, die Claviere so weit in die Orgel hinein geleget werden, daß das unterste Clavier nicht über die Vorderwand der Orgel heraus geht, und dagegen hierbey das Pedal doch gar nicht, oder nur sehr wenig in die Orgel hineingeschoben wird. Einige Orgelbauer geben vor, daß es nicht gut aussähe, wenn der Kasten, der die Claviere umgiebt und verschließt, vor die Orgel heraus ragte, und derselben gleichsam einen kleinen Bauch machte. Vom Pedale aber sagen sie, daß wenn es weiter in die Orgel hineingerückt wäre, der Organist nicht auf die Pedalclaves sehen könnte. Wie ungereimt aber dieses sey, fällt gleich in die Augen. Denn wenn der Organist, bey einer solchen Anlage, auf dem obersten Claviere spielen will, so muß er sich vorwärts bücken, und folglich kann er auf dem Pedale nichts als einzelne langsame Töne anschlagen. Denn wer recht auf dem Pedale spielen will, muß ganz gerade sitzen. Welcher Organist aber die Pedalclaves ohne darauf zu sehen, ja gar im Finstern, nicht richtig treffen kann, der verdient weder den Namen noch das Amt eines Organisten.

Und solchen Herren zu Gefallen wollte man eine Orgel in diesem Stücke so verhunzen, daß kein rechtschaffener Organist, ohne große Unbequemlichkeit, was gescheutes darauf spielen kann? Entweder muß, zumal bey dreyen und mehrern Clavieren, die nicht über die Orgel herausragen, auch das Pedal weiter hineingerückt werden: oder man muß den vermeynten Uebelstand, daß wenigstens das unterste, und die Hälfte vom mittelsten Claviere vor die Vorderwand der Orgel hervorrage, sich gefallen lassen. So haben es die Alten gemacht, wie z. Ex. an den Orgeln zu St. Thomas und zu St. Nicolai in Leipzig, auch in Berlin an der von Urp Schnittkern erbaueten Orgel bey St. Nicolai, und überhaupt an den meisten alten großen Orgeln zu sehen ist. So macht man es auch heutiges Tages noch an den neuesten Orgeln in Frankreich, wie aus Abrissen davon kann wahrgenommen werden. Welcher Fehler ist wol an einer Orgel größer als der, wenn man, sie mag auch noch so viele und noch so schöne Stimmen haben, nicht alles was man will, und was man vermag, bequem darauf spielen kann?

§. 350.

Ob es schon ein großer Fehler ist, wenn die claves insgemein allzu tief fallen; so ist es doch am schlimmsten, wenn die chromatischen so tief fallen, daß sie sich in den Diatonischen gar verbergen. Da muß man auf manchen Orgeln fast die Diatonischen mit

berühren,

the third manual up from the bottom for any length of time on many organs with long keys. Anyone who is in the habit of holding his fingers properly will know that he need not stretch any finger straight out while playing. What need is there, then, of such long keys? As regards the width of the keys, it is common knowledge that especially in the Mark [Brandenburg] the keys are narrower than elsewhere, and yet no one has yet gotten his fingers caught between the semitones. Are there such giants in Thuringia? One organist who wore very wide shoes had the pedals of his organ (on which he couldn't play much anyway) placed so far apart that if anybody else had tried to play any more on that pedalboard than the bass notes indicated for the little finger of the left hand, he could easily have ruptured himself. The French make even their harpsichord keys shorter than the Germans—and rightly so—and nevertheless no one has yet complained about it. Above all, the semitones must be somewhat narrower on top than at the bottom. The late Kapellmeister [J.S.] Bach required this, and for the same reasons mentioned above, he also preferred short keys on organs. We must allow Mr. Adlung this his opinion on this point, in consideration of his other considerable merits, although at the same time we are not obliged to concur with it, or to accept it as gospel.

It is also a major fault to recess the keyboards far into the organ [case], as happens in many new organs, especially those with 3 manuals, so that the lowest keyboard does not protrude beyond the forward wall of the organ [case], while on the other hand recessing the pedal not at all, or only a bit, into the organ [case]. Some organbuilders allege that it does not look good for the enclosure that surrounds the keyboards to protrude out in front of the organ [case], making a little bulge in it. Concerning the pedal, however, they say that if it were shoved further into the organ, the organist could not look at the pedal keys. It is immediately apparent, however, how absurd this is. For if the organist wants to play on the uppermost keyboard with such a layout, he has to lean forward, and consequently he cannot play anything on the pedals except isolated sustained tones. For anyone who wants to play the pedals correctly must sit absolutely erect. Any organist who cannot hit the correct pedal notes without looking at them (in the shadows, at that!) deserves neither the name nor the position of organist.

Should these parts of an organ be so botched up just to please these gentlemen [i.e., the organbuilders], so that no proper organist can play skillfully on it without great discomfort? Either the pedal must be further recessed, especially when there are three or more keyboards that do not protrude beyond the organ [case], or one must put up with what I consider the nuisance of having at least the lowest and half of the middle keyboard protrude beyond the forward wall of the organ [case]. Earlier generations did it this way, as may be seen, e.g., in the organs at St. Thomas and St. Nicolai in Leipzig, also in the organ built by Arp Schnitger at St. Nicolai in Berlin, and in general in most large old organs. It is still done today in the newest organs in France, as may be perceived from sketches of them. What greater fault could there be in an organ, no matter how many beautiful stops it might have, than being unable to play comfortably on it anything one wishes and is capable of? [Agricola]

§. 350.

Although too deep a keyfall is a major fault, it is worst of all when the chromatic keys fall so deep that they disappear entirely between the diatonic ones. Then, on many organs, one is almost forced to play the diatonic keys along with them, if one wants to depress them fully. To be sure, the chromatic [keys] can be adjusted somewhat higher

berühren, wenn jene völlig niederfallen sollen. Man kann ja, um diesen Fehler zu verhüten, die Chromatischen desto höher machen. Daß aber die Claves insgemein nicht tief fallen sollten, werden diejenigen am besten wissen die mit dergleichen geplagt sind. Wenn der Fehler in der Windlade ist; so kann man es hernach nicht ändern: denn wollte man die Schrauben an den clauibus nachlassen; so würde nicht satt Wind in die Cancellen gehen: folglich würde das Werk unrein klingen. Daher ist dahin zu sehen, daß die Ventile gleich Anfangs recht gemacht werden; denn dadurch werden solche Fehler verhütet. Noch schlimmer ists, wenn ein clauis tief fällt, der andere aber nicht. Es thut ein Orgelmacher wohl, wenn er die claues in einer gewissen Höhe anschraubt und nach solcher Höhe stimmt. Und damit durch die Aenderung dieser angenommenen Höhe nicht etwan mit der Zeit die Stimmung verdorben werde; so mache er ein Brett, oder Leiste, so unter die Claves passet, wenn sie die rechte Höhe haben, und überlasse solches Brett oder Leiste, dem Organisten, daß er seine Claviere darnach auf oder abwärts schraube; so wird das Werk reine bleiben. Ich habe auch angetroffen, daß eine palmula tiefer gefallen ist, als die andere, welches noch schändlicher ist. Auf solchen Clavieren kann nie was rechtes herausgebracht werden. Die Claviere sollen auch nicht klappern, ohne was wegen des Angehänges nicht anders seyn kann. Wo die Löcher zu den Stiften zu weit sind, da rasseln die Claviere gern. Ein Orgelmacher hat demnach dahin zu sehen, daß er diesen, und andere vorhin erwähnte Fehler verhüte.

§. 351.

Kurze Oktaven sind auch ein Hauptfehler an Orgeln. Man lasse oben, bis ans c, nichts mangeln, und unten mache man die Anlage so, daß Cis, Dis, Fis und Gis dabey sind. Das Cis zwar wird noch nicht überall gemacht, doch aber die andern. Wo neue Orgeln gebauet werden, thut man wohl, wenn man auch in diesem Stücke auf eine Vollkommenheit bedacht ist, und das große Cis im Manuale und Pedale mit anleget: denn es thut bey heutiger Spielart sehr gute Dienste, und man kann dasselbe so wenig als einen andern clauem der untersten Oktave entbehren. Ob das Hauptmanual solle oben oder unten liegen, ist oben bereits erinnert worden, s. §. 279. Das Clavier soll vornen seyn, und durchgehends keine Subsemitonia bekommen. Sie kosten viel, und doch schaden sie mehr, als sie nutzen. Wer die Temperatur verstehet, der wird sich in solche Quackeley nicht verlieben. Man findet aber solche Subsemitonia noch; und haben manche Orgeln mehr, manche weniger davon. In der Orgel zu St. Marien Magdalenen in Hamburg sind in jeder Oktave ein Paar Subsemitonia. (Doch ist sie schon 1629. gebauet worden.) Eben so hat auch die Stockholmer Orgel in jeder Oktave zwey dergleichen, u. a. m.

§. 352.

Wenn die Claviere weit einwärts geleget werden, nach der Lade zu; so kommen die Abstrakten weit vor, folglich werden solche Claviere nicht so tief fallen, als andere: hingegen

in order to prevent this fault. Those that are plagued with them will know better than anyone else that, generally speaking, the keys should not fall [too] deep. If the fault lies in the windchest,* it cannot be altered after the fact, since if the screws on the keys are loosened, insufficient wind would enter the [wind] channels, and consequently the instrument would sound out of tune. From this we may perceive that right from the start the pallets must be made correctly, for in this way such faults will be prevented. It is even worse if one key has a deep fall and the next one not. Organbuilders would do well to screw the keys up to a certain height and tune [the instrument with] them at that height. And so that this chosen height does not shift and in time ruin the tuning, they should make a board or a strip that fits under the keys when they lie at the correct height, and leave this board or strip with the organist, so that thereafter he may screw his keys up or down; in this way the instrument will stay in tune. I have also encountered [situations where] one key falls deeper than the others, which is even more disgraceful. Nothing can be executed properly on such keyboards. The keys also ought not to clatter, except for the unavoidable noise caused by the action points. Where the holes for the pins are too large, the keys are likely to rattle. Accordingly an organbuilder must see to it that he prevents this fault, as well as the others previously mentioned.

§. 351.

Short octaves† are also a major fault in an organ. Nothing‡ should be missing at the top [of the keyboard], right up to c‴, and at the bottom the layout should be arranged so that C#, D#, F# and G# are present. To be sure, the C# is not built everywhere, but the others certainly are. Wherever new organs are to be built, it would be best to aim for completeness in these components as well, and to include the lowest C# in the manual[s] and in the pedal. It is very useful in today's style of playing, and is as indispensable as any other key in the lowest octave. I have already discussed in §. 279 above whether the main manual should be placed on the top or on the bottom. The keyboard should be forward,§ and should not have subsemitones at any point [in its compass]. They cost a lot, and are more of a hindrance than a help. Anyone who understands temperament will not become enamored with such quackery. Such subsemitones are, however, still to be found in many an organ, some with more, some with less. In the organ at St. Mary Magdelene in Hamburg there are two subsemitones in each octave (but [this organ] was built way back in 1629).¶ The organ in Stockholm‖ likewise has two of them in each octave, etc.

§. 352.

If the keyboards** extend deep into the organ in relation to the chest, then the trackers are placed far toward the fronts of them. Consequently such keyboards do not

* i.e., the pallet design necessitates a deep keyfall.

† an arrangement normally applied to the lowest octave of keys on an organ or other keyboard instrument. The keyboard appears to begin at E, but in fact that lowest note sounds C. Low F# sounds D, G# sounds E, and then the diatonic keys ascend as usual up to B-flat, which is the first chromatic note. From there the keys usually ascend chromatically. Short octaves were common in keyboard instruments until the dawn of the 18th century.

‡ i.e., no notes.

§ This cryptic remark may mean that the keyboard should be placed on the front of the case (as opposed to the sides or the back), or it may mean that the keyboard should not be recessed into the case (in which case §. 352 could be considered a further explanation and refinement of the statement).

¶ See Mattheson/Niedt, p. 180.

‖ See *ibid.*, p. 198.

** i.e., the key levers.

gegen wenn man so weit herausrückt; so kommen die Abstrakten weiter einwärts zu stehen, folglich fallen die Claviere tiefer: doch sind sie leichter zu spielen. Nun ist beydes gut; aber nicht zugleich zu erhalten; daher man das mittlere wählt, und die Abstrakten nicht allzuweit hinterbringt. Daß beyde Wahrheiten aus der Struktur der Theile fließen, wird in der Mechanik erwiesen, weil die claues wie Hebebäume können betrachtet werden, bey welchen, wenn das hypomochlium unter der einen Extremität liegt, die Potenz um so viel stärker wird, um wie viel das pondus von ihr nach dem hypomochlio zu stehet. Hingegen muß sie auch einen größern Bogen beschreiben, als sonst, wenn das pondus soll gehoben werden. [67]) Ferner sollen die Stifte von Meßing seyn, in welchen die palmulae laufen, so auch im Pedale; denn eisern Drat rostet gern, und ist nicht so glatt als Meßing. Das obere Clavier muß können heraus gehoben werden, daß man kann zu dem andern kommen; sonderlich wenn an den Koppeln etwas verderbt ist.

§. 353.

Das Pedal muß abermals nach der gewöhnlichsten Art ausgedehnet seyn. In Rothenstein, einem Dorfe ohnweit Jena, habe ich ehedessen ein Pedal gesehen, da die Palmulen so enge und schmal waren, daß wenigstens der 3te Theil ihrer Breite abgieng. Da muß man es erstlich gewohnt werden. Man verliert aber dabey die Gewißheit im Treten, und gehört folglich dieser Umstand unter die Fehler einer Orgel, die man zu verbessern hat. [68]) Die Pedalclaves müssen auch mit meßingenen Stiften versehen seyn, worinne sie hinten laufen; sie müssen in die gefütterten Scheiden accurat passen, daß sie nicht beym Auf- und Niedergehen klappern, auch nicht auf die Seite schwanken. Man legt es am besten so an; daß das mittlere c perpendiculär unter dem mittlern c des Manuals liege, s. §. 29. Manche wollen es unter das cis haben: aber ich sehe nicht ein, warum? denn da ich mich mitten vor das Clavier setze, warum sollte ich nicht im Pedale eine Oktave auf der einen, die andere auf der andern Seite haben? Das Scheidenbrett, wie auch das ganze Pedal, soll etwas weit hinein gelegt werden, weil man sonst, wenn man auf dem Pedale was besonders machen will, nicht fortkommen kann. Denn es müssen die Füße zuweilen hinter einander weggehen, und dazu hat man alsdann nicht Raum genug. Wollte man sich helfen durch Abrückung der Bank; so käme das Manual so weit ab zu liegen, welches auch eine Unbequemlichkeit im Spielen verursacht, und nicht zu rathen ist. Solche Spieler zwar, die im Pedale nicht viel Wesens machen, haben dergleichen nicht nöthig: allein man muß so bauen, daß es sich für allerley Leute schickt.

§. 354.

[67]) Sind die Orgeln zu schwer nieder zu drücken; so kann man auch nie manierlich spielen, und man ist genöthiget die Triller und Mordenten insgesammt wegzulassen.

[68]) Ein großer Fehler ist es auch, wenn ein Pedalclavis nicht so tief fällt, als der andere. Werkmeister merkt dergleichen Fehler an in Organo grüningensi, §. 16.

fall as deep as others. On the other hand, if the [keyboards] are shifted further out, then the trackers are attached further inwards.* Consequently the keys fall deeper—but they are easier to play. Now both of these [alternatives] are good, but both cannot be had at the same time. Thus it is best to choose a happy medium, and not attach the trackers too far back. [The study of] mechanics proves that both of these facts are the result of the structure of the components, since each key may be considered as a lever resting on a fulcrum at one extremity. The lever's power becomes stronger the closer the weight stands to the fulcrum; on the other hand, it [i.e., the lever] must also describe a larger arc if the weight is to be lifted.[67] Furthermore, the pins in which the keys move should be of brass, in both [the manuals and in] the pedal, since iron pins rust easily and are not as smooth as brass. The upper keyboard must be capable of being lifted out to allow access to the other [keyboard], in particular when something is out of order in the couplers.

* i.e., further back on the key levers.

§. 353.

Once again, the pedal must be laid out according to the usual dimensions. A while ago I saw a pedal[board] in Rothenstein, a village not far from Jena, where the [pedal] keys were so crowded and narrow that the pedalboard was no more than a third of its [usual] width. First of all, one has to become accustomed to [the unusual dimensions]. But in addition one is never secure in pedaling. Consequently this situation must be considered a fault in an organ, that needs to be corrected.[68] The pedal keys must also be provided with brass pins at their outer ends, in which they travel. They must fit exactly into the lined sheaths, so that they do not rattle as they move up and down, and do not shift from side to side. It is best to lay out the pedalboard so that its middle c† lies directly under the manual middle c′; see §. 29. Many would like to center it under c#, but I do not understand why. For if I place myself in the middle of the [manual] keyboard,‡ why should there not be one octave of pedals on one side of me and the other on the other side.§ The sheath-board (Scheidenbrett¶), as well as the entire pedalboard, must be amply recessed, since otherwise one cannot make any headway when attempting to play anything significant on the pedals. For sometimes one foot must pass behind the other, and then there is not enough room to do it. If one tries to help the situation by moving the bench, then the manuals would lie too far away; this also causes discomfort in playing, and is not advisable. To be sure, players who cannot do much with the pedals do not need such an arrangement—but an organ must be built to suit all types of people.

† i.e., tenor c.
‡ i.e., presuming that the compass is 4 octaves, C-c‴, with middle c exactly in the middle.
§ i.e., presuming that the pedal compass is 2 octaves, C-c′, with the tenor c located in the middle.
¶ Here Adlung seems to be referring to the pierced board through which the levers of the pedal keys pass into the organ case. Adlung describes this board in Vol. I, §. 27 & 28, but refers to it as "das Kerbenbrett."

[67] If an organ's key action is too heavy, it is impossible to play elegantly, and one is constrained to omit the trills and mordents entirely. [Albrecht]

[68] It is also a major fault if one pedal key does not fall as deep as another. Werkmeister mentions this same fault in his *Organum gruningense*, §. 16. [Albrecht]

§. 354.

Die Abstrakten des Pedals sollen auch inwendig seyn, weil man sie sonst mit den Knien zerdrücken würde. Zwar kann es ohne dies nicht geschehen, wo das Manual nicht durch dieselben andas Pedal verknüpft wird; doch soll man auch in dem Falle sie inwendig anbringen. Die Federn sollen von Meßing seyn, und zwar von gleicher Stärke, und in gleicher Anzahl; denn sonst wirdeine palmula schwer zu treten, die andere aber leicht, welches ein großer Fehler bey dem Pedale und Manuale ist. In großen Werken findet man oft 2, 3 und mehrere Federn unter einer palmula; doch muß man sie durchgängig überein machen, sonst wo die eine palmula 1 Feder, die andere 2 u. s. w. hat, da ists ein Zeichen, daß entweder die Federn nichts taugen, oder die Ventile nicht gut passen. In Görlitz zu St. Petri und Pauli sind 7 Federn unter einer palmula. Wie es aber ein Fehler ist, wenn das Manual allzutief hineinfällt, also taugt es auch nichts, wenn das Pedal allzutief hinunterfällt. Doch aber muß es tief genug fallen, daß die Ventile sich weit genug aufziehen, und das Werk satt Wind habe. Die Pedalbank soll beweglich seyn, daß jeder Spieler sie ab- und beyrücken könne, wie ers am liebsten hat; deswegen aber darf sie nicht umfallen. Sie soll auch ihre Füße zu beyden Seiten über das Pedal hinaus strecken, sonst wird durch etwas Verrücken ein Geheul verursacht, wenn die palmulae sich an den Füßen stoßen. Man macht sie itzo auf beyden Seiten schief, s. §. 29. und verwahret sie rund herum, daß etwas darein verschlossen werden kann. Die Anzahl der Palmulen endlich anlangend, so macht man sie nach dem Manuale; doch habe ich auch gefunden, daß, obgleich im Manuale kurze Oktave gewesen, man doch das Pedal vollständig gemacht hat. Etliche Orgelbauer haben die Mode, das C anstatt das Dis zu setzen, und unten das Pedal mit D anzufangen: aber dies taugt nichts. Man bleibe bey der Ordnung, und fange mit C an, und ende es oben mit c̄. Kann man es haben; so thue man noch oben c̄is und d̄ dazu. Es ist diese Sache so neu nicht, sondern man findet diesen Umstand an gar vielen alten Orgeln, daß sie nämlich noch einige palmulas über das c̄ haben. Es kosten auch die Pfeifen dazu nicht gar viel, weil sie nicht gar groß werden. Zu Eisenach gehet das Pedal bis ins c̄, und hält 29 palmulas in sich; zu Weissenfelß reicht es gar bis ins f: das ist aber überflüßig. (**)

(**) Ich wüßte nicht warum es überflüßig wäre. Zu gewissen Arten von Pedalstücken ist es vielmehr sehr gut.

§. 355.

Wie die Registerknöpfe anzubringen, ist schon §. 335. erinnert worden. Hier melde ich noch, daß es mit den eisernen Registern nicht fein sey, wenn sie auf- und abwärts geschoben werden, weil es so ein arges Klappern verursacht, zumal wenn das Registerziehen eilig ist. Auch merke ich noch dieses an, daß es nicht übel gethan sey, wenn die Register zu jedem Claviere mit Farben unterschieden werden. Denn es kann nicht allezeit die Reihe geschlossen werden, daß keins in der benachbarten Reihe zu stehen käme nach der Eurythmie, da es einem doch Verwirrung verursacht, wenn man zuerst ein solches Werk spielt. So sind in Görlitz die Register mit Farben unterschieden, jedes

§. 354.

Furthermore, the pedal trackers must be inside* [the case], since otherwise they would be crushed by the knees. To be sure, this cannot happen if there are no trackers that couple the pedal to the manual;† but even in that case [all the pedal trackers] should be built inside [the case]. The springs should be of brass; they should all have the same tension, and there should be the same number of them [for each pedal key]. Otherwise one key will be difficult to tread, while another will be light, and this is a major fault in the pedal as well as in the manual. In large instruments one often finds 2, 3 or more springs under one [pedal] key; but the number must be consistent throughout. Where one key has 1 spring, another 2, etc., it is a sign that either the springs are inferior or the pallets do not fit well. At St. Petri & Pauli in Görlitz there are seven springs under each [pedal] key.‡ Just as it is a fault, however, when the manual keyfall is too deep, it is also unsatisfactory if the pedal keys travel too far. But they must travel deep enough to open the pallets fully and give the instrument enough wind. The organ bench should be movable, so that every player can move it forward or back as he prefers; for this reason, it must be stable. Its side supports must extend beyond the pedalboard on both sides; otherwise it may cause ciphering when it is shifted and the supports strike the keys. Both the side supports are now built at a slant, and the bench should be enclosed on all sides, so that things may be locked up in it. Finally, the number of keys [per octave] should be equivalent to those in the manual;§ but I have also found that pedal [divisions] are made complete even if there is a short octave in the manuals. Some organbuilders follow the practice of putting C in place of D#, and beginning the pedal at the bottom with D, but this is unsatisfactory. The normal arrangement should be preserved, beginning with C at the bottom and ending with c′ on top. If possible c# and d′ should be added on top. This is not such a new practice; indeed, one finds that quite a number of old organs have several [pedal] keys above c′. The pipes for it cost very little, since they are not very large. At Eisenach the pedal extends upward to e′ and has 29 keys; at Weissenfels it even goes up to f—but that is excessive.(**)

(**) I do not know why it should be [considered] excessive. On the contrary, for certain types of pieces that require the pedals it is very good. [Agricola]

§. 355.

I have already mentioned in §. 335¶ how the stopknobs should be arranged. Here I will add that it is not good if they are made of iron, since then they create such an annoying clatter when they are shoved in and out, especially if this is done quickly. I will also mention that it is not a bad idea to differentiate the stops of each division by color. For it is not always possible to contain [each division] in one row, without for the sake of eurythmy placing some stops in a neighboring row. But this creates confusion for someone when playing such an instrument for the first time. Thus at Görlitz the stops are differentiated by color, each according to its manual.‖ If in addition a sign of the

---

* i.e., they must be covered by a knee panel.

† i.e., only these trackers are located far enough forward that the organist's knees could reach them.

‡ Boxberg, p.[10]; Boxberg reports that the pedals are therefore rather hard to depress.

§ See §. 351.

¶ incorrect citation; it should read "§. 345."

‖ See Boxberg, p.[10].

nach seinem Claviere. Wollte man über dies auf den Clavieren ein gleiches Zeichen machen, daß man sogleich sehen könne, welche Farbe jedem Claviere respondire; so wäre es auch gut, und nicht zu verwerfen.

§. 356.

Wir kommen auf die **Windlade**, deren Theile Kap. 3. erzählet worden; allda dieselbe zweyerley war, nämlich die **Springlade** und die **Schleiflade**. Jene sind sehr alt, und wurden ehedessen fast überall gemacht, sonderlich in Holland. Nachdem man aber die Schleifladen accurat machen gelernet, und bey solchen nicht soviel Incommoditäten vorkommen, als bey jenen; so sind sie bey uns fast gar abgekommen, und die Holländer folgen hierinne auch nach. Die Springladen haben dies voraus, daß man kein Durchstechen hört: aber sie haben viel incommoda bey sich, welche **Werkmeister** erzählt in der **Orgelprobe** Kap. 17. und 18. S. 39., welche ich hersetzen will, weil man bey der Probe die Fehler einer Springlade darnach erkennen und beurtheilen kann. Er sagt: „Nicht jeder Orgelmacher kennt sie; und sie wollen einen fleißigen Arbeiter „haben. Denn bald bleibt ein Druckel stehen, bald schwinden die Stöcke, bald die „Keilleisten, worunter die Stöcke befestiget, bald kann eine Feder abspringen, wel„ches gar oft geschieht, bald kann ein Druckel bey dem Ventile vorbey treten, bald „kann ein Ventil nicht just wieder vortreten und decken, bald werden die Drückel „nicht gleich gebohret, daß sie alsdann mit dem Parallel vollens krumm geschlagen „werden: bald gehen die Parallelen zu hoch in die Höhe, daß die Drückel (ach lei„der) herausspringen; bald sind die Federn gar zu schwach, daß die Druckel stecken, „und die Ventile offen bleiben, bald springen die Federn gar heraus: bald fällt et„was unter die Ventile. Summa, wo vielerley Arbeit ist, da fället öfters was „zu verbessern vor. Nun ist viel mehr Arbeit und Gekrickele in den Springladen, als „in den Schleifladen, darum ist in den Springladen öfter etwas zu bessern, als in den „Schleifladen. So werden auch mehrentheils die Ventile in Springladen mit weißem „Bleche auf die Stöcke geheftet: wenn denn das Blech rostet, so frißt der Rost das „Leder entzwey, dann haben die Herrn Orgelmacher wieder etwas zu thun, welches „ihr Vortheil, und der Kirchen und Gemeine Schaden. Darum sollen zu solcher Be„festigung meßingene und nicht eiserne Bleche genommen und getaucht werden."

§. 357.

Die andere Art der Springladen, davon **Werkmeister** l. c. S. 41. etwas schreibet, und meldet, daß man die Stöcke könne heraus nehmen, so daß die Pfeifen auf einem besondern Stocke stehen bleiben, hat dies incommodum, daß, weil der obere Stock veste ist, und nicht mit Schrauben dirigirt wird, der Wind durchgehet, wenn sich das Wetter ändert; und wären auch schon Schrauben da, wer will stets dabey sitzen, wenn sich das Wetter ändert? Sonst kann man von der Windlade, auch von der Springlade **Prätor**. T. II. p. 107. u. f. nachschlagen, welcher zeigt, woher sie entstanden.

§. 358.

same [color] could be set on the keyboard, so that one could see immediately which color corresponds to which keyboard, that would also be good and unobjectionable.

§. 356.

Next we come to the windchest, whose components were described in Chapter 3. There [we stated that there] were two types, namely the spring chest and the slider chest. The former are very ancient, and were formerly built almost everywhere, especially in Holland. After builders learned to make slider chests accurately, however, [spring chests] have become almost totally obsolete in this area, and the Hollanders are also following suit, since slider chests do not have as many inconveniences as spring chests. Spring chests have the advantage of never having runs, but they have many drawbacks. Werkmeister describes these in his *Orgelprobe*, Chapters 17 & 18, p. 39[f.], and I will reproduce [his remarks] here, since thereby one can recognize and evaluate the faults of a spring chest when examining [a new organ]. He says: "Not every organbuilder knows how to build them; they require a competent craftsman. For sometimes a sticker gets stuck, sometimes the toeboards shrink, or the wedges that fasten down the toeboards, sometimes a spring flies off (this happens quite often), sometimes a sticker slips past the pallet, sometimes a pallet fails to reseat itself and seal properly. Sometimes the stickers are not precisely aligned, and then they are bent entirely out of shape by the pallet rods; sometimes the pallet rods rise too high above the chest, so that the stickers (alas!) fly out. Sometimes the springs are so weak that the stickers jam and the pallets stay open; sometimes the springs fly out entirely. Sometimes something falls under the pallets.* In sum, where there is a complicated mechanism, there is more often something to repair. Since there is much more handiwork and intricate detail in a spring chest than in a slider chest, there is consequently more often something to repair in them than in a slider chest. For example, the pallets in spring chests are usually fastened to the toeboards with tin-plated sheet iron; then when the metal rusts, the rust corrodes the leather.† Then the gentlemen who build organs again have something to do, which is to their advantage and to the loss of the church and parish. Therefore tin-plated brass and not tin-plated sheet iron should be selected and used for this kind of fastening."

* keeping them from closing.

† This statement may be referring to the pallet hinges or to the leather linings of the chest.

§. 357.

Werkmeister writes something about the other type of spring chest in the *Orgelprobe*, p. 41, reporting that [with this second type] the pipes are mounted on a separate toeboard [above the main one] and the toeboards can be removed. But this system has the drawback that, since the upper board is in a fixed position and cannot be adjusted by screws, the wind escapes as the weather changes. And even if there were screws, who would want to have to tend them constantly with every change in the weather? Concerning the windchest as well as the spring chest, one may also consult Praetorius [*Syntagma musicum*] Vol. II, pp. 107f; this [source] indicates whence they originated.

§. 358.

Wir bleiben also bey der Schleiflade, und erinnern hierbey hauptsächlich, daß zu allen Windladen das dürreste Holz zu nehmen sey. Die Schleiflade muß accurat passen, und recht egal gearbeitet seyn. Man pflegt sie zu beledern; allein ich wünschte, man machte sie so accurat, daß sie auch ohne Leder keinen Wind durchstechen ließe. Denn das Leder reibt sich ab, rollt sich zusammen, und machet Ungelegenheiten. Billig muß die Lade auch ohne Leder die Probe halten. Die Unterschiede in der Lade, welche die Cancellen von einander unterscheiden, müssen, wie die Lade, von Eichenholze seyn, und auf allen Seiten wohl antreten, sonst marschiret der Wind aus einer Cancelle in die andere, und sticht durch. Das ist, wenn ich z. Ex. den clauem a angeschlagen, so gehet der Wind in die Cancelle a, aus derselben aber gehet etwas davon in die benachbarte Cancelle durch solche Ritzen, und bläßt den darneben liegenden clauem an, doch sehr schwach, weil es wenig Wind ist; man hört es aber doch. Und das ist ein Fehler. Ist ein Register gezogen, so hört man es zuweilen deutlich; sind mehrere gezogen, so wird der wenige Wind allzusehr zertheilt, und behält deswegen keine Kraft, eine Pfeife klingend zu machen. Wer nun probiren will, ob eine Lade durchsteche, der muß ein Register ziehen, und einen clauem nach dem andern anschlagen.

§. 359.

Die ganze Windlade muß wohl mit Leim ausgegossen seyn; denn das Holz ist porös, und durch die subtilen Poros marschirt Wind: daher man das Ausgiessen ja nicht unterlassen darf. Einige machen eine besondere Masse dazu; welches aber den Orgelmachern verbleiben mag. Von des Casparini inventiösen Invetriatur ist §. 38. gesagt worden. Ein Fehler ist, wenn ein Fundamentbrett gemacht wird. Was das sey, ist §. 37. zu lesen. Es hat viel Incommoditäten bey sich. Denn es zieht sich oft mit den Schrauben, und verwirft sich in verändertem Wetter, alsdann stichts durch. Man spünde die Cancellen lieber zu. In der Beschreibung der grüningischen Orgel §. 21. hat Werkmeister diese Gedanken, weil sich daselbst dieser Fehler auch geäussert. Die Register, oder Parallelen, müssen recht accurat aufliegen, daß darunter kein Wind von einem Loche zum andern ziehe. (Wenn das geschiehet, werden die Stöcke nach und nach schwarz, als ob sie geräuchert wären.) Die Löcher derselben, wie auch der Spünde, sollen wohl ausgebrannt und rund seyn, daß sie das Leder nicht abreiben.

§. 360.

Damit die Parallelen sich nicht so weit aufthun, so sollen sie oben und in der Mitte mit starken meßingenen Stiften versehen seyn. Sie müssen von rechtem guten Holze seyn, und zwar von dem Holze, davon die Dämme gemacht sind. Ordentlicherweise nimmt man recht gesundes und ausgedorrtes Eichenholz dazu. Denn wenn dazu zweyerley Holz genommen wird, und das Wetter wird verändert, so schwellen die Register und Dämme nicht zugleich, oder nicht auf einerley Art. Wenn das Holz der Dämme im

§. 358.

Thus we will stay with the slider chest, above all mentioning about it that the most completely cured wood should be used for all the windchests. The slider chest must fit together precisely, and must be perfectly fashioned. It is customary to cover them with leather, but I would like them to be made so precisely that they are absolutely air-tight without leathering them. For the leather gets abraded or bunched up and creates problems. The chest simply must be able to stand the test without leather. The dividers in the chest that separate the channels from each other must be of oak, like the chest [itself], and must fit tightly at all its edges; otherwise the wind passes from one channel into another and runs. That means that if I strike the key a, for example, the wind passes into channel a, but some of it passes through some cracks into the neighboring channel, and makes the adjacent note sound. Even though the sound is very weak, since the amount of wind is very little, it is still audible, and that is a fault. If one stop is drawn, it may at times be heard clearly; if several are drawn [at once], though, then the small amount of wind is distributed so widely that it does not maintain enough force to make a pipe sound. Anyone who wants to test whether a chest has runs should draw one stop and play one key after another.

§. 359.

The entire windchest must be thoroughly impregnated with glue. This is because wood is porous, and wind passes through the tiny pores; thus [the builder] must not fail to impregnate [the chest]. Some [builders] make a special substance for this purpose, but this [matter] is better left to the organbuilders. Casparini's ingenious *Invetriatur* has already been mentioned in §. 38. It is a mistake to make a table (consult §. 37 to find out what that is). It has many drawbacks, such as becoming distorted from the screws or warping with changes in the weather, and then running. It is better to cover the channels with sponsels. Werkmeister also advances this idea in his description of the organ at Gröningen, §. 21,* since this fault also manifested itself there. The stops, or sliders, must fit very precisely on top, so that no wind runs from one [slider] hole to another—if that happens, then the toe-boards eventually become black, as if they were smoked. The [edges of the] holes in them [i.e., the sliders], as well as those in the sponsels, should be thoroughly burned out and rounded, so they do not abrade the leather.

* See also §. 23 of this source, the *Organum gruningense redivivum*.

§. 360.

In order that the sliders do not move too far, they should be provided with strong brass pins on top/at one end and in the middle.† [The sliders] must be made of very good wood, indeed of the same wood that the spacers are made of. Normally very sound and well-cured oak wood is used to make these. For if two kinds of wood are used, the sliders and the spacers do not swell at the same time or to the same degree when the weather changes. If the wood employed for the spacers swells more in damp weather,

† Adlung may be referring to the practice of cutting an oblong hole in the middle of a slider, into which a pin that is driven into the chest projects; thus the pin would prevent the slider from travelling too far in either direction. "In the middle" may refer to the mid-point in the width of the slider, rather than in its length. Cf. also §. 36 in Vol. I, which states that sliders are stopped by pins driven into the end of the chest.

feuchten Wetter mehr aufschwillt; so werden die darauf ruhenden Stöcke weiter von den Parallelen entfernet, daß der Wind nicht alle aus den Parallelen in die Stöcke gehet, sondern sich zerstreuet. Alsdann sind die Register allzuleicht zu ziehen. Wenn eben das Holz der Dämme im dürren Wetter mehr einfeucht oder schwindet, als die Parallelen; so setzen sich die Stöcke auch schärfer auf die Parallelen, daß man sie fast nicht erziehen kann. Diesem Uebel abzuhelfen muß man mit dem Schraubenzwinger die Stöcke höher oder niedriger schrauben können. Wenn die Parallelen mehr schwellen, als die Dämme, so ists mit dem Registerziehen verkehrt; denn da sind sie im feuchten Wetter schlimm zu ziehen. Schwinden sie mehr, so sind sie gut zu ziehen. Also begreift man hieraus, wie es zugehe, daß in einer Orgel die Register im nassen Wetter schwer zu ziehen sind, im trockenen aber gut; In der andern Orgel hingegen im guten Wetter schwer, im feuchten aber leicht. Wenn aber einerley Holz zu den Dämmen und Parallelen genommen wird; so schwellen und schwinden sie zugleich, und folglich bleibt der Stock immer gleich weit von ihnen entfernet; folglich sind die Register immer gleich schwer zu ziehen, ohne was etwan die Feuchtigkeit verursacht, als welche alles rauch macht. ⁶⁹) Es müssen aber auch die Dämme so gemacht werden, daß die Seite des Holzes, die am Baume in der Höhe gestanden, itzo nicht aufwärts zu stehen komme. Denn aufwärts schwillt das Holz nicht, schwindet auch wenig; aber wohl geschiehet beydes in die Breite und Dicke. Die Parallelen werden auch so gelegt, daß der Theil, der an dem Baume in die Höhe gieng, hier auf der Seite sey. Folglich müssen die Dämme auch so seyn.

§. 361.

Es geschiehet oft, wenn ein Register gezogen wird, daß das andere sich von freyen Stücken wieder zurück ziehet. Quaer: Wie gehet das zu? Resp. Es sind auf der Lade ordentlich zwey Parallelen hart an einander zwischen den Dämmen. Ist nun das Wetter feucht, und sie klemmen sich etwas; so wird eins das andere mit sich ziehen. Eine Parallele wird aber von der rechten, die andern hingegen von der linken Seite her aufgezogen; folglich kann eine die andere mit sich führen. Es kann auch wol kommen, daß sich die Stifte der Wellen und Arme an einander hängen, und dergleichen Umstand verursachen. Ferner ist ein Fehler, wenn die Schrauben nicht jeden Stock an die Lade heften: oder wenn dieselben von Eisen sind, weil es im feuchten Wetter feucht wird, und die Lade anhebt zu faulen; auch rosten sie, daß man dieselben mit dem Schraubenzwinger nicht kann herum drehen. Die Stöcke sollen nicht zu groß werden, daß man sie sammt den Pfeifen bequem abheben könne. Auch ists gut, wenn auf einem Stocke nur die Pfeifen eines Registers stehen: es müßten denn die Pfeifen oder die Lade gar zu klein seyn. (**)

(**) Oder es müßten gewisse doppelte Register das Gegentheil erfordern. Siehe z. Er. Seite 229 und 245. des 1sten Bandes.

§. 362.

⁶⁹ Welchem noch beyzusetzen, wenn das Holz zu den Registern sich verwirft.

then the toeboards that rest on them will be raised further from the sliders, and then all the wind will not pass through the slider [holes] and into the toeboard [holes], but will become dispersed.* In this case the stop[knobs] are too easily drawn. If, however, the wood employed for the spacers contracts or shrinks more than the sliders in dry weather, then the toeboards will sit more heavily on the sliders, making them almost impossible to pull. In order to remedy this malady, it must be possible to tighten or loosen the toeboards with a screw-clamp.† If [on the other hand] the sliders swell more than the spacers, then the reverse situation prevails when drawing stops; in that case they are difficult to pull in damp weather, and if they shrink more [than the spacers in dry weather], then they are easy to pull. From this one may understand how it happens that in one organ the stops are difficult to pull in wet weather, but easy in dry, while in another organ, on the other hand, they are difficult in good‡ weather, but easy in damp. If, however, the same kind of wood is used for both spacers and sliders, then they swell and shrink equally, and consequently the toeboard always stays the same distance from them. As a result, the stops are always equally difficult to pull, except when dampness gets into them and makes everything uneven.[69]§ The spacers must also be made so that the grain of the wood is not vertical, since wood swells and shrinks vertically hardly at all, but it does swell horizontally in all directions. The grain of the wood used for the sliders is made to lie horizontally, and thus the spacers must follow suit.

* thus causing runs.

† See §. 463, Vol. II, p. 81.

‡ i.e., dry.

§ "als welche alles rauch macht." Here "rauch"="rauh." Thus the sense of the statement is that dampness causes all the wooden parts of the stop action to swell and become distorted; thus they become difficult to pull, no matter how carefully they have been built.

§. 361.

When one stop is drawn, it often happens that another [stopknob] retires all by itself. Question: How does that happen? Answer: On the chest there are ordinarily two sliders right next to each other between the spacers. If the weather is damp, and they bind each other a bit, then one will draw the other along with it. One slider, however, is drawn from the right side, while on the other hand the other is drawn from the left. Consequently one can draw the other with it. It may also happen that the pins of the rollers and arms [of the stop action] catch on each other, and cause the same situation. Furthermore, it is a fault if the screws do not fasten every toeboard to the chest, or if the [screws] are made of iron, since [iron] gets damp in humid weather and the chest commences to rot. [The screws] also rust, and then it is impossible to turn them with the screw-clamp. The toeboards should not be so large that one cannot remove them with the pipes on them. It is also good for the pipes of only one stop to stand on a toeboard, unless the pipes or the chest are simply too small.(**)

(**) Or unless certain doubled registers require the contrary. See, e.g., page 229¶ and 245‖ of the first volume. [Agricola]

[69]) To which may be added, "if the wood in the sliders warps." [Albrecht]

¶ Agricola is referring to the Vox humana on the Hauptmanual of the organ in the Stadtkirche in Gera, with doubled pipes (one a reed, the other a flue) for each note on the same toeboard; see the stoplist of this organ in Chapter 10.

‖ Agricola is referring to the Contrabass in the Pedal at the Jena Stadtkirche, with a 32′ stopped pipe and a 16′ open for each note on the same toeboard; see the stoplist of this organ in Chapter 10.

und Fehlern einer Orgel.

§. 362.

Man muß um die Lade herumgehen können des Stimmens wegen; auch daß man die Stöcke allenthalben schrauben könne; sonderlich muß man können zu den Ventilen kommen, weil man bald nöthig hat eins davon gleich zu rücken, bald es von der darauf gefallenen Unreinigkeiten zu reinigen, bald die Federn zu corrigiren. ꝛc. Die Lade muß auf guten Balken liegen: auch keine spanische Reuter oder schwedische Stiche haben. Dadurch versteht man die Schnitte und Stiche, die man in die Lade macht, damit wenn der Wind durchsticht, er dadurch auswärts gehe, und nicht in die Pfeifen komme, oder doch geschwächt werde. Wie dieses ein Zeichen ist, daß die Lade nicht accurat gemacht worden; so hat man es für einen Hauptfehler anzusehen, der dem Orgelmacher nicht zu gute gehen darf. Der Wind ist edel, und darf man ihn nicht von der Lade leiten.

§. 363.

Der Windkasten muß ebenfalls accurat werden, und zwar von uraltem Holze, das gar nicht quillt; auch soll er mit dem Leim wohl ausgegossen werden. [70] Wundert man sich, daß man alle Poros vor dem Winde verschlossen haben will; so bedenke man, daß es kein gemeiner Wind sey, sondern ein solcher, der durch so starke Gewichte in den Windkasten und in die Windlade gezwungen wird, daß man da die Luft fast greifen kann. Bey dergleichen force bricht er durch, wo auch nur die geringsten Oefnungen sich finden. Wenn die Lade sehr breit ist; so ist es wohl gethan, wenn auf beyden Seiten Windkasten und Ventile angeleget werden, daß der Wind in gehöriger force und Behändigkeit alle Register anblasen könne. Die Ventile in dem Windkasten müssen auf der breiten Seite, oder oben, wohl beledert werden, daß sie accurater decken und nicht so sehr klappen. Das Leder muß aber auf jedem Ventile für sich von gleicher Dicke seyn, sonst würden nicht alle Theile des Ventils vest anschliessen. Es soll das Leder auch nicht zu kalkigt oder salpeterisch seyn, weil solches die Feuchtigkeit an sich ziehet. Die Ventile müssen von leichtem Holze gemacht werden, und zwar von solchem Holze, das sich nicht verwirft, oder krumm wird. Etliche wollen dem Verwerfen damit vorbauen, wenn sie die Ventile mit Schrauben befestigen. So ist es im Stifte Maria in Erfurt und in Zimmern supra. Wenn man da ein Ventil abnehmen will; so ist es zwar etwas mühsam, die Schrauben erst auszuziehen; allein diese Incommodität ist so groß nicht, daß man nöthig hatte, diese Invention deswegen zu verachten. Ich lobe sie vielmehr; ob ich gleich nicht in Abrede seyn will, daß ein accurater Meister, wenn er gut Holz nimmt, und es wohl traktirt, das Verwerfen auch ohne dies verhüten könne. Es muß nämlich die Breite der Flamme des Holzes nicht die obere Fläche des Ventils seyn, sondern auf die Seite fallen. Sie sollen unten conisch, oder spitzig zugehen: denn wenn sie breit sind; so legt sich der Wind allzuscharf dargegen, und machet, daß sie sich schwer aufziehen. Ein solch Werk heißt sodann: Windzähe.

§. 364.

---

[70] Das Gegentheil hiervon bemerkt **Werkmeister** in Organo grüningensi §. 23. als einen Fehler.

§. 362.

One must be able to get around on the chest for the purpose of tuning, and also so that one can adjust the screws of the toeboards at all points. In particular the pallets must be accessible, since it is necessary at times to shift one of them right away, or to cleanse it from dirt that has fallen upon it, or to adjust the spring, etc. The chest must lie on solid beams, and must not have any bleed grooves or holes.* These terms refer to the grooves and punctures that are made in the chest to allow the wind to escape when it runs, thus keeping it from getting into the pipes or at least weakening it.† Since this is a sign that the chest is not accurately constructed, it must be considered a major fault, and one ought not let the organ builder get away with it. Wind is precious, and it ought not be allowed to escape from the chest.

* These are mentioned in Vol. I, §. 256, where they are also called "Laufgraben"; see also §. 444 below.

† i.e., so that it cannot cause a pipe to sound; see §. 444.

§. 363.

The pallet box must likewise be meticulously [crafted], and indeed of thoroughly cured wood that will not swell at all. It must also be thoroughly impregnated with glue.70) If anyone wonders why all the pores must be sealed to the wind, just consider that it is no ordinary wind, but is forced into the palletbox and the windchest by such a heavy weight that one can almost take hold of the air.‡ Under such pressure it forces its way through even the tiniest openings. If the chest is very wide, it is good to place pallet boxes and pallets on both sides, so that the wind may feed all the stops with the proper strength and uniformity. The pallets in the pallet boxes must be thoroughly covered with leather on their wider side, i.e., on top, so that they fit more snugly and do not clatter so much. The leather on each individual pallet must be of the same thickness, otherwise not all areas of the pallet will seal tightly. The leather also must not have too much lime or saltpeter, because these attract dampness. The pallets must be made of lightweight wood, and of a variety that does not warp or become crooked. Some have tried to guard against warping by fastening the pallets with screws.§ That is how they are at St. Mary's Cathedral in Erfurt and in Zimmern supra.¶ If one wishes to remove a pallet in those places, it is somewhat troublesome at first, to be sure, to remove the screws; but this inconvenience is not so great as to warrant scorning this invention on its account. On the contrary, I praise it, although I cannot deny that a meticulous master can prevent warping without it, if he uses good wood and treats it well. The broad grain of the wood must not be on the upper surface of the pallet, but on the side. [The pallets] must be beveled or pointed underneath, for if they are broad, then the wind presses too heavily against them and makes them difficult to pull.‖ An instrument with this characteristic is called "tough-winded."

‡ i.e., it is so thick and compressed.

§ See §. 366 below.

¶ See the stoplists of these organs in Chapter 10.

‖ i.e., makes the action hard to play.

---

70) Werkmeister in his *Organum gruningense*, §. 23, cites the opposite of this as a fault.** [Albrecht]

** Werkmeister, *Organum gruningense*, §. 23, says: "The impregnation with glue was also very scanty [i.e., in the organ at Gröningen], and thus no small amount of wind escaped.

§. 364.

Wenn die Ventile nicht allzubreit, sondern schmal und desto länger sind; so wird das Clavier auch leichter zu spielen. Hingegen wird es etwas tief fallen müssen. Wenn das Angehänge weit hinten nach der Feder zu angehänget wird; so wird ein Clavier abermal schwer zu drücken: hingegen aber braucht es nicht tief zu fallen, und doch wird das Ventil sich weit aufthun. Wenn aber das Angehänge weit vor kömmt; so wird es zwar leichter zu spielen, aber das Clavier muß auch tiefer fallen, wenn das Ventil sich weit genug aufthun soll. Man nimmt von beyden commodis etwas. Hieraus folgt, daß alle Angehänge gleich weit vom Ende angemacht werden müssen, daß die palmulae überein zu drücken sind, und daß ein Ventil so weit aufgehe als das andere. Die Demonstration ist fast wie oben §. 352.

§. 365.

Die Federn sollen von Meßing seyn, daß sie nicht rosten, und dabey ihre Kraft behalten. Nicht zu schwach: denn obgleich das Clavier dadurch leichter zu spielen ist, so heulet es doch zuweilen, weil, bey schwachen Federn, die Ventile nicht recht decken: aber auch nicht zu stark, weil alsdann das Clavier schwer zu spielen wird. Damit ein clavis so leicht sey, als der andere: so müssen sie zwar insgesammt wohlgezogen seyn, und nach ihrer Elasticität frisch anschlagen; doch muß eine so stark seyn, als die andere. Noch weniger ist zu dulden, wenn ein Ventil eine, das andere zwo Federn hat. Das zeuget von der Unrichtigkeit der Ventile. Wo ein clavis schwach, der andere schwer zu drücken ist, da mag der beste Künstler nichts gutes spielen. Also sind gar viel Ursachen vorhanden, warum ein Clavier nicht so zu traktiren ist, wie das andere. 71) Die Stifte, zwischen welchen die Ventile aufgehen, dienen dazu daß diese sich nicht auf die Seite begeben. Es sollen dieselben von Meßing seyn, nicht zu kurz, daß die tief aufgezogenen Ventile nicht darauf treten; nicht krumm, sonst bleiben die Ventile stecken. Eben deswegen dürfen sie nicht allzunahe stehen, daß die Ventile ihre Spielung haben. Wenn man die Art des Casparini haben kann, davon §. 38. steht, daß zu jedem clave ein besonderer Kanal ist, deren jeder sich in dem Ventil endet, und welche durch das Ventil zugleich aufgemacht werden; so müssen die Ventile in die Quere aufgezogen werden, s. davon §. 41. Dies ist zu recommandiren. (**) Auf solche Art sind die Baßventile zun Predigern in Erfurt, und in Niedernissa gemacht worden.

(**) Andere Kunstverständige sagen, daß eben deswegen die Görlitzer Orgel so gar schwer zu spielen ist.

§. 366.

Die Beutelchen oder Säckchen müssen nicht zu kurz seyn, sonst thun sie diejenigen Dienste nicht, die sie thun sollen. (conf. §. 41.) Der Windkasten wird von vornen

---

71) Die Federn müssen auch gerade unter den Ventilen eingesetzt seyn, sonst geben sich die Ventile auf eine Seite, und schaben sich nach und nach in die Stifte. S. Werkmeisters Organum grüningense §. 22. und 24.

Chap. XIII. Concerning the Merits

§. 364.

If the pallets are not too wide, but narrow and thus proportionately longer, then the keys will be easier to play. On the other hand, they will travel deeper. If the trackers are connected far to the rear [of the pallet] toward the spring, then the keys will again be difficult to depress, but on the other hand they will not travel so deep before fully opening the pallet. If they are connected right at the front [of the pallet], the keys will be easier to play, to be sure, but they will also have to travel deeper in order to open the pallet wide enough. One should find a happy medium. It follows from this that all the trackers must be connected an equal distance from the end [of the pallet], so that the keys have the same touch, and all the pallets open equally wide. The proof of this is almost the same as in §. 352 above.

§. 365.

The springs should be of brass, so that they keep their strength and do not rust. [They should] not be too weak; for then although the keyboard will be easier to play, it will sometimes cipher, since with weak springs the pallets will not seal properly. But [they should] not be too strong, since then the keyboard will be difficult to play. In order that one key is as easy to play as another, [the springs] must all be well tempered and rebound with vigorous elasticity. But they must all be equally strong. It is even less tolerable if one pallet has one spring and another has two. That is evidence of unevenness in the pallets. Even the finest artist cannot play well if one key is easy to depress and the next one difficult. Thus many reasons may be given why one keyboard may not be played like another[71] The pins between which the pallets move serve to keep the pallets from shifting to one side. They should be made of brass, not so short that the fully open pallets catch on them, and not crooked, otherwise the pallets get stuck. For the same reason they must not stand too close together, so that the pallets have some play. If it is possible to have the sort [of pallets] like Casparini's that are discussed in §. 38, where every note [of every stop] has a separate channel that ends at the pallet and where [all the channels] are opened simultaneously by the [same] pallet, then the pallets must be drawn open sideways; q.v. §. 41. This [system] is to be recommended.(**) This is the way the pedal pallets at the Predigerkirche in Erfurt and in Niedernissa* are made.

* There is no listing for an organ in this place, either in Adlung's book or in the other sets of stoplists he integrates into his list.

(**) Other experts in this art say it is for this very reason that the organ at Görlitz has such a heavy action. [Agricola]

§. 366.

The pouches must not be too short, otherwise they do not function as they ought (cf. §. 41.). The pallet box is provided with a bungboard at the front, with rings or straps

---

[71] The springs must also be positioned upright under the pallets, otherwise the pallets will twist to one side and the pins will gradually abrade them. [Albrecht]

vornen verspündet, doch so, daß durch angebrachte Ringe, oder Riemen, die Spünde können heraus gezogen werden, wenn man zu den Ventilen kommen will. Gar fein ists, wenn man die Windkasten von unten her öfnet, daß man die Ventile besser heraus nehmen und mit den Händen richten könne; da denn anstatt daß man die an den Ventilen hinten angeleimten Leder an den Kasten oben anleimet, gar artig ist, wenn man sie durch Bretterchen anschraubt, daß man allezeit das verlangte Ventil ausnehmen und einsetzen könne. So ists im Dom zu Erfurt, und zu Zimmern supra. Siehe, was dieses Umstands wegen §. 363. beygebracht worden. Ein Fehler bey den Spünden ist, wenn sie nicht wohl beledert werden, und daher den Wind zum Theil durchlassen; auch wenn sie nicht mit Vorschlägen versehen sind: denn da kann die Gewalt des Windes sie heraus treiben, wenn sie eingedorret sind. Ein Windkasten muß, wenn er lang ist, viel Spünde haben. In den Kasten gehet der Wind durch Röhren oder große Kanäle. Wenn diese nicht weit genug sind, so ist der Zufall des Windes zu schwach, und im vollen Werke klingt die Orgel unrein; auch schlagen nicht alle Pfeifen in der Tiefe in gehöriger Geschwindigkeit an, womit sodann das so verhaßte Schwanken verknüpft ist; welches auch geschiehet, wenn die Cancellen zu klein sind, und doch viele und große Stimmen darauf zu stehen kommen. Am besten ists, man läßt den Wind durch mehr als eine Oefnung in den Kasten fallen. conf. §. 363.

§. 367.

Wir kommen aufs Eingeweide der Orgel, das Pfeifwerk ausgenommen. Da treffen wir verschiedene Windröhren oder Windführungen an. Etliche gehen nach dem Windkasten zu, andre aber gehen von der Windlade anderwärts wohin. Also gehen etliche nach denen im Gesicht stehenden Pfeifen, Sonnen, Statüen, Stern ꝛc. etliche nach inwendig stehenden Pfeifen. Denn zuweilen leidet die Breite der Lade nicht, eine große Stimme unmittelbar auf die Stöcke zu setzen, und doch soll sie darauf: da setzt man auf die Stöcke Röhren, so lang als nöthig, und auf die Röhren die Pfeifen, da dann die Röhren schief stehen, und oben aus einander gehen, eine da= die andere dorthin; da haben die Pfeifen Raum. Es steht dieses nicht fein, und ist auch schädlich: aber Noth hat kein Gesetz. Daraus sieht man, wieviel daran liege, eine Orgel recht auszubreiten. Alle Windführungen und Röhren sind entweder von Holz oder Metall; alle müssen auf beyden Seiten recht passen, und aus diesem Grunde werden sie mit Leder versehen. Das Holz dazu mus recht dürre seyn, sonst bekommen sie Ritzen und halten keinen Wind. Sie sollen wie andere hölzerne Windführungen nach der Lade mit Leim ausgegossen seyn.

§. 368.

Die Abstrakten müssen sonderlich von gutem geschmeidigem Holze seyn, daß sie sich nicht verwerfen: sonst ist das Clavier nie gerade. Sie sollen auch leicht seyn, und daher weder breit noch dicke, daß sie unter dem Windladenventil keine so starken Federn erfordern, dadurch die Claviere schwer zu drücken sind. Wenn sie sehr weit in die Höhe gehen;

affixed to it so that the board can be pulled out to allow access to the pallets. It is especially advantageous to be able to open the pallet boxes from underneath, so that the pallets may be more easily removed and adjusted by hand. Then, instead of glueing the leather attached to the back side of the pallets onto the top of the box,* it is particularly handy to screw them on with strips of wood, so that any pallet may be removed or inserted at any time. This is how it is at the Cathedral in Erfurt and at Zimmern supra; see what has been said about this matter† in §. 363. It is a fault for the bungboards not to be totally faced with leather, for then they let some of the wind escape; also if they are not provided with stays, since then the wind pressure can force them out when they become dried out.‡ If a pallet box is long, then it must have a number of bungboards. The wind reaches the pallet box through tubes or large ducts. If these are not wide enough, then the supply of wind is insufficient, and the full organ sounds out of tune; also not all of the bass pipes speak with the proper promptness. This [situation] is also connected with that odious wobble that happens if the channels are too small to support many large stops. It is best for the wind to enter the pallet box through more than one opening; cf. §. 363.

* i.e., the underside of the grid.

† i.e., what must be observed in facing the pallets with leather.

‡ and thus shrink.

§. 367.

We come now to the internal components of the organ, with the exception of the pipes. First we encounter various wind tubes or conduits. Some lead to the pallet box, others however proceed from the windchest elsewhere. That is, some go to the pipes, suns, statues, zimbelsterns, etc., that stand in the façade, and others to [offset] pipes located inside [the case]. For sometimes the width of the chest does not allow a large stop to stand directly on the toeboards, even though it should. In that case tubes of whatever length necessary are set into the toeboards, and the pipes sit on the tubes. Since the tubes lie at a slant and spread out from each other atop [the windchest], one going here and another going there, the pipes thus gain the [necessary] space. This does not look well and is likewise detrimental, but necessity knows no law. From this one may perceive just how important it is to give an organ adequate space. All of the wind ducts and tubes are made either of wood or metal; they must all fit exactly at both ends, and for this reason they are provided with leather. The wood used for them must be thoroughly cured, otherwise they crack and do not hold wind. Following the example of the windchest, all of the wooden wind ducts must be impregnated with glue.

§. 368.

The trackers in particular must be made of good, flexible wood, so that they do not warp; otherwise the keyboard will never be level. They should also be light-weight, and thus neither wide nor thick, so that they do not require such strong springs to be placed under the pallets, making the keys hard to depress. If they are very long and

gehen; so pflegen sie etliche in ein Kammbrettchen, oder sogenannten Kamm s. §. 48. zu legen, daß sie nicht schwanken oder schottern. Einige pflegen sie auch mit Federn zu versehen, die sie helfen in die Höhe ziehen. Da man hernach durch das Clavier 2 Federn für eine zu ziehen hat. An die Claviere müssen sie mit Schrauben von Meßing angemacht seyn. s. §. 51. Die Registraturwellen sollen stark, und von dürrem Holze seyn, mit kurzen Armen, daß die Register nicht so weit heraus gehen; doch wo sie gar zu kurz, und die manubria gar zu wenig heraus gehen, da sind sie schwer zu ziehen. Drey bis 4 Zoll ist der gemeinste Lauf. s. §. 346. Die Schiebstangen müssen auch ihre gehörige Stärke haben, daß sie beym Herausziehen und Einschieben der Register nicht nachgeben und Unlust erwecken.

§. 369

Die Wellenbretter sollen fein gerichtet seyn, daß die Wellen nicht dichte zusammen stoßen, auch nicht nahe am Brette liegen, sonst quillt das Holz, und eins hindert das andere, daß es alsdann heulet, oder es fällt Staub dazwischen. Darum ist nicht zu verwerfen, wenn die Wellenbretter gesetzt, oder gar die Wellen im Rückpositive unten angebracht werden, damit der Staub nicht schade. Etliche machen gar keine Wellenbretter, sondern disponiren die Wellen auf einem starken eichenen Rahmen; und da müssen die Claviere fein beständig bleiben. Etliche wollen gar ohne Wellen durch Winkelhaken das Angehänge herbey bringen. Etliche wollen, man solle die Wellenbretter verkehren, und die Wellen quer herüber legen, so müßte das Clavier auch gleich und gerade liegen bleiben. Aber es ist noch gefährlicher: denn wenn das Holz zusammen schwindet, wird es die Wellen zwischen ihren Stiften so vest zusammen halten, daß alle Claviere stecken bleiben, wo nicht sattsame Spielung gelassen wird. Die Wellen, welche lang sind, müssen auch stark seyn, sonst biegen sie sich. Gut ists auch, daß in einen Wellenarm 2 oder 3 Löcher gebohret werden, daß man kann nachgeben: die Löcher aber dürfen nicht zu weit seyn, daß die da innen laufende Stifte nicht rasseln. Wenn man die Wellen von langen dünnen eisernen Stangen machet; so werden sie nicht so stark wie die hölzernen, nehmen auch nicht so viel Raum ein, und ist sonderlich zu recommendiren, wo viel Wellenbretter anzulegen sind, und man zu allen, (wenn sie nämlich von Holz gemacht werden sollten) nicht Raum hat. Es findet sich dies an der Görlitzer Orgel. s. oben §. 50.) Hölzerne Wellen dürfen keine Aeste haben, sonst verwerfen sie sich wenn das Wetter sich ändert. Mehr füge ich vom Eingeweide nicht hinzu. Ein jeder Orgelmacher verfertige alles so, daß dadurch eines jeden Stückes Endzweck erreichet wird; so ist es gut, und er wird Segen und Ehre von seiner Arbeit haben. Die Theile selbst sind Kap. 4. erzählet worden.

§. 370.

Es folgen zum 4ten die Bälge und Windführungen, deren Struktur und Theile Kap. 5. bekannt gemacht worden. Es müssen heut zu Tage lauter Spanbälge seyn,

tall, some [builders] follow the practice of fitting them into a guide rail, the so-called "comb" (see §. 48), so that they do not wobble or shake. Some [builders] are accustomed to fitting them with springs as well, that help pull them upward, but then [the player] must pull against two springs for each key. They must be attached to the keys with brass screws; see §. 51. The stop-trundles should be strong, made of cured wood, with short arms so that the stop[knobs] do not come out so far. But if they are too short, and the stopknobs come out too little, then they [i.e., the stopknobs] are difficult to draw. The most usual distance is between 3-4 inches; see. §. 346. The trace rods must also be of an appropriate strength to keep from bending and becoming annoying when the stops are drawn and retired.

§. 369.*

The roller boards must also be meticulously fashioned, so that the rollers do not lie so close as to strike each other, or lie too near the board; otherwise one interferes with the other when the wood swells or dust falls between them, thus causing [the pipes to] cipher. Therefore there is nothing wrong with the roller boards being shifted (gesetzt†) or even with mounting the Rückpositiv rollers underneath [the rollerboard], so that dust cannot cause any harm. Some [builders] do not construct any roller board at all, but arrange the rollers on a strong oaken frame; then the keyboards are forced to remain in good alignment. Some believe in directing the trackers with squares, omitting rollers entirely. Some feel that the direction of the wood grain in the roller boards should be shifted and the rollers set across the grain; in this way the keyboard is also forced to lie straight and even. But this creates an even greater danger; for if the wood shrinks together, then the rollers bind so tightly between their pins that all the keyboards get stuck, unless ample play is left. The rollers that are long must also be stiff, otherwise they bow. It is also good to bore 2 or 3 holes in a roller arm, so that one can control the tension [of the tracker]. These holes must not be too big, however, so the pins that move within them do not rattle. If the rollers are made of long, thin iron rods, then they are not as thick as wooden ones and do not take up as much space; this is especially to be recommended where many roller boards have to be constructed, and there would not be enough room for them all if they were made of wood. These [iron rollers] are to be found in the Görlitz organ‡ (see §. 50 above). Wooden rollers must not have any knots, otherwise they will warp when the weather changes. This is enough about the internal components. Let every organbuilder construct everything so that the final purpose of each part may be achieved; it is good thus, and he will reap blessing and honor from his handiwork. The parts themselves have been described in Chapter 4.

§. 370.

In fourth place§ follow the bellows and wind ducts, whose structure and components have been described in Chapter 5. Nowadays there should be only wedge bellows,

* Parts of this section are taken almost verbatim from chapter 7 of Werkmeister's *Orgelprobe*, including a number of vague expressions that Adlung does not attempt to clarify.

† = "versetzt?"; in this regard, see Vol. I, §. 49 & 50.

‡ See Boxberg, p.[9.]

§ i.e., the bellows and wind ducts are the fourth of the internal components that Adlung began to describe beginning in §. 367.

seyn, d. i. solche, die nur eine Falte haben. Ehedessen waren die Faltenbälge stark im Gebrauch: aber dieseben führen dieses incommodum bey sich, daß, so oft eine Falte sich legt, man es in der Orgel spührt. Die Spanbälge nun müssen von gutem Holze und wohl gearbeitet seyn; auch gießt man sie mit der §. 38. gedachten Masse wohl aus, sonst würde sich der Wind verschleichen. Sie sollen groß genug seyn; und macht man sie ißo ordentlich, 5′ breit und 10′ lang; oder 6′ breit und 12′ lang. Sie müssen weit genug aufgehen, daß sie satt Wind fangen. Es hat Werkmeister in der Orgelprobe Kap. 1. S. 2. das nöthigste von den Bälgen beygebracht. Doch das weite Aufthun betreffend, ist noch etwas dabey zu gedenken. Weil die Bälge vornen unbeweglich aufliegen; so muß nothwendig die aufgezogene obere Platte einen Zirkel beschreiben, oder einen Bogen, als ein Stück des Zirkels. Je höher der Bogen gehet, desto weniger hat das Balggewicht seine force, weil es alsdann seine Schwere mehr nach dem centro zu exercirt, welches in solchem Falle weiter vornen ist. Denn gesetzt, es gienge der Bogen durch einen Quadranten oder 90°, daß also die obere Platte perpendiculär stünde, gesetzt ferner, wenn das Gewicht fest anhienge, daß es nicht herunter fiele; so würde es nicht die Platten zusammentreiben, sondern stille stehen, weil es nach dem Centro drückt, die linea directionis aber durch den Ort geht, wo der Balg veste liegt. Je kleiner aber der Bogen ist, desto weniger verliert das Gewicht von seiner force die Platten zusammen zu treiben, weil aus der Mechanica mathemat. in der Lehre de Vecte bekannt, daß je näher die Kraft (so hier das Gewicht ist) dem hypomochlio kömmt, (welches der Ort ist, wo der Balg stille liegt) desto weniger ist ihre Kraft; und je höher der Balg aufgehet, desto näher kömmt das Gewicht nach diesem Orte. Derowegen nicht rathsam ist, daß ein Balg alzuweit sich aufthue. Dann wo das Gewicht nicht stets mit gleicher force die Blätter zusammen drückt, ist auch der Wind nicht von gleicher Macht; folglich wird das Pfeifwerk bald höher, bald tiefer klingen: Und das taugt nichts. [72] Allein man muß doch den Balg auch einen ziemlichen Bogen aufgehen lassen, sonst muß man alle Augenblicke treten, welches abermals nichts nützt. Nun fragt es sich: Was zu thun?

§. 371.

Der Bogen kann nicht vermieden werden; also muß man auf Mittel denken, wodurch der Wind in einer Gleichheit bleibt. Da recommandire ich mit Werkmeistern, daß man den Balg, an dem Ende wo die weiten Falten sind, niedriger lege, als an dem andern Ende. Besser aber ists, man macht recht große Bälge. Die haben viel Wind, weil sie lang und breit sind, und brauchen so hoch nicht aufzugehen, als kleinere. Ferner so beschreiben die großen Bälge einen großen Zirkel; in einem großen Zirkel ist die Krümme einer gewissen Höhe so merklich nicht, als die Krümme derselben Höhe in kleinen Bogen ist. Z. Er. wenn ein Bogen gerissen wird, dessen Semidiameter, oder Linie von dem Bogen nach dem Centro nur 4′ lang ist, und die obere Platte gehet nur eine Elle

---

[72] Hierbey lese man das 20ste Kapitel in **Werkmeisters** Orgelprobe nach.

i.e., those that have only a single fold. In times past multi-fold bellows were widely used, but these have the shortcoming that every time a fold collapses it may be perceived in [the sound of] the organ. Wedge bellows must be carefully fashioned of solid wood, and thoroughly impregnated with the substance mentioned in §. 38; otherwise the wind will seep through them. They must be large enough—normally they are made 5′ wide and 10′ long, or 6′ wide and 12′ long. They must rise far enough to capture ample wind. Werkmeister has imparted the most essential [information] about bellows in his *Orgelprobe*, Chapter 1, p. 2[f.]. Concerning the extent of the rise, though, there is something else to keep in mind. Since the bellows plates are inseparably joined at the front end, then the upper plate must of necessity, as it rises, describe a circle, or an arc (a segment of a circle). The higher the arc rises, the less force the bellows-weight has, since it exerts its weight more toward the center (which in this case is further forward). For, given that the arc passes through a quadrant or 90°, so that the upper plate stands perpendicular [to the lower], and given further that the weight is firmly fastened to it and cannot fall off, then the weight would not force the plates together, but remain still, because it would be pressing toward the center, with its line of travel proceeding to the point where the bellows is immobile. The smaller the arc is, the more force the weight retains to force the plates together, since in mechanical mathematics the theory of vectors proves that the closer the force (in this case, the weight) comes to the fulcrum (here the place where the bellows plates are fastened), the less force it has; the higher the bellows rises, the nearer the weight approaches this point. For this reason it is not advisable for a bellows to rise too high. For wherever the weight does not press the plates together with the same force, there the wind will not have the same pressure, and consequently the pipes will fluctuate between sounding sharp and sounding flat—that will not do.[72)] Yet the bellows must be allowed to travel a reasonable distance as it rises, or they must be pumped constantly, which once again is unacceptable. Now the question arises: What should be done?*

* i.e., how should these conflicting demands be reconciled?

§. 371.

The arc cannot be avoided, and thus one must consider a means by which the wind can remain at a constant [pressure]. Thus I recommend, [in agreement] with Werkmeister,† that the end of the bellows, where the wide folds are, should be set lower than the other end.‡ It is better, however, to make really large bellows; they hold a lot of wind because they are long and wide, and do not need to rise so high as small ones. Furthermore, large bellows describe a large circle, and in a large circle the curve at a given height is not as noticeable as the curve of a smaller arc at the same height. For example, sketch an arc whose radius (the line from the arc to the center) is only 4′ long; by the time the upper plate rises only a yard, the arc will already reach about 30°. That is al-

† *Orgelprobe*, Chapter 20.
‡ see also §. 373.

[72)] In this regard, consult Chapter 20 of Werkmeister's *Orgelprobe*. [Albrecht]

Elle hoch in die Höhe; so wird der Bogen doch ohngefehr 30° halten. Das ist schon eine merkliche Krümme. Wenn aber die obere Platte 12' lang ist, und beschreibt einen Bogen, so, daß sie 1 Elle hoch steigt, wird der Bogen ungefähr 5° austragen. Aber 5 Grade in einem Bogen haben keine gar merkliche Krümme, und die Differenz der Distanz des Gewichtes vom Centro des aufgezogenen und des zugegangenen Balgs bedeutet nicht viel, und hat mit der Länge keine Proportion, daß eine solche Linie fast für eine gerade Linie kann gehalten werden. Also weicht das Gewicht nicht weit von dem vordern Theile der untern Platte nach dem hintern Theile, wo die Platten zusammen sind; und da man sich das centrum eines Bogens vorstellet, also verliert es wenig von seiner force, die Platten zusammen zu treiben. Deswegen regardiren viele weiter auf nichts, und verwerfen die Gegengewichte. So sagt z. Er. Werkmeister S. 46. der Orgelprobe, daß die Faltenbälge keine Gegengewichte hätten, wol aber die Spanbälge; doch müsse man sie nicht zu stark machen: Auch könne man ohne dieselben die Bälge heutiges Tages machen, daß der Wind nicht über 1 Grad abfalle, obschon der Balg sehr hoch aufgienge, und das könne man durch Roßadern zwingen. Solche Bälge hätten ihr Gegengewicht bey sich, man möchte sie legen, wie man wollte; zumal weil man sie itzo schief legte. Man wird auch wol ehe 10 Orgeln ohne Gegengewichte finden, als eine mit demselben. Hier in Erfurt ist dergleichen zun Reglern.

§. 372.

Nun ist die Frage: Was ist davon zu urtheilen? Ich antworte, daß es auf eine solche Kleinigkeit im Winde eben nicht ankomme, zumal da doch selten die Bälge im Treten zugleich in der Höhe, und die andern, welche fast ausgelaufen, den Wind völlig geben, daß also die Schwäche des einen nicht völlig bemerkt wird. Unterdessen sind diejenigen nicht zu tadeln, welche auch diese Kleinigkeiten nicht aus der Acht lassen, sondern loben die Gegengewichte, und bringen sie bey den Orgeln an, zumal bey solchen, wo die Bälge nicht gar groß sind. Nur rathe ich, daß man sie recht mache. Wer in Mathematicis, und sonderlich in Mechanicis nicht versirt ist, der gebe ein solch Ding nicht an. Man muß nach richtigen principiis messen; die Differenzen der Distanzen, und wieviel das Gewicht von seiner force verliert, daraus rechnen; und hernach, da der Balg immer tiefer kömmt und augenblicklich in der Kraft zunimmt, die Gegengewichte auch also einrichten, daß ihr Ziehen augenblicklich abnehme.

Es wird, wie §. 72. kürzlich erwähnet worden, hinter jedem Balge eine Säule aufgerichtet, ein Pflock durchgesteckt, an welchem Stricke herunter hangen, und unten an diese wird ein Backstein oder dergleichen angemacht. Von der obern Platte des Balges gehen auch Stricke herab: die an solches Gewicht bevestiget sind. Wenn der Balg aufgezogen wird, so zieht er dieses Gewicht mit in die Höhe, und wenn der Balg niedergehet, so ziehet dies Gewicht den Balg mit nieder. Oder man macht zwischen aufgerichteten Säulen ein Holz an einer Welle beweglich, etliche Schuh lang, hohlet es aus, daß ein darauf gelegtes Gewicht nicht herabfalle, und läßt es gleichfalls mit dem Balge auf

ready a considerable curve. If however the upper plate is 12′ long, and describes an arc as it rises one yard, the arc will amount to about 5°. In an arc, 5 degrees form a curve that is hardly noticeable, and the difference in the weight's distance from the center in the expanded and collapsed bellows is of little significance, hardly anything in relation to the length; such a line* can almost be considered straight. Thus the weight does not move far from the forward edge of the lower plate toward the rear edge (where the plates meet), and, as may be understood by imagining the center of the arc, thus it looses little of its power to force the plates together. For this reason many [organbuilders] disregard any other [means of equalizing the bellows' pressure], and reject counter-weights. For example, on p. 46[f.] of the *Orgelprobe* Werkmeister says that the multi-fold bellows had no counter-weights; wedge bellows may indeed have them, but they must not be made too powerful. Also [he says that] nowadays bellows may be made without them whose wind [pressure] does not deviate by more than 1 degree, no matter how high the bellows expands; this may be accomplished by using horse veins.† [He also says that] such bellows have their own built-in counter-weights, no matter how they are placed, especially since nowadays [lower plates] are set at an angle.‡ To be sure, for every organ with counter-weights one is likely to find 10 organs without them. Here in Erfurt they may be found in [the organ of] the Reglerkirche.

* i.e., the shallow arc.

† i.e., to make the bellows especially air-tight; see Vol. I, §. 59.

‡ See the second sentence of this paragraph, above.

§. 372.

Now we may ask: What conclusions are to be drawn from this? I hold that such a trifling deviation in the wind is insignificant, especially since the bellows are seldom at the same point in their cycle when they are in operation; the weakness of one [that is fully expanded] is little perceived, since others that are more nearly exhausted are producing full wind [pressure]. Nevertheless one should not criticize those who do not wish to dismiss these trifles, and thus favor counter-weights and build them into their organs (especially those whose bellows are not very large). I would only advise that they be made correctly. Anyone who is not well-versed in mathematics, and particularly in mechanics, ought to refrain from designing them. They must be laid out according to correct principles. From these [principles] one must determine the differences between the distances, and how much of its force the weight will lose, and then adjust the counter-weights accordingly to begin to slacken their counter-pull to exactly the degree that the bellows increases in weight as it falls.

I have already mentioned briefly in §. 72 that [to construct counter-weights] a post must be erected behind each bellows. Through it passes a peg on which cords hang down. A brick or some such [weight] is attached to the bottom [of the cords]. Other cords hang from the upper plate of the bellows, and are attached to this same weight. As the bellows is raised, it draws the weight upward with it; as the bellows falls, the weight draws the bellows downward with it. Alternatively, two posts are erected, with an axle running between them. On this axle moves a piece of wood, several feet long. The wood is hollowed out to hold a weight so that it does not fall off. This piece of wood

auf und abgehen. Es mögen die Bälge hoch oder niedrig liegen, so können dennoch die Gegengewichte alle in einer Reihe liegen. Nun muß man eine accurate Windprobe dabey haben, daß man sieht, wieviel der Wind steigt und fällt, wenn der Balg hoch oder niedrig aufgezogen wird, und das Gegengewicht muß soviel helfen ziehen, als das Gewicht des Balgs, wenn er hoch aufgezogen ist, weniger drückt: Und da der Balg, je mehr er wieder herabsteigt, allzeit den Wind völliger giebt, wie die Windprobe (davon weiter unten zu reden) zeigt; so muß das Gegengewicht allzeit, indem es mit herabgehet, soviel weniger ziehen, als das Balggewicht heftiger drückt. Es kann dies nicht anders seyn; daher man das Gewicht sowol in der justen Höhe zu hängen hat, daß es präcise so hoch aufgehe, als es nöthig: es muß aber auch die proportionirte Schwere haben, daß es nicht zu viel oder zu wenig ziehe. Und da die Bälge alle gleich aufgehen; so macht man sie darinne alle gleich. Diese Art durch die Windprobe sie accurat anzubringen, ist mechanisch. Man könnte aber durch Abmessung der Bogen, und solche Dinge, die etwas in die Mathesin sublimiorem laufen, die Sache ausmachen; aber ich will der Kürze wegen dieses nicht berühren.

§. 373.

Wenn in die aufgerichtete Säulen viel horizontale Löcher gebohret werden; so kann man den Pflock oder Welle erhöhen oder erniedrigen, wie man will. Ein Fehler ist bey solchen Gegengewichten, wenn sie zu gänge sind um diese Wellen, weil sie dadurch von ihrer Schwere etwas verlieren. Wo sie sich nach der Zeit durch das Reiben Luft gemacht; so wächst ihre Schwere: man muß daher auf ihre Aenderung bedacht seyn. Ein Hauptfehler ist auch, wenn sie nicht präcise so viel ziehen helfen, als der Schwere des Balggewichtes abgegangen; Und, da man von den Back= oder andern Steinen so accurat nichts ab= und zuthun kann, daß es recht gleich käme; so haben mir die jenaischen Gegengewichte, die Herr Bach daselbst in der Stadtorgel angegeben, besser gefallen. Da ist in einem weiten Ritze der aufgerichteten Säule an einer Welle ein Quadrant bevestiget, in dessen Rande von aussen herum eine Riefe ist, darinn der Strick gehet, und den Quadranten mit sich herum nimmt. An den Quadranten ist ein Stück Holz von gewisser Länge, welches, wenn der Quadrant herum gehet, sich in die Höhe begiebt. Unten an dem Fusse des Quadranten ist ein Kasten eingeschnitten, und mit Sand ausgefullet, auch mit einem Schiebdeckel wieder verwahret, das nichts herausfalle. Wenn man nun findet, daß zu viel darinne sey; so kann man nach Proportion ohne Mühe etwas heraus thun. Ist das Gegengewicht zu leichte; so thue man Sand hinein, bis es accurat passet. Die Gegengewichte stehen eher stille, als die Bälge sich ganz zuthun, weil, wenn der Balg fast zu ist, der Bogen und die Differenz der Schwere gar nichts austrägt, und also ein Ziehen des Gegengewichts nicht nöthig ist. Daß aber das Gegengewicht mehr ziehen muß, wenn es hoch stehet, als wenn es fast unter sich hängt, ist klar aus dem, was §. 370. gesagt ist. Das Centrum desselben ist die Welle; je weiter nun das Gewicht von der Linie, die von dem Centro desselben nach dem

rises and falls with the bellows. Then all the counter-weights can lie in a row, no matter whether the bellows are placed high or low. It is necessary to have an accurate wind gauge at hand, in order to see to what extent the wind fluctuates as the bellows rises and falls, and [in order to insure] that the counter-weight helps pull to the degree that the bellows weight (when it is in a higher position) exerts less pressure. And since the bellows produces more and more pressure as it falls (as the wind gauge shows—we will say more about this below*) thus the counter-weight must pull proportionately less and less as it falls with it. This is exactly how it must be, and so the weight must be hung at just the right height to rise exactly as high as necessary, and it must have the proportionate weight to exert just the right amount of pull. And since the bellows all rise to the same height, all of the [counter-weights] must be made exactly the same. The method of positioning them accurately by means of the wind gauge is a mechanical one. It is possible to determine the matter by measuring the arc and by procedures that tend somewhat toward higher mathematics, but for the sake of brevity I will not treat these.

* in §. 442.

§. 373.

If a number of holes are bored at equal heights in [each of] the upright posts, then the peg or the axle may be raised or lowered at will. Such counter-weights are faulty if they fit too tightly/loosely? on the axles, for in that way they lose some of their weight. If they have become worn down and slack in the course of time, then their weight increases. Thus one must be attentive to their deterioration. It is also a major fault if they do not help pull exactly in proportion to the decrease in the bellows weight. Since it is not possible to add or subtract very accurately from bricks or other stones to achieve precise adjustment, I am more in favor of the counter-weights in the organ of the Jena Stadtkirche that were designed by Mr. [Johann Nikolaus] Bach, [the organist] there. There we find a quadrant† fastened on an axle inserted in a wide slot on an upright post. There is a groove around the outer edge of the quadrant, and into it fits a cord that pulls the quadrant, turning it. Affixed to the quadrant is a piece of wood of a given length that rises up as the quadrant turns. A compartment is hollowed out in the base of the quadrant, filled with sand and covered with a sliding top to keep any of the sand from falling out. If one discovers that there is too much sand in it,‡ then one may remove whatever amount is necessary without trouble. If the counter-weight is too light, then sand may be added until it is accurately adjusted. Counter-weights move less and less as bellows collapse, since the arc and the difference in weight amounts to absolutely nothing when the bellows is almost closed, and thus the pull of the counter-weight is not necessary.§ From what has been said in §. 370, however, it is clear that the counter-weight has to exert more pull when it is raised than when it is hanging almost straight down. The center [of the counter-weight's pull] is the axle. The further the weight departs from the line that is drawn from the center of the axle to the center of the earth, i.e., straight

† i.e., a quarter of a circle.

‡ i.e., it is too heavy.

§ Here Adlung is speaking as if the lower bellows plate were lying horizontally, not on an incline as he advises in §. 371.

Centro der Erde, d. i. gerade unterwärts, gezogen wird, wegkömmt, desto schwerer ist es, oder desto mehr ziehet es; je näher es dabey ist, desto weniger wird es den Mangel des Balgs ersetzen. Am weitesten kann es weg seyn, wenn es 90° abstehet, oder situm horizontalem hat: so hoch kömmt es aber nicht, weil der Balg nicht so hoch aufgehet. Doch genug von den Gegengewichten; weil ohnedies viele nichts davon halten. Ich lasse jedem seine Meynung. Das einzige will ich nur noch erinnern, daß man 2 oder 3 und mehrfältigen Bälgen keine Gegengewichte geben kann. Um aber ohne Gegengewichte den Wind desto gleicher zu erhalten; so legen etliche die Bälge hinten, wo sie aufgehen, tiefer als vornen, und in diesem Falle ist das beste, wenn die Vertiefung die Hälfte der Höhe im Aufthun austrägt. Man besehe dieses Umstands wegen die Orgel in Alach.

§. 374.

Es müssen die Bälge ferner einen feinen gleichen, sanften, langsamen Gang haben, daß man nichts sonderliches von Poltern höre, als was der motus nothwendig mit sich führt. Man siehet leicht, daß wenn gespielet wird, sie geschwinder gehen, als sonst; doch dürfen sie nicht allzusehr laufen, weil es sonst ein Zeichen ist, daß der Wind sich wo verschleiche. Trost, in der Beschreibung der Weissenfelßischen Orgel, sagt S. 17. daß er den ganzen Glauben, alle 3 Verse, oder über 180 Takte, könne spielen, ehe die 3 Bälge ausliefen, wo sie mit einander getreten sind: doch müsse man nicht zu viel 16füßige Stimmen zusammenziehen. Zwar sagen etliche, daß große Pfeifen nicht viel Wind brauchten, nämlich nicht mehr, als durch die enge Straße zwischen dem Kern und Labio durchkommen könnte. Allein ich sehe nicht, wie das folgt: die Oefnung ist klein, und geht nicht viel mehr Wind durch, als bey einer andern; ergo braucht die Pfeife wenig mehr Wind. Denn solche Pfeifen haben große Füße, die müssen bey dem Anschlagen der Pfeife erst ganz ausgefüllet werden mit Winde, daß er darinne zusammen gedrückt ist, als in der Lade. Von hölzernen Pfeifen ließe ich es paßiren, weil da meistentheils ein langes Röhrchen auf der Lade stehet, welches den Wind zu solcher Oefnung führt, ohne daß nöthig wäre, so viel Wind in den Fuß zu thun. Haec obiter. Von den Bälgen ist weiter zu merken, daß sie nicht schüttern dürfen, welches geschieht, wenn man sie langsam aufzieht, da das Ventil nicht stets offen bleibt, sondern auf- und zuschlägt, daß es rasselt. Sie sollen nicht knarren, weil dies in der Kirche sehr häßlich ist, und wohl vermieden werden kann, theils wenn die beyden Platten accurat mit einander verbunden sind, an dem Orte wo sie zusammen bleiben, theils wenn der Calculaturclavis recht gemacht wird. Sie sollen den Wind fein schnell in sich ziehen, sonst wird der Balg nicht voll, wenn man etwas geschwinde tritt. Es trägt sich dies oft zu, wenn der Balg groß, das Fangventil aber etwas zu klein ist, und merkt man es bald, wenn nach dem Aufziehen des Balges er ein Fleck geschwinder wieder herabgehet, als hernach. Daraus siehet man, daß ein Theil leer gewesen. Doch wollte ich nicht rathen, das Blatt des Fangventils zu groß zu machen, oder allzubreit: weil dergleichen Blätter sich leicht verwerfen.

downward, the heavier it becomes, or the more pull it exerts. The nearer it is [to that line], the less capable it is of replacing weight lacking in the bellows. The furthest it can be from the line is 90°, a horizontal position; but it never gets that high, since the bellows never rises that far. But enough about counter-weights, since many people do not think much of them anyway. Everyone is entitled to his own opinion. I want to mention only one other thing: counter-weights may not be used with bellows having 2, 3 or more folds. In order to maintain the steadiest possible wind pressure without counter-weights, some [builders] set the back end of the bellows, the end that rises, lower than the front end.* In this case, it is best if it is lowered one half the distance of its maximum rise. As an example of this situation, inspect the organ at Alach.

* Adlung has already suggested this in §. 371.

§. 374.

The bellows, furthermore, must have a precisely even, gentle, slow movement, so that no noticeable thumping/clattering is heard beyond what arises in the normal course of movement. It is easy to see that they move more quickly when the organ is being played—but they ought not operate too quickly, since that is a sign that wind is escaping somewhere. In his *Beschreibung der Weissenfelßischen Orgel*, p. 17, Trost says that he is able to play the entire Creed,† all three verses—over 180 measures—before the 3 bellows are exhausted (providing they are trod at the same time), but that not too many 16′ stops may be drawn together. Some say, to be sure, that large pipes do not need much wind, no more than can pass through the narrow passage between the languid and the lip. But [let me say] in passing I do not see how this [proposition] follows: [i.e.,] the opening is small and not much more wind passes through it than through other [smaller pipes], therefore the pipe needs little more wind. Consider that such pipes have large feet that must first be completely filled with wind, to the same pressure as prevails in the chest, before the pipe will speak. I will grant [the proposition] in the case of wooden pipes, since there is usually a long slender tube that stands on the chest and guides the wind to the opening‡ without requiring so much wind to fill the feet. With regard to the bellows, it should further be noted that they ought not shake; this happens when the valve does not stay open as the bellows is slowly raised, but flops open and shut, creating a rattle. The bellows also ought not creak, since this [sounds] horrid in the church, and can easily be avoided, partly by joining both plates together precisely and partly by making the bellows pole correctly. They ought to draw in the wind nice and quickly; otherwise the bellows will not fill up if they are pumped quickly. This often happens with a large bellows whose intake valve is somewhat too small; it is easily noted if the bellows falls a bit more quickly just after it has been raised than subsequently. This betrays the fact that it was partially empty. I would not advise, however, making the feeder valve lid too large or too wide, since large ones easily become warped. It is better to

† i.e., the hymn "Wir glauben all' an einen Gott," Martin Luther's versification of the Creed. The passage from Trost reads: "Indeed, by treading all three bellows I can make it through the entire "Glauben," all three verses, over one hundred eighty measures; but one must not draw all the stops (das gantze Werk) at the same time, or too many heavy 16′ stops."

‡ i.e., the lip.

werfen. Besser macht man die Oefnung so, daß durch die Mitte eine Leiste bleibt, und macht darauf zwo Klappen neben einander, die sich zugleich auf- und zuthun. Das ganze Fangventil, sammt dem Rahmen, soll man billig ausheben können, daß man hinein kommen könne in den Balg, wenn etwas zu flicken vorfällt. Es sollen die Bälge auch den Wind wohl halten, wozu die Leimtränke viel hilft.

§. 375.

Sie sollen auch nicht über das Lager zu weit hinaus liegen, sonst heben sie sich leicht von dem Kanale los. Ihre Blätter sind ordentlich aus 2" dicken Bohlen, mit Zimmerholz und Schrauben wohl verwahrt. Wenn die Roßadern vergessen werden, so dauren sie nicht lange: wenn aber diese gar eingebohrt und mit hölzernen Nägeln und Leim eingenagelt werden, ists noch besser, sagt Werkmeister l. c. Sie müssen auch mit Leisten beschlagen seyn, daß das Leder sich nicht abfitschele. Sie werden mit weisgahrem Rindleder, oder an dessen Statt mit doppeltem Schafleder beledert. Sie sollen mit Querbalken belegt seyn, daß sie nicht aus einander gehen: denn sie müssen gar viel Gewalt vertragen können. Sie sollen nicht zu sehr schwanken, welches gutentheils verhindert wird, wenn das Pedal besondere Bälge bekömmt. Der Wind muß bey allen vollkommen gleich seyn, welches durch die Windprobe zu erfahren, davon unten §. 442. Das Kanalventil muß auch groß genug seyn, und bey einem wie bey dem andern; auch darf dessen Klappe nicht zu ungelenk seyn, und auch bey allen von einerley Art. Sind sie nicht groß genug; so ist der Zufall des Windes nicht stark genug. Ist eins größer, als das andere; so bläset ein Wind stärker, als der andere, und hält durch die Macht die Klappe des andern Balges an, daß kein Wind herauskommt; folglich kann der eine Balg nicht laufen, bis der andere fertig ist. Daher es oftmäls kömmt, daß ein Balg steht, bis der andere ausgelaufen, welches also ein Fehler ist. So auch, wenn eine Klappe gänger ist, als des andern Balges; weil des andern Wind nur etwas stark drücken darf, so ist der Balg ohne Bewegung.

§. 376.

Es geschiehet zuweilen, daß ein Balg anhebt innerlich zu rasseln, zumal wenn er fast ausgelaufen hat, und zwar auf die Art, wie er rasselt, wenn man langsam tritt, und das Fangventil sich stets auf- und zuschlägt, oder wie ein Tremulant schlägt. Ich habe dies an einigen Orgeln observiert, und gern die Ursache wissen mögen. Endlich bin ich auf die Gedanken gerathen, daß die Ursache, welche eben dieses bey dem Fangventil verursacht hat, auch hier sey. Dort ist die äussere Luft, die die Klappe einwärts drückt: die inwendige Luft widersteht der äussern mit fast gleicher Stärke, daher das Ventil bald auswärts, bald aber einwärts getrieben wird, daß es zittert. So wird auch bey dem Tremulanten durch den Wind das Gehäuse bald gehoben, bald durch das äussere Gewicht niedergedrückt. Wenn also hier der Wind in der Lade nach dem Kanale zu der Klappe treibt, so muß eben ein solch Zittern entstehen. Und dies kann nicht vermieden

werden,

make the opening with a strip dividing it in the middle, and then to make two flaps next to each other that open and close simultaneously. The entire feeder valve, together with its frame, should be easily removable, to allow access to the bellows' interior in case anything needs to be repaired. The bellows ought also to hold the wind tightly; impregnating them with glue helps insure this.

§. 375.

The bellows also ought not extend very far out beyond the frame, otherwise they are likely to become separated from the wind duct. Their plates are normally made of 2" thick planks, well secured with heavy timbers and screws. If the horse veins* are omitted, then they will not be very durable; Werkmeister† says it is even better to drill them through and fasten them on with wooden pegs and glue. They must also be covered with strips to keep the leather from coming loose. They are to be covered with tawed cows leather, or with a double layer of sheep's leather in its place. They should be fitted with crossbraces so that they do not crack open, since they must be able to withstand a lot of stress. They ought not to shake a lot; this can be prevented in large measure by providing the pedal with its own separate bellows. All of them must have exactly the same wind pressure, which is ascertained with the wind gauge (discussed in §. 442 below). The duct valves must also be large enough, and identical for each bellows. Their flaps must not be too stiff, and must be of the same type for each bellows. If they are not large enough, then the supply of wind will not be sufficient. If one is larger than another, then one source of wind will have greater pressure than another, and its force will keep the flap of the other bellows closed, thus trapping its wind. As a result, one bellows will not be able to operate until the other is exhausted. Thus it often happens that one bellows is immobile until the other is exhausted; this is a fault. It is likewise a fault if one flap is looser than that of another bellows, because as soon as the other [bellows'] wind presses a bit heavily, the [first] bellows stops moving.

* see Vol. I, §. 59.
† *Orgelprobe*, Chap. 1.

§. 376.

At times it happens that a bellows begins to rattle internally, especially when it is almost exhausted. This rattling is of the sort that arises when the bellows are being pumped slowly and the intake valve keeps flapping open and closed, or it resembles the beating of a tremulant. I observed this in several organs, and became very curious as to the cause of it. Finally I hit upon the idea that the same circumstance that causes this [rattling to happen] with the feeder valve‡ is also at work here. In that case it is the exterior air that presses the valve inward; the air inside resists that outside with almost the same [degree of] force, and thus the valve is driven first outward and then inward, so that it flutters. The tremulant§ is likewise first raised by the wind and then depressed by the exterior weight [that rests on it]. In this case, the [internal] fluttering must arise from the wind in the chest forcing its way back through the duct to the flap. And this

‡ see §. 374.

§ see §. 200.

werden, es sey denn der Wind in allen Bälgen vollkommen gleich, die Ventile nach dem Kanale von einer Größe, und die Klappen gleich gänge. Man spührt es auch, weil man, wenn ein solcher Balg allein getreten wird, kein Geklappere vernimmt. Will jemand einwenden, daß dies sodann auch geschehen müsse, wenn der Balg hoch stehet, und nicht allein wenn er niedrig stehet, dem dienet zur Antwort, daß der Wind, wenn der Balg fast zugegangen, viel schwächer ist als sonst. Doch mag endlich einer Zweifel dabey machen, wie er will; Genug, daß diese Sache ein Fehler ist, und bey der Probe nicht darf vergessen werden.

§. 377.

Es sollen die Bälge starke und recht lange Calcaturclaves haben, welche auf einer Quersäule aufliegen, und in eisernen Nägeln beweglich sind. Diese Quersäule soll viel weiter nach dem hintern Theile des Clavis liegen, als nach dem vordern Theile; weil solchergestallt die Bälge leichter zu treten werden. Denn ich setze, es wäre die Säule just in der Mitte, das Gewicht ruhete auf dessen hintern Enden, die Potenz, die es in die Höhe bewegen sollte, stünde vorn am Ende: wenn nun die Potenz nicht mehr und nicht weniger Gewicht oder Gewalt hat, als das hintere Gewicht; so wird keins das andere bewegen, wie bey einer Waage geschiehet. Ist aber die Potenz vornen mächtiger, als das Gewicht, so wird sie das Gewicht aufwärts heben, wenn sie, wie bey der Waage geschiehet, die andere Seite niederdrückt. Das Gewicht der Bälge aber ist oft sehr schwer; folglich muß die Potenz, oder der Calcant, in dem Falle auch schwer seyn: etwan ein Kerl von 15, 20, ꝛc. Jahren. Bey kleinen Bälgen können auch Knaben die Bälgen treten. Es muß aber der Calcant um ein merkliches schwerer seyn, daß er das Gewicht ohne Mühe heben könne. Also wenn das Gewicht ½ Centner hält, muß er wenigstens 30 Pfund, oder noch mehr darüber wiegen. Denn die Materie der Maschine resistirt ohne dies. Wenn ich aber setze, daß die Zwerchsäule weiter vorwärts als hinterwärts läge; so würde das Gewicht um so vielmal schwerer seyn, als vielmal die hintere Distanz die vordere übertrift. Z. Ex. ich setze, das Gewicht wäre 50 Pfund; aber es läge vom hypomochlio oder Zwerchsäule noch eins so weit weg, als der Calcant von der Zwerchsäule ist; so wird auch dessen Schwere noch eins so groß, und hält 100 Pfund. Will also der Calcant den Balken halten; so muß er 100 Pfund schwer seyn, und daß ers bewege, auch ob resistentiam materiae, noch etwan 30 Pfund darüber. Wäre hingegen der Calcant noch einmal so weit vom hypomochlio, als das Gewicht; so wird seine halbe Schwere das Gewicht heben können. Daraus sieht man, daß man durch die Lage des hypomochlii machen kann, daß Bälge von dem stärksten Manne nicht können ertreten werden, und durch eine andere Lage kann sie das kleinste Kind von der Stelle bringen. Wo es nun sich zuträgt, daß der Raum zu kurz ist; so muß man das hypomochlium oder den Querbalken desto weiter hinten anlegen, sonst tritt es sich schlimm. Doch wird dabey eine größere Höhe erfordert, als sonst. Denn wenn der Querbalken gleich mitten unter dem Calcaturclave

liegt;

cannot be avoided unless the wind pressure from all the bellows is exactly equal, the valves to the ducts are of the same size, and the flaps offer equal resistance. This theory is corroborated by the fact that one perceives no rattling if one of these bellows is pumped alone. If anyone objects that this would also have to happen when the bellows is expanded, and not only when it is exhausted, here is the reply: the wind from a bellows that is almost exhausted is much weaker than it would otherwise be. In the end, let anyone doubt this as he will; suffice it to say that this situation is a shortcoming, and ought not to be overlooked in the examination [of the new organ].

§. 377.

The bellows ought to have strong and rather long bellows poles, that rest upon crossbeams* and move between iron nails.† The crossbeams should lie much further toward the far end of the pole‡ than toward the near end, since the bellows will then be easier to pump. For let us suppose that the beam were exactly in the middle, with the weight resting on its far end and the force that is to raise it on the near end. If the force had the same weight or power as the weight on the far end, then neither would move the other, as happens with a scale. If the force on the near end is mightier than the weight, then it would raise the weight by pressing down on the opposite end, as happens with a scale. The weight of the bellows, however, is often very heavy, and consequently the force—the pumper—in that case must also be heavy, say, a fellow 15 or 20 years old. [Younger] boys may pump the bellows, too, but the operator must be considerably heavier [than the weight of the bellows] in order to be able to raise it without difficulty. Thus if the weight amounts to half a hundred-weight, then his weight must be at least 30 pounds or more greater,§ since the material of the apparatus offers some degree of resistance as well. Let us suppose, on the other hand, that the crossbeam lies further forwards¶ than back; then the weight would be heavier in proportion to the amount by which the rear section exceeds the forward one. Let us suppose, for example, that a 50 lb. weight lay twice as far from from the fulcrum (the crossbeam) as the pumper. It would then require twice as much weight on the other end to balance it, i.e., 100 pounds. If the operator is to stay the pole, then he must weigh 100 pounds. In order to move it, he must weigh 30 pounds more, due to the resistance of the apparatus. If, on the other hand, the pumper were twice as far from the fulcrum as the weight, then half of his weight would be able to raise the weight on the other end. This should make it clear than one position of the fulcrum will make it impossible for the strongest man to pump the bellows, while another position will allow the smallest child to move it. Where it turns out that there is insufficient room [for a long bellows pole], then the fulcrum must be placed all the further toward the far end, otherwise the bellows will be very difficult to pump. But this situation requires a longer path of travel‖ than otherwise. For if the crossbeam lies exactly under the middle of the bellows pole, then the

* i.e., the crossbeam serves as a fulcrum.
† i.e., the nails prevent the poles from slipping to one side or another.
‡ i.e., the end furthest from the operator, nearest to the bellows.

§ Here Adlung is still presupposing that the midpoint of the bellows pole is resting on the crossbeam.
¶ i.e., toward the pumper.

‖ at the operator's end of the pole.

liegt; so geht vorn der Clavis so weit nieder, als der Balg sich hinten in die Höhe giebt. Je weiter das hypomochlium vorkömmt, desto kleiner ist der Fall des Clavis gegen das Aufthun des Balgs. Je weiter es hinten liegt, desto tiefer fällt der Clavis. Ich will drey Figuren zeichnen, da bey der ersten das hypomochlium mitten liegt; bey der andern weiter hinten; bey der dritten weiter vorn. Man sehe die hiebeystehenden Fig. 1. 2. 3.

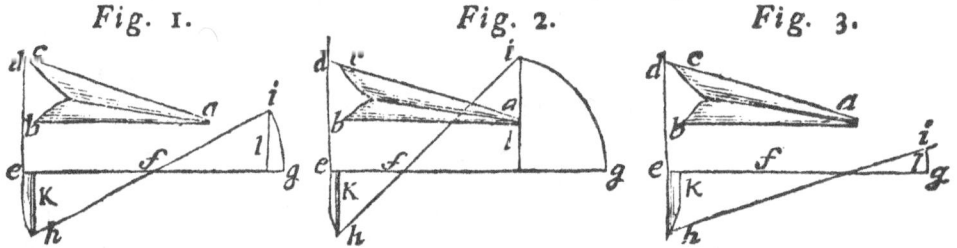

a c b ist der Balg aufgezogen; *d e* die Stange die ihn hebt; oder wenn der Clavis über dem Balge liegt, so zieht sie ihn; *e f g* ist der Calcaturclavis, so in *f* im hypomochlio veste liegt. Wenn nun bey der ersten figur der Balg zugehet; so muß die Stange sammt dem Clave eben so weit herunter, als die obere Platte: diese gehet von *c* nach *b*. Dergleichen Distanz giebt auch die Linie *k* an, da der Clavis von *e* nach *h* gehet. Der Fall des Clavis ist hinten allezeit einerley, das hypomochlium *f* mag stehen, wo es will: aber wenn der Balg zugehet; so sieht man, wie hoch vorn in der andern figur der Clavis von *g* nach *i* in die Höhe muß, nämlich noch eins so hoch, als in der ersten, weil die Distanz vom hypomochlio *f* bis *e* nur halb so groß ist, als die von *f* nach *g*. Hingegen die dritte figur ist wieder anders. In eben der Zeit nun, da das Gewicht von *b* nach *c* geht, muß die Potenz von *i* nach *g* gehen. Da nun fig. 2. der Weg von *i* nach *g* noch eins so groß ist; so muß auch die Potenz noch eins so geschwinde laufen. Wie sich aber diese Zeit verhält zu jener Zeit, so verhält sich die Kraft gegen jenes pondus. Ergo ist auch die Kraft der Potenz noch eins so stark. Fig. 3. ist eben das, doch alles umgekehrt. (vid. Mechanicam mathematicorum.)

§. 378.

Damit der Balg einmal soweit aufgehe, als das anderemal, oder durch das allzuhohe Aufziehen nicht zerrissen, oder aus seiner Stelle gehoben werde; so muß man nun nach der vorigen Rechnung im Balghause oben und unten abzeichnen, und mit Leisten unterscheiden, wie weit jeder Clavis fallen und steigen soll. Es muß der Clavis, zumal wenn er vorn einen großen Bogen beschreiben soll, um ein ziemliches aus dem Balghause hervorragen, sonst, weil er einen Bogen macht, kömmt er unten oder oben soweit hinein, daß man nicht wohl treten kann. Je länger der Clavis ist, und je weiter das hypomochlium hervor gelegt wird, desto größer wird der Bogen, und desto weiter muß es hervorragen. Doch, wenn es zuweilen überflüßig hervorragt, ist es ein Vortheil für den

forward edge of the pole goes as far down as the back end of the bellows rises. The further forward the fulcrum moves [toward the operator], the less distance the pole must travel to lift the bellows. The further away it lies, the greater distance the pole must travel. I will sketch three figures, the first showing the fulcrum lying in the middle, the second lying further away, the third further forward; note figures 1, 2 and 3 below.

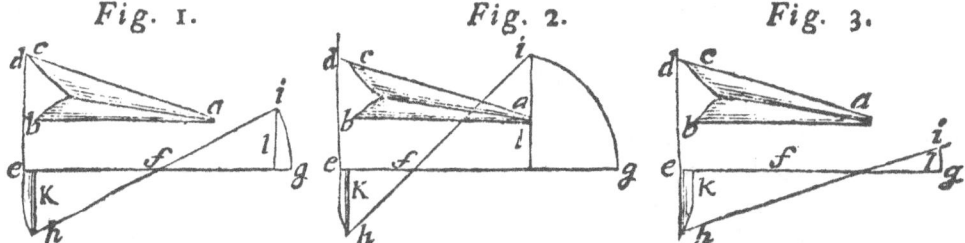

a c b is the expanded bellows; *d e* is the rod that shoves it up it (or if the pole is situated above the bellows, then the rod pulls it up); *e f g* is the bellows pole that is fastened to the fulcrum at *f*. In figure 1, if the bellows collapses, then the rod together with the pole must fall the same distance as the upper plate, from *c* to *b*. The line *k* indicates that same distance, since the pole travels from *e* to *h*. The distance the pole travels at its far end is always the same, wherever the fulcrum *f* stands. But [the arc] *g* to *i* in figure 2 illustrates how high the pole must travel when the bellows closes, i.e., twice as high as in figure 1, since the distance from the fulcrum *f* to point *e* is only half as great as that from *f* to *g*. Figure 3 illustrates just the opposite situation. [In all three cases,] in the same time that the weight travels from *b* to *c*, the force [at the other end] must move the pole from *i* to *g*. Since in figure 2 the distance from *i* to *g* is is twice as great, thus the force must also move twice as fast. The force is related to the weight as the speed at one end of the pole is related to the speed at the other. Thus the force exerted by the operator is twice as great. Figure 3 illustrates the same situation in reverse (refer to the mechanics of mathematics.)

§. 378.

So that the bellows always rises to the same height and is not torn apart or lifted out of position by being pulled too high, it is necessary to indicate in the bellows chamber* the upper and lower limits of the pole's travel, figured according to the principles given above, and to mark them off with boards. The bellows pole must protrude a considerable distance beyond the bellows chamber, especially if it must trace a large arc at the forward end; otherwise in making the arc it will move so far inward that it just cannot be pumped. The longer the pole is, and the further forward the fulcrum lies, the larger the arc will be and the further the bellows pole must extend. It is to the opera-

* "Balghaus:" this word means both "bellows chamber" and "bellows frame," since the bellows framework was commonly covered with boards, turning it into an enclosed chamber, to prevent any possible damage to the bellows.

den Calcanten, wenn er nahe auf die Spitze des Clavis tritt, weil seine Potenz vermehrt wird, wie aus dem vorhergehenden §pho fließt.

§. 379.

Das Balghaus muß an einem bequemen Orte liegen, da die Luft nicht allzufeuchte, oder die Sonne und Wärme nicht allzupenetrant ist. Jenes macht, daß der Leim weich wird, und das Leder verdirbt: dieses aber daß die Blätter schwinden, und die Bälge Luft kriegen. Untern den Dächern liegen sie gar nicht gut, denn da ist die Hitze groß; sondern an einem Orte, da es mit Mauren meistens verbauet ist, sonderlich in den Thürmen. Man muß das Balghaus rund herum verwahren und verschliessen, daß kein Schade daran geschehe durch Stiche ins Leder, Verruckung der Gewichte, u. d. gl.; und wenn einer nur eine Hand voll Pflaumfedern unter das Ventil hält; so ziehen sie sich mit hinauf und zerstreuen sich in die Pfeifen, daß man sie sobald nicht wieder davon saubern kann. Eine Thür muß daran seyn, daß man geschwind hinein kommen könne, wenn etwas mangelbar worden. Der Calcant muß eine Bank bekommen, oder Treppen, zwischen den Bälgen, darauf er in die Höhe steigt, sonderlich wenn sie hoch aufgehen: auch ist die Bank besser, weil er geschwinder von einem zum andern kommen kann. Oben ist ein Riegel, daran er sich hält, daß er nicht herunter falle; der aber nicht höher seyn muß, als eine Mittelperson erreichen kann, von dem Orte an gerechnet, da der Calcaturclavis unten aufschlägt. Was sonst noch §. 67. erwähnet worden ist, daran liegt nicht viel; und von den Haken halte ich auch nicht viel.

§. 380.

Die Kanäle sollen recht weit seyn, (doch nach Proportion der Orgel und der Bälge) damit der Zufall des Windes desto stärker sey. Deswegen auch wol der Wind aller Bälge vorher in einen weiten Kanal geführet wird, aus welchem zu jeder Lade besondere Röhren gehen: sonst gehets so, daß wenn ich einen großen clauem etlichemal hintereinander anschlage, der Wind nicht allezeit so geschwinde da ist, und etliche wol gar aussen bleiben, sonderlich wenn dabey die Ventile zu enge sind. Doch, wenn die Cancellen allzuweit sind, kann der Wind sie auch nicht so geschwind ausfüllen. Folglich kann man auf solchen Orgelwerken keine geschwinde Noten spielen. Was bey dem Windkoppel in diesem Falle zu observieren, das folgt unten §. 442. Das Holz zu den Kanälen muß auch recht dürre seyn; sie müssen mit Leim auch wohl ausgegossen werden, und sind über dies mit Leder und Pergament wohl zu verwahren. Sie dürfen nicht auf einem feuchten Boden zu liegen kommen, und wo sie etwan an offenen Orten liegen müssen, daß man darüber hingehet, müssen sie mit Brettern wohl bekleidet werden, daß ihnen kein Schade geschehe. Zu den Kanalventilen muß man auch kommen können.

§. 381

tor's advantage if it extends an excessive distance outward, since in pumping the near end of the pole his force is increased, as may be deduced from the previous paragraph.

§. 379.

The bellows chamber must be located in a favorable spot where the air is not too damp and the sun's warmth does not penetrate too much. The former makes the glue soft and rots the leather; the latter makes the [bellows] plates shrink and the bellows leak. They do very poorly under the eaves, for it is very hot there; rather they should be in a place that is mostly enclosed by [stone or brick] walls,* especially in towers. The bellows chamber must be secured and closed off on all sides, so that no damage occurs through puncturing the leather, shifting the weights, etc. If someone holds just a single handful of down feathers† under the [intake] valve, they will be drawn in with the air and scattered among the pipes, and it will be a long time before the pipes can be cleared of them. There must be a door into the bellows chamber, allowing quick access if something is out of order. The treader must have a bench or a set of stairs between the bellows, on which to climb, especially if [the poles] rise up high. A bench is better, because it allows him to get more quickly from one bellows to another. On top there is a rail for him to hold on to to keep from falling; it must be no higher, however, than a person of average height can reach (figuring from the bellows pole's lowest point of travel). The other matters mentioned in §. 67 are of little importance. I also think very little of hooks.‡

* i.e., not directly under the roof.

† "Pflaumfedern" = Flaumfedern.

‡ i.e., to latch the bellows down and prevent their unintended operation; see §. 67.

§. 380.

The wind ducts must also be quite ample (albeit in proportion to the organ and the bellows), so that the wind supply is powerful enough. For the same reason, the wind from all the bellows ought first to be directed into one broad duct, from which separate conduits pass to each chest. Otherwise when one low key after another is played, the wind is not always immediately available, and some pipes simply do not speak, especially if in addition the pallets are too narrow. If, however, the wind channels are too broad, then the wind cannot immediately fill them up, and consequently it is impossible to play rapid passages on organs that have them. §. 442 below describes what to note about the *Windkoppel* in connection with this situation. The wood used for the ducts must also be thoroughly cured; it must be impregnated with glue, and then completely covered over with leather and parchment. They must not be laid on a damp floor, and if they happen to lie in an exposed location where people have to pass over them, they must be carefully shielded with boards so that no damage is done to them. The duct valves must also be accessible.

und Fehlern einer Orgel.

§. 381.

Von den Ventilen der Kanäle an den Bälgen ist schon §. 375. etwas gedacht worden, nämlich daß sie gleich schwehr aufgehen sollen, sonst bleibt der Balg stehen, dessen Ventil schwerlich zugehet; indem die andern Bälge das Ventil vollends zurücke treiben, obschon dieser Balg mehr Gewichte hätte als die andern. Doch sagt Werkmeister daß man oft nicht wisse, warum ein Balg stehen bleibt, bis die andern ausgelaufen sind. Wenn die Ventile gar zu gern aufgehen; so tremuliren sie, wovon §. 376. auch geredet worden. Werkmeister in Organo grüningensi §. 71. [73]) entdeckt ein loses Stück der Orgelmacher, da sie oft in die Hauptkanäle heimliche Ventile machen, dadurch man die Kanäle zu dem oder jenem Clavier zum Theil versperren kann, daß der Wind nicht hinreicht im vollem Werke. Das thun sie, damit sie die alte Windlade zu sich nehmen, und die Leute bewegen wollen, eine neue machen zu lassen. Das ist was gottloses!

§. 382.

Nun kommen wir auf das Pfeifwerk überhaupt. Denn jedes Register besonders zu betrachten, wäre zu weitläuftig, und kömmt doch meistens darauf hinaus, daß jedes so klinge, wie es nach dem 7ten Kapitel des 1sten Bandes hat klingen sollen. Es sollen die Pfeifen ihre rechte Legirung haben, und nicht von allzugeringen Metalle seyn, sonst dauren sie nicht lange. Der Schärfe wegen giebt man zuweilen den Mixturen besser Metall. Z. Er. in Merseburg §. 309. sind sie alle von Zinn. Im Gesichte nimmt man Zinn; oder wenig Bley darunter. Werkmeister sagt in der Orgelprobe S. 67. zwey Theile Zinn und ein Theil Bley gebe ein gut Metall. Mann könnte auch gering Metall nehmen, und dasselbe durch den regulum erhöhen und verbessern, daß es so weiß und hart werde, als Zinn; aber ein jeder könne den Regulum aus dem Antimonio nicht herausbringen; sey auch der Gesundheit schädlich. Etliche wollten es durch Marcasit verbessern; es sey aber nichts. Haec ille. [74]) Wie man eine gute Farbe gebe, ausser solchen Dingen, ist bekannt. Etwas davon wird im 28sten Kapitel zu lesen seyn.

§. 383.

Man wird gewahr, wie auch Werkmeister in Organo grüning. angemerkt, daß der Salpeter die Pfeifen nicht weiter angreift, als an den Füßen, da der Wind hineinschlägt, und solche Materie sich ansetzt, welche die Füße zermalmet: und wo ein Werk gar zu viel Bley hat, kann es wol in 24 oder 30 Jahren zu Grunde gehen. Ich habe
dabey

---

[73]) Auch in der Orgelprobe Kap. 24. S. 59. der Herr Verfasser hat dieser Betrügerey schon oben §. 74. Erwähnung gethan.

[74]) Was Mizler in diesem Stücke für ein Geheimniß zu entdecken versprochen, vermittelst welches das Bley beynahe dem Zinne gleich, und das Zinn wie Silber zu machen, lieset man im vierten Theile des ersten Bandes der musikalischen Bibliothek, S. 45; und aus ihm hat es auch der Hr. Verfasser angeführt in der Anleitung. S. 528.

§. 381.

Concerning the valves on the bellows into the ducts, it has already been mentioned in §. 375 that they must all open with equal ease. Otherwise the bellows whose valve is stiff will stop moving, since the other bellows will press this valve completely closed, even if the first bellows were to be driven by a weight greater than the others. Werkmeister says, however, that the reason why one bellows will not move until the others are exhausted is often not known.* If the valves open far too easily, then they flutter; §. 376 also speaks about this. In §. 71 of his *Organum gruningense*[73] Werkmeister discloses a roguish trick [perpetrated by] organ builders; they often install secret ventils in the main duct, by which the ducts to this or that division may be partially blocked, rendering the wind insufficient for the full organ. This they do in order to take the old windchest for their own use, and thus induce the people to have a new one made. That is a wicked deed!

§. 382.

Now we come to a general commentary on the pipework. Considering each stop separately would be too lengthy, and it usually works out that each of them sounds just as it has been described in Volume 1, Chapter 7. Pipes should be given their proper alloy, and not be made of inferior metal, otherwise they will not last long. Mixtures are at times made of better metal for the sake of brilliance; for example, in Merseburg they are all made of tin (see §. 309). Façade pipes are made of [pure] tin, or at least tin [alloyed] with a bit of lead. On p. 67[-68] of the *Orgelprobe* Werkmeister says that two parts tin and one part lead produce a good [pipe] metal.† [He says that] a metal of poorer quality may be used, and upgraded and improved by the *regulus*,‡ so that it [the metal] becomes as white and hard as tin; but not everybody can extract the *regulus* from antimony, and the process is also a health hazard. Some have tried to improve it with marcasite,§ but that does not work. So says Werkmeister.¶ [74] It is well known how to produce a pleasing color without such methods; there is some information on this in Chapter 28.‖

§. 383.

It should be noted, as Werkmeister has mentioned in his *Organum gruningense*,** that saltpeter does not attack any parts of the pipe other than the feet, where the wind bursts in and deposits materials that corrode the feet.†† If [the pipework of] an instrument contains too much lead, it can disintegrate completely in 24 or 30 years. In

---

[73] as well as in the *Orgelprobe*, Chap. 24, p. 59[f.]. The author [i.e., Adlung] has already made mention of this deceit above in §. 74. [Albrecht]

[74] In the Fourth Part of Volume I of Mizler's *Musikalische Bibliothek*, p. 45, one may read concerning this matter that [Mizler] has promised to reveal a secret, by means of which lead may be made almost like tin, and tin may be made like silver; Adlung has quoted him on p. 528[-529] of the *Anleitung [zu der musikalischen Gelahrtheit]*. [Albrecht]

---

* This statement is to be found neither in the *Orgelprobe* nor in the *Organum gruningense redivivum*.

† Here Adlung works a subtle improvement on Werkmeister, who states that a good metal for pipes inside the organ is 2 parts lead to one part tin; a higher grade metal for principals is half lead and half tin, but principals are better yet if they have 2 parts tin to one part lead.

‡ Here again, as in §. 369, Adlung borrows a term directly from Werkmeister, pp. 67-8, that is unclear in the original; it apparently refers to a substance refined out of antimony.

§ i.e., iron disulfide.

¶ i.e., this is the end of this particular reference to Werkmeister (*Orgelprobe*, p.67).

‖ *Orgelprobe*, p. 182 (in the original edition).

** §. 39.

†† Adlung expands on this matter in Chap. 28, pp. 173f.

dabey gedacht, ob es nicht rathsam sey, daß man zu den Füßen Zinn, oder doch recht gut Metall nehme, besser als zu den Pfeifen, denn so wäre ja dem Unheil abgeholfen, und man hätte den Profit, daß das Pfeifwerk sich auch nicht so leicht setze, weil gut Metall härter ist, und die Last der Pfeife eher tragen kann, als Bley. Es kostet dies auch nicht viel: denn auswendig ist ohnedies alles gut; inwendig aber braucht man keine großen Füße. Ich dächte, der Vorschlag wäre gut. Bey geringerem Metalle könnte man die Füße stärker machen. Hierbey aber sind einige andere Meynung. Sie geben vor, wenn die Füße an den Pfeifen in gleicher Dicke, (oder gar noch dicker) mit den obern Körpern wären; so gäben die darauf stehenden Pfeifenkörper nicht so einen guten Klang von sich, wären auch nie so gut zu intoniren, als wenn sie dünner wären. Wer Lust hat, der untersuche es. Ich habe mich von der Richtigkeit dieses Vorgebens bis daher noch nicht überzeugen können.

§. 384.

Die Pfeifen sollen oben sein rund seyn; nicht eingebogen oder was angehänget: denn das zeigt an, daß die Mensur nicht richtig, oder die Pfeifen verschnitten seyn. Es stehet auch schändlich, wenn sie einer zusammengedruckten Pfaffenmütze gleichen, oder als wenn sie von jungen Hunden oder Katzen zerknauset wären. (s. Trosts Weissenfelßische Orgelbeschreib. S. 22.) Sie sollen auch nicht ausgeschnitten seyn; auch an den Füßen keine Löcher haben, noch eingeknippen seyn. Beydes verräth die Unrichtigkeit der Lade, und will man dadurch das Durchstechen verhindern. Denn wenn wenig Wind ohnedies in die Pfeife kömmt; so wird er über dieses zum Theil durch solches Loch abgeführet, daß das, was zum Labio kömmt, nicht stark genug ist, einen Sonum zu machen. Sie sollen auch Oeschen oder Haken haben, daß sie angehänget werden, und nicht umfallen, wenn sie nicht in Pfeifenbrettern stehen können. s. §. 94. Item Werkmeisters Organum grüningense §. 14. Die Pfeifen sollen nicht zu dünne geschunden seyn; denn wenn man sie angreift, so drückt man Narben hinein; auch werden sie allzugeschwinde warm wenn man sie stimmt und etwan in die Hand nimmt, daher sie auch unrein werden. Hierzu kömmt noch, daß solche Pfeifen oft niemals zur Intonation zu bringen sind, weil sie zittern, und das ganze Corpus sich mit bewegt und mit schnurrt. Hier aber muß nicht die Materie klingen, sondern die Capacität muß den gewissen Sonum geben, indem die fractio aëris in dem labio geschiehet. Auch frißt es der Salpeter eher durch. f Werkmeisters Orgelprobe. Kap. 2. it. Trosts Weissenfelßische Orgelbeschreibung S. 22. Ich habe oft gesehen, daß man die Pfeifen mit Bändern umwinden mussen, um ihr Zittern zu hemmen, und die Intonation zu befördern. Das ist aber gar nicht zu verantworten.

§. 385.

Es sollen die Pfeifen wohl und glatt gehobelt seyn; die rothe Farbe, die beym Löthen daran geschmieret worden, soll abgewaschen seyn. Die Fusse mussen stark seyn, daß sich das Pfeifwerk nicht setze. (conf. §. 383.) Die Labien und Aufschnitte sollen recht

this connection it has occurred to me that it might be advisable to use tin, or at least very high quality metal, for the feet, rather than for the [bodies of the] pipes, since in that way this calamity might be remedied, with the additional advantage that the pipes would not be so prone to settle, since high-quality pipe metal is harder and better able to bear the weight of the pipe than lead is. There would not be much [extra] cost, since all the façade [pipes] are of fine [tin] anyway, and the pipes inside the case do not need large feet. I would think this suggestion might be a good one. The feet could be made stronger even when using inferior metal; but there is a difference of opinion on this point. Some assert that if the feet of pipes were of the same thickness as (or even thicker than) the bodies of the pipes above them, then those pipe bodies would not produce as fine a sound and would be more difficult to voice than if the feet were thinner. Let anyone who wishes investigate this. Up to this point I have not been able to convince myself of the validity of this assertion.

§. 384.

The pipes should be exactly round on top, not bent in and with nothing attached to them; these [faults] indicate that the scale of the pipes is incorrect, or that they were poorly cut. It looks disgraceful when they resemble a pinched-up priest's cap, or as if they had been gnawed by puppies or kittens (see Trost's *Ausführliche Beschreibung deß... Orgelwercks...zu Weissenfels*, p. 22*). Neither ought they to be cut out, nor have little holes in the feet, nor be pinched in.† These [faults] betray an inaccurately built chest, and are intended to prevent running or bleeding. For if a little wind manages to get into a pipe, it is channeled off in part by such a hole, so that whatever reaches the lip is not strong enough to produce a sound. [The pipes] also ought to have eyelets or hooks so that they may be attached [to a pipe rack] and not topple over (provided they cannot stand in rack boards; see §. 94; also Werkmeister's *Organum gruningense*, §. 14). The pipes ought not to be made too thin; otherwise they get dented when someone takes hold of them. They also become warm too quickly when someone picks them up to tune them, and thus get out of tune. In addition, such pipes often can never be voiced properly, since they vibrate and their whole body quivers and buzzes. In this case, it is not the material that should be sounding, but the interior air column should produce a given sound arising from the air striking the lip. Furthermore [when the pipes are too thin] saltpeter corrodes them sooner; see Werkmeister's *Orgelprobe*, Chap. 2; also Trost's ... *Beschreibung deß...Orgelwercks zu Weissenfels*, p. 22). I have often seen pipes that had to be wound round with tape to inhibit their vibrating and promote [good] voicing. That is simply irresponsible.

* Here, as elsewhere, when Adlung cites a source, he often quotes it almost verbatim without using quotation marks.

† "eingeknippen" = eingekniffen.

§. 385.

The pipes should be planed thoroughly smooth, and the red size spread on for soldering should be washed off. The feet must be strong to keep the pipe from settling.‡ The lips and cut-ups should be absolutely neatly formed, not as if someone had knawed

‡ cf. §. 383.

recht sauber seyn, und nicht, als hätte man sie mit den Zähnen zerbissen. Sie sollen nicht ehe Bärte haben, bis es solche Register sind, die dergleichen haben müssen; als: Quintatön, Gedackt u. d. gl.; hingegen, wenn die Violdigamba dergleichen hat, so ists ein Zeichen, daß der Meister sie nicht accurat gemacht habe. So auch in andern. Ob sie Bärte bekommen müssen, ist aus dem 7ten Kapitel zu ersehen. Die Gedackten haben dergleichen; auch etliche offene Stimmen, wenn sie nämlich gar zu enge Mensur haben, als z. Ex. das Salcional. Die Pfeifen sollen im Gießen ihre richtige Länge und Weite bekommen, weil es ein Fehler ist, wenn man anflicken muß. Sie sollen auch mit Silberloth wohl und veste gelöthet seyn, daß keine Löcherchen bleiben. Wenn das Loth nicht veste ist; so zerdrückt man die Pfeife gar leicht im Stimmen. Wenn der Kern nicht wohl gelöthet ist; so rauschet und fladdert die Pfeife. Der Kern aber muß recht nach geraden Winkel aufs allergenaueste eingesetzt werden.

§. 386.

Wenn die Pfeifen Sandlöcher haben; so zittern sie. Die Sandlöcher kommen aber daher, wenn sich in den Gießladen Sand unter das Metall mischet. Etliche Orgelmacher gießen deswegen die Blätter auf Asche; etliche aber auf Leinwand, davon §. 88. zu lesen. Bey gedeckten Pfeifen sollen sonderlich die Hüte vest anliegen, daß sie nicht sinken und Unreinigkeiten verursachen. Wenn die gedeckten Pfeifen filpen; so sind sie entweder nicht weit genung aufgeschnitten, oder der Kern liegt zu hoch. Wenn er in offenen Pfeifen so gelegt wird, daß man unter demselben nur als ein Haarbreit hinsehen kann; so ists gut. In metallenen Pfeifen kann man den Kern etwas biegen; aber im Holze ists schwer zu verbessern. Auch ists ein Fehler wenn das Blech, da der Ausfall über den Kern gehet, nicht gerade ist; da man denn mit einem Intonirbleche ihm helfen muß. Jede Pfeife soll die Mensur haben, die ihre im 1sten Bande, Kap. 7. gezeigte Natur der Länge und Weite nach erfordert. Sonderlich kann man bey den Mensuren unterschiedlicher Claviere eine sich wohl ausnehmende Veränderung anbringen. Doch davon s. §. 272. Dazu man noch thun kann, was in der Altdresdener Orgel ist; da ist nämlich das Oberwerk um eine Sekunde enger mensurirt, als das Hauptmanual: das Pedal aber ist noch weiterer Mensur. Die enge Mensur klingt schöner, s. Prätorius Tom. II. P. IV. cap. II. doch macht man in der obern Oktave die Pfeifen gemeiniglich weiter, daß sie sich besser intoniren lassen. Es sollen alle Pfeifen ihren richtigen Aufschnitt haben, wie auch frisch und äqual ansprechen.

387.

Ein Fehler ist, wenn in einem und ebendemselben Register eine Pfeife schwach, die andere aber stark klingt. Das zeigt an, daß eine stumpf geschnitten sey; und dem kann nicht geholfen werden, wenn man nicht an die obere Lefze was anlöthen kann. Doch besser ists, man macht die ganze Pfeife anders. Man muß den Aufschnitt nach dem Zirkel machen, und bey jeder Pfeife die Höhe nach der Breite rechnen. Doch NB. manchmal

them with his teeth. They ought not to have beards, unless they are stops that require them, such as the Quintatön, Gedackt, and the like. On the other hand, if a Viola da Gamba has them, then it is a sign that the builder did not fashion it meticulously. The same holds true for the other [stops]. Chapter 7 will indicate which stops ought to have beards. Gedackts have them, as do some open stops that have a very narrow scale, such as, for example, the Salcional. The pipes should receive their proper length and width when they are cast, since it is a fault if they have to be patched together. They should also be firmly soldered with silver solder, so that no gaps remain. If the solder is not firm, then the pipes get crushed easily when they are tuned. If the languid is not well soldered, then the pipe sizzles and flutters. The languid must be inserted precisely at a right angle.

§. 386.

If the pipes have sand holes, then they vibrate. Sand holes are the result of sand getting mixed into the metal during pouring. For this reason, some organ builders cast the pipe sheets on [a bed of] ashes, and some on a sheet of canvas; consult §. 88 about this. Concerning stopped pipes in particular, the caps should fit tightly, so that they do not drop and cause out-of-tuneness. If stopped pipes misspeak (filpen*), they are either not cut up far enough, or their languid is positioned too high. In open pipes [the languid] should be positioned so that the lower lip is just a hairs-breadth below it. With metal pipes the languid can be bent to some degree, but with wooden ones it is difficult to adjust. It is also a fault if the lower lip that directs the wind stream over the languid is not straight; this has to be corrected with a flue tool. Every pipe should have the scale that its character requires, according to its length and width, as described in Vol. I, Chap. 7. In particular, it is possible to achieve exceptional variety among the various divisions by means of scaling; concerning this, see §. 272. Furthermore, one might follow the example of the organ in the church in Dresden Neustadt,† in which the Oberwerk is scaled two pipes narrower than the Hauptwerk, while the pedal is scaled more widely.‡ Narrower scaling produces a more beautiful sound (see Praetorius [*Syntagma musicum*], Vol. II, Part IV, Chap. II[, p. 143], but pipe scales normally increase in the upper octave, to allow for better voicing. All the pipes should be given their proper cut up; they should have a lively and consistent speech.

* see also §. 84 and Chap. 28, p. 180

† i.e., the Dreikönigskirche, that received a new organ in 1711.

‡ by implication more widely than the Hauptwerk; the stoplist in Mattheson's Appendix to Niedt's *Musicalische Handleitung*, p. 170, lists the *Haupt-manual* as being of wide scale, the *Oberwerck* as being scaled two pipes narrower (um eine Secunde mensuriret) than the *Haupt-manual*, and the *Pedal* as having a very wide scale.

§. 387.

It is a fault if within the very same stop one pipe sounds soft and the next one loud. That indicates that one has been cut up until it is dull; this cannot be amended without soldering something onto the upper lip. But it is better to make the whole pipe over. The cut up must be done by using a compass and calculating the height [of the cut up] of each pipe according to its width. But take note! It might often seem as though one

mal deucht einem, als klinge eine Pfeife anders, weil sie an einem andern Orte stehet, und weil etwan zwischen einer Pfeife und unsern Ohren mehr stehet, das den Schall wo andershin leitet, als bey der andern. Daher kann es kommen, daß uns an diesem Orte eine Pfeife schwach klinget, welche an einem andern Orte einen stärkern Laut von sich giebt. Will man in solchem Falle recht urtheilen; so muß man die Pfeifen herausnehmen, und sie gegeneinander hören. Es sollen die Pfeifen auch geschwind ansprechen, und sich nicht überschreyen in die Quinte oder Oktave, welches ein großer Fehler ist, und oft bey enge mensurirten Pfeifwerke gemerkt wird; als bey der Violdigamba, Violon, ꝛc. Wer die Kunst weis, einen Silberklang zu machen, der weis was schönes. Was sonst noch für gute Dinge bey der Intonation zu merken, die findet man §. 93.

§. 388.

Ein Fehler ist auch endlich, wenn nicht jede Stimme von der Materie gemacht ist, die im Contrakte benennet worden. Werkmeister Kap. 9. der Orgelprobe, sagt: Man hält von dem Pfeifwerke am meisten, so in den sonis grauioribus oder großen clauibus und Stimmen von weiterer Mensur, in den kleinen von engerer ist, als die radices proportionum es mit sich bringen. Denn dieses klingt lieblich und scharf, jenes prächtig und gravitätisch. Doch daß jede Stimme ihre Art bekomme; daß auch eine Aequalität sey, und die großen die kleinen nicht übertreiben. Und Kap. 13. sagt er: Wenn zwey Consonanzen vor sich reine klingen; so hört man, wenn man sie zugleich greift, oft eine Dissonanz dabey, als wäre eine dritte Pfeife da, und ist doch kein Durchstechen; sondern wenn die Proportion der Pfeife nicht in acht genommen worden, daher man eine zerschneiden, und sie der Weite nach, der andern gleich machen muß, nach Proportion. Dies ist eben aus dem Grunde herzuleiten, woraus das fließt, was er Kap. 15. sagt, daß die unproportionirten Körper nicht könnten zusammen rein gestimmet werden.

§. 389.

Von den Schnarrwerken überhaupt hat mehrgedachter Werkmeister im 4ten Kapitel der Orgelprobe noch etwas. Nämlich: das die Körper ihrer Art nach groß genug seyn sollen, sowol was die Länge als auch die Weite anbelanget. Denn obwol die Tiefe bey kleinen Körpern auch erhalten wird; so ist doch die Gravität nicht da. Wenn sie in den großen clauibus sehr weit sind; so überschreyen sie den Diskant. Auch geschiehet dies zuweilen, wenn der Zufall des Windes ungleich ist;[75] auch sind etwann die Blätter und Mundstücke nicht gleich; oder eins ist gerade und das andere nicht; oder eins ist weit, und das andere enge. Die Pfeifen müssen nicht zu enge stehen des vielen Stimmens wegen; und muß man auch die Schnarrwerke stimmen, die hinter den vördersten stehen. Die Stiefel müssen weit seyn, daß die Blätter nicht anstoßen. Starke Blätter sind beständiger, als die schwachen: sie müssen aber durch alle claues

---

[75] Dieses Fehlers wegen ist es gut, wenn man in den Ventilen den Schnarrwerken den Wind durch Unterschiede zumisset.

pipe sounds different because it is standing in another place, and because more [obstructions] that deflect the sound elsewhere may be standing between our ears and one pipe than another.* Thus it may happen that a pipe sounds soft to us from one location, while the same pipe produces a bold sound in another location. In order to judge correctly in such a case, it is necessary to remove the pipes and compare their sounds.† The pipes must also speak promptly, and not overblow to the fifth or octave, which is a major fault often noted in narrow-scale pipes such as the Viola da Gamba, the Violon, etc. Anybody who knows how to create a silvery tone has mastered a beautiful art. For other good voicing characteristics to take note of, consult §. 93.

* Adlung discusses a related matter, i.e., why a pipe may sound good when the listener is located in one place, and poorly when the listener is at another, in Chap. 28, p. 170f.

† e.g., to put them both near each other on the same chest

§. 388.

Finally, it is also a fault if not every stop is made of the material specified in the contract. In Chap. 9‡ of the *Orgelprobe*, Werkmeister says: "In general, bass pipes and lower pitches of a broader scale and trebles of a narrower scale are considered best, according to a *radices proportionum* (geometrically proportional scheme); the treble then sounds pleasing and bright, and the bass splendid and sonorous. But stops should be even throughout their compass, according to their required character, and the bass pipes should not overpower the trebles." And in Chapter 13§ he says that if two pipes sounding a pure consonant interval in themselves are played together, a dissonance is often heard with them, as if there were a third pipe sounding. This is not the result of a run; rather the proper proportion of [one of] the pipes has been disregarded. One of them should be cut open and its width made to match the other, heeding the [correct] proportion. The root of this fault is the same one described by [Werkmeister] in Chapter 15, i.e., bodies that are out of proportion cannot be brought into pure tune with each other.¶

‡ p. 21.

§ p. 30.

¶ Werkmeister states this in Chap. 15, p. 36, in connection with reed stops.

§. 389.

The oft-cited Werkmeister has more to say in Chapter 4‖ of the *Orgelprobe* about the reeds in general, namely that the resonators should be large enough, in keeping with each particular variety, both as regards length and width. For although fractional-length resonators can attain a low pitch, they will have no gravity. [He also says** that] if the resonators of bass pipes are very wide, they will overpower the treble; this also sometimes occurs if the wind supply is unsteady,75) or perhaps if the tongues and shallots do not match, or if one is straight and another not, or one is broad and another narrow. Because they must be tuned frequently, [reed] pipes must not stand too close together; after all, the reeds that stand behind the one in front also have to be tuned. The boots must be wide enough that the tongues do not strike them. Heavy tongues are more durable than weak ones:†† but they must have the same proportion throughout the en-

‖ p. 7f.

** p. 8.

†† i.e., thick tongues are more durable than thin ones.

---

75) Because of this fault it is a good thing to distribute [part of] the wind at the pallets for the reeds by means of dividers.‡‡ [Albrecht]

‡‡ i.e., to place a divider in each channel separating the wind source for the reeds from that of the flues.

und Fehlern einer Orgel.

claues gleiche Proportion haben, daß sie sich mit einander in die Höhe oder in die Tiefe ziehen, weil dies ein Zeichen ihrer Accuratesse ist. Die Krücken müssen stark seyn; gleichgebohret, daß sie just auf dem Blatte liegen. Sie müssen nicht zu veste und nicht zu lose stehen. Und weil bisweilen etwas an den Krücken zu bessern, diese aber sich wegen der Haken nicht heraus ziehen lassen; so sind andere auf den guten Einfall gerathen, daß sie die Krücken ohne Haken machen, und an dessen Statt sie mit Schrauben versehen. So ist z. Ex. die Erfurtische Domorgel, und die Posaune in Alach gemacht. (s. auch oben §. 105.) Die geschlagenen Krücken pflegen leicht umzufallen, sonderlich wenn sie gar schmal sind. Es stehet auch fein, wenn die Krücken in gleicher Länge sind, oder nach Proportion ab- und zunehmen. Die meßingenen rosten nicht so bald, als die eisernen; doch stehen sie nicht so veste. Die eisernen verstaniolt man, daß sie nicht rosten. Die stählernen würden dadurch die Härte verlieren, daher man es bey diesen unterläßt. Kann man Schrauben haben, zumal bey größern Schnarrwerken, ists desto besser. Zu Gera (§. 301.) und zu Jena (§ 302.) findet man Krücken und Schrauben zugleich, welches was schönes ist. Der Annehmlichkeit halben sollen die Mundstücke auch enger Mensur seyn. s. Prätor. l. c. In den Stiefeln sollen die Mundstücke veste stehen, daß sie beym Stimmen nicht herausfallen. Die meßingenen Mundstücke sind die beständigsten. Sie werden auch wol mit Metall gefüttert, welches darauf gelöthet wird, daß die Blätter nicht zu sehr knastern. Nicht gut ist, wenn man die hölzernen Stöcke in metallenen Stiefel setzet: denn wenn das Holz schwindet: so treibet der Wind die Pfeifen heraus: quillt es aber; so zerspringen die Stiefel. Bey großen Registern werden die Stöcke an die Stiefeln angehangt, daß sie nicht heraus fallen; bey kleinen sollte es aber noch mehr geschehen, weil oft der Wind, noch mehr aber das Aufwärtsschlagen der Krücke sie abzieht. Daher in Zimmern supra mir gefällt, daß der Cornetbaß und Trompete angeschraubet sind; denn so stehen sie veste im Stimmen. Die großen Mundstücke z. Ex. im Posaunenbasse, füttert man am besten mit Leder, daß sie nicht zu sehr knastern. Hierzu ist das lohgahre Leder besser, als das weißgahre: denn dieses zieht viel Feuchtigkeit an sich, welche den Leim abweicht, und leicht abfällt. Man pflegt auch wol hölzerne Mundstücke zu machen, wie bey dem Posaunbasse geschehen zu St. Thomä in Erfurt, it. zu Zimmern supra.

§. 390.

An allen hölzernen Pfeifen ist es als ein Fehler anzusehen, wenn sie mit der Leimtränke nicht wohl ausgegossen sind, weil der Wind sich verschleicht. Sind die Pfeifen ganz von Holz; so ist es eine Vollkommenheit für sie, wenn sie können einen metallenen Klang bekommen, wie Casparini in Görlitz gemacht. Dazu hilft die Leimtränke etwas: Imgl. wenn man hart Holz nimmt, als Birnbaum u. dergleichen; auch wenn man die Kerne und labia mit Zinn belegt, wie §. 301. zu Gera am Gedackt 4′, und beym Principal 8′ zu sehen: doch wenn es nicht ausdrücklich bedungen wird; so macht es
keiner

tire range of the stop, so that they are consistent* from treble to bass; this is a sign of their being precisely crafted. The tuning wires must be strong and precisely bored so that they fit snugly against the tongue; they must fit neither too tightly nor too loosely. And since the tuning wires sometimes need fixing but cannot be removed because of the hooks,† others have hit upon the happy idea of making tuning wires without hooks, replacing them with screws instead. The ones at Erfurt Cathedral are made in this way, for example, as is the Posaune at Alach (see also §. 105 above). Tuning wires that are struck‡ are prone to bend easily, especially if they are very thin. It looks neat if the tuning wires are all of the same length, or increase and decrease proportionally. Brass ones do not rust as quickly as iron ones, but they are not as stiff. Iron ones are plated with tin to keep them from rusting, but this is not done to steel ones, since it would make them lose their strength. If it is possible to have screws,§ this would be better, especially in the case of large reed stops. At Gera (§. 301) and at Jena (§. 302¶) there are tuning wires together with screws, which is really very fine. For the sake of a pleasing [tone] the shallots ought to be of narrow scale (see Praetorius, l.c.‖). The shallots should fit tightly into the boots, so that they do not fall out while being tuned. Brass shallots are the most durable. Shallots may also be plated with pipe metal that is soldered on, to prevent the tongues from rattling so loudly. It is not good to put wooden blocks** into metal boots, for when the wood shrinks the wind forces the pipes out [of them], and when it swells the boots burst. In large stops the blocks are attached to the boots to keep them from falling out; this should be done all the more to small pipes, since often the wind (or even more likely the upward beating of the tuning wires] drives them out. Thus I am pleased to see that at Zimmern supra the [blocks of the] pedal Cornet [2′] and the Trompete [8′]†† are screwed onto [the boots]; in this way they keep their tune. The large shallots, e.g., those in the pedal Posaune, are best covered with leather, to keep them from rattling too much. Tanned leather is better for this than tawed, for the latter attracts dampness, loosening the glue and causing [the leather] to fall off. Some [builders] are in the habit of making wooden shallots, as is the case with the pedal Posaune at St. Thomas in Erfurt and likewise at Zimmern supra.

§. 390.

It is to be considered a fault for wooden pipes not to be thoroughly impregnated with a solution of glue, since [otherwise] the wind seeps through [the pores of the wood]. If the pipes are entirely of wood, it is a great merit if they can be made to sound like metal, as Casparini has done at Görlitz.‡‡ The glue solution helps somewhat in this regard, as does using hard wood such as pearwood or the like. Plating the languid and lips with tin (as seen in the Gedackt 4′ and Principal 8′ at Gera, §. 301§§) also helps; but no [organ builder] will do this unless it is specifically contracted. Being able to unscrew

* i.e., in their voicing.

† i.e., at the top of the wire, the end opposite the contact point with the tongue.

‡ to adjust them—i.e., wires with hooks.

§ i.e., in addition to tuning wires.
¶ See the stoplists of both organs in Chapter 10.
‖ p. 143.

** The word Adlung uses here is *Stöcke* (toe boards), a term taken directly from Chapter 4 of Werkmeister's *Orgelprobe*, on which much of this section is based. By comparing the context of this passage with §. 104, (Vol. I, p. 66), it seems reasonably certain that what Adlung means, both here and in the following sentence, is *Köpfe* (blocks)

†† on the *Hauptmanual*; see the stoplist of this organ in Chapter 10.

‡‡ See Boxberg, p.[11.]

§§ See the stoplist of this organ in Chapter 10.

keiner. Eine gute Invention ist auch, da man die labia der hölzernen Pfeifen kann abschrauben, daß man ihnen desto besser zu aller Zeit helfen könne. So ist z. Ex. der Subbaß 16′ zu St. Thomä in Erfurt gemacht.

Was die gekoppelten Stimmen anlangt, so ist §. 276. schon erinnert, daß der Wind vom Pedale und Manuale müsse gleich stark dahin geführet werden. Sonst aber ist wegen des Pedals noch zu erinnern, daß die Art, da man die Manualventile auf die eine, die Pedalventile aber auf der andern Seite anbringt, (wie §. 127. weitläuftig gesagt worden) folgende Incommodität bey sich führe. Wenn man es nicht zieht, sondern im Manuale spielet; so drückt die force des Windes die Pedalventile auf, und der Wind wandert in den Pedalwindkasten; daher entstehet oft der Fehler, daß wenn man in der Tiefe spielt, das Werk schluckt, und die obigen Pfeifen schlagen nicht an, weil der Wind nicht zureicht. diesem gehet man entgegen durch die andere Art, da die Ventile an einer Seite angebracht werden. s. §. 127. Welche Art man aber erwählet; so wollte ich rathen, daß die Pedalabstrakten so gemacht würden, daß sie durch den Zug abgehänget werden, damit sie bey schwachem Spielen nicht stets mit rasseln, als welches ein besonderer Fehler ist.

Das XIV. Kapitel.
Von der Temperatur der Orgeln.

Inhalt:

§. 391. Von der Temperatur und Proportionen überhaupt. §. 392. insonderheit, und wie sie gefunden. §. 393. Alle Quinten sind nicht reine zu stimmen. §. 394. auch helfen die Subsemitonia nichts, sondern man muß temperiren. §. 395. Kircherus hat davon geschrieben. §. 396. item Werkmeister. §. 397. Prätorius; Neidhardt. §. 398. Mattheson; Bümler, ꝛc. §. 399. Wieviel durch die Temperatur einzutheilen. §. 400. Wie dieses von etlichen verschiedentlich geschehen. §. 401. Ob man die Temperatur durch das Monochord solle auf die Orgeln bringen? §. 402. Die Incommoda dabey, §. 403. welche Hr. Neidhardt selbst erfahren. §. 404. Von dem ersten Grund-Sono der Orgel. §. 405. Die Temperatur geschieht besser nach 2 Pfeifen. §. 406. Wie sie nach dem Gehör geschehe. §. 407. Was man für ein Register nimmt. §. 408. Die Terzen können Richter seyn §. 409. Wie andere Instrumente zur Temperatur klingen. §. 410. Von Kammerregistern. §. 411. Etliche temperiren durch Dissonanzen. §. 412. Der Grundton sey nach der am meisten recipirten Art.

§. 391.

Es werden allhier zween Haupttheile zu machen seyn. Wir wollen nämlich I. von der Temperatur überhaupt etwas gedenken. II. das gesagte auf die Orgel appliciren, weil es ein Hauptfehler ist, wenn die Orgel nicht recht temperirt und gestimmt ist.

the lips of wooden pipes, in order to be able to adjust them at any time, is also a good invention. For example, this is how the Subbass 16′ [in the organ] at St. Thomas in Erfurt is made.

Concerning stops with a *Windkoppel*,* §. 276 has already mentioned that the wind must be conducted at equal pressure to both pedal and manual. With regard to [stops of this construction that sound in] the pedal, it must furthermore be noted that the method of putting the manual pallet on one side and the pedal pallet on the side opposite (as has been described in detail in §. 127) is accompanied by the following weakness: when [the pedal drawknob] is not drawn, then the force of the wind forces the pedal pallet open when the manual is played, and the wind passes into the pedal pallet box. Thus there often arises the fault that when the lower pipes are played the instrument gulps/gasps and the treble pipes do not speak, because there is insufficient wind. This [fault] may be prevented by the second method [of construction], in which both pallets are placed on the same side; see §. 127. Whichever method is chosen, I would recommend that the pedal trackers be able to be uncoupled by a stop mechanism, so that one does not hear a constant rattling when the organ is being played softly, which is a definite fault.

* i.e., stops with two pallet boxes, one for the manual and one for the pedal.

Chapter XIV.
Concerning Organ Temperament.

Contents:

§.391. Concerning temperament and [interval] proportions in general. §.392. Specifically, how they were discovered. §.393. All fifths are not to be tuned pure. §.394. Subsemitones are of no value; an instrument must be tempered. §.395. Kircher has written about this. §.396. Likewise Werkmeister. §.397. Praetorius; Neidhardt. §.398. Mattheson; Bümler, etc. §.399. The proper distribution when tempering. §.400. The various systems of temperament. §.401. Should the monochord be used when tempering the organ? §.402. The inconveniences connected with it. §.403. These have been experienced by Mr. Neidhardt himself. §.404. Concerning the basic pitch of an organ. §.405. Tempering succeeds better with two pipes. §.406. How to do it by ear. §.407. Which stop to use. §.408. Thirds may be used to check accuracy. §.409. How other instruments sound in comparison to the temperament. §.410. Concerning stops at chamber pitch. §.411. Some use dissonances to set a temperament. §.412. The basic pitch should correspond to that most commonly prevailing.

§. 391.

Here we must divide the subject into two parts. First, we must consider to some degree temperament in general, and second, apply the discussion to the organ, since it is a major fault for organs not to be tempered and tuned correctly.

Kap. XIV. Von der Temperatur der Orgeln.

Die Temperatur überhaupt betreffend, so wird mancher Anfänger nicht gleich begreifen, was dadurch zu verstehen: welchem also folgendes zur Nachricht dienen kann: Wenn eine Pfeife von beliebiger Länge und Weite genommen wird; so hat dieselbige ihren gewissen, und nach der Länge und Weite determinirten Klang, so und so tief. Zum Exempel, ich nehme die Pfeife 8′ lang, (vom labio an) und von der Principalweite; so giebt sie C an. Will nun der Orgelmacher andere Sonos haben, höher oder tiefer; so muß er wissen, wieviel die Pfeife länger oder kürzer [76] werden müsse, als jene war. Nun hat man gefunden, wie die Soni sich gegen einander verhalten, und wie die Pfeifen eine gewisse Länge und Weite gegen einander haben müssen; welche Proportion die Orgelmacher auf ein Brett zeichnen, vom C bis $\bar{\bar{c}}$. So auch mit den Sayten: denn wenn ich einer Sayte, die etwan C giebt, einen Steg unter setze, und dadurch den dritten Theil abnehme; so giebt sie die Quinte an: nehme ich die halbe Länge; so ist es eine Oktave, u. s. w. Diese Proportiones oder Verhältnisse der Sonorum gegen einander hat man in gewissen Zahlen ausgedruckt, und hat von der 1. angefangen, da allezeit die doppelte Zahl eine Oktave bedeutet. Wenn also 1′ das $\bar{\bar{c}}$ wäre; so ist die Zahl doppelt genommen 2′; das giebt $\bar{c}$; diese wieder doppelt 4′, ist c; diese wieder doppelt 8′, ist c; diese nochmal doppelt 16′, ist C, ꝛc. Oder von unten auf: wenn eine Sayte (die also nur 1 Theil hat) C giebt; so theile ich sie mit einem untergesetzten Stege in 2 gleiche Theile, dann giebt mir ein jeder von diesen Theilen c an, als die Oktave. Theilt man jeden Theil wieder in 2 Theile; so giebt jeder neue Theil $\bar{c}$ an, weil sodann die ganze Sayte in 4 Theile getheilet ist. Theilt man jedes Theilchen weiter in 2 gleiche Theile, so giebt es $\bar{\bar{c}}$, sodann ist die ganze Sayte in 16 gleiche Theilchen getheilet, davon ein jedes allein $\bar{\bar{c}}$ angiebt. Also wenn ich die Zahl 3 habe, und nehme das Duplum 6; so ist es eine Oktave höher, als jene. Ist nun die 3 $\bar{f}$ gewesen; so giebt 6 f, 12 F, ꝛc. Oder herunterwärts: wenn 12 F ist, so ist die Hälfte 6 f; wieder die Hälfte 3 $\bar{f}$; wieder die Hälfte 1½ $\bar{\bar{f}}$; wieder die Hälfte ¾ $\bar{\bar{\bar{f}}}$, ꝛc. So geht es in allen Zahlen.

§. 392.

Fraget man: wie man diese Proportiones der Oktaven und anderer Intervallen gefunden? So dient zur Antwort, daß dieses nicht auf einmal geschehen. Den ersten Ursprung leitet man von dem **Pythagoras** her; (conf. Nicomachus, ein Musicus Pythagoraeus, pag. 10. ex edit. Meibom. Und aus ihm **Neidhardts** Temperatur des Monochordi S. 8. u. f.) welcher in der Schmiede von ohngefähr eine Harmonie der Hämmer angemerkt, daher er ihre Schwere erforscht, und sothane Proportiones, wo nicht alle, doch zum Theil, entdeckt haben soll. [77] Uns gehet es weiter nichts

---

[76] Auch weiter und enger.

[77] Daß man dieses Vorgeben nicht anders, als ein Mährchen anzusehen habe, beweiset der berühmte Herr Kapellmeister **Scheibe** im kritischen Musikus, S. 16. in einer gelehrten

Chap. XIV. Concerning Organ Temperament

With regard to temperament in general, many a beginner will not comprehend immediately what is meant by it. Thus the following may serve as an introduction. If we take a pipe of a given length and breadth, this [pipe] will sound at its own particular pitch, determined by its length and width. As an example, I shall take a pipe 8′ long (from the lip upward), of principal scale; this pipe produces a C. If the organbuilder wants other pitches, either higher or lower, he has to know how much longer or shorter [76] than the first the pipe must be. Now it has been discovered how pitches are related to each other, and what relative length and width each pipe must have over against the others. Organ builders indicate these proportions on a board, from C to c‴. The same holds true with strings; for if I place a bridge under a string that sounds, let us say, C, thereby shortening it by one third, it will sound the fifth [above the C]. If I choose [to divide it in] half, then it will sound an octave [above C], etc.. These proportions or relations between pitches have been expressed by certain numbers, beginning with 1; twice the number always indicates an octave [lower]. Thus if 1′ is a c‴, twice that number is 2′ and sounds c″; twice the latter is 4′, c′; twice that 8′, c; again twice that, 16′, C, etc. Or moving upward from the bottom: if a string (that is one entire unit) sounds C, and I divide it into two equal parts by placing a bridge under it, then each of these two sections will produce for me a c, i.e., the octave. If each of these sections is again divided into two parts, each of those new parts will sound c′, since then the entire string is divided into 4 sections. If each subdivision is once again divided into two equal parts, each will sound c″; when the whole string is divided into 16 [equal] parts, each one of them alone will sound c‴. Likewise, if I begin with the number 3 [as the putative length of the string] and double it, making 6, then the latter is an octave lower* than the former. If the 3 is an f′, then 6 will sound f, 12: F, etc.. Or conversely, if 12 is F, then half of it, 6, is f; half of that, 3, is f′; half of that, 1½, is f″; half again, ¾, is f‴, etc.. The procedure operates like this with all numbers.

* Adlung reads "höher" (higher).

§. 392.

If anyone should ask, "How were these proportions for octaves and other intervals discovered?," here is the answer: this did not happen all at once. The origin is attributed to Pythagoras (cf. *Nicomachus, ein musicus Pythagoraeus*, p. 10, from the edition by Meibom,† and excerpts from him in Neidhardt's *Temperatur des Monochordi*, p. 8ff.), who, noting by chance a harmonious sound produced by hammers in a forge, investigated their weights, and is said to have discovered some, though not all, of these proportions.[77] We will not concern ourselves further with this, since enough has been

† Meibom, Marcus, *Antiquae musicae auctores septem*. Amsterdam: Elzevirius, 1652.

---

76) as well as [how much] broader or narrower. [Albrecht]

77) The noted Kapellmeister Scheibe, in a learned and extensive note on p. 16‡ of his *Kritischer Musicus*, proves that one must consider this pretense as nothing more than a legend, offering such reasons that no one could fail to agree. [Albrecht]

‡ The note begins on p. 12 and extends to p. 16.

nichts an, weil man genug Schriften von diesen Materien hat, und wenn wir es wollten ausführen, würde es ein besonderer Traktat werden, da es doch einem Organisten und Orgelmacher weiter zu wissen nicht nöthig, als wie etwan eine Orgel oder ander Instrument zu temperiren ist. Wir wollen die Proportiones nur hersetzen, wie sie an sich anfänglich gewesen ist. Die Oktave ist zu dem untern Tone wie 2 zu 1. Das ist, wenn eine Sayte einen gewissen Sonum giebt, und man theilt die Sayte in 2 Theile; so giebt ein Theil davon die Oktave; wie §. 391. gesagt. Die Quinte ist wie 3 zu 2. Das ist, wenn eine Sayte getheilet wird, durch den Zirkel und einen untergesetzten Steg, in 3 Theile, so geben die 2 Theile die Oktav, den 3ten Theil dazu gethan, giebt die Quinte. (unterwärts) Die Quarte hat die Proportion wie 4:3. Die große Terz wie 5:4. Die kleine Terz wie 6:5. Die Sekunde wie 9:8. Die große Sexte wie 5:3. Die große Septime wie 15:8. Die kleine Sexte wie 8:5. Die kleine Septime wie 9:5.

§. 393.

Ob die Stimmung einer Pfeife reine sey, kann man so genau nicht hören, daß nicht ein Pünktchen zuweilen fehlen sollte; doch hört man es bey den Oktaven und Quinten accurater, als bey andern, als bey welchen man ein Zittern vernimmt, wenn sie nicht reine sind. Nach den Oktaven aber kann man nicht temperiren, weil man nicht aus der Stelle käme, sondern immer auf c bliebe, wenn ich da angefangen. Daher ist man auf die Quinten gefallen, weil bey den noch übrigen Intervallen die Schwebung oder das Zittern nicht so vernommen wird, wie bey ihnen. Wenn wir nun die Quinten wollten reine stimmen, daß keine mehr zitterte; so würde die proportio sesquialtera oder 3 gegen 1 vollkommen seyn: aber wenn alle Quinten durch wären, und ich wieder auf den Anfangsclavem käme; so würde die letzte Quinte viel zu klein werden. Wollte ich die erste wieder ändern; so würden die andern wieder falsch, und so in infinitum. Auch würden die Oktaven nicht treffen. Ließ ich es stehen, so würden die kleinen Terzen zu niedrig, und die großen Terzen zu hoch.

§. 394.

Wollte man es durch Subsemitonia verbessern; so würde es viel Geld kosten, zumal in großen Orgeln: auch wurde es dem Organisten viel Verdruß machen, und doch wäre es Flickwerk, darauf man nicht durch den Zirkel gehen könnte, und was für incommoda mehr damit verknüpft sind. Subsemitonia aber nennet man, die eingeschobenen Claves, da man 2 cis, 2 gis, ꝛc. hat; wiewol man die andern anders nennet, daher des, as, ꝛc. entstehet. Es gehet auch diese Sache in infinitum, und kömmt nie zur Reinigkeit. Man ist deswegen schon vor Alters her auf eine Temperatur bedacht gewesen; dadurch man verstehet, wenn dasjenige, was in der letzten Quinte mangelt, nach Proportion eingetheilet wird, so, daß es nicht eine Quinte allein einbußen musse,

son-

und weitläuftigen Anmerkungen, mit solchen Gründen, welchen Niemand den Beyfall versagen kann.

written about these matters; if we wished to elaborate on it, it would turn into a separate treatise, but it is really not necessary for an organist or organbuilder to know anything more about it other than how to temper, say, an organ or some other instrument. Here we will only set forth the proportions in their original [untempered] form. The octave is to its fundamental as 2:1; that is, if a string produces a given pitch, and that string is divided into two parts, one part will produce the octave, as has been said in §.391. The fifth is as 3:2; that is, if a string is divided into 3 parts by measuring it off with a compass and placing a bridge under it,* then the 2 parts will produce a tone, and when the third part is added in it will produce the fifth below it. The fourth has the proportion 4:3. The major third is as 5:4; the minor third as 6:5; the second as 9:8; the major sixth as 5:3; the major seventh as 15:8; the minor sixth as 8:5; and the minor seventh as 9:5.†

* i.e., dividing it into 2 parts versus 1 part.

† The proportions Adlung gives for the less fundamental intervals are Pythagorean; they only approximate the actual proportions.

§. 393.

It is not possible to hear precisely whether the tuning of a pipe is exactly correct; an occasional small error is unavoidable. Yet it may be heard more precisely in octaves and fifths than in other [intervals]; in the former a flutter is perceived if they are not exactly in tune. It is not possible to set a temperament using octaves, however, since one would never leave the same spot, remaining on c if that were the starting point. Thus people have turned to the fifths, since the beating or fluttering is not so perceptible in the rest of the intervals as in these. If I were to tune the fifths pure, so that none of them fluttered, then the *proportio sesquialtera* or 3:1 would be exact; but when I had passed through all the fifths and returned to the key where I started, [I would find] the final fifth much too small. If I were to return and alter the first [fifth], then the next would again be wrong, and so forth *ad infinitum*. Neither would the octaves correspond.‡ If I let it§ stand, then the minor thirds would be too narrow and the major thirds too wide.

‡ i.e., if all the fifths were tuned pure.

§ i.e., the circle of perfect fifths.

§. 394.

Using subsemitones to improve the situation would cost a great deal of money, especially in large organs, and would also cause the organist much vexation; and yet they would only be a patch-up job, since they would not permit [the organist] to pass through the circle of fifths,¶ together with all the other inconveniences coupled with this limitation. Subsemitones are the name for the recessed keys, so that there are 2 c sharps, two g sharps, etc.; although the second [key of the pair] is given a different name, whence [the expressions] d flat, a flat, etc., arise. This could also go on *ad infinitum* without ever reaching perfect tuning. Thus [musicians] began to be concerned about temperament a long time ago; by that [term] is meant that the amount lacking in the final fifth is distributed proportionately so that no one fifth must suffer [the lack],

¶ i.e., to modulate.

sondern es müssen die andern auch sich etwas nehmen lassen, daß der Verlust hernach nirgends so empfindlich wird.

§. 395.

Wie man aber das Bischen eintheilen soll, darinne stimmen die Autores nicht überein, und fehlt nicht viel, daß nicht so viel Meynungen sind, als Autores, die von der Temperatur geschrieben; welches alles ich allhier ohnmöglich durchgehen und ausführen kann: sondern ich will etliche Schriftsteller anführen, wo man von der Temperatur weitläuftige Nachricht findet. Doch werden es neuere Schriftsteller seyn, welche dann und wann die alten allegiren, daß man diese aus jenen nach und nach auch kann kennen lernen: denn ich will gar wenig von diesen Sachen in dem gegenwärtigen Kapitel beybringen.

Athanasius Kircherus, ein bekannter Jesuit, dessen schon oben §. 12. gedacht worden, hat in Musurgia universali, siue arte magna consoni & dissoni, im 3ten Buche de harmonicorum numerorum doctrina gehandelt, da er alle proportiones beschreibt und eintheilet, von pag. 82. bis 158. Da weiset er auch, wie man in der Arithmetica harmonica oder Musica operiren solle: denn die musikalischen Rechnungen sind viel anders, als die andern. Im 4ten Buche pag. 159 bis 210 hat er de diuisione Monochordi geometrica gehandelt: denn das Monochord kömmt hier am meisten in Betrachtung, als worauf mit dem Zirkel alles abgemessen wird. Es hat aber dieses Werk nicht ein jeder, indem es 10 bis 12 Rthlr. kostet; auch kann man diese Sachen aus kleinen Schriften fast noch besser fassen, und jenes Buchs wol entbehren.

§. 396.

Andreas Werkmeister, der wegen verschiedener Traktate bekannter ist, als daß ich viel von ihm sagen sollte, hat auch von der Temperatur geschrieben, und zwar in seiner Harmonologia, welche 1702 in 4to herausgekommen, S. 37. 39. 223. Item in den Paradoxaldiscursen, die nach seinem Tode 1707. heraus kamen, Kap. 13. 14. 23. Jt. in Hypomnematibus musicis Kap. 9. 10. S. 29. u. f. Ex professo aber hat er diese Sache abgehandelt in der musikalischen Temperatur, welche 1691. in 4to ans Licht getreten. In seinen übrigen Schriften hat er auch nicht unterlassen, dieser Sache hin und wieder Erwähnung zu thun. Z. Er. in der Orgelprobe Kap. 32. S. 78. u. f. In Organo grüningensi rediuiuo §. 51. bis 64. In Hodego mus. mathemat. curioso. Da ist genug davon zu lesen, wie auch vom Monochord.

§. 397.

Noch älter, als **Werkmeister**, ist **Michael Prätorius**, der in seinem Syntagmate musico Tom. II. Part. IV. cap. 3. pag. 149 — 158. davon handelt, wie eine Orgel nach der Temperatur zu stimmen sey. Er macht aber kein großes Aufsehen. Dies ist auch von **Trosten** zu sagen, der in der Beschreibung der Weissenfelsischen

Chap. XIV. Concerning Organ Temperament

but rather the others must also relinquish a bit, so that the loss is thereafter not so perceptible in any given spot.

§. 395.

Authors are not in agreement, however, as to how that small amount should be distributed, and there are almost as many opinions as authors who have written about temperament. It is impossible for me to go through and elaborate on all of it here; rather I will cite a number of authors where one may find extensive information about temperament. These will be more recent authors who refer to the ancient [sources] now and then, however, so that one may gradually become acquainted with the latter through the former, since I intend to say very little about such matters in this chapter.

Athanasius Kircher, a noted Jesuit already mentioned in §.12 above, has dealt with the doctrine of harmonic numbers in the third book of his *Musurgia universalis, sive ars magna consoni et dissoni*, pp. 82-158, where he describes and classifies all the proportions. There he also shows how to proceed with harmonic arithmetic, or music, since musical calculations are far different from others. In Book IV, pp. 159-210, he has dealt with the geometrical division of the monochord; here it is mostly the monochord that comes under consideration, on which everything* is measured off with a compass. Not everyone has his work, however, since it costs 10-12 Reichsthaler; it is possible to comprehend such matters almost better from shorter writings, and dispense with this book altogether.

* i.e., all the interval proportions.

§. 396.

Andreas Werkmeister, who is too well known through various treatises to require much more to be said about him, has also written about temperament in his *Harmonologia [musica]* that was published in quarto in 1702, pp. 37, 39 [and 140, §.] 223; likewise in the *[Musicalische] Paradoxal-Discourse* that appeared in 1707 after his death, Chapters 13, 14 and 23; likewise in *Hypomnemata Musica*, Chapters 9, 10 [ff.], p. 29f.† He has dealt expressly with this subject, however, in his *Musicalische Temperatur*, that appeared in quarto in 1691. He has not refrained from mentioning this subject here and there in his other writings, either: e.g., in the *Orgelprobe*, Chapter 32, pp. 78ff.; in *Organum gruningense redivivum*, §.51-64; and in *Hodegus musicae mathematicae curiosus*.‡ These sources provide an ample amount to read on this [topic], as well as on the monochord.

† This should read "p. 26f."

‡ Chap. 22, pp. 58-62.

§. 397.

Even earlier than Werkmeister is Michael Praetorius, who in his *Syntagma musicum*, Vol. II, Part IV, Chap. 3, pp. 149§-158 has dealt with how an organ should be tuned according to a temperament. He makes no big thing of it, however. The same may be said of Trost, who also deals with this subject in his *Beschreibung der Weissenfelßischen*

§ This should read "148".

Schloßorgel S. 31 — 40. auch davon handelt. Mit besonderm Vorsatz und Bedacht hat Wolfgang Caspar Prinz von der Temperatur gehandelt im satyrischen Componisten, und zwar im 7ten Kapitel des 3ten Theils. Item in seinen Exercitationibus musicis theoretico-practicis curiosis. Am allerbekanntesten aber ist wol Herr Johann Georg Neidhardt, ehemaliger Königl. Preuss. Kapellmeister in Königsberg, welcher 2 Traktate blos von der Temperatur geschrieben; den einen Ao. 1706. unter den Titul: Beste und leichteste Temperatur des Monochordi; den andern nennet er Sectionem canonicis harmonici, und kam Ao. 1724 zum Vorschein, da er als Kapellmeister in Königsberg stand; da hingegen der erstere in Jena herauskam, da der Verfasser noch ein Studiolus Theologiae daselbst war. Nach der Zeit sind auch noch dessen gänzlich erschöpfte mathematische Abtheilungen des diatonischen temperirten Canonis monochordi im Druck erschienen, wovon Anno 1734. die 2te Auflage zu Königsberg und Leipzig in 4to herausgekommen. Er schreibt kurz, und muß einer, zumal des andern Traktats wegen, schon aus der mathesi sublimiori einige fundamenta haben, der sie mit Nutzen lesen will.

§. 398.

Der Herr von Mattheson hat in seiner **Organistenprobe**, und zwar in der **theoretischen Vorbereitung**, die Proportionen der Intervallen auch vorgetragen. Ausser diesem und den vorigen Schriftstellern von der Temperatur sind noch folgende anzuführen. Als: Sinn, welcher in Temperatura practica davon gehandelt. Bümler, von dessen Temperatur s. Matthesons Crit. Mus. Tom. I. pag. 52; wobey man conferiren kann, was Neidhardt in Sectione Canonis harmonici S. 28. u. f. anmerkt, und hierbey abermal die Crit. Mus. Tom. II. pag. 234. Der Altdorfische Mathematikus Treu hat auch eine Disputation geschrieben de divisione monochordi; daß ich des Zarlino, Didymi, Ptolomäi, rc. welche älter sind, nicht gedenke. Was Bulyowsky de Dulicz, Kirchenrath des Marggrafen zu Badendurlach, und Professor Philosophiä am Gymnasio, davon geschrieben, liefet man in Matthesons Crit. Mus. Tom. II pag. 246.[78] Beyläufig ist zu merken, daß von diesen Proportionen oder Zahlen der Streit entstanden über die Frage: Ob die Ohren, oder die Zahlen in der Musik den Wohl- oder Uebelklang beurtheilen sollen? Hiervon hat am allerausführlichsten gehandelt der Herr von Mattheson im forschenden Orchestre.

§. 399.

Von der Temperatur nun selbst zu reden; so fragt sichs erstlich: Wieviel der letzten Quinte mangele, und wieviel also den übrigen Intervallen abzuzwacken? Dieses zeigt Neidhardt in Temperat. Monochordi pag. 29; da er die

---

[78] Da der Herr Verfasser hier nicht einmal die Hälfte derjenigen Schriftsteller angeführet, die von dieser Materie geschrieben; so wird der **geehrteste Leser** wohl thun, wenn er das 5te Kapitel der **Anleitung zu der musikalischen Gelahrtheit** mit diesem Vortrage verbindet, allwo auch von allen hierher gehörigen Schriften vollständige Nachricht ertheilet wird.

Chap. XIV. Concerning Organ Temperament

Schloßorgel, pp. 31-40. Wolfgang Caspar Prinz has dealt with temperament with particular good judgment and circumspection in Chapter 7 of the third part of his *Satyrischer Componist*,* as well as in his *Exercitationes musicae theoretico-practicae curiosae*. Without doubt the best known of all is Mr. Johann Georg Neidhardt, former Royal Prussian Kapellmeister in Königsberg, who has written 2 treatises solely on temperament; one appeared in 1706 in Jena, while the author was still a student of theology there, under the title *Beste und leichteste Temperatur des Monochordi*, and the other, called *Sectio canonis harmonici*, appeared in 1724 while [Neidhardt] was Kapellmeister in Königsberg. His *Gänzlich erschöpfte mathematische Abtheilungen des diatonischen temperirten Canonis monochordi* eventually appeared in print as well, of which the second printing was published at Königsberg and Leipzig in quarto in 1734. He writes economically, and anyone who wishes to read them to his profit (especially the second treatise) must already be grounded in higher mathematics.

* pp. 67-76.

§. 398.

Mr. von Mattheson has also presented the proportions of the intervals in his *Organistenprobe*, specifically in the *theoretische Vorbereitung*.† In addition to him and the above-mentioned authors on [the subject of] temperament, the following remain to be mentioned, to wit: Sinn, who has treated it in his *Temperatura practica*; Bümler (concerning his temperament, see Mattheson's *Critica musica*, Vol. I, p. 52[f.]; one may compare this with what Neidhardt states in his *Sectio Canonis harmonici*, p. 28ff, and also with [Mattheson's] *Critica musica*, Vol. II, p. 234); Treu, the mathematician from Altdorf, has also written a disputation *De divisione monochordi*; not to mention the more ancient writings of Zarlino,‡ Didymus,§ Ptolomaeus,¶ etc. One may read in Mattheson's *Critica Musica*, Vol. II, p. 246[f.][78] what Bulyowsky de Dulicz, *Kirchenrath* of the Margrave of Badendurlach and Professor of Philosophy at the Gymnasium, has written about it. It should be noted in passing that with regard to these proportions or numbers, a controversy has arisen over the question, "Which ought to pass judgment on harmony or discord in music, the ears or the numbers?" Mr. von Mattheson has discussed this matter in the greatest detail in his *Forschende Orchestre*.‖

† "Theoretical Preliminaries;" pp. 85ff.

‡ Gioseffo Zarlino discusses temperament in *Le istitutioni harmoniche* (1558), *Dimostrationi harmoniche* (1571) and *Sopplimenti musicali* (1588).

§ A Greek music theorist of antiquity. While none of his writings are extant, his ideas on temperament are discussed in Ptolemy's Harmonics.

¶ Claudius Ptolemy, a Greek mathematician and music theorist of antiquity. His three-volume *Harmonics* (mid-second century, A.D.) had great influence on subsequent music theorists.

‖ This is indeed the main topic of the book.

§. 399.

Speaking of temperament proper, the first question that arises is: "How much does the final fifth lack, and thus how much must be subtracted from the other intervals."** Neidhardt shows this in his [*Beste und leichteste*] *Temperat.* [*des*] *Monochordi*,

** i.e., how is the comma to be distributed among all the fifths within the circle of fifths.

---

[78] Since the author has not mentioned here even half of the authors who have written on this matter, the honored reader would do well to read in conjunction with this passage the fifth chapter of [Adlung's] *Anleitung zu der musikalischen Gelahrtheit*, where is imparted a complete report on all the writings about this subject. [Albrecht]

Quinten besonders addirt, und sagt: 531441 — 4096 sey die Summa der Quinten; it. die Oktaven addirt er auch besonders, deren Summa 128 — 1. ist. Diese von jenem subtrahirt bleibt 531441 — 524288. übrig, um wieviel die Quintensumma größer ist, als die Summa der Oktaven, welcher Excreß ein Comma (80 — 81.) und noch 32805 — 32768. austrägt. Die Art diesen Excreß einzutheilen ist bey den meisten Autoren verschiedentlich; theils weil sie meinen, es müßten die Modi variiren nach ihren verschiedentlich proportionirten Intervallis; theils weil sie sich um die gemeinsten Modos mehr, als um die andern, z. Ex. fis, cis, gis, ꝛc. bekümmert.

§. 400.

Didymus machte es also, und machte eine Sekunde größer als die andere, so, daß c d war wie 9 zu 8; d e wie 10 zu 9; f g wie 9 zu 8: g a wie 10 zu 9; a h wie 9 zu 8. Also ist der kleinere Ton 10 — 9 gegen den größern 9 — 8 um 80 — 81, oder ein Comma kleiner, s. davon Neidhardts Temperatur, S. 21. und f. Aber es sind viel Unreinigkeiten darinnen, weil der kleinen Terz d f ein Comma fehlt, dahingegen die Quarte A D ein Comma zu viel hat. s. l. c. S. 25. Prinz hat andere principia, als welcher nur auf die gemeinsten Modos regardirt. Werkmeister hat es also: Es sollen alle Quinten um den 12ten Theil eines Commatis herunter schweben. Denn weil ein Comma übrig wäre, und man in der Oktave 12 Quinten hätte, als:

c g. g d. d a. a e. e h. h fis. fis cis, cis gis. gis dis. dis b. b f. f c;
1. 2. 3. 4. 5. 6. 7. 8. 9. 10. 11. 12.

so könnte jede Quinte den 12ten Theil fahren laßen, und wären sodann alle Quinten gleich; folglich würden die andern Intervallen auch gleiche Schwebung behalten, so, daß alle kleine Terzen ¼ eines Commatis abwärts schwebten, und alle große Terzen ⅔ aufwärts. In den Anmerkungen über den Generalbaß will er doch, daß man die gemeinsten Modos etwas laße reiner seyn. Dessen principiis, ist, wiewol etwas accurater, Neidhardt gefolget; und bey diesen kann man auch ziemlich bleiben: unterdessen ist doch das Bisgen vergessen, welches §. 399. über das Comma übrig war, welches bey Neidhardten in der Quinte fis cis fehlt, welche also um ein Schisma zu kleine gerathen, dies heißt: der Wolf, s. Neidhardt l. c. S. 73. u. f. weil die Wölfe heulen; und eine unreine Orgel gleichermaaßen. Wo gar das obgedachte Comma fehlt, ist es der alte Wolf; das Schisma aber macht nur einen jungen Wolf aus. (Prätorius schreibt: Wulff.) Von Orgelwölfen sagt Trost in der Beschreibung der Weißenfelsischen Schloßorgel folgendes, und berichtet, daß die Alten einen Wolf genennet hätten, wo die Pfeifen keine rechte Proportion hätten, und also nicht zur Reinigkeit zu bringen wären. Solche Wölfe könne man nicht vertreiben, man müsse denn die Pfeifen wegwerfen.

§. 401.

Neidhardt hat in Sectionis canonis auch das Schisma mit eingetheilet. Es fragt sich nun weiter: wie man diese Temperatur auf den Orgeln anbringt? Da

Chap. XIV. Concerning Organ Temperament 53

p. 29, where he adds up the fifths separately and says that [the ratio] 531441/4096 is the sum of the fifths; he likewise adds up the octaves separately, whose sum is 128/1. The latter [ratio] subtracted from the former yields the excess 531441—524288, the amount by which the sum of the fifths is greater than the sum of the octaves. This excess amounts to [the syntonic] comma (80/81*), 32805/32768.† Most authors differ on the method of distributing this excess, partly because they believe that the keys should vary according to their differently proportioned intervals, partly because they are more concerned about the most common keys than about the others, e.g., f#, c#, g#, etc.

§. 400.

This is how Didymus did it: he made one second greater than the next, so that c-d was as 9 to 8, d-e as 10 to 9, f-g as 9 to 8, g-a as 10 to 9, a-b as 9 to 8. Thus the lesser interval, 10 to 9, is smaller than the greater interval, 9 to 8, by 80/81,‡ or a comma; in this regard see Neidhardt's *Temperatur [des Monochordi]*, pp. 21f. But this system harbors many impurities, since the minor third d-f is a comma too small, while on the other hand the fourth A-D is one comma too large; see l.c., p. 25. Printz§ follows another formula that takes into account only the most common keys. This is what Werkmeister suggests:¶ each of the fifths should beat a twelfth of a comma low; since there is one comma too many, and there are 12 fifths in the octave,|| namely

c͡g g͡d d͡a a͡e e͡b b͡f# f#͡c# c#͡g# g#͡d# d#͡bflat bflat͡f f͡c;
1.   2.   3.   4.   5.   6.   7.   8.   9.   10.   11.   12.

thus each fifth could relinquish a twelfth part, and then all of the fifths would be equal. [Werkmeister continues by saying that] consequently the other intervals would also beat equally, with each of the minor thirds beating ¾ of a comma low and each of the major thirds ⅔ high.** In his *Anmerkung über den Generalbaß*,†† on the other hand, he holds that the most common keys should be made somewhat purer. Neidhardt has followed his [i.e., Werkmeister's] formula, albeit rather more precisely; one may pretty much adhere to it. But in the meanwhile the minute excess above the comma (see §.399) that was lacking in Neidhardt's formula in the fifth f#-c#, which turned out to be a Schisma too small, has been forgotten; this is known as the "wolf" ‡‡ (see Neidhardt, l.c., p. 73f., where he says that wolves howl, and so do out-of-tune organs). Where the entire comma discussed above is lacking, this is the "old wolf";§§ the Schisma, on the other hand, causes only a "young wolf"¶¶ (Praetorius spells the word "Wulff"||||). Concerning organ-wolves, Trost in his *Beschreibung der Weissenfelsischen Schloßorgel**** reports that in former times a "wolf" described a situation in which the pipes did not have the proper proportion and thus could not be brought into tune; [he says that] such "wolves" cannot be gotten rid of, and the pipes must be discarded.

§.401.

In his *Sectio canonis* Neidhardt has factored the Schisma as well into the distribu-

---

* Sic; the ratio should properly read "81/80."

† Prof. Raymond H. Haggh, my colleague on the University of Nebraska-Lincoln music faculty, has kindly prepared the following explanation of this matter: Various theoretical solutions offered to derive equal or unequal temperaments proceed from Pythagorean tuning based on the pure octave (2/1), the pure fifth (3/2) and the pure fourth (4/3) as a point of departure. Adlung here derives the Pythagorean comma, 531441/524288, the difference between enharmonic notes in the system by the addition of a spiral of perfect fifths, for example, built on C and ending on B#: (3/2) to the 12th power = 531441/4096. His ratio 128/1 results from (2/1) to the 7th power, seven pure octaves above the assumed reference note C; subtracting 128/1 from 531441/4096 (B# in frequency is higher than C) is obtained as follows: 531441/4096 × 1/128 = 531441/524288, the Pythagorean comma, which has the value of 23.5 cents. 81/80 is the Didymic or syntonic comma (a difference of 21.5 cents), found, for example, between like intervals in the Pythagorean and just intonation systems. The minute difference between the Pythagorean and Didymic commas is expressed in the ratio 32805/32768, known in tuning theory as the Schisma.

‡ Sic; should read "81/80."

§ *Phrynis*, Part 3, Chap. 7, pp. 67-76.

¶ in the *Paradoxal=Discourse*, Chap. 13, p. 66.

|| i.e., in the circle of fifths.

** Prof. Raymond Haggh again offers the following explanation: To Didymus, a theorist of late Antiquity, is reputed a system of just intonation, and the ratios given at the beginning of this paragraph are those of that system. A great failing of the system is the fifth D-A which has a ratio of 40/27; consequently the minor third lacks a comma (81/80) and the fourth is too large by the same comma. A characteristic way of obtaining an equal temperament is by dividing the Pythagorean comma into twelve parts and shrinking each fifth by that amount. At one point in the process, in order to obtain a closed system, an enharmonic change must take place; Adlung chooses D# as that place, making it equivalent to E flat. Since each fifth is reduced by 1/12th of a Pythagorean comma, the process is cumulative; the small numbers under the intervals shown indicate the number of twelfths a particular fifth has been reduced as compared with the note C, the note that serves as a point of departure.

†† in an appendix, "Kurzer Unterricht und Zugabe, wie man ein Clavier stimmen und wohl temperiren könne" ["Brief Instruction and Supplement on how to Tune and Well-temper a Keyboard Instrument"].

‡‡ The term for the ill-sounding effect evident in certain intervals that results from the more severe tuning systems.

§§ 29 i.e., the comma that results from a severe meantone temperament (e.g., ¼-comma).

¶¶ i.e., such a slight out-of-tuneness that it hardly "howls" at all.

|||| *Syntagma musicum*, Vol. II, p. 155; this remark is purely parenthetical, and has nothing to do with the substance of the discussion.

*** pp. 35-36.

fallen die meisten auf das Monochordum, und wollen die Orgeln darnach temperiren. Das Wort ist von μόνος, η, ον, eins, und χορδή eine Sayte, zusammen gesetzt, weil man nur eine darauf zu ziehen braucht. Es ist ein langes schmales Kästchen, etwan 4 Finger breit und hoch. Die Länge ist willkürlich, doch je länger es ist, desto leichter ist die Eintheilung. Es kann 4′ oder auch 8′ lang seyn. Die mehrsten aber werden 2′ lang gemacht. Man spannt daran die Sayte, und theilet die Intervalle mit dem Zirkel auf der Decke des Kastens ein, und zeichnet sie mit Linien oder Punkten. Ein darunter gesetzter Steg giebt hernach den Sonum, wenn ich ihn bald auf dies, bald auf jenes abgezirkelte Pünktchen drücke, und das Stück der Sayte anschlage. Canon ist auch so viel, als Monochordum. Mehr mag ich davon auch nicht beybringen. Man lese die angeführten Autores, sonderlich Neidhardts Temperat. Monoch. c. IX. p. 70. allwo er das **Monochord** hinlänglich beschrieben.

§. 402.

Wenn man nun stimmen will, so giebt man der Seyte, wie sie an sich ist, nach der Trompete oder Chorpfeife, die gehörige Tiefe oder Höhe, etwan c. Hernach nimmt man den Steg und setzt ihn unter das g, das ist, unter den Punkt, welcher ein Stück der Seyte abschneidet, das g angiebt; hernach immer auch unter die andern Intervalle, und stimmt die Pfeifen nach der Seyte. Aber ich finde doch etliche incommoda bey dieser Temperatur. Erstlich müßte man beständig die Seyte an sich probiren, ob sie mit dem ersten Clave noch reine sey: denn eine Seyte verstimmt sich leicht; und zum andern schickt sichs sehr übel, daß man eine Pfeife nach einer Seyte stimmen will. Denn beyde haben einen allzuverschiedenen Klang, und ihr Tremuliren oder Beben wird nie gleich. Ja, wenn die Seyte angeschlagen wird, so wird sie etwas höher, als wenn sie sich fast wieder zur Ruhe neiget, daher sie nie gleiche Schwebung haben kann. Und ob es schon wenig austräget, so ist es doch etwas. Denn durch den Anschlag wird die Seyte etwas gegen die Latera beweget, daß sie einen, wiewol mit dem Gesichte nicht wohl zu erreichenden Triangel macht, in welchem aber die längste Seyte nie so groß ist, als die übrigen 2 zusammen genommen. Und es mag dem seyn, wie ihm will; genug daß es nicht angehet, wie die Erfahrung lehrt.

§. 403.

Denn eben diesem Herrn **Neidhardt** ist es in Jena arriviret. Als die Stadtorgel daselbst gebauet worden, und gestimmet werden sollte, war er noch daselbst ein Studiosus, und gab sich beym Rathe an, daß er wolle die Orgel temperiren, weil Herr **Bach** es für sich nicht erlauben durfte. Der Rath wollte nicht dran, und sorgete, es möchte nicht gerathen, und wollte den Schaden ersetzt haben, falls es nicht geriethe. Endlich nahm Herr **Bach** ein Gedackt in einem Claviere, und Herr **Neidhardt** eins im andern: Jener stimmte seins nach dem Gehör; dieser mathematisch und nach dem Monochord, das er bey sich hatte. Als man es hernach mit den Ohren untersuchte, wollte des Herrn **Neidhardts** Gedackt nicht klingen: aber des Hrn. **Bach** seins klang.

Neid.

tion. The question further arises, "How is this temperament to be applied to organs?" For this most people resort to the monochord, suggesting that organ temperaments should be set by it. The word is constructed from [the Greek] monos, h, on, "one" and cordh, "a string", since it is strung with only a single [string]. It is a long, narrow box, about 4 finger[widths] broad and high. Its length is immaterial; but the longer it is, the easier it is to divide.* It may be either 4′ or 8′ long, but the majority are built 2′ long. A string is stretched upon it, and the intervals are divided off on the box's sounding board with a compass and marked with lines or dots. A bridge placed under the string allows it to produce a tone when it is stopped at one or another of the points indicated and the [resulting] section of the string is struck. "Canon" is the same as "monochord". I will not mention any more about it; one may consult the authors cited, in particular Neidhardt's *Temperatur des Monochordi*, c. IX, p. 70, where he he gives an adequate description of the instrument.

* i.e., to stop the string accurately.

§. 402.

If you want to tune [an organ], first tune the string [of the monochord] in and of itself to the desired pitch, according to a trumpet† or a pitch pipe, let us say, c. Next one takes the bridge and places it under the g, that is, under the dot that divides off a section of the string that produces g. Next come each of the other intervals in turn, and each pipe is tuned to the string. I find, however, several inconveniences with this [method of] temperament. First, one must constantly keep testing the string itself to make sure it is still in tune with the first note, for a string goes out of tune easily. In the second place, a string is very ill-suited for tuning a pipe, since the two have very different sounds, and their wavering or beating will never be alike. Indeed, when the string is struck it is somewhat higher than when it has almost stopped vibrating, and thus it never maintains the same vibration. And even though [this difference] amounts to very little, it is nevertheless there. For by striking the string it is set into vibration from side to side, so that it creates an arc, though this is not visible to the naked eye, in which the longest side is never as large as the sum of the two remaining sides. Let anyone say what he will; suffice it to say that it‡ does not work, as experience teaches us.

† i.e., presuming that the organ is intended to play in an ensemble with this instrument.

‡ i.e., tuning an organ using the monochord.

§. 403.

[The truth of] this [assertion] was brought home to Mr. Neidhardt himself while he was in Jena.§ He was a student there when the organ at the Stadtkirche was being built and was about to be tuned. He applied to the council to be allowed to set the temperament for the organ, since Mr. [Johann Nikolaus] Bach¶ was not in a position to grant this permission himself. The council did not agree to this, fearing that it would not be successful; they wanted an assurance that the damage would be covered in case it did not succeed. Finally Mr. Bach took a Gedackt on one manual and Mr. Neidhardt took one on another. The former tuned his by ear, while the latter tuned mathematically using the monochord that he had with him. When the work was subsequently put to the listening test, Mr. Neidhardt's Gedackt did not sound well, but Mr. Bach's did.

§ as a student.

¶ The organist of the Jena Stadtkirche, and Adlung's former organ instructor.

Kap. XIV. Von der Temperatur der Orgeln. 55

Neidhardt konnte das Temperiren nicht verwerfen, nach dem Gehöre; wußte aber nicht, wie es zugieng, und wollte behaupten, mathematice müßte es besser seyn. Allein man ließ einen den großen Glauben aus dem B moll singen, der ohne Temperatur nach seiner Kehle sang, und auch die Bachischen Claves traf. Man muß also auch mit auf die Kehle des Menschen sehen, als in welche Gott die Töne einmal gelegt hat. Herr Neidhardt mußte es also lassen anstehen; Herr Bach aber temperirte nach dem Gehöre fort, und gieng ihm wohl von statten, gerieth auch alles wohl.

§. 404.

Ein besserer Vorschlag wäre es, wenn man Pfeifen nach Pfeifen stimmte und temperirte. Doch kann man so viel Pfeifen nicht bey sich führen. Oder, wenn man auch solche hätte, die einmal alle reine nach der Temperatur gemacht wären, so ist der Wind nicht immer gleich: denn einmal bläset man mit dem Munde stärker, als das andere mal: folglich ist der Sonus einmal höher, als sonst, und also ist auch das Schweben nicht einerley: folglich nutzt es gleichfalls nichts. Man siehet es sogar an der Chorpfeife; die haben die Orgelmacher, nach welcher sie der Orgel den ersten Sonum geben, daß sie mit den andern Orgeln überein werden soll: gleichwol trift es oft nicht ein, weil ihr Wind einmal stärker ist, als das anderemal; folglich kann eine Orgel wol eins oder mehr Commata höher werden, als die andere. Also wäre zu wünschen, daß man hierinne was beständiges hätte, welches ja wohl angienge. Denn man könnte auf einem Stocke eine Pfeife bevestigen, von ziemlicher Größe, und unter den Stock einen Balg legen, der beständig und einerley Gewicht und Wind hätte, welches durch die Windprobe allezeit von neuem zu erforschen: so gäbe alsdann die Pfeife einmal wie das andermal ihren langen und beständigen Klang, daß man die erste Orgelpfeife darnach rein stimmen könnte. Wollte einer sagen, daß es doch im veränderten Wetter sich ändere, weil eine metallene Pfeife im warmen Wetter höher gehe als sonst, wie man siehet, wenn man die Pfeife mit der warmen Hand angreift, daß sie höher wird, hernach aber wird sie wieder tief: So wollte ich den Rath geben, daß man die Pfeife nur in die Orgel stelle, daß sie gleiche Wärme mit den Orgelpfeifen bekäme; und ob sie gleich im warmen Wetter etwas höher wurde, so gehet es doch den andern Orgelpfeifen auch so, und im kalten Wetter werden sie sich schon wieder erniedrigen. Wollte man aber die Stimmpfeife an einem wärmern Orte haben, als die Orgelpfeifen; so könnte wol das Werk im Tone etwas zu hoch kommen. Nach der Trompete den ersten Ton anzugeben ist, wegen des ungleichen Windes, gleichfalls nichts.

Man stimmt die Orgeln im Chorton, wie man es itzt nennt, welcher 1 oder $1\frac{1}{2}$ Töne höher ist, als Kammerton. Sonst hat man es umgekehrt, und ist Kammerton höher gewesen, als Chorton, und man hat die Orgeln im Kammerton gestimmt, welcher also geheissen, weil man ihn bey der Tafel in Zimmern zur Frölichkeit gebraucht, daß man die Vokalisten schonen könnte. Besiehe hievon mit mehrerem Prator. Syntag. T. II. P. II. c. II. pag. 14. Wie hoch aber unser Chorton sey, ist wegen der Varietät

nicht

Chap. XIV. Concerning Organ Temperament

Neidhardt could not object to setting a temperament by ear, but did not know how it worked, and continued to insist that it had to be better when done mathematically. But then they had someone sing one of the verses of the chorale "Wir glauben all an einen Gott" in the key of b-flat minor; this person sang directly from his throat, without [any concern for] temperament, and he produced the same pitches as Mr. Bach's temperament. Thus one must take into consideration the human voice, in which God admittedly has placed the [various] pitches. Mr. Neidhardt therefore had to let the matter rest; Mr. Bach however continued to set temperaments by ear, which proceeded smoothly and turned out successfully.

§. 404.

It would be a better suggestion to tune and temper pipes from [other] pipes. It is impossible, however, to carry so many pipes around. And even if they were all available and were all actually tempered exactly correctly, the wind pressure is not always the same, since one blows through one's mouth with greater force one time than the next, and consequently the pitch is sharper one time than the next. Thus the beating is not the same, and consequently it is useless. This may even be noted with the pitchpipe; organbuilders carry these to give the first pitch for an organ, so that it will correspond in pitch to other organs. This seldom succeeds though, since their breath is more forceful one time than the next, and consequently one of their organs may be as much as one or more commas sharper than another. Thus it would be desirable to have for this purpose something consistent, and this could indeed be possible. For one could fasten a pipe of a suitable size onto a toeboard, and place under the toeboard a bellows that provided a consistent wind pressure. This [pressure] could be constantly checked by the windgauge, and in this way the pipe would produce time and time again a prolonged* and consistent sound, by which one could tune the first organ pipe precisely. Someone might object that this [pitch] would change with the weather, since a metal pipe gets sharper in warm weather; hold a pipe in your warm hand, and you will see that it rises in pitch, but subsequently† it returns to its original pitch. Thus I would advise simply placing the pipe‡ within the organ, so that it gets to be the same temperature as the organ pipes. Even though it would go somewhat sharp in warm weather, so would the other organ pipes as well, and they would again sink to the lower pitch in cold weather. If one were to place the tuning-pipe in a warmer place than [that of] the organ pipes, however, then the instrument might well be somewhat too high in pitch. One ought not to set the first pitch by a trumpet, again because of inconsistent pressure [of the breath].

Organs are tuned in choir pitch, as it is now called, which is 1 or 1½ steps higher than chamber pitch. But it should have been the other way around; chamber pitch should be higher than choir pitch, and organs should be tuned in chamber pitch (this gets its name from being used at table in chambers for entertainment), so that vocalists might be spared.§ In this regard see (among others¶) Praetorius's *Syntagma musicum*, Vol. II, Part II, Chap. II, p. 14.‖ It is not possible to state the exact pitch of our choir

---

* i.e., not subject to decay, as the sound of a plucked or struck string.

† i.e., after being set down.

‡ i.e., the device Adlung is proposing should be used to set the first pitch.

§ the extra exertion of singing at a higher pitch. In the 18th century, chamber pitch was essentially used for instrumental performance (chamber music, for entertainment), while choir pitch was used for church music that was primarily vocal.

¶ "mit mehrerem;" this might also mean "with further information."

‖ The chapter begins on p. 14, but the reference to lower pitch being helpful to singers is on. p. 15. Prætorius discusses choir pitch and chamber pitch on pp. 15-16.

nicht zu melden, und wird auch hierinnen wol schwerlich eine Einigkeit zu hoffen seyn. Mr. Sauveur in Frankreich hat einen gewissen Sonum determiniren wollen, dadurch man in der ganzen Welt einerley Stimmung erhalten könnte. Er verwirft die Chorpfeifen, weil 1) die Materie derselben veränderlich ist; 2) weil der Wind des Blasenden ungewiß ist; 3) weil auch eine Orgelpfeife, die noch richtiger ist, als jene, keinen Ton überein von sich giebt. Er giebt auch Anschläge, wie die Vibrationen einer Orgelpfeife durch ein Uhrwerk zu zählen sind, und statuirt Sauveur, daß der Ton, der in einer Sekunden-zeit 100 Vibrationen machte, der tonus fixus in der ganzen Welt seyn könnte. Allein es ist nicht angegangen; und dürfte das Zählen nicht von allen so leicht können verrichtet werden. S. Histoire de l'Academie Royale de l'année 1700; woraus es Herr Mattheson im forschenden Orchestre, P. I. c. 4. §. 10. S. 428. anführt. Wer sonst nicht weis, was Vibrationen sind, der kann unten im 28sten Kapitel etwas davon lesen.

§. 405.

Aber was zu thun mit der fernern Temperatur, wenn nun der erste Sonus da ist? Antw. Von dem jenaischen Herrn Bach habe ich ehedessen folgenden Vorschlag gehört, der mir auch gefallen hat. Nämlich: Man solle eine Pfeife nehmen, durchaus von einer Weite; sich einen Cylinder drehen lassen, der just in die Pfeife passet, und in die Pfeife kann gesteckt werden. Die Pfeife wird auf einen Stock gesetzt, und ein guter beständiger Balg darunter gelegt, der den Wind einmal wie das andere mal giebt, und man steckt den Cylinder in die Pfeife, daß sie gedeckt wird, da denn der erste Ton, wenn der Cylinder ein klein wenig darinne steckt, der erste Ton der Orgel werden kann, etwan anstatt der Trompete oder Chorpfeife, und kann man die Pfeife schon darnach einrichten. Man macht aber auf diesem Cylinder oder Stöpsel die Abtheilungen nach dem Maaßstabe, so wie sie ist nach dem Monochord gemacht worden, klebt entweder das Papier um den Stöpsel, oder zeichnet alles mit dem Zirkel auf den Stöpsel selbst. Wenn man nun stimmen will, so drückt man den Stöpsel allezeit weiter hinein nachdem die Abtheilung ist, und stimmt so fort vom c bis h, wie die Hemitonia in der Ordnung folgen; denn da braucht man nicht durch Quinten zu stimmen. Meynet man, es werde in einer Pfeife der Stöpsel allzutief hinein kommen; so mache man zwo Pfeifen neben einander, da die eine etwan im c, die andere im g oder f anhebt. Da darf jede nur eine Quarte höher werden durch den Stöpsel. Die andere Pfeife müßte aber etwas enger werden, und auch kürzer; daher auch die Abtheilung darauf anders wird. Beyde Pfeifen aber müssen stark seyn. Wenn dies geschehen; so kann man nach einem solchen Instrument 1000 Orgeln temperiren, und kann man es aus einer Orgel in die andere tragen. Doch muß die Abtheilung richtig seyn. Trift es einmal zu, so trift es allemal; und so hat die Pfeife einen langen sonum, daß man das Schweben einer Pfeife gegen die andere recht hören kann. Es muß aber zum Stöpsel gut Holz genommen werden, das nicht schwindet oder quillt; sonst läßt es entweder den Wind neben sich durch, oder zerdrückt die Pfeife; auch muß er vollkommen rund, und durchaus von gleicher Dicke seyn.

§. 406.

Chap. XIV. Concerning Organ Temperament

pitch, however, due to the variety,* and any unity in this regard is scarcely to be hoped for. The Frenchman Mr. Sauveur† wanted to set a specific pitch by which a standard tuning might be established throughout the entire world. He rejected pitchpipes, because 1.) the materials they are made of are variable; 2.) the breath of the one who blows them is uneven; 3.) even an organ pipe, which is yet truer than a [pitchpipe], does not produce an exactly constant pitch. He gives beats‡ by which the vibrations of an organ pipe are to be timed, and Sauveur decrees that the pitch that is produced by 100 vibrations per second should be a universal standard pitch. But this has not caught on; not everyone finds it easy to carry out his timing [procedure]. See the *Histoire de l'Academie Royale de l'annee 1700*, from which Mr. Mattheson quotes in his *forschende Orchestre*, Part I, Chap. 4, §.10, p. 428[f.]. Anyone who does not know what vibrations are may read something about them below in Chapter 28.§

* of choir pitch standards in use.
† See note in Chap. 28, p.175 below.
‡ presumably vibrations per second.
§ p. 166 below.

§. 405.

What is to be done about the rest of the temperament, however, once the first pitch has been set? Here is the answer: I heard the following suggestion a while ago from Mr. [Johann Nikolaus] Bach in Jena, which I thought a good one, to wit: take a pipe of uniform width,¶ and then have a cylinder turned that fits into the pipe precisely and can be inserted into the pipe. Set the pipe upon a toeboard, and put a good, stable bellows‖ under it, one that provides the same wind pressure at all times.** Insert the cylinder into the pipe, stopping it in such a way that the first pitch, the one that results from the cylinder being inserted a very short distance into the pipe, can become the first pitch for the organ, replacing, say, a trumpet or pitchpipe. Then a pipe can be tuned according to it. The cylinder or stopper, however, is divided according to a ruler, just as is done on the monochord; then either paper [strips] are glued to the stopper,†† or lines are drawn on the stopper itself with a compass. When you are ready to tune, keep pushing the stopper in from one dividing line to the next, tuning each note in this way from c to b, one half step after another. This method obviates tuning by fifths. If anyone thinks that the stopper would have to go too deeply into one single pipe, he can construct two pipes side by side, the first commencing, say, at c and the other at g or f. Then each of them need rise only a fourth in pitch by means of the stopper. The second pipe must, however, be of somewhat narrower scale, and also shorter, and thus the dividing lines‡‡ must be different.§§ Both pipes, though, must be strong. If this method were adopted, then a temperament could be set for 1,000 organs with such an instrument, and it could be carried about from one organ to another. But the dividing lines must be accurate. If it is once correct, then it will be correct from then on; and since it employs pipes that produce protracted tones, one can hear properly the beating of one pipe against another. But good wood must be used for the stopper, wood that does not shrink or swell; otherwise it would either let the wind escape around it, or it would squeeze open the pipe. It must also be perfectly round, and of a uniform thickness throughout.

¶ i.e., perfectly cylindrical.
‖ i.e., a winding system.
** cf. §.404.

†† to mark the divisions.

‡‡ on its cylinder.
§§ than the first pipe's cylinder.

Kap. XIV. Von der Temperatur der Orgeln

§. 406.

Will man ohne ein solches Instrument die Temperatur unternehmen; so kann man durch Quinten stimmen, und man lasse sodann alle den 12ten Theil eines Commatis abwärts schweben. Solchergestallt kann man vom $\bar{c}$ anheben, und es nach der Chorpfeife rein stimmen: zu $\bar{c}$ stimmt man $\bar{g}$ rein, doch mit der Schwebung; zu $\bar{g}$ macht man g reine; (die Oktaven schweben nicht) zu g das $\bar{d}$, jedoch $\frac{1}{12}$ abwärts schwebend; zu $\bar{d}$, $\bar{a}$ schwebend; zu $\bar{a}$ stimmt man a reine; hierzu die Quinte $\bar{e}$, $\frac{1}{12}$ abwärts schwebend; hierzu $\bar{h}$, $\frac{1}{12}$ abwärts schwebend; hierzu h reine; hierzu $\overline{fis}$, $\frac{1}{12}$ abwärts schwebend; hierzu fis reine; hierzu $\overline{cis}$, $\frac{1}{12}$ abwärts schwebend; hierzu $\overline{gis}$, $\frac{1}{12}$ abwärts schwebend; hierzu gis reine; hierzu $\overline{dis}$; $\frac{1}{12}$ abwärts schwebend; hierzu $\bar{b}$; $\frac{1}{12}$ abwärts schwebend; hierzu b reine; hierzu $\bar{f}$, $\frac{1}{12}$ abwärts schwebend. Nun wären wir fertig, wenn nur noch zu $\bar{f}$ $\bar{\bar{c}}$ gestimmt wird. Hernach probire man $\bar{\bar{c}}$ gegen das anfänglich gestimmte $\bar{c}$, ob es vollkommen reine sey. Ist dieses; so wird die Temperatur meistentheils gut seyn, wenn nur die Quinten nicht allzusehr verfehlt worden. Wo aber das $\bar{\bar{c}}$ $\bar{c}$ unrein sind; so ist entweder $\bar{\bar{c}}$ zu hoch gegen $\bar{c}$, oder zu niedrig. Ist es zu hoch; so hat man die Quinten noch zu groß genommen: also gehe man zurücke und lasse sie etwas abwärts, daß sie endlich in eine Gleichheit kommen, und doch das $\bar{\bar{c}}$ und $\bar{c}$ reine werden. Ist es zu tief; so hat man den Quinten, wo nicht allen, doch etlichen, allzuviel abgebrochen: also muß man denselben nachhelfen. Es ist also kein Wunder, daß die Temperatur eine mühsame und langsame Sache ist; denn den 48sten oder 60sten Theil von einer Sekunde merkt das Gehör nicht so bald; zumal bey Ungeübten. Es ist von der Stimmung durch Quinten die Redensart: Quintam accipere entstanden, welche bey den Musikern soviel bedeutet, als: böse oder zornig werden, weil die Quinte in der Stimmung uns so viel vexirt. De Chales T. III. p. 20. Propos. 14. sagt: musici dicuntur *quintam accipere*, dum irascuntur, eo quod quinta saepe ipsis bilem moveat. Hingegen hat man nur eine Oktave also zu stimmen, die übrigen Claves stimmt man Oktavenweise.

§. 407.

Am besten ists, man nimmt das Principal 8′ dazu, wo man es hat, und temperirt es, und fängt vom $\bar{c}$ an. Denn größer ist es nicht fein, weil die Pfeifen allzutief brummen. In der Höhe hat man auch keinen so vernehmlichen sonum; auch trägt also ein Comma gar zu wenig aus. Das Principal, als das Hauptregister, hat auch besser Metall, und verstimmt sich sobald nicht. Man darf auch, wo etliche Claviere sind, nur eins temperiren; die andern werden nach jenem gestimmt. Damit man aber auch nicht so hoch steige; so gehe man desfalls zuweilen eine Oktave abwärts. Also sollte vorhin zu $\bar{g}$ das g erst reine gemacht werden; zu diesem aber wird das d gestimmt; und so weiter.

Chap. XIV. Concerning Organ Temperament

§. 406.

If you want to undertake setting a temperament without such an instrument, you may tune by fifths, and in that case each [of the fifths] should beat a twelfth of a comma low. Using this method, one may begin at c′, tuning it precisely according to a pitchpipe. Then g′ is tuned to the c′, but with the beating; then g is tuned pure to g′ (octaves should not beat); then d′ to g, though beating a 1/12 [of a comma] low; then a′ to d, with beats; then a to a′, pure; then e′ to a, beating 1/12 low; then b′ to e, beating 1/12 low; then b to b′, pure; then f#′ to b, beating 1/12 low; next f# to f#′, pure; next c#′ to f#, beating 1/12 low; next g#′ to c#′, beating 1/12 low; then g# to g#′, pure; then d#′ to g#, beating 1/12) low; then b flat′ to d#′, beating 1/12) low; then b-flat to b flat′, pure; and finally f′ to b-flat, beating 1/12 low. At that point we would be finished, except for tuning c″ to f′. Next c″ needs to be tested against c′ that was tuned at the beginning, to see if it is exactly in tune. If it is, then the temperament is for the most part good, as long as none of the fifths is too false. If, however, c″ is not in tune with c′, it may be either too high or too low. If it is too high, then the fifths have been made too wide; then one must go back and make them a bit narrower, so that they finally become uniform, while allowing c″ to c′ to be pure. If it is too low, then one has made the fifths too narrow (perhaps not all, but just some of them); then they have to be touched up. Thus it is no wonder that setting a temperament is a slow and troublesome process, since one's hearing, especially if it is inexperienced, does not so readily perceive a [beat with a duration of a] 48th or a 60th of a second. It was from tuning by fifths that the saying originated, "Quintam accipere," which means among musicians "to become cross or angry," since tuning fifths is so annoying. De Chales, Vol. III,* p. 20, Propos. 14, says, "musici dicuntur quintam accipere, dum irascuntur, eo quod quinta saepe ipsis bilem moveat."† On the other hand, there is only one octave to be tuned in this way; the remaining notes are tuned by octaves.

* Tract 22, "Musica."

† "Musicians say "quintam accipere" when they are angry because the fifth always irritates them."

§. 407.

It is best to take the 8′ Principal, if there is one, for this [purpose],‡ if there is one, and to set a temperament on it, beginning with c′. The pitch is not as perceptible in the bass, because the lower pipes rumble too much. The higher pitches in the treble are also not easily perceptible, and there the comma amounts to almost nothing. The Principal, being the main stop, is also made of better metal, and does not go out of tune so quickly. Where there are several keyboards, a temperament must be set on only one of them, and the others tuned to it. In order to keep from rising too high [in the treble], one should occasionally drop down an octave. Thus for example, if g has first been tuned pure to g′ above§ [in §.406], then d′ is tuned to it, and so forth.

‡ i.e., to set a temperament.

§ see §.406.

§. 408.

Weil es aber verdrüßlich, wenn man ganz durch ist, wieder zurück zu gehen; so kann man die Terzen zu Richtern annehmen. Nämlich, wenn man im Temperiren auf einen Clavem fällt, der zu dem vorhergehenden eine Terz ausmacht; so schlägt man ihn mit solchem Clave an, und hört, ob sothane Terz (wenn sie groß ist) $\frac{2}{3}$ aufwärts schwebe; oder (wenn sie klein ist) ob sie $\frac{3}{4}$ eines Commatis abwärts schwebe. Also wenn ich gestimmt habe $\bar{c}$ $\bar{g}$; $\bar{g}$ $\bar{\bar{g}}$; $\bar{g}$ $\bar{\bar{u}}$; $\bar{d}$ $\bar{\bar{a}}$; $\bar{\bar{a}}$ $\bar{\bar{e}}$: so ist das $\bar{\bar{e}}$ eine Terz zu dem schon gestimmten $\bar{c}$. Und zwar eine große Terz. Diese muß $\frac{2}{3}$ aufwärts schweben. Trift es nicht ein; so muß man die gestimmten Quinten wieder durchgehen, und ändern. So ist auch eben das $\bar{\bar{e}}$ zu dem gestimmten $\bar{g}$ die kleine Terz, unterwärts zu zählen: da müssen diese beyden Soni auch unreine seyn, so, daß $\bar{g}$ $\frac{3}{4}$ abwärts schwebe. So verhält sichs auch mit andern. Man darf folglich nicht erst ganz durch stimmen. So auch in folgendem. Also wenn zu $\bar{c}$, $\bar{h}$ gestimmet wird; so kann man probiren, ob $\bar{h}$ gegen $\bar{g}$ $\frac{3}{4}$ aufwärts schwebe, ꝛc. Diesen Proceß zu temperiren lese man mit etwas mehrern Umständen in Neidhardts Temperatur, S. 102. Imgl. in Werkmeisters Anmerkungen zum Generalbasse. Es kommt bey dieser Sache auch viel auf die Uebung an.

§. 409.

Wie nun die Temperatur in der Orgel höchst nöthig ist; also muß sie auch mit allem Fleiße gemacht werden, und leide man ja nicht, daß man einen modum wolle reiner haben, als den andern, sondern man lasse sie alle gleich machen, der Transposition wegen; auch damit die andern modi nicht allzu unbrauchbar werden. Wollte jemand fragen: **Wie klingen aber die Trompeten, Waldhörner und andere Instrumente dazu?** Antw. Besaytete Instrumente können so gestimmt und gegriffen werden; daß die Temperatur angehet. Es ist daher nicht recht, wenn man alle Quinten und alle Sayten auf andern Instrumenten so reine stimmt, als es möglich. Man sollte ebenfalls $\frac{1}{12}$ Commatis fehlen lassen; und so auch im Greifen. Bey Blaßinstrumenten, wo man die Töne durch Löcher hat, als bey Flöten, Oboen, ꝛc. kann der Mechanikus auch die Löcher nach der Temperatur einrichten. Was aber die Trompeten und Waldhörner anlanget; so geht es nicht an, daß man sie temperiren wollte. Unterdessen, da die Temperatur so nöthig und nützlich ist; so ist es doch besser, sie einzuführen, als der Trompeten wegen sie wegzulassen. Wem die Trompete nicht gefällt, wie sie denn bey einer reinen Temperatur jämmerlich klingt, der lasse sie weg. Ein Waldhorn kann durch den Wind noch eher etwas gezwungen werden, als die Trompete. (**)

(**) Hier ist nur die Kleinigkeit erst auszumachen, ob die Trompete, von denen, die sie recht zu blasen verstehen, nicht auch reiner geblasen werden kann, und wird, als insgemein von Unerfahrnern geschieht.

§. 410.

Wenn Kammerregister in der Orgel sind; so braucht man sie nicht von neuem zu temperiren, sondern man läßt sie so lange ungestimmt, bis im andern Claviere auch etliche

Chap. XIV. Concerning Organ Temperament

§. 408.

Since, however, it would be anoying to [have to] go back after completing the entire [circle of fifths], the [intervals of] thirds may be adopted as guides. That is, when one reaches a note while setting a temperament that forms a third with a note that has already been tuned, one should play them together and listen whether the said third (if it is major) beats 2/3 [of a comma] high, or (if it is minor) if it beats 3/4 of a comma low. Thus if c'-g', g'-g, g-d', d'-a', a'-a [and] a-e' have already been tuned, then the e' is the third above the c' that has already been tuned—a major third, to be precise. This [interval] must beat 2/3 [of a comma] high. If this does not prove to be the case, then one must again pass through the already-tuned fifths and adjust them. The e' is likewise a minor third below the already-tuned g'. These two pitches [when played together] must also not be perfectly in tune, but the g' should be 3/4 [of a comma] low. The same holds true for the rest [of the circle of fifths]. Consequently one must not tune straight through.* Here is a similar instance: if b' has been tuned to e', then one may test whether [the interval] b'-g' beats 2/3 [of a comma] high. One may read about this process of setting a temperament in somewhat greater detail in Neidhardt's *Temperatur [des Monochordi]*, p. 102, as well as in Werkmeister's *Anmerkungen zur Generalbaße*.† Experience also counts a great deal in this matter.

* i.e., without occasionally checking for accuracy.

† See §.400 above.

§. 409.

Since setting a temperament in an organ is absolutely necessary, it must be done with great diligence. One ought not to put up with anyone who wants one key to be more in tune than another, but one should have them all tempered equally; this is because of transposition, and also so that the other keys do not become unusable. If anyone should ask how trumpets, horns, and other instruments will sound against it, here is the answer: string instruments can be tuned and fingered to conform to a temperament. Thus it is improper to tune all strings on other instruments‡ by fifths as pure as possible. One should likewise tune the fifths ½ of a comma short, and finger them in a similar manner. A craftsman can arrange the holes of wind instruments that produce pitches by stopping holes, such as flutes, oboes, etc., according to a temperament. Tempering horns and trumpets does not work. But since temperament is so necessary and useful, it is better to introduce it anyway than to leave it out§ because of the trumpets. Anyone who does not like the sound of a trumpet—and it does sound wretched against an equal temperament—should leave it out. [The pitch of] a horn can be somewhat more easily adjusted by the breath than [that of] a trumpet.(**)

‡ i.e., other than the organ.

§ i.e., to retain a meantone temperament.

> (**) Only one minor matter should be verified in this regard: whether it is possible that a trumpet can be—and is—played more in tune by someone who knows how to play it well than usually happens with someone who is inexperienced. [Agricola]

§. 410.

If there are stops at chamber pitch within an organ, it is not necessary to temper them from scratch. Rather they should be left untuned until some stops on another key-

liche Stimmen reine sind: nach denselbigen kann man sie hernach stimmen, so, daß man allezeit eine Sekunde tiefer nimmt, daß das Kammer c dem b gleich werde; cis dem h, u. s. w. Oder wenn man es $1\frac{1}{2}$ Ton erniedrigen will; so wird das c dem a gleich, cis dem b, u. s. f. Wo man kein Principal 8' hat, kann man 4' nehmen; doch muß man bey solcher Temperatur in der Tiefe bleiben. Wo man aber Principal 16' nimmt, muß man in der Höhe bleiben, nach §. 407.

§. 411.

Noch dies will ich gedenken, daß andere nicht gerne durch die Quinten temperiren, weil $\frac{1}{12}$ Comma gar zu leicht verfehlt wird; sondern sie stimmen lieber durch Dissonanzen; und wenn sie c haben, so stimmen sie die Secunde, große Quarte und Sexte dazu, weil in Dissonanzen auch eine kleine Unreinigkeit besser gemerkt wird, zumal wenn der ganze Tritonus maior $\frac{6}{4}$, wie man den Griff nennet, dabey ist. Item sie nehmen 2, 4, 7, wenn sie dann 2, 4, ♮ nehmen, und hernach 3, 5, ♭7; so haben sie so wol die kleine als große 7. Und so ist c, d, e, fis; f, g, a, b, h schon gestimmt: denn bey dem Griffe $\frac{7}{2}$ nimmt man die kleine Quarte f. Also ist noch cis, dis und gis übrig. Man darf aber nur d nehmen, und die ♮ mit der 4, 2, dazu klingen lassen, so wird cis, als die ♮, bald rein werden. Nimmt man zu d die $\frac{6}{4}$; so wird gis, als die 4, auch rein werden. Stimmt man zu h, welches schon reine ist, die Oktave unterwärts, und schlägt zu solchem die $\frac{7}{5\times}$ an; so wird in dem Griffe das dis auch reine werden. Bey dieser Stimmung kann man den Vortheil haben, daß man nicht so viel in Oktaven stimmen muß, und also, wenn ja was versehen wäre, nicht so viel Corrigirens nöthig ist. Zuletzt kann man entweder die Quinten durchgehen, und hören, ob sie erträglich schweben, oder man probire die Temperatur so, daß man aus allen Tönen spiele.

§. 412.

Endlich erinnere ich noch einmal, daß man ja die Orgel nach der einmal eingeführten üblichsten Art stimme, ich meine, was den ersten Sonum anbelanget, damit man nicht der Orgel zu Gefallen neue Instrumente kaufen müsse. Wären in einer Kirche zwo Orgeln; so versteht sich dies von selbst, daß deren Temperatur und Stimmung einander vollkommen gleich seyn müsse.

board are in tune. Then [the former] can be tuned to the latter by always playing a second lower, so that the chamber-pitch c is the same as [the choir-pitch] b flat, c# is the same as b, etc. Or, if chamber pitch is to be 1½ steps lower, then c will be the same as a, c# the same as b flat, etc. If there is no 8′ Principal, then the 4′ [Principal] may be used, but one must stick to the lower register in tempering it. If it is a 16′ Principal [that is to be tempered], then one must stick to the treble, in accord with what was said in §. 407.

§. 411.

Let me mention in addition that others do not like to set a temperament using fifths, because 1/12 of a comma is all too easy to get wrong, but would prefer to tune by dissonances. Beginning with c, they tune the second, the tritone and the sixth to it, since a small degree of out-of-tuneness is more easily noticed in dissonances, especially if the complete *Tritonus major* 6/4/2,* as this chord is called, is sounding. They likewise play 2, 4 and 7; if they tune 2, 4, +7 and then 3, 5, -7, then both the minor and major seventh are in tune. Thus c, d, e, f#, f, g, a, b-flat, and b are already tuned (the 7/4/2 chord contains the f a perfect fourth [above c]), and only c#, d# and g# remain. But one need only begin with d, playing the 2, 4, and +7 with it, and then c#, the major seventh, is quickly in tune. By playing 6/4#/2 together with d, then g#, the #4, gets in tune. By tuning the octave below b (the latter already being in tune), and playing with it the 7/5/3#, the resulting chord will allow the d# to get in tune. This method of tuning has the advantage of not requiring so much tuning by octaves, and thus not so much correcting when something has been overlooked. All that is left is to proceed through all of the fifths,† listening whether their beating is tolerable, or [alternatively] testing the temperament by playing in all keys.

* i.e., the dominant seventh chord in its third inversion.

† i.e., to check the completed temperament.

§. 412.

Finally let me mention yet again that an organ should be tuned according to the most usual way prevailing—here I am referring to setting the first pitch—so that it is not necessary to buy new instruments just for the sake of the organ. If there are two organs in the same church, it goes without saying that their temperament and tuning must be absolutely the same.

Das XV. Capitel.
Von der Stimmung der Orgeln.

Inhalt:

§. 413. Wann man stimmen solle? §. 414. Von dem Stimmhorn. §. 415. Wie bey Flötwerken die offenen Pfeifen erhöhet oder erniedriget werden? §. 416. Der Wind muß gleich seyn. §. 417. Wornach jede Stimme zu stimmen. §. 418. Von der Terz und Quinte. §. 419. Von gemischten Stimmen überhaupt. §. 420. insonderheit. §. 421. ein Vortheil. §. 422. Von gedeckten Flötwerken. §. 423. Von Schnarrwerken. §. 424. Wie ein Clavier nach dem andern zu stimmen? It. wenn die Pfeifen zittern. §. 425. Vom Pedale. §. 426. Von der Onda maris, und andern Anmerkungen.

§. 413.

Allhier soll kürzlich gezeiget werden wie man nach verrichteter Temperatur ferner stimmen solle. Da erinnere ich zuvörderst, daß man weder die Temperatur noch das übrige Stimmen eher anfahen solle, als bis die Orgel ganz fertig ist, auch bis das Schnitzwerk, welches nahe um die Pfeifen herum ist, angeheftet worden: denn dadurch wird oft eine Unreinigkeit verursachet. Wenn aber die Temperatur richtig ist; so bleibt man bey solchem Register, welches man zu temperiren angefangen, und stimmt alles durch Oktaven, auf- und abwärts, vom C bis $\bar{c}$. Und da die Oktaven gar nicht schweben dürfen; so ist diese Stimmung desto leichter. Je langsamer eine Pfeife tremulirt, desto reiner ist sie: wenn sie aber gar inne stehet, daß gar kein Zittern mehr gehöret wird; so ist sie völlig reine.

§. 414.

Das Stimmen geschiehet mit dem Stimmhorne, welches von Holz ist, oder von Meßing; oder das Holz ist mit Meßing überzogen. Es ist dasselbe in forma coni, an einem Ende spitzig, am andern breit und dabey hohl; etwan so: ▽ Wenn man nun große Pfeifen damit stimmen soll; so muß es selbst auch groß seyn: bey kleinen Pfeifen ist es klein. Doch die gar großen Pfeifen drückt man lieber mit der Hand aus- und einwärts. Wenn man stimmt; so lasse man die Pfeife stehen, wie sie stehet, und rühre sie nicht an: denn sie wird in der Hand gleich warm, und dadurch etwas höher. Stimmt man sie alsbald, und sie wird nach der Stimmung wieder kalt: so wird sie wieder tiefer, folglich unrein. Wenn aber eine Pfeife abgehoben werden muß, weil sie etwan nicht recht anspricht; so muß man sie eine Zeitlang stehen und wieder kalt werden lassen, ehe man sie stimmt.

§. 415.

Chapter XV.
Concerning Tuning Organs.

Contents:

§.413. When should one tune? §.414. Concerning the tuning cone. §.415. How should open flue pipes be raised or lowered [in pitch]? §.416. The wind must be steady. §.417. What to tune each stop to. §.418. Concerning the Terz and Quinte. §.419. Concerning compound stops in general. §.420. [Concerning] specific [compound stops]. §.421. A benefit. §.422. Concerning stopped flue registers. §.423. Concerning reeds. §.424. How should one division be tuned according to another? [What to do] if pipes vibrate. §.425. Concerning the pedal. §.426. Concerning the Onda maris, and other remarks.

§. 413.

Here I shall briefly indicate how to continue tuning once a temperament has been set. First of all, let me mention that one should neither begin to set a temperament or do any other tuning until the organ is completely finished, even until the carving has been attached, since it fits close around the pipes and affixing it after tuning often causes out-of-tuneness. But when the temperament is correct, then stick with the stops that were first tempered, tuning all [the rest] by octaves, up and down, from C to c‴. And since octaves must not beat at all, this [part of the] tuning is all the easier. The slower a pipe beats, the more in tune it is. When it is completely "in", so that no more beating is heard, then it is perfectly in tune.

§. 414.

Tuning is done with a tuning cone made of wood or brass, or of wood overlaid with brass. It is made in the shape of a cone, pointed at one end, broad and hollowed out at the other, something like this: If large pipes are to be tuned with it, then it must also be large, and if it is to be used with small pipes, then it is small. The largest pipes, however, are better bent in or out by hand. When pipes are being tuned they should be left where they are and not touched, since they get warm right away in one's hands and thus go sharp. If they are tuned thus and again grow cold after tuning, then they go flatter and consequently out-of-tune. If a pipe must be lifted out, though, perhaps because it does not speak properly, then it must be left sitting a while and allowed to grow cold again before it is tuned.

Kap. XV. Von der Stimmung der Orgeln. 61

§. 415.

Wenn bey Flötwerken, die oben offen sind, die Pfeifen zu tief sind; so steckt man die Spitze des Stimmhorns hinein, und drückt sie aus einander. Trägt die Tiefe viel aus, daß es nicht angehet, sie also in die Höhe zu bringen; so schneidet man ihr etwas rund herum ab, doch gar behutsam, daß man die Pfeifen nicht verschneide. Je größer die Pfeifen sind, desto größere Stücke kann man abnehmen: und da bey einer 2füßigen Pfeife, wenn ein halber Ton zuviel wäre, wenig darf abgeschnitten werden; so kann in gleichem Falle bey der 16füßigen 8mal so viel abgenommen werden. Ist aber die Pfeife allzuhoch; so ist sie entweder im Gusse zu kurz gerathen, oder man hat sie verschnitten. Da ist kein ander Mittel, als daß man etwas anlöthe, oder (welches gemeiner ist) die Pfeife oben mit dem hohlen Theile des Stimmhorns zusammen drücke; welches letztere auch mit der Hand geschehen kann: oder auch daß man etwas einhänge; oder ein Theil der Pfeife durch ein Blech zudecke. Doch gehöret dies mit unter die Fehler.

§. 416.

Es muß bey der Stimmung der Wind in den Bälgen just abgewogen seyn: auch müssen die palmulae gleich weit und völlig niedergedrückt werden, sonst wird eins hoch, das andere tief. Und da auch daran viel liegt, daß die Ventile gleich weit aufgehen; so muß das Clavier bey der Stimmung vollkommen gleich geschraubet seyn, sonst wird das Werk allezeit unreine, wenn das Clavier hernach erst recht geschraubet wird. Besiehe hierbey was §. 350. gerathen worden.

§. 417.

Wenn das Principal gestimmt ist; so stimme man zuvörderst die Oktaven reine, da man nur zu dem Principal 8′ die Oktave 4′ ziehen und solche stimmen kann. Hier merke man eine allgemeine Regel: Wenn man Register zusammen stimmt, die allzuweit von einander abstehen; so hört man die Schwebung so eigentlich nicht. Also wollte ich nicht rathen, daß man die Oktave 2′ oder 1′ nach dem Principal 16′ oder 8′ stimmen sollte. Sondern man stimme entweder die Register nach ihres Gleichen, d. i. 8′ zu 8′; 4′ zu 4′, ꝛc. Oder nach solchen, die eine Oktave höher oder niedriger sind, als sie. Zum Ex. die Oktave 2′ nach 4′, u. s. w.

§. 418.

Nach den Oktaven kömmt man auf andere offene einfache Stimmen, und zwar werden die Violdigamben, Gemshörner, und andere Oktavstimmen also, wie der vorige Sphus angiebt, gestimmet. Die Quinten anlangend, mit allen ihren Arten, gedeckte und offene, werden 5 Töne höher gestimmet, als die Oktavstimmen, so, daß der untere Clavis im Principal c, aber in der Quinte g angiebt, ꝛc. Die Quinte 6′ stimmt man nach Principal oder (welches allezeit eins ist) Oktave 8′. Die Quinte 3′ aber am besten nach der Oktave oder Principal 4′; doch geht 8′ auch

H 3 endlich

§. 415.

If a flue pipe that is open on top is too low [in pitch], then the point of the tuning cone is inserted into it and [its top] is pushed outward. If it is so low that this does not suffice to bring it up to pitch, then a bit has to be snipped off all around [the top rim], but very carefully so as not to cut off too much. The larger the pipe is, the larger the piece that may be removed; only a little bit needs to be snipped off a 2' pipe if it is a half step too low, but in the same situation 8 times as much has to be taken off a 16' pipe. If the pipe is too sharp, however, then it has either been made too short in casting, or too much has been snipped off it. Then there is nothing else to do but to solder something on it, or (as is more commonly done), to press the top rim of the pipe inward with the hollowed-out part of the tuning cone. This last operation may also be done by hand. It is also possible to suspend something [in the pipe], or to cover a portion of the pipe with a [partial] metal [lid]. But this must be considered a fault.

§. 416.

The wind from the bellows must be perfectly steady when tuning, and the keys must also be depressed the same distance, completely to the bottom. Otherwise one [pipe] will be sharp and the next flat. And since it is also very important that the pallets open the same distance, thus the keyboard must be adjusted perfectly evenly. Otherwise, if the keyboard is subsequently adjusted to be even, the instrument will constantly be out-of-tune. In this connection note what has been suggested in §.350.

§. 417.

The octaves should be tuned immediately after the [8'] Principal has been tuned, by drawing the 4' Oktave with the 8' Principal and tuning it. Here take note of a general rule: if stops that are far apart from each other [in pitch] are tuned together, it is difficult to hear the beating properly. Thus I would not advise tuning the 2' or 1' Oktave from the 16' or 8' Principal. Rather, each stop should be tuned to its equivalent, i.e., 8' to 8', 4' to 4', etc. Or [each stop should be tuned] to one that is an octave higher or lower that it is, e.g., the 2' Oktave to the 4' etc.

§. 418.

After the Oktaves come the other single open stops; thus the Violdigambas, the Gemshorns and other octave-sounding stops are tuned as the paragraph above indicates. Concerning quints of all sorts, stopped and open, all of them are tuned 5 steps higher than the octave-sounding stops; thus the lowest note of the Principal sounds c, but the Quint sounds g, etc. The 6' Quinte is tuned to the Principal, or to the 8' Oktave (which amounts to the same thing). The 3' Quinte, however, is best tuned to the

endlich an. NB. Es werden die Quintregister vollkommen reine gestimmt, ohne Temperatur, so daß ein jeder Clavis gegen die Oktavstimme desselbigen Clavis eine völlige reine Quinte hören lasse, ohne daß sie um $\frac{1}{12}$ eines Commatis abwärts schweben sollte. Daher sie mit den Oktavstimmen fast wie eine Pfeife klingen, auch in der Orgel tolerirt werden, da sie sonst unter dem Spielen verboten sind. Die Terzen, wenn solche vorkommen, werden auch vollkommen rein gestimmt, ohne Temperatur. Man nimmt aber lauter große Terzen. Ob sie rein sind, kann nicht wohl gehöret werden, wenn nicht die Quinte dabey ist, welche man also dazu ziehen kann.

§. 419.

Es folgen die gemischten Stimmen. Wie es nun überall bey der Stimmung nicht zu rathen, daß man mehr Register dazu ziehe, wenn man etwas stimmt; sondern man stimmt eins nur nach einem, damit man die Schwebung höre: so ist auch bey allen gemischten Stimmen das Schreyen vieler Pfeifen nichts nütze. Deswegen muß man Dämpfer haben, sie damit schweigend zu machen. Man nimmt dünne Hölzer, und macht unten ein Paketchen Werg daran, steckt sie in die Pfeife, und belegt den Aufschnitt mit dem Werg, so schweiget die Pfeife. Es kömmt aber nie eine Pfeife über 3 zu dämpfen: denn obschon bey Mixturen 4′ vorkömmt; so stimmt man doch die größte Pfeife zuerst, welche man also nicht braucht zu dämpfen. Hat man sie alle stumm gemacht bis auf eine, nämlich die größte; so zieht man eine Oktavstimme dazu, nach der Vorschrift §. 417. und stimmt die größte reine; hernach kömmt man an die andern, und dann so fort, bis zur kleinsten. Die gestimmten braucht man eben nicht wieder zu dämpfen, weil sie eben die Schwebung nicht verderben werden.

§. 420

Also wird die Sesquialter, wenn sie 3fach ist, ebenfalls gestimmt. Die Terz und Quinte wird gedämpft; die Oktave 4′ wird nach Principal 8′ oder (in dessen Ermangelung) nach 4′ gestimmt; hernach die Quinte dazu, alsdann die Terz; und das ist ein Clavis. Hernach gehe man zum andern clave, und verfahre damit so fort, bis man durch ist. Ist sie 2fach; so stimmt man die Quinte 3′ am besten nach Oktave 4′, sodann auch die Terz. Das Terzian ist gleicher Art; weil da die Quinte erst kann nach Oktave 4′ gestimmt werden, (ob sie wol kleiner ist als die Terz,) und man hernach besser mit der Terz fortkommen kann; hernach nimmt man die Terz und stimmt sie vollkommen rein. Die Rauschpfeife wird auch so gestimmt; da liegt aber nichts daran, ob man die Quinte oder Oktave erst nehme. Ist die Quinte 3′, so stimmt man sie nach Oktave 4′; dann die Oktave dazu. Die Mixturen, Scharp, Cymbel, Koppel u. d. gl. werden auch so gestimmt, daß man sie alle bis auf eine Pfeife dämpft, und so fort stimmt.

§. 421.

Oktave or to the 4′ Principal, but in the end an 8′ will work, as well. N.B. The quint stops are tuned exactly pure, without being tempered, so that each note sounds a perfectly pure fifth in relation to the octave-sounding stops of the same note, and does not beat a 1/12 of a comma low. Thus [when combined] with the octave-sounding stops they sound almost like one pipe, and so they are tolerated in the organ,* while otherwise they are forbidden in performance. The Terzes, if there are any, are also tuned perfectly purely, without being tempered. By these are meant exclusively major thirds. It is not possible to hear if they are in tune without the Quint being present,† and thus it may be drawn for that purpose.

* i.e., the perfect fifths they create in harmonic progressions.

† This is not precisely correct, but drawing the quint does make it easier to perceive whether the third is in tune.

§. 419.

Now we come to the compound stops. Just as it is never advisable to draw several stops when tuning, but to tune them singly in order to hear the beating, likewise the screaming of many pipes in compound stops is also a hindrance. Therefore dampers must be used to silence them.‡ [For this purpose] one takes thin wooden sticks and fastens a wad of tow on them, inserting them into the pipe so that the cut-up is covered by the tow, and thus the pipe is silenced. No pipe over 3′ is ever dampened, however, for although 4′ ranks do appear in mixtures, the largest pipes are tuned first and thus do not need to be dampened. When all [the pipes of the mixture] except one, i.e., the largest, have been silenced, an octave-sounding stop is drawn with it, according to the directions in §.417, and it is tuned pure. Each of the other ranks is then tuned in turn, ending with the smallest. It is not necessary to dampen again the ones that have been tuned, since they will not disturb the beating.

‡ i.e., the pipes that are not being tuned at the moment.

§. 420.

The Sesquialter, if it is 3 ranks, is tuned in a like manner. The Terz and Quinte are dampened. Then the 4′ Oktave§ is tuned to the 8′ Principal or, in its absence, to the 4′ [Oktave]; next the Quinte is added in, and finally the Terz, thus completing [all the pipes sounding on] one key. One then moves to the next key and proceeds in this way through the entire compass. If [the Sesquialter] is 2 ranks, then it is best to tune the 3′ Quinte to the 4′ Oktave, and then the Terz as well. The same method is used for the Terzian. In it the Quinte may first be tuned to the 4′ Oktave (even though it is smaller than the Terz), and then it is easier to deal with the Terz. After [tuning the Quinte] the Terz is added and tuned pure. The Rauschpfeife is also tuned in this way; it does not matter whether the Quinte or Oktave is tuned first. If the Quinte is 3′, then it should be tuned to the 4′ Oktave, and then the [2′] Oktave should be added. The mixtures, Scharp, Cymbel, Koppel, and the like, are also tuned like this, by damping all the pipes but one and then tuning one by one.

§ i.e., the one in the Sesquialter; see §.190.

Kap. XV. Von der Stimmung der Orgeln. 63

§. 421.

Ueberhaupt ist es ein Vortheil beym Stimmen, wenn man einen Claven um den andern auslässet: denn die Pfeifen stehen Wechselsweise, bald zur linken, bald zur rechten Seite. Damit man nun nicht stets müsse hin und wieder laufen; so stimme man C, D, E, Fis, Gis, Ais, c, ꝛc. bis ins $\bar{\bar{c}}$. Hernach gehe man auf die andere Seite, und stimme auch Cis, Dis, F, G, A, H, cis, ꝛc. bis $\bar{h}$. Und obschon in jedem Thurme die Pfeifen zuweilen auch nicht nach der Ordnung stehen, so darf man doch so weit nicht darnach laufen. Wo mehr Personen sind, kann einer treten, der andere drückt die Palmuln nieder, bis der Stimmer pocht, zum Zeichen es sey rein, und er solle weiter gehen. Wo nur eine Person stimmen soll; so ist nöthig, daß sie durch ein Stück Bley, oder dergleichen, die Palmuln niederdrücke, und wenn ein Clavis reine, dasselbe weiter verlege.

§. 422.

Die gedeckten Flötwerke überhaupt werden also gestimmt: wenn sie zu hoch stehen; so zieht man den Deckel etwas in die Höhe, weil dadurch die Pfeife länger wird. Wo man aber zu Ende ist, und die Pfeife ist doch noch allzuhoch; so ist sie durch Ansetzung eines Stücks zu verlängern. Ist sie zu tief, so schlage man den Deckel vester auf, daß die Pfeife kürzer werde: wo man aber nicht weiter kann, so schneide man etwas von der Pfeife ab. Sind es hölzerne Pfeifen; so zieht man, wenn die Pfeife tiefer werden soll, den Stöpsel weiter heraus: hinein drückt man ihn, wenn die Pfeife höher werden soll. Sind die Stöpsel oder Deckel (welche letztern man auch Hüte nennt. §. 107.) allzugänge, daß sie sich leicht wieder verschieben; so umwinde man bey den Metallenen die Pfeife, bey Hölzernen aber den Stöpsel mit Leder, bis alles accurat passe.

§. 423.

Die Schnarrwerke sind entweder mit Schrauben oder Krücken. Bey den Schrauben bedient man sich eines Stimmschlüssels, der wie unsere Stimmhämmer aussiehet, und drehet die Schraube zur Rechten oder zur Linken, nachdem man die Pfeife höher oder tiefer haben will. Die Krücken aber werden hineinwärts geschlagen: denn dadurch drückt man das Blatt besser an das Mundstück, daß weniger Wind hinein kömmt. Ziehet man aber die Krücke heraus; so geschiehet das Gegentheil; und die Pfeife wird tiefer. (conf. §. 105.) Die Schnarrwerke stehen hinten, und man stimmt sie auf die letzte, indem sie durch das hin- und wieder gehen gar leicht wieder verstimmt werden.

§. 424.

Will man die andern Claviere nach dem obern stimmen, so ziehe man das Koppel, und stimme erst das Principal nach dem obigen reine; hernach kann man die übrigen Stimmen nach dem Principale stimmen. Doch wenn das Principal allzuklein, Er. 2′ wäre, und wäre doch Gedackt 8′ da, so thut man am besten, man koppelt

die

Chap. XV. Concerning Tuning Organs

§. 421.

In general it is an advantage to omit every other note when tuning, for the pipes stand in alternation, first on the left and then on the right side. To obviate the necessity of running back and forth from side to side, one should tune C, D, E, F#, G#, A#, c, etc., up to c‴. Then one should go to the other side and tune C#, D#, F, G, A, B, c#, etc., up to b″. Then even though the pipes do not always stand in order in every tower,* it is not necessary to move so far to reach them. If there are a number of persons [involved in the tuning], one can tread [the bellows] while another depresses the key, until the tuner raps as a sign that [the pipe] is in tune and he is ready to go on [to the next pipe]. If only one person is doing the tuning, then he must depress the keys with a lead weight or something similar, transferring it to the next key when the note is in tune.

* Here Adlung is referring to pipes that stand in the façade.

§. 422.

The stopped flutes are generally tuned in this way: if they are too sharp, then the cap is drawn upward a bit, since in doing this the pipe is made longer. When it has been pulled up as far as it can go, however, and the pipe's [pitch] is still too sharp, then the pipe must be lengthened by an extension. If the pipe is too flat, the cap should be pushed further down, making the pipe shorter. If it cannot go in any further, then some of the pipe must be cut off. If the pipes are of wood, then the stopper should be drawn further out to make the pipe flatter, and pushed [further in] to make it sharper. If the stoppers or the lids (which are also called caps; see §.107) are too loose, so that they easily shift out of place, then the metal pipes should be wrapped with leather; or if the pipes are wooden, the stoppers should be wrapped with leather to make everything fit snugly.

§. 423.

Reeds are [tuned] either by screws or tuning wires. If there are screws one makes use of a tuning key, that looks like our tuning hammer, and turns the screw right or left, according to whether the pipe should be sharper or flatter. Tuning wires, however, must be driven in; in that way, the tongue is pressed more tightly against the shallot, so that less wind can pass between them. By drawing the tuning wire outward, the opposite happens, and the pipe becomes flatter (cf. §.105). The reeds are located at the back [of the chest], and are tuned last, since they are easily put out of tune again by [the tuner] moving about.

§. 424.

If the second manual is to be tuned to the one above it, the coupler should be drawn and the Principal tuned pure to the one on the upper manual. After that the other stops may be tuned to the Principal. But if the Principal is too high-pitched, e.g. 2′, and there is an 8′ Gedackt to be tuned, then it is best to couple the manuals and

die Claviere, und stimmt sie nach einer größern Stimme des andern Claviers, nach der Vorschrift §. 417. Wenn ohngefehr ein Clavis eines Registers nicht wohl anschläget, oder zittert; so kann man darnach die andere Pfeife nicht stimmen, und muß also ein ander Register nehmen. Z. Er. die Violdigamba 8' stimme ich nach Principal 8'; ist aber eine Pfeife im Principale falsch, so stoße ich es ab, und stimme solchen clauem nach Oktave 4'.

§. 425.

Kömmt man an ein Clavier das nicht gekoppelt werden kann; so hält man beyder Claviere Palmuln zugleich an, entweder mit dem Finger, oder mit Bleygewicht. Das Pedal anlangend; so stimmt man nach dem Principal 8' des Hauptmanuals erst eine Oktave 8', da man etwan das Pedalkoppel zieht, und das Pedal alleine antritt, oder ein Gewicht darauf legt: oder man hält den Manualclavem zugleich an. Nach 8' stimmt man die 16- und 4füßigen Stimmen; nach 16' die 32füßigen; nach 4' die 2füßigen. Z. Er. nach der Oktave 4' das Cornet 2'. Das andere, was dabey zu wissen, ist bey den Manualen schon erinnert. Die Schnarrwerke habe ich oft alleine gestimmt, so, daß ich mit einer Hand durch die Abstrakten das Ventil des Windkastens aufgezogen, (nämlich wo man dazu kommen kann) mit der andern aber habe ich die Schnarrwerke gestimmt. Aber ich wollte rathen, daß man lieber das Pedal anträte, oder wo die Personen mangeln, daß man ein Gewicht darauf legte. Denn mit der Hand zieht man ein Ventil weiter auf, als das andere, und dadurch werden die Pfeifen einmal stärker angeblasen, als das andere mal; folglich wird da im Spielen keine Reinigkeit seyn. Der Posaunenbaß 16' wird von etlichen nach dem Subbaß 16' gestimmet: mir aber gehet es mit der Oktave 8' besser von statten, weil man die Schwebung besser hört; auch weil von offenen Pfeifen präsumirt wird, daß sie länger reine bleiben, als gedeckte, deren Stöpfel und Deckel sich zuweilen verrücken.

§. 426.

Und soviel ist bey dem Stimmen zu erinnern vorgekommen. Daß die Onda maris etwas über die andern Stimmen schweben müsse, erkennet ein jeder aus deren Natur, davon oben §. 173. gesagt worden. Es trägt sich oft zu, daß unter dem Stimmen eine Pfeife fladdert, filpet, auch wol gar nicht anschlägt, und was solcher Sächelchen mehr sind: allein das gehört eigentlich nicht zum Stimmen, sondern davon wird Kap. 18. etwas beygebracht. Durch das viele Schreyen werden die Ohren fast unempfindlich, daher der Stimmende eine geringe Schwebung nicht so gut vernimmt, als einer, der unten vor der Orgel stehet, oder etwas von den Pfeifen entfernet ist. Also ists am besten, man probirt seine Stimmung vor der Orgel. In der Stimmung paßiren manchmal wunderliche Dinge. So habe ich z. Er. sehen den Posaunenbaß 16' nach der Mixtur stimmen. Allein wie hört man da die Schwebung? — Die Ursache ist, weil nicht ieder die Schwebung weis.

Das

Chap. XV. Concerning Tuning Organs

tune it from one of the larger stops of the other manual, according to the instructions in §.417. If perchance one note of a stop speaks poorly, or vibrates, one cannot tune the other pipe according to it, and thus must draw another stop. Let us say, for example, that I am tuning the 8′ Violdigamba from the 8′ Principal; if one of the pipes in the Principal is faulty, then I retire the stop and tune that note from the 4′ Oktave.

§. 425.

If one happens upon a manual that cannot be coupled, then one must hold the keys of both manuals down at the same time, either with the fingers or with a lead weight. In the case of the pedal, the 8′ Oktave should first be tuned from the 8′ Principal of the main manual, either by drawing the pedal coupler and playing the pedal alone, or by setting a weight on it;* or one could hold both down at the same time. The 16′ and 4′ stops are tuned from the 8′, the 32′ from the 16′, and the 2′ from the 4′ (e.g., the 2′ Cornet from the Oktave 4′). Anything else necessary to know has already been mentioned in [discussing the method of tuning] the manuals. I have often tuned the reeds by myself, by grasping the tracker with one hand (that is, if I can reach it) and pulling the pallet in the windchest open, and then tuning the reeds with the other. But I would advise depressing the pedal,† or if the personnel is lacking, setting a weight on it. For with one's hand, one draws one pallet further open than another, and thus the pipes are allowed more wind one time than the next; consequently the organ is always out of tune when it is played. Some tune the 16′ Posaunenbass from the 16′ Subbass, but this is accomplished more successfully with the 8′ Oktave, since this makes the beating more audible; it is also expected that open pipes hold their tune better than stopped ones, whose stoppers and caps at times shift.

* i.e., the note in the main manual.

† The fact that Adlung advises depressing the pedal and not the manual keys reflects the particular situation with his organ in Erfurt (several reed stops are available in both manual and pedal, on separate stopknobs; see the stoplist of this organ in Chapter 10); but it also indicates that by now the majority of the reeds found on organs are in the pedal.

§. 426.

This is what needs to be remembered about tuning. Everyone understands that the Onda maris by nature must beat a bit sharp to the other stops, as has been said above in §.173. It often happens in tuning that a pipe flutters, misspeaks/overblows, simply does not speak at all, or has some other minor problem, but that has nothing to do with tuning; rather, Chap. 18 has something to say about this. All that din‡ makes the ears almost insensitive, and therefore the tuner does not perceive a negligible beating as well as one who stands below in front of the organ, or who is some distance from the pipes. Thus is is best to check the tuning in front of the organ. All sorts of strange things happen in tuning. For example, I have seen the 16′ Posaunenbass being tuned from the Mixture. But how is it then possible to hear the beating? The reason [for such odd practices] is that not everyone knows [about listening for] beating.

‡ i.e., from the tuning.

Das XVI. Kapitel.
Von der Ueberlieferung und Probe der Orgeln.

Inhalt:

§. 427. Man muß die Orgeln probiren. §. 428. Es ist für den Orgelmacher gut. §. 429 Die Schriften bey diesem Kapitel. §. 430. Personen bey der Probe §. 431. 432. Ob Orgelmacher oder Organisten die Probe thun sollen? §. 433. Sie soll nicht partheyisch geschehen. §. 434. Die Kosten dabey. §. 435. Ob man einen Probisten in Bestallung zu nehmen habe? §. 436. Man muß dabey die Wahrheit sagen dürfen. §. 437. Man nehme Zeit dazu. §. 438. Man geht nach dem Contrakte. §. 439. Man thue alles bescheiden. §. 440. Man examinire die Claviere. §. 441. den Wind, ob er hinreicht. §. 442. ob er gleich sey? und dessen Zufall stark genug? §. 443 Ob die Bälge schwanken? § 444. Ob die Lade richtig? §. 445 Wie das Durchstechen in den Cancellen zu finden. §. 446 Das äusserliche Durchstechen. §. 447 448 449. Ob das Pfeifwerk richtig? §. 450. Ob ein Werk windsiech sey? § 451. Ob die Materie der Pfeifen richtig? §. 452. sonderlich bey metallenen Pfeifen. §. 453. Man kann es nicht daran sehen. §. 454. ob eine Pfeife eher anspreche als die andere? §. 455. Von der Mensur. §. 456. andere Remarquen. §. 457. Unrichtige Mensur. §. 458. Was nach der Probe anzufangen?

§. 427.

Nun sind wir endlich mit der Orgel in so weit fertig, als sie zur Vollkommenheit zu bringen ist. Es folgen aber noch einige Kapitel, welche die Orgel angehen, darunter das von der Orgelprobe nicht das geringste ist. Wollte man der Arbeit etlicher Orgelmacher schlechterdings trauen; so würde manche Kirche im Orgelbau betrogen werden. Denn da man zuweilen eine große Nachläßigkeit dieser Leute merkt, da doch ihre Arbeit gemeiniglich eine Censur ausstehen muß; was würde es werden, wenn man ihre Arbeit gar nicht untersuchte? Also sind die Consistoria, Rathsherrn und Inspektores zu loben, welche ein neugebautes Werk visitiren lassen, ob es nach dem Contrakte verfertiget worden.

§. 328.

Auch ist es für den Orgelmacher sicherer, wenn er sein Werk probiren, und nach dem sich ein Zeugniß von seiner Arbeit geben läßt, damit nicht ein unverständiger Organist das Werk verderbe, und dem Künstler hernach die Schuld gebe. Man muß aber einen Theil des Geldes inne behalten, bis nach der Probe; sonst fragen manche nicht viel darnach, und lassen die gefundenen Fehler unverbessert. Findet man aber, daß die Arbeit gut gerathen ist; so verhalte man dem Orgelmacher seinen verdienten Lohn nicht.

Chapter XVI.
Concerning the Delivery and Examination of Organs

Contents:

§.427. Organs must be examined.. §.428. This is good for the organbuilder.. §.429. The literature pertaining to this chapter.. §.430. Persons present at the examination.. §.431. 432. Whether organbuilders or organists should carry out the examination.. §.433. It should be conducted impartially.. §.434. The expenses involved.. §.435. Whether an examiner should be under contract.. §.436. One must be free to speak truthfully.. §.437. [Sufficient] time should be allowed for it.. §.438. One must proceed according to the contract.. §.439. One must maintain modest behavior.. §.440. The keyboards must be examined.. §.441. [Likewise] the wind, whether it is sufficient.. §.442. Is it steady? Is the supply ample enough? §.443. Do the bellows shake? §.444. Are the chests properly [constructed]? §.445. How to detect running in the channels.. §.446. External runs.. §.447. 448. 449. Are the pipes properly [made]? §.450. Is the instrument wind-starved? §.451. Are the pipes [made] of the proper material? §.452. Especially the metal pipes? §.453. The examination cannot be superficial.. §.454. Does one pipe speak more promptly than another? §.455. Concerning the scaling.. §.456. Other remarks.. §.457. Incorrect scaling.. §.458. What to do after the examination.

§. 427.

Now we have arrived at the point in our discussion of the organ when it is brought to completion. Several other chapters that concern the organ will follow, however, among which the one concerning the examination of the organ is by no means the least important. If one were to trust unquestioningly the work of some organbuilders, many a church would be defrauded in its organ's construction. Since these people exhibit at times great carelessness, even though their work must ordinarily undergo critical scrutiny, how would it be if their work were not examined at all? Thus consistories, town councillors and inspectors are to be praised for having a newly built organ checked over to ascertain if it has been constructed in accordance with the contract.

§. 328. [i.e., 428.]

It is also safer for the organbuilder to have his worked checked, and then be given a certificate attesting to his workmanship, so that no ignorant organist can subsequently damage the instrument and then put the blame on the builder. A portion of the money must be held back until after the examination, though, or otherwise many [builders] will not show much concern afterwards, and will leave unrepaired the faults that have been uncovered. If it is ascertained, however, that the work has turned out successfully, then no one should withhold from the organbuilder the wage he has earned.

Kap. XVI. Von der Ueberlieferung

§. 429.

Bey diesem Kapitel hat man etliche sonst schon allegirte Schriften nachzulesen. Werkmeister hat von dieser Materie, wie bekannt, in der Orgelprobe mit Vorsatz gehandelt. Es gehört auch dessen Beschreibung der grüningischen Orgel hierher, da er die Fehler nennt, welche man darinne gefunden: er erzählt auch, wie man sie probirt. Matthäus Hertel hat auch eine Orgelprobe geschrieben, deren Prinz Meldung thut, in der historischen Beschreibung der edlen Sing= und Klingkunst, Kap. 12. §. 83. Da erzählt er, daß ein anderer dieses Werkchen mit Verschweigung des wahren Autoris unter seinem eigenen Namen in den Druck gegeben. Etliche haben gemeynet es wäre des Werkmeisters Orgelprobe: aber Prinz widerleget es, und rettet Werkmeisters Ehre, in der Vorrede des Phrynidis. Hertels Traktat heißt: Examen Organi pnevmatici. Prinz entschuldiget den Herausgeber, als möchte er den wahren Autorem nicht gewust haben. Allein, gesetzt es sey also, so ziemet sichs doch nicht, seinen Namen einer Schrift vorzusetzen, wenn man nichts dabey gethan hat. Werkmeister selbst beschweret sich hierüber in der Vorrede zur musikalischen Temperatur, welche nach der ersten Edition der Orgelprobe 1691. herausgekommen, und sagt, es sey eine Calumnie, und geschehe ihm hierinne zu viel. Er habe dergleichen Arbeit nie gesehen, als etwan $\frac{1}{2}$ Bogen worinnen ein guter Freund einem Tyroni entworfen, wie ein solches Examen müsse beschaffen seyn, so aber Kinderpossen gewesen, ꝛc. Er habe viele Orgeln examinirt, bauen sehen, auch selbst bauen und renoviren lassen; sey gereist, und habe die Defecta aufgesucht, ꝛc. und werde ja so wol Augen, Ohren und Vernunft gehabt haben, als ein anderer, u. s. w. Sollte mirs bey gegenwärtigem Traktat auch also gehen, wie dem ehrlichen Werkmeister; so würde ich mich auf eben solche Art defendiren. Denn was ist das für ein Schluß: der schreibt etwas, welches vor ihm der und der schon angemerkt, ergo hat ers aus ihm genommen? Wenn ich nun die Orgel betrachte; so ist es ja wol möglich, daß ich den und jenen Defekt oder Vollkommenheit wahrnehme, den ein anderer auch wahrgenommen hat, ohne das ich von ihm oder seinen Schriften die geringste Erkenntniß habe. Jedoch habe ich, allem vorzubeugen, fast alles allegirt, was ich in andern gedruckten Büchern gefunden; ob mir schon die Sache eben so gut bekannt gewesen, als solchen Schreibern. Ich will also lieber andern dies und jenes zuschreiben, ob ich es gleich ohne sie gewußt; als ein plagiarius heißen. Johann Caspar Trost, sen. hat auch seine Anmerkungen in der Beschreibung der Weißenfelßischen Schloßorgel, Kap. 7. S. 53. u. f. Er hat ein Examen Organi pnevmatici contra sycophantas mit unterschiedlichen Kupfern ediren wollen. s. Walthers musikal. Lexikon S. 620. Janowka in claue p. 94. hat auch etwas weniges davon. Anderer zu geschweigen. [79]) Es deucht mir aber nöthig zu seyn, daß ein künftiger Organist Gelegenheit suche, eine Orgelprobe mit anzusehen, indem er dadurch beherzt wird, es nachzuthun; auch sieht er, was da vorgehet.

§. 430.

---

[79] Mehrere Autores findet man angeführt in des Hrn. Verfassers Anleitung S. 337 — 342. Die mehresten sind auch schon im ersten Kapitel dieses Buchs bekannt worden.

Chap. XVI. Concerning the Delivery

§. 429.

In connection with this chapter one must consult a number of treatises that have already been cited. Werkmeister has expressly treated this matter, as is well-known, in his *Orgelprobe*. His *Organum Gruningense redivivum* should also be mentioned here, since he enumerates the shortcomings that were found in that organ. He also relates how it was examined. Matthäus Hertel has also written an *Orgelprobe* which Prinz mentions in his *Historische Beschreibung der edlen Sing= und Klingkunst*, Chap. 12, §.83.*. There he relates that someone else has printed the work under his own name, withholding [the name of] the true author. Some thought that he was referring to Werkmeister's *Orgelprobe*, but Prinz refuted that and rescued Werkmeister's honor in the preface† of his *Phrynis*.‡ Hertel's treatise is entitled *Examen Organi pneumatici*. Prinz excused the one who published it as not having known the true author. Yet be that as it may, it hardly seems proper to put one's name at the head of a treatise if one has had nothing to do with its creation. Werkmeister himself complains about this matter in the preface to his *Musikalischen Temperatur*, published after the first edition of the *Orgelprobe* (1691), saying that it was calumny, and it had caused him much grief. [The preface states that] he never saw such a work, except for perhaps ½ a sheet on which a good friend had sketched for an amateur what should take place in such an examination, nothing more than childish nonsense. [He further states that] he has examined many organs, has watched them being built, and had them built and rebuilt himself; he is well traveled, has sought out the faults, and has eyes, ears and good sense just like anyone else. If the same thing should happen to me in connection with this present treatise as happened to honest Werkmeister, I would defend myself in exactly the same way. After all, what kind of reasoning is that? Just because he writes something that this or that one has already noted, does that mean that he has taken it from them? If I am considering the organ, it is indeed possible that I might perceive this or that defect or merit that someone else has also perceived, without my having the least acquaintance with him or his writings. Nevertheless, in order to safeguard myself [against any of this], I have cited almost everything I have found in other published books, even though I was just as well-versed in the matter as those authors. I would rather ascribe this or that to others, even though I knew it already without them, than be called a plagiarist. Johann Caspar Trost, Sr.,§ also has excellent observations in his *Beschreibung der Weißenfelßischen Schloßorgel*, Chap. 7, p. 53f. He had intended to publish an *Examen Organi pneumatici contra sy[n]cophantas* with various copper plates; see Walther's *musikal. Lexicon*, p. 620. Janowka also has a little bit on the subject in his *Clavis*, p.94; not to mention others.[79]. It seems to me to be necessary, though, that an aspiring organist seek the opportunity to sit in on an organ examination, since that will encourage him to emulate it; he would also see what happens during it.

* p. 149.

† Preface to Part I of the 1696 edition, entitled "An den Leser."

‡ *Phrynis Mitilenæus, oder Satyrischer componist*...

§ Should read "Jr."

[79] A number of [other] authors are to be found mentioned in the author's *Anleitung*, pp. 337-342. Most of them have already been mentioned in the first chapter of this book. [Albrecht].

und Probe der Orgeln.

§. 430.

Die Personen, welche dabey nöthig, sind folgende: 1) der Orgelmacher, welcher das Werk verfertiget. 2) Einer oder etliche, die es examiniren. 3) Einer der die angemerkten Fehler getreulich aufschreibt, damit sie den Inspectoribus zur Verbesserung können übergeben werden. Es muß aber dieser Schreiber, so, wie der, welcher die Probe verrichtet, unpartheyisch und ehrlich seyn, sonst läßt er das beste auffen, und die Kirche wird sodann sammt der Gemeinde betrogen. Man nehme lieber zween Schreiber, und ein paar Deputirte von der Gemeinde, auch wol vom Consistorio, oder vom Rathe. Ohne was sonst noch zuläuft. Doch, was denjenigen anlangt, der die Probe verrichten soll, ist noch was zu erinnern.

§. 431.

Es fragt sich nämlich hier: Ob ein Orgelmacher, oder ein Organist die Orgel probiren solle? Es handelt von dieser Frage Werkmeister in der Orgelprobe Kap. 1. §. 1. Sonst habe ich auch einmal gesehen, daß einer dergleichen Probe verrichtet, der seiner Profeßion nach ein Pastor war, nie aber einen Organisten abgegeben, sondern er wußte nur etwas auf dem Clavier. Aber dergleichen kommen hier gar nicht in Consideration. Es gehört mehr dazu als sich dieser Herr Pastor vorgestellet. Ein Concept von einer Predigt zu schreiben würde ihm ohnfehlbar beßer gelungen seyn, als die unternommene Probe. Man hätte ihm zurufen sollen: manum de tabula! — Es kanns zwar auch einer verrichten, der kein Organist ist; aber er muß doch die Principia davon in Kopfe haben, dergleichen bey dem Pastor nicht war: denn er wußte nichts von allen dazu gehörigen Dingen. Was unsere Frage anlanget; so müssen wir betrachten, wie weit ein Organist oder Orgelmacher sich zur Probe schickt, oder nicht, und was bey jeden für Commoda und Incommoda sich finden. Ein Orgelmacher weis die mechanischen Griffe am besten, sonderlich die Mensuren. Er weis, was sonst für Schnitzer hier und da sich zu finden pflegen, weil er vielleicht selber hinter der Thür gesteckt. Beydes ist einem Organisten, (das Wort nehmen wir nun stets in weitläuftigerm Verstande, daß es auch den in sich schließt, der die Organistenkunst verstehet, ob er gleich keiner ist) als einem Organisten, so wohl nicht bekannt. Dieser hingegen, der mehr mit dem Klange zu thun hat, und die Veränderungen anmerken kann, die bey veränderlichem Wetter paßiren, kann beßer wissen, was aus diesem oder jenem Versehen ins künftige für Unheil entstehen werde. Bis dato werden die commoda fast gleich seyn; und wenn man solche hat, die nichts von des andern seiner Wissenschaft besitzen, scheint es fast nöthig, beyderley Personen dazu zu ziehen. Wollte man sagen, es gäbe keine Organisten, die nicht wissen sollten, was in der Orgel paßirte, weil sie stets damit umgingen; der beliebe doch zu erwägen, daß an manchen Orten ein Organist sich so wenig um seine Orgel bekümmert, so, daß auch der Orgelmacher alle Festage den Posaunenbaß stimmen muß. Mancher hat auch in seiner Orgel wenig Stimmen; wie kann er von den andern ihm unbekannten urtheilen?

J 2 §. 432.

§. 430.

The persons whose presence is required are as follows: 1) the organbuilder who has built the instrument; 2) one or more [persons] who will examine it; 3) someone who faithfully writes down the faults that are noted, so that they may be turned over to the Inspectors to insure their repair. This scribe, however, just like the person who carries out the examination, must be impartial and honest; otherwise he will leave out what is most important, and then the church together with the parish will be defrauded. It is preferable to use two scribes, plus a few deputies from the parish and even from the consistory or the town council, in addition to any others who might be present. As concerns those who are to carry out the examination, though, there is yet more to keep in mind.

§. 431.

Here the question arises, "Ought it be an organbuilder or an organist who examines the organ?". Werkmeister discusses this question in his *Orgelprobe*, Chap. I, p. 1. One time I witnessed an examination conducted by a person who was a pastor by profession; he had never served as an organist, but only knew a bit about the keyboard. Such people as this should never even come under consideration. There is more to it than this good pastor could ever imagine. He would undoubtedly have succeeded better in writing a sermon than in undertaking such an examination. Someone should have called out to him, "Manum de tabula!"* One who is not an organist can carry it out, to be sure, but he must have an understanding of the principles involved. This the pastor did not have—he knew nothing about matters pertaining to it. To address the question above, we must consider to what degree an organist or an organbuilder is suited for such an examination, and what the advantages and disadvantages of each one are. An organbuilder has the best understanding of mechanical concepts, especially scaling. He knows what sort of blunders are likely to be committed in various places, because he himself perhaps has a few of them hidden in his past. Neither of these matters is very familiar to an organist as such (we are using the word "organist" always in the broad sense of the term, to include those who understand the art of the organist, whether or not they are practicing organists). The organist, on the other hand, who deals more with the sound [of the instrument], and can take note of the variations that come about with the changes in the weather, has a better understanding of what sort of trouble will arise in the future from this or that error. Up to this point the advantages are almost equal, and when the only people available are those who know nothing of the other's area of expertise, it would seem almost necessary to bring in both persons. Anyone who suggests that every organist should know what goes on inside an organ, since they are always involved with it, should realize that in many places the organist is so ignorant of his organ that the organbuilder must even tune the pedal Posaune for every feast day. Many an organist also has only a few stops in his organ; how is he to evaluate others† that are unknown to him?

---

* "Take your hands off the table!"— i.e., don't concern yourself with that which you know nothing about.

† i.e., ones in a larger organ somewhere else that he may be called upon to examine.

§. 432.

Man kann aber heut zu Tage zuweilen solche Organisten haben, welche in der Orgelmacherey sich zugleich eine gute Wissenschaft zuwege gebracht haben, daß, ob sie wol keine Orgel bauen können, sie dennoch von allen Dingen, die in der Orgel paßiren, richtig zu urtheilen wissen. Sie kennen die Register auch, und en fin was etwan in diesem Traktate zu der Organisten Unterrichte vorgetragen wird. Solche schicken sich dazu, daß sie allein eine Probe verrichten. Nicht weniger aber sind Orgelmacher, welche Orgeln in Bestallung haben, daran sie alles observiren können, was bey Aenderung des Wetters, oder sonst von dem Organisten besonders angemerkt wird, geschickt, ohne Organisten ein Werk zu probiren; zumal wenn sie spielen können, und in der Mathematik, Physik und dergleichen Wissenschaften etwas wissen. Welcher ist unter diesen beyden zu erwählen? Ich sage: der Organist. Und so ist es anjetzo fast durchgehends eingeführt. Denn bey den Orgelmachern findet sich noch das Incommodum, daß einer immer andere Principia hat, als der andere, daher er des andern Arbeit gerne tadelt. Es kömmt auch gemeiniglich der Neid dazu; daß einer den andern zu verachten sucht, um dessen Verdienst an sich zu ziehen: weswegen auch ein Orgelmacher nicht gern den andern über seine Arbeit läßt; weil sie beyderseits gar leicht in Affekt gerathen können, wobey sodann viel unnöthiges Raisonniren mit unterläuft: anderer Excesse nicht zu gedenken.

§. 433.

Man hüte sich aber vor partheyischen Probisten. Denn wenn der Organist es mit dem Orgelmacher hält; so thut er das Maul zu rechter Zeit nicht auf, extenuirt die Fehler, oder sagt sie gar nicht. Zumal wenn ihm etwas für seine unzeitige Freundschaft versprochen wird. Am besten wird dem Unheil vorgebogen, wenn man solche Personen zur Probe nimmt, die so genaue Bekonntschaft nicht haben mit dem Orgelmacher; auch können deswegen etliche genommen werden, die einander auch selbst nicht recht bekannt sind: da muß sich doch einer vor dem andern fürchten, und was einer nicht anmerkt, das entdeckt der andere. Und alle wird sie der Orgelmacher so geschwind nicht auf seine Seite ziehen; zumal, wie ich wol rathen wollte, wenn man es dem Orgelmacher nicht auf die Nase bindet, wer die Probe verrichten soll. Man setzt ihm also einen Tag kurz vorher, und kömmt unversehens mit solchen, von denen er dergleichen sich nicht vermuthet. Man verfehle aber nicht in der Wahl. Zuweilen fällt man unbesonnener Weise auf Organisten, die ihrer Kunst wegen sonderlich berühmt sind, und bekümmert sich nicht darum, ob sie den Orgelbau verstehen, oder nicht, welches doch zuweilen bey ihnen am meisten fehlt.

§. 434.

Will jemand sagen: das kostet viel Geld, wenn deren etliche, und noch dazu so auseriesene Personen, sollen zur Probe einer Orgel gerufen werden; dem dienet zur Antwort, daß solches nicht zu ändern sey. Entweder man lasse eine Probe gar unterwegens; oder ver-

§. 432.

Nowadays, however, organists are sometimes available who have also achieved a good understanding of organbuilding, so that, even though they are not able to build an organ, they nevertheless know how to evaluate correctly everything that takes place in an organ. They are also familiar with the stops; in sum, with everything that has been explained in this treatise to instruct an organist. Such people are suited to carry out an examination by themselves. No less suited to examine an instrument unaccompanied by an organist, though, are those organbuilders who have contracts to take care of organs, in which they can observe everything—changes related to the weather or anything else—that might otherwise be noted only by an organist. This is especially true if they are able to play and know something about mathematics, physics and other such sciences. Which one of these two is to be chosen? I say, "The organist." And this is almost exclusively the way it is set up these days. For there is yet another disadvantage with organbuilders: one always has different principles than another, and thus is quick to censure the other's work. It generally comes down to jealousy; one tries to malign another in order to steal his business. This is why one organbuilder is reluctant to let another inspect his work, since both of them get emotional about it, and then a lot of unnecessary arguing goes on, not to mention other excesses.

§. 433.

One should guard against biased examiners. For when the organist is in league with the organbuilder, then he never opens his trap at the right time, excusing the faults or remaining silent about them. This is especially true if he has been promised something for his sudden friendship. This trouble is best prevented by choosing for the examination persons who do not have a very close acquaintance with the organbuilder. For the same reason, several may be chosen who do not know each other very well. Then each one must be wary of the other, and what one does not note the other will discover. And it will not be so easy for the organbuilder to entice them all over to his side, especially if (as I would advise) one is not so quick to tell the builder who is to carry out the examination. One should set a date with him shortly in advance, and then appear unexpectedly with persons whom he could not be sure [would conduct the examination]. But do not choose unwisely!. Sometimes organists are rashly chosen who are famous for their art, without troubling to investigate whether or not they understand organbuilding; often it is the thing they are the weakest in.

§. 434.

Anyone who says that it costs a lot of money to summon several persons, and distinguished ones to boot, to examine an organ, should be told that this is unavoidable. Either the examination should be dispensed with altogether, or it should be conducted

verrichte sie recht. Eine Orgel wird nicht alle Jahre verändert, so wie man etwan mit andern Sachen stets umsetzen kann. Man muß also behutsam verfahren. Werkmeister erzählt in Organo grüningensi rediuiuo, daß die Probe desselben Werks von 53 Personen verrichtet worden, welche theils Organisten, theils andere Musici gewesen. Der ganze Haufe der Probisten bekam 3000 Rthlr. Da siehet man, was man sonst an die Orgelproben gewendet. Heutiges Tages will man nicht gerne etliche Thaler daran wenden, da der Probist die Kleider verdirbt, Staub genug in sich frißt, und sich dabey oft Feinde macht, auch von seinen Verrichtungen zu Hause vieles versäumt. s. Werkmeisters Orgelprobe S. 68. Doch gar zu viel Personen sind bey einer Probe nichts nütze; es hindert nur einer den andern. Zwey oder drey rechtschaffene Männer berufen, und dieselben redlich und nicht so schlecht bezahlt, ist viel besser. Ich kenne Schulmeister, welche in dem Orgelbau wohl bewandert sind, und diesfalls zu einer Probe wohl zu gebrauchen wären. Aber die siehet man nicht mit einem Auge an. Der große Ruhm eines Organisten macht alles aus. Noch eins: Mancher versteht die Sache gut, aber er hat nicht das Herz, die Wahrheit zu sagen. Das taugt auch nichts. Noch merke ich an, daß einer, der sich zu dergleichen Verrichtungen mit Nutz und sich selbst zum Ruhm will brauchen lassen, die Baukunst, und sonderlich die Mechanik, wohl verstehen müsse, wenn er von allen Theilen einer Orgel ein gesundes Urtheil fällen will.

§. 435.

Hier fällt mir die Frage ein: ob es rathsam, in einem Lande einen Mann allein in Bestallung zu nehmen, daß er alle Orgeln probiren solle? Meine Antwort darauf ist diese: Wenn in einer Stadt einer ist, der das Werk recht verstehet, dabey aber auch ehrlich ist; so thut man nicht übel, wenn ihm die Probe aller Orgeln aufgetragen wird. Man muß ihn aber darüber beeydigen, daß er der Kirche zum Schaden nichts verschweigen, oder dem Orgelmacher heucheln wolle. Deswegen kann doch bey wichtigen Werken noch anders woher jemand dabey seyn.

§. 436.

Es soll die Probe nicht angestellet werden, es sey denn alles fertig, auch die Stimmung, daß es nicht hernach heisse, es solle erst gemacht werden. Denn auch die Stimmung muß mit examinirt werden. Man muß dem Probisten alle Freyheit lassen, seine Meynung zu eröfnen. Sonst habe ich wol mehr als einmal gehört, daß die Inspektores selbst denselben gebeten, etwas gelinde mit dem Orgelmacher zu verfahren: entweder weil sie von demselben ein ansehnlich Accidens (etwan ein Clavier oder Clavessin) erhalten oder zu hoffen hatten; oder wegen Bekantschaft; oder, damit die Gemeinde nicht rebellisch würde, und das rückständige Geld nicht zahlte, wofür sie doch gut geworden. Aber das heißt nichts. Mit gutem Gewissen kann der Probist ihnen nicht Gehör geben; vielweniger kann er dem Orgelmacher auf deren Bitte ein gut Zeugniß aufsetzen, wenn er keins merititret, weil dadurch auch andere Kirchen betrogen werden. Noch schlimmer

properly. An organ is not soon altered the way other things may be changed around, and so one must proceed with caution. In his *Organum gruningense redivivum*[*] Werkmeister relates that the examination of this instrument[†] was conducted by 53 persons, of whom some were organists and some were other musicians. The whole crowd of examiners received 3,000 Reichsthaler. This will show what others have spent on examining organs. Nowadays nobody wants to put out a number of Thalers;[‡] after all, an examiner ruins his clothing and swallows plenty of dust, often making enemies in the process and neglecting many of his duties at home; see Werkmeister's *Orgelprobe*, p. 68. But it is not useful [to involve] a great many people in an examination; one only gets in another's way. It is far better to summon two or three upright men, paying each of them a just and generous fee. I know schoolteachers who are quite knowledgeable about organbuilding, and in that case they also might well be used for an examination. But no, [people] such as these do not even rate a second glance. If an organist has a great reputation,[§] that is all that counts. One more comment: many a one understands the matter well, but does not have the courage to speak the truth. Such people are also worthless. But let me state that a person who seeks to make himself useful in such work and to do himself credit must understand well the art of organbuilding, and especially the mechanics of it, if he wishes to pronounce sound judgment on all the components of an organ.

[*] pp. 9-12.
[†] i.e., the one in the Palace at Gröningen; see this stoplist in Chapter 10.
[‡] i.e., to spend a lot of his own money on being an examiner. Adlung continues by listing the disadvantages of the task, including certain financial ones; if the examiner were to undertake the work without compensation, he would inevitably incur certain expenses that would have to come out of his own pocket.
[§] i.e., as a virtuoso.

§. 435.

Here the question occurs to me: would it be advisable to appoint a single man to examine all the organs in a territory? This is my answer: if there is someone in a city [within the region] that understands the instrument properly, and in addition is also honest, then it would not be a bad idea to commission him to examine all the organs. But he must be bound with an oath that he will not withhold anything that would be a detriment to the church, or try falsely to flatter the organbuilder. For that reason a person from somewhere else can be present at [the examination of] important instruments.

§. 436.

The examination should not be arranged until everything is completed, including the tuning, so that it need not later be said, "This should have already been done." For the tuning must be part of the examination. The examiner must be allowed complete freedom to express his opinion. More than once I have heard that the Inspectors themselves have asked the examiner to be a bit lenient with the organbuilder, either because they have received or hope for a handsome bonus from him (say, a clavichord or a harpsichord), or because of connections; or so that the congregation does not become rebellious and refuse to pay the money yet owed, which they will then have to make good on. But that will not do. The examiner cannot in all good conscience be swayed by them; far less can he provide the organbuilder a good reference at their bidding if he does not merit it, because other churches will thereby be defrauded. What Werkmeister

ist es, was Werkmeister in Organo grüning. erzählt, daß, da einer die Wahrheit bey der Probe reden wollen, er einen Küchenschilling dafür aushalten müssen. Wenn Inspektores, oder andere, das Werk nur wollen gelobet haben; so ist nicht nöthig, Fremde dazu zu holen: diese Kunst können sie selber. Aber das heißt nicht censirt oder probirt. Für dergleichen Compliment bedanke ich mich!

§. 437.

Wer das Capitel von den Vollkommenheiten und Fehlern einer Orgel gelesen, und merkt, was noch soll gesagt werden, der wird leicht beurtheilen können, wie viel Zeit zu dem Actu gehöre. Oft ist in einer Stunde das ganze Werk fertig: aber was kann man da examiniren? Wie kann man alle Stimmen, und alle Claves jeder Stimme, probiren? Ein oder mehr Tage sollten bey großen Werken dazu genommen werden: Gemeiniglich aber ist man vergnügt, wenns bald und geschwinde vorbey geht, daß man fein bald zur Fresserey kömmt; da läßt man sich es eher gefallen, etwas länger auszuhalten, als bey der Orgelprobe. Werkmeister sagt in der Orgelprobe, Kap. 17. in etlichen Stunden ist es nicht ausgerichtet. Und da ich ebenfalls die Erfahrung auf meiner Seite habe, so sage ich ein Gleiches.

§. 438.

Was die Probe selbst anlanget; so nimmt man den Contrakt vor sich, und untersucht, ob demselben in allen Stücken genug gethan worden. Der Orgelmacher muß vom Anfange bis zum Ende dabey seyn. Ist ein Fehler vorhanden; so läßt man denselbigen aufzeichnen. Allezeit aber kann man den Orgelmacher fragen, warum er dies oder jenes nicht so oder so gemacht? Vielleicht hat er was bessers gefunden, als die Contrahenten verlangt, das kann man folglich für keinen Fehler ansetzen. Ist der Contrakt weitläuftig; so geht das Examen freylich besser von statten, und kann man den Orgelmacher desto eher überführen. Daher ich Kap. 9. gerathen, das vornehmste mit vorzuschreiben. Ist aber solches nicht geschehen (wie, leider! oft geschieht, daß auch die gemeinsten und nothwendigsten Dinge nicht bemerkt werden;) so muß man das Kapitel von den Vollkommenheiten und Fehlern einer Orgel vor sich nehmen, und darnach alles untersuchen: dabey man aber die nothwendigen Dinge von denen zu unterscheiden hat, die nur des Staats oder der Commodität wegen gemacht werden. Auf jene dringt man billig, auf diese aber nicht, wo sie nicht ausdrücklich vorgeschrieben worden.

§. 439.

Ueberhaupt muß man nicht nur sehen auf den itzigen Zustand der Orgel, wie man sie nämlich bey der Probe befindet; sondern auch auf das, was sich künftig zutragen werde. Darauf gründet sich, daß man untersuchen muß, ob das Holz recht durre sey? ob es zu den Parallelen und Dämmen einerley? ꝛc. Denn da verspürt man anfänglich so leicht keine Fehler: wohl aber bey Veränderung des Wetters. Man müßte denn ein Werk zweymal probiren, bey oder nach einer Durrung, und nach feuchtem Wetter noch

relates in his *Organum gruningense** is even worse, that someone had to endure a kick in the pants for daring to speak the truth in an examination. If the Inspectors or others only want to have the instrument praised, then it is not necessary to bring in strangers to do it; this is an art they can manage for themselves. But doing it does not amount to a critique or an examination. I want nothing to do with this sort of complimenting!

§. 437.

Anyone who has read the Chapter "Concerning the Merits and Faults of an Organ"† and who notes what is about to be said will easily be able to judge how much time this task takes. Often the entire instrument is gone over in one hour: but how much examining can take place in that short time? How is it possible to test all the stops, and all the notes of each stop? Examining large instruments should take a day or more—but normally everybody is content to get it over quickly and get on with the eating.‡ They would rather spend more time at that than at the examination of the organ. In Chap. 17 of his *Orgelprobe* Werkmeister says, "It cannot be accomplished in several hours."§ And since I for my part am experienced as well, I say the same thing.

§. 438.

With regard to the examination itself, with the contract at hand one investigates whether it has been adequately fulfilled in all particulars. The organbuilder must be present from start to finish. If a fault is discovered, it should be recorded. One may ask the organbuilder at any time why he did or did not do this or that. Perhaps he has discovered something superior to what the other contracting party¶ required, and consequently this cannot be counted as a fault. The examination will of course be even more successful, and the organbuilder all the easier to convince, if the contract is detailed. Thus in Chap. 9 I advised that all the principal considerations be prescribed in it. If this has not been done (alas, how often it happens that even simplest and most necessary things are not noted), then the chapter on the merits and faults of an organ‖ needs to be kept at hand, and everything investigated according to it. In doing this, though, one must distinguish the things that are necessary from those that have been done only for the sake of display or convenience. One must simply insist on the former, but not on the latter unless they have been expressly prescribed.

§. 439.

In general, not only must the present condition of the organ as it is discovered in the examination be taken into consideration, but also those things that might happen in the future. That is the reason for checking if the wood is thoroughly cured, and if the same wood is used for the sliders and the spacers. For such faults are not easily detected at the outset, but become very evident with a change in the weather. An instrument ought then to be examined twice, once during or after a dry spell, and once

---

* §.13.

† Chapter XIII above.

‡ i.e., the final banquet celebrating the successful completion of the examination; see §.458.

§ "... in etlichen Stunden ist es nicht ausgericht." The use of bold type for this statement suggests that it is a direct quote; that is not the case, although Chapter 17, p. 38, does indeed contain words to this effect.

¶ i.e, the church.

‖ Chapter XIII above.

noch einmal. Dies wäre keineswegs was ungereimtes. Nur Schade, daß es nicht Mode ist! — Man mache aus einer Mücke keinen Elephanten. Ich will damit so viel sagen: wo geringe Fehler vorkommen, die leicht und ohne besondere Unkosten können corrigiret werden, die auch keinen Einfluß in das Verderben des Werks selbst haben; so mache man kein allzugroß Wesen davon: (conf. Organ. grüning. §. 74.) Wie man denn überhaupt alles mit der größten Bescheidenheit vorzutragen, und den Orgelmacher darüber zu vernehmen hat, daß er sehe, man rede aus Liebe zur Wahrheit, und nicht aus Affekten, oder aus Haß gegen ihn, oder seine Erfahrung und Auctorität vor andern sehen zu lassen; wie dergleichen ridicula capita zuweilen angetroffen werden. Was man auch vorbringt, dazu setze man hinlängliche Gründe und Ursachen, damit man die Umstehenden und den Orgelmacher überführe, man habe ein Ding nicht ohne Ursach erinnert.

§. 440.

Man untersuche: ob Holz= Eisen= und alle Metallarbeit gut sey? ob das Elfenbein und Ebenholz richtig? das letztere erfährt man, wenn von etlichen palmulis bald aus der, bald aus jener Oktave, in allen Clavieren etwas abgeschnitten wird, doch hinten, daß man es nicht merkt, oder Schaden thut. Denn wo es nur schwarz gebeitzt ist, da wird man die Farbe bald abkratzen können. Man observirt: ob die palmulae ihre ausgedungene Zahl haben, it. ihre Größe; (dies kann durch den Zirkel geschehen,) ob die palmulae schwer zu drücken? ob man sonderlich die Mordenten und Tremuletten machen könne, daß man nicht saurer darauf arbeiten müsse, als die, so in Westphalen den sogenannten Bumpernickel kneten? (s. Trost l. c. S. 63.) Ob eine schwerer, als die andere, zu drücken? Und wenn dieses ist, muß man untersuchen: ob eine Feder im Windkasten stärker, als die andere? oder ob ein Ventil 2 Federn habe? welches nicht zu leiden, und die Unrichtigkeit des Ventils anzeigt; und was dergleichen mehr. Man kann das 13 Kapitel dieses Traktats vor sich nehmen, und darnach urtheilen.

§. 441.

Ferner untersuche man: ob der Wind stark genug sey? Dazu hat man eine Windprobe vonnöthen, deren Beschreibung im folgenden Kapitel zu finden. Diese Windprobe füllet man mit Wasser, stecket die gläserne Röhre an gehörigen Ort; steckt das Instrument in das Löchelchen des Windkanals, das sich dazu schickt, und hält den Maaßstab an die gläserne Röhre, daran man absiehet, wie hoch der Wind das Wasser treibe. Nachdem eine Kirche groß ist, nachdem sind auch starke Werke nöthig, folglich auch starker Wind. Denn je stärker der Wind ist, desto stärker schreyet die Orgel. Aber man muß sich auch nach dem Pfeifwerke richten. Gut Pfeifwerk kann auch einen stärkern Wind vertragen, als geringes und dünnes. Ist nun der Wind allzuschwach; so hat man destomehr Ursach, zu forschen: ob es etwann geschehen, weil das Pfeifwerk nicht viel nutz ist? Auch spühret man bey starkem Winde das Durchstechen der Lade mehr, daher es ein Zeichen einer übel abgerichteten Lade ist

again after damp weather. This is in no way an absurd suggestion. What a pity that it is not customary! One should not make a mountain out of a molehill. I will say this much: wherever there are minor faults that may be corrected easily and without undue expense, and that also do not have an adverse effect on the instrument itself, then one ought not to make a big fuss about them (cf. *Organum gruningense*, §.74). One ought then to carry out the entire operation in complete moderation, and to question the organbuilder about it [in such a way] that he sees one is speaking out of love for the truth and not impulsively or out of hatred toward him, or to flaunt one's experience and authority before others (one encounters such foolish people at times). Anything that is brought up should be supported with sufficient reason and cause, in order to convince those present as well as the organbuilder that the matter has not been mentioned idly.

§. 440.

One should investigate whether the wood- and iron-work, as well as all the metal-work, is good, and whether the ivory and ebony have been properly [applied to the keys]. In this regard. The latter may be ascertained if bits have been cut off some of the keys, in one octave or another and on all manuals, but at the back so that it cannot be noticed or damaged. For where [a key] is only stained black, the stain can easily be scratched off it.* Observe whether the number of keys are as contracted, and whether their size is correct (this may be achieved with dividers). Is the key action heavy? Can mordents and trills be played without working at it harder than those who knead pumpernickel [bread] (as it is called) in Westphalia (see Trost, l.c., p.63)? Is one key harder to depress than another? If so, one must investigate whether one spring is stronger than another in the pallet boxes, or whether one pallet has two springs. This should not be tolerated, since it shows an error has been made in the pallets (and other shortcomings as well). The 13th chapter of this treatise may be kept at hand and used to judge such matters.

* thus revealing the organbuilder's deceit.

§. 441.†

One should further investigate whether there is sufficient wind. For this a windgauge is needed; it will be described in the next chapter.‡ This windgauge is filled with water and the glass tube is inserted at the proper place. The gauge is inserted into the little hole in the wind duct that is designed for this purpose, and a ruler is held next to the glass tube to see how high the wind forces the water. The larger the church, the louder the instrument must be and consequently the stronger the wind, since the greater the wind pressure, the louder the organ sounds. But the pipe work plays a role in this, as well. Good pipes can endure a heavier wind pressure than poor, thin[-walled] ones. But if the wind [pressure] is too weak, then there is even more reason to investigate it. Is it perhaps so because the pipe work is of poor quality? Runs in the chest are also more [easily] detected when the wind [pressure] is heavy, and thus it is a sign of an inaccurately built chest if the wind [pressure] is too weak. Various organs

† Much of this paragraph is taken from Chapter 25 of Werkmeister's *Orgelprobe*.
‡ §.460.

ist, wenn der Wind allzuschwach ist.   Etliche Orgeln haben 15°, 20°, 30°, 40°, 45° bis 50°   Das ist, der Maaßstab wird in Grade getheilet, die Länge von 6 Zoll etwann in 60 Grade, (wiewol man es nicht bey allen überein antrift) so treibet dann der Wind das Wasser zuweilen 15 oder 20 solcher Theile oder Grade hoch; welches aber ein elender Wind ist.   30° geht noch mit.   35° oder 40° ist der beste. Denn ein gar zu großes Geschrey ist nicht anmuthig, und verderben die Orgeln desto eher.   Wo große Stimmen sind, da ist ohnedieß ein stärkerer Wind vonnöthen, als bey kleinern, weil dessen Zufall sonst zu schwach wird.

§. 442.

Mit eben der Windprobe erforschet man, ob des einen Balges Wind præcise so stark sey, als des andern.   Wenn ein Balg das Wasser im Glase höher treibt, als der andere; so ist der Wind nicht gleich.   Man muß dabey jeden Balg ganz alleine treten lassen.   Folglich muß man durch Abnehmen oder Zulegen das Gewicht der Bälge ändern, bis der Wind gleich wird.   De Chales l. c. Prop. 13. sagt, er habe gefunden, daß bey Tretung zweyer Bälge der Wind stärker worden, als bey einem, und folglich auch der Sonus höher: deswegen solle man den Wind in ein Receptaculum bringen (ehe er in die Orgel kömmt) dessen Loch, wo es den Wind in die Orgel schickt, viel kleiner seyn solle, als ein Loch eines Balges, so würde bey einem Balge satt Wind seyn, bey den beyden würde das Loch den Wind zum Theil abhalten.   Aber dieß Vorgeben ist nicht gar zu richtig: man mache nur den Wind gleich durch die Windprobe, was gilts, es wird sich kein Unterschied finden, ob man einen oder mehr Bälge tritt.   Daß aber die Windröhren weit seyn müssen, daß der Zufall des Windes stark genug werde, ist ohne dieß an gehörigem Orte schon erinnert.   Ist der Wind in allen vorhandenen Bälgen just abgewogen, und gleich gemacht; so muß man nachhero untersuchen und forschen, ob auch der Zufall des Windes stark genug sey. Dies erfährt man auf folgende Art: man zieht das volle Werk, und spielt scharf, greift viel zusammen, auch im Pedale tritt man, wo es sich schickt, die Palmuln doppelt, und merkt dabey genau, ob die Schärfe da sey; imgleichen, ob das Werk reine bleibe, wenn vorher alle Stimmen, einzeln betrachtet, reine gewesen. Ist das Werk falsch, so ist der Wind jetzo gewiß schwächer, als da man mit wenigen Stimmen spielte: folglich fällt der Wind nicht in gehöriger Menge in die Cancellen, daß er soviel Pfeifen anblasen könnte.   Hierher gehört auch, und ist gewissermaaßen ebendas, wenn die großen Pfeifen den kleinern den Wind rauben.   Dies erfährt man, wenn man im vollen Werke in der untern Oktave läuft; (oder, wenn das Pedal keine eigene Bälge hat, kann man im Pedale laufen) unterdessen aber in den obern Oktaven hält.   Wenn sodann die kleinern Pfeifen anfangen zu schluchzen, oder bleiben wol gar aussen; (welches auch geschiehet, wenn man in den obern palmulis läuft) so ist es abermals ein Zeichen von dem oben angezeigten Fehler.   Solchem Mangel ist nicht leicht abzuhelfen: und wo dergleichen Knoten vorkommen, da sieht es übel aus mit dem Orgelmacher.   Wo ein **Windkoppel**

have 15°, 20°, 30°, 40°, 45° or even 50°. This means that the ruler is divided into degrees, 60 degrees over about 6 inches (although there is no universal standard in this). Sometimes the wind drives the water 15 or 20 of such sections or degrees high, but that is a feeble wind. 30° is acceptable. 35° or 40° is the best. For too loud a roar is not pleasant and causes the organ to deteriorate faster.[*] A heavier wind [pressure] is of course necessary when there are large stops than when there are little ones, because otherwise there is not an ample supply of wind.

[*] perhaps due to greater wear on the wind system.

§. 442.

This same wind gauge is used to investigate whether the wind from one bellows is exactly as strong as that from another. If one bellows drives the water in the glass [tube] higher than another, then the wind is not equal. For this [test] each bellows must be pumped totally by itself. Thereafter the weights on the bellows must be either decreased or increased until the wind is equal. De Chales, *l.c.*,[†] Prop. 13, says he has discovered that pumping two bellows makes the wind stronger, and thus the pitch higher, than [pumping] one; therefore the wind should be conducted into a reservoir before it reaches the organ, and the hole through which wind is dispatched into the organ should be much smaller than the holes from the bellows; thus one bellows will provide enough wind, but the hole will partially restrain the wind when both are in operation. But this theory is not really correct. The wind need only be made equal using the wind gauge, and then it makes no difference whether one or more bellows is being pumped. It has already been mentioned at the appropriate spot[‡] that the wind ducts must be wide so that there is an ample supply of wind. If the wind is exactly balanced and made equal from all available bellows, one must then investigate and determine whether the supply of wind is ample. This is done in the following way. One draws all the stops and plays staccato, playing full chords, pedal included (where appropriate), doubling notes, and in doing so one takes careful note whether the brilliance is still there, and also whether the instrument stays in tune (provided that each individual stop is already in tune). If the instrument sounds out of tune, then the wind is assuredly weaker than when only a few stops were being played. Consequently an ample quantity of wind to feed all those pipes is not reaching the channels. Here should also be included (since it is to some degree the same [shortcoming]) large pipes robbing wind from smaller ones. This may be detected by playing runs in the lowest octave on full organ (or if the pedal has no separate bellows, runs may be played in the pedal) while holding octaves in the treble. If the smaller pipes then begin to gulp or do not sound at all (this also happens if runs are played on the treble keys), then it is once again a sign of the fault indicated above. Such a defect is not easily remedied, and where such difficulties appear they do not speak well of the organbuilder. If there is a *Windkoppel* on

[†] Vol. III, Tract 22.

[‡] cf. §.366 and §.380.

pel vorhanden, da das Manual ins Pedal gebracht wird, da muß man untersuchen: ob der Wind auch äqual sey? oder ob vielleicht dadurch das Werk unrein werde? Man spiele etwan mit dem Claviere, welches gekoppelt werden kann; doch allein, und ohne Koppel, und observire, ob es reine sey. Alsdann ziehe man das volle Pedal, und das Koppel dazu. Wo man nun hier eine Unreinigkeit antrifft; so ist der Wind falsch durch das Koppel. Denn wenn das völlige Manual reine ist, und das Pedal mit demselben Manuale, und es wird nach der Ziehung des Koppels unrein; so muß nothwendig der Fehler im Windkoppel seyn.

§. 443.

Man untersuche ferner: ob die Bälge allzusehr schwanken? Und dies geschiehet also: einige Probisten treten bey die Bälge und observiren; einer setzt sich auf die Orgel und spielt hackend, vollstimmig, im Pedale und Manuale, mit vollem Werke. Da wird man sehen, ob die Calcaturclaves so große Sätze und Sprünge auf- und abwärts machen. Geschiehet dieses; so ists ein Fehler. Es gehen aber dabey viel Betrügereyen vor, und kann man von einer Orgel nicht reden, wie von der andern. Denn man tritt ordentlich bey die Calcaturclaves, wenn man observiren will, welche aber nicht bey allen Orgeln gleich weit in die Höhe gehen, obschon die Bälge gleichviel abwärts gegangen; welches aus dem klar ist, was §. 377. vorgetragen worden, dessen Nutzen sich hier zeigt. Also kann ein Orgelmacher nur kurze Claves machen; oder er kann die Mittelsäule weit hervor legen; so wird man das Fahren der Bälge um viel weniger merken. Besser thut man, wenn man bey die Bälge selbst tritt, und observirt genau, was sich damit zuträgt. Auch entstehet hier ein Unterschied unter großen und kleinen Bälgen. Denn gleich wie diese durch starkes Spielen und viel Stimmen eher erschöpft werden, als jene, also müssen sie auch stärker in die Höhe fahren. Am meisten ist hier zu merken, daß das simple Auffahren des Calcaturclavis, oder das Herniederfahren des Balges von dem Schwanken wohl zu unterscheiden ist. Jenes kann nicht verboten werden, weil es natürlich ist, daß ein Balg mehr Wind verliehrt, folglich sich schneller setzt, wenn viel Stimmen auf einmal ihm den Wind benehmen, als wenn man alles verschliesset, indem man hackend spielt. Das Schwanken aber ist ein Fehler, wenn dabey der Calcaturclavis in die Höhe fähret, und hernach wieder etwas herunter. Oder wenn der Balg abwärts fähret, und hernach wieder aufwärts. Dieses muß bey der Probe als ein Fehler angemerkt werden; denn es zeigt eine große Unrichtigkeit in der Windlade an. Die Bälge selbst misset man nach der Länge und Breite, und erkundiget sich, ob etliche ins Pedal besonders gehen oder nicht, nachdem es bedungen worden. Doch bey dem Messen darf man die rheinländischen Schuhe, welche ½ Elle halten, nicht mit dem geometrischen verwechseln, welche größer sind. Ordentlich versteht man im Contrakte die erste Art.

§. 444.

Man examinire auch die Windlade, ob sich schwedische Stiche darinne finden, oder sonst ein Fehler, (conf. §. 362.) da man die Lade nicht richtig gemacht, daher sie durchsticht.

and Examination of Organs

the organ by which manual [stops] are brought to the pedal, then one must also investigate whether the wind is equal;† or does it perhaps make the instrument [sound] out of tune? One should [begin by] playing, say, the manual that can be coupled, but by itself, without the coupler, and observe whether it is in tune. Then the full pedal should be drawn together with the *Windkoppel*. If any out-of-tuneness is encountered in this procedure, then the wind is being disturbed by the coupler. For if the manual is in tune when all the stops are pulled and the pedal is in tune with it, and it becomes out of tune when the coupler is drawn, then the defect must of necessity be in the *Windkoppel*.

§. 443.

Furthermore, one should investigate whether the bellows shake too much. This is done as follows: several examiners stand next to the bellows and watch, while another sits at the organ and plays big choppy chords on both manual and pedal on the full organ. Then it becomes obvious if the bellows-pole makes large jerks and jumps up and down. If this happens, it is a defect. Much deceit is connected with this, however, and no two organs are alike. To observe this it is usual to stand next to the bellows-poles, but these do not rise the same distance in every organ, even though the bellows travel the same distance; this is clear from what has been explained in §.377, whose usefulness is revealed here. Thus an organbuilder may make only short poles, or he may set the fulcrum-post far forward,‡ and then the bellows' travel§ will be far less noticeable. It would be better to stand next to the bellows themselves and take careful notice what is occurring. Here there also arises a difference between large and small bellows. For since the latter are exhausted sooner than the former by loud playing and thick textures, they must therefore rise more forcefully. In this connection it is most important to distinguish the normal rise of the bellows-pole or the collapse of the bellows from their shaking. The former cannot be prevented, since it is natural for a bellows to lose more wind and collapse more quickly if a thick texture suddenly deprives it of wind than if the player blocks [the wind] by playing abruptly. Shaking is a defect, however, if it causes the bellows-pole to rise and then to fall somewhat again, or [if it causes] the bellows to fall and then to rise again. In the examination this must be noted as a defect, for it indicates a major error in the windchest. The bellows themselves must be measured [to ascertain] their length and width, and it must be determined if some of them feed the pedal separately, according to the requirements of the contract. In measuring, though, it is important not to confuse the Rhineland foot (which contains ½ a yard) from the geometric [foot], which is larger.¶ Contracts ordinarily presume the first type.

§. 444.

The windchest should be examined for any bleed grooves or any other defect (cf. §.362), since the chest has runs because it is not properly constructed. In order

---

* There are two pages numbered 71 and two pages numbered 72 in vol. 2.

† i.e., when the stops are drawn and played in the manual, and then drawn and played in the pedal.

‡ i.e., away from the bellows.

§ i.e., any motion the bellows makes, including any shaking.

¶ See §.78.

sticht. Um nun dieses Durchstechen zu verwehren, so schneidet man Ritzen in die Lade, welche diesen Namen führen, sonst auch Laufgraben und spanische Reuter genennet werden. Sie sehen also aus: \| \/ und wie man sie sonst machet. Will man diese Fehler finden; so schraube man bald hinten, bald vorn, etliche Stöcke ab, welches der Orgelmacher leiden muß, obschon etliche darüber brummen. Ingleichen wollen die Orgelmacher das Durchstechen verwehren, (was das heiße, steht §. 358.) wenn man die Pfeife unten kneipt, oder durchbohrt; (conf. §. 384.) daher der Probist bald da bald dort Pfeifen ausheben und besichtigen kann. Man sieht leicht, daß man dieses nach examinirter Stimmung thun müsse, weil man sonst dadurch leicht etwas verstimmt. Ich meynte, es gienge eben so gut, ob man den Fuß kneipte, oder ob man mit einem Instrumente im Loche, worinne die Pfeife steht, etwas einschnitte, daß der Wind gleichfalls darneben heraus kommen könne. Ob es einer schon prakticirt, weis ich nicht. Ein Probist kann also auch observieren, ob die Löcher recht rund sind? Alle Pfeifen, und alle Stöcke kann man wol nicht abheben; doch sollte man es mit mehrern thun, als es insgemein geschiehet, um den Orgelmachern eine Furcht einzujagen. Die Fliegenschnäpper und Sternlöcher sucht man auch auf.

§. 445.

Man probire übrigens, ob die Lade durchsteche; also: man nehme nur ein Register, und zwar ein kleines, das nicht viel Wind wegnimmt, und spiele ganz langsam in lauter großen Terzen, oder gehe sie vielmehr also durch, und observire, ob eine dritte Pfeife sich hören lasse. Denn die Orgeln sind ordenlich also disponirt, daß ein Clavis, z. Ex. c im Thurme zur Rechten steht, und zwar zur rechten Hand, der ander cis im Thurme zur linken Hand, etwan nach der linken Hand; die dritte d wieder im rechten Thurme, aber gegen die linke Hand des davor sitzenden Organisten: also liegt ihre Cancelle nicht neben der vorigen; die 4te dis im Thurm der linken Hand, doch nach der Rechten des Organisten: diese Cancelle liegt auch nicht neben der vorigen, die im Thurme war. Der 5te liegt wieder zur Rechten im rechten Thurme: also liegt diese Cancelle neben der ersten. Daraus sieht man, daß man durch große Terzen gehen müsse, wenn man observiren will, ob der Wind in die benachbarte Cancelle schleiche? doch noch besser hört man es, wenn man, bey ietzt erzählter Positur der Pfeifen, (denn sie ist nicht allezeit so) durch kleine Sexten geht, da zwischen zwo angeblasenen Cancellen eine leer steht, welche also von beyden Seiten etwas Wind bekommen kann, wenn die benachbarten Cancellen nicht wohl verwahret sind, daher auch das Durchstechen eher gehöret wird in der leeren Cancelle. Durch Terzen aber zu gehen ist alsdenn rathsam, wenn ein Thurm diese figur hat: .·.·. oder: ·.·.· nicht aber: .·.·. ; auch wenn

man

to prevent these runs, grooves that bear this name† are incised into the chest; they are also called *Laufgraben* and *spanische Reuter*. They assume these shapes, among others: \\ \/ In order to detect these defects, someone should loosen some of the toe-board screws, sometimes in front, sometimes at the back. The organbuilder must allow this, even though some of them grumble about it. Organbuilders likewise try to prevent runs (for the meaning of this term see §.358) by nipping/pinching the bottom of the pipe, or puncturing it (cf. §.384); therefore the examiner may lift out pipes here and there and look them over. It is easy to see that this should be done after the tuning has been examined, since in doing it it is easy to put something out of tune. I would think it would work just as well whether one nips/pinches the foot or makes a little incision with a tool in the toe-hole in which the pipe sits; in either case the wind could escape at the side of [the pipe]. But I do not know whether someone actually practices [the latter]. An examiner may also observe whether the toe-holes are perfectly round. It is of course impossible to remove all the pipes and all the toe-boards, but it should be done with several of them, something that is commonly done to give the organbuilder a fright. One should also look for *Fliegenschnäpper* and *Sternlöcher*.‡

§. 445.

Moreover, the chest should be tested for runs, in this way: a single stop should be drawn, a little one that does not use much wind, and someone should play a series of major thirds very slowly, or rather play through every one of them [on that stop], and note whether [with any of them] a third pipe also sounds. For organs are ordinarily laid out with one pipe, e.g., c, at the right side of the right tower, the next, c#, at the left side of the left tower, the third, d, again in the right tower, but at the left side of it (thus its channel does not lie next to the previous [pipe]); the fourth, d#, at the right side of the left tower (this channel also does not lie next to the previous pipe in that tower). The fifth [pipe] again sits at the right side of the right tower, and therefore its channel lies next to that of the first pipe. This makes it clear that it is necessary to proceed by major thirds if one wishes to ascertain whether wind is seeping into the neighboring channel. One may hear it even better, though, by proceeding by minor sixths (providing that the arrangement of the pipes is described above--but it is not always so). Then there is an empty channel between the two that are being winded, and therefore some wind may enter from both sides if the neighboring channels are not well sealed; thus it is more likely that running may be heard in the empty channel. But it is advisable to move by thirds if a tower has this shape: or this: but not this: ; it is likewise

---

* There are two pages numbered 71 and two pages numbered 72 in vol. 2.

† i.e., *schwedische Stiche*; but elsewhere (§.362) *schwedische Stiche* seems to refer to bleed holes, while *spanische Reuter* seems to refer to bleed grooves. See also §.256.

‡ Both of these are types of incisions in the chest to bear off unwanted wind and prevent runs. On pp. 349-50 of his *Anleitung zu der musikalischen Gelahrtheit*, Adlung writes: "Inaccurate craftsmen attempt all sorts of tricks to bear off the unwanted wind, such as *spanische Reiter*, *Fliegenschnäpper*, or other incisions, *Sternlöcher*, holes in the feet of pipes, nipped/pinched pipes, and whatever other unacceptable tricks they can dream up." Adlung describes *Sternlöcher* in his *Anleitung*, p. 538: star-shaped holes (instead of perfectly round ones) in which the pipe feet rest, creating tiny channels to let the wind escape. He does not describe *Fliegenschnäpper*, but the context suggests they are some variety of scoring/bleed groves; cf. §.256.

man die größte Pfeife eines jeden Thurmes zur untersten annimmt, und sodann in Terzen fortgehet.

§. 446.

Eine andere Art des Durchstechens ist, wenn ein schwaches Pfeifen vernommen wird, da doch kein Register offen ist. Und dies zeigt an, daß die Lade auswendig, oder die Parallelen nicht just seyn, und daß die Parallelen nicht allewege vest aufliegen: daher der in den Kanälen sich findende Wind unter den Parallelen sich hinschleicht, und ein Singen verursachet. Dies erfähret der Probist, wenn er alle Register zudrückt, (doch recht accurat, daß die Löcher nicht etwas vom Winde naschen) und drückt mit den Armen, oder, welches besser ist, durch ein Brett alle Claves eines Claviers nieder, sowol die chromatischen, als auch die diatonischen, und läßt die Bälge treten, und observirt alsdann, ob sich ein Zischen oder Klingen hören läßt. Denn auch das Zischen zeigt an, daß der Wind unter den Parallelen durchwandere. Dieses thue man bey jeder Lade besonders, sowol im Manuale, als auch im Pedale. Doch ist ein loses Stück der Orgelmacher hier nicht zu verschweigen. Denn manche (nicht alle) haben in dem Hauptkanal ein heimlich Ventil, dessen §. 381. schon gedacht worden, (wiewol dort ein anderer Gebrauch desselben gemeldet worden) wenn sie nun sehen, daß das Durchstechen auf besagte Weise soll untersuchet werden; so schließen sie dadurch den Wind von der Lade aus: dadurch vergeht ihr das Zischen und Durchstechen. Aber dieser Betrügerey geht man entgegen, wenn man dies unversehens thut, und erst mit dem vollen Werke spielt, um zu hören, ob der Wind völlig da sey, und unterdessen befiehlt, daß alles, was den Orgelmacher angehet, und er selbst, vor die Orgel trete, und alsdann diese Probe anstelle, damit keiner den Wind versperren könne, wenn auch gleich ein heimlich Ventil da wäre. (NB. Wo Ventile unter den Registern sind, die müssen bey der Probe aufgezogen werden, sonst kommt kein Wind zur Lade.) Könnte man nicht erhalten, daß bey der Probe der Orgelmacher, und was sonst verdächtig ist, bey dem Probisten zugegen seyn müßten; so könnte man unter der Probe zuweilen ein klingend Register herausziehen, um zu vernehmen, ob der Wind noch in der Lade sey. Soviel ist hierbey noch zu bedenken, daß, wenn diese Probe im dürren Wetter geschiehet, es allzuleer nicht wol abgehe, und muß man sich also darinne wohl bescheiden, daß man dem Orgelmacher keinen Verdruß mache, um etwas, das nicht zu ändern ist. Denn das Holz verwirft sich und schwindet in einer großen Dürre, und wenn es viele Jahre alt wäre. Darum habe ich oben gerathen, solche Dinge 2mal zu probiren; nämlich in feuchtem und dürrem Wetter.

§. 447.

Ferner untersuche man die Temperatur, da man das Principal allein probiren kann. Man gehe durch Quinten, oder spiele aus allerhand Tönen, um zu hören, ob ein Modus so rein sey, als der andere. Hernach gehe man das Principal ganz durch, und zwar durch Oktaven. Was sich auch hier für unreine Pfeifen finden, die werden

[advisable] to proceed by thirds if the largest pipe of each tower is used as the lowest [note].

§. 446.

Another type of run produces a weak whistling when [a note is played and] yet no stop is drawn. This indicates that the outer walls of the chest or the sliders are not precisely [made], and that the sliders do not fit tightly everywhere; thus the wind in the channels seeps out under the sliders, causing a whistling noise. An examiner may determine this by pushing in all the stops (being careful to do that completely so that the holes do not nibble a bit of the wind), and depressing all of the keys of a manual, the chromatic as well as the diatonic, with his arms, or even better, with a board; then he should have the bellows pumped, and observe whether any hissing or tinkling may be heard. For hissing also indicates that the wind is passing under the sliders. This [procedure] should be done with each chest separately, both manual and pedal. Here, though, we ought not to pass over a roguish trick of organbuilders in silence. Many of them (not all) have a secret ventil in the main wind duct; this has already been mentioned in §.381, although there a different use for it was described. If they see that the method stated above is about to be used to check for runs, they close off the wind from the chest with it, and thus the hissing and running disappears. But this deceit may be countered by proceeding without warning, playing first on the full organ to hear if the wind is fully present, and at the same time ordering that everything connected with the organbuilder, as well as he himself, move in front of the organ; then this test may be carried out without anyone being able to shut off the wind, even if there were a secret ventil (NB. If the ventils are controlled by stopknobs, these must be drawn for the test, otherwise no wind will enter the chest). If it is impossible to keep the organbuilder and anything else suspicious in the presence of the examiner for the test, then [the examiner] may occasionally draw one of the sounding stops during the test to check if wind is still in the chest. This must also be kept in mind: if this test is being conducted in dry weather, the examination might not proceed without problems, and one must be more easily satisfied, in order to spare the organbuilder any dismay over something that cannot be avoided. For wood warps and shrinks in very dry weather, no matter how many years old it is.* For that reason I have advised above† that such things should be tested twice, both in damp as well as in dry weather.

* i.e., how well it is cured.
† in §.439.

§. 447.

Furthermore, the temperament should be tested by testing the [8'] Principal alone. One should proceed through [the circle of] fifths, or play in all sorts of keys, to hear if one key is as pure as another. Next the Principal should be entirely gone through in octaves. Any out-of-tune pipes found [in these tests] should also be noted

zur Correktion angemerkt. Für allen Dingen untersuche man, ob das Werk im richtigen Chortone stehe; es wäre denn, daß es im Contrakte ausdrücklich ausbedungen worden, daß es Kammerton seyn sollte. Hernach gehe man alle Stimmen durch, und halte sie gegen das Principal, ob sie alle vollkommen rein sind. So auch mit den gemischten Stimmen. Bey diesen letztern aber hat man genau zu observiren, ob etwan etliche Pfeifen nicht anschlagen, oder vielleicht gar an den Labien verdruckt worden, weil die Intonation nicht von statten gehen wollen. Bey Sesquialtern, Rauschpfeifen, Koppeln, ꝛc. kann man es bald hören: aber nicht so gut bey Mixturen, Scharpen und Cymbeln, da man also dann und wann die Pfeifen ausheben und mit dem Munde anblasen kann, um dadurch gewiß zu vernehmen, ob sie klingen. Also sieht man, was von Rechts wegen für Zeit zur Probe eines Orgelwerks erfordert wird. Bey dem Examen kann man auch, (wie es billig seyn muß) anmerken, ob eine Pfeife staddert, silpet, sich etwan in die Oktave oder Quinte überschreyet; welche Fehler allerdings geändert werden müssen: oder wo es nicht angeht, so muß der Orgelmacher neue Pfeifen hinsetzen. Bey Schnarrwerken kann man die Reinigkeit nicht so genau verlangen, weil sie sich leicht verstimmen. Es liegt auch nichts daran, weil dieselben allezeit können gestimmt werden.

§. 448.

Bey eben diesem Examen kann man aufmerken: ob eine Pfeife stärker oder schwächer klinge, als es die Natur des Registers erfordert? It. ob jedes Register seiner Natur und Eigenschaft gemäß klingt? Hierbey erinnere ich, daß wenige Organisten fremde Orgeln beschauet haben, daher sie auch nicht wissen, wie z. Er. Bärpfeife, Krumhorn, Salcional u. a. m. zu klingen pflegen. Wenn nun einer dergleichen nie gehöret hat, wie kann er deren Natur wissen? Andere Register haben von Instrumenten den Namen: allein man kann wenige vollkommen gleich machen. Hat nun einer sie nicht anderswo etlichemal gehöret, wie kann er davon urtheilen? Will er sagen es gleicht dem Instrumente nicht völlig, wovon es den Namen hat; so wird er mit seiner Censur ausgelacht: denn das kann man nicht verlangen. [80]) Hierher gehört auch, daß man untersu-

[80]) Zur Ergänzung dessen, was der Hr. Verfasser vorgetragen, will ich noch folgendes hinzufügen: Man hat nämlich hierbey wohl zu überlegen, daß ein Register mit dem andern, theils was die Materie, theils auch was die Arbeit betrifft, vollkommen gleich seyn kann; demohngeachtet kann es doch wol kommen, daß es nicht so klingt, als das, welcher der Probiste gehöret, und nach welchem er ebendasselbe in einer andern Orgel beurtheilen will. Denn überhaupt kann sowol die Kirche, als auch die Lage der Orgel, wie auch der Ort, wo das Register in der Orgel seine Stellung erhalten, den Klang verändern; sonderlich aber trägt der Wind sehr viel hierzu bey. Denn wenn die Stimmen in diesem Werke nicht just eben den Wind haben, als in jenem; so klingen sie einander nicht vollkommen gleich. Oder wenn der Wind an einem Orte weiter zu einer Stimme geleitet wird; so wird sie so stark auch nicht klingen, als wo derselbe nicht weit darnach gehen darf. Diejenigen, welche aus der Physick die Lehren von der Luft verstehen, werden die Richtigkeit dieser Sache leicht einsehen, ohne daß ich nöthig hätte, dasjenige aus der Natur, Elasticität und Drücken der Luft zu beweisen, was ich hier gesagt habe.

for correction. Above all the instrument must be examined to determine if it is tuned in proper *Chorton*, unless it has been expressly stated in the contract that it should be in *Kammerton*. Next all the stops should be gone through, comparing them against the Principal to ascertain if they are perfectly in tune. The same goes for the compound stops; in testing these one must carefully observe whether there may be some pipes that do not speak, or whose lips may even have been pressed shut because they could not be successfully voiced. In Sesquialteras, Rauschpfeifen, Koppeln, etc., this can be heard immediately, but not as readily in Mixtures, Scharffs and Cymbels, and therefore pipes should be removed now and then and blown by mouth to perceive for sure if they are sounding. Thus one may see just how much time is rightfully required to examine an organ. During the examination it should (and simply must) be noted whether any pipe flutters, misspeaks, or perhaps overblows at the octave or fifth. Such defects must of course be rectified; or if this cannot be done, then the organbuilder must supply new pipes. It is not possible to demand that the reeds be precisely in tune, since they so easily go out of tune. This is of no great consequence, since they may be tuned again at any time.*

* i.e., they are easier to get to and to tune than the flue pipes.

§. 448.

In the same examination it can be noted if one pipe sounds louder or softer than the nature of the stop requires; likewise if each stop sounds in conformity with its nature and character. In this regard let me mention that few organists have inspected organs other than their own, and thus they are not familiar with, for example, what a Bärpfeife, a Krumhorn, a Salcional, etc., are supposed to sound like. If somebody has never heard such stops, how can he know what their nature is? Some stops get their names from instruments, but few can be made to sound identical to their namesakes. Now if someone has not heard such a stop several times somewhere else, how can he make any judgment about it? Should he assert that it does not sound exactly like the instrument for which it was named, his criticism would be ridiculed, since no one can demand such a thing.[80] It is also a part of the examination to determine whether any pipe within a given stop

[80] To supplement what the author has expounded, I would like to add the following: in this regard one must consider that even though one stop may be absolutely identical to another in materials and workmanship, it may well be that it nevertheless does not sound like one that the examiner has heard and according to which he must now evaluate the same stop in another organ. Speaking in general, the church, the location of the organ and also the place where the stop lies within the organ case can alter the sound; and in particular the winding may contribute a great deal to this [difference]. For if the stops in one instrument do not have exactly the same winding as in another, then the two of them will not sound exactly alike. Or if the wind has to be conducted further to one stop, then it will not sound as loud as another where the wind need not go as far. Those who are familiar with physics and understand the theory of air will easily see the correctness of this assertion, without making it necessary to prove it from the character, the elasticity and the pressure of air. [Albrecht].

tersuche: ob eine Pfeife in einem und ebendemselben Register stärker klinge, als andere? Wo man dieses antrift, da hat man Ursach deswegen zu reden, weil es ein großer Fehler ist. Wenn endlich die Pfeifen stärker klingen, als die Natur des Registers erfordert; so kann man sie leicht im Labio weiter verschneiden, daß sie stumpfer gehen: aber wenn sie zu schwach lauten, und sind schon verschnitten; so ist ihnen nicht wohl zu helfen, und der Orgelmacher ist anzuhalten, diesen Fehler durch andere Pfeifen zu verbessern. Ich habe Orgelmacher gehört, welche bey schwachen Pfeifen sagten: **Das Register bringt es so mit sich.** Sagte man: warum ist die andere stark im Klange? So war die Antwort: **Man könne es den Leuten nicht stark genug machen.** Das war listig!

§. 449.

Bey dem Stärkerklingen einer Pfeife für der andern hat man eine Cautel zu merken, die §. 387. auch berühret worden, daß nämlich unsere Ohren zuweilen betrogen werden; man trete also bey die Pfeife; oder hebe sie aus und höre sie besonders. Alle Pfeifen jedes Registers sind besonders zu examiniren. Wobey noch anzumerken: ob dieselben in der gehörigen Geschwindigkeit anschlagen? doch in scharfen Registern, und engen offenen Mensuren kann man die Geschwindigkeit nicht fordern, wie bey den andern, wo man der Pfeife die Schärfe nicht nehmen will. Also schlägt die Violdigamba, wenn sie recht enge ist, so geschwinde nicht an, als andere Stimmen. [81])

§. 450.

Man untersuche auch: ob das Werk windsiech sey? das ist: ob eine Stimme der andern den Wind raube? Dieß geschiehet, wenn die Cancellen zu enge, die Ventile zu schmahl, und folglich der Zufall des Windes nicht stark genug ist; daher der Wind in die großen Pfeifen nicht hinreicht, wenn die andern auch ihren Theil davon nehmen. Dieses erfährt man, wenn man bey der Probe alle Stimmen gegen das Principal, oder unter sich, einzeln als reine befunden, hernach aber etliche, oder alle zusammen zieht, und eine Unreinigkeit bemerkt. Denn ist eine jede Stimme für sich reine, so muß auch das volle Werk reine seyn, wenn der Wind nicht fehlt.

§. 451.

Man visitire das Pfeifwerk, erstlich: ob jede Stimme, und alle Pfeifen derselben von der Materie gemacht worden, die im Contrakte benennt ist? Bey dem Metalle examinire man dessen Güte, oder ob es so gemischt, wie es vorgeschrieben? Dieß kann der Zinngießer am besten thun? Doch wissen Organisten die Art es zu erforschen zuweilen auch. Sie thun es bisweilen durch Probiersteine. Ich wollte es auch durchs Wasser finden: denn ich wollte eine Pfeife nehmen, die z. E. von purem Zinn seyn sollte, und wollte sie wiegen. Hernach wollte ich ein Stück anderes gutes Zinn nehmen von gleichem Gewicht, und ein Gefäß mit Wasser anfüllen, das Zinn hinein legen,

---

[81]) Die **Quintatön, Salicional,** ingl. **Fugara,** thun es auch nicht.

sounds louder than others. Where one encounters this, then one must inquire into the reason for it, since it is a major defect. If the pipes do indeed sound louder than the nature of the stop requires, their lips may easily be cut up higher, so they become duller. But when they sound too soft and are already cut up, then they are beyond alteration, and the organbuilder should be bound to remedy this defect by [supplying] other pipes. I have heard of organbuilders who say of soft pipes, "It is inherent in the stop." When someone asked why another [pipe] had a loud sound, the answer came, "It is impossible to make it strong enough for [these] people." That was deceitful!

§. 449.

There is a *caveat* to note if one pipe sounds louder than another, and it has already been touched upon in §.387: namely, our ears are sometimes fooled. It is necessary to move close to the pipe, or to remove it and listen to it separately. All the pipes of each stop should be tested separately, noting whether they speak with appropriate promptness. But in keen stops, ones that are open and of narrow scale, the same promptness as other stops cannot be required without robbing the pipe of its keenness. Thus a Violdigamba, if it is really of narrow scale, will not speak as promptly as other stops.[81]

§. 450.

It is also necessary to investigate whether the instrument is wind-starved, that is, does one stop rob the wind from others? This comes about from the channels being too narrow, the pallets too small, and the resulting lack of a sufficiently strong wind supply. Thus the wind is not sufficient for the large pipes if the others are also using their share of it. This [fault] becomes evident if, in the course of the test, one has checked all the stops against the Principal or against each other and has found them to be in tune, but subsequently detects out-of-tuneness in some [combination] of them, or in all of them together. For if each stop by itself is in tune, then the full organ must also be in tune, unless there is insufficient wind.

§. 451.

One should inspect the pipes [to ascertain] first if every stop, and all the pipes of every stop, are made of the materials specified in the contract. In examining the metal pipes the quality of the metal should be tested, or whether the alloy is as prescribed. This can best be done by a tinsmith, but sometimes organists know the method of investigating this as well. It is sometimes done with a touchstone. I would also find [the alloy] by means of water, by taking, for example, one pipe that is supposed to be of pure tin and weighing it. After that I would take a piece of solid tin from elsewhere that weighs the same [as the pipe being examined], and then fill a vessel with water

---

[81] The same goes for the Quintatön, Salicional and Fugara. [Albrecht].

legen, und zusehen, wie hoch das Wasser gestiegen. Hernach nehme ich es wieder heraus, und lege die Pfeife hinein. Wenn sie gleiche Schwere hat wie das Stück Zinn, und auch einerley Materie ist mit demselben, daß kein Bley drunter ist; so sind alle ihre Theile zusammen genommen so groß, als das Stück Zinn; folglich muß das Wasser davon eben so hoch steigen, als vorhin. Steiget es nicht so hoch; so ist Bley drunter. Der Kern zwar wird von Bley gemacht, und also kann man eine gar zu geringe Discrepanz wohl negligiren. Der Grund dieser Sache ist, weil das Zinn viel leichter ist, als Bley; folglich muß der Zinnklumpen gleiches Gewichtes viel größer seyn, als das Bley. Also steigt bey eben so schwerem Zinn das Wasser höher, als beym Bley. Man kann kurze Pfeifen nehmen, damit das Gefäß nicht allzulang seyn dürfe: doch nehme man deren etliche, weil bey vielen die Differenz merklicher wird. Ich könnte auch ausrechnen aus der verschiedenen Höhe des Wassers, wie viel Bley bey einem Pfunde Zinn sey. Denn man kann so viel Pfeifen von eben dem Register noch ins Wasser legen, bis das Wasser gleiche Höhe bekömmt, als bey dem Stucke Zinn. Das nachgelegte wiegt man besonders. Und dieses ist die Schwere des Bleyes. Z. E. es wäre das Stück Zinn 12 Pfund schwer; etliche Pfeifen welche eben so schwer wiegten, trieben das Wasser nicht hoch genug; man thäte noch andere Pfeifen hinein, bis das Wasser die Höhe bekäme; die nachgelegten Pfeifen hielten zusammen 3 Pfund. Wie viel Loth Bley wird unter einem Pfunde seyn? Antw. 3) $1\frac{2}{4}$ giebt 3 Pf. Ueberschlag; was 1 Pf.?

Fac. $\frac{1}{4}$ Pf. oder 8 Loth Ueberschlag; und so viel ist Bley drunter. Nun gäbe es noch was zu rechnen; aber es wird mir zu weitläuftig. Man denke der Sache selbst weiter nach.

§. 452.

Bey metallenen Pfeifen mache man es eben so. Man nehme etliche Pfeifen, wiege sie, und lege sie ins Wasser; Thue sie heraus, und mache das Gefäß wieder so voll, wie zuvor; (weil leicht etwas verschüttet werden können, oder an den Pfeifen kleben blieben) man lege so viel Metall hinein, (nämlich von solchem Metalle, wie man es ausgedungen, da man Zinn und Bley mischen kann). Wenn das Wasser bey den Pfeifen nicht so hoch gestanden, als bey dem Stück Metalle, welches doch dem Gewicht nach jenem gleich ist; so ist bey den Pfeifen mehr Bley, als bey dem Stück Metalle. Folglich hat man den Betrug entdeckt. Man kann ein länglicht Gefäß nehmen, damit man das Steigen des Wassers merklicher mache. Man versuche es auch mit großen Pfeifen; auch mit mancherley Registern, weil es die Orgelmacher bey einem oft mehr prakticiren als bey dem andern. Bey dem Wägen der Pfeife wäre zwar auch noch etwas zu erinnern: aber ich muß mich der Kürze befleißigen. Genug, daß man generatim den Betrug auf vorher gezeigte Art entdecken kann. Sollte man bey den Pfeifen mehr Zinn antreffen, (welches aber nicht leicht zu vermuthen) als man ausgedungen; so ists kein Fehler, sondern ist für die Orgel gut. Auf gleiche Art

and set the tin in it, noting how high the water rises. Next I take it out and lay the pipe in the water. If it is equal in weight to the piece of tin and is also of identical material with it, without any lead being mixed into it, then its total substance is the same size as the piece of tin; consequently it will cause the water to rise to the same height as the first time. If it does not rise as high, then lead is mixed in with the tin. To be sure, the languid is made of lead, and thus one may ignore a minor discrepancy. The reason behind this phenomenon is that tin is much lighter than lead, and consequently a lump of tin must be much larger than a piece of lead of the same weight. Thus with a piece of tin the water will rise higher than with a piece of lead of the same weight. Short pipes may be used to keep the vessel from having to be so long; but the test should be run with several pipes together, since the difference becomes more noticeable the greater the mass. I could also compute from the different heights of the water just how much lead was mixed into a pound of tin, by setting more pipes of the same stop into the water until it reaches the same height as that reached by the piece of tin. Then the additional pipes are weighed separately; they will amount to the weight of the lead. For example, if the piece of tin weighs 12 pounds and some pipes of the same weight do not force the water high enough, then other pipes should be added until the water reaches the proper height. If these added pipes together amount to 3 pounds, what is the alloy of lead mixed into one pound? Answer: roughly 3 pounds = 3/12 or ¼ [lead]; thus 1 pound would be ¼ pound or roughly 8-weight* lead. There is yet more figuring that could be done, but it would be too lengthy for me to do here. You may think the matter through for yourself.

§. 452.

This is how it is done with pipes made of pipe metal: several pipes are weighed and then placed in the water. Then they are removed and the vessel is again filled to the previous point (since some [of the water] may easily get spilled or cling to the pipes). Next the same quantity of pipe metal [as contained in the pipes] is placed [in the water], pipe metal of the alloy of tin and lead that has been contracted for. If the water does not rise as high when the pipes are placed in it as it does with the quantity of metal, even though they are of the same weight, then there is more lead in the pipes than in the quantity of metal. Cheating has thus been uncovered. An oblong vessel may be used, in which the rising of the water becomes more noticeable.† This should be tried with large pipes as well, and also with a number of stops, since organbuilders follow this practice more often with some stops than with others. There are other things to keep in mind when weighing the pipes, but I must endeavor to be brief. It is enough to state that in general this deceptive practice may be exposed by the method indicated above. If pipes of a greater tin content than contracted for are encountered (though this is hardly to be expected), this is no fault, but is to the good of the organ. The same

* "8-weight" does not seem to make sense in this context. See Agricola's note on this matter in Chap. 6, §.87, where he contradicts Adlung's explanation of this term, calling it "totally incorrect."

† i.e., the vessel, being of approximately the same dimensions as the pipes, need have only a relatively small amount of water in it. Since there is then a lesser proportion of water to metal, the water will rise higher when displaced.

und Probe der Orgeln.

Art kann man finden, ob die Pfeifen von englischem Zinne einen Zusatz bekommen haben. Oder man nimmt einen Form, und Metall von der bedungenen Art, gießt eine Kugel, feilt sie oben am Engusse glatt ab; hernach schneidet man Metall von einer Pfeife, gießt davon auch eine Kugel in eben denselben Form, und feilt sie auch glatt. Nun wiegt man beyde: wo die letzte schwerer wiegt, als die erste; so ist mehr Bley drunter, als sich gehört. Den Form muß man etwas groß machen, weil dadurch diese Probe desto merklicher wird.

§. 453.

Ich habe eine Probe mit angesehen, da man die im Gesicht stehenden Pfeifen nur besahe, und ein wenig anfühlte; darauf ließ der Probiste seine völlige Approbation von sich hören. Quasi vero; als könnte man es so eigentlich den Pfeifen ansehen; eben als wenn sie nicht durch Kunst eine Zinnfarbe bekommen könnten. Und was das Anfühlen anlangt; so kann eine bleyere Pfeife durch die Kunst gehärtet werden. Und was macht man mit dem innern Pfeifwerk?

§. 454.

Man visitire auch: ob das Pfeifwerk allzudünne gehobelt? Dieß erfährt man, wenn man die Pfeifen angreift. Drücken sich beym Angreifen leichtlich Gruben hinein; so ists ein Zeichen, daß das Metall zu dünne geschunden. Trost l. c. hat angemerkt, daß einige das allzudünne Pfeifwerk durch folgende unerlaubte Manier vor dem Umfallen verwahren wollen. Sie löthen nämlich inwendig metallene Spreitzen in die Pfeifen, daß sie, da sie vor Elend und Schwäche kaum stehen können, nicht umstürzen. Eine solche gespreizte Pfeife kann niemals recht klingen. Man sehe, ob etliche Stimmen, oder einzelne Pfeifen Bärter haben, denen sie etwan nicht zukommen? It. ob die rothe Farbe wieder abgewaschen? ob sie fein Zirkelrund sind? nicht eingebogen; nichts eingehängt ꝛc. Man untersuche auch: ob die Löcher der Windlade und Parallelen recht auf einander treffen, und zwar alle zugleich? Man ziehe desfalls ein Register ganz langsam heraus, halte die Palmuln nieder, und höre, ob ein Clavis eher klingt, als der andere; als welches, wenn es bemerkt wird, ein Fehler ist, weil, wenn ein Loch das untere eher berührt, dasselbe auch etwas über dasselbe hintreten wird, wenn die andern Löcher völlig offen sind; folglich wird dadurch der Wind ungleich. Doch wenn die großen Claves fein nach der Reihe eher anheben, als die kleinen; so ist es nicht unrecht: denn die Löcher sind größer, als bey den kleinen. Sollten alle Löcher zugleich an die Löcher der Windlade anrühren, daß sie zugleich anfiengen zu klingen; so würde hernach das kleine Loch der Parallele über das kleine der Windlade hinlaufen, ehe das große ganz über das untere große tritt. Denn die Parallele gehet oben so weit fort, als unten, da doch augenscheinlich ist, daß das eine Extremum des großen Lochs eine weitere Reise hat nach dem andern Extremo des

untern

method may be used to reveal whether the pipes have received a good admixture of English tin. Or pipe metal of the sort contracted for can be [melted and] poured into a mold, making a ball, and the sprue may be filed off smooth. Next pipe-metal may be cut from a pipe and a ball cast in the very same form; it should also be filed off smooth. Then both balls should be weighed. If the latter weighs more than the former, then it contains more lead than it should. In this test the mold must be rather large to reveal the difference clearly.

§. 453.

I have witnessed a test in which the examiner only inspected the façade pipes and handled them a bit; thereupon he declared his full approval. As if that were possible! —one could hardly [test an organ by] merely looking at the pipes; it could well be that they have been artificially painted the color of tin. And as regards feeling [the pipes], a lead pipe may be artificially tempered. And what about the pipework inside the case?

§. 454.

One should also inspect whether the pipework has been planed too thin. This may be discovered by handling the pipes. If in taking hold of them dents are easily pressed into them, it is a sign that the builder has scrimped on the metal. Trost, l.c.,* has noted that some [builders] try to prevent such thin pipes from falling over in the following illicit manner: they solder metal stays on the insides of the pipes, so that they do not topple over, even though they are so miserably weak they can hardly stand. A pipe thus propped up can never sound properly. One should observe whether some stops or individual pipes [within a stop] have beards that they perhaps should not have. Has all the red size been washed off? Are the pipes perfectly round? Are they straight? Are any of them hung up? The holes in the windchest and the sliders should also be examined to see if they match precisely, and all at exactly the same point. To do this, one stop should be drawn very slowly while the keys are being depressed. One should listen if one note sounds sooner than another. If this is noticed, then it is a defect, because if one of the holes reaches the one beneath it sooner, it will also move somewhat beyond it when the other holes are fully open, and thus it will not receive full winding. But if the large pipes begin to speak one after the other in a neat sequence, this is not improper. For their holes are larger than those of the small pipes. If all the holes reached the holes of the windchest simultaneously, so that they began to sound at the same instant, then the small holes in the sliders would subsequently pass beyond those in the windchest before the large holes had moved entirely over the ones beneath them. After all, a slider moves as far at one end as at the other, and thus it is apparent that one edge of a large hole [in the slider] has further to travel to the other edge of the hole

* pp. 22 & 65.

untern Lochs, (also muß es eher anheben drüber zu treten) als das eine Extremum des kleinen Lochs nach dem andern. Genug ists, wenn sie zugleich zu Ende kommen, und wenn die Löcher recht gerade über einander stehen.

§. 455.

Die Mensur der Pfeifen wollen etliche mathematisch ausmessen, z. E. Trost, in der mehrmals angeführten Beschreibung der Weissenfelsischen Schloßorgel, S. 61: aber man merke, daß die Orgelmacher ihr Pfeifwerk nicht allezeit nach den musikalischen radical proportional Zahlen einrichten. Sie geben ja auch in der Höhe etwas zu, daß die kleinen Pfeifen besser zur Intonation können gebracht werden; in der Tiefe aber nehmen sie der Weite etwas ab, daß der Klang anmuthiger wird: auch ändert die Temperatur die Proportion.

§. 456.

Man leide nicht, daß ein Ventil mehr Federn habe, als das andere: ingleichen, daß eine Pedalpalmul mehr, als eine, Feder habe. Bey Schnarrwerken gebe man genau Achtung auf die Größe der Körper. Denn obwol die Tiefe ohne große Körper kann erhalten werden; so mangelt doch z. E. dem Posaunenbasse die Gravität, wenn er 16 füßig seyn soll, und doch kaum 9 oder 10 Schuhe lang ist. Bey Schnarrwerken untersuche man: ob die Blätter proportionirt sind. Davon stehet §. 389. Zu einer Zeit siehet man es nicht; wol aber wenn man es in verändertem Wetter wieder durchgehet. Wenn ein Balg dem andern den Wind raubt, oder knarrt; so ist es auch als ein Fehler anzumerken.

§. 457.

Wenn zwo Pfeifen in Consonanzen für sich rein sind, und sie werden zusammen gegriffen; so sind sie oft so, daß sie eine Dissonanz, als die 3te Pfeife, hören lassen. Das kömmt daher, weil sie gegen einander nicht die rechte Proportion haben; daher der Orgelmacher anzuhalten, eine Pfeife zu zerschneiden, und anders zu machen, daß sie die ihr gehörige Proportion gegen die andere bekomme. Bey dem Eingeweide der Orgel regardirt man sonderlich: ob alles von Meßing sey, wie es etwan bedungen worden? Das übrige, was bey der Probe zu beobachten, kann man im 13ten Kapitel dieses Buchs finden. Alles hier zu wiederholen, erachte für unnöthig. Zuweilen hat der Orgelmacher mit der Probe nichts zu thun, wenn nämlich ein Baudirektor alles nach seinem Sinne hat machen lassen: denn alsdann hat man es mit ihm zu thun.

§. 458.

Wenn diese Dinge alle untersuchet worden; so übergiebt man die gefundenen Fehler den Inspektoren schriftlich, und sagt ihnen, welche zu corrigiren sind, oder nicht. Die zu corrigiren sind, muß der Orgelmacher verbessern, und eher bekömmt er das rückständige Geld nicht. Wenn aber hernach der Probiste wieder visitirt ob alles geändert worden,

beneath it, and thus it must begin to pass over it sooner than one edge of a small hole to the [further] edge of the one beneath it. It is sufficient if they reach their positions simultaneously, with the holes lined up directly one over the other.

§. 455.

Some try to measure the scale of the pipes mathematically, e.g., Trost in his frequently cited *Beschreibung der Weissenfelßischen Schloßorgel*, p. 61.* But take note that organbuilders do not always dispose their pipes according to the musical radical proportional numbers.† They add a bit in the treble, so that the smaller pipes can be voiced more easily, but in the bass they decrease the width somewhat so that the sound becomes more agreeable. Temperament also alters the proportion.

* This should read "p. 66."

† i.e., using an exact proportion; cf. §.388.

§. 456.

One pallet should not be permitted to have more springs than another, nor should one pedal key have any more than one spring. Precise attention should be paid to the size of reed resonators. For although low pitches may be attained without large resonators, the Posaunenbass, e.g., will be lacking in gravity if it is supposed to be 16′ and yet is barely 9 or 10 feet long. Reed tongues should be inspected to make sure they are in proportion; this has already been discussed in §.389. This may not be noticed at a given time,‡ but will be evident when it is re-examined after a change in the weather. If one bellows robs wind from another, or creaks, this is also to be noted as a defect.

‡ i.e., the first time the organ is examined; see §.439.

§. 457.

If two pipes forming a pure consonance with one another are played together, it often happens that they create a dissonance, as if a third pipe were sounding. This comes about because they do not have the proper proportion in relation to each other. Therefore the organbuilder is to be required to alter one of the pipes and make it differently, so that they attain the proper proportion to each other. In [examining the] interior of the organ special attention should be paid to whether all [the metal parts] are of brass, if that is what has been contracted for. Everything else that should be observed during an examination may be found in Chapter 13 of this book; I do not consider it necessary to repeat it all here. Sometimes the organbuilder is not involved in the examination at all, as when a director has had everything built according to his ideas. Then [the examiner] must deal with him.

§. 458.

After all these things have been examined, the defects that have been discovered are submitted to the Inspectors in writing, indicating whether they are to be corrected or not. The organbuilder must repair those that are to be corrected, and should not receive the money held in reserve§ until he does. If a later time, after the examiner

§ i.e., for payment to the organbuilder after the terms of the contract have been certified as fulfilled.

worden, und er befindet es richtig; so bekömmt er sein Geld. Kommen aber Fehler vor, die nicht können corrigirt werden, ohne die ganze Lade zu ändern, und der Orgelmacher will nicht dran; so kann er es nicht verargen, wenn man dafür ein Stück Geld inne behält: oder bey der Obrigkeit Hülfe sucht, daß er es auf seine Unkosten ändern müsse. Z. E. Wenn der Zufall des Windes zu schwach, da denn der Fehler in den Cancellen steckt, welche zu enge sind ꝛc. da muß er die Lade ändern. Hat er endlich alles recht gemacht; so fertiget der Probiste ein Testimonium aus, und giebts dem Orgelmacher zur Versicherung, daß nicht unwissende Organisten etwas verderben, und dem Künstler die Schuld geben. Nach der Probe bekömmt der Probist sein Geld, und mit den Orgelmachergesellen noch eine besondere Discretion; die letztern bekommen an manchen Orten auch wol noch so viel guten Wein zum besten, als die größte Pfeife in sich faßt; alle zusammen aber bekommen zum Beschluß ordentlich einen Schmauß.

Das XVII. Kapitel.
Von der Windprobe, und andern mechanischen Instrumenten eines Organisten.

Inhalt:

§. 459. Was man in diesem Kapitel zu suchen. §. 460. Von der Windprobe. §. 461. Von der Federzange. §. 462. Von dem Stimmschlüssel. §. 463. Von dem Schraubenzwinger. §. 464. Von den Cylindern; it. Vom Intonirblech.

§. 459.

Dieses Kapitel wird gar kurz werden. Denn wir wollen hier nicht beschreiben, was ein Orgelmacher für Instrumente nöthig hat, wenn er eine Orgel bauen will, als deren eine ziemliche Menge ist; sondern es sollen hier nur kürzlich die wenigen Instrumente beschrieben werden, welche ein Organist braucht, wenn er dasjenige gehörig besorgen will, was im folgenden Kapitel von der Erhaltung der Orgeln vorkömmt.

§. 460.

Sonderlich ist die Windprobe deutlicher zu beschreiben; wiewol es Werkmeister bereits gethan in der Orgelprobe, Kap. 25. S. 63. Der Erfinder derselben soll Christian Förner seyn, wie Trost von ihm meldet in der Weissenfelß. Orgelbeschr. S. 5. u. f. [82]) Erstlich wird in Kästchen gemacht von Metall, 2 oder 3 Zoll lang,

---

[82]) Ein gleiches bezeuget Herr Johann Georg Ahle in der Unstruhtinne, oder musikalischen Gartenlust, S. 24. aus D. Joh. Olearii Einweihungspredigt, der Anno 1667. zu

again inspects whether everything has been set right, he finds it all in order, then [the builder] receives his money. If, however, defects appear that cannot be corrected without altering the entire chest, and the organbuilder is not willing to do this, then he he has no right to become angry if part of the money is withheld, or if the authorities are asked to intervene in an attempt to force him to set things right at his own expense. For example, if the wind supply is too weak, and the fault lies in the channels being too narrow, then he must alter the chest. If in the end he has righted everything, then the examiner draws up a testimonial, giving it to the organbuilder as insurance that no ignorant organist will ruin some [part of the instrument] and blame it on the craftsman. After the test the examiner receives his payment, and also a special bonus together with the journeymen. In many places the latter also receive as much wine of the finest quality as the largest pipe will hold. And at the conclusion everyone together is ordinarily treated to a banquet.

Chapter XVII.
Concerning the Windgauge and other Mechanical Tools of [Use to] an Organist.

Contents:

§.459. What to be found in this chapter. §. 460. Concerning the wind gauge. §.461. Concerning the spring forceps. §. 462. Concerning the tuning key. §.463. Concerning the screw clamp. §.464. Concerning the cylinders; also the lip tool.

§. 459.

This chapter will be very brief. In it we do not intend to describe the sorts of tools that an organbuilder needs to build an organ, since there are so many of them. Rather you will find here only a brief description of the few tools that an organist needs to take proper care of those things to be presented in the following chapter on the maintenance of an organ.

§. 460.

In particular, the wind gauge must be described in greater detail, even though Werkmeister has already done this in his *Orgelprobe*, Chap. 25, p. 63. Christian Förner is said to have invented it; Trost reports this about him in his *Beschreibung der Weissenfelßischen Schloßorgel*, p. 5f.[82] First a box is constructed of metal, 2 or 3 inches long and

---

[82] Mr. Johann Georg Ahle attests to the same in his *Unstruhtinne, oder musikalischen Gartenlust*, p. 24, citing Dr. Joh. Olearius's Dedicatory Sermon for the organ built in the year 1667 in the

lang, und halb so breit und tief. Es wird aber nicht allein viereckicht, sondern auch rund gemacht. Hier wird ein Kanal oder kurzes Röhrchen von Metall aufgelöthet, jedoch gekröpft, also: ⌐, daß, wenn ein rund Loch in den Windkanal gebohret wird, man das Kästchen an diesem Röhrchen könne daran stecken. Hierneben wird ein ander kürzer Kanälchen gesetzt, worauf man eine gläserne Röhre bevestiget ist, die in dem Diametro etwann $\frac{1}{4}$" hält. (Zuweilen macht man sie auch enger.) Man kann dergleichen leicht zu sehen bekommen. Werkmeister hat sie in Kupferstich vorgestellt bey seiner Orgelprobe. Ich habe dieß auch gethan auf der dritten Tabelle in meiner Anleitung zu der musikal. Gelahrtheit. Fig. 23. u. 24.; dabey muß man aber, um alles gehörig einzusehen, den 240. §phum gedachter Anleitung bedächtig nachlesen. Das blosse Anschauen machts allein nicht aus. Das Kästchen füllet man mit Wasser voll. Wenn man es nun an den Windkanal steckt; so wird durch den Wind der Bälge das Wasser in der gläsernen Röhre in die Höhe getrieben. Wenn man nun den Maaßstab dran hält: so erfährt man, ob bey einem Balge der Wind so stark sey, als bey dem andern; wovon §. 441. schon etwas gedacht. Dadurch kann der Organist auch den Wind wieder gleich machen, wenn das Gewicht der Bälge, oder das Gegengewicht verrückt worden. Ein Kind von wenig Jahren kann das Wasser aus der Windprobe blasen; und hingegen so ein schwer Balggewicht nicht, sagt Werkmeister l. c. und Trost l. c. Doch vielleicht rede ich im 28sten Kapitel etwas von diesem Phänomeno.

§. 461.

Kalbleder muß man auch bey der Hand haben, weil der Wind zuweilen Ausgänge findet. Folglich auch Leim und Hausenblasen Pfundleder braucht man zu Schrauben. Die Federzange ist ein sehr nöthig Instrument, weil die Ventilfedern im Windkasten damit zu bessern und einzusetzen sind. Aus diesem Endzwecke sieht man, daß sie zwar eben so gemacht werden kann, als andere Dratzangen, nämlich mit 2 Spitzen; aber sie muß sehr lang seyn, weil man sehr weit hinter reichen muß. $\frac{1}{2}$ Elle kann genug seyn; doch richtet man sich nach der Breite des Windkastens. Sonst kann auch eine ordentliche Dratzange nicht wohl entübriget werden, als mit welcher man die Stifte und den andern Drat in der Nähe besser traktiren kann, als mit der Federzange.

§. 462.

Der Stimmschlüssel ist fast wie ein Stimmhammer, und kann auch bey der Stimmung eines Claviers gebraucht werden; aber ein Stimmhammer kann nicht so gut bey einer Orgel gebraucht werden, wo etwan der Posaunenbaß zu schrauben ist: denn

Halle in der Domkirche von oben gedachtem **Christian Förner** erbaueten Orgel; welche Predigt: **Das fröliche Halleluja**, betitelt wird.

80   Chap. XVII. Concerning the Windgauge and other Tools

half as wide and deep (it may not only be made rectangular, however, but also round). To it is soldered a conduit, a short metal tube, but at a right angle, like this:

When a round hole is bored into the wind duct [of an organ], this box may be plugged into it by means of this tube. Next to it [on the metal box] is placed another short conduit, on top of which is fastened a glass tube, about ½ inch in diameter (sometimes it is made even narrower). It is easy to find an illustration to take a look at; Werkmeister has depicted it on the copperplate in his *Orgelprobe*.* I have also done this on the third chart† in my *Anleitung zu der musikalischen Gelahrtheit*, Fig. 23 & 24. In connection with it, however, one must carefully consult §.240‡ of the said *Anleitung* in order to understand everything properly; merely looking at it will not suffice. The box is filled with water. Then when it is plugged into the wind duct, the wind from the bellows forces the water up the glass tube. By holding a ruler beside it, one can determine whether the wind from one bellows is as strong as from another (something about this has already been mentioned in §.441). By means of it, the organist can also restore the wind pressure to equality if a bellows weight or a counterweight has gotten shifted. Both Werkmeister, *l.c.*§ and Trost, *l.c.*¶ relate that a young child can blow the water out of the wind gauge, while on the other hand a heavy bellows weight cannot. Perhaps I will speak somewhat on this phenomenon in Chapter 28.‖

* on the frontispiece; the box depicted there is round.
† facing p. 542.
‡ pp. 542f.
§ *Orgelprobe*, Chap. 25, p. 64.
¶ p. 6.
‖ Adlung makes no mention of this in Chapter 28.

§. 461.

One must also have calf leather at hand,** since the wind at times finds ways to escape. And consequently [one must have] also glue and isinglass. Heavy leather is also needed for screwing.†† The spring forceps is a very necessary tool, since the pallet springs in the windchest may be adjusted and inserted with it. Its purpose makes it clear that, although it can be made just like other pliers, with two prongs, these [prongs] must nevertheless be very long, since it is necessary to reach very far back [into the pallet box]. Half a yard [long] is sufficient; but the length should be determined by the depth of the pallet box. Furthermore, ordinary pliers are certainly indispensable, since they are handier than the spring forceps when working with the pins and other wire [components] at close range.

** to patch wind leaks.
†† See §.469.

§. 462.

The tuning key is almost like a tuning hammer, and can also be used for tuning a [stringed] keyboard instrument. But a tuning hammer cannot be used so well in [tuning] an organ in which there may be a Posaunenbaß that needs to be screwed [to tune

Cathedral Church at Halle by the abovementioned Christian Förner; this sermon bears the title *Das fröhliche Halleluja*. [Albrecht]

denn er ist oben allzubreit, daß man ihn vor der Pfeife, ohne Absetzen, nicht wohl herumdrehen kann. Den Stimmschlüssel macht man deswegen nur oben etwas breit, daß man ihn fassen und umdrehen kann.

Es sind auch viel Schrauben in der Orgel von Messing oder Eisen, welche man mit dem Meißel oder dergleichen breiten und scharfen Instrumenten aus- und enziehen kann. Wenn man in die obersten Stockwerke will, versteht es sich ohne dieß, daß man mit Leitern und Treppen versehen seyn müsse. Das Stimmhorn ist oben §. 414. beschrieben worden, und muß ein Organist dergleichen auch haben, große und kleine. Die Hüte der Gedackte niederzuschlagen, kann mit einem Holze geschehen, und ist nichts besonders dazu nöthig.

§. 463.

Die Veränderung des Wetters macht zuweilen, daß die Stockschrauben auf der Lade müssen anders geschraubet werden, wozu man aber mit der Hand nicht allezeit kommen kann; daher ist sonderlich der Schraubenzwinger nöthig. Dieses ist ein lang eisernes Instrument, oben etwas breit, daß man es mit der Hand wohl regieren kann, unten aber hat es wenigstens 2 starke Spitzen, wie eine Gabel, in der Weite, daß die Schraubenköpfe just dazwischen treten können. Wenn man nun drehet; so muß die Schraube mit herum, weil der Diameter von einer Ecke zur andern länger ist, als die Weite der Spitzen. Wenn man 3. Spitzen dran macht, ist es noch besser. Ob die Schrauben in allen Orgeln gleich breite Köpfe haben, weis ich nicht. Man läßt den Schraubenzwinger nach seiner Orgel machen: sonsten, wo die Köpfe kleiner wären, würde er sich um dieselben drehen lassen, ohne sie mit herum zu führen: wären sie breiter; so müßte man mit den Spitzen einstechen und sie forttreiben, welches aber nicht gut von statten gehet. Die 3 Spitzen müssen nicht in gerader Linie stehen, sondern einen Triangul vorstellen, aber keinen gleichen, sondern so, daß sie auf einem Viereck (wie die Schraubenköpfe sind) an 3 Seiten anliegen.

§. 464.

Unter die Claviere ist ein Brett nöthig, darnach man die Clavierpalmuln schraubt: wovon §. 350. etwas gedacht worden. Durch das Angreifen werden zuweilen Gruben in die Pfeifen gedruckt. Deswegen sind die hölzernen Walzen oder Cylinder nöthig, womit man sie wieder einrichtet. Wenn man deren etliche hat, nämlich ein ganz kleines zu den kleinsten Pfeifen, ein anders zu den mittlern Pfeifen, und ein etwas starkes; so hat man genug, weil es eben nicht nöthig, daß sie gleich in die Pfeifen passen. Das Intonirblech dient die Labien bey der Intonation zu richten. Wer aber damit nicht recht gut umzugehen weiß, der lasse diese letzte Verrichtung lieber an den Orgelmacher.

it], since the top of it is so wide that it cannot very well be turned without removing the pipes. For that reason the top of the tuning key is made only moderately wide, so that one can grasp it and turn it.

There are also many screws in an organ, of brass or iron, that one can screw in and out with a chisel* or some other such broad and sharp instrument. If one wants to get into the highest chest, it goes without saying that ladders and steps must be available. The tuning cone has been described above in §.414, and an organist must also have some of these, both large and small. Tapping down the caps of stopped pipes may be done with a [stick of] wood, and no special [tool] is needed for it.

* i.e., using it as a screwdriver. As painful as this comment may be to modern woodworkers, the translation is correct.

§. 463.

A change in the weather sometimes necessitates that the toe-board screws be adjusted differently. Since they are not always accessible to the hand, a screw-clamp is especially necessary. This is a long iron tool, somewhat broad at the top to allow the hand to control it well; at the bottom it has at least two strong prongs, like a fork, spread apart so that the heads of the screws fit precisely between them. When they are turned, the screw is forced to turn with them, since the diameter from one edge [of the screw] to the other is greater than the spread of the prongs.† It is even better if [this tool] has three prongs. Whether all screws in organs have heads of equal size, I do not know. [An organist] should have the screw-clamp made to fit [the screws of] his organ. Otherwise, if the heads should turn out to be smaller, [the screw-clamp] would keep turning around them without twisting them. And if they were broader, then one would have to shove the prongs into them and force them to turn, which does not work very well. The three prongs must not stand in a straight line, but form a triangle—not an equilateral one, but one that will fit onto three sides of a square (which is the shape of the screw heads).

† Adlung is speaking here of wooden screws (cf. §.44) that have square heads (cf. the last sentence of this paragraph).

§. 464.

It is necessary to have a rail to place under the keyboards to determine the level at which the keys must be adjusted; this has already been mentioned in §.350. Sometimes dents are pressed into the pipes by handling them. For this reason wooden rollers or cylinders‡ are necessary, to put them back into shape. It is sufficient to have a few of them: a very small one for the smallest pipes, another for the pipes of moderate size, and a rather hefty one, since it is not really necessary that they fit into the pipes exactly. The lip tool serves to adjust the lips during voicing. But anyone who is not very skillful in using one had better leave this final adjustment to the organbuilder.

‡ i.e., mandrels.

Das XVIII. Kapitel.
Von der Erhaltung und Reparatur der Orgeln.

Inhalt:

465. Es gehört dieß für Orgelmacher. § 466. Organisten müssen etwas dafür bekommen. § 467. Sie sollen die Orgeln nicht ruiniren helfen durch ihre Hitze. §. 468. Was zu thun, wenn die Register übel zu ziehen? §. 469. Wenn die Palmuln niederfahren ohne das es heulet? §. 470. Wenn es dabey heulet §. 471. Wenn es heulet ohne daß sie niederfallen §. 472. Wie das zerbrochne Koppel zu bessern §. 473 Wenn das Pedal heulet. §. 474. Von Druckwerken. §. 475. Wenn sich die Palmuln verwerfen. §. 476 Vom Durchstechen. §. 477 Wie sonst die Pfeifen zu bessern. §. 478. Der Calcant soll sanft treten ꝛc. §. 479. §. 480. Noch andere Fehler der Bälge, wie sie zu heben. §. 481. Schluß.

§. 465.

Dieses Kapitel wird auch nicht lang werden, weil die vorigen einem Organisten so viel Licht geben können, daß allhier nur etwas weniges darf beygebracht werden. Ein Organist zwar, als Organist, hat mit der Besserung der Orgel nichts zu thun, sondern er bekümmert sich um sein Spielen; daher man ihn auch dazu nicht zwingen kann, daß er die vorfallenden Fehler bessern solle: sondern das gehört für die Orgelmacher, welchen ich auch dadurch ihren Verdienst nicht abschneiden will. Vielmehr rathe ich, daß man einen Orgelmacher in Bestallung nehme, der die vorfallende Schäden zu rechter Zeit bessere, das Werk in der Stimmung erhalte, u. s. w. Diesen habe ich nicht Ursach zu zeigen, wie sie sich dabey zu verhalten: denn sie wissen es besser, als ich. Allein an vielen Orten kann man keine Orgelmacher haben; oder man hat sie nur selten, etwan auf hohe Feste, da doch unter der Zeit oft etwas vorfällt, das dem Organisten Verdruß machet. Es ist also gut und lobenswerth, wenn in solchem Falle der Organist solche Fehler selbst verbessern kann.

§. 466.

Wie man aber einem Orgelmacher, der das Werk selbst gebauet, diese Commißion lieber aufträgt, als einem andern, und wo etwan ausserordentliche Fälle vorkommen, ihm ausser seinem Bestallungsgelde es besonders bezahlt: also ist auch nöthig bey dem Organisten, daß man auf seine Geschicklichkeit sehe. Denn man muß ihm von Rechtswegen seine Mühe auch bezahlen, und jährlich Bestallungsgeld geben; folglich muß man auch sehen, ob er die Sache verstehe, und nicht, anstatt die Orgel zu verbessern, dieselbe verderbe. Nachdem die Orgeln wichtig sind, nachdem giebt man auch Bestallungsgeld. Es ist nicht zu viel, wenn dafür 4. 6. 8 und mehr Rthlr. gezahlt werden. Verstehet also der Organist die Sache; so kann er zu aller Zeit den Schaden verbessern,

der

Chapter XVIII.
Concerning the Maintenance and Repair of Organs.

Contents:

§.465. This is a job for the organbuilder. §.466. Organists should receive some recompense [for doing it]. §.467. [Organists] should not hasten the ruin of organs by playing violently. §.468. What to do if the stops are difficult to pull. §.469. ...if the keys drop but there is no cipher. §.470. ...if a key has dropped and there is a cipher. §.471. ...if the organ ciphers without any key having dropped. §.472. How to repair a broken coupler. §.473. [What to do] if the pedal ciphers. §.474. Concerning sticker mechanisms. §.475. [What to do] if the keys become warped. §. 476. Concerning running. §.477. How to repair pipes. §.478. The bellows pumper should pump gently, etc. §.479. §.480. Other faults in the bellows and how to remedy them. §.481. Conclusion.

§. 465.

This chapter will likewise not be lengthy, since what has already been said will so enlighten an organist that only a few minor matters need to be mentioned here. To be sure, an organist as such has nothing to do with the repair of the organ; rather he should concern himself with his playing. Therefore no one can force him to repair any defects that occur; rather this is a matter for the organbulder, and it is also not my intention to deprive him of his livelihood. Rather I would counsel that an organbuilder be retained under contract, to repair in a timely fashion whatever damage occurs, to keep the instrument in tune, etc. I have no reason to show [organbuilders] how to do their job, for they know it better than I. But in many places an organbuilder is seldom or never available, perhaps only for the main holy days—but something often goes wrong in the meantime to cause the organist annoyance. Thus it is good and praiseworthy if in such a situation the organist himself can repair such problems.

§. 466.

But it is better to entrust this duty to the organbuilder who built the organ than to another, paying him a special [fee] above and beyond his maintenance contract if extraordinary situations should arise. It is also necessary and only right to recognize an organist's skill [in repairing the organ] and pay him for his trouble by giving him a yearly maintenance fee. Consequently it must be ascertained whether he understands what is involved, and does not damage the organ instead of repairing it. The amount of the maintenance fee is determined according to how important* the organ is. 4, 5, 6 or more Reichsthaler is not too much to pay. If an organist understands the job, then

* i.e., how large and complex.

Kap. XVIII. Von der Erhaltung und Reparatur der Orgeln. 83

der sich etwan eräuget: folglich verdient er solch Geld redlich. Manche knauserichte Kirchväter denken, sie wollen die Kirche reich machen, wenn sie solches Geld zurück behalten: wenn aber irgend ein kleiner Schade wo geschiehet; so kann derselbe nach und nach der Orgel so großen Tort thun, daß nachhero die Kirche doppelte Kosten anwenden muß, wenn alles wieder in guten Stand kommen soll. Sind aber die Kirchen arm, und es fallen solche Fehler vor, die ohne besondere Unkosten können geändert werden; so sollen Organisten sich nicht entziehen, sondern es umsonst machen. Christliche Vorsteher einer Kirche oder Gemeinde werden nicht unterlassen, die Gutherzigkeit des Organisten auf andere Weise vielfältig zu belohnen.

§. 467.

Organisten sollen nicht nur die Orgeln verbessern, wenn ohngefähr ohne ihre Schuld ein Mangel sich aussert; sondern sie sollen sich auch sonderlich hüten, daß sie dieselbe nicht durch Unachtsamkeit verderben. Daher das erste ist, daß sie im Spielen sich moderiren, und nicht so ungestüm auf der Orgel herumdreschen. Denn dadurch werden die Säckchen im Windkasten zerrissen; die Ventile werden allzusehr abwärts geschnellt, daß sie auf die Stifte springen; der Drat wird zerzerrt; die ledernen Schrauben an den Abstrakten halten nicht, u. d. gl. Und was soll denn endlich das gräuliche Dreschen auf dem Manuale, oder das unbändige Trommeln auf dem Pedale helfen? Manche wollen sich damit zwar groß machen; aber wer dergleichen Posituren ansiehet, der muß drüber lachen, wenn manche Organisten die Hände und Arme aufheben und so damit ausholen, als wollten sie einen pohlnischen Ochsen todtschlagen. Man kann ja ohne dergleichen närrische Grimmassen geschwinde spielen: man darf sich nur das sanfte Wesen im Spielen angewöhnen. Das Pedal, wenn es zu hart aufgetreten wird, schlägt an, und macht ein ärger Rasseln, als es klingt.

§. 468.

Wenn die Register nicht wohl zu ziehen sind; so brauche man ja keine Gewalt daran, sondern man wandere mit dem Schraubenzwinger (s. §. 463.) in die Orgel, und schraube die Stöcke höher. Sind sie allzuleicht zu ziehen; so schraube man sie vester an. Die Ursach kann man §. 360. lesen. Wollte man im ersten Falle Gewalt brauchen; so würde man leicht die Stifte der Registraturwellen biegen und zerbrechen, auch die Arme derselben würden leichtlich zum Zerbrechen genöthiget werden. Im letzten Falle darf man auch nicht das Anschrauben vergessen, weil sonst der Wind unter den Parallelen weg gehet. [83)]

§. 469.

Es trägt sich oft zu, daß etliche Claviere freywillig niederfallen, entweder ganz, oder zum Theil. Da observire man, ob sie, wenn ein Register gezogen ist, heulen, oder nicht.

L 3

[83)] Der Wind schleicht sich in diesem Falle auch gern zwischen den Parallelen und den Stöcken hin. Diesem muß man also durch das Anschrauben entgegen kommen.

he can repair a defect at any time he notices one; consequently he justly merits such a fee. Many stingy church elders think they are enriching the church by avoiding paying such a fee. But when some small defect arises somewhere, it can gradually do the organ so much injury that the church must later spend double the money to restore everything to good condition. If a church is poor, though, and defects arise such as can be repaired without extra expense, then the organist should not shirk it, but do it free of charge. Christian wardens of a church or parish will not fail to repay the generosity of the organist many times over in other ways.

§. 467.

Organists ought not only to repair organs when defects accidentally arise through no fault of theirs, but they ought also to be especially careful that they do not damage them through carelessness. Thus it is essential that they play moderately and not thrash around violently on the organ, for this will rip the pouches in the pallet boxes, yank the pallets too far down, causing them to spring off their pins, pull apart wires, strip the leather nuts on the trackers, and such. And what good does this horrid thrashing on the manuals or unrestrained tromping on the pedals really do? Some [organists] want to make themselves look important by doing it; but anyone who witnesses such posturing can only laugh at it, to see some organists throwing up their hands and arms and swinging them about as if they were trying to beat a Polish ox to death. One can certainly play rapidly without making such foolish grimaces; it just takes getting used to a quiet demeanor in playing. If the pedal is too heavily trod, it clatters* and makes an annoying rattle when it sounds.

* i.e., wood strikes wood.

§. 468.

If the stops cannot be drawn easily, one should not use force on them, but merely take a screw-clamp, go on back into the organ, and loosen the toeboard screws. If [the stops] are too easily drawn, then the screws should be tightened. §.360 explains the reason for this. If one were to use force in the former instance, then the pins in the stop rollers could easily get bent and break; even the [roller] arms themselves could easily be forced until they break. In the latter instance, tightening the screws certainly ought not to be ignored, since otherwise the wind will escape under the sliders.[83]

§. 469.

It often happens that several keys drop of their own accord, either partially or entirely. Then one must observe whether or not they cipher when a stop is drawn. If

---

[83] In this instance the wind is also likely to escape between the sliders and toeboards. Therefore this must be prevented by tightening the screws. [Albrecht]

nicht. Wo sich das letzte zuträgt; so wird etwan die lederne Schraube nachgegeben haben zwischen der Palmul und den Abstrakten, welche man also nur wieder aufschrauben kann: Oder wo sie ausgelaufen und unbrauchbar worden, nehme man ein Stück Pfundleder, schneide es in eben die Form und steche mit der Pfrieme ein Loch durch, so enge, daß nur das meßingene Schräubchen der Abstrakte dahinein treten kann, hernach schraube man dasselbe gehörig an, so ist der Fehler corrigirt. Hat sich aber die Palmul gesenkt; so schraubt man sie in die Höhe, den andern gleich, nach dem Maaße, davon §. 350. gesagt ist. Wenn aber die Abstrakten mit Drat, nicht mit Schrauben, an die Claves gebunden; so kann man mit der Dratzange es so lange biegen und drücken, bis der Fehler verbessert ist: ist der Drat gar entzwey; so mache man einen andern an, der den andern gleich ist.

§. 470.

Wenn die Palmuln aber abwärts fallen, und man vernimmt ein Heulen solcher Clauium; so wird etwan zwischen die Palmuln etwas gefallen seyn, welches man mit einem Federkiel leicht removiren kann. Ist es im obern Claviere; so stosse man es nicht durch, sondern hole es heraus, sonst fällt es in das andere Clavier, dazu man nicht gut kommen kann. Oder es haben sich die Abstrakten verwickelt; oder es ist etwas in das Wellenbrett gefallen, daß die Welle ihre Spielung nicht hat. Nach diesen Dingen hat man sich umzusehen. Oder die Ursach ist, weil das Ventil nicht deckt, indem vielleicht etwas drauf gefallen. Da kann man nur den Windkasten öfnen bey dem Spunde, und das Ventil mit einer Feder abkehren. Wenn es noch nicht decken will; so ist vielleicht die untergelegte Feder daran Schuld, als welche etwas zu schlaf geworden, oder gar ausgetreten. Und dieses kann vermittelst der Zange leicht verbessert werden. Es könnte auch geschehen seyn, daß die Ventile auf den Stiften sitzen geblieben, wenn sie stark geschnellt worden und die Stifte kurz sind, und da kann man sie leicht wieder an ihren Ort bringen. Oder es sind die Ventile zwischen den Stiften gequollen, und drücken sich, und bleiben daher offen stehen. Da kann man nur die Stifte etwas auf die Seite drücken. Oder es liegt sonst ein Ventil nicht glatt an, wegen übler Arbeit.

§. 471.

Geschiehet es aber zuweilen, daß ein Heulen entstehet, und die Palmuln stehen doch in ihrer Höhe; so ist etwann eine Palmul allzuhoch geschraubt. Dieß erfährt man leicht, wenn man sie tiefer schraubt. Denn die Palmuln, wenn sie hoch geschraubt werden, stossen oben an, ehe das Ventil recht zu ist. Legt sich das Heulen nach geschehenen Niederschrauben nicht; so gehe man sogleich nach dem Windkasten, und sehe, ob das Ventil etwann sich verworfen habe; d. i. ob es von seinem Orte auf die Seite gewichen. Man merkt dieses gleich, wenn man es gerade rückt, und andrückt, als wodurch das Heulen gestillet wird. Hat es sich verworfen; so schmiere man hinten Leim an, und drücke das Ventil bey dem Leder in die Höhe, richte es gleich, und lasse es wieder trocknen, ehe man es wieder braucht.

§. 472.

the latter is the case, then the leather nut between the key and the tracker may have slipped, and then one need only screw it on again. Or if it is worn out and unusable, take a piece of heavy leather, cut it into the same shape, and pierce a hole in it with an awl, small enough so that the little brass screwthread on the tracker can just fit into it. Then screw it on properly, and the defect is corrected. If the key is too low, then screw it up to the height of the other ones, using §.350 as a guide. If the trackers are attached to the keys with wire, however, and not with screws, then pliers may be used to bend and compress the wire to whatever length necessary to repair the fault. If the wire is broken, then another must be attached that is just like the rest.

§. 470.

If a key drops and causes a cipher, however, then something may have fallen between the keys; this may easily be removed with a feather quill. If it happens in the upper manual, then it should not be forced through, but drawn out, otherwise it will fall into the other* keyboard, which is not easily accessible. Or the trackers may have gotten entangled, or something may have fallen into the roller board, causing the roller to lose its play. These things must be checked out. Or the reason may be that the pallet is not properly seating, perhaps because something has fallen on it. Then the only thing to do is to open the bungboard into the pallet box and brush off the pallet with a feather. If it still will not seat properly, then the problem may be that the spring under it has gotten too slack, or has come out entirely, and this can easily be corrected by means of pliers. It could also be, if the pins are short and the pallet has been yanked hard, that it has gotten caught on its pins, and then it can easily be put back into position. Or the pallet may have swollen and gotten stuck between the pins, thus sticking open. Then the pins need only be pressed a bit to the side. Or [a pallet] may just not be seating itself properly due to poor workmanship.

* i.e., the lower.

§. 471.

Sometimes it happens that a cipher arises even though none of the keys has dropped. Then it may be that a key is adjusted too high. This may easily be tested by screwing it lower. For when the keys are screwed too high, they then strike [the thumper board] before the pallet is completely shut. If the cipher does not cease when the key is screwed lower, then one should proceed immediately to the pallet box to see whether perchance the pallet has gotten twisted, i.e., whether it has turned to one side. This may be ascertained right away if setting it straight and pressing [upward] on it silences the cipher. If it has gotten twisted, then spread the back end of it with glue, press the pallet upward against the leather (setting it into its proper position), and allow it to dry before using it again.

Kap. XVIII. Von der Erhaltung und Reparatur der Orgeln. 85

§. 472.

Mit dem Koppelziehen nehme sich ein Organist in Acht, daß, wenn es ein Schiebekoppel ist, er die Hand nicht auf dem obern Claviere habe, sonst stößt er die Klötzchen ab. Welches auch geschiehet, wenn die Palmuln nicht hoch genug geschraubt sind, daß auch die Hölzerchen nicht auf einander treten, sondern vor einander stossen, und bey gebrauchter Gewalt eins zerbricht, weil sie nur angeleimt sind. So lange solches abgebrochne Klötzchen liegen bleibt wie zuvor, entstehet kein Heulen: wo es sich aber auf die Seite begiebt, und man spielt das Oberwerk, so heulet es. Man merkt es bald, weil man es theils hört, ob was entzwey bricht, theils aber daran, daß man das Heulen auf dem andern Claviere spürt, da man doch auf dem obern spielt. *Quaer:* wie hilft man? *Resp.* Man spiele unterdessen auf dem untern Claviere. Nach dem Gottesdienste schraube man alle Abstrakten des Oberwerks von ihren Palmuln, schraube auch das Clavier allerwegen loß, und wenn der Fehler an einer Palmul des mittlern oder untern Claviers ist; so hebe man das Oberclavier heraus. Alsdann nehme man die Palmul des andern heraus, und leime das Klötzchen an gehörigem Orte wieder an, lasse es trocken werden, und setze hernach alles wieder in vorigen Stand. Gehen etwan die Abstrakten gleich hinter den Abstrakten des Oberclaviers, daß die Stifte durch die obern Palmulas gehen; so müssen alle Abstrakten losgeschraubet werden, daß man das obere Manual herausheben könne. Ist aber der Schade im Obermanuale; so schraubt man nur die einzige schadhafte Palmulam von der Abstrakte loß, macht inwendig die Querleiste, worunter die Enden der palmularum sich bewegen, loß, und nimmt die palmulam heraus, leimt es wieder an, und setzt alles wieder in vorigen Stand. Es hat viel Mühe, daher hüte man sich die Hand auf das Clavier zu legen im Koppelziehen. Aber auf das untere von den zweyen darf man wol greifen; da kann es keinen Schaden thun. So wäre auch dem Heulen abgeholfen.

§. 473.

Wenn das Heulen im Pedale gehört wird; so hat man auf eben diese Dinge zu merken, welche oben §. 470. und 471. angemerkt worden. Doch kann es sich auch zutragen, daß die Feder unter der Palmul schlaff wird, oder abfällt, oder gar zerbricht. Da kann man im ersten und letzten Falle eine neue Feder machen, die Querleiste über dem Pedal loß machen, und die Palmul heraus nehmen, folglich ohne besondere Mühe den Fehler verbessern. Ist die Feder nur abgefallen; so steckt man sie wieder an. Auch entstehet ein Heulen, wenn die Bank an eine Palmul anstößt; da kann man sie nur wegrucken.

§. 374.

Wenn in Druckwerken aus dem übelgeschraubten Clavier ein Heulen entstehet, oder wenn man sonst dieselben Claviere will gerade schrauben; so schraubt man unter dem Claviere ein Brett loß, daß man zu den Stangen kommt, und zu den Schrauben; oder wie man sonst kann dazu kommen. In großer Dürrung trägt sichs oft zu, daß
man

Chap. XVIII. The Maintenance and Repair of Organs 85

§. 472.

An organist should be careful not to depress any keys on the upper manual while drawing a shove-coupler, otherwise he will shear off the coupling blocks. This can also happen if the keys are not adjusted high enough; then the coupling blocks do not simply make contact, but rather collide with each other, and since they are merely glued on, one of them breaks if force is used. As long as a coupling block that has broken stays in the same position no cipher will arise, but when it gets turned on its side, then the organ will cipher when the Oberwerk is being played. This is soon detected, in part by hearing something break apart, and in part by noticing a cipher on the other manual while one is playing on the upper one. Now the question arises, what to do? The answer: for the time being keep on playing on the lower manual. After the worship service unscrew all of the Oberwerk trackers from their keys, and also unscrew the keyboard on all sides, and then (if the defect is in a key of the middle or lower keyboard), lift out the upper keyboard. Then remove the [broken] key from the other keyboard and glue the coupling block back onto its proper place; let it dry, and then put everything back as it was. If perchance the trackers pass directly behind the trackers of the upper manual, so that the pins pass through the upper keys, then the trackers must be unscrewed in order to be able to lift out the upper manual. If the defect is in the upper manual, then unscrew only the one defective key from its tracker, loosen from the inside the thumper board under which the ends of the keys move, and remove the key. Glue [the coupling block] back on, and put everything back as it was. This is a lot of trouble; therefore be careful not to place a hand on a key when drawing the coupler. But one may play on the lower of the two manuals, of course, without doing any damage. This is how to fix the cipher.

§. 473.

If a cipher is heard in the pedal, then check out the same things that were noted in §.470 and 471 above. But it may also happen that a spring under a [pedal] key becomes weak, or falls out, or breaks entirely. In the first and last instances, one can make a new spring, then loosen the cross-strip across the pedals and remove the key, and thus repair the defect without any special effort. If the spring has merely fallen out, then insert it again. A cipher may arise from a key rubbing against the bench; in that case simply move [the bench] away [from it].

§. 374. [i.e., §. 474.]

If a cipher occurs in a manual with a poorly adjusted sticker mechanism, or if otherwise one wants to adjust such a keyboard straight, then unscrew a board underneath the keyboard in order to get at the key shafts and the screws; or do anything else necessary to get at them. It often happens that during a prolonged drought it is hardly

man die Palmuln kaum so hoch schrauben kann, daß die Ventile durch sie aufgezogen würden, weil die Abstrakten zu lang geworden. Dies ist wol möglich, weil alsdann die Balken, worauf die Lade ruht, schwinden, und folglich sich die Lade setzt, also, daß die Abstrakten zu der geringern Höhe etwas zu lang sind. Da kann man nicht wol helfen, es sey dann, daß man etwas an den Abstrakten wollte abnehmen. Oder man muß es stehen lassen, bis sich das Wetter ändert. Da wird es sich selbst corrigiren. Doch wenn sich die Balken setzen sollten; so würde das ganze Clavier es spüren. Daher andere sagen, es habe sich das Schraubenmütterchen gegeben: allein so könnte man es ja wieder zurechte schrauben. Es muß wol zuweilen eine andere Ursach seyn, z. Ex. daß sich etwan eine verworfen, u. s. w.

§. 475.

Es geschiehet auch wol, daß im dürren Wetter die Claves sich verwerfen, und entweder auswendig oder inwendig an einander stoßen, und solchergestalt hängen bleiben, und ein Heulen verursachen. Ob das Heulen davon entstehe, kann man leicht erfahren, wenn man nur die Palmuln in die Höhe hebet, und siehet; ob es sich dadurch stillen läßt. Auch sieht man wol, ob sie sich reiben. Da kann man etwas abschaben, daß sie ihre Spielung wiederbekommen. Oder man lege einen feuchten Lappen in- und auswendig auf das Clavier; so wird es in einer Nacht sich wieder zurechte ziehen.

§. 476.

Spüret der Organist ein Durchstechen; so drücke er alle Register besser einwärts. Denn zuweilen sind die Register nicht völlig abgezogen, da es kein Wunder ist, wenn solcher Fehler sich spüren läßt. Ein gleiches geschiehet, wenn sie nicht recht aufgezogen werden, wobey man zugleich eine Unreinigkeit der Orgel vernimmt. Doch dieses gehet an, wenn die Register gut abzuziehen sind; wo nicht, so muß man erst die Stöcke anders schrauben. Ob dies die Ursache des Fehlers sey, kann man leicht abnehmen. Wenn aber die Register recht stehen, und dergleichen sich doch hören läßt; (da doch die Ventile recht decken,) so ist es ein solches Durchstechen, da der Wind aus einer Cancelle in die andern marschirt. Im ersten Falle müßte man aus der Noth eine Tugend machen, und Stiche in die Lade anbringen, wovon §. 362. geredt worden: denn ein anders ist, ob man den Orgelmacher wegen solcher Fehler reprimandirt; ein anders aber zu Abwendung einer größern Incommodität eine kleinere über sich nimmt. Wo es aber nicht allezeit so ist, sondern nur etwan im dürren Wetter; so lasse man es uncorrigirt; es wird sich schon selbst ändern. Ist die Cancelle nicht Schuld daran, sondern die Parallele hat sich verworfen; so habe ich sehen etliche Tropfen Wasser in das Loch des Stocks schütten, dadurch das Heulen sich gestillet hat. Doch muß man das Register zuziehen. Denn wo die Löcher alle über einander stehen; so läuft das Wasser in die Lade, allwo es aber nichts nütze ist. So aber, wenn es auf die Parallele fällt, und sie anfeuchtet, kann sie dadurch sich wieder gleich ziehen. Ich habe zwar auch gesehen, daß man es oben durch

possible to screw the keys high enough to make them open the pallets, since the trackers have gotten too long. This is indeed possible, because then the beams on which the chest sits shrink, and consequently the chest settles, so that the trackers are a bit too long for the lesser height. This is impossible to repair, unless one wishes to remove a section of each tracker. Otherwise it must be left alone until the weather changes. Then it will correct itself. But if the beams have settled, then it would be perceived throughout the entire keyboard. Therefore others say that a screw nut has given way; if this is indeed so, then it could be adjusted properly. At times, of course, there have to be other reasons for it, e.g., that [a tracker] has gotten warped, etc.

§. 475.

It may also happen that in dry weather the keys become warped and rub against each other either outside or inside;* in this way they get stuck and cause a cipher. It is easy to find out whether the cipher is a result of this, by simply lifting the keys upward and noting whether this silences the cipher. In doing this one also notes whether they are rubbing. In that case one may shave off a bit to give them their play again. Or a damp cloth may be laid on top of the keyboard, both inside and out, and the keys will pull back into place overnight.

* i.e., either the keys themselves or the key levers that extend into the case behind the thumper board.

§. 476.

If an organist detects any running, then he had better shove all the stops completely in, since sometimes the stops are not entirely off, and in that case it is no wonder that such a defect shows up. Something similar happens in that when they are not entirely pushed in the organ is perceived to be out of tune. But this only applies if the stops can be pushed in fully. If they cannot, then the toeboards must first be adjusted differently. It is easy to perceive if this is the cause of the defect. If, however, the stop[knobs] are all in the proper position and [the running] is still heard (even though the pallets are properly seated), then it is the sort of running in which the wind is forcing its way from one channel into another. First of all, then, a virtue must be made of necessity, and punctures must be made in the chest, as was discussed in §.362. For it is one thing to reprimand an organbuilder because of such defects, but quite another to adopt a lesser evil to cure a greater one. Where it does not happen all the time, however, but perhaps only in dry weather, then it should be left uncorrected; it will take care of itself. If the channel is not at fault, but rather the slider has become warped, then I have seen someone shake several drops of water into the hole in the toeboard; that took care of silencing the cipher. But the stop must first be shut off. For if the holes are all lined up, then the water would run into the chest, where it is of no use. But if it falls onto the slider and dampens it, then it can cause it to come straight again. Indeed, I have also seen someone shake it down into the top of the pipe instead of removing

durch die Pfeifen geschüttet; anstatt daß man dieselbe abheben, und es in das Loch des Stockes schütten sollen. Hat man da etwan gedacht, das Wasser werde durch die Pfeife in den Stock fallen; so ifts eine große Einfalt: denn es fallt auf den Kern. Und so viel thut man nicht hinein, daß es durch die Ritze unter den Kern laufen sollte. Vielleicht aber hat sich die Pfeife hernach schwerlicher anblasen lassen, daß also die Schwäche des Windes es nicht ausrichten können, und das Durchstechen aufhören müssen. Ich habe aber dies nie probirt. Thäts es etwas; so gienge es in beyden Fällen an: es möchte das Durchstechen von der Cancelle oder Parallele herrühren. Wie denn auch für beyde Fälle gebraucht wird, wenn man in den Fuß der Pfeife ein Löchlein bohret, daher die Pfeife alsdann mehr Wind erfordert, wenn sie klingen soll; oder wenn man sie unten kneipt, 2c. s. §. 384. Es sind dies zwar Dinge die unter die Fehler gehören; aber aus zweyen Uebeln wählt ein Verständiger doch das geringste. Man treffe aber auch die rechte Pfeife, dabey man nur den Sonum anmerken, und auf dem Claviere erforschen kann, welcher Clavis es sey; hernach hat man nur noch zu untersuchen, welches Register das Durchstechen thue. 84)

§. 477.

Zuweilen will eine Pfeife nicht ansprechen; oder sie filpet; oder sie überschreyet sich in die Quinte und Oktave. Davon kann man vielerley Ursachen anführen; folglich muß man auf mancherley Art dem Fehler suchen abzuhelfen. Man hebe die Pfeife heraus, (wenn sie nicht gar zu groß ist) und richte das Labium anders, ein- oder auswärts, mit einem Messer. Oder, wenn vielleicht etwas zwischen den Kern gefallen; so kann man es wegschaffen. Man kann auch den Kern selbst von dem etwan daraufgefallenen Staube oder Kothe reinigen. Vielleicht liegt auch der Kern zu hoch; in diesem Falle drücke man ihn abwärts. Ist alles auf diese Art richtig, und die Pfeife sladdert; so wird der Kern an einem Orte sein Loth verlohren und eine Oefnung bekommen haben; das löthe man wieder zu. Tremulirt die Pfeife noch; so hat sie ein Sandlöchlein. Wenn man das finden kann; so nehme man den Sand heraus, und löthe das Loch wieder zu. Wo das auch nicht hilft; so lasse man eine andere Pfeife machen. Dabey ist gewöhnlich, die Pfeife auszuheben, und nach der Correction durch Anblasung mit dem Munde zu probiren, ob sie richtig anspreche, daß man des vielen Einsetzens nicht vonnöthen habe. Allein das will mir so schlechterdings nicht gefallen, weil unser Athem sehr feucht und warm ist, wodurch die Höhe und Tiefe sehr verändert wird. Stimmt man sogleich; so wird hernach, wenn die Pfeife wieder kalt ist, der Ton wieder anders. Also müßte man sie erst eine Zeit lang stehen lassen, welches verdrüßlich; ja durch die bloße Wärme der Hand wird sie höher. Es hat Christian Förner, da er die Ulrichsorgel in

---

84) Das Durchstechen geschieht auch, wenn die Ventile nicht gerade gehobelt sind, daß sie an etlichen Oertern Wind durch lassen. Da ifts am besten gethan, wenn man sie herausnimmt, und ändert.

Chap. XVIII. The Maintenance and Repair of Organs

the pipe and shaking in into the hole in the toeboard. That person was grossly naïve to think that the water would fall through the pipe into the toeboard, since it falls on the languid. And one never shakes enough into [the pipe] to make it flow through the slit and beneath the languid. Perhaps, however, the pipe subsequently has more trouble speaking, so that the weak stream of wind* cannot manage to accomplish it, and the running is forced to stop. I have never tried this. If it accomplished anything, it would apply in both cases, whether the running originated from the channel or the slider. It is useful in either case for a little hole to be bored in the foot of the pipe, or for a snippet to be cut out of it at the bottom [of the foot], whereby the pipe requires more wind to speak; see §.384. To be sure, these are things that are to be considered as faults, but a sensible person will choose the lesser of two evils. But make sure to treat the right pipe, by noting the pitch and then experimenting on the keyboard to find out which note it is. Thereafter it is also necessary to investigate which stop is doing the running.[84]

* caused by the running.

§. 477.

At times a pipe will not speak, or it misspeaks, or it overblows at the fifth or the octave. A number of causes could be cited for this, and consequently one must try out a number of ways to remedy the defect. Lift out the pipe (if it is not too large) and adjust the lip differently, either in or out, with a knife. Or perhaps something may have fallen between the languid [and lip]; then just remove it. Or the languid itself may be cleansed from any dust or filth that may have fallen onto it. Perhaps the languid is positioned too high; in this case it should be pressed downward. If all of these things are as they should be, and the pipe [still] flutters, then the languid may have lost its solder somewhere and gotten a hole; it should be soldered shut again.† If the [tone of the] pipe still flutters, then it may have a little sand-hole.‡ If it can be found, then remove the sand and solder the hole shut again. If that does not help either, then a new pipe should be made. In this connection it is usual to lift out the pipe and, after making the correction, to blow it by mouth, testing whether it speaks properly, so that it is not necessary to keep taking it out and putting it back in. But I am not entirely in favor of this practice, since our breath is very moist and warm, and greatly affects the pitch [of the pipe]. If it is tuned immediately, then subsequently, when the pipe cools off again, its pitch is different. Therefore it is necessary to let it sit a while, which is annoying. Indeed, the very warmth from the hands makes it sharper. Christian Förner discovered

† cf. §.385.
‡ cf. §.88 & §386.

---

[84] Running also occurs if the pallets are not planed flat, so that they let the wind enter at various points. In that case it is best to take them out and modify them. [Albrecht]

in Halle gebauet, einen überaus nützlichen modum erfunden, daß bey währender Stimmung die Pfeifen nicht mit dem Munde dürfen intonirt werden. s. Trosts Beschr. der Weißenfelßer Schloßorgel, S. 8; der aber das Inventum nicht communicirt. Meines Erachtens schickte sich ein besonderer Balg mit einem Windkästchen am besten dazu, darauf ein Loch gemacht werden müßte, um die Pfeife hinein zu setzen, daß sie angeblasen würde. Denn wenn man die Orgelpfeifen stimmen will, werden sie ohnedieß auf ihre Lade gesetzt. Es möchte jemand fragen: wie das Loch seyn solle; groß oder klein? (zu jenem schicken sich kleine Pfeifen nicht, und zu diesem werden die großen nicht passen.) Dem dient zur Antwort, daß man auf solches Loch eine starke vollkommen runde metallene Röhre könnte setzen, und zwar in conischer Figur, unten sehr enge, und nach und nach weiter, etwann also: ; so würden die kleinen und großen Pfeifen mit den Spitzen ihrer Füße hineingehen. Man könnte deren auch wol zwo neben einander setzen, damit eins für die sehr großen diene, daß die Röhren nicht allzulang werden dürften. Den Wind könnte man dem Winde in der Orgel gleich machen, nach der Windprobe, weil bekannt, daß manche Pfeife wohl anschlägt mit starkem Winde, da sie es hingegen mit schwachem Winde nicht thun würde. Andere wollen schwachen Wind haben. Wie man sonst bey der Stimmung verfahren soll, wenn dabey etwas unrein geworden, ist Kap. 15. beygebracht. Hat man durch das Angreifen Gruben in die Pfeifen gedruckt; so kann man durch den Cylinder (davon §. 464. gemeldet) dieselben wieder wegbringen. Ist durch das Drücken der Labien etwas vom Loth aufgeborsten; so löthe man es nach der ordentlichen Art.

§. 478.

Die Bälge nehme ein Organist wohl in Acht: Und wie er an der ganzen Orgel alles verschlossen halten soll; so sollen die Bälge auch verwahret seyn, daß keiner einen Schabernack daran beweisen könne. Es soll ein Calcant dazu seyn, der der Sache gewohnt ist. Denn wenn man bald diesen bald jenen drüber läst; so kann man nicht sicher seyn, daß nichts verdorben werde. Alle Calcanten sind von dem Organisten anzuhalten, daß sie die Bälge fein sanft niedertreten. Denn durch das ungestüme Fahren thut man den Bälgen großen Schaden. Sie reissen oft entzwey; heben sich von ihren Canälen loß, 2c. Er soll sie auch alle treten, so, daß nicht ein Balg allzusehr bearbeitet werde, der andere aber nicht: denn deswegen läßt man viel Bälge machen. Er soll auch nicht immerfort darauf herumtummeln, sondern sie auslaufen lassen. Doch damit die Bälge nicht verwechselt werden, sondern daß von den Pedalbälgen sowol als von den Manualbälgen jederzeit Wind da sey; so kann man die eine Art mit gewissen Zeichen von der andern unterscheiden.

§. 479.

an exceedingly useful method while he was building the organ in the Ulrichskirche in Halle, whereby the pipes need not be sounded by the mouth while constantly being tuned, but he did not reveal this discovery; see Trost's *Beschreibung der Weissenfelßer Schloßorgel*, p. 8. In my opinion a separate bellows together with a miniature windchest would be best suited for this task. A hole would have to be made into the top of it, to set the pipe in so it could be blown. For if organ pipes are to be tuned, they have to be set on their windchest anyway. Perhaps someone will ask, "Should the hole be large or small?"— the former is not suited for small pipes, and the large pipes will not fit into the latter. Here is the answer: upon such a hole there could be set a strong metal tube, perfectly round, but cone-shaped, i.e., very narrow at the bottom and growing gradually wider, something like this: 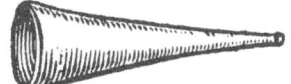 In this way the feet of either small or large pipes would fit into it. It would also be possible to set two of these next to each other, so that one could serve for the very large [pipes] without the tube needing to be made so long. The wind pressure could be made the same as that of the organ, using the wind gauge, since it is well known that some pipes speak well on heavy pressure that would not do so on a light pressure. Other pipes, on the contrary, need to have a light wind pressure. Chapter 15 describes how otherwise to proceed with tuning if anything has gotten out of tune. If dents have been pressed into the pipe from handling it, these may be removed with a mandrel (as reported in §.464). If in pressing the lips some of the solder breaks out, it should be re-soldered according to the proper method.

§. 478.

An organist should pay careful attention to the bellows. Just as he should keep everything on the whole organ locked up, so also should he secure the bellows so that no one can play a prank on them. It is also necessary to have a bellows pumper who is familiar with the job. For if first this one and then that one is allowed to do it, one can never be sure that nothing will be damaged. The organist should admonish every bellows pumper to pump the bellows nice and gently, since they can be badly damaged by operating them violently. They often rip apart, or come loose from their ducts, etc. [The pumper] should also pump them all, and not work one bellows too hard while ignoring another; after all, that is why a number of bellows have been provided. He ought also not to run constantly from one to another, but let them exhaust themselves. So that he does not get confused [when pumping] the bellows, however, but keeps both pedal and manual bellows supplying wind, one type may be distinguished from the other by special signs.

§. 479.

Wenn der Wind an dem Balge ein Loch gemacht, oder wenn er sonst wo an einem Kanale durchmarschirt; so kann der Organist mit Leim und Leder den Schaden leichtlich gut machen. Und weil der Fehler auch daher entstehen kann, wenn die Mäuse über die Bälge gerathen; so kann er sowol ins Balghaus, als in die Orgel, Mäusepulver setzen, daß solches Ungeziefer der Orgel nicht schade. Wenn die Balken knarren, kann er sie mit Baumöhl zur Ruhe bringen. Wenn ein Balg den Wind aus dem Kanale in sich zieht, oder dem andern Balge den Wind raubt; so ist der Schade am Kanalventile. Man erfährt dieß leicht. Denn es werden bey Tretung eines solchen Balges die andern geschwinde in die Höhe fahren. Sobald man dieses merkt; so bald muß man solchen Balg ad interim ungetreten lassen, und hernach den Balg vom Kanal abheben, so wird man finden, daß das Ventil am Kanal entweder gar abgerissen; (da man es wieder anleimen kann) oder es ist krumm; da macht man es anders) oder, welches das gemeinste ist, es ist etwas dazwischen gefallen. Wenn man das wegschaft; so ist dem Mangel abgeholfen. Daraus folgt auch dieß, daß ein Organist unter die Bälge nicht so viel Unreinigkeit kommen lassen dürfe, weil, wenn der Balg tief liegt, er mit Gewalt alles samt der Luft in sich zieht, welches hernach das Kanalventil irre macht, oder gar in den Windkasten und in die Pfeifen kömmt. Wenn aber allen Bälgen, die zu ebenderselben Lade gehören, ein gleiches wiederfährt, daß sie nämlich nach dem Treten geschwind in die Höhe fahren, und keiner raubt dem andern den Wind; so wird entweder der Kanal an der Lade entzwey seyn, oder, welches öfters geschiehet, es wird ein Spund an dem Windkasten herausgefahren seyn, welchen man alsdann wieder hineinschlagen, mit Leder vestmachen, und mit Vorschlägen verwahren kann, daß ihm der Vorwitz davon zu hüpfen ein andermal vergehe. Wenn jedes Clavier oder Lade besondere Ventile hat; so kann man dasjenige zudecken, wo der Fehler ist, und unterdessen die andern Claviere oder Laden brauchen. Wo aber keine sind, oder doch zum ganzen Manuale nur eins, und zum Pedale auch nur eins; da wird gleich das ganze Manual oder Pedal, folglich die ganze Orgel eine Zeit lang unbrauchbar. Deswegen ich oben so gerathen, viel Ventile zu machen; man braucht sie allerwegen.

§. 480.

Wenn das Gewicht eines Balges verdorben worden; so kann der Organist durch die Windprobe denselben den andern Bälgen wieder gleich machen. Wenn der Balg sich vom Kanale gehoben; so hebe er ihn wieder drauf. Ob dieß geschehen, sieht man gleich, wenn der Balg augenblicklich wieder in die Höhe fährt, und doch den andern Bälgen den Wind nicht raubt, und den andern wiederfährt dergleichen nicht. Zuweilen aber kann sich dieser Umstand auch zutragen, wenn der Balg sich nicht abgehoben, sondern wenn die Balgventile nicht decken, und nach dem Treten offen bleiben, daß der Wind wieder herauswandert, wo er hinein gekommen, weil etwann was dazwischen sich gesetzt, oder die Ventile sich verworfen. Beydes ist leicht zu ändern. Von dem Rasseln des

Chap. XVIII. The Maintenance and Repair of Organs

§. 479.

If the wind has forced a hole in a bellows, or if it is escaping from a duct anywhere, the organist can easily repair the damage with glue and leather. And since this defect can also arise from mice getting into the bellows, he can set out rat poison both in the bellows chamber as well as in the organ, to keep such vermin from damaging the organ. If the bellows creak, he can quiet them [by lubricating them] with olive oil. If one bellows is drawing wind back in from the duct, or robbing wind from another bellows, the fault lies in the duct valve. It is easy to find out about this, since when one of the bellows is pumped the others move quickly upwards. As soon as this is noticed, that bellows should be put out of operation for the time being. Later on it should be lifted off the wind duct, and this will reveal that the valve leading to the duct has either torn off completely (in which case it may be glued on again) or has gotten crooked (in which case it should be properly adjusted). Or even more commonly, something has fallen into it [that impedes its closing]. When the [object] is removed, the defect is remedied. Thence it follows that an organist ought not to allow so much filth to accumulate under the bellows, since when the bellows is exhausted [and then lifted], it forcibly draws everything into it along with the air. Such [foreign objects] later foul the duct valve, or even get into the pallet box and the pipes. But if all the bellows that belong to the same chest react identically when they are pumped, i.e., they rise rapidly* without any one of them robbing wind from the others, then either the wind duct has come apart at the chest or, as more often happens, one of the pallet-box sponsels has fallen out. This may again be driven in, fastened with leather, and secured with latches, to prevent its inclination to pop out a second time. If each keyboard or chest has a separate [cut-off] ventil, then the one that is defective may be shut off, and the other keyboard or chests may be used in the meantime. If there are no [separate ventils], however, or only one for all the manuals together and also one for the pedal, then all the manuals or the pedal, and thus the entire organ, will be unusable for a time. This is the reason I have recommended above† making many ventils; they are useful in all sorts of ways.

* i.e., the bellows poles rise without offering any resistance.

† Vol. I, §.74.

§. 480.

If a bellows weight has been disturbed, the organist can again equalize it with the other bellows by using the windgauge. If a bellows has come loose from the duct, he should connect it again. One can determine that this has happened if the bellows pole rises instantly but does not rob wind from the other bellows, and this does not happen with the other bellows. Sometimes this same situation can happen not from the bellows coming loose, but from the bellows valves not shutting tightly, and remaining open after being pumped, so that the wind again rushes out where it entered. Something may have propped the valve open, or the valve may have become warped. Either problem is easy to repair. §.376 mentions something about the duct

Kanalventils ist §. 376. etwas angemerkt, und ich dächte, wenn man den Wind vollkommen gleich machte, so sollte dieser Fehler zu heben seyn.

§. 481.

Es sind noch mehr Dinge zu corrigiren, welche theils aus dem 13. Kapitel leicht zu erkennen, theils von einem verständigen Organisten ohne besondere Mühe können entdeckt und verbessert werden. Gut ist es, wenn ein Organist etwas von der Schreinerkunst versteht: denn es reissen manchmal z. E. die Arme der Wellen ab, oder es geht ander Holzwerk zu Grunde. Kann man nun nicht gleich einen solchen Profeßionisten haben; so will es die Noth erfordern, daß der Organist selbst Hand anlege, und solche Arbeit übernehme.

Wenn der Defekten sich nach und nach allzuviel einschleichen; so muß zuweilen eine Hauptreparatur vorgenommen werden. Z. E. wenn die Bälge schadhaft werden, indem das Leder sich nach und nach abgerieben; wenn die Windführungen den Wind nicht wohl halten; wenn die Unreinigkeit des Werks allzugroß wird rc. rc. Hierbey haben die Kirchenvorsteher, oder der Organist in deren Namen, fast auf eben die Dinge zu sehen, worauf bey Verdingung einer neuen Orgel oben gesehen worden. Wenn es der Organist selber verrichten kann und will; so ist es gut: doch muß er es ex officio noch weniger thun, als daß er einzelne Defekte corrigirt; daher muß man ihm solches besonders bezahlen. Dieß erfordert die Billigkeit. Kann oder will er aber nicht; so suche man sich einen feinen gewissenhaften und verständigen Orgelmacher aus, und übergebe es demselben, welches entweder Tageweise, oder überhaupt verdungen wird. Bey beyden ist nöthig, daß der Organist die Inspektion habe, und NB. die Defekte wohl verstehe, wo sie sind, wieviel deren sind, wie sie zu corrigiren, ob es mühsam und langwierig, sie zu ändern rc. sonst machen gewissenlose Orgelmacher allerhand Händel. Da bringen sie die Sache ins weitläuftige; stellen sich, als wären noch so viel Defekte vorhanden; als koste es sehr viel Zeit und Mühe, dieselbigen zu ändern; ja sie thun, als wäre es noch so gefährlich, da doch zuweilen es was leichtes ist. Denn ein anders ist ein großer Defekt, ein anders aber ists, ob er leicht zu verbessern, oder nicht. Ein großer Defekt ist, z. E. wenn ein Balg dem andern den Wind entziehet. Wer da nicht weis, wie es damit zugehet, der wird sich leichtlich viel Geld abschwatzen lassen, und der Orgelmacher kann sich stellen, als würde es ihm noch so sauer. Wer aber aus dem §. 479. eines bessern unterrichtet ist, der wird sich keine Nase machen lassen. Und so gehts mit vielen Defekten. Große Mangel können zuweilen in kurzer Zeit geändert werden: also kann man dafür soviel nicht bezahlen. Werkmeister meldet in Organo Grüningensi §. 69. daß einige Orgelmacher sich gerühmet, daß sie, da ein Ventil sich auf einen Stift geschlagen, (wovon oben §. 470.) einen Ducaten für solche Reparatur gefodert und bekommen, welches doch in ½ Viertelstunde geändert werden kann. Es sollten solche Dinge jeden Organisten reizen, das Studium mechanicum zu traktiren, um nicht die Kirchen, und auch zuweilen sich selbst, so schändlich betrügen zu lassen.

Andere

Chap. XVIII. The Maintenance and Repair of Organs

valve rattling, and I should think that if the wind were perfectly equalized, then this defect would be done away with.

§. 481.

There are yet other things to correct, some of which may easily be recognized through [familiarity with] Chapter 13, while others may be discovered and repaired by any knowledgeable organist without particular effort. It is good if an organist understands something about woodworking, since the arms of the rollers sometimes break off, or something else wooden breaks down. If a professional is not immediately available, then necessity demands that the organist himself take a hand in it and undertake the work.

If too many defects gradually accumulate, then it is sometimes necessary to undertake a major repair. For example, the bellows may become dilapidated from the leather gradually being worn away, or the wind ducts may no longer contain the wind, or the instrument gets too far out of tune. In this the church superintendents, or the organist as their representative, need to keep in mind almost the same things that were noted above* in connection with contracting for a new organ. If the organist himself is willing and able to carry it out, that is fine; but he should even less be expected to do this *ex officio*† than to repair isolated defects. Thus he must be paid extra for such [an undertaking]. Fairness demands that this be so. If however he is unwilling or unable, then a conscientious and knowledgeable organbuilder must be sought out, and the work must be entrusted to him; this may be contracted either by the day or as a whole. In either case it is necessary for the organist to conduct the inspection, and—take note!—to understand thoroughly the defects, where and how many they are, and how to correct them, and whether it is troublesome and tedious to fix them. Otherwise unscrupulous organbuilders make all sorts of [extra] business [for themselves]. They prolong the job, pretending there are so many defects present that it will cost a great deal of time and effort to repair them. Indeed, they act as if it were something very dangerous, when it may only be something minor. For it is one thing for there to be a major defect, but quite another whether it is easily repaired or not. For example, it is major fault if one bellows robs wind from another. Anyone who does not know how this happens may easily let himself be talked out of a lot of money, and the organbuilder can make it look like it will cost him a lot of hard work. But anyone who has learned better from §.479 will not allow himself to be fooled. This is how it is with any number of defects. Major flaws can sometimes be repaired in no time at all, and therefore one need not pay all that much for it. In his *Organum gruningense*, §.69, Werkmeister reports that some organbuilders boast about demanding and getting a ducat for repairing a pallet that has gotten caught on a pin (see §.470 above), a problem that can be repaired in less than 10 minutes. Such things as this ought to be an incentive for every organist to undertake the study of mechanics, in order to prevent the church (and sometimes himself as well) from being so shamefully swindled.

* in Chap. 9

† i.e., without pay.

Kap. XVIII. Von der Erhaltung und Reparatur der Orgeln. 91

Andere machen Defekte, damit sie lange was zu thun haben mögen. Sie schmeissen weg, was gehen will, und halten sich auf, wo sie können; ja, wie schon Werkmeister in der Orgelprobe S. 59. klagt, sind manche so gewissenlose, daß sie (wie auch §. 381. schon von mir ebenfalls gemeldet worden) den Wind aus dem Kanal zum Theil ausschließen, und hernach vorgeben, es tauge die Lade nichts, damit sie was zu thun haben mögen. Siehe auch was er in Organo grüning. §. 71. hat. Daß ich anderer Dinge nicht gedenke. Also hat man sehr behutsam zu verfahren, daß man nicht berückt werde.

Gemeiniglich haben neue Orgelwerke, wenn sie einige Jahre gestanden, solcher Reparatur nöthig, weil das Pfeifwerk sich etwas setzt, das Holz, so dürre man es auch genommen, schwindet u. s. w. zuweilen wird man dazu durch andere Zufälle genöthiget, wie z. E. vor etlichen Jahren der Wind ein Stück vom Kirchthurm in die Reglerorgel zu Erfurt warf. Bey der Arbeit selbst muß der Organist beständig seyn, daß nichts obenhin gemacht werde, oder daß bey der Stimmung der gemischten Stimmen nicht etliche Pfeifen zugedruckt werden: Imgleichen daß die Temperatur ganz von vorn an richtig gemacht werde ꝛc. Man pflegt zuweilen bey dergleichen Reparaturen in den Stimmen etwas zu ändern, wenn man nämlich etwas anders hinein, an dessen Statt aber etwas anders heraus haben will. Diese Stimmen darf man in solchem Falle so hoch nicht anrechnen, als wenn man neue Orgeln bauet: denn man macht hier keine Stöcke, keine Registraturen, keine Löcher ꝛc.: auch hat man vom alten Register oft die Materie entweder völlig oder zum Theil zu dem verlangten neuen. Ja oft kan man die alten Pfeifen nur aufschneiden, kürzer oder enger machen, und sie wieder zulöthen: so ist es fertig. Das kann so viel nicht kosten, als wenn alles neu gearbeitet wird.

Zuweilen macht man zu einem Werke neue Bälge, wobey entweder der Wind den vorigen vollkommen gleich ist oder nicht. Bey dem ersten Falle kann man, wo das Werk sonst nicht unrein gewesen, die Stimmung unterlassen; im andern Falle aber muß man das Werk völlig wieder temperiren und durchaus stimmen, weil bey Veränderung des Windes sich auch die Höhe und Tiefe ändert.

Auf was für Art aber die Defekte zu corrigiren, muß der Orgelmacher wissen. Größtentheils ists auch Kap. 18. zu lesen: wie man denn auch nachzuschlagen hat, was Werkmeister in der Grüning. Orgelbeschr. §. 30. u. f. meldet, da die Art und Weise deutlich gezeiget wird, wie vielen Hauptmängeln abzuhelfen. Z. E. die Pfeifen, die keine Oeschen haben, müssen dergleichen bekommen; die aufgesprungenen Pfeifen werden wieder gelöthet. Ist der Zufall des Windes nicht stark genug gewesen; so vergrößere man die Windgänge und verwahre sie, nebst den Bälgen, wohl, damit das Stoßen und Schwanken des Werks unterbleibe. Auch kann man noch einen neuen Windkasten auf der andern Seite anlegen, und neue Ventile drein bringen. Sind die Pfeifen zerstochen; so löthe man sie, nach verwehrtem Durchstechen, zu. Sind die Löcher in den Schleifladen scharf; so suche man sie durch einen kolbichten Bohrer glatt zu machen, daß sich die Register desto besser ziehen lassen. Ist das Leder weg; schabt so mache man anders hin. Die Cancellen der Lade kann man auch aufmachen, und das unnutze Spaziergehen

Chap. XVIII. The Maintenance and Repair of Organs

Other [organbuilders] make defects in order to increase the work for them to do. They throw away things that still work, and make delays wherever they can. Indeed, as Werkmeister has already complained in his *Orgelprobe*, p. 59, many of them are so unscrupulous that they partially block the wind from the duct (as I have also reported in §.381) and then pretend that the chest is good for nothing, so that they may have something to do—see also what Werkmeister says in his *Organum grüningense*, §.71—not to mention other things. Thus it is necessary to proceed with great caution, to keep from being taken in.

It is usual for new organs to need such repairs a few years after they have been built, since the pipes have settled a bit, or the wood shrinks, no matter how dry it was when procured, etc. Sometimes other occurrences force such repairs, such as the wind casting a piece of the church tower into the Reglerkirche organ at Erfurt a few years ago. The organist himself must be in constant attendance while the work is in progress, so that nothing is done superficially, no pipes of the compound stops are pinched shut while they are being tuned, and also that the temperament is done correctly right from the beginning. It is normal sometimes to make some changes to the stops while such repairs are being carried out, if [the organist] wants to have them removed and others put in their place. In such a case these stops should not be priced as high as when a new organ is being built, since here no toeboards, no stop mechanism, no [toe] holes, etc., are being made, and furthermore the builder is often given the material from the old stops either partially or entirely in exchange for the new ones desired. Indeed, the old pipes often need only be cut off, made shorter or narrower and re-soldered, and the job is done. That ought not to cost as much as if everything were being made from scratch.

At times new bellows are made for an instrument. In this case, the wind pressure is either exactly equivalent to the former [bellows], or it is not. In the first instance re-tuning may be dispensed with, providing the instrument has not otherwise gotten out of tune; in the second instance, however, the instrument must be completely re-tempered and thoroughly tuned, since its pitch will be altered with the change in wind pressure.

The organbuilder must know, however, the proper method of correcting defects. One may read about this for the most part in Chapter 18; but then one should also consult what Werkmeister says in his *Organum gruningense*, §.30f., where ways to repair many major flaws are clearly indicated. For example, pipes that have no hooks must be given them, and pipes that have split open must be re-soldered. If the supply of wind has not been ample enough, then the wind ducts must be enlarged and made good and tight, together with the bellows, so that there is no more jolting or wobbling in the instrument. A new pallet box may also be added on the other side, and new pallets constructed in it. If the pipes are perforated, then after preventing any running* they should be soldered shut. If the holes in the slider chest are ragged, then one should attempt to make them smooth with a blunt drill, so that the stops are more easily drawn. If the leather has been worn away, then it should be replaced with new. The channels

---

* i.e., repairing any runs in the chest; see §.476 above.

ziergehen des Windes von einer Cancelle zur andern durch das Verleimen und Ausstreichen verbieten. Sind die Schrauben nicht mehr veste; so bohre man sie anders ein. Sind die Ventile des Windkastens zu klein; so reisse man den Windkasten ab, haue größere Oeffnungen in die Cancellen, wenn es möglich, und lege größere Ventile drauf. Sind die Stöhrfedern nicht gut oder gleich; so mache man andere. Alles gieße man wieder mit Leim aus. Sind die Pfeifen gedruckt; so richte man sie wieder ein. Mangeln etliche, oder taugen gar nichts; so mache man neue. Sind etliche von oben her verschnitten; so löthe man neue Stücke drauf. Hat der Salpeter die Füsse gefressen; so mache man neue dran. Ist etwann eine Stimme gar nichts nuß; so mache man sie ganz neu. Alles stimme man reine. Ist Koth, oder solches Zeug, in die Pfeifen gefallen; so reinige man die Pfeifen wieder. Haben sich die Palmuln des Manuals hohl gegriffen, oder die Palmuln des Pedals abgetreten; so mache man neue, oder versehe sie mit neuen Platten, besonders im Manuale. Ist sonst noch was entzwey; so verbeßre man es.

Zuweilen richtet man bey dergleichen Reparatur einen förmlichen Contrakt vorher auf; zuweilen aber giebt man nach vollendeter Arbeit, was der Künstler verdienet hat.

Das XIX. Kapitel.
Von der Historie der Orgeln.

Inhalt.

§. 482. Die Schriftsteller hiervon. §. 483. Wer die Orgeln erfunden? §. 484. Wann sie erfunden worden? §. 485. Anfänglich waren sie schlecht. §. 486. Wann das Pedal erfunden worden? it. von den alten Clavibus und Bälgen. §. 487. Nach und nach verbesserte man alles. §. 488. Der Register werden immer mehrere gemacht.

§. 482.

Dieses Kapitel ist so nöthig nicht, daß es nicht sollte können ausgelassen werden. Doch zur Zugabe soll nur etwas weniges davon gemeldet werden. Denn wenn wir darinne wollten weitläuftig seyn; so könnte man beybringen, wie ein Stück nach dem andern aufkommen. Aber was hat man für einen besondern Nutzen davon? zumal da man von wenigen rechte Gewißheit hat. Es hat diese Materie Prätorius Tom. I. p: 143. lateinisch, und Tom. II. p. 89. sequ. deutsch vorgetragen, da man sich allenfalls Raths erholen kann. Aus ihm hat Werkmeister in den nach seinem Tode herausgekommenen Paradoxaldiscursen S. 83. u. f. das nöthigste eingeschaltet. Johann Caspar Trost, jun. hat in der Beschreibung der Weissenfelsischen Schloßorgel Kap. I. auch versprochen, diese Materie ausführlich abzuhandeln: aber bis hierher ist sein Versprechen unerfüllt geblieben. Die Historie der Orgeln hat auch wohl zusammen gefasset

M. Gott-

of the chest may also be opened, in order to halt the useless leakage of the wind from one channel to another by smearing them with glue. If the screws are no longer tight, then new ones should be screwed in to replace them. If the pallets in the pallet box are too small, then the pallet box should be dismantled, larger opening should if possible be chiseled into the channels, and larger pallets should be placed on them. If the pallet springs are either not good or uneven, then others should be made. Everything needs to be re-coated with glue. If the pipes are pressed shut, they should be re-straightened. If anything is defective or worthless, it should be replaced with a part newly made. If any [pipes] are cut too short on top, new pieces should be soldered onto them.* If saltpeter has corroded the feet, then they must be given new ones. If any stop is simply useless, then it should be made over. Everything should be well tuned. If filth or any sort of matter has fallen into the pipes, then they need to be cleaned again. If hollows have been worn into the manual keys, or if the pedal keys have been worn away, then new ones must be made, or they must be re-covered with new slips, especially the manuals. If anything is broken, it should be repaired.

* to lengthen them.

Sometimes a formal contract is drawn up in advance of such repairs; sometimes, however, the craftsman is paid what he has earned after the work has been completed.

Chapter XIX.
Concerning the History of Organs.

Contents:

§.482. Writers on this subject. §.483. Who invented organs? §.484. When were they invented? §.485. Originally they were inferior. §.486. When was the pedal invented, as well as the ancient [type of] keys and bellows? §.487. Everything was gradually improved. §.488. The number of stops has kept on increasing.

§. 482.

This chapter is not so necessary as to be indispensable. But I will now report just a bit about the subject, as a bonus. For if I were to go into detail about it, I could relate how one part after another came into existence. But of what particular use would that be, especially since no one is absolutely certain about most of it. Praetorius has reported on this matter in [his *Syntagma musicum*,] Vol. I, p. 143[f.] (in Latin) and Vol. II, pp. 89f. (in German), so that one may always consult him if need be. Werkmeister has interpolated the most important passages from Praetorius into his *Paradoxal-Discourse*, published after his death, on pp. 83f. Johann Caspar Trost, Jr., also promised in his *Beschreibung der Weissenfelßischen Schloßorgel*, Chap. I,* that he would give a detailed account of this matter, but up to now his promise has remained unfulfilled. Gottfried Kretschmar,

* p. 3.

Kap. XIX. Von der Historie der Orgeln. 93

M. Gottfried Kretschmar, Pastor Primarius zu Görlitz, in der Einweihungspredigt der Görlitzer Orgel, davon §. 11. dieses Traktats Anzeige geschehen.

§. 483.

Man weis nicht, wer die Orgeln zuerst erfunden; worüber Polydorus Vergilius klagt Lib. I. de rerum inuentoribus, cap. XV. da er spricht. at auctor nostri tam concinni organi non proditur, cum magna eius nominis iactura. Lib. III. cap. ult. denkt er wieder hieran. Wie man ohnedieß in uhralten Zeiten so accurat in der Historie nicht war, wie heut zu Tage: Also ists kein Wunder, wenn sie auch in Anmerkung des Erfinders der Orgel saumselig gewesen, zumal da sie damals nicht so viel hat zu bedeuten gehabt.

§. 484.

Da man nun den Erfinder nicht weis; so ist auch nicht zu verwundern, wenn die Historienschreiber sich um die Zeit nicht vergleichen können, zu welcher die Orgeln aufgekommen. Man lieset beym Volat. lib. XXII. daß der Pabst Vitalianus sie in die Kirchen eingeführet, ohngefähr Anno 660. nach Christi Geburt. Andere sagen Anno 820. wären sie gebraucht worden; noch andere Anno 997. Ja, etliche sagen, daß zur Zeit Thomä Aquinatis die Orgeln noch nicht im Gebrauch gewesen, der doch im 13ten Jahrhundert erst gelebet. Aber von diesen wird die Erfindung der Orgeln gar zu neu gemacht; indem aus andern Geschichtschreibern zu ersehen, daß sie weit älter sind, und daß sie ohngefahr im 6ten oder 7ten Jahrhundert erfunden worden, und da hat man sie auch bald in der Kirche gebraucht. Zwar möchte jemand einwenden, als habe man zu Davids, des Israelitischen Königs Zeiten, schon Orgeln gehabt, sintemal deren in den Psalmen gedacht wird. Allein daran wird von andern gar viel ausgesetzt, und was aus dem Hebräischen עוגב zu machen, ist §. 16. berühret worden. M. Kretschmar l. c. hat hiervon verschiedenes beygebracht, da er sagt, sie wären ohne Zweifel alt, ob aber Salomo zu seiner Zeit im Tempel eine so herrliche Orgel gehabt, dergleichen man nicht mehr finde, wie die Rabbinen vorgeben, und in Ermangelung dergleichen Werks sich lieber gar keines bedienen wollen, mögen sie ausmachen. (conf. Lundii jüdische Heiligthümer Lib. IV. c. IV. no. 11. p. m. 746. b.) Hernach führt er an, zu welcher Zeit ohngefähr die Orgeln im Neuen Testament eingeführet worden, welches man daselbst lesen mag. Wer weis übrigens, was das für Instrumente gewesen sind, welche man für Orgeln halten und ausgeben will? Vielleicht den Haupttheilen nach ganz andere, als unsere. Doch davon mag ich nicht viel reden. Sollte David unsere Orgeln sehen, was würde er sagen?

§. 485.

Wie aber alle Erfindungen anfänglich den Grad der Vollkommenheit nicht haben welchen sie nach der Zeit erlangen; (quia inuentis facile est aliquid addere) so ist es auch sonderlich mit den Orgeln ergangen, wie aus Prätorii Tom. II. c. III. sequ. p 93. lequ. u. aus Werkmeisters Paradoxaldiscursen, Kap. 6. zu ersehen ist. Denn Anfangs machten

Chap. XIX. Concerning the History of Organs.

Senior Pastor in Görlitz, has also summed up the history of organs in his dedicatory sermon for the Görlitz organ, about which notice is given in §.11 of this treatise.

§. 483.

No one knows who first invented organs. Polydorus Vergilius laments this in Book I of his *De rerum inventoribus*, [Book V,] Chap. XV, saying: *at auctor nostri tam concinni organi non proditur, cum magna eius nominis iactura.** He mentions this once again in the final chapter of Book III.† But at any rate history was not recorded in ancient times as accurately as it is today, and thus it is no wonder that [ancient historians] were negligent in noting who invented the organ, especially since there was nothing very significant about it at that time.

* "but the inventor of our much celebrated organ is not known, due to the grave loss of his name."

† i.e., Chap. 18.

§. 484.

Since the inventor is not known, it is also no surprise that historians cannot agree on the time at which organs came into existence. *Volat. lib. XXII*‡ records that Pope Vitalianus introduced them into the church in approximately the year 660 A.D. Others say that they were in use in the year 820, and yet others say 997. Indeed, some say that organs were not yet in use at the time of Thomas Aquinas, who did not live until the 13th century. But these set a far too recent date for the organ's invention, since other historians reveal that they are far older, and that they were discovered approximately in the 6th or 7th century, and then quickly came into use in the church. To be sure, someone might object that organs were already in existence in the time of David, King of Israel, since they are mentioned in the Psalms. But other [scholars] have found a great deal to take exception to in this opinion, and §.16 has already discussed how to interpret the Hebrew עוגב. Mr. Kretschmar, l.c., has imparted various information about this, saying that they [i.e., organs] are without doubt ancient, but it is no longer possible to know whether there was a magnificent organ in the Temple in Solomon's day, as the rabbinic writings§ allege; lacking such an instrument, the [ancient rabbis] assert that they prefer to have none at all (cf. Lundius, *Jüdische Heiligthümer*, Book IV, Chap. IV, no. 11. p.m. 746.b.). Later on [Kretschmar] indicates the approximate date at which organs were introduced in the New Testament;¶ the reader may consult this source for himself. Anyway, who knows what sort of instruments there were that were being considered as and called organs?—perhaps ones that were completely different than ours in their essential features. But I do not want to discuss this matter further. What would [King] David say if he were to see our organs?

‡ Volaterranus, Raphael, *Commentariorum Urbanorum Raphaelis Volaterrani, octo & triginta libri.* Basel: Froben, 1544, Book XXII, p. 251.

§ The "Arakin" treatise of the Babylonian Talmud. See: Jean Perrot, *The Organ from its Invention in the Hellenistic Period to the end of the Thirteenth Century.* London: Oxford University Press, 1971, pp. xx-xxi.

¶ i.e., into the Christian Church.

§. 485.

No invention, however, possesses at the outset the degree of perfection that it eventually attains (since it is easy to add something to what is already invented), and this is especially true of the organ, as may be learned from Praetorius's [*Syntagma musicum,*] Vol. II, Chap. IIIf., pp. 93f., as well as from Werkmeister's *Paradoxal-Dis-*

94   Kap. XIX. Von der Historie der Orgeln.

machten sie gar kleine Werke, die in der Höhe der Kirchen als Schwalbennester klebten, auch keine Register oder Parallelen hatten; sondern wenn mehr Pfeifen auf einem clave stunden, so klungen sie alle zugleich. Es waren also die Orgeln damals von solcher Beschaffenheit wie unsere Mixturen sind. Die größten Pfeifen setzten sie voran zum Schein. Sie klungen scharf. Auch hatten sie keine Hemitonia, oder chromatischen Claves, und der diatonischen waren auch wenige, so, daß das ganze Clavier etwan eine oder 1½ Oktaven groß war. Die Palmuln waren erschrecklich breit, so, daß 9 Claves, die wir jetzo mit einer Hand erreichen können, damals wol anderthalb Ellen Raum eingenommen, welche auch schwer zu drücken waren, daß man sie mit den Fäusten niederdrücken mußte, davon noch die Redensart: die Orgel schlagen, bekannt ist, die aber heutiges Tages nicht mehr gilt: denn wir schlagen keine Orgeln mehr, sondern wir spielen sie. Etliche Orgelclaviere waren so angelegt: h c d e f g a h c d e f; etliche: c d e f g a b c d e f g a; etliche wieder anders. Und obwol nach Timothei Milesii Zeiten bald die Claves in der Musik dergestalt erhöhet worden, daß man 14 und 15 Claves bekommen; so findet man doch, daß sie nicht in den Orgeln so bald eingeführet worden. Die Ursache lese man in Prätorii Tomo II. p. 95.

§. 486.

Vor drittehalb hundert und mehr Jahren ist auch das Pedal erfunden worden von einem Deutschen Bernhardo, der Anno 1470 es nach Venedig gebracht. Dieß Pedal hatte nur acht Claves h c d e f g a h. Die Claves der Manuale waren etwan so: ⌣ oder ⌣. Hernach hat man auch mehrere Claviere gemacht, da eins mit der rechten Hand geschlagen wurde, und der Diskant hieß, da man bloß die Melodie des Chorals drauf hatte; das andere aber mit der linken Hand, welches der Baß hieß, und anstatt des Pedals gebraucht wurde. Die alten Blasbälge waren gar elend. Sie waren klein, daher man deren gar viel brauchte. Sie legten keine Gewichte drauf, sondern der Calcant mußte drauf treten und sie niederdrücken; mit dem andern Fuß zog er den benachbarten Balg zugleich in die Höhe. Daher zu 2 Bälgen ein Calcant, zu 24. aber 12 gehörten. Das muß sehr sauber gegangen seyn! denn die Personen haben nicht gleiche Schwere; folglich giebt es nicht gleichen Wind. s. Prator. l. c. S. 105. Er hat daselbst alles im Risse vorgestellet. Die Windlade betreffend, so hatte man weder Schleif- noch Springladen, weil man keine Register hatte. Hernach ist die Springlade erfunden worden, da man die Pfeifen hat wollen absondern. Also sind die Springladen was altes, und schon etliche 100 Jahre gebraucht worden. s. Prätor. l. c. S. 107. u. f.

§. 487

Nach und nach ist man immer weiter gekommen, und man hat auch die chromatischen Claves erfunden; die Palmuln auch immer schmahler gemacht, bis sie itzt auf einen

Zoll

Chap. XIX. Concerning the History of Organs.

course, Chap. 6.* For in the beginning only very small instruments were made, that clung to the heights of churches like swallows' nests. These organs had no stops or sliders, rather when there were a number of pipes for one key, they all sounded at the same time. Thus the organs of that time were constituted like our mixtures are.† The largest pipes were placed in front for appearance's sake. They sounded shrill. They had no *Hemitonia*, or chromatic keys, and there were also only a few diatonic ones, so that the entire keyboard had a compass of about one or 1½ octaves. The keys were frightfully wide, so that 9 keys, [a compass] that we can now reach with one hand, would easily have occupied a space of 1½ yards. They were also difficult to depress, so that it was necessary to do it with the fists, giving rise to the still familiar expression, "to beat the organ"—but this does not hold true any more today, since we no longer beat organs, but play them. Some organ keyboards were arranged like this: b natural c d e f g a b natural c d e f; some like this: c d e f g a b-flat c d e f g a; while others followed another [scheme]. And although soon after the time of Timotheus Milesius the number of notes [Claves] used for music had been increased to the point that there were 14 or 15 of them, yet one soon discovers that they were not so readily introduced into organs. For the reason, read Praetorius [*Syntagma musicum*], Vol. II, p. 95.

* This should read "16."

† i.e., a *Blockwerk*.

§. 486.

The pedal was discovered 350 years ago or more by a German, Bernhardo, who brought it to Venice in the year 1470. This pedal had only 8 keys: b natural c d e f g a b natural. The manual keys were shaped somewhat like this ⌣ or ⌣ .

Subsequently the number of keyboards was increased to two. One, called the treble, was beaten with the right hand, and upon it was played only the melody of the [Gregorian] chant. The other, called the bass, [was played] by the left hand, and used instead of the pedal. The old-time bellows were deplorable. They were small, and thus a great many of them were needed. No weights were set on them; rather the bellows treader had to tread upon one of them and press it down, while at the same time lifting the neighboring bellows with the other foot. Therefore there were 2 bellows per pumper, or 24 for 12 pumpers. What a mess that must have been! Since the personnel do not all weigh the same, consequently the wind pressure is unsteady; see Praetorius, l.c., p. 105.‡ There he has depicted all of this in a plate. As for the windchest, there were neither slider nor spring chests, since there were no stops. Subsequently the spring chest was discovered, since it was deemed desirable to divide up pipes.§ Thus spring chests are something ancient, and have already been in use some 100 years;¶ see Praetorius, l.c., pp. 107f.

‡ This should read "p. 103."

§ i.e., into stops.

¶ counting from Prætorius' day.

§. 487.

The instrument gradually developed further, and chromatic keys were also invented. The keys were also made smaller and smaller until by now they have been

Kap. XIX. Von der Historie der Orgeln. 95

Zoll abgesetzt worden. Man hat ferner immer mehrere Oktaven gemacht; mehr Claviere u. s. w. Die Stimmen hat man immer nach und nach von einander gesetzt; daher dann die Register entstanden. Vor ein Paar 100 Jahren hat man auch andere Stimmen gemacht, als: Spitzflöten, Schnarrwerke u. d. gl. Im Pedale ist man auch immer weiter gegangen, daß man endlich von C angefangen und bis zum c̄ fortgefahren, dabey die alten das Cis und Dis nicht hatten: aber anjetzo werden sie, sonderlich das Dis, überall gemacht. Das Cis und D thut man bisweilen hinzu, bisweilen nicht. Auch hat man endlich die schönen Spanbälge gemacht, und die Gewichte erfunden.

§. 488.

Wer die große Menge der Stimmen bedenkt, muß sich wol billig über den Fleiß der Künstler heutiges Tages verwundern. Zwar vor anderthalb hundert und mehr Jahren haben sie schon sehr viel solcher Stimmen gehabt, wie Prätorii Orgeldispositionen zeigen: aber jetzo hat man deren noch mehr, als Glöckleinton, Vox Humana, Violdigamba, Fugara u. s. w. die man damals nicht gekannt hat; und täglich entdeckt man der Stimmen noch mehr. Von wem aber, und zu welcher Zeit, dieses und jenes Stück entdeckt worden, ist hier nicht auszuführen, weil ich keine vollkommene Historie der Orgeln allhier liefern, sondern nur ein Paar Worte lallen wollen, daß ein Liebhaber der Musick wenigstens so viel wisse, daß die alten Orgeln nicht so gewesen, als die unsrigen heutiges Tages. Mehr suche man in Prätorii 2tem Tomo, und andern in diesem Traktate hin und wieder bekant gemachten Schriften. Daß Christian Förner aus Wettin im vorigen Säkulo die Windprobe (einige schreiben auch Windwaage) erfunden, ist §. 460. gemeldet worden.

Das XX. Kapitel.
Von den andern Instrumenten, die ein Organist zu kennen nöthig hat, überhaupt: Item von Positiven insonderheit.

Inhalt.

§. 489. Der Endzweck dieses und der folgenden Kapitel. §. 490. Alle Instrumente sind mir noch nicht bekannt. §. 491. Ich will sie einen nicht machen lehren. §. 492. Sie sind nicht einerley Art. §. 493. Von der Benennung der Positive. §. 494. Wie groß sie seyn dürfen. §. 495. Etliche präsentiren sich wie ein Tisch. §. 496. Was man dabey zu beobachten. §. 497. Etliche haben ein Instrument bey sich. §. 498. Besondere Art des Balgziehens. §. 499. Prätorii Positiv. §. 500. Beschluß des vorigen.

§. 489.

Es würde meine Musica mechanica sehr unvollkommen seyn, wo die bisherige Traktation, welche bloß auf die Orgeln gerichtet gewesen, das einzige darinnen seyn sollte, da doch ein Organist noch mehr Instrumente kennen und können muß, welche

reduced to one inch. Furthermore, more and more octaves were added, more keyboards, etc. The ranks have gradually been divided off one from another, and this is how stops originated. Several hundred years ago other stops* began to be made, such as Spitzflutes, reeds, and such. The pedal was also constantly expanded, until it now finally extends from C to c′. In earlier days the [pedal] C# and D# were missing, but now they are built everywhere, especially the D#. The [pedal] c#[′] and d[′] are sometimes added, sometimes not. Finally the fine wedge-shaped bellows began to be made, and [bellows] weights were invented.

* i.e., stops other than principals.

§. 488.

Anyone who considers what a great quantity of stops there are cannot help but admire the diligence of today's craftsmen. It is true that 150 or more years ago a great many of these stops were already in existence, as Praetorius's organ stoplists† show, but nowadays there are even more of them, such as Glöckleinton, Vox Humana, Violdigamba, Fugara, etc., that were unknown in earlier times. And more stops are being discovered every day. It is not my intention to go into when and by whom this or that item was discovered, because I am not furnishing here a complete history of the organ, but only intend to babble a few words to help an admirer of music at least realize that old organs were not the same as those today. More about this subject may be found in the second volume of Praetorius's [*Syntagma musicum*‡] and in other writings mentioned here and there in this treatise.§ It has already been reported in §.460 that Christian Förner of Wettin invented the windgauge in the past century (some also call it "Windwaage").

† in the *Syntagma musicum*, Vol. II, pp. 161-203.

‡ Vol. II, Part III, pp. 81-118.
§ i.e., the *Musica mechanica organœdi*.

Chapter XX.
Concerning other Instruments in general that an Organist needs to be familiar with, and in particular Positivs.

Contents:

§.489. The purpose of this chapter and the one following. §.490. Not all instruments are yet known to me. §.491. It is not my intention to teach anyone how to make them. §.492. They are not all of the same sort. §.493. How the Positiv got its name. §.494. How large they ought to be. §.495. Some have the appearance of a table. §.496. What to observe about them. §.497. Some contain an Instrument.* §.498. A special method of pumping the bellows. §.499. A Positiv described by Praetorius. §.500. Conclusion to the above [paragraph].

* see §.540.

§. 489.

My *Musica mechanica* would be very incomplete if the previous discussion, which was directed solely toward the organ, were the only one in it. For an organist must be familiar with and be able to play other instruments as well, and thus these

also mit gutem Rechte allhier in einige Erwägung zu ziehen. Wenn ich zwar sollte die Instrumente alle beschreiben, welche aus der Wissenschaft des Claviers ihren Grund herleiten; so würde ich die wenigsten dürfen unberührt lassen. Denn das getraue ich mir zu behaupten, daß ein rechter Clavierverständiger die meisten Instrumenta musica für sich erlernen könne, wenn die Zeit und Uebung dazu kömmt: allein so weit will ich allhier nicht ausschweifen, sondern bloß bey denen bleiben, die mit der Orgel auch in der Struktur eine nähere Verwandtschaft haben, daß sie entweder mit vielen Pfeifen oder mit dem Claviere versehen sind; das letzte aber wird insbesondere in Betrachtung gezogen.

§. 490.

Wie aber die Künstler die Mechanik heut zu Tage überall hoch treiben, und solche Dinge erfinden, da man nicht meynen sollte, daß Menschenhände dergleichen machen könnten; also wächst auch die Anzahl solcher Instrumente noch immer, von welchen wir anjetzo reden. Folglich kann niemand von mir verlangen, daß ich von allen eine Beschreibung geben solle. Ja auch nicht einmal diese, welche man heut zu Tage allbereit erfunden, werden von mir alle erzählet werden, weil mir alle noch nicht bekannt, und auch in andern Ländern manches anzutreffen, welches bey uns nicht zu finden ist.

§. 491.

Es möchte mancher bey den folgenden Kapiteln mit der Kürze nicht zufrieden seyn, zumal wenn er darinne eine völlige Nachricht gesucht, wie ein jedes zu machen, wie mit dem Zirkel und Maaßstabe alles abzutheilen und die Mensuren zu messen: allein wie eine jedwede Schrift nach dem Endzwecke des Schreibers zu beurtheilen; so wolle der geneigte Leser es auch bey dieser Schrift beobachten. Mein Endzweck ist, einem Organisten, oder andern Liebhaber des Claviers eine Wissenschaft von den Theilen der Instrumente überhaupt beyzubringen; imgleichen, was ihre Vollkommenheiten und Fehler sind, daß er sich im Urtheilen und Wählen in Acht nehmen könne; it wie solche Instrumente zu brauchen und zu erhalten. Wollte ich aber hier lehren, wie man dergleichen zimmern sollte; so würde ich mich dabey ganz anders bezeigen müssen. Aber das ist mein Vorsatz weder bey der Orgel, noch bey den nachgesetzten Instrumenten, gewesen.

§. 492.

Es sind solche Instrumente nicht einerley Art. Denn einige gehen in den Haupttheilen nichts oder wenig von der Orgel ab, da sie mit Pfeifen, Windladen, Bälgen, Clavieren, rc. gemacht sind: etliche aber gehen gar sehr ab, daß sie der Orgel in wenig Stücken gleichen, nur daß sie, wie jene, ein Clavier haben. Und dieser natürlichen Ordnung wollen wir für dießmal folgen: und weil uns die Theile der Orgel noch im frischen Andenken sind; so wollen wir gleich die Instrumente dazu fügen, welche ihr am nächsten kommen.

§. 493.

ought rightfully to be considered here, too. To be sure, if I were to describe all the instruments that are originally based on the science of the keyboard, then only a very few would go unmentioned. For I dare say that anyone truly knowledgeable about the keyboard could learn most musical instruments by himself, given time and practice. Here, however, I will not spread myself so thin, keeping rather only to those that are closely related in their structure to the organ, in that they are either provided with many pipes or with a keyboard; but the latter will be given particular attention.

§. 490.

Since mechanical craftsmen have everywhere developed their art nowadays to such a high degree of perfection, and invented such things as one would hardly think possible from human hands, thus the number of such instruments about which we are now about to speak continues to grow. Consequently no one can require of me that I give a description of every one of them. Indeed I will not even tell about all those that have been discovered up to this point, since I am not yet familiar with all of them; and there are many to be encountered in other lands that are not to be found among us.

§. 491.

Some people will not be satisfied with the brevity of the following chapters, especially if they seek from them a detailed report of how to make each [instrument], how to measure off everything with a compass and ruler and how to measure the scales. But since every written work ought to be judged according to its author's purpose, I beg the gracious reader to observe [this precept] with this work as well. My purpose is to give general instruction in the science of the components of instruments to an organist or to other admirers of the keyboard; likewise [to impart] what their virtues and faults are, so that [an organist] may be able to keep them in mind when evaluating and selecting; as well as [to teach] how to use and maintain such instruments. If I had intended to teach how to build them, then I would have had to express myself entirely differently. But that has not been my intention either with regard to the organ or with regard to those instruments that follow it.*

* i.e., in this treatise.

§. 492.

Such instruments are not all of the same sort. For some deviate little, if at all, from the organ in their principal components, in that they are made with pipes, windchests, bellows, keyboards, etc.. Others, though, deviate very widely indeed, resembling the organ only in that, like it, they have a keyboard. For now we will follow this natural order, and since the components of the organ are now fresh in our minds, we will immediately proceed to the instruments that resemble it most closely.

it. von Positiven insonderheit.

§. 493.

Am wenigsten geht von der Orgel ab das sogenannte Positiv, als welches bloß in der Größe von jener unterschieden, deswegen es auch von den Italienern Organo piccolo, d. i. eine kleine Orgel, genennet wird. Daher ist es auch die Mode, daß in der Orgel das eine geringere Werk das Positiv heißt, und zwar das Rückpositiv, wenn es im Rücken steht; Brustpositiv, wenn es voran, doch unten, gebauet ist; Oberpositiv, wenn dessen Windlade über den andern steht. Wer wollte zweifeln, daß diese Positive nicht eben die Theile hätten, als die andern Claviere. Die kleinen Orgeln auf den Dörfern führen deswegen oft auch diesen Namen, oder wo sonst kleine Werke stehen. Das Wort Positiv ist von ponere setzen. Warum dieser Name ihnen insbesondere gegeben sey, weis ich nicht. Die großen Werke, welche doch ebenfalls auch hingesetzt werden, wie jene, führen dennoch diesen Namen nicht, sondern man nennet sie, wie überall bekannt, Orgeln.

§. 494.

Es haben diese Positive, wie gesagt, die Haupttheile mit der Orgel gemein, nämlich die Pfeifen, Windlade, Register, Claviere, Bälge, ꝛc. und alles geht auch eben so zu, als in den Orgeln. Da sie nun bloß an der Größe unterschieden; so fragt sichs: wie klein das Positiv seyn müsse, daß es also genennet werden könne? Antw. Man siehet auf die offenen Stimmen in solchen kleinen Werken. Wenn deren größtes, oder das sogenannte Principal nicht größer ist, als 2′ Ton; so heißt es insgemein ein Positiv: wo aber dasselbe größer ist; so ist es eine Orgel. Und so hat man zu Prätorii Zeiten diesen Unterschied allbereits bestimmt. Man lese deßfalls nach, was er Tom. II. Synt. P. IV. c. I. p. 123. davon vorgetragen. Aber zuweilen nennt man andere Werke auch also, sonderlich in Orgeln, da das Positiv oft 4′ Ton ist.

§. 495.

Da nun die Theile eines Positivs fast einerlei mit den Theilen der Orgel sind, zumal wenn die Pfeifen aufwärts stehen; so wäre wol überflüßig, wenn ich sie erzählen wollte, da es bey der Orgel allbereits geschehen; sondern ich lasse es dabey bewenden, und erzähle nur, was man noch für besondere Arten der Positive zu machen pfleget. Es giebt solche, die in Form eines Tisches sich präsentiren, da das Tischblat sich schieben läßt, daß das Clavier zum Vorschein kömmt. Bey diesen Positiven liegen die Pfeifen hinterwärts. Dergleichen habe ich gesehen, unter welchen das eine einen doppelten Balg hatte; die Pfeifen waren von Holz; der Register waren 2, eins 8′, das andere 4′, beyde gedackt. Das eine, nämlich das Gedackt 8′ ließ sich stets hören; aber die gedackte Oktave 4′ konnte durch einen Zug abgezogen werden, welcher diese Form hatte:

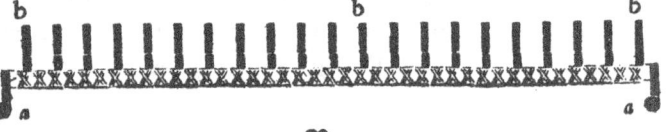

§. 493.

The instrument that deviates the least from the organ is the so-called Positiv, which differs from it only in size; for this reason the Italians call it *organo piccolo*, i.e., "little organ." Thus it is also customary that the lesser division in an organ is called the Positiv, and indeed the Rückpositiv if it is located behind [the organist's] back, the Brustpositiv if it is in front [of the organist] yet underneath [the Hauptwerk], or the Oberpositiv, if its windchest stands above the others. It is obvious that such Positivs have the same components as the other manuals. For this reason small village organs also bear this name, or wherever else small instruments are to be found. The word "Positiv" comes from [the Latin verb] *ponere*, "to place." Why this name was given to them* in particular, I do not know. It is commonly known that large instruments, that are also stationary just like them, nevertheless do not bear this name, but are called "organs."

* i.e., small organs.

§. 494.

As we have said, these Positivs share the same principal components in common with the organ, namely pipes, a windchest, stops, keyboards, bellows, etc., and everything works the same as in organs. Since they differ merely in size, the question arises: how small must a Positiv be to be called such? The answer: in such small instruments the open stops are the determining factor. If the largest of these, the so-called Principal, is not larger than 2′ pitch, then [the instrument] is usually called a Positiv; if this stop is larger, then it is an Organ. This distinction was already established in Praetorius's day. In that regard, consult his statements in Vol. II of the *Syntagma*, Part IV, Chap. I, p. 123. But sometimes other instruments† are so designated, especially in organs, since the Positiv is often at 4′ pitch.

† i.e., organs that do not share the distinguishing characteristic of a Principal that is 2′ or smaller.

§. 495.

Since the components of a Positiv are almost identical to those of an organ, especially if the pipes stand erect, it would be superfluous for me to enumerate them, since this has already been done in connection with the organ. Rather I will let the matter rest after relating only what particular types of Positivs it is customary to build. There are those that assume the appearance of a table, in which the tabletop slides back to reveal the keyboard. In such Positivs the pipes are set at the back.‡ I have seen [instruments] such as this, among which one had a double bellows; its pipes were wooden, and it had two stops, an 8′ and a 4′, both stopped. One of them, namely the 8′ Gedackt, was permanently on, but the stopped 4′ Oktave could be shut off by a mechanism that took this form:

‡ i.e., facing away from the player.

Diese Zacken b b b traten in die Löcher des Windbehältnisses, (weil die Windlade nicht auf der breiten Seite liegen konnte, sondern auf der schmahlen) und waren mit Faden und Leder umwunden, daß sie einander gleich waren. Sie waren rund, und kaum halb so dicke als ein Finger: und wenn man sie an der Welle vermittelst der Knöpfe *a a* herum drehete; so giengen sie einwärts, und jeder Zacke hielt den Wind von der dazu gehörigen Pfeife ab.

§. 496.

Diese sind bequem zu brauchen, weil man sie forttragen kann; zumal da sie als ein Tisch uns anderweitige Dienste thun können. Mit dem doppelten Balge geht es auch an, daß einer allein ohne Calcanten sich kann lustig machen, wenn er nur gewohnt ist, accurat zu treten, daß der Wind nicht mangele. Wollte man zweene kleine Bälge nehmen, deren Calcaturclaves vorgiengen, daß man sie selber treten könnte; so würde das spielen etwas mühsam werden, ja, manchem Spieler würde es gar unmöglich seyn, etwas gescheides vorzubringen, wenn er sich selbst Wind machen sollte. Das Gedackte 8' kann zur Musik wohl gebraucht werden, welches ich ohnedieß bey allen Positiven für nothwendig erachte. Man muß hierbey in Acht nehmen, daß man die Register nicht ganz heraus drücke, oder die Zacken abbreche, oder einen dicke und den andern dünne mache, sondern durch Faden und Leder mache man sie recht passend, daß kein Wind neben denselben herauskommen kann. Wollte man ein Pedal daran machen; so könnte man sich zwar besser darauf üben: doch würde es der Mühe nicht werth seyn, es wäre denn, daß man es nur an das Manual heftete. Und da dürften wol Wellen nöthig seyn, daß man durch die schiefen Faden die Palmulen nicht auf die Seite ziehe. Es müssen aber, wenn man die Kosten sparen will, nicht eben Abstrakten, Schrauben, und dergleichen Dinge, daran gemacht werden, sondern durch guten Bindfaden kann ein gleiches zu Stande kommen.

§. 497.

Ferner habe ich ein Positiv, fast von gleicher Art, gesehen, dabey die Pfeifen in die Höhe stunden, und oben drauf war ein Instrument gemacht, welches von ebendemselbigen Claviere regieret wurde. Da nun das Positiv selbst Register hatte; so konnte man solche alleine brauchen, oder man konnte sie wegthun, und das Seyteninstrument alleine spielen, weil solches durch einen Registerzug konnte gestillet, und wieder zum Klange gebracht werden, wie unten bey dem Clavicymbel zu sehen ist. §. 528. Hätte man ein Clavicymbel wollen drauf bringen; so wäre dessen Spitze allzuweit hinaus gegangen. Wie das zugehe, ist leicht zu begreifen. Denn die Docken können hinter den Pfeifen hinunter auf die Clavierpalmuln reichen, wie bey dem Clavicymbel geschiehet. Was bey solchem insonderheit zu beobachten, das wird unten bey dem Instrumente, Kap. 22. beygebracht werden. Die Fehler, Erhaltung u. s. w. sind wie bey den Orgeln. Es können solche Positive überhaupt nicht wohl in die Stuben gesetzt werden,

The teeth b b b fit into holes into the wind reservoir (since the windchest could not lie lengthways, but sideways), and were wrapped with thread and leather, so that they were identical [in size]. They were round, and barely half the thickness of a finger; and if one rotated them on their axle by means of the knobs a a, then they moved inward, and each tooth blocked the wind from its assigned pipe.

§. 496.

[Positivs] are convenient to use because they are portable, especially since they can do us further service as a table. If they have a double bellows, it is also possible to play at will alone, without a bellows pumper, as long as [the player] is accustomed to pumping precisely so there is always sufficient wind. If the instrument had two small bellows whose poles protruded, allowing [the player] to pump by himself, then it would be somewhat troublesome to play; indeed, some players would find it absolutely impossible to produce anything decent if they had to provide the wind for themselves. The 8′ Gedackt is well suited for [playing continuo in ensemble] music; at any rate I consider that [stop] a necessity for every Positiv. Be careful not to pull the stops out hard, or to break off the teeth, or to make one thick and the next thin. Rather by using twine and leather they should be made to fit precisely, so that no wind can escape around them. If one were to add a pedal to [the instrument], then it would indeed be all the more suited for practice; but this would not be worth the trouble, unless it were only attached to the manual. And this might well make rollers necessary, to prevent the keys from being pulled sideways by the slanting cords. If economy is a necessity, however, not even trackers, screws and such things have to be made for it, but rather the same result may be achieved with good-quality twine.

§. 497.

Furthermore, I have seen a Positiv of almost the same sort, in which the pipes stood up top,* and above them was built an Instrument,† operated from the very same keyboard. Since the Positiv was controlled by its own stops, it could be used by itself, or it could be shut off, allowing the stringed instrument‡ to be played by itself, since it could also be silenced by a stopknob or again be made to sound (as may be seen below in §.528 in connection with the harpsichord). If one had wanted to set a harpsichord above it, then its pointed tail would have hung over too far. How it§ works is easy to comprehend. The jacks could extend downward behind the pipes to the keys, as is the case with the harpsichord. Chapter 22, in which the Instrument is discussed, will relate what in particular to pay attention to. The faults, maintenance, etc.¶ are the same as the organ's. Such Positivs most assuredly cannot be placed in living quarters, where

* i.e., above the keyboard; this seems to be a remark that distinguishes this placement of pipes from that described in §.495 & 496, i.e., table positivs.

† see §.540.

‡ i.e., the Instrument.

§ i.e., this combination of a Positiv and an Instrument.

¶ after having described a combination Positiv/Instrument, Adlung now returns to speaking specifically about the Positiv.

werden, wo die Kälte und Wärme beständig abwechselt, weil ihre Höhe und Tiefe sodann gar oft verändert wird. Es sind dergleichen Positive für wenige Thaler zu machen, weil man ordentlich hölzerne Pfeifen dazu nimmt, die man entweder viereckicht macht, oder sie aushöhlt, daß sie rund werden: und andere Kostbarkeiten kommen nicht dazu. Wenn sie in etliche Stockwerke getheilet sind; so läßt es sein, und ist gut, wenn man sie kann von einander nehmen. So habe ich eins gesehen, welches in 3. Stockwerke getheilt war. Im untersten waren die Bälge; auf dieses war nur ein Gehäuse gesetzt mit den Wellen, Claviere, Abstrakten ꝛc. welches man abheben konnte, wenn man nur die Abstrakten vom Claviere loßmachte, als welche an der Windlade bleiben müssen, welche nebst dem Pfeifwerke im obersten Stockwerke war, und das auch allein abgenommen werden konnte.

§. 498.

Wenn man metallene Pfeifen macht, und zwar etwas kleine; so kann man die Positive schreyend machen. Sonst habe ich noch mancherley Positivarten gesehen, die ich aber nicht anführen mag, weil ein jeder Orgelmacher nach seinem Kopfe diese und jene Invention machet, da denn des Beschreibens kein Ende seyn würde. Zuweilen setzt man ein Regal mit darauf. Zuweilen hat man anstatt des Calcaturclavis eine andere Invention, daß man bessern Raum haben möge. Man bevestiget nämlich an die obere Platte des Balges einen Strick, und oben in die Decke oder Säule eine Rolle, darauf der Strick zu liegen kömmt. Auf der Seite, wo der Calcaturclavis hätte sollen heraus gehen, machet man ein Loch und zieht den Strick durch, an welchem man hernach den Balg mit der Hand ziehen kann. Oder man macht an das Ende des Stricks eine Stange, deren unteres Ende in einer Welle bevestiget wird, und daran zieht man den Balg auf. Darneben kann eine kleine Kette angemacht werden, samt einem Schlosse, um den Balg anzuschliessen, daß niemand spiele, wenn wirs nicht haben wollen.

§. 499.

Eine besondere Art des Positivs hat Prätorius in Syntagm. T. II. P. II. C. 48. pag. 79. seqq. beschrieben. Weil dasselbe Buch nicht in aller Handen ist, will ich seine Worte ganz hierher setzen. Sie heissen so: „Dieses alte Positiv (welches er nämlich damals gesehen und im Risse vorgestellt) ist von sauberer und subtiler Arbeit, von einem Mönche gemacht, so dem Könige in Dännemark Christiano IV. zugebracht worden. In demselben sind nur einerley Pfeifen, nemlich ein offen Principälgen von 2′ Ton, und wiewol nur 38 Claves von F bis $\bar{\bar{a}}$ da sind, so sind doch der Pfeifen noch eine Oktave drüber, oben in der Mitte des corporis in die Runde herum gewunden gesetzt. Zu solcher einzigen Partie Pfeifen sind 3. Register; 1. zum rechten Ton der untersten Pfeifen; das andere zur Quinte; das dritte zur Oktave drüber, und kann ein jedes Register vor sich selbst alleine und absonderlich gebraucht werden, daß also in einerley Pfeifen auf einem clave 2. und auch 3. discreti soni, als nemlich neben dem rechten Tone die Quinte und Oktave sich hören lassen. Wie solches zugehe, lasse ich einen verständigen

the constant alternation of warm and cold [temperatures] would cause their pitch to vary continually. Such Positivs can be made quite cheaply, since they are normally provided with wooden pipes, either rectangular or round* and hollowed out, and other expensive components need not be used. It is a good thing and a convenience if they are divided into a number of levels that may be taken apart. Thus I have seen one that was divided into three levels; in the lowest was the bellows, and on it a case was set containing only the rollers and trackers, the keyboard, etc. This [case] could be lifted off merely by disconnecting the trackers from the keyboard; they then had to remain attached to the windchest which, together with the pipes, was in the uppermost level, and which could also be removed by itself.

* i.e., turned on a lathe.

§. 498.

If the pipes are made of metal and are rather small, then a Positiv may well be shrill.† Moreover I have seen any number of types of Positivs, but I will not cite them all, since each organbuilder thinks up this or that invention, and there would be no end of describing them. At times a Regal is included with [the other ranks]. Instead of a bellows pole there is sometimes another invention that takes up less space. Namely, a cord is fastened to the upper plate of the bellows, and above it a roller is fastened on [the underside of] the lid or on a post, over which the cord passes. A hole is made on the side [of the instrument], where the bellows pole would have protruded, and through it is threaded the cord; then it may subsequently be used to draw up the bellows by hand. Or a rod is affixed to the end of the cord, whose lower end is fastened to an axle, and the bellows is lifted by pulling [the rod]. A chain may be attached next to [the rod], along with a lock, to fasten the bellows closed and keep anyone from playing it except when desired.

† This translation suggests a pejorative meaning for "schreyend," but it is possible that Adlung intends just the opposite, i.e., "sharp" or "ringing." There is no context or further development of the remark that would make it clear.

§. 499.

Praetorius has described a special type of Positiv in his *Syntagma*, Vol. II, Part II., Chap. 48, p. 79f. Since this book is not always available, I will reproduce his entire text here. It reads like this:‡ "This old Positiv§ (which [Praetorius] had at that time seen and depicted in a sketch] is of fine and delicate workmanship. It was made by a monk, and then brought to King Christian IV of Denmark. There are only a few pipes in it, namely a small open Principal at 2′ pitch; and even though there are only 38 keys, from F to a″, there is an extra octave of pipes, set high in the middle of the case and wound about in the shape of a circle. From this single batch of pipes are derived 3 stops: the first at the proper pitch of the lowest pipe, the second at the fifth [above], and the third at the octave above. Each stop may be used alone by itself, separate from the others, so that from the same pipes two or even three distinct pitches may be heard from each key, namely the unison, the fifth and the octave. I will leave it to a qualified organbuilder to judge how such a thing works, and would only wish that a craftsman might undertake to reproduce such an instrument. There is yet another clever feature in this little instru-

‡ Adlung again reproduces the essence of Praetorius's text without quoting it directly. The passage in question is in Praetorius, Vol. II, p. 80.

§ i.e., the one Praetorius had seen at that time and provided a plate of; the plate is No. I in the "Theatrum Instrumentorum" at the end of Vol. II.

Orgelmacher judiciren, und wollte wünschen, daß ein Künstler solch Werk nachzumachen sich unternehmen wollte. Uiber das ist auch dieses noch ein Kunststucke an diesem Werklein, daß es, wenn die eine Hälfte des Bleyes oder Gewichten, (so dieserwegen von einander zertheilet und halbiret seyn) von den Blasbälgen genommen werden, gar ein sanften stillen Resonantz, gleich den Querflöten, von sich giebt, und sich nicht anders hören läßt, als wenn ein Stimmwerk Querflöten zusammen accordirt und geblasen würde." So weit Prätorius. Man sieht also, daß man heut zu Tage nicht allein klug ist. Ich stelle mir diese Sache also vor, daß durch besondere Windführungen eine Pfeife hat können von dreyerley Orten her Wind haben: wenn nun z. E. der Clavis die größte Pfeife hat klingend gemacht; so kann durch eben das Ventil der Wind durch eine Röhre in die Cancelle der Quinte kommen seyn, welche also auch mit geklungen, so auch in die Cancelle der Oktave. Durch Register haben die Röhren können verdeckt werden. Deswegen hat eine Oktave Pfeifen mehr seyn müssen, als Palmuln gewesen, das die obere Oktave auch eine andere Oktave bekommen. Also hat nicht eine Pfeife dreyerley Sonos gehabt. Daß durch den geschwächten Wind auch der Sonus geschwächt worden, ist auch wol zu begreifen.

§. 500.

Sollte jemand im Rathen glücklicher seyn, als ich, dem will ich es gerne gönnen: genung, daß ich vorgestellet, wie dergleichen möglich sey.

Das XXI. Kapitel.
Von allerhand Regalen.

Inhalt.

§. 501. Ihre Struktur. §. 502. Ihr Nutzen. §. 503. Man macht sie mit hölzernen Pfeifen; it. in Form eines Buchs. §. 504. Man könnte mehrerley Regale machen.

§. 501.

Dieses Kapitel wird sehr kurz werden, weil in dem 7ten Kapitel das vornehmste schon berühret worden. Zwar wird daselbst eigentlich von den Regalen in den Orgeln geredet; allein das meiste geht auch an ausser der Orgel. Der Name ist, wie daselbst §. 183. gemeldet, von Rex, ein König. Die Ursach lese man daselbst nach. Ausser der Orgel hat man nämlich die Regale gar vielfältig, und kommen solche der Struktur nach den Orgeln, wie die Positive, noch am gleichsten. Sie haben eine Windlade, Bälge, Clavier, Pfeifen, ꝛc; nur daß man sie ordentlich mit hölzernen oder meßingenen Pfeifen versieht, welche sehr klein, dabey entweder offen, oder gedeckt sind, diese aber an den Seiten Löcherchen haben, dadurch der Schall heraus gehet.

Es

ment: if half the lead weights (which have been divided in half just for this purpose) are taken off the bellows, then the instrument produces a gentle, quiet tone, similar to a traverse flute, and sounds just like a consort of traverse flutes being blown and sounded together." This is the end of the quote from Praetorius. Thus it is evident that it is not only we moderns who are clever. I imagine this situation as one pipe getting wind from three sources by means of separate wind ducts; if, for example, a key has caused the largest pipe to speak, then a tube leading from the same pallet can permit the wind to enter the channel that sounds the fifth, causing it to sound as well; the same procedure could produce the octave. The tubes could be shut off by stops. That must have been the reason for the extra octave of pipes beyond the number of keys, to serve the additional octave of notes. Thus each pipe did not produce three different sounds. It is also easy to understand how a weaker wind pressure could produce a weaker tone.

§. 500.

If anyone should be possessed of more ample information than I,* I do not begrudge it him in the least; at least I have explained how such a thing would be possible.

* i.e., concrete information as to how the Positiv described by Praetorius actually works.

Chapter XXI.
Concerning Regals of all Types.
Contents:
§.501. Their structure. §.502. Their use. §.503. They are made with wooden pipes, in the shape of a book. §.504. Various types of regals could be made.

§. 501.

This chapter will be very brief, since Chapter 7 has already dealt with the most important matters.† It was regals found in organs that were being discussed there, to be sure, but most of what was said also applies [to regals] that are independent from [larger] organs. As reported in §.183 above, the name comes from [the Latin] Rex, a king (refer to this paragraph for the reason). There are many different types of regals that exist independent from the organ, and, like the positiv, their structure very closely approximates that of the organ. They have a windchest, bellows, keyboard, pipes, etc.—but they are normally furnished with wooden or brass pipes that are very small. They may be either open or stopped; in the latter case the pipes have small holes in their sides, in order to let the sound escape. They are reed [pipes], and consequently it

† see §.183.

Es sind Schnarrwerke, und folglich sieht man leicht, wie sie zu stimmen sind. **Prätorius** meynt, ausser der Orgel könnte man sie **Regalwerke,** in derselben aber **Regalpfeife,** zum Unterschiede, benennen: aber das ist jetzo nicht Mode.

§. 502.

Sie dienen zur Musik in den Zimmern, oder an solchen Orten, da man keine Orgeln hat, als welche sich nicht forttragen lassen. Wollte man Clavicymbel brauchen; so klingt es zwar angenehmer: allein sie sind etwas zu stille, wo sie nicht 2 oder 3 Chöre Seyten haben, auch continuiren sie den Klang nicht; auch reissen die Seyten bisweilen, und verderben das Spiel, wenn es am besten hergehen soll. Aus diesem Grunde verdienen die Regale einiges Lob. Denn wegen des Klanges wollte ich sie für meine Person wenig achten. Damit sie bequem können fortgetragen werden; so legt man die Pfeifen meistens hinterwärts, zuweilen aber stehen sie auch aufwärts, weil sie ohnedieß oft kaum Fingers lang sind. Das ganze Werk wird sodenn in einen länglicht viereckichten Kasten gemacht; die Bälge kann man auch abnehmen, auch das Gestell, oder Tisch, worauf es ruhet, kann allein fortgetragen werden. Man kann sie mit 2 Bälgen machen, die eine andere Person hinten aufhebet, oder die der Spieler mit 2 Beinen wechselsweise tritt. Man kann auch durch einen Doppelbalg diese Mühe verringern. Dieß ist die ordentliche Art von Regalen.

§. 503.

In der Organographia prætoriana p. 73, (woraus es **Mattheson** allegirt in den **Anmerkungen zum Nied Kap. 10.**) wird von einem Regalwerklein etwas gemeldet mit hölzernen Pfeifen, welches nicht allein von gutem, stillem und lieblichem Resonanz ist, sondern auch gar leicht und bequem von einem Orte zum andern fortzubringen seyn soll. Wenn ich (sagt **Mattheson**) ein solches bekommen könnte, möchte ich mich mit dem Regal wieder aussöhnen. Man hat noch mehr Inventionen von Regalen. Unter andern ist nicht allzu unbekannt, daß man es in der Form eines Buchs in Folioformat zuweilen verfertiget, da man aus 2 Theilen das ganze Werk und das Clavier bestehen läßt, und es hernach zusammen legt. Die Bälge sind auch dabey, und dienen dem Buche zu Pappen. Auf solche Weise sind sie sehr bequem fortzutragen. Die ersten Regale in der Gestalt eines Foliantens hat ein Nürnbergischer Orgelmacher, Namens **Georg Voll,** gemacht, welcher bereits 1565. gestorben, wie solches **Walther** aus **Doppelmayers** historischen Nachricht von den Nürnbergischen Künstlern, S. 290. anführt. Ein solches Regal stellt einen ordentlichen Folianten vor, ist 2 bis 3 Hände breit dicke. Der thut sich in der Mitte von einander wie ein Buch. Da liegt das Clavier drinne, in jeder Seite die Hälfte, welches man heraus nimmt und accurat zusammen setzt, so ist unter dem Clavier gleich die Windlade dabey; die Pfeifchen auch, doch gar klein. Das Buch wendet man hernach um, und legt es hinten an, so sind es die Blasbälge, und die beyden Tafeln geben die 2 Oberplatten, davon man die Bälge in die Höhe hebt. Inwendig

Chap. XXI. Concerning Regals of all Types

is easy to see how they are tuned. Praetorius* suggests that they could be referred to as "Regalwerke" when independent from the organ, but as "Regalpfeife" when a part of the organ, in order to distinguish them; but that is not the custom at present.

*Syntagma musicum, Vol. II, p. 73.

§. 502.

They are of service for ensemble music in chambers, or in places where there are no organs that are portable. It would sound more pleasant, to be sure, if a harpsichord were used, but their sound is rather too quiet unless they have 2 or 3 choirs of strings. Furthermore, their tones also cannot be prolonged, and at times their strings also break and ruin the performance at the most crucial moment. For these reasons regals deserve some degree of praise. But because of their sound I personally have little regard for them. In order that they may be conveniently transported, their pipes are usually laid horizontally.† But sometimes they also stand upright, since they are barely the length of a finger anyway. The entire instrument is then built into an oblong rectangular case; the bellows may also be detached, and the stand or table on which [the instrument] sits may also be transported separately. They may be made with 2 bellows, pumped either from behind by a second person, or alternately with both legs by the player himself. This effort may be reduced by using a double bellows.‡ This is the usual type of regal.

† i.e., stretching backward from the keyboard.

‡ probably a variety of feeder bellows.

§. 503

In Praetorius's [*Syntagma musicum*, Vol. II, *De*] *Organographia*, p. 73 (which Mattheson refers to in his notes to Niedt, Chapter 10§) there is some report of a small regal with wooden pipes, not only of good, quiet and lovely tone, but also said to be extremely easy and convenient to transport from one place to another. "If I," says Mattheson, "could get such an instrument, I might once again become reconciled with the regal." A good deal of inventiveness has been applied to regals. Among other things, it is rather well known that they are at times built in the shape of a book the size of a folio: the whole instrument and the keyboard are constructed as two separate sections, which are then put together. The bellows are also part of the ensemble, serving as the covers of the book. They are very convenient to transport [when built] in this fashion. A Nuremberg organbuilder by the name of Georg Voll was the first to build regals in the shape of a book;¶ this man died back in 1565, as Walther‖ cites from Doppelmayer's *Historische Nachricht von den Nürnbergischen Künstlern*, p. 290. Such a regal resembles an ordinary folio volume, being 2 to 3 handbreadths thick. It opens up from the middle like a book. The keyboard lies within, half on either side, which is taken out and carefully fitted together; the windchest is directly under the keyboard, and the pipes as well, all of them very small. The book is then turned around and attached at the back, becoming the bellows; both covers end up being the 2 top boards by which the bellows is expanded. Inside is the intake valve. The book is about a half ell in

§ Niedt, *Musikalischer Handleitung*, Part II, p. 114, note i.

¶ Such an instrument is sometimes referred to as a "Bible regal," due to its shape. There is an illustration in Praetorius, *Syntagma Musicum*, Vol. II, "Theatrum Instrumentorum," Plate IV/2.

‖ Johann Gottfried Walther, *Musikalisches Lexikon*, p. 641.

102   Kap. XXII. Von dem Clavicymbel, Clavicytherio, Spinet,

wendig ist das Fangventil. Die Breite des Buchs ist etwann eine halbe Elle. Die Gewichte muß man besonders nebenher tragen. Die Bälge werden von einem gehoben; oder man macht eine Stellung, so, daß sie der Spieler selbst tritt.

Man kann auch 2. solche Schnarrstimmen beysammen haben, etwann eins 16′ Ton, das andere 8′; oder 8′ und 4′ Ton, und was man sonst hierinnen nach Belieben erdenken möchte. Auch kann eine gedeckte oder offene Pfeife dabey seyn; doch da wurde es groß werden. Sonst ist schön, wenn eine Stimmpfeife dabey zu finden, die accurat das c nach dem Orgeltone angiebt, und die man durch einen besondern Zug klingend machen kann, wann und wie lange man will.

§. 504.

Wir haben im 7ten Kapitel so vielerley Arten der Regale namhaft gemacht, als: Trichterregal, Geigen= oder Jungferregal, Apfelregal, Cymbelregal, Singendregal u. d. gl. und wundert mich, warum man nicht zur Lust die Pfeifen nach einer Art machen läßt, welche anmuthiger, als die gewöhnliche Art, klingt. Doch ist die Ursach wol, weil die Pfeifen bey den meisten mehr Raum wegen der Weite und Länge einnehmen, als die ordinären Regale, und folglich nicht so bequem zu gebrauchen sind.

Das XXII. Kapitel.
Von dem Clavicymbel, Clavicytherio, Spinet, Instrument, Arpichord, und Cembal d'Amour.

Inhalt:

§. 505. Beschreibung des Clavicymbels. §. 506. Das Corpus. §. 507. Die Claviere. §. 508. Die Decke. §. 509. Die Tangenten. §. 510. Die Seyten. §. 511. Die Register. §. 512. Die Anschlagfedern. §. 513. Von dem leichten Spielen. §. 514. Lautenzug. §. 515. Transponirclavicymbel. §. 516. Ziehclavecins. §. 517. Clavecins mit 2 Clavieren. §. 518. eine andere Art. §. 519. deren Stimmung. §. 520. Die Veränderung durch die Luft. §. 521. Abputzen der Seyten. §. 522. Wie man darauf zu spielen habe. §. 523. Vom Holze der Decken. §. 524. Wie das Drücken des Steges zu verhüten. §. 525. Der Erfinder des Clavecin. §. 526. mehr Namen desselben. §. 527. Was Kircher davon hat. §. 528. Vom Claviorgano und Pantalonischen Cymbal. §. 529. Cristofali Clavecin. §. 530. dessen Eigenschaften. §. 531. 532. 533. 534. dessen Theile und Abriß. §. 535. Der Ort verändert den Klang der Clavecins. §. 536. Die Sayten schlagen mit einer gewissen Sympathie an. §. 537. 538. Clavicytherium. §. 539. Spinet. §. 540. Instrument. §. 541. Arpichord. §. 542. Cembal d'Amour.

§. 505.

Diese Stücke haben fast einerley Art: derowegen wollen wir sie allhier zusammen fassen. Das Clavicymbel betreffend, so nennen die Franzosen dasselbe Clavecin, oder Clavessin. (beydes liefet man clavessäng.) Es ist ein mit gelben oder weißen
Dratseyten

width. The [bellows] weights have to be carried separately along with it. The bellows are pumped by another, or a stand is made so that the player may pump them himself.

It is also possible to have two such reed ranks together, say, one 16' pitch and the other 8', or any other arrangement one might care to think up. A [rank of] stopped or open [flue] pipes can also be added, but then [the instrument] becomes large. Moreover, it is very nice if a pitch pipe is included, that sounds *c* accurately according to the pitch of the organ,* and that can be made to sound by a separate stop, when and as long as desired.

* i.e., another organ in the church or chamber that is not portable, as is the regal.

§. 504.

In Chapter 7 we have mentioned so many kinds of regals by name, such as *Trichterregal*, *Geigen-* or *Jungferregal*, *Apfelregal*, *Cymbelregal*, *Singendregal*, and such, that I am surprised no one has been inclined to make pipes of a sort that sound more agreeable than the usual type. The reason is probably that in most cases the pipes [would] take up more space because of their width and length† than ordinary regals, and consequently they would not be as convenient to use.

† i.e., only larger pipes could produce the type of sound more agreeable to Adlung.

Chapter XXII.
Concerning the Harpsichord, Clavicytherium, Spinet, Instrument, Arpichord and Cembal d'Amour.*

* A number of passages from this chapter and others following are translated in Frank Hubbard's book, *Three Centuries of Harpsichord Making*. (Cambridge: Harvard University Press, 1967), together with informative annotations.

Contents:

§.505. Description of the harpsichord. §.506. The case. §.507. The keyboards. §.508. The soundboard. §.509. The jacks. §.510. The strings. §.511. The stops. §.512. The quills §.513. Concerning a light playing [action]. §.514. The buff stop. §.515. Transposing harpsichords. §.516. Harpsichords [with mechanisms for] shifting [stops]. §.517. Two-manual harpsichords. §.518. Another variety. §.519. Their tuning. §.520. Change due to weather. §.521. Cleaning the strings. §.522. How to play on them. §.523. Concerning the wood for the soundboard. §. 524. How to relieve the pressure of the bridge [on the soundboard]. §.525. The inventor of the harpsichord. §.526. Other names for the instrument. §.527. What Kircher says about it. §.528. Concerning the claviorganum and Pantaleon. §.529. Cristofali's harpsichord.† §.530. Its characteristics. §. 531, 532, 533, & 534. Its components, and a sketch. §.535. Location alters the tone of harpsichords. §.536. The strings vibrate with a certain sympathy. §.537 & 538. The clavicytherium. §.539. The spinet. §.540. The "instrument". §.541. The arpichord. §.542. The cembal d'amour.

† i.e., Cristofori's pianoforte.

§. 505.

All these instruments are very similar, and therefore we will treat them all together here. Concerning the harpsichord, the French call it *Clavecin* or *Clavessin* (both are pronounced "clavissäng"). It is an instrument strung with brass or steel wire strings

Dratsenten bezogenes Instrument. (Hier nehme ich das Wort generatim für ein musikalisches Instrument, da es im Gegentheil unten §. 540. insbesondere einer gewissen Gattung zugeeignet wird.) Es ist vom Clavicytherio und dem eigentlich sogenannten Instrument darinnen unterschieden, daß dessen Seyten von vornen hinterwärts gezogen sind, oder von dem Claviere an bis in die Spitze; da das Clavicytherium perpendikular in die Höhe gehet mit allen Seyten: bey dem Instrument aber gehen die Seyten von der rechten Hand zur Linken, wenn man vor der Tastatur sitzt. Das Spinett hat weniger Oktaven als vier; ist also davon auch leicht zu unterscheiden. Im weitläuftigen Verstande nennen einige alle diese Werke Spinette.

§. 506.

Wir merken bey dem Claveçin oder Clavicymbel erstlich das Corpus. Dasselbige ist zuweilen von weichem Holze; aber die von hartem Holze sind beständiger. Sie werden vornen bey den Claviertasten breit gemacht, so, daß die gewöhnlichen vier oder (welches besser ist) fünf Oktaven Raum haben; hinten aber gehet es ganz spitzig zu, fast wie ein rechtwinkelichter Triangul. Die Mahlereyen, Fournierarbeit u. d. gl. stehen in des Künstlers Belieben. Ihre Höhe ist etwann $\frac{1}{2}$ Elle; doch geben etliche etwas zu, etliche nehmen der Höhe etwas ab. Wenn jenes geschiehet; so klingen sie gravitätischer und pompichter: dieses aber verursachet mehr Lieblichkeit. Es mögen die Seiten von weichem oder hartem Holze seyn; so macht man den Boden doch von Tannenholz, um den Klang zu befördern. Denn bey dem Klange, und der Bewegung der Luft, wird sowol die Decke als auch der Boden einigermaassen bewegt; doch liegt an der Decke mehr, als an dem Boden. Vornen bleibt es offen, daß man das Clavier hinein bringe.

§. 507.

Dieses Clavier nun ist wie bey der Orgel, und besteht aus 4 Oktaven; zuweilen hat man auch 5 Oktaven. Und ich wollte rathen, dergleichen Instrumente niemals anders, als mit 5 Oktaven, zu machen, weil gar viel Claviersachen darnach gesetzt sind, welche man mit 4 Oktaven nicht wohl spielen kann. Ich erinnere dieses ein= für allemal, und es ist dieser Umstand nicht nur bey dem Clavicymbel, sondern auch bey dem Clavikord und Clavicytherio nicht aus der Acht zu lassen. Die Claviere liegen alle parallel bis ein Fleck hinter. Eine Viertelelle, oder etwas drüber, kann wol genug seyn; das äuserste wo man spielt, nicht mitgerechnet. Hinten leimet man Leder oder Tuch auf eine iede Palmul, daß die herabfallenden Docken kein Klappern verursachen, wenn sie unmittelbar auf das Holz fallen. Hinten laufen sie in Ritzen wie die Palmuln der Clavikordien, auch liegen sie hinten auf einem Rähmen, der abermal mit Tuch überzogen werden kann. [85] Vornen laufen oder bewegen sie sich in Stiften, welche in einen

Zwerch=

---

[85] Oder man macht keine Stifte hinten an, sondern läßt die Palmulen sich zwischen zwey Dratspitzen bewegen, daß sie hinten frey sind. Diese Art, deucht mir, ist heut zu Tage gewöhnlicher, und bekannter, als die oben vom Hrn. Verfasser angeführte.

(here I am using the word "instrument" to mean a musical instrument in general, while in §.540 below, on the other hand, it is applied specifically to a certain type). It is distinguished from the clavicytherium and the actually so-called "instrument" in that its strings stretch from front to back, or from the keyboard toward the tail, while all the strings of the clavicytherium are strung perpendicularly from bottom to top, and those of the "instrument" stretch from right to left (if one is sitting at the keyboard). The spinet has fewer than four octaves, and thus it is easily distinguished [from the others]. In the broad sense some call all these instruments "spinet".

§. 506.

Let us first take note of the case of the *claveçin* or harpsichord. It is sometimes made of soft wood, but those of hard wood are more durable. At the front where the keys are they are built broad, so that they normally have space for four or (even better) five octaves; but at the back they come to a point, almost like a right triangle. Painting, veneers, and the like, are at the discretion of the builder/an artist. Their depth is about half an ell, but some are a bit deeper, others a bit more shallow. If the former is the case, then they sound more weighty and pompous, while the latter causes a more delicate sound. Whether the sides are of soft or of hard wood, the bottom board is made of fir wood to improve the tone. For when sound is produced and sets the air moving, then both the soundboard as well as the bottom board are to some degree set into motion; but more depends on the soundboard than on the bottom. The instrument remains open in front to allow the keyboard to be installed.

§. 507.

Its keyboard is like that of the organ, consisting of 4 or sometimes even 5 octaves. I would advise never to build such an instrument with less than 5 octaves, since a great deal of keyboard music is composed in such a way that it cannot very well be played with 4 octaves. I will mention this now once and for all, for this situation must be taken into account not only with the harpsichord, but also with the clavichord and clavicytherium. The keys all lie parallel, extending back to a [given] point [within the case]. A quarter of an ell or a bit more may well be sufficient, not counting the exterior portion upon which one plays. Leather or cloth is glued on the back of each key, so that the jacks do not create a clatter by falling back directly onto [bare] wood. At the rear they travel in slots, like the keys of clavichords; at the back end they also rest in a frame, that likewise may be covered with cloth.[85] At

---

[85] It is also possible to omit the pins* at the rear, and to allow each key to travel between two wire prongs, thus leaving it free at the rear. It seems to me that this method is more common and familiar nowadays than that described above by the author. [Albrecht]

* i.e., the slips that move in the slots.

Zwerchrahmen geschlagen sind, der von einem Ende des Clavessin bis zum andern reicht, und unbeweglich ist.

§. 508.

Alsdann macht man die Decke über das ganze Clavessin von subtilem Tannenholze. Denn dieß Holz ist leichter, als das meiste andere, daher es durch die Luft am leichtesten beweget wird, folglich auch den Klang am besten befördert. Es muß aber recht dürre seyn, sonst würde es im dürren Wetter schwinden und springen, und durch die daher entstehenden Ritze der Klang nachgehends gehemmet werden. Der Boden (so nennt man auch zuweilen diese Decke) wird in die Seiten eingefalzet: vornen liegt er auf, und da wird von der rechten Hand an bis nach der Spitze ein Steg gelegt, nicht weit von dem Seitbrete, darüber legt man hernach die Seyten. Noch weiter gegen die Seiten werden auch so wie auf demselben Stege Stifterchen eingeschlagen, daran man die Seyten hängt. Vorn bey dem Clavier wird für jede Seite ein Wirbel von starkem eisernen Drat, oder von geschlagenem Eisen, eingeschlagen. Diese müssen fein stark gemacht werden, daß sie sich nicht biegen, und auch desto vester stehen. Unter denselben muß ein Balke von Eichenholze bevestiget werden, darein sie durch die Decke reichen, damit sie vester stehen. Meßingene Wirbel stehen so gut nicht. Vor diesen Wirbeln liegen die Seyten noch auf einem Stege.

§. 509.

Nicht weit von diesem Stege geschiehet der Anschlag durch die Docken. Dieses sind dünne Hölzerchen, von hartem Holze gearbeitet, etwann den 10ten Theil eines Zolles in die Dicke, und ohngefähr Fingers breit. Die Länge ist so, daß sie unten auf jeder Palmul aufstossen, und durch die Decke bis fast an die Seyten reichen. Damit sie aber in ihrer Ordnung recht perpendicular stehen bleiben; so wird in die Decke ein sogenanntes Sieb eingelegt, welches etwann diese Form hat:

Durch dieses Sieb gehet jede Docke, daß sie nicht auf die Seite fallen kann. Oben ist die Docke eingeschnitten, etwann so: in die eine Oefnung bey b wird ein Stückchen Tuch gelegt, daß es, wenn die Docke wieder abwärts gehet, auf die Seyten falle, und den Schall dämpfe; in die andere bey a wird die Zunge gebracht. Dieses subtile Hölzchen wird um ein durchgeschlagen Stiftchen bewegt, und oben mit einer Feder versehen, welche die Länge bekömmt, daß sie unter die Seyte reicht und sie anschlägt. Hinten bekömmt die Zunge eine Säuborste anstatt einer Springfeder. Diese muß etwas stark seyn. Dieß sind die Theile, die man am meisten zu merken hat.

§. 510.

the front they travel or move on pins hammered into a stationary cross-frame* that stretches from one side of the harpsichord to another.

§. 508.

Next the soundboard (die Decke) of thin fir† wood is built across the entire harpsichord, since this wood is lighter than most others and is thus most easily set into motion by the air; consequently it propagates the tone the best. It must, however, be thoroughly cured, or else it will shrink and split in dry weather, and thereafter the sound will be hampered by the resulting cracks. The soundboard (Boden) (at times it is also called by this name) is rabbeted into the sides [of the case]; it is supported at the front, and from the front right side back to the tail there extends a bridge, not far from the side wall [of the case], over which the strings are subsequently drawn. Even further toward the sides little pins are driven in (as is also the case on the aforementioned bridge), and the strings are hitched onto them. In front next to the keyboard wrest pins of heavy iron wire or forged steel are driven [into the wood], one for each string. These must be made good and strong, so they do not bend and also so that they grip more firmly. An oaken beam‡ must be secured under them, into which they extend after passing through the soundboard,§ so that they grip more firmly. Brass pins do not hold very well. The strings are drawn across yet another bridge¶ in front of these pins.

§. 509.

Not far from this [last-mentioned] bridge [i.e., nut] lies the point where the strings are plucked by the jacks. These are thin slips of wood, fashioned out of hardwood, about a tenth of an inch in thickness and a fingersbreadth wide. They are [made] long enough to reach from each key below, upon which they strike [as they fall], up through the soundboard‖ and right next to the strings. So that they remain standing perpendicularly in a row, a so-called "sieve"** is set into the soundboard, that looks something like this:

Each jack passes through this jack guide, which prevents it from shifting from side to side. The jack is slotted at the top, something like this: In slot b is wedged a bit of cloth, that falls onto the string when the jack drops and dampens the sound. Into slot a is inserted the tongue. This is a thin piece of wood that pivots on a little pin driven through it†† and is fitted at the top with a quill, long enough to reach under the string and pluck it. At the rear of the tongue there is a pig bristle serving as a spring; this must be quite strong. These are the components that one must be the most familiar with.

---

* Here Adlung seems to be referring to the balance rail.

† or "spruce."

‡ i.e., the wrest plank.

§ i.e., after passing through a veneer of soundboard wood glued to the upper surface of the wrest plank.

¶ i.e., the nut.

‖ Adlung seems to be describing an arrangement, not uncommon in early German harpsichords, in which the soundboard continues all the way to the front of the wrest plank (which is sometimes "hollow" so the soundboard is resonant under the nut). See, for example, the description of such a harpsichord at the *Bayerisches Nationalmuseum*, Munich, described in: John Henry van der Meer, "A Little-Known German Harpsichord," in: *Early Keyboard Studies Newsletter* (Westfield Center, Easthampton, MA), Vol. V, No. 3 (March 1991), pp. 8ff.

** i.e., the jack guide, a strip with slots to receive each jack.

†† The pin is then anchored in either side of the slot in the jack.

§. 510.

Ich will aber noch mehr davon reden, weil ich hernach mich darauf berufen werde, wenn ich zu den andern Instrumenten komme. Nämlich, die Seyten sind von gehärtetem Drate, entweder weiß, oder gelbe. Jene sollen etwas annuthiger klingen und besser halten; diese aber rosten nicht, und halten folglich desto länger. Ich für meine Person ziehe lieber gelbe Seyten auf. In den obern clavibus müssen sie zart seyn; hernach steigt deren Dicke nach und nach bis ans Ende. Wie hoch aber die Numern seyn sollen, kann man so genau eben nicht bestimmen. Etliche Claveßins lassen stärkere Seyten zu, als andere. Auf etlichen kann man das $\bar{\bar{c}}$ mit No. 8. beziehen; aber andere wollen No. 9. auch wol 10. haben. Kleiner taugen sie nicht viel, weil der Klang schwach wird. Wollte man die Ursach wissen; so ist solche darinne zu suchen, daß die Claveßins nicht einerley Größe haben; oder daß auf einem die Distanz der Seyte, von deren Angehänge bis zu dem Stege, größer ist, als bey andern, daher man schwächere Seyten nehmen muß. Denn eine lange starke Seyte kann so hoch nicht gezogen werden, als wenn sie kürzer wäre. Ich wollte rathen, wenn ja des Klanges halben die Claveßins etwas länger gemacht würden, daß man doch die Stege darnach setzte, daß die Seytenlänge nicht zu groß würde. Die Proportion allhier auszuführen, wird zu weitläuftig. Ein Orgelmacher theilt es überhaupt so ein, daß ins C etwann No. 1. kömmt. Besser aber ist es, man nimmt stärkere Seyten in der Tiefe, die man aber klafterweise kaufen muß. Will man sie spinnen, etwann von unten herauf bis ins c; so wird der Baß desto gravitätischer. (**) Man kann dieß leicht zu sehen bekommen und lernen. Ich halte mich deswegen dabey nicht auf. Das ist zu merken, daß mancher Orgelmacher, oder Künstler, den Seyten eine etwas schwächere Proportion giebt, als sie ordentlich vertragen können. Z. E. ich bezöge ein Claveßin, und oben in $\bar{\bar{c}}$ hielte es wol No. 9. nicht aber 8; im $\bar{c}$ bis $\bar{\bar{c}}$ 8, nicht aber 7, u. s. w; so thäte ich wohl, wenn ich oben im $\bar{\bar{c}}$ No. 10. nähme, und anstatt 8. No. 9, anstatt 7. No. 8. ꝛc. weil es im feuchten Wetter so leer nicht abgehet, daß es sich nicht sollte aufwärts ziehen, da denn die Seyten leicht springen und neue Arbeit und Verdruß verursachen. Wenn aber ein Claveßin also bezogen wird, daß es ohne Gefahr einen halben Ton in die Höhe gehen kann; so ist man sicher. Man schreibe aber die Anfangs gebrauchten Nummern von oben bis unten auf, damit, wenn was zerreißt, man die rechte Numer wieder aufziehe, weil es ein Fehler ist, wenn eine Seyte schwach, die andere aber stark ist.

(**) Aber die Federkielen reiben das übersponnene gar zu bald ab. Daher halten viele nichts von gesponnenen Saiten auf Claveßins.

§. 511.

Etliche Clavicymbel sind einchöricht, andere haben 2 Seyten auf jedem Clave; noch andere 3. Die Struktur der einfachen ist die vorhin beschriebene. Wenn sie 2chöricht sind; so werden 2 Reihen Docken neben einander gesetzt daß also ein Clavis deren 2 in die Höhe hebt, und deren eine die Seyte auf der einen Seite, die andere aber die Seyte auf der andern Seite anschlägt. Also stehet die Feder der einen Docke gegen

§. 510.

I would like to discuss this matter further, however, since I shall subsequently refer back to it when I am speaking about the other instruments. To continue: the strings are of tempered wire, either steel or brass. The former are said to sound somewhat more pleasant and to be more durable; the latter, though, do not rust, and consequently last all the longer. I personally prefer to string with brass. In the upper register they must be thin, with their thickness gradually increasing as they descend. It is not possible to specify all that precisely, however, what gauge the strings should be. Some harpsichords will stand thicker strings than others. On some it is possible to string c''' with no. 8, but others will demand no. 9 or even 10.* They are not much use smaller than this, since their sound is weak. If anyone wants to know the reason for this, it lies in the fact that harpsichords are not all the same size, or that on one the distance between where the strings are attached† and the bridge is greater than on others, and thus thinner strings must be used. For a long, thick string cannot be drawn as tight as one that is shorter. If for the sake of the tone a harpsichord were indeed to be made somewhat longer, my advice would be nevertheless to position the bridge so that the strings would not be all that long. It would be too lengthy to elaborate on the proportion‡ here. An organbuilder would distribute it so that no. 1 would probably be used for C. It is better to use thicker strings for the low notes; these, however, must be bought by the span.§ If they are overspun, say from the bottom up to c, then the bass will be all the more weighty (**) It is easy to get to see this and learn about it; therefore I will not dwell on it. Take note that many organbuilders or craftsmen give the strings a somewhat thinner proportion than they can normally tolerate. For example, if I were stringing a harpsichord that would tolerate no. 9 at c''' but not 8, and no. 8 from f''[?] to c'' but not 7, etc., then I would be well advised to use no. 10 for the upper c''', and no. 9 instead of 8, no. 8 instead of 7, etc., because in damp weather [the instrument] will inevitably go sharp,¶ since then the strings break easily and create more work and bother. If however a harpsichord is strung so that it can be tuned a half step higher without any risk [of breaking a string], then one is safe. The [gauge] numbers that are used when first [stringing the instrument] should be recorded, from top to bottom, so that when something breaks it may be replaced with the proper size, since it is a fault if one string is thin and the next is thick.

(**) But the quills wear away far too quickly the wire that is wound on; thus many people do not think much of overspun strings on harpsichords. [Agricola]

§. 511.

Some harpsichords have one choir [of strings], while others have two strings for each key, and yet others three. The structure of single-choir instruments is that described above. If a [harpsichord] has two choirs, then two rows of jacks are set parallel to each other, so that one key lifts both of them; one of them then plucks the string on one side, while the other plucks the string on the other side. Thus the quills of the

---

* Adlung's gauge system seems to have been the usual continental system, also used in France; for an explanation of this system, see: Hubbard, pp. 207ff.; also G. Grant O'Brien, "Some Principles of Eighteenth Century Harpsichord Stringing and their Application," in: *The Organ Yearbook*, Vol. XII (1981), pp. 160-175.

† sic; Adlung must mean the distance between the nut and the bridge, i.e., the speaking length.

‡ i.e., of string size to length.

§ or fathom (i.e., about 6 feet). Adlung seems to suggest that the larger string sizes were purchased not on spools (as were smaller sizes), but in short lengths.

¶ Concerning this suggestion, Hubbard (p. 281, n. 113) says:
... the process of drawing steel into fine wires seems to produce a structure composed of a hard sheath around a softer core. This sheath is always roughly equal in thickness, and thus occupies a larger percentage of the diameter of a thin string than of a thick one. Therefore, a thin string will actually stand a slightly higher pitch than a thick one ....
The phenomenon that thinner strings are relatively stronger (i.e., have greater tensile strength) is known in metallurgy as "tensile pickup."

die rechte, und der andern gegen die linke Hand. Diese Art ist die gemeinste, weil, wo nur eine Seyte ist, dieselbe leicht zerreist, daß der Clavis hernach gar nicht klingt. Daß die Stärke des Tons doppelt so groß seyn müsse, als bey einem einfachen Claveßin, verstehet sich von selbst. Damit man aber es auch schwächer machen könne, oder daß man besser stimmen möge; so werden die §. 509. Siebe (deren nun zwey neben einander liegen) so gemacht, daß man sie kann etwas hin und her bewegen. Dieß geschiehet vermittelst der herausragenden Ecken, welche die Registerzüge vorstellen. Auch sind inwendig zuweilen Eisen eingesteckt, woran man dieß auch verrichten kann.

Wenn beyde Register auf einer Seite sind; so ziehet man eines heraus, das andere drücket man hinein, wenn alle Seyten klingen sollen. Ist eins auf der rechten und das andere auf der linken Seite; so werden beyde auswärts gezogen, oder bey andern einwärts gedrückt, wenn sie gehen sollen. Sollen sie schweigen; so thut man das Gegentheil. Soll das eine schweigen; so zieht man auch darnach. Wo 3. Chöre Seyten sind, da stehen 3 Docken auf jedem Clave. Allein die 3te Seyte ist ordentlich eine 4fußige Oktave, die nicht über den vördersten Steg weggehet, sondern durch denselben, daß also die Docken etwas tiefer anschlagen müssen, als die andern 2 Docken. Anders schickt es sich nicht. Dergleichen 3fach bezogene Claveßins gefallen mir wohl; sie schlagen brav durch. Wo sie aber ein Mechanikus nicht accurat zu machen weis; so sind sie etwas schwer zu spielen. Allein, wenn es geschwinde gehen soll, kann man das 3te Register schon wegziehen. Ich habe etliche dreychörichte Claveßins bespielet, die sehr leicht zu spielen waren, daraus ich gemerkt, daß es sehr wohl möglich sey, dergleichen Claveßins eine leichte Traktation zu verschaffen, wenn man nur die Vortheile weis.

§. 512.

Man merke weiter die Federn, die man zum Anschlage nimmt bey allen Claveßins und dergleichen Instrumenten. Gänsefedern würden zu weich seyn, und nicht scharf genug schlagen Bisweilen habe ich Fischbein gebraucht: allein es bricht bald, und ist auch gar zu hart. Die Straußfedern gehen noch eher an; doch sind sie auch allzu hart zu spielen; und wenn das ist, so reissen die Seyten leicht entzwey. Am besten sind die Rabenfedern, wenn man die stärksten aussucht und anmacht. Man schmieret sie mit Baumöhle, daß sie zähe werden, und so leicht nicht springen oder knicken. Es gehöret großer Fleiß dazu, daß man die Federn alle überein abkneipe, daß sie alle gleich geschwind zurückprallen; it. daß man sie alle gleich stark mache, weil es ein Hauptfehler ist, wo ein Clavis härter zu drücken ist, als der andere; imgleichen daß man sie alle hoch genug an die Seyten bringe, damit die Claviertasten nicht so tief fallen müssen. Einige haben was beständigers anbringen wollen, als die Federn sind, weil dieselben doch zuweilen matt werden, oder sich abnutzen, daß man bald da, bald dort etwas bessern muß. Sie haben ein etwas starkes gelbes Drat durch die Federöffnung gesteckt, so hinten in einem subtilen meßingenen Blätchen veste ist, welches an die Docke angeheftet, und durch das Drat zurückgetrieben wird, aber auch zugleich das Drat wieder

zurück

one jack face right, while those of the other face left. This is the most common type [of harpsichord], since if there is only one [choir of] strings and one breaks (which easily can happen), then the key will not produce any sound at all. It is self-evident that its sound is twice as loud as harpsichords with one choir. But in order for it to be made softer, as well as for convenience in tuning, the jack guides described in §.509 (of which there are now two, lying parallel to each other) are so constructed that they can be moved back and forth a bit. This is done by means of the ends that protrude [from the cheek piece or spine of the harpsichord], that serve as stops. Sometimes iron [levers] are installed inside, by which this can also be achieved.

If both stops are on the same side [of the harpsichord case], then one should be drawn out and one pushed in, in order for both stops to sound. If one [stop] is on the right and the other on the left side, then both are drawn out (or, on other harpsichords, pushed in) in order to play. If the strings are to be silent, then the stops must be drawn in the opposite direction; the same holds true if one stop is to be silent. If there are three choirs of strings, then three jacks rest on each key. The third string, however, is ordinarily a 4-foot octave, that does not pass over the bridge nearest [the keyboard], but through it; thus its jacks must pluck somewhat lower than the other two. It is not proper to do it any other way. I am indeed fond of such triple-strung harpsichords; they have a fine, penetrating tone. But if a craftsman does not know how to build them precisely, then they have a rather heavy touch. In rapid passages, of course, the third choir may be retired. I have played some three-choired harpsichords that had a very light touch, from which I note that it is certainly possible to provide such harpsichords with a light action, providing that one knows the proper procedures.

§. 512.

Furthermore, it is necessary to take note of the quills that are used to pluck all harpsichords and like instruments. Goose quill would be too soft, and not pluck sharply enough. At times I have used fishbone;* it soon breaks, though, and is altogether too hard. Ostrich feathers work better, but they also cause too heavy a touch, and if that is the case, then the strings easily break in two. Raven quill is the best of all, if the strongest ones are sought out and installed. They should be coated with olive oil to make them tough and keep them from snapping or splitting so easily. It requires a great deal of diligence to snip off all the quills to exactly the same length, so that they all spring back equally quickly. The same holds true for making them all the same strength; it is a major fault if one key is harder to depress than the next. The same also holds true for setting them [i.e., the quills] near enough to the strings, so that the keys do not have to fall so deep [before the quill plucks the string]. Some [builders] have tried installing something more durable than quill, since in time the latter does get dull or wears out, requiring repair here and there. These [builders] have inserted a rather strong brass wire through the quill hole, fastened at the back into a thin brass tongue attached to the jack; this tongue is forced backward by the wire, but then immediately pushes the wire back [into position for plucking], just like a quill. It is easier

* i.e., whalebone (baleen).

zurückdrückt wie eine Feder. Man kann es besser weisen, als beschreiben. Allein es hat den Klang so reine nicht befördert, als die Federn, weil durch den Anschlag die Seyte schon zu singen anhebt, ehe das Schnellen geschiehet. Derowegen verfertiget man iho kein Claveßin von dergleichen Art. Mizler erzählt im 2ten Theile des ersten Bandes der musikal. Bibliotheck, S. 76. daß in Anspach ein geschickter Orgelmacher, Namens Wiclef, eine besondere Erfindung habe, daß man der Rabenkiele in den Docken der Clavicymbel entübriget seyn könne. Er macht nämlich kleine Maschinen, da Meßing mit dabey ist, welche so lange, als das Clavicymbel selbst, dauren, und die Seyten hell und lieblich anschlagen, und man des beschwerlichen Kielens überhoben ist.

§. 513.

Ich habe von berühmten Mechanicis Clavicymbel gesehen, welche leicht zu spielen waren, und wo die Palmuln wenig gefallen, welches beydes eine schöne Tugend ist. Dieß liegt meistens in der Accuratesse der Federn; imgleichen wenn der hintere Theil der palmularum hinter dem Stifte gegen dem vordern nicht zu schwer ist. Genug erachtete ich es zu seyn, wo sie in æquilibrio stünden, da dann eine geringe Force nöthig wäre, durch Druckung des vordersten Theils den hintern Theil samt der Docke zu heben. Oder wo der hintere Theil lang und schwerer werden muß; (welches letztere nicht eben nöthig, weil man in der Dicke schon abnehmen kann) so mache man den vordersten auch etwas schwerer.

§. 514.

Uiber den Docken liegt eine Leiste mit Tuch gefüttert, damit die Docken nicht zu hoch oder gar heraus springen, und doch auch durch ihr Anstossen nicht pochen. Wenn etwas zu corrigiren vorfällt; so kann man die Leiste wegnehmen. An dem Stege ist zuweilen ein Lautenzug, da durch dessen Schiebung das daran gemachte Tuch oder dergleichen in die Höhe tritt und die Seyten dämpft, daß sie wie Darmseyten klingen. Ich habe auch gesehen, daß man zwischen dem Stege und zwischen den Docken noch durch ein Sieb eine Reihe Docken angebracht, welche man oben mit Tuch verticaliter beklebt, und dieß dämpfte die Seyten auch, weil diese Docken durch einen Zug alle zugleich an die Seyten gerückt wurden, und nach Gefallen wieder hinweg. Es gefällt mir dieses noch besser als jene Art. Die Docken, damit sie inwendig sich auf keine Seite lenken, gehen eben durch dergleichen Sieb, wie auf der Decke ist.

§. 515.

Zuweilen trift man Trausponirclavicymbel an, welche Invention gar fein ist, sonderlich für die, welche nicht im Stande sind alle Generalbässe in alle Töne zu transponiren, da doch solches zuweilen nicht wohl zu vermeiden ist. Durch Schiebung des Claviers bey solchen Claveßins kann ich Chorton haben; it. einen halben oder ganzen Ton, oder auch $1\frac{1}{2}$ Töne tiefer, welches der rechte Kammerton ist; auch wol $\frac{1}{2}$ Ton über Chorton. In solchem Falle ist nöthig, daß man mehr Chöre Seyten aufzieht, als Palmuln sind, damit die äusersten, wenn sie fortgerückt werden, auch Seyten haben.

to demonstrate this than to describe it. But it does not produce as pure a sound as quill, since the attack causes the string to begin to vibrate before the pluck takes place. For this reason no harpsichords of this type are now being made. Mizler in the second part of the first volume of his *Musikalische Bibliotheck*, p. 76, relates that a skillful organ-builder from Ansbach by the name of Wiclef has a remarkable invention, by which the raven quill in the jacks of harpsichords may be dispensed with. He makes small devices, of which brass is one component, that last as long as the harpsichord itself, and pluck the strings brightly and pleasingly;* one is thus spared the onerous [task of] quilling.

* There is a harpsichord in the Bayerisches Nationalmuseum in Munich with a set of brass jacks that may correspond to the ones Mizler mentions; see: John Henry van der Meer, "A Little-Known German Harpsichord," in: *Early Keyboard Studies Newsletter* (a publication of the Westfield Center for Early Keyboard Studies), Vol. V, No. 3 (March 1991), p. 11.

§. 513.

I have seen harpsichords [built] by renowned craftsmen that had a light touch as well as a shallow keyfall, both of which are fine virtues. Precision in fashioning the quills is by-and-large responsible for this, as well as the back part of the keys (behind the pins) not being too heavy in relation to the forward part. I consider it sufficient for them to be balanced, since then only a slight force is necessary when depressing the forward part in order to lift the back part together with the jack. Or, if the back part has to be long and heavier (which is really not necessary, since it can always be made thinner [than the front]), then the front part can also be made somewhat heavier.

§. 514.

Above the jacks lies a board† lined with cloth, so that the jacks do not jump up too high or fly out altogether, and yet also do not thump when they strike. If there is something [about the jacks] that needs correcting, then the board may be removed. Next to the bridge [i.e., nut] there is sometimes a buff stop, which, when it is shifted, lifts up the piece of cloth attached to it and dampens the strings, making them sound like gut strings. I have also seen a row of jacks installed between the bridge [i.e., nut] and the jacks, again in a jack guide, at the top of which are glued upright [pieces of] cloth.‡ These also dampen the strings, in that by means of a hand stop the jacks are all raised up to the strings or lowered from them, at will. I am more in favor of this [arrangement] than the former. So that the jacks do not shift to one side or the other internally, they pass through the same [sort of] jack guide that is in the soundboard.

† i.e., the jack rail.

‡ i.e., dampers.

§. 515.

Sometimes one encounters a transposing harpsichord,§ an excellent invention, especially for those who are not in a position to transpose every figured bass [realization] to any key (indeed, this sometimes cannot be avoided). By shifting the keyboard of such harpsichords it is possible to play at choir pitch as well as at pitches a half step, whole step, or even 1½ steps lower [than choir pitch] (the last-named is the true chamber pitch), or even a ½ step above choir pitch. In this case¶ it is necessary to string a greater number of sets of strings than there are keys, so that the ones at either end [of the keyboard] still have strings to play when they are shifted. Thus a few [sets of

§ There is such a harpsichord (thought to be Thuringian) at the Bach-Haus in Eisenach. It has a hollow wrest plank and a buff stop, just as Adlung has described earlier in this chapter.

¶ i.e., with a transposing harpsichord.

108　Kap. XXII. Vom dem Clavicymbel, Clavicytherio, Spinet,

Also bleiben ja einige leer stehen, auch so viel Docken. Die Struktur selbst ist diese: Das ganze Clavier wird in einen viereckichten Rahmen eingefaßt, doch so, daß es nicht an die Seiten anstoße. Das setzt man so hinein; folglich kann man das ganze Ding im Claveßin unter den Docken weg hin und her schieben, welche Docken, daß sie nicht im Wege stehen, in dem innern Siebe eingeschnitten werden, daß sie nie herunter fallen können. Zwischen das Manual und die Seiten setzt man Klötzerchen, oben oder unten, ein, die man alsdann wieder heraus nimmt, wenn man das Clavier rückt. Wenn nun die Docken alle stehen bleiben, und die Palmuln werden gerückt; so kömmt der Clavis C unter die Docke Cis oder D; Cis unter D; D unter Dis. ꝛc. Oder wenn es nur etwas abwärts geschoben wird, so tritt c̄ unter h̄; h̄ unter b̄; b̄ unter ā, u. s. w. Oder wenn man weiter schiebt, so kömmt c̄ unter b̄ oder ā; h̄ unter ā oder g̅i̅s̅ ꝛc. Prätorius gedenkt Tom. II. P. II. cap. 40. pag. 65. eines Clavicymbels, welches man 7mal transponiren könne, so, daß der Clavis c stehe zuweilen unter c, cis, des, d, es, dis, e. Darunter sind etliche Subsemitonia, als wovon er viel hält. s. pag. 63. c. 40. l. c. dieß nennet er perfectissimum instrumentum.

§. 516.

Wir sind noch lange nicht fertig. Ich will es ein für allemal ausführen, daß ich hernach desto kürzer gehen könne. Anstatt der Register habe ich einsten einmal ein solch Clavier gesehen, welches man konnte aus- und einwärts schieben. Es war dreychöricht. Wenn nun die Palmuln an beyden Seyten zugleich in einer gewissen Weite gezogen wurden; so schlug nur die eine Reihe Docken an, welches die hinterste war; die andern wurden nicht bewegt. Zog man es anders; so schlugen die mittlern Docken allein; wiederum schlugen die vordersten allein; wiederum schlugen die hintersten und mittlern zusammen an; ein andermal schlugen die hintersten und vordersten zusammen; wiederum die mittlern und vordersten. Endlich schlugen alle 3 Reihen zugleich an alle Seyten. Dieses hat mir wohl gefallen. Denn bey den Registern ist die Incommodität, daß sie zuweilen sich nicht recht ab- oder anziehen, daher eine Feder itzo anders anschlägt, als vorhin. Wie aber das vorgesagte zugehe, ist leicht zu begreifen. Ich stelle mir die hintersten Theile der Palmulen durchgeschnitten vor: oder sie können an der Seite ausgeschnitten werden. Die Docken werden gemacht, daß dieselben nicht abwärts fallen. Eine Palmul sieht ohngefähr also aus:

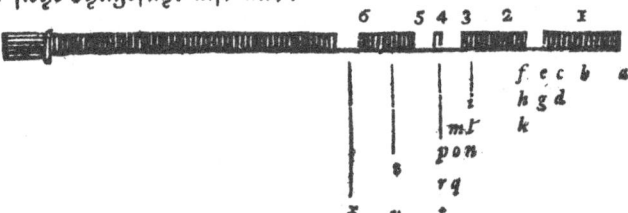

Hier sieht man ganz einfältig die Möglichkeit, da z. E. wenn a b c unter den 3 Docken sind, alle 3 Seyten klingen: rücke ich ein wenig; so kömmt d e f unter die Docken,

108   Chap. XXII. The Harpsichord, Clavicytherium, Spinet,

strings] are always out of use, plus an equal number of jacks. The structure itself is as follows: the whole keyboard is enclosed within a rectangular frame that [fits within the case] without touching the sides. It is set into the case, and consequently the entire assembly can be pushed from side to side under the jacks, right inside the harpsichord. In order not to stand in the way, the jacks are notched in at the inner jack guide,* so that they can never drop down. Small blocks are inserted between the keyboard and the sides, either above or below, that are removed when the keyboard is shifted. If the jacks all remain stationary and the keys are shifted, then the key C moves under the jack C# or D, C# under D, D under D#, etc. Or if they are shifted just a bit downward, then c''' moves under b'', b'' under b-flat'', b-flat'' under a, etc. Or if the keyboard is shifted further, then c''' moves under b-flat'' or a, b'' under a'' or g#'', etc. In [his *Syntagma musicum*,] Vol. II, Part II, chapter 40, p. 65, Praetorius makes mention of a harpsichord that can be transposed to seven different pitches, so that the key c may stand at times under c, or under c#, d-flat, d, e-flat, d# and e. Among these are several sub-semitones, which he is much in favor of; on p. 63 [& 65], chap. 40, *loc. cit.*, he calls this *perfectissimum instrumentum* [the most perfect instrument].

* i.e., they are dogleg jacks.

§. 516.

We are still far from finished. I intend to deal with everything at length, so that I can be all the more brief later on. I once saw a keyboard that could be shifted in and out, making stops unnecessary. The [harpsichord] had three choirs. If both sides† of the keyboard were shifted simultaneously to a certain position, then only one set of jacks would pluck, the ones at the rear; the other [jacks] were not moved. If it were shifted to a different position, then only the middle jacks would pluck; at another spot only the front jacks plucked, or the rear plus middle, or the rear plus front, or the middle plus front. Finally, [at one spot] all three rows plucked all the strings together. This pleased me very greatly, since the stop [levers] have this inconvenience, that they sometimes do not engage or release properly, and thus the quill plucks differently than it did before. It is easy to conceive how the [arrangement] described above works. Visualize the rear section of a key in cross-section (the notches can also be made in the side [of the key]). The jacks are so constructed that they do not drop down [into the notches].‡ Thus conceived, a key looks something like this:

† i.e., endblocks.

‡ i.e., they are dogleg jacks.

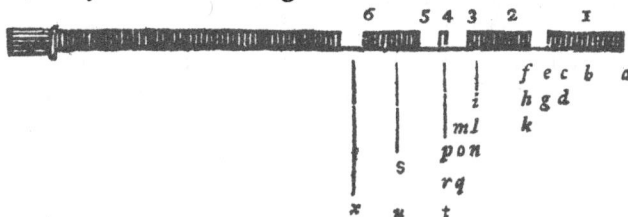

Here the various possibilities are represented quite simply. If abc are under the 3 jacks, then all 3 strings will sound; if I move [the key] a bit, then def will be under the

Docken, da denn e schon ausfällt, als die mittelste Docke, die neben der Palmul weggehet. Rückt man weiter; so steht unter den Docken ghi, da fällt g, die hinterste Docke, weg. Hernach (itzo schieben wir immer einwärts) folgt klm, da fällt m weg, als die vörderste Docke. Alsdann folgt nop, da, wie man sieht, nur n die hinterste klingen muß. Bey qrs klingt die vörderste, und bey tux die mittlere. Wo man dieses bey zweychörichten Clavicymbeln appliciren wollte; so würden nur 3 Veränderungen heraus kommen. Nämlich 1) beyde zusammen, 2) die vordere allein, und 3) die hintere allein. Prätorius sagt, (wie es denn wohl möglich ist) er habe vierchörichte gesehen, und unter denenselben eins, so zwo äqual Seyten gehabt (das heißt bey ihm 8 Fuß Ton) und eine Oktave, auch eine Quinte. Diese 3te und 4te Seyte dürfen die Länge nicht bekommen, wie die 8 füßigen; also müssen sie gegen den Seiten einen nähern Steg bekommen. Die zwo 8 füßigen stehen ordentlich, und ihre Seyten liegen auf beyden Stegen; (wo man sie spinnt, können sie 16′ werden) aber die Oktave und Quinte gehen unten durch den vordersten Steg, und da also der niedrig anschlagenden Docken auch 2 seyn müssen, so schlägt eine gegen die rechte, und die andere gegen die linke Hand. Wenn dieß recht gemacht wird; so schlägt es nicht eben gar zu schwer an. Wollte man dabey das Clavier vorbesagter maaßen rücken; so kämen 13 Veränderungen heraus. Aber dieses Ziehen und das Transponiren habe ich noch nie beysammen gesehen; ich sollte aber auch dieß für möglich halten, wenn man nur unter den viereckichten Rahmen, der vor- und hinterwärts kann geschoben werden, noch einen Rahmen legte, den man samt dem ganzen Clavier auf- und niederschieben kann. Kann es jemand mit einem Rahmen machen; so ist es auch gut. Die vorbesagten 7fachen Veränderungen habe ich von dem Jenaischen Herrn Bach angebracht gefunden.

§. 517.

Man kann auch ein Clavicymbel-Corpus mit zwey Clavieren machen, damit ihrer zwey spielen können. Man macht nämlich die Länge gewöhnlicher maaßen, ohne daß man etwann 1′ oder etwas weniger drüber nimmt. Aber die Breite wird durchaus überein in forma quadrati oblongi. Alsdann macht man auch die Decke durchaus; doch wird oben darüber ein Unterschied gemacht von einer Ecke zur andern von a nach b, etwann also:

So präsentirt dieß ein doppelt Clavessin, deren das eine das Clavier von a nach c hat; das andere aber von d nach b. Das übrige wird gemacht, wie bisher gesagt worden. Wollte man aber das eine Clavier auf der Seite haben, etwann zwischen a d; so würde es ein Instrument werden, dessen wir hernach gedenken wollen.

§. 518.

jacks, and then e, the middle jack that rises above the key, drops out [of operation]. If [the key] is moved further, then it sits under the jacks ghi, and then g, the rear jack, drops out [of operation]. Subsequently come klm (the keyboard continues to be shifted inward), and then m drops out, the front jack. Thereafter follow nop, at which (as can be seen) only n, the rear jack, sounds. At qrs the front jack sounds, and at tux the middle one. If this [mechanism] were to be applied to a harpsichord with two choirs, then only 3 variations would result, namely 1) both together, 2) the front [jack] alone, and 3) the rear one alone. Praetorius* says (and this is indeed possible) that he has seen [harpsichords with] four choirs, among them one that had two "äqual" choirs (by that he means 8′ pitch), and an octave, as well as a quint. These third and fourth [sets of] strings cannot be as long as the 8-foot [sets], and thus they have to have a closer bridge. The two 8-foot [choirs] are located in the usual position, and their strings lie across both bridges (if they are overspun, they could be at 16′ pitch), but the octave and quint pass under and through the front bridge [i.e., nut]. Since there must also be 2 jacks that pluck at a lower level, one plucks to the right and the other to the left. If this is built properly, it will not even have too heavy a touch. If in addition it is desired that a keyboard [of a harpsichord] of the magnitude just described be able to shift, then 13 variations would result. I have never seen the shifting and transposing [mechanisms] combined. I should think, though, that such a thing would be possible, by simply placing a second frame under the rectangular frame that can be shifted forward and backward; this second frame would make it possible to shove the entire keyboard [mechanism above it] from one side to the other. If anyone can accomplish this with a single frame, all the better. I have seen the seven-fold variation described above put into operation by Mr. [Johann Nicolaus] Bach from Jena.

* *Syntagma musicum*, Vol. II, p. 63.

§. 517.

It is also possible to build a harpsichord case with two keyboards, so that the two of them can play together. An instrument of normal length is built, or perhaps a foot or so longer. But its width is constant, thus forming a rectangle. A soundboard is placed across the entire [instrument], but a divider is built on top of it from corner a to corner b, something like this:

This then forms a double harpsichord, one of whose keyboards extends from a to c and the other from d to b. Everything else is build as described above. If, however, one of the keyboards were to be placed on the side, say between a and d, [the harpsichord belonging to] that keyboard would become an "instrument", which we will talk about later on.†

† See §.540.

§. 518.

Man kann aber die Clavicymbel auch so machen, daß 2 oder 3 Claviere übereinander stehen: da denn am besten ist, wenn aller Claviere Docken auf einerley Seyten schlagen. Was das helfe, und wie es möglich, daß dabey doch ein Clavier stärker klinge, als das andere, wird hernach bey den **Lautenwerken** Kap. 25. vorkommen. Doch geht es auch an, daß jedes Clavier besondere Seyten habe, wo zumal der Claviere zwey sind. Denn es können die Docken des andern neben den übrigen Docken stehen, und zwar etwas niedriger, da sie denn, wenn es zweychöricht seyn soll, auf beyden Seiten anschlagen, wie es oben war, wenn drey oder mehr Docken neben einander stunden. Bey der Gattung könnte man auch ein Koppel anbringen. Denn man könnte das obere Clavier machen, daß es sich schieben liesse, und das übrige würde alles wie bey einem Orgelkoppel dieser Art. Dabey ist nöthig, daß die Palmuln hinten nicht anstehen durch Stifte, sondern daß sie nur zwischen 2 Stiften sich bewegen; wie ich denn dergleichen öfters gesehen habe. Es ist mir aber auch ein Breitenbachisches Claveßin mit 2 Clavieren vorgekommen, das dreychöricht war. Es bestand aus Oktave 4′, 8′, und die gesponnenen Seyten hielten 16′. Es reichte aber ins F unter Contra, also bis in 24′. Die Oktave 4′ nebst 16′ war bey dem untern Claviere. Jene lag tiefer, hatte auch ihren besondern Steg, und reichte weder vor an die andern Wirbel, noch hinter an den krummen Steg, sondern der krumme Steg war ein ziemlich Spatium weiter vor besonders, doch niedrig, daß die andern Seyten 8′ und 16′ darüber hin liefen, ohne ihn zu berühren. Hinter dem niedrigen Stege waren in die Decke Stifte geschlagen, daran die 4füßigen Seyten hiengen, und reichten vor an den geraden Steg, an welchen eine besondere Reihe Wirbel eingeschlagen war (nothwendig ist an dem Orte eine eichene Querstrebe unter der Decke) zwischen den andern Seyten woran diese gewunden wurden. Diese wurden von den hintersten Docken durch das untere Clavier regiert, und gaben einen artigen Resonanz von sich. Das Oberclavier regierte durch die vordersten Docken eine 8füßige Seite: Und daß man die Stärke beym Unterclaviere haben könnte; so konnten diese Claviere auch zusammen gekoppelt werden, doch anders, als vorhin gesagt, daß durch Schiebung des obern das untere mit niedergedruckt würde, und da man sodann oben spielen muß; sondern das obere schob man, und spielte auf dem untern, so gieng das obere auch mit, denn die untern Palmuln haben die obern in die Höhe; welches durch Anleimung solcher Hölzeichen oben und unten geschehen kann, wie bey dem Orgelkoppel. Und eben so kann man sie auch mit drey Clavieren machen. Die Claviere selbst sind so, daß das obere die vordersten Docken hebt; das andere geht etwas weiter hinter, und hebt die andern.

§. 519.

Was das **Stimmen** betrift; so muß man, wie bey der Orgel, erst einen Sonum gewiß haben, nach einem gewissen Instrumente. Hernach folgt die Temperatur, wie bey der Orgel: das übrige wird alsdann durch Oktaven gestimmt. Man merke dabey,

§. 518.

It is also possible to construct harpsichords with 2 or 3 manuals, one above the other; with this arrangement it is best if the jacks of all the keyboards pluck the same [choir of] strings. Chapter 25 on the *Lautenwerk* will discuss of what value this is and how it is possible that one keyboard can nevertheless sound stronger than another.* But it is also feasible to provide separate strings for each keyboard, especially if there are [only] two keyboards. Then the jacks of the second [keyboard] can stand next to the other jacks, and indeed somewhat lower, since if there are two choirs the jacks must pluck on opposite sides, as was the case above† if three or more jacks were to stand next to each other. With this type‡ it is also possible to install a coupler, by making the upper keyboard so it can be shifted; everything else would then be just like a coupler of this sort on an organ. Then it would be necessary that the rear end of the key not be held in place by pins,§ but move between two pins; I have seen this sort [of construction] quite often. I have also encountered a two-manual harpsichord made in Breitenbach¶ that had three choirs. It consisted of Octave 4′, [unison] 8′, together with overspun strings that produced a 16′ pitch. It extended down to F below low C, though, all the way down to the 24′ [pitch].∥ The Octave 4′ plus the 16′ were on the lower keyboard, the 4′ [choir of strings] lying beneath [the 16′] and also having its own separate bridge [i.e., nut]. The 4′ did not extend as far as the other wrest pins in front, nor as far as the curved bridge at the rear. Rather it had its own curved bridge, a good deal further forward, yet low, so that the other strings of the 8′ and 16′ [choirs] passed over it without touching it. Behind the low bridge, pins were driven into the soundboard, upon which the 4′ strings were hitched (at that spot an oaken wrestpin rail is required beneath the soundboard**). Those strings then extended forward to the straight bridge [i.e., the nut], at which a separate row of wrest pins was driven in between the other strings; [the 4′ strings] were wound on these pins. They were operated from the lower keyboard by the furthest [row of] jacks, and gave forth a pleasing tone. The upper keyboard operated the 8′ strings with the nearest [set of jacks]. So that the loudest sound could be produced by the lower keyboard, the manuals could be coupled together, but not as described earlier (where by shifting the upper keyboard the lower one would be depressed by it, thus making it necessary to play on the top manual), but by shifting the upper keyboard and playing the lower, then the upper played along with it. For the lower keys lifted [the back ends of] the upper keys upward; this was achieved by gluing small wooden blocks on the top [of the lower key-levers] and the bottom [of the upper ones], like an organ coupler. An instrument with three manuals can be made in just the same way. The keyboards themselves are placed so that the upper one lifts the front row of jacks, while the second reaches somewhat further back and lifts the others.††

§. 519.

Concerning tuning, it is first necessary to establish a pitch, as with the organ.‡‡ Next a temperament is set, as with the organ,§§ and then everything else is tuned by octaves. In this regard, note that if the wrest pins slip, then they need to be hammered in

* See §.559.

† See §.516.
‡ i.e., a two-manual harpsichord.

§ extending out of the back end of each key-lever.

¶ Hubbard (p. 267, n. 65) identifies only two makers who might have built the instrument Adlung saw: Johann Heinrich Harrass (d. 1714) and H.W. Langguth. Dieter Kricheberg attributes the "Bach" harpsichord in Berlin to Harrass; see: Dieter Kricheberg and Horst Rase, "Beiträge zur Kenntnis des Mittel- und Norddeutschen Cembalobaus um 1700," in: *Studia Organologica, Festschrift für John Henry van der Meer...*, ed. Friedemann Hellwig (Tutzing: Hans Schneider, 1987), pp. 285ff.

∥ i.e, to the pitch than an open organ pipe 24′ long would produce: FFF.

** i.e, the part of the soundboard over the (hollow) wrest plank.

†† The sentence previous to this one must be considered parenthetical. This final sentence, then, does not refer to an instrument with three manuals, but continues to describe the two-manual instrument made in Breitenbach.

‡‡ See §.402 and §.404.
§§ See §.406, 408 and 411.

wo die Wirbel nicht stehen wollen, so schlage man sie hinein: wenn man die Seyten aufziehet; so winde man sie nicht so tief, daß sie bis in die Decke reichen, doch auch nicht so hoch, sonst liegen sie nicht auf dem Stege veste auf, und wird dadurch verursacht, daß die Seyten sich losheben; imgleichen daß der Wirbel nicht so gut stehet, sondern sich biegt; jenes macht, daß die Seyten den Steg und die Decke zu sehr drücken, und einen großen Triangul machen, oder wenigstens einen Winkel, wo sie auf dem Stege liegen, daher sie eher reissen. Denn da sie krumm gehen, werden sie nicht nur etwas geknickt, sondern sie werden auch länger. Man muß sich dahero im Abzeichnen der Wirbel hüten, daß die Seyten nicht zu krumm herumgehen dürfen; genug ists, wenn sie so viel auf die Seite gehen, daß sie auf dem Stege vest an dem Drate liegen. Von der Stimmung der Clavicymbel hat Kircherus in Musurgia etwas Lib. VI. Part. II. c. I. pag. 462. Da er durch den Zirkel geht §. 3. §. 4. hat er sonst gar curiös gehandelt von der Proportion der Seyten, und wäre es gut, sagt er, wo jeder Clavis seine besondere Dicke hätte. Er hat auch eine Tabelle davon samt dem Diametro der Seyten. Dieß merke ich noch an, daß die Seyten besser halten, wenn ich sie (zumal wo sie bey den Stiften und Wirbeln merkliche Winkel machen) in die Höhe ziehe, ehe ich sie über ihren Stift und gehörige Stelle bringe, als wenn sie in den Winkel sollen gelegt, und in die Höhe gebracht werden. Die Stimmung muß auch geschehen kurz zuvor ehe man es braucht, und nicht eher muß man es an den Ort tragen, wo man es nöthig hat, als wenn die Musik gleich angehen soll.

§. 520.

Denn sonst wird die veränderte Luft, oder wo es etwann feuchter ist, es bald verstimmen. Wo der Ort wahrscheinlicher Weise feuchter ist, als der, wo man es gestimmt; so lasse man es bedeckt, sonderlich wo Rasen ist. Oder man müßte es eine gute Zeit vorher dahin tragen, und wenn es sich erst verzogen, es hernach nochmals reine stimmen. Die Nacht ist kühler, als der Tag, folglich wird dieselbe leicht eine Veränderung verursachen. Denn die Decke ist gar anzüglich und spannt sich; auch nehmen die Seyten die feuchte Luft an, und dehnen sich auseinander.

§. 521.

Es ist auch gut, daß man die Seyten abpuße, wenn sie rosten, sonderlich wenn es weisse sind. Dieses ist nöthig, wenn solche Werke an feuchten Orten stehen; derowegen sie in feuchten Stuben nichts nütze sind. Das Abpußen geschiehet mit Bimmstein; auch wol im Nothfalle mit Kreide. Ohne Noth reisse man die alten Seyten nicht ab: sie halten die Stimmung weit dauerhafter, und klingen besser als die neuen. Wenn zuweilen eine Seyte nicht in der Höhe bleibt, da doch der Wirbel veste stehet, so wird sie nicht scharf genug um den Wirbel gewunden seyn: oder man hat die Seyte nicht scharf genug gedrehet beym Angehenge, daher sie sich wieder aufzieht.

further. When stringing a harpsichord, be careful not to wind the strings so far [down the wrest pin] that they reach the soundboard; this causes the strings to press too heavily on the bridge and the soundboard by creating a triangle* or at least an angle where they lie on the bridge; thus the strings are more prone to break. Be careful also not to string them so high that they do not lie firmly across the bridge, causing the strings to lift off it and the pins to be more prone to bend. When strings are drawn at an angle,† they not only get somewhat bent, but they also get stretched. Thus in positioning the wrest pin one must guard against the strings being positioned at too great an angle; it is sufficient for them to angle off just enough to rest firmly against the pin on the bridge [i.e., nut]. Kircher says something about tuning the harpsichord in his *Musurgia*, Book VI, Part II, chap. I, p. 462. After he has passed through the circle [of fifths] in §.3, he has something very curious to say about the proportion of the strings.‡ He says it would be good for [the string of] each key to have its own thickness. He gives a table§ for this, containing the diameter of the strings. Furthermore, let me mention that the strings are less likely to break (especially if a considerable angle is created between the [bridge] pins and the wrest pins) if they are tightened before being laid in place over their respective pins, rather than first being set at an angle and then tightened. An instrument must be tuned just before it is used, and should not be carried to the spot where it is needed until just before it is to be played.¶

* i.e., between the string and the soundboard.

† Here Adlung is speaking about strings bending off to one side.

‡ in §.4, p. 463.

§ p. 464.

¶ The spot Adlung seems to have in mind may well be outdoors; cf. the second sentence of §.520.

§. 520.

Otherwise the change in temperature and humidity will quickly put it out of tune. If the spot is likely to be more humid than the place where it is tuned, then it should be left covered, especially if it is sitting on a lawn. Alternately, it should be brought to its destination a good while in advance, and only when it has become acclimated should it again be tuned. Nighttime is cooler than daytime, consequently the shift [from one to another] can easily cause a change [in tuning]. The soundboard, you see, is very absorbent and expands; the strings also absorb the damp air and become slacker.

§. 521.

It is also good to clean the strings if they are rusty, especially if they are iron/steel. This is necessary if such instruments sit in damp places, and for this reason they do not do well in damp rooms. The cleaning is done with pumice, or in cases of necessity with chalk. Old strings should not be ripped out unless it is necessary, since they hold their tune far longer and sound better than new ones. If a given string does not hold pitch, even though its wrest pin fits tightly, then it may not be wound tightly enough around the wrest pin, or the string was not wound tightly enough at the hitchpin; thus it needs to be re-strung.

§. 522.

Das Spielen auf solchen beseyteten Instrumenten ist anders, als auf der Orgel. Man muß sich mehr der Brechungen und dergleichen befleißigen, als daß man die Claves zusammen oder allzulangsam anschlägt; denn die Seyten hören bald auf zu klingen. Kircherus l. c. p. 465. sagt, daß Toccaten, Sonaten, Ricercaten u. d. gl. sich am besten dazu schickten. Man muß aber auch fein sanfte spielen, und durch ungestümes Dreschen nicht die Seyten vergeblich zersprengen.

§. 523.

Das Holz zu der Decke muß nicht fettigt seyn. Es pflegen dahero einige Instrumentmacher solche Bretterchen, welche sie zu Decken brauchen wollen, zuvor wohl auszusieden, welches in einer Braupfanne am füglichsten geschehen kann. Alsdann leimt man sie accurat zusammen. Dicker dürfen sie nicht seyn, als etwann den 16ten Theil eines Zolles, damit die Decke sich leichter bewegen lasse und zum Zittern gebracht werde. Wenn man etwas auf den Steg legt; so wird der Klang stiller, weil das Zittern so frey nicht geschehen kann. Wenn man sonst auf die Decke etwas legt, z. E. einen Schlüssel oder sonst etwas; so rasselt es: woraus man siehet, die Decke müsse durch den Anschlag stets in Bewegung gebracht werden. Man findet, daß neue Clavicymbel (wiewol es bey den meisten musikalischen Instrumenten eintrift) nicht so angenehm und scharf klingen, als wenn sie eine Zeitlang gespielet worden. Die Haupturfach ist, weil das Holz immer dürrer und leichter wird. Daher etliche nicht unrecht thun, wenn sie alte Kasten ꝛc. dazu nehmen, die man lange Zeit an dürren Orten liegend gehabt, daß sie recht haben ausdorren können. Auch pflegt man die Decke im Basse etwas dicker zu machen, der Gravität wegen. Unter die Decke kömmt ein Wiederhalt zu stehen.

§. 524.

Da nun das Drücken des Steges auch das Zittern der Decke verhindert, dieses aber mit der Zeit etwas abnimmt; so kann endlich der Klang sich verbessern. Allein, sollte es wol nicht möglich seyn, was die Stege anlangt, eine Aenderung zu machen? Ich stelle mir solches nicht unmöglich vor. Und zwar könnte man anstatt des vordern Steges ein breites Eisen in beyde Seiten bevestigen, welches nicht gar auf die Decke reichte, daher auch dieselbe nicht drückte. Oben müßte es etwas dünne seyn, daß man Kerben hinein feilen könnte, anstatt der Stifte, darinne die Seyten veste liegen. Von Holz dergleichen zu machen, dürfte wol nicht rathsam seyn. Sollte sich das Eisen etwas der Länge wegen in der Mitte biegen wollen; so kann man von unten herauf durch die Decke einen Enthalt oder Pfeiler unter setzen, welches der Decke wenig schadet, da ja Oeffnungen genug auch bey den Docken sind, und man auch sonst Oeffnungen auf die Decke machen muß, in runder Form, oder wie man will. Der andere Steg auf der Seite hinauf könnte auch weggebracht werden, wenn man die Seyten an das Seitbrett anhienge, und durch eiserne Arme einen erhabenen eisernen Steg anbrächte, wo man nicht beyde Stege behalten, die Decke aber auf der Seite und unten nicht gar

§. 522.

Playing on this sort of stringed instrument is different than playing on the organ. One must endeavor to use more arpeggios and such, rather than striking the keys together or playing too slowly, since the strings cease vibrating right away. Kircher [in his *Musurgia*], *loc. cit.,* p. 465 [§. I], says that toccatas, sonatas, ricercars and such are best suited for the instrument. It is necessary to play nice and gently, though, so as to avoid breaking the strings needlessly by thrashing about violently.

§. 523.

The wood for the soundboard must not be oily. Some instrument makers, therefore, are in the habit of thoroughly boiling the boards that they intend to use for the soundboard; this is most conveniently accomplished in a brewer's cauldron. Next they are glued together precisely. They cannot be any thicker than about a sixteenth of an inch,* to allow the soundboard to be set into motion and vibrate easily. If something is set on the bridge, then the sound becomes quieter, since vibration is hindered. If something is laid on the soundboard, e.g., a key or some such, then it rattles; it is clear from this that the soundboard is always set in motion by plucking the string. You will observe that new harpsichords (as is the case with most musical instruments) do not sound as agreeable and brilliant as those that have been played a while. The main reason for this is that the wood keeps getting dryer and lighter. Thus some [makers] are not doing anything improper by using old boxes, etc., for [soundboards], wood that has been left lying in dry places for a long time and has thus had a chance to dry out thoroughly. It is customary to make the soundboard somewhat thicker in the bass, for the sake of gravity. A cross-brace is placed under the soundboard.

* See Hubbard, p. 274, note 91.

§. 524.

While pressure from the bridge also hinders the vibration of the soundboard, this decreases with time, and thus the tone ultimately gets better. With regard to the bridge, would it not be possible, though, to do things differently? I do not consider such a thing to be impossible: instead of the nearer bridge [i.e., the nut], a long iron [rod] could be anchored to both sides [of the case], that did not reach completely down to the soundboard, and thus did not press on it. It would need to be somewhat narrow on top, so that notches could be filed into it (instead of pins), in which the strings would fit tightly. Making such a device of wood would not be advisable. If the piece of iron were to sag in the middle due to its length, then a support or prop could be set under it, passing through the soundboard. This would do very little harm to the soundboard, since there are already plenty of holes in it for the jacks, and holes (either round or in whatever shape desired) have to be made in the soundboard anyway.† The other bridge next to the [bent] side could also be lifted off [the soundboard], by attaching the strings to the case wall and then mounting an iron bridge resting on iron posts, if one did not wish to retain both bridges, but did not wish to let the sound-

† i.e., rose holes or sound holes.

an die Stege wollte gehen lassen. Dabey ist dieses nicht zu vergessen, daß, da auf solche Art zwischen dem Stoße der Seyten und der Decke keine Gemeinschaft ist, man wenigstens von solchem erhabenen Stege eine sogenannte Stimme auf die Decke führen müßte, um dadurch das Zittern zu befördern; doch drückt solche Stimme so viel nicht, als der ganze Steg thun würde, wenn er auf der Decke durchgängig aufläge. Die vorgedachte Oeffnung anlangend; so ist sie etwas bedenklich, wenn sie auf der Decke angebracht wird, sowol bey diesem, als andern Instrumenten: denn es fällt Staub hinein. Mir deucht, man thue wohl, wenn man oben alles zuläßt, und vornen eine Oeffnung macht vermittelst etlicher kleiner Löcherchen. Denn eine Oeffnung muß seyn; sonst wenn die Luft eingesperrt ist, bewegt sich das corpus nicht frey, daher es nicht lange nachklingt, und über dieses so ist der Klang ganz stumpf und ohne alle Lieblichkeit. Ich habe Clavicordien gesehen, die von ausnehmend schönem Klange waren die aber oben auf der Decke keine Oeffnung oder sogenannten Stern hatten. Diese Observation, nebst etlichen andern, ist aus Matthesons Critica musica Tom. II. P. VIII. im 22sten Stück, da eine Beschreibung des Scipionis Maffei von einem besondern Clavicymbel ist (davon hernach) nebst etlichen dergleichen Anmerkungen. Sonst ist unten Kap. 26. bey Beschreibung des Claviskords noch verschiedenes zu finden, das hier nicht stehet, doch aber allhier mit Nutzen nachzulesen und zu brauchen ist.

§. 525.

Lasset uns doch dabey fragen: wer der Erfinder dieses schönen Instruments sey? Wenn wir Prinzens historische Beschreibung der edlen Sing- und Klingkunst aufschlagen; so lesen wir im 10ten Kapitel, §. 14. daß der bekannte Mönch Guido Aretinus nebst dem Claviford auch das Clavessin erfunden, wie auch noch andere dergleichen Instrumente. Wenn dieß wahr ist; so werden sie gewiß Anfangs gar einfältig gewesen seyn. Polidorus Vergilius de inuent. rerum Lib. III. c. 18. sagt ausdrücklich, der inuentor der monochordorum & clauicymbalorum sey uns ganz unbekannt. Seine eigenen Worte sind: Item alia id genus sunt, quæ monochordia, clauicymbala, varieque nominantur, eorum tamen aeque inuentores magno quidem suæ gloriæ damno in nocte densissima debitescunt. Ich will mich in diese Sache nicht einlassen, weil mir bis dato nicht Gelegenheit gegeben worden, die fontes zu untersuchen, woraus Prinz seine Nachricht genommen.

§. 526.

Es handeln sonst von dem Clavessin auch andere Auctores; doch meistens sehr kurz. Wir wollen aber doch allhier noch etwas davon anführen, um dasjenige noch daraus zu lernen, was bisher noch nicht berühret worden. Prätorius T. II. P. II. c. 39. pag. 63. sagt: etliche nennen es Gravecymbalum; etliche einen Flügel wegen der Figur; etliche einen Schweinskopf, (sed male) weil es spitzig ist. Cap. 40. pag. 63. handelt er de Clauicymbalo vniuersali siue perfecto; dadurch ein solches Instrument

board extend to the [bent] side and not quite up to the bottom of the bridge. In this regard it should not be forgotten that, since this procedure would provide no connection between the vibration of the strings and the soundboard, it would be necessary to run a so-called soundpost between the raised bridge and the soundboard, to stimulate its vibration. Such a soundpost, however, would not exert as much pressure as would a bridge lying across the entire width of the soundboard. Concerning the [sound]hole mentioned earlier: it is questionable whether it ought to be put into the soundboard, in this as well as other instruments, since dust falls through it. It seems to me it would be a good thing to leave [the soundboard] covering everything on top, and to open up the front by means of several small holes.* For there has to be an opening; otherwise the air is trapped and the case does not vibrate freely. Therefore the instrument does not resound very long, and furthermore the tone is completely dull and without charm. I have seen clavichords that had an exceedingly lovely tone, yet had no opening, or so-called "Rose" through the top of the soundboard. This observation,† together with several others, is from Mattheson's *Critica Musica*, Vol. II, in the 22nd section‡ of Part VIII, where there is a description by Scipione Maffei of an unusual harpsichord§ (more about this later¶) together with a number of similar remarks. Furthermore, with the description of the clavichord in Chapter 26 below, various other comments may be found that are not recorded here, but may profitably be consulted and applied here.

* i.e., holes in the belly rail.

† i.e., the suggestion to omit the opening in the soundboard, found in Mattheson's *Critica Musica*, vol. II, Part VIII, pp. 340-41. The intervening sentences appear to be a parenthetical statement expressing Adlung's experience in the matter.

‡ see: Mattheson, *Critica Musica*, Vol. II, p. 321 (bottom); cf. *ibid.*, p. 345 (bottom).

§ i.e., Cristofori's pianoforte. Maffei's description is found on pp. 335-342 of Mattheson's *Critica Musica*, Vol. II.

¶ §.529f.

‖ p. 109.

§. 525.

Let us ask, moreover, who the inventor of this beautiful instrument is. If we consult Prinz's *Historische Beschreibung der edlen Sing- und Klingkunst*, we read in Chapter 10, §.14,‖ that the well-known monk Guido d'Arezzo invented the harpsichord as well as the clavichord, together with yet other instruments of this kind. If this is true, then at the beginning it must certainly have been very crude indeed. Polidorus Vergilius, in his *de rerum inventoribus*, Book III, Chap. 18, expressly says that the inventor of monochords and harpsichords is totally unknown to us. His exact words are: *Item alia id genus sunt, quae monochordia, clavicymbala, varieque nominantur, eorum tamen aeque inventores magno quidem suae gloriae damno in nocte densissima debitescunt* [There are also others of that kind, that are variously called clavichord and clavicymbel, but their inventors are likewise, in fact, consigned to deepest obscurity due to the grave loss of their remembrance]. I will not get involved in this matter, since up until now I have not had the opportunity to investigate the sources from which Prinz took his information.

§. 526.

There are yet other authors who treat the harpsichord as well, but mostly very briefly. Here, however, I will cite some of their information, to learn from it about things that have not yet been touched on here. Praetorius [in his *Syntagma musicum*,] Vol. II, Part II, chap. 39, p. 63, says: "Some call it *Gravecymbalum*; other a Flügel** because of its shape; others a pig's head because it comes to a point (but this is crude)." In Chap. 40, p. 63, he discusses the "universal or perfect harpsichord" (*Clavicym-*

** i.e., wing, referring to its shape.

ment verstehet, worauf man das genus chromaticum spielen kann. Er will die Subsemitonia mit eingeflickt wissen: allein diese sind bey unserer heutigen Temperatur überflüßig. Mattheson im Orchestre I. P. III. cap. III. §. 4. nennt diese Clauicembali (welches Italienisch ist; und Cembalo bedeutet ein gleiches) französisch Clavessins, oder Clavecins, auch Flügel oder Steertstücke, und giebt ihnen den Preis vor allen Instrumenten. Sonst besinne ich mich, daß er ibid. §. 3. durch Clavier auch das Clavessin, nicht aber die Orgel, verstehet, und ziehet es, wo nicht der Orgel selbst, (wie es doch fast scheinen sollte) doch den andern Instrumenten vor. Man lese, was er allda sagt.

§. 527.

Kircherus in *Musurgia* beschreibt das Clavicymbel auch L. VI. P. II. Cap. I. pag. 453. seqq. Das Clavier daran nennet er abacum oder tastaturam. Die Wirbel heissen bey ihm claues. Die Stege vorn nennet er prismata triangularia; den krummen Steg auf der Seite prisma coruilineum. Die Docken führen bey ihm den Namen der Subsiliorum. Die anschlagenden Federn heissen plectra pennacea. Er sagt ib. §. 2. daß die Italiener die Docken oder subsilia saltarelli, die Franzosen aber Sauteraux nenneten. (dieß Sauterau kommt her von sauter, in die Höhe springen. s. Frisch Lex. gall. an dessen Statt de Chales sauterelle sagt. Prop 36.; da er sonst die Docken auch pinnas nennt. Prop. 34.) Die Zunge heißt epiglottis. Die Feder festuca ex penna coruina vel aquilina. (aus Raben= oder Adlersfedern). Das übrige ist theils da gewesen, theils kömmt es unten vor. Die Spinete, Clavicytherium ꝛc. nennt er auch daselbst zuweilen Clavicymbel. Etwas weniges hat aus ihm Janowka beygebracht in Claue pag. 39. Der musikalische Trichter hat Kap. X. nur so viel davon, daß man es einen musikalischen Flügel nenne, und sey es lieblich; doch aber wandelbar. Das letzte ist gewiß: denn man wird es doch nie so beständig machen, als Pfeiffwerke sind. Die Docken nennt er Tangenten, von *tangere*, anrühren. De Chales Mund. math. T. III. p. 217. hat auch was davon, und nennets Fidiculare organon.

§. 528.

Wenn das Clavicymbel oder Spinet, bey einem Positive zu finden; so heißt es Clauiorganum. Die Sache selbst ist Kap. 20. §. 497. schon berühret: bey Kirchero aber in Musurgia l. c. cap. 42. pag. 67. it. in *Ribouii* Enchirid. mus. pag. 155. findet man diesen ihm beygelegten Namen. Wollte man eine solche clavicymbalische Struktur zu einem Pedale erwählen; so hiesse es: Clavicymbelpedal; doch davon handelt unten das 26ste Kapitel. Es kömmt auch der pantalonische Cembal vor; allein ob dieß schon mit unserm Instrument gleichen Namen führt; so ist es doch kein Clavier, welches ein Organist (qua talis) spielen köune; derowegen will ich es allhier nicht beschreiben. Es heißt sonst auch Pantalon, und ist den Hackbrettern etwas gleich, doch mit fleischernen Seyten bezogen; ist schwer, doch schön. Conf. Orch. I. Part. III. cap. III. §. 17. Der Name ist von dem großen Meister **Pantalon**, der sonst

Chap. XXII. The Harpsichord, Clavicytherium, Spinet,

balum universalis sive perfectum), by which he means an instrument on which chromatic pieces can be played. He wants to see subsemitones mixed in with it, but with our modern temperament these are superfluous. Mattheson in his [*Neu=Eröffnete*] *Orchestre I*, Part III, chap. III, §.4,* calls these [instruments] "*clavicembali*" (which is Italian; "*Cembalo*" means the same thing), clavessins or *claveçins* in French, as well as Flügel or Steertstücke,† and praises them above all other instruments. Moreover I recall that in §.3 of the same source‡ he also uses "Clavier" to mean the clavessin, but not the organ, preferring it (and not the organ itself, as one would think) above all other instruments. Consult what he has to say there.

§. 527.

Kircher also describes the harpsichord in his *Musurgia*, Book VI, Part II, Chap. I, pp. 453ff. He calls its keyboard "abacus" or "tastatura." His word for wrest pins is "claves." The forward bridge [i.e., nut] he calls "prismata triangularia," and the curved bridge on the side "prisma corvilineum."§ In his book the jacks bear the name "subsilia." The quills that pluck are called "plectra pennacea." In §. 2 he says that the Italians call the jacks or "sublilia"¶ "saltarelli," while the French call them "Sauteraux" (the word "Sauterau" is derived from "sauter," "to leap into the air;" see Frisch, *Lex. gall.*;|| de Chales,** Prop. 36, uses "sauterelle" instead, but elsewhere, in Prop. 34, he calls the jacks "pinnae"). The tongue is called "epiglottis," the quill "festuca ex penna corvina vel aquilina ([shaft_of] raven's or eagle's feather). The rest†† has in part already been presented; in part it will appear below. The spinet, clavicytherium, etc., he sometimes refers to there as a "harpsichord" (Clavicymbel). Janowka in his *Clavis*, p. 39, has also incorporated a small part of the information he‡‡ gives. In *Der musikalische Trichter*, Chap. 10[, p. 90, Fuhrmann] mentions only that it is called a "musikalischer Flügel,"§§ and that it is charming though unstable [in pitch]. The latter is certainly true; it can never be made as stable as pipes. The jacks he calls "Tangenten," from *tangere*, "to touch." De Chales also has something about it in his [*Cursus seu*] *mund. math.*, Vol. III, p. 217, calling it "Fidiculare organon."

§. 528.

If a harpsichord or spinet is found as part of a positive [organ], then [the resulting instrument] is called a Claviorganum. This matter has already been mentioned in Chap. 20, §.497. In Kircher's *Musurgia*¶¶ [it is treated] in Chap. 42, p. 67; likewise in Ribovius' *Enchirid. mus.*,|||| p. 155, this name is found assigned to it. If one were to choose the harpsichord's structure for a pedal, then it would be called "Clavicymbelpedal;" but this is treated in Chapter 26 below.*** There is also such a thing as Pantalon's Cembalo,††† but although it bears the same name as the instrument we are discussing, it is nevertheless not a keyboard instrument that an organist (as such) could play. Therefore I will not describe it here. It is also called Pantaleon, and resembles to some degree the dulcimer, though strung with gut strings. It is difficult [to play], but beautiful; cf. [Mattheson's *Neu-Eröffnete*] *Orchestre* I, Part. III, chap. III, §.17.‡‡‡ It

---

* p. 262.

† Probably the German equivalent of the Dutch *staartstuk*, "tail piece;" cf. the translation of a passage from Quirinius van Blankenburg's *Elementa musica* (The Hague, 1739), in: Hubbard, p. 237.

‡ p. 256f.

§ Kircher has "prismata... curvilinea."

¶ sic; the word should be "subsilia."

|| Johann Leonhard Frisch, *Noveau dictionnaire...françois-allemand et allemand-françois*. Leipzig: Gleditsch und Sohn, 1712.

** *Cursus seu mundus mathematicus*, Vol. III, Tract 22.

†† i.e., other information from Kircher.

‡‡ referring ostensibly to Kircher.

§§ i.e., a "musical wing."

¶¶ This should read "Praetorius's *Syntagma musicum*."

|||| L. Ribovius, *Enchiridion musicum*. Königsberg: 1638.

*** see §.603.

††† The Panteleon, a type of dulcimer developed by Pantaleon Hebenstreit in 1697; one of the forerunners of the piano.

‡‡‡ p. 280.

Hebenstreit heißt. Siehe etwas weitere Nachricht von diesem Instrumente in Matthesons Critica Musica Tom. II. pag. 236. da Kuhnau davon redet in einem Briefe an Mattheson; auch pag. 248. ist noch verschiedenes davon. Uns geht es demnach itzo nichts an.

§. 529.

Die Bogeninstrumente haben den Vortheil für den Clavieren, daß man das forte und piano darauf haben kann, welches das schönste mit in der Musik ist. Da hat man sich nun besondere Mühe gegeben, ob es bey Clavieren nicht auch möglich zu machen. Daher ist das Geigenwerk entstanden, davon im folgenden Kapitel zu reden. Wo aber 2 Claviere sind, da kann man auch wenigstens eins piano haben. Es hat auch ein Claviermacher, Namens Bartolomeo Cristofali, aus Padua gebürtig, der bey dem Großherzoge von Florenz in Diensten gestanden, eine Art des Clavesins von ordinärer Größe erfunden, deren Beschreibung wir vom Marchese Scipio Maffei, nebst einigen Betrachtungen über die musikalischen Instrumente, in welscher Sprache haben; die aber König ins deutsche übersetzt, und Mattheson in Crit. Mus. Tom. II. p. 335. seq. eingerückt hat (**). Weil nun dasselbige mit einem Claviere regieret wird; so will ich es allhier mit einschalten.

(**) Daß der Herr Christoph Gottlieb Schröter, Organist an der Hauptkirche in Nordhausen, sich die Erfindung dieses Instruments zueignet, ist, eines gewissen Sendschreibens desselben an den Hrn. Hofrath Mizler, nicht einmal zu gedenken, auch vornehmlich, und mit vielen Umständen im 139, 140, und 141sten Briefe der kritischen Briefe über die Tonkunst, zu lesen. Es würde sehr unbillig seyn, an der Wahrheit dessen, was ein Mann, wie der dessen Rechtschaffenheit nichts einzuwenden ist, (und für einen solchen ist Hr. Schröter bekannt,) und noch dazu mit so vielen besondern Umständen, und öffentlich sagt, zu zweifeln. Unterdessen ist doch damit noch nicht ausgemacht, ob Hr. Cristofali schlechterdings nicht auch auf ähnliche Gedanken hätte gerathen können, und ob er nothwendig sich der Erfindung des Hr. Schröter hätte müssen bedienet haben. Um dieses zu entscheiden müßte man untrüglich wissen: 1) nicht allein, wenn Hr. Cristofali wenigstens das erste dieser Instrumente verfertiget hätte, sondern auch wenn er angefangen hätte, auf dessen Erfindung zu denken. Dieses zu erfahren ist mir vor der Hand nicht möglich. Es würde aber sehr viel dazu helfen, wenn man wissen könnte, in welchem Jahre der Marchese Scipio Maffei die vom Hrn. Hofrath König ins Deutsche übersetzte Beschreibung davon gemachet hätte. Dies kann ich itzo auch nicht untersuchen. 2) Müßte man vom Hrn. Gottfried Silbermann eine Erklärung auf sein Gewissen haben, nach welchem Modelle, oder nach welcher Angabe er die Verfertigung des ersten dieser Instrumente in Deutschland angeleget habe. Diese Erklärung hat Hr. Silbermannen niemand bey seinem Leben abgefordert: und itzo ist er schon seit einigen Jahren todt. Folglich ist dieser 2te Punct vollends gar unmöglich. Und doch würde damit nicht erwiesen seyn, ob Hrn Schröters Erfindung nicht vorher nach Italien hätte können gekommen seyn. Das müßte vielmehr durch Gegeneinanderhaltung der angeführten ersten Forderung, wenn sie erfüllet werden könnte, mit Hrn. Schröters Nachricht und Beschreibung heraus gebracht werden.

Indessen, es möchte nun diese Untersuchung ausfallen wie sie wollte, würde sie dem Hrn. Schröter doch nach der genauesten Billigkeit nicht den geringsten Nachtheil bringen. Denn, da

gets its name from the great master Pantalon, also called Hebenstreit. For somewhat more detailed information about this instrument, see Mattheson's *Critica Musica*, Vol. II, p. 236[f.], where Kuhnau speaks of it in a letter to Mattheson; there is also more about it on p. 248. Accordingly it does not concern us here.

§. 529.

The bowed instruments have this advantage over the keyed ones, that it is possible to play loudly and softly on them, a thing that is most beautiful in ensemble music. Therefore people have taken special pains to see if such a thing might be possible for keyboard instruments. This is how the *Geigenwerk* came into being, about which the following chapter speaks. If there are two manuals [on a harpsichord], then it is possible to make at least one of them soft. A keyboard [instrument] maker by the name of Bartholomeo Cristofali* [sic], born in Padua and in the service of the Grand-duke of Florence, has also invented a type of harpsichord† of ordinary size, a description of which we have in Italian from the Marquis Scipio Maffei,‡ together with several observations on musical instruments. König has translated it into German, and Mattheson has inserted it into his *Critica musica*, Vol. II, pp. 335f.(**) Since this instrument is operated by means of a keyboard, I will include it here.

(**) Mr. Christoph Gottlieb Schröter, organist at the principal church in Nordhausen, claims to have invented this instrument. One may read about this matter chiefly in the 139th, 140th and 141st letters of [Marpurg's] *Kritische Briefe über die Tonkunst*,§ where a many details are given, not to mention a certain communication from Schröter to Privy Councillor [Lorenz Christoph] Mizler.¶ It would be very unfair to doubt the truth of a statement made by a man whose integrity is unquestioned (and Mr. Schröter is recognized as such a man), especially when it is stated publicly with so many specific details. Meanwhile it has not been determined whether Mr. Cristofori necessarily had to have made use of Mr. Schröter's invention, or whether he simply hit upon similar ideas. In order to decide this, it would be necessary to know infallibly: 1) not only if Mr. Cristofori had at least built the earliest of these instruments, but also when he had begun to think about his invention. For the present it is not possible to determine this. It would be very helpful in the matter, though, if one could know the year in which the Marquis Scipio Maffei had written the description of the instrument that was translated into German by Privy Councillor König. This I also cannot investigate at present. 2) It would be necessary to have from Mr. Gottfried Silbermann a declaration, on his word, as to which model or whose specifications he based the construction of the first of these instruments in Germany on. No one ever requested such a declaration from Mr. Silbermann during his life, and by now he has been dead for several years. Consequently this second point is altogether quite impossible. And yet even it would not rule out the possibility that Mr. Schröter's invention had not reached Italy at some earlier time. Rather that would have to be accomplished by a comparison of the first question above, if that could be answered, with Mr. Schröter's report and description.

Nevertheless, however this investigation might come out, in all fairness it would not put Mr. Schröter at the least disadvantage. Since he had already begun to think about his

---

* Adlung reports Cristofori's name as "Cristofali", an error stemming from Maffei's description, mentioned below in §.529. I have corrected the spelling each time the name appears subsequently in the text.

† Here, of course, Adlung is beginning to report the invention of the fortepiano. A clear distinction in terminology between the harpsichord and fortepiano became common only at the end of the 18th century.

‡ Scipione Maffei, *Giornale de' letterati d'Italia*, Venice, 1711. Parenthetically, it should be noted that Maffei's description differs somewhat from the action of the three surviving Cristofori instruments.

§ Vol. III, pp. 81-104.

¶ Schröter's letter of Sept. 22, 1738, which Mizler printed in his *Musikalische Bibliothek*, Vol. 3, No. 3 (Leipzig, 1747), pp. 473ff.

da er im Jahre 1717 angefangen hat auf seine Erfindung zu denken, und am 11 Febr. 1721. sie am königlichen Hofe in Dresden gezeiget hat: so ist schwer zu glauben, daß er, als ein Schüler auf der Kreutzschule in Dresden, Gelegenheit gehabt haben sollte Nachrichten von den neuesten Erfindungen in Italien zu bekommen. Uberdieses, so hat die in dem 140sten kritischen Briefe, vom Hrn. Schröter angegebene Vermehrung der Saiten in der Höhe, da nämlich vom Contra F bis cis, 2 Saiten, vom d bis $\bar{\bar{h}}$ 3 Saiten, und von $\bar{\bar{h}}$ bis $\bar{\bar{g}}$ 4 Saiten: oder vom Contra F bis h zwo, vom $\bar{c}$ bis $\bar{\bar{g}}$ aber drey Saiten auf das gedachte Instrument sollen gezogen werden, wie mich dünkt, einen großen Vorzug in Ansehung der durchaus gleichen Stärke, vor denen welche Hr. Silbermann und seine Nachfolger verfertiget haben, als welche durchgehends auf jedem Clave nur mit zwo Saiten bezogen, und folglich, der Natur der Dinge gemäß, in den höhern Tönen nicht ganz so stark klingen können, als in den tiefern. Anderer Vortheile der Schröterschen Erfindung mehr zu geschweigen.

Ich halte also für das beste: in diesem Stücke nichts entscheiden zu wollen. Hiernach bitte ich auch die Anmerkung, welche ich S. 212. des 1. Bandes dieser Musica mechanica in der 4. u. f. Zeilen gemacht habe, zu erklären. Denn ich habe da, bey diesem unentschiedenen Zweifel, nach der gemeinsten Meynung gesprochen. Indessen bemerke ich doch noch, daß Hr. Adlung schon S. 561 seiner Anleit. zur mus. Gelahrth. dieser Schröterschen Einwendungen Erwähnung gethan hat.

Da dieses Instrument aber, es mag es nun erfunden haben wer da will, sonderlich in der Art, wie es Hr. Silbermann in seinen letzten Zeiten, und desselben gleichfalls nun verstorbener Vetter, der Commißionsrath Silbermann in Dresden, u. s. w. dargestellet haben, gar große Schönheiten und Annehmlichkeiten besitzet; wenn man auch den etwas schwächern Laut in der Höhe übersehen will: als in welchem Stücke Hrn. Schröters Angabe, mit Vermehrung der Saiten in der Höhe, nach der größten Wahrscheinlichkeit einigen Vorzug haben muß: so halte ich es nicht für überflüßig noch etwas zur Geschichte desselben hier beyzubringen.

Herr Gottfr. Silbermann hatte dieser Instrumente im Anfange zwey verfertiget. Eins davon hatte der sel. Kapelm. Hr. Joh. Sebastian Bach gesehen und bespielet. Er hatte den Klang desselben gerühmet, ja bewundert: Aber dabey getadelt, daß es in der Höhe zu schwach lautete, und gar zu schwer zu spielen sey. Dieses hatte Hr. Silbermann, der gar keinen Tadel an seinen Ausarbeitungen leiden konnte, höchst übel aufgenommen. Er zürnte deswegen lange mit dem Hrn. Bach. Und dennoch sagte ihm sein Gewissen, daß Hr. Bach nicht unrecht hätte. Er hielt also, und das sey zu seinem großen Ruhme gesagt, für das beste nichts weiter von diesen Instrumenten auszugeben; dagegen aber desto fleißiger auf Verbesserung der vom Hrn. J S Bach bemerkten Fehler zu denken. Hieran arbeitete er viele Jahre. Und daß dies die wahre Ursache dieses Verzugs sey, zweifele ich um so viel weniger: da ich sie selbst vom Hrn. Silbermann aufrichtig habe bekennen hören. Endlich, da Hr. Silbermann wirklich viele Verbesserungen, sonderlich in Ansehung des Tractaments gefunden hatte, verkaufte er wieder eins an den Fürstlichen Hof zu Rudolstadt. Dies ist vermuthlich eben dasselbe dessen Hr Schröter im 141sten krit. Briefe, S. 102. gedenkt. Kurz darauf ließen des Königs von Preussen Maj. eines dieser Instrumente, und als dies Dero allerhöchsten Beyfall fand, noch verschiedene mehr, vom Hrn Silbermann verschreiben. An allen diesen Instrumenten sahen und hörten sonderlich die, welche, so wie auch ich, eines der beyden Alten gesehen hatten, sehr leicht, wie fleißig Hr. Silbermann an deren Verbesserung gearbeitet haben mußte. Hr Silbermann hatte auch den löblichen Ehrgeiz gehabt, eines dieser Instrumente, seiner neuern Arbeit, dem seel. Hrn. Kapellmeister

invention in the year 1717 and had demonstrated it at the royal court in Dresden on Feb. 11, 1721, it is difficult to believe that as a student at the Kreuzschule in Dresden he would have had an opportunity to get information about the latest inventions in Italy. Furthermore it seems to me that the increase in strings in the treble, as indicated by Mr. Schröter in the *Kritische Briefe über die Tonkunst*, no. 140, i.e., stringing the instrument in question with 2 strings from FF to c#, 3 from d to b-flat', and 4 from b' to g''', or [alternatively] with two from FF to b and three from c' to g''', is far superior with respect to a consistent strength [of tone] throughout the compass to those that Mr. Silbermann and his successors have built, which are strung throughout with only two strings per note and thus naturally cannot have as strong a tone in the treble as in the bass. Not to mention other merits of Schröter's invention.

Thus I consider it best not to pronounce judgment in this matter. Furthermore, may I be permitted to comment on the note that I made on p. 212 of Vol. I, line 4f., of this *Musica mechanica*. There I was speaking according to the prevailing opinion on this unsettled dispute. In the meantime I note that on p. 561 of his *Anleitung zu der musikalischen Gelahrtheit* Mr. Adlung has already made mention of Schröter's objections.

This instrument, however, especially in the version that Mr. Silbermann produced toward the end of his career, as well as his now deceased cousin,* the *Commißionsrath* Silbermann in Dresden, etc., possesses truly great beauty and charm, no matter who its inventor may have been, provided one is willing to overlook its somewhat weaker tone in the treble (in this regard it must be granted that Mr. Schröter's direction to increase the strings in the treble has in all probability some merit). Therefore I do not consider it superfluous to impart some of its history here.

* actually his nephew, Johann Daniel Silbermann, who became Gottfried Silbermann's heir; see: Ernst Flade, *Gottfried Silbermann* (Leipzig: VEB Breitkopf & Härtel [c.1953]), p. 87.

In the beginning Mr. Gottfried Silbermann built two of these instruments, one of which the late Kapellmeister Joh. Sebastian Bach saw and played. He praised, indeed admired its sound, but criticized its weak tone in the treble and its heavy action. This greatly affronted Mr. Silbermann, who could not stand for any of his work to be criticized. Accordingly he was angry with Mr. Bach for a long time; yet his conscience told him that Mr. Bach's criticism was not unfair. He thus considered it best, and this must be said to his great credit, not to issue any more of these instruments, but rather to apply himself all the more diligently to improving the faults noted by Mr. J.S. Bach. He worked on this for a number of years. I doubt all the less that this is the true reason for this postponement, since I have heard Mr. Silbermann himself honestly admit it. Finally, after Mr. Silbermann had devised many improvements, especially with regard to the sensitivity of touch, he again sold one to the ducal court at Rudolstadt. That instrument is presumably the very one that Mr. Schröter mentions in [Marpurg's] *Kritische Briefe über die Tonkunst*, no. 141. Shortly thereafter His Majesty the King of Prussia placed an order with Mr. Silbermann for one of these instruments, and when it received enthusiastic approbation, he ordered several more. Especially those who, like me, had seen one of the two earlier instruments saw and heard very readily just how assiduously Mr. Silbermann must have labored to improve all these instruments. Mr. Silbermann also had the commendable ambition to show one of these instruments, his more recent work, to the

meister Bach zu zeigen und von ihm untersuchen zu lassen; und dagegen von ihm völlige Gutheißung erlanget.

Indessen hatten auch andere geschickte Instrumentmacher, noch ehe Hr. Silbermann mit seiner neuern Arbeit hervor getreten war, obwohl nach einer etwas verschiedenen Anlage der Clavierregierungen, an dieser Art von Instrumenten gearbeitet. Wie sie manchem gerathen seyn mögen, weis ich nicht zu sagen. Doch scheint mir die Arbeit des Hrn. C. E. Friderici, eines Mannes der immer die feinste Erfindung mit der glücklichsten Ausarbeitung zu verbinden gewohnt ist, auch in dieser Art, vorzüglich bemerkenswerth.

Dieses habe ich, wenigstens der Geschichte dieses Instruments wegen, hier anzuführen für nöthig gehalten. Im übrigen nehme ich an dem ganzen Streite über den eigentlichen Erfinder dieses Instruments, über das was noch daran hätte verbessert und nicht verbessert werden können und sollen, und wessen Anweisung man bey diesen Verbesserungen hätte folgen oder nicht folgen sollen, weiter nicht den geringsten Antheil.

Dies aber wird mir noch zu sagen oder zu wünschen erlaubt seyn, daß doch einmal ein geschickter Instrumentmacher sich entschließen möchte, wenigstens die vom Hrn. Schröter angegebene Vermehrung der Saiten nach der Höhe zu, wieder zu versuchen. Ich dächte die Möglichkeit dieses Unternehmens könnte man Hrn. Schrötern nun auf sein Wort glauben.

Daß aber die unten folgende Beschreibung des Hrn. Adlung nicht ganz so ist, wie Hr. Silbermann wenigstens in den neuern Zeiten diese Instrumente eingerichtet und gearbeitet hat, kann jeder sehen, der Gelegenheit hat ein neueres Silbermannisches Piano forte einwendig zu untersuchen.

§. 530.

Es klingt angenehmer, wenn man sich davon entfernt. (Dies ist bey den meisten Instrumenten zu merken; auch bey der Orgel. Die Ursachen mag ich allhier nicht ausführen.) Einen schwächern oder stärkern Ton auf diesem Instrumente anzugeben, liegt blos an dem verschiedenen Nachdrücken, womit ein Clavierspieler den Anschlag berühret: so gehts wie auf einem Violoncello. So stark wie andere Claveßins geht es nicht, und ist ein Kammerinstrument, und daher zu keiner starken Musik zu gebrauchen. (**) Es will einen Meister haben, der sich fleißig darauf geübt haben muß, wenn er sich mit Beyfall und Vergnügen will hören lassen.

(**) Man hat es gleichwohl einsmals in Berlin in der Oper mit gutem Erfolge gebraucht.

§. 531.

Anstatt der gewöhnlichen Springerchen, (das sind die Docken) welche andere Clavicymbel mit der Feder berühren, ist allhier ein Register von Hämmerchen, welche von unten auf die Seyten anschlagen, und oben mit starkem Elendsleder bedeckt sind. Ein jedes Hämmerchen wird durch ein Rädchen beweglich gemacht, und diese Rädchens stehen in einem Kammförmigen Holze verborgen, als worinnen sie reihenweise eingelegt sind. Nahe an dem Rädchen und unter dem Anfange des Stiels an dem Hämmerchen befindet sich eine hervorragende Stütze, welche von unten zu angestoßen wird, und die das Hämmerchen in die Höhe treibt, daß es die Seyte nach dem Maaße und der Stärke desjenigen Schlages anstößt, welcher von der Hand des Spielers herkommt, wodurch er nach Belieben einen starken und schwachen Ton angeben kann. Man kann auch

desto

[now-]deceased Kapellmeister J.S. Bach and to let him examine it, and it now gained his complete approval.

In the meantime other skillful instrument makers had also been working on this type of instrument, though with a somewhat different arrangement for the key action, even before Mr. Silbermann came forth with his more recent work. How many of them have had any success, I cannot say. But it seems to me that the work of Mr. C. E. Friderici,* a man who is always accustomed to combine the highest [degree of] inventiveness with the highest quality of workmanship, is in this type [of instrument] also pre-eminently worthy of note.

* Christian Ernst Friderici (1709-1780), who worked in Gera.

I have held it necessary to record all this here, at least for the sake of this instrument's history. Beyond that I do not take the slightest interest in the whole contest over the actual inventor of this instrument, or over what could and should have been improved on it or not, and whose instructions should or should not have been followed for these improvements.

I beg to be allowed, however, to state or to wish that a skilled instrument maker might resolve at least once again to investigate increasing the [number of] strings in the treble as indicated by Mr. Schröter. I should think that one could take Mr. Schröter at his word concerning the feasibility of this undertaking.

Anyone who has had the opportunity to examine a more recent Silberman pianoforte internally (einwendig†) can see, however, that Mr. Adlung's description following below does not entirely tally with the way Mr. Silbermann has designed and constructed these instruments, at least in more recent times. [Agricola]

† i.e., "inwendig".

§. 530.

[The fortepiano] sounds more pleasant when [the listener] is at a distance from it (note that this holds true for most instruments, including the organ; I do not wish to elaborate on the reasons here). Producing a softer or louder sound on this instrument is purely the result of the player's exerting different amounts of pressure when attacking [a key]; it is the same on a violoncello. It is an instrument for chamber music, not getting as loud as other harpsichords, and thus is not to be used in any loud musical ensemble.(**) It requires an accomplished performer, one who has practiced diligently on it, if he wishes to be heard with approval and pleasure.

(**) It was nevertheless used once quite successfully in the opera at Berlin. [Agricola]

§. 531.

In place of the usual devices that spring upward (i.e., the jacks), that pluck other harpsichords with quills, this instrument has a series of small hammers that strike the strings from below. These hammers are covered on top with heavy moose leather. Each hammer turns upon a little wheel imbedded in a row into a comb-shaped wooden [rack]. Beneath the hammer shaft, near the point where it leaves the wheel, is located a protruding post that is struck from beneath. This impels the hammer upward so that it strikes the string with the degree of force given it by the finger (von der Hand) of the player, thus producing a loud or soft sound at will. It is possible to play all the more

desto stärker spielen, weil das Hämmerchen den Schlag ganz nahe an seiner Einnagelung empfähet: Nahe am Mittelpunkte des Bezirks, so weit nämlich sein Umkreis gehet, in welchem Falle ein jeder mäßiger Anschlag eine plötzliche Herumdrehung des Rades verursachet, also, daß von dem Schlage an das Hämmerchen unter dem äusersten Theile der vorgedachten herausstehenden Stütze, sich ein hölzernes Züngelchen befindet, welches auf einer Hebe ruhet, so, daß es von derselben in die Höhe gehoben wird, wenn der Spieler den Anschlag berührt. Dieses Züngelchen oder Zäpfchen liegt aber doch nicht auf der Hebe, sondern ein wenig erhaben, und ist eingefaßt in 2 dünne Seitenstützchen, wovon auf jeder Seite eins befindlich ist. Weil aber nöthig war, daß das Hämmerchen die Seyte gleich wieder verlasse, so bald sie berühret werden, und sich gleich wieder absondere, ob schon der Spieler die Hand von dem Anschlage noch nicht wieder weggenommen; so war nöthig, daß besagtes Hämmerchen augenblicklich wieder in die Freyheit gesetzt würde, an seine Stelle zurückzufallen. Daher ist das Züngelchen, so ihm den Druck giebt, beweglich, und solchergestalt zusammen gefügt, daß es in die Höhe geht und vest anprallt. Aber so bald der Schlag gegeben, plötzlich wieder abschießt, d. i. vorbey gehet, und sich, so bald als der Schlag geschehen, herumwendet, zurückkehrt, und sich wieder unter das Hämmerchen verfügt.

§. 532.

Diese Wirkung hat der Künstler durch eine Feder von meßingenem Drat zuwege gebracht, die er an der Hebe bevestiget, und welche sich ausdehnt, mit der Spitze unter dem Züngelchen antrift, und indem sie einigen Widerstand giebt, dasselbe antreibt, und an einem andern meßingenen Drate bevestiget hält, der vest, und aufwärts derselben gerade entgegen stehet. Durch diese stete Befestigung die das Zünglein durch die Feder hat, welche drunter ist, und durch die Einfügung auf beyden Seiten, stehet es veste, oder giebt nach, wie es erfordert wird. Damit die Hämmerchen auch in dem Zurückprallen nach dem Anschlage nicht wieder aufhüpfen, und an die Seyten zurück stoßen können; so fallen sie, und liegen auf kreutzweise geschlungenen seidenen Schnürchen, die solche ganz ruhig auffangen. Der Ton muß auch wieder verschwinden, weil jede von oftgemeldeten Heben ein Schwänzchen hat, und auf demselben nach der Reihe ein Register von Springerchen befindlich, die nach ihrem Gebrauch Dämpfer genennet werden könnten. Sobald der Griff geschehen, berühren diese die Seyten mit dem Tuche, welches sie auf der Spitze haben, und verhindern das Nachzittern.

§. 533.

Es ist auch ein Riß dabey in der Critica Musicae Matthesonii, etwann auf die Art wie Tab. III. Fig I. zu sehen. Wobey ich erinnere, daß ich nicht eben alles just nach dem Zirkel gerissen habe; Genug, daß man einigermaaßen sehen soll, wie es zugehe. A bedeutet die Seyte. B den Boden zu dem Claviere oder zu dem Anschlage. C sind die Claviere oder ersten Heber, welche mit dem Pflöckchen die andern in die Höhe treiben.

D das

118   Chap. XXII. The Harpsichord, Clavicytherium, Spinet,

forcefully, since the hammer receives the attack very near to where it is anchored [in the wheel]: near to the midpoint of its radius. In this case any moderate attack causes a sudden rotation of the wheel, in this way: beneath the point on the outer edge of the aforementioned protruding post where the hammer is struck, there is a little wooden tongue* (Züngelchen) that rests upon a lever, and is driven upward when the player initiates the attack. This little tongue or peg, however, does not rest upon the lever, but is raised a bit above it, cradled in two thin lateral supports, one on each side. Since however it is necessary that the hammer retreat from the string the instant it has struck it, even though the player has not yet lifted his hand from the keys, thus it is necessary that the said hammer is instantaneously again set free to fall back to its [original] position. Thus the tongue that gives it thrust is movable, and constructed in such a way that it flies upward and strikes [the post on the hammer shaft] sharply. But as soon as the blow is delivered, it instantly flies past [the post] and changes direction, returning and again coming to rest under the hammer.

* i.e., the escapement jack.

§. 532.

The builder has accomplished this action by means of a brass wire [spring] fastened to the lever, whose point stretches out to contact the bottom of the tongue. By providing a certain amount of resistance, it forces the tongue up tight against another brass wire that stands upright and right next to it. By the tongue's constant stabilization from the spring under it, and by its confinement on both sides, it remains stationary or responds, as required. To keep the hammers from bouncing up and striking the strings again after rebounding from the attack, they fall to rest upon silken chords strung crosswise that catch them very gently. The sound is forced to cease by giving each of the abovementioned levers an extension, upon which are found a row of upright posts that in view of their use could be called dampers.† As soon as a chord has been released, these devices touch the strings with the cloth that is affixed to the tops of them, and prevent [any further] vibration.

† i.e., speaking from the viewpoint of harpsichord dampers, that are quite different in their appearance.

§. 533.

Furthermore a sketch [of this action] may be found in Mattheson's *Critica musica*,‡ resembling the one that can be seen in Table III, Fig. I.§ In connection with it, let me mention that I have not sketched everything according to precise measurements; it is sufficient to see in general how it works. A signifies the string; B the bottom of the keyboard or keyfall. C is the key or the first lever that pushes the second one upward with the small block. D is the block that delivers the attack. E is the

‡ see Vol. II, p. 339.

§ This sketch may be found between pp. 170 & 171 of Vol. I. It is copied directly from Mattheson.

D das Pflöckchen, Zäpfchen, oder Holzschuh an den Anschlag. E Die zweyte Hebe, wo auf jeder Seite eins von den Nebenstützchen vest gemacht ist, die das Züngelchen halten. F der Angel oder Stift in der andern Hebe. G das bewegliche Zünglein, welches, wenn es mit der andern Hebe sich in die Höhe schießt, auf das Hämmerchen stößt. H die Nebenstützen auf beyden Seiten, worinn das Züngelchen eingefalzt ist. I ein vester meßingen Drat, oben an der Spitze breit geschlagen, der das Zungelchen veste hält. L eine Feder von meßingen Drat, die unter dem Züngelchen liegt, und es gegen dem vesten Drate angestoßen hält, den es hinten hat. M das Kammholz, wo in der Reihe die Hämmerchen eingelegt sind. N das Rädchen an den Hämmerchen, welches in dem Kammholze verborgen liegt. O Das Hämmerchen, so von unten her durch das Züngelchen angestoßen die Seyte mit Elendsleder anschlägt, womit es oben bedeckt ist. P. die kreuzweise geschrenkten seidenen Schnürchen, zwischen welchen die Stiele der Hämmerchen aufliegen oder ruhen. Q. Das Schwäuzchen der zweyten Hebung, das sich nieder giebt, wenn sich die Spitze erhebt. R. Das Register oder die Reihe Springerchen oder Dämpfer, die, sobald der Angrif andrückt, sich herab verfügen, und die Seyte frey lassen, hernach gleich wieder an ihren Ort springen, um den Schall zu hemmen. S. Der völlige Querbalke zur Verstärkung des Holzkammes.

§. 534.

Ueber dieß alles ist noch zu merken, daß die Leiste, wo die Wirbel gesetzt werden, die die Seyten halten, wie sie in andern Clavicymbeln unter den Seyten selbst ist, hier über denselbigen zu stehen kömmt, und die Wirbel darunter hangen, daß die Seyten von unten her vestgemacht werden, weil es nöthig war, mehr Platz unten zu gewinnen, damit das ganze Griffwerk hinein gehen könnte. Die Seyten sind viel stärker, als die gemeinen, und damit die Schwere dem Boden nicht schaden möge, so sind sie nicht auf demselbigen bevestiget, sondern etwas höher angebracht worden. Wo ein Geklappere entstehen könnte, da ist es durch Leder oder Tuch verhindert worden, sonderlich in den Löchern, wo die Nägel oder Stifte durchgehen, wo alles mit Elendsleder ausgefüttert ist, daß der Stift durch dasselbe hervor kömmt. Mehr kann ich davon nicht sagen, als ich gelesen, weil ich es nicht selbst gesehen. Begreift jemand hieraus nicht, wie es zugehe, daß das forte und piano zu haben sey, dem kann ich weiter nicht helfen. Er mag Gelegenheit suchen es zu beschauen.

§. 535.

Endlich ist überhaupt anzumerken, daß bey Clavicymbeln und andern besenteten und unbesenteten Instrumenten der Ort viel hilft, wo es gespielet wird. Denn wenn derselbe also gebauet ist, daß es von allen Ecken her schallet, und ein Echo giebt; so wird die Delicatesse und Stärke der Instrumente viel zunehmen. Wenn man nun solche Instrumente kauft, oder ästimirt; so muß man sich dadurch nicht betrügen lassen, und eins dem andern des Klanges oder Nachsingens wegen vorziehen, wenn der verschiedene Ort dem einen einen Vorzug giebt, den es anderswo nicht haben würde.

second lever, on each side of which supports are affixed that hold the tongue. F is the pivot or pin in the second lever. G is the movable tongue that strikes the hammer when the second lever thrusts it upward. H are the supports on both sides in which the tongue is cradled. I is the stationary brass wire, the top end of which is pounded flat, that holds the tongue stationary. L is a brass wire spring lying under the tongue and pressing it firmly against the stationary wire behind it. M is the wooden rack into which the row of hammers is set. N is the little wheel connected to the hammer, the wheel that is imbedded in the wooden rack. O is the hammer that strikes the string with moose leather (with which it is covered) when it is struck from beneath by the tongue. P are the silken cords strung crosswise, upon which the shafts of the hammers lie or rest. Q is the extension of the second lever that drops when the other end [of the lever] rises. R is the row of upright posts or dampers, that drop the instant the fingers attack the keys, allowing the strings [to vibrate] freely; thereafter they immediately spring back into their [former] position, to dampen the sound. S is the heavy crossbrace that reinforces the wooden rack.

§. 534.

In addition to all of this, it must be mentioned that in this instrument the wrest plank, into which the wrest pins that hold the strings are driven, sits above the strings with the wrest pins hanging downward, while on other harpsichords it is beneath the strings. Thus [on the pianoforte] the strings are attached beneath it, since it is necessary to gain more space beneath to allow the entire action to be fitted in. The strings [of this instrument] are much thicker than usual, and, to keep their tension from harming the soundboard, they are not attached directly to it, but are mounted somewhat higher.* Anywhere a clattering might arise is fitted with leather or cloth to prevent it,† especially in the holes through which pass the nails or pins; in the latter everything is faced with moose leather, so that the pin protrudes up through it. I cannot report anything more about it than I have read, since I have never seen it in person. If there is anyone who does not conceive from my description how it is possible to produce a *forte* and *piano*, I cannot provide any further help. He should seek an opportunity to inspect the instrument.

§. 535.

Finally it should be noted in general in connection with harpsichords and other stringed as well as non-stringed instruments that the place they are played plays a vital role [in their tone]. If the room is built so as to reflect sounds from all sides and to produce an echo [i.e., reverberation], then the power and delicacy of the instrument will increase a great deal. In buying or evaluating such instruments, then, one must not allow oneself to be deceived into preferring a certain instrument due to its sound or resonance, when a given place lends it an advantage that it would not have somewhere else.

---

* Adlung (per Maffei) is describing Cristofori's construction in which the hitchpin rail and exterior case wall are independent from the soundboard.

† i.e., bushing.

§. 536.

Es schlagen auch die Seyten cum sympathia, (wie es etliche nennen, die noch Anbeter der qualitatum occultarum sind) das ist, bey dem Anschlagen einer Seyte läßt sich eine andere nicht angeschlagene zugleich hören, wenn sie eingestimmt ist. Wenn nun in einem großen Zimmer mehrere Claveßins stehen, und eins davon wird gespielt; so lassen sich die andern zugleich mit hören, und mehren das Nachsingen und die Harmonie. Es geschiehet solches durch die Bewegung und Anstoßung der Luft. Denn wenn ich setzte, daß durch den oder jenen Ton die Luft so und so stark gestoßen werde; so wird auch diese Luft keine andere Seyten leicht irritiren, als die einen gleichen Stoß, oder doch einen proportionirten annehmen können, d. i. die eingestimmt sind, und mit jenen consoniren. Einige meynen, so subtil als die Luft auch immer sey, so könnte man doch vielerley Arten der Lufttheilchen statuiren, da die Bewegung der einen Art diesen sonum, die Bewegung der andern Art einen andern sonum hervorbrächten, und soviel man sonos-hätte, soviel wären auch Arten der Luft. Eine Art wäre fähig eine Seyte von der und jener Länge und Dicke anzustoßen, welches die andern Arten nicht könnten; hingegen hätten die andern Arten ihre Kraft in andern Seyten von anderer Dicke und Länge, welche die erste nicht hätte. ꝛc. Wir lassen dem Erfinder diese Gedanken, und stellen es an seinen Ort: wenigstens sind dergleichen Arten noch nicht bewiesen, und die Sache ist schwer zu begreifen; wiewol ohnedieß in der Lehre vom Klange uns noch viel verborgen ist. Besser gefällt mir der Vortrag des de Chales Tom. III. Prop. 2. welcher folgende Gedanken hat: Wenn die Luft die Pfeife oder Seyte in Bewegung bringt von dieser oder jener Größe, und dieser motus tremulus geht in der Luft fort, und trift ein ander corpus an, welches mit dem vorigen concordirt, so muß er selbiges auch in eine zitternde Bewegung bringen, eben deswegen, weil die Luft noch eben die force hat wie zuvor, und also Körper von einerley Proportion mit eben der force bewegen kann. Z. E. Wenn ein corpus sich zum andern verhält wie 1 zu 1; so muß der andere Körper mit klingen. Denn der eine Körper repetirt bey jeder Vibration das Stoßen der Luft und durch diese das Anstoßen des andern Körpers, und so werden diese 2 Körper immer motu recto mit einander sich bewegen, und wird nicht geschehen, daß wenn der eine dorthin stößt, jener hieher stoße. Denn wenn sie einander conträr stoßen, so destruirt eine Vibration die andere. So wird auch solches Mitklingen angehen, wenn die Vibrationen in ihrer Geschwindigkeit sich verhalten wie 2 gegen 1, und zwar so, daß der zuerst angestoßene Körper 1. Vibration macht, in der Zeit, da der andere deren 2 macht: so gehts auch an. Denn wenn des ersten Vibration hinwärts geht, so geht des andern seine motu recto hin und her; geht der ersten tremor wieder zurück, so geht des andern seine auch hin und her, doch nicht wider einander; folglich hindert keiner den andern. Hätte aber der erste Körper 2, der andere 1; so würden sich die Vibrationen hindern: denn, wenn des ersten seine andere Vibration nach dem andern zu anhebt, so kommt der andere zum erstenmal zurück, dem ersten entgegen, und hindert einer den andern. Fragt man: welcher

Chap. XXII. The Harpsichord, Clavicytherium, Spinet,

§. 536.

Strings vibrate sympathetically (as some say who are still ardent admirers of occult properties*), that is, when one string is struck another that has not been struck begins to sound simultaneously, provided they are tuned to the same pitch. If there are several harpsichords in a large room, and one of them is played, then the others will sound along with it, increasing the resonance and the harmony. This [phenomenon] is the result of the motion and impact of air. Given that such and such a pitch strikes the air this or that strongly, then that air is not likely to excite any other string than one that can accept an equivalent stroke and harmonize with it, one that is proportionally related, i.e. tuned to the same pitch. Some believe that despite the air's thinness, it is possible to assert that it is divided into many types; the motion of one type would produce one sound, the motion of a second another sound, and there would be as many types of air as there were sounds. One type would have the capacity to excite a string of such and such a length and thickness, a capacity that other types did not possess. On the other hand, other types would hold power over strings of other thicknesses and lengths that the first [category] would not have. We will leave these thoughts to their author and set them aside. In any event such types are not yet proven, and the matter is difficult to comprehend; and moreover much in the theory of sound remains as yet hidden from us. The explanation offered by de Chales [*Cursus seu mundus mathematicus*], Vol. III, [Tract 22,] Prop. 2, is more satisfactory to me; it runs as follows: if air sets a pipe or string of such and such a size in motion, and this vibrating motion is launched into the air and encounters another object that it concords with, then it must set that same [object] into a vibrating motion, for this reason, that the air has just the same force as at the outset, and thus can move objects of the same proportion with the same force. For example, if one object is related to another as 1:1, then the second object has to sound with it. For the one object repeatedly strikes the air with every vibration, and by striking the second object both objects will continue to move in exact conformity with each other. When one strikes in a certain way, then the other will not strike in opposition to it, for if they were to strike contrary to each other, then one vibration would cancel out the other. Such a sympathetic vibration would also happen if the vibrations were related to each other as 2:1, in this way: the first body, when struck, would make one vibration in the time that the other would make two. While the vibration of the first was going in one direction, then the other's would be going both backward and forward in conformity with it. While the first's vibration was returning, then the second's would again be moving both backward and forward. Neither would be moving contrary to the other, and consequently neither would hinder the other. But if the first object had 2 [vibrations] to the second's one, then the vibrations would be impeded, since when the second vibration of the first [object] encountered the second [object], then the second would be returning for the first time, in contrary motion to the first, and one would impede the other. Should the question arise, which of

---

* This parenthetical remark may be directed against musicians who still subscribed to the remnants of mystical Neo-platonism, ideas that were still alive in Germany through the first half of the eighteenth century in figures such as Athanasius Kircher, Andreas Werckmeister and (perhaps) J.S. Bach. It is yet another indication of Adlung's progressive "scientific" orientation.

welcher von beyden alsdann schweigen wird? so ist die Antwort, derjenige wird fort: klingen, der zuerst angestoßen worden. Doch ich mag hierinn nicht so weitläuftig seyn. Es denke jeder selber nach. Wenigstens ist das vernünftiger, als wenn man sich schlechthin auf die Sympathie beruft, da doch kein Mensch sagen kann, worinnen das Ding bestehe. Vom Echo mag ich itzo gar nichts reden, sondern ich will den Leser verweisen auf des Kircheri *Musurgiam*, allwo derselbe im 4ten Theile des 9ten Buchs davon gar curiöse Dinge aus der Physik und Mathematik beygebracht hat. Er nennt diese Abhandlung phonocampticam, von φωνὴ, vox, und κάμπτω, reflecto, (Im letzten Kapitel dieses Buchs habe ich auch etwas davon angeführt.) Ich besinne mich, an einem gewissen Orte gelesen zu haben, daß einstens ein Zimmer so angelegt worden, daß die Ecken und Seiten den Schall sehr stark reflectirt; da man nun in jede derer vier Ecken ein Claveßin gesetzt, vollkommen überein gestimmt, und auf dem einen gespielet hat, man nicht gewußt, welches eigentlich klinge, indem man bey einem jeden, zu welchem man gegangen, den rechten Klang anzutreffen vermeynet. Es hat dieses durch das Echo und durch die Action der Luft von einer Seyte zur andern gar wohl geschehen können. Es folgt wenigstens soviel hieraus, daß, wenn ein Clavier oder Claveßin gut nachsingen solle, man es stets reine halten und oft stimmen müsse.

§. 537.

Wir gehen vom Clavicymbel fort zu dem Clavicytherio. Was bisher gesagt worden, das wird sich auch meistens hierauf schicken, weswegen ich hier solches nicht wiederhohlen, sondern mich auf die vorige Traktation berufen will. Es ist aber ein Clavicytherium von dem Clavicymbel darinn unterschieden, daß es in die Höhe spitzig zu gehet; in den Haupttheilen aber ist es ein wirklich Clavicymbel, deswegen es auch oft mit darunter verstanden wird. Es hat sonst vom Clavicytherio geredt Prätorius Tom. II. cap. 41. pag. 66; woraus man abnehmen kann, daß diese Struktur und Benennung schon damals gebräuchlich gewesen sey. Nach dem hat Kircherus in *Musurgia* Lib. VI. Tom. I. pag. 454. der Strucktur nicht aber des Namens erwähnet, als der sie mit unter den Clavicymbeln beschreibet. Er sagt: Non desunt, qui dicta instrumenta (clauicymbala) ita ordinant, ut harpam uerius quam clauicymbalum referant; chordæ enim non horizontalem situm, sed uerticalem obtinent. Huiusmodi instrumenti frequens in Germania usus est; commoda enim sunt, quia parum loci occupant, & seruiunt ad ornamentum conclauium: duplicem præterea usum habent & Harpæ & clauicymbali. Das ist: „Es sind einige, „welche die besagten Instrumente so verfertigen, daß sie der Harfe ähnlicher sehen, „als einem Clavicymbel; denn die Seyten haben keine horizontale Lage, sondern sie „gehen in die Höhe. Dergleichen Instrumente werden in Deutschland stark gebraucht; „denn sie sind bequem, weil sie wenig Raum einnehmen, dienen auch den Zimmern „zur Zierde: über dieß haben sie einen doppelten Gebrauch, da sie an statt der Harfe „und

them would then be silent, the answer is that the one to continue sounding would be the one that was struck first. But I do not wish to go on at length about this. Everyone should think it through for himself. In any event that is more reasonable than simply making reference to "sympathy" without anyone being able to say what it consists of. I also do not wish to discuss [the phenomenon of] echo at all, but rather refer the reader to Kircher's *Musurgia*, Book 9, Part 4,* where the author has explained very curious things about it from [the viewpoint of] physics and mathematics. He has entitled his discussion *phonocamptica*, from φωνή, *vox* [voice] and κάμπτω, *reflecto* [to reflect] (I have also mentioned something about this in the final chapter of this book†). I remember having read in a certain place that there was once a room laid out in such a way that the corners and sides were highly reflective; when harpsichords perfectly in tune with each other were placed in each of its four corners, and someone played on one of them, it was impossible to tell which of them was actually sounding, since the actual sound [source] seemed to be whichever one the listener was standing next to. This could very well have come about through echo and through the action of the air from one string to another. At any rate one may conclude from this that if a clavichord or harpsichord is to resonate well it must be tuned often and always be kept in tune.

* Vol. II, pp. 237f.

† i.e., Chap. 28, pp. 269f.

§. 537.

Let us turn from the harpsichord to the clavicytherium. Most of what has already been said applies here as well, and for that reason I will not repeat it here, but refer to the previous discussion. A clavicytherium is different from a harpsichord in that its [case] rises vertically to a point. In its major components, though, it is in reality a harpsichord, and thus is often grouped together with it. Praetorius has already spoken about the clavicytherium in [*Syntagma musicum*,] Vol. II, chap. 41, p. 66[-67]; from this discussion one may perceive that this structure and designation were already current at that time. Following him, Kircher in his *Musurgia*, Book VI., Vol. I, p. 454, describes the structure as he is discussing harpsichords, without however mentioning the name. He writes: *Non desunt, qui dicta instrumenta (clavicymbala) ita ordinant, ut harpam verius quam clavicymbalum referant; chordæ enim non horizontalem situm, sed verticalem obtinent. Hujusmodi instrumenti frequens in Germania usus est; commoda enim sunt, quia parum loci occupant, & serviunt ad ornamentum conclavium: duplicem præterea usum habent & Harpæ & clavicymbali.* Translation: "There are those who construct the said instruments‡ in such a way that they look like a harp rather than a harpsichord; the strings do not lie horizontally, but they rise vertically. Such instruments are much in use in Germany, since they are convenient in that they occupy little space and also serve to decorate the room. Moreover they have a double use in that they may be used as a substitute for both harp and harpsichord." [Fuhrmann's] *Musi-*

‡ i.e., harpsichords.

„und des Clavicymbels dienen können." Der Musikalische Trichter hat im 10ten Kapitel etwas weniges davon. Es heißt daselbst: „Clavicytheria sind Clavicymbel „in die Höhe wie eine Harfe. Ist ein unbeständig Aprilleninstrument, und hocket „bald hie, bald da." Diese Unbeständigkeit anlangend; so wird sie wenig größer seyn, als des Claveßins. Wenn ein Clavicytherium auf die Art dauerhaft gemacht wird, als ich oben bey dem Claveßin erfordert; so wird die Unbeständigkeit größtentheils wegfallen, und nicht mehr Ungelegenheit verursachen als ein Clavicymbel. Jedoch wird dieß für jenem ein großes zum voraus behalten.

§. 538.

Die Struktur anlangend; so liegt das Clavier horizontal, die Seyten aber gehen in die Höhe, und die Tangenten oder Docken sind auch horizontal, und ist übrigens alles wie ein Clavicymbel eingerichtet. Kircherus l. c. hat es im Risse vorgestellet.

§. 539.

Es folget das Spinet, welches in der Große und Form von dem Clavicymbel abgehet. Es bekömmt nämlich nur 2 oder 3 Oktaven; oder wenn man ja die 3 obersten Oktaven vollkommen macht: so ist doch im Gegentheil die unterste nur eine kurze Oktave. Die Seyten liegen alle von der rechten Hand zur linken, daher es hintenaus nicht spitzig, sondern etwas rund, oder oval aussiehet; oder man macht es in Forma trapezii, wie es auch Kircherus hat Iconismo IV. Fig. III. Tom. I. fol. 455. etwann also:

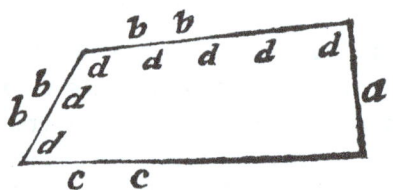

Bey *a* werden die Wirbel eingeschlagen; bey *b* werden die Seyten an die Stiftchen gehenkt, und über einen Steg gelegt. Die Decke geht, wie bey den andern, durchaus; die Docken aber gehen von *d* an nach *a* zu, und werden sie ordentlich nur einchöricht. Diese Spinette gehen kindisch, wie der Musikalische Trichter l. c. anmerkt, und dabey meldet, daß sie eine Quinte oder Oktave höher gestimmt würden als Chorton. Die Seiten werden sehr kurz. Ueberhaupt, es wird wie ein Instrument, davon in folgenden §. zu reden. Die Italiener nennen es auch Spinetto, s. den Musikal. Trichter l. c; auch Spinettino. Dieß könnte das eigentliche Spinet seyn, jenes aber das sogenannte Instrument. Vergleiche Kircheri Musurgia l. c. pag. 454. Tom I. da er es auch unter die Clavicymbel zählt. Er schreibt ihnen 18 Palmuln zu, welches also noch viel kleiner wäre, als unsere Spinette sind. Uebrigens ob schon die Form anders ist, als bey den vorigen; so ist doch die Struktur einerley, und die Tangenten schlagen eben so an, wie bey den vorigen: da denn

122 Chap. XXII. The Harpsichord, Clavicytherium, Spinet,

kalischer-Trichter has a bit about it in chapter 10[, p. 90]. There it reads: "Clavicytheria are harpsichords that rise vertically like a harp. It is an unstable, inconstant* instrument, and gets hung up† here and there." With regard to its instability, it is little more so than a harpsichord. If a clavicytherium is durably made according to the method that I have called for above in connection with the harpsichord, then the instability will be negligible, causing no more inconvenience than a harpsichord. Nevertheless the harpsichord has many advantages over the clavicytherium.

* i.e., as April weather.

† i.e., experiences mechanical difficulties.

§. 538.

Concerning its structure, the keyboard lies horizontally, but the strings rise vertically. The jacks are also horizontal, but the rest is all laid out like a harpsichord. Kircher, *l.c.*, represents it in a drawing.‡

‡ *Iconismus* IV, fig. II, following p. 454 of Vol I.

§. 539.

Next comes the spinet, that deviates in size and shape from the harpsichord. That is, it has only 2 or 3 octaves, or if the three upper octaves are made complete, then the lowest is only a short octave in contrast. The strings all stretch from right to left, and therefore it does not come to a point in the back, but is rather round or oval; or it may be made in trapezoidal shape, as in Kircher (*Musurgia*), Iconismus IV, Fig. III, Vol. I, folio 455,§ rather like this:

§ following p. 454.

The wrest pins are driven in at [letter] *a*; at *b* the strings are looped around the pins and laid over a bridge. The soundboard, as with other [harpsichords] lies under the entire instrument, but the jacks extend from *d* to *a*, and there is normally only one set of strings. Such spinets sound childish, as [Fuhrmann] remarks in his *Musikalischer-Trichter, l.c.*;¶ he also reports that they are tuned a fifth or octave higher than Chorton. The strings get very short. In general it is like an "instrument", which will be discussed in the next paragraph. The Italians call it "spinetto" or "spinettino"; see *Musikalischer-Trichter*, l.c.‖ The latter could refer to the spinet proper, with the former referring to the so-called "instrument"; cf. Kircher's *Musurgia, l.c.*, Vol. I, p. 454, where he includes it among the harpsichords. He assigns 18 keys to it, and thus it would be far smaller than our spinets. Although the shape is different from the preceding [harpsichords], nevertheless the construction is identical, with the jacks plucking

¶ p. 90. Fuhrmann writes that the instrument is suited "for proper little ladies."

‖ ibid.

denn die bisher erzählten Vollkommenheiten großen Theils sich hier appliciren laffen. Weiter halte ich mich billig dabey nicht auf, weil es sich nicht der Mühe verlohnt, zumal da auch Prätorius Tom. II. P. II c. XXXVIII. davon handelt, aus welchem noch anzumerken, daß sie (wie auch der Trichter sagt) eine Oktave oder Quinte höher giengen ꝛc.; sonderlich daß sie in England Virginal, in Frankreich Espinette, in den Niederlanden Clavicymbel, und in Deutschland Instrument genennet werden. Die Franzosen sagen auch Epinette. Sonst führt es auch noch den Namen Magadis, und Pectis. s. Prätor. T. III. P. III. c. V. pag. 121.

§. 540.

Es folgt das Instrument. Dieß Wort heißt überhaupt ein Ding, womit man je was ausrichten kann; ein Werkzeug. In der Musik wird es für allerhand Gattungen musikalischer Instrumente genommen. Ißo nehmen wir es für eine besondere Gattung der Claviere und Clavessins, da die Seyten, wie bey dem Spinett, auch von der rechten Seite nach der linken gezogen werden. Das übrige ist alles den vorigen Clavieren gleich, und differirt es vom Spinet darinn, daß es so viel Palmulen hat, als die Clavessins sonst haben. Zwar habe ich noch keins gesehen, welches mehr als 4 Oktaven gehabt: allein wer wollte es wehren, wenn man vieles dabey applicirte, was bey dem Clavicymbel angemerkt worden. Sie werden ordentlich mit sehr tiefen Körpern gemacht, daher sie so pompös klingen. Sie sind meistens einchöricht; doch wollte ich rathen sie zweychhöricht zu machen. Es werden dieselbigen, zwar etwas breit werden; allein wie muß man thun, wenn man Clavikordien will bundfrey machen. Ißo sind diese Instrumente fast verachtet; doch wenn sie recht gemacht werden, und dasjenige beobachtet wird, was von den Clavicymbeln ausgeführet worden; so sind sie nicht zu verachten, und eben so gut als jene zu gebrauchen. Das Wort Instrument, weil es in so weitläuftiger Bedeutung genommen wird, schickt sich nicht gar zu wohl hieher, wie Prätorius Tom. II. P. II. c. XXXVII. p. 62. anmerkt, allwo dies Clavier auch Symphonia genennet wird, und Tom. III. P. III. c. V. p. 121. nennet er es, so, wie das Spinet, Magadis, Pectis und Virginal.

§. 541.

Es gedenket Prätorius l. c. pag. 67. Tom. II. des Arpichordi, welches wenig besonderes hat, weil nur bey einer Symphonia oder Virginal (i. e. Spinetto oder Instrumento) durch sonderliche Züge von Meßingshäflein unter den Seyten ein harfenirender Resonanz entsteht, daher es den Namen bekommen. Es kömmt wenig vor, weswegen ich es hier nur obiter erwähne. Man könnte ohnedieß noch mehrere Inventionen erdenken, und bey Clavicymbeln anbringen: aber von Poßibilitäten, die ich noch nicht wirklich practicirt gefunden, will ich nicht reden.

§. 542.

Cembal d'Amour wird von mir nur des Nachschlagens wegen hierher gesetzt, weil ich selbst keine besondere Nachricht davon habe. Es gedenkt dieser Invention die

Instrument, Arpichord and Cembal d'Amour.

in just the same way. Thus the merits already described by and large apply here. I will not dwell further on it; it would not be worth the trouble, especially since Praetorius has discussed it in [*Syntagma musicum,*] Vol. II, Part II, chap. XXXVIII.* Take note from that [discussion] that they sound an octave or fifth higher ([Fuhrmann in his *Musikalischer-*] *Trichter*† says the same thing); but especially that in England they are called "virginal", in France "espinette", in the Low Countries "clavicymbel", and in Germany "instrument". The French pronounce it "epinette". In addition it also bears the name "magadis" and "pectis"; see Praetorius, Vol. III, Part III, chap. V, p. 121.‡

* p. 62.

† p. 90.

‡ Because this volume is falsely paginated from p. 104-128, the page is numbered 141, but it is actually 121.

§. 540.

Next comes the "instrument". In a general sense this word means "a thing with which something is accomplished," or "a tool." In music it is applied to all sorts of categories of musical instruments. At present we use it for a specific category of keyboard instrument and harpsichord in which the strings, like the spinet, are strung from right to left. In all other ways it is identical to the keyboard instruments [discussed] previously, differing from the spinet only in that it has as many keys as a normal harpsichord. True, I have never yet seen one that has had more than 4 octaves, but there is nothing to prevent anyone from applying most of the characteristics already noted in connection with the harpsichord.§ They are ordinarily made with very deep cases, and therefore sound full and rich.¶ Most of them have a single choir [of strings], but I would advise making them with two. That would make them rather wide, to be sure, but after all that is the way clavichords have to be if they are unfretted. These instruments are now almost scorned, but if they are made properly, and if the suggestions made [above] in connection with harpsichords are heeded, then they are of just as much use as the latter, and should not be despised. The word "instrument", since it has so many different meanings, is not very well suited to it; Praetorius mentions this in [*Syntagma musicum*], Vol. II, Part II, chap. XXXVII, p. 62, where this keyboard instrument is also called "symphonia"; in Vol. III, Part III, chap. V, p. 121, he also calls it "magadis," "pectis" and "virginal," just like the spinet.

§ i.e., it would be possible for it to have 5 octaves, as Adlung advises in §.507.

¶ cf. §.506.

§. 541.

Praetorius, *l.c.*,∥ p. 67, makes mention of the arpichord, [an instrument] that is hardly unique, since it is merely a "symphonia" or "virginal" (i.e., a "spinetto" or "instrument") that has a special mechanism of little brass hooks under the strings that give it a harp-like sound; this is how it gets its name. It is relatively rare, and therefore I will only mention it in passing. Any number of additional inventions could be dreamed up and applied to harpsichords, but I will refrain from discussing possibilities that I have not actually seen in practice.

∥ i.e., Vol II.

§. 542.

I am including the cembal d'amour here only for the sake of completeness, since I have no specific information on it. Mr. Mattheson mentions this invention in his

124 **Kap. XXII. Von dem Clavicymbel, Clavichtherio Spinet,**

Critica Musica des Herrn von Mattheson Tom. II. pag. 243. Die Beschreibung aber ist nicht dabey. Wer Gelegenheit hat, es auf Reisen zu sehen, wird es nicht vorbey lassen. Der Erfinder desselben ist der berühmte Herr Silbermann, aus Straßburg. Etwas mehrers findet der geneigte Leser in meiner Anleitung §. 251. S. 563. u. f. welches ich hier nicht wiederholen mag; wie ich denn überhaupt bitten will, bey diesem und den folgenden 3. Kapiteln gedachte Anleitung mit vor Augen zu haben. (**)

(**) Ich füge hier, weil dies Instrument, einiger kleinen Unbequemlichkeiten die es mit sich führet, und denen vielleicht, bey weiterem Nachsinnen noch abgeholfen werden kann, ungeachtet, doch wohl verdienete, bekannter und gebräuchlicher zu seyn, eine Abzeichnung und eine kurze Beschreibung desselben bey, wie sie mir von einem geschickten Instrumentmacher, der die Silbermannischen Cembals d'Amour öfters gesehen, und sich ihre Einrichtung und ihren Bau wohl gemerket hat, ist mitgetheilet worden. Wenn diese Beschreibung auch nicht für jeden hinreichend seyn sollte ein solches Instrument darnach zu verfertigen; so wird doch ein geschickter Arbeiter auch hieraus schon sehr viel abnehmen können: da zumal, auch im Kleinen, die rechte Meusur dabey beobachtet ist. Gewiß wird diese Beschreibung genug seyn, um einen richtigen Begriff vom ganzen Instrumente zu geben.

Ich halte dieses um so viel mehr für nöthig, weil ich den Riß, auf welchen sich die **Anleitung**, nach Matthesonen, beruft, in den Breslauischen Samlungen alles Nachsuchens ungeachtet nicht habe finden können; und daraus schlüße, daß er nicht in dieselben geliefert worden seyn muß, ob man es gleich versprochen hatte.

Es gehöret das **Cembal d'Amour**, wie Hr **Adlung** S. 564 der **Anleitung zu d. m. G.** mit Recht saget, nicht zu der Gattung der **Clavicymbel** sondern zu der Gattung der **Clavichorde**. Die Seyten sind doppelt so lang als die auf ordentlichen Clavichorden. Anstatt daß der Tangent auf den Clavichorden die Seyte nicht weit vom Ende linker Hand berühret, so berührt er hier die Seyte just in der Mitte. Und diese Berührung muß auch, um reiner und richtiger Stimmung willen, ganz genau in der Mitte der Seyte geschehen. Uebrigens sind die Tangenten auf den Tasten, und die Tasten selbst, eben so gestaltet wie die in den Clavichordien. Jede Seyte giebt also hier auf beyden Seiten den Klang.

Um dieses zu erhalten, folgt ganz natürlich, daß das Griffbret nicht wie bey den Clavichorden auf der Seite linker Hand, sondern fast in der Mitten, doch, um der hohen Seyten willen, etwas mehr nach der rechten Hand zu, liegen müsse. Ferner müssen, wie eben hieraus auch folgt, auf beyden Seiten **Decken** oder Resonanzboden, und Stege seyn: Doch ist die Decke rechter Hand kleiner und auch von einer andern Form, als die auf der linken Hand.

Anstatt daß auf den ordentlichen Clavichorden die Seyten durch ein zwischen denselben durch geflochtenes und also festsitzendes langes aber schmales Stück Tuch gedämpft werden: so liegen hier die Seyten zu beyden Seiten des Tangentens nur auf zweyen Stückchen Tuchs auf, welche auf besonders dazu angebrachten **Stöckchen**, nicht aber an den Seyten fest gemacht sind. In diesen Stöckchen bewegen sich die Tasten in einem Einschnitte, wie auf den Clavichorden. Wenn nun also ein Tast angeschlagen wird, so hebt er die Seyte etwas in die Höhe; die folglich, weil sie alsdenn ganz frey ist, einen stärkern, und, so viel nämlich einer solchen Seyte möglich ist, länger anhaltenden Klang von sich giebt, als eine Clavichordseyte; und alsdenn erst wieder gedämpft wird, wenn sie, nach Aufhebung des Fingers vom Tasten, wieder auf das Tuch zurück fällt.

Weil

Chap. XXII. The Harpsichord, Clavicytherium, Spinet,

Critica musica, Vol. II, p. 243,* but does not include a description of it. Anyone who has the opportunity to see one while traveling should take advantage of it. Its inventor is the famed Mr. Silbermann of Strassburg.† My gracious readers will find something more [about this instrument] in my *Anleitung*, §.251, p. 563f., which I will not bother to repeat here; thus I beg them in general to consult the said *Anleitung*, in connection with this and the following three chapters.(**)

* note b.

† The inventor is in fact Gottfried Silbermann of Saxony.

> (**) Since this instrument deserves to be more well-known and common, in spite of a few imperfections that it exhibits (which with continued reflection it may well be possible to remedy), I am including here a drawing and a short description of it, as imparted to me by a skilled instrument maker who has frequently seen Silbermann's cembalo d'amour and taken careful note of its layout and construction. If this description is not sufficient for someone to build such an instrument from it, a skillful craftsman will at least be able to derive a good deal from it, especially since [the sketch] is drawn exactly to scale, albeit in miniature. This description will surely be sufficient to furnish a proper conception of the entire instrument.
>
> I consider this all the more necessary, since I have been unable, despite an intensive search, to find the sketch that the *Anleitung* refers to‡ (following Matthesons§) in the *Breslauer Sammlungen*, and thus conclude that it was never submitted there, even though this was promised.
>
> The cembal d'amour, as Mr. Adlung correctly states on p. 564 of the *Anleitung zu der musikalischen Gelahrtheit*, belongs not to the category of harpsichords but to the category of clavichords. The strings are twice as long as those of ordinary clavichords. Unlike the tangents on a clavichord that contact the strings not far from their left ends, [the tangents] on this instrument strike the strings exactly in the middle. And this contact, in order to insure perfectly accurate tuning, must indeed occur absolutely precisely in the middle of the string. Otherwise the tangents on the key [levers] and the keys themselves, are shaped exactly like those in a clavichord. Thus each string produces a sound from both sides.
>
> In order to make this possible, it of course follows that the keyboard must be placed not on the left side, as in clavichords, but almost in the middle, yet somewhat more to the right for the sake of the treble strings. It likewise follows that there must be soundboards and bridges on both sides, but the soundboard on the right is smaller and of a different shape than that on the left.
>
> Instead of the strings being dampened by a long, narrow length of cloth threaded snugly between them, as on an ordinary clavichord, the strings [on this instrument] rest on both sides of the tangents only on two lengths of cloth that are attached to small posts placed there especially for that purpose. The strings, however, are not attached to the cloth. The keys, [operating] like those in a clavichord, move within a notch in these posts. Thus if a key is struck, it lifts the string a bit; the string, which is then completely free [to vibrate], consequently produces a louder and, insofar as is possible from such a string, longer lasting sound than a clavichord string. It is then dampened only when it falls again onto the cloth, after the finger has released the key.

‡ on p. 564. Ernst Flade (among others) has located the sketch; see: Flade, *Gottfried Silbermann; ein Beitrag zur Geschichte des deutschen Orgel- und Klavierbaus im Zeitalter Bachs* (Leipzig: VEB Breitkopf & Härtel [1953]), plate facing p. 230.

§ *Critica Musica*, Vol. II, pp. 243 and 380.

Instrument, Arpichord und Cembal d'Amour. 125

Weil die Seyten viel länger sind als die auf den Clavichorden, und in der Mitte angeschlagen werden, folglich auf beyden Seiten frey sind; so können sie viel mehr als auf dem Clavichorde durch eine sanfte Bewegung des Tasts, bebend gemacht werden. Doch kann hierbey durch allzustarkes Niederdrücken, die Seyte sehr leicht gar zu hoch klingend werden. Und eben dies ist die größte noch nicht gehobene Unbequemlichkeit dieses Instruments, deren ich oben gedacht habe. Uebrigens sind die Seyten, wie auf den Clavichorden, rechter Hand durch Wirbel aufgezogen, und linker Hand vermittelst kleiner Oesen an kleinen Stiftchen befestiget. Daß der Platz unter den Tasten, so wie auf den Clavichorden, leer seyn muß, wird man von sich selbst begreifen.

Alles dieses wird man sich noch leichter und deutlicher vorstellen können, wenn man den *Fig. I.* befindlichen Abriß dieses Cembals d'Amour, im Ganzen, und die bey *Fig. II.* befindliche Abzeichnung eines besondern Theils desselben, betrachtet.

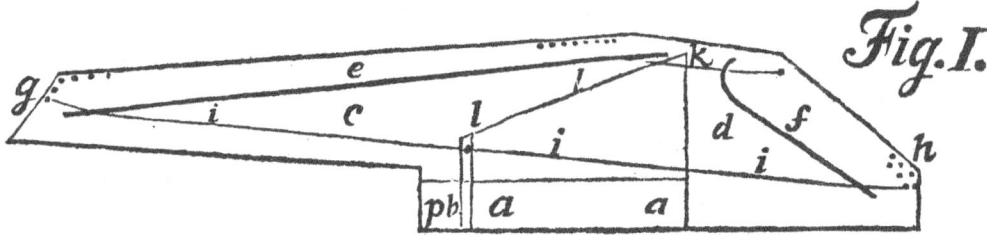

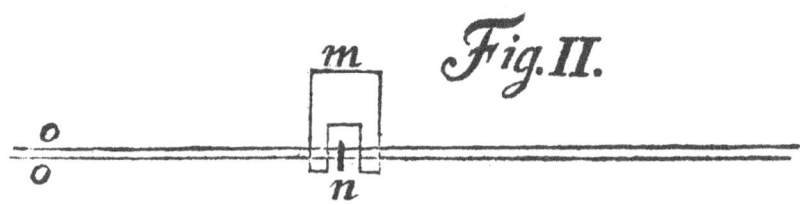

a a ist das Griffbret oder das Clavier.
b. ist ein einzelner Taste, und zwar einer der tiefern.
c. d. sind die beyden Decken oder Resonanzboden.
e. f. sind die zween Stege auf denen die Seyten ruhen.
g. die Stifte an welchen die Seyten angehängt sind.
h. die Wirbel.
i. i. i. ist die tiefste Seyte.
k. eine der hohen Seyten.
l. l. die Reihe der oben mit Tuch bekleideten Klötzchen, auf welchen die Seyten aufliegen, und in deren jedem der dazu gehörige Taste sich endiget, und, wie bey dem Clavichorde, vermittelst eines aus ihm am Ende hervorragenden hölzernen oder fischbeinernen schmahlen Stiftchens in einem Einschnitte sich auf und nieder bewegen kann.
p. ist das Kästchen, am Ende des Griffbrets zur linken Hand: so wie bey den Clavichordern.

Since the strings are much longer than those on clavichords and, being struck in the middle, are thus free on both sides, they can be made to produce a much more pronounced tremolo* than on a clavichord, by gently moving the key. In doing this, however, the string can very easily be made to sound too sharp by pressing on it too hard. It is precisely this that is this instruments's greatest unsolved imperfection, of which I spoke above. Furthermore the strings are strung on wrest pins on the right side, as in clavichords, and are hitched to small pins on the left side by means of small loops. It goes without saying that the space under the keys must be vacant, just as in clavichords.

It will be possible to envision this all the more easily and clearly by examining the sketch of the cembal d'amour seen in its entirely in Fig. I, together with a detail of a certain part of it found in Fig. II.

*i.e., *Bebung*.

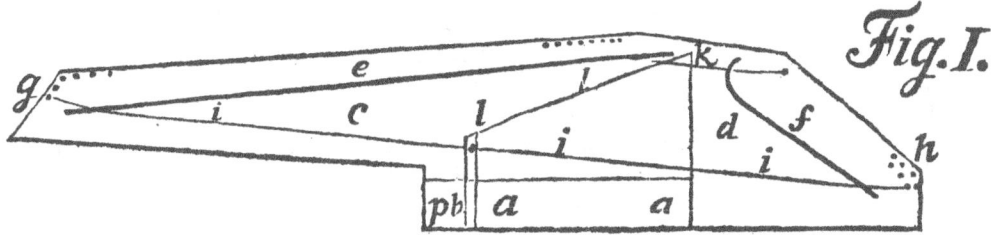

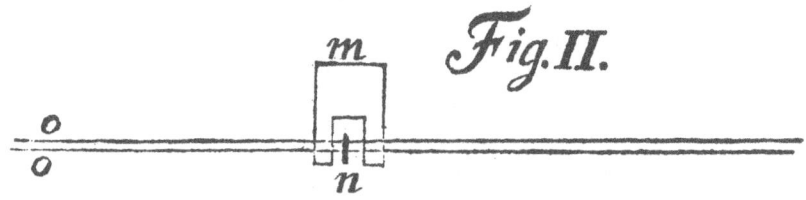

a-a is the keyboard.
b. is a single key, more specifically one of the bass ones.
c. d. are the two soundboards.
e. f. are the two bridges on which the strings rest.
g. the pins on which the strings are looped.
h. the wrest pins.
i.i.i. is the lowest string.
k. one of the treble strings.
l.l. the row of small posts covered on the top with cloth, on which the strings lie. In each of them the key that belongs to it terminates, and as in the clavichord, can move up and down in a notch by means of a narrow pin of wood or fishbone protruding from its end.
p. is the [tool] box at the bass end of the keyboard, just as in clavichords.

Bey *Fig. II.* ist eins von denen bey *l. L* in der Reihe angedeuteten Klötzchen einzeln und größer vorgestellet. *m.* ist das Klötzchen selbst; *n.* der meßingene auf dem Taste stehende Tangent. *oo.* sind zwo aufgezogene Seyten. Diese Klötzchen sind, wie schon gedacht worden, oben mit Tuche bekleidet.

Man sieht also hieraus, daß die Vorzüge dieses Cembals vor dem Clavichorde eigentlich darinn bestehen, daß es 1.) einen stärkern Laut hat als das Clavichord, ob es gleich nicht so stark als ein Clavicimbel klingen kann, sondern zwischen beyden gleichsam das Mittel hält. 2.) Hält es den Ton länger aus; folglich kann noch singender darauf gespielet werden als auf einem Clavichord. 3.) Hat es auch in Ansehen der, durch den Anschlag der Tasten hervorzubringen möglichen, verschiedenen Stärke oder Schwäche des Tons vor dem Clavichord noch etwas voraus: worinn es jedoch einem Piano-Forte noch sehr nachstehet. Man muß aber jedes Ding nach seiner Art beurtheilen.

Noch merke ich an, daß der Herr **Hähnel** in Meißen, einsmals ein dergleichen Cembal verfertiget hat, wobey er dadurch, daß er neben jeden Tangenten auf beyden Seiten zween meßingene starke Stifte gesetzt, die man nach Belieben durch einen Zug an und abschieben konnte, den Klang der sogenannten Cälestin- oder Pantalonclavichorde, und zwar in viel mehrerer Stärke als auf diesen, hervorbringen konnte. Eben dieser Herr **Hähnel** hatte auch eine mit Tuch bezogene lange Leiste angebracht, welche man nach Belieben über dem einen oder dem andern Sangboden auf die Seyten legen, und dadurch die Hälfte der Seyten dämpfen konnte, so daß der Klang einem ordentlichen Clavichorde ähnlich wurde.

Das XXIII. Kapitel.
Vom Violdigambenwerke, Claviergamba, Geigenwerk und Leyer.

Inhalt.

§. 543. Auctor und Eigenschaften des Violdigambenwerks. §. 544. dergleichen beschreibt auch Prätorius. §. 545. Inhalt dessen. §. 546. die Seyten sind fleischern. §. 547. von der Leyer.

§. 543.

Dieses Kapitel soll uns, wie auch die folgenden, nicht so lange aufhalten als das vorige. Es folgt nämlich zu betrachten das **Violdigambenwerk**, mit welchem das **Geigenwerk** wie auch die **Claviergamba** einerley bedeuten, wie die Wörter selbst anzeigen. **Geigeninstrument** und **Geigenclavicymbel** ist eben das. In der Critica Musica Matthesoniana Tom I. pag. 254. wurde unter den neuen Zeitungen von musikalischen Sachen aus Ilmenau am Thüringer Walde 4 Meilen von Erfurt geschrieben, daß (etwan Anno 1722.) der dasige Organist Johann Georg Gleichmann ein ganz neues Instrument erfunden, welches er eine **Claviergamba** genennet, weil es in einem vollkommenen Claviere bestehet, das zu jedermanns Verwunderung die ordentliche Violdigamba nicht nur natürlich imitiret, als ob sie mit dem Bogen

Fig. II depicts, singly and enlarged, one of the posts indicated [in Fig. I] in the row from *l.-l. m.* is the post itself; *n.* the brass tangent as it contacts the string; *o-o.* are the two strings stretched [across the post]. These posts are covered on top with cloth, as has already been mentioned.

One may see from this that the merits of this cembal over the clavichord consist in 1.) its ability to produce a louder sound than a clavichord, although it cannot get as loud as a harpsichord, but holds the mean between them; 2.) its ability to sustain the sound longer; thus it can be played in a more singing fashion than a clavichord; 3.) its ability to produce a louder or softer tone by striking the keys, although in this it exceeds the clavichord only to a certain degree, and falls far short of a pianoforte. Each thing should, however, be judged according to its own standard.

In addition let me remark that Mr. Hähnel in Meissen once constructed just such a cembal that could produce the sound of the so-called cælestin- or pantalonclavichord, but even louder than this instrument, by placing two strong brass pins on either side of each tangent that could be engaged or released by a stop at will. This same Mr. Hähnel also installed a long strip covered with cloth that could be placed upon the set of strings over one or the other soundboard, by which half of the strings could be dampened, rendering the sound similar to an ordinary clavichord. [Agricola]

Chapter XXIII.
Concerning the Violdigambenwerk, Claviergamba, Geigenwerk and Hurdy-gurdy.

Contents:

§.543. The inventor and the characteristics of the Violdigambenwerk. §. 544 Praetorius describes this instrument. §.545. What Praetorius says about it. §.546. It has gut strings. §.547. Concerning the hurdy-gurdy.

§. 543.

This chapter, as well as the one following, will not detain us as long as the previous one. Its intent is to consider the Violdigambenwerk, a term with which Geigenwerk as well as Claviergamba are synonymous (as the words themselves indicate). Geigeninstrument and Geigenclavicymbel are also the same thing. In Mattheson's *Critica Musica*, Vol. I, p. 254, among the news about musical matters from Ilmenau in the Thuringian Forest, 4 miles* from Erfurt, it was reported that the organist there, Johann Georg Gleichmann, had invented an entirely new musical instrument, in about the year 1722. He called this instrument a Claviergamba, since it consisted of a complete keyboard that to everyone's astonishment not only faithfully imitated an actual violdigamba as though it were being stroked with a bow, but also could be played with

---

* The length of a mile varied greatly from place to place in the eighteenth century; nevertheless this distance cannot be correct. Ilmenau is approximately 40 km. from Erfurt.

Bogen gestrichen würde; sondern auch wegen seiner unglaublichen Niedlichkeit und beweglichen Intonation überaus galant traktirt werden kann, indem es augenblicklich und ohne die geringste Veränderung des Instruments forte und piano hören zu lassen eingerichtet ist.

§. 544.

Was der Herr Gleichmann für eine besondere Invention dabey habe, ist mir nicht bekannt worden. Sonst aber kann man den Bogenstrich durch Räder imitiren, daß man dabey das Clavier spielt. Wenn dabey weiter nichts angebracht worden, als dieß; so wäre es so neu nicht, und hat man schon längst dergleichen gehabt. Bey den Clavieren hat man freylich die Delicatesse nicht, die man bey dem Bogenstriche haben kann durch das forte und piano, welches so vielerley Grade leidet. Daher ist diese neue Invention zu loben. Die Struktur dieser Werke hat schon Prätorius in Syntag. Tom. II. P. II. c. XLIV. pag. 67. bis 72. beschrieben, woraus ich das vornehmste hierher setzen, das übrige aber dem Leser daselbst nachzusuchen überlassen will.

§. 545.

Das Geigenwerk, Geigeninstrument, oder Geigenclavicymbel ist wie ein ander gemeines Clavicymbel, und ist von einem Bürger in Nürnberg, Hans Hayde, erdacht worden. Galiläus und andere sagen, es sey schon vorher erdacht gewesen. Es hat anstatt der Tangenten 5 oder 6 stählerne Räder, mit Pergament glatt überzogen, und mit Colophonio oder Oleo spicæ vel lauendulæ bestrichen. Die Räder werden durch ein groß Rad und unterschiedliche Rollen unter dem Sangboden liegend mit beyden Füssen von dem Organisten selbst unten an der Erde regieret, oder auch wol mit Händen von einen Calcanten oben an der Seyte gezogen, daß die Räder in vollem Schwange gehen und bleiben müssen. Wenn ein Clavis vorn gedruckt wird; so rührt die Seyte an ein Rad, und klingt als ob sie mit einem Geigenbogen gestrichen würde. Die groben Seyten sind dick Meßing, fast so dicke, als die große auf dem Basse. Dieß dient dazu, daß ein Componist alle Affekten piano oder forte nach Gefallen ausdrücken kann, nachdem er den Clavem stark niederdrückt, welches bey andern Clavicymbeln nicht angehet, auch nicht einmal bey den Orgeln. Auch kann man eine lange Note aushalten, wie auf der Orgel; man kann ein Echo machen, als wären unterschiedliche Stimmen da; man kann es auch als eine Leyer oder Cyther brauchen zur Lust. Es werden auch Pauken durch ein Register mit angebracht. Doch will es eine starke Uebung haben, daß man des Tretens gewohnt werde, und eine leichte Hand habe, daß man nicht so eintappe. So viel aus dem Prätorio.

§. 546.

Man wird auch aus der Beschreibung nicht völlig klug in dieser Sache; daher man sich die Mühe geben und darnach reisen muß, da man denn diese Beschreibung gegen des Hrn. Gleichmanns Arbeit halten kann, um zu sehen, ob es etwas neues, oder nur etwas erneuertes sey. Soll es ein Violdigambenwerk, oder Clavier=

Chap. XXIII. Concerning the Violdigambenwerk, etc. 127

exceeding charm because of its incredible delicacy and nimble speech, in that it was disposed so as to play loudly or softly at any moment, without the slightest adjustment to the instrument.

§. 544.

The specific type of invention that Mr. Gleichmann had developed is unknown to me. It is possible, though, to imitate a bowstroke by means of wheels operated from a keyboard. If this was the extent of the invention, then there is nothing very new about it; this sort of thing has been around for a long time. It is of course not possible to achieve the delicacy with a keyboard that one can with a bowstroke that permits so many gradations of loudness and softness. Therefore this new invention is worthy of praise. Praetorius has already described the structure of this instrument in his *Syntagma musicum*, Vol. II, Part II, chap. XLIV, pp. 67–72. I will reproduce the most important things he says, leaving the reader to look up the rest for himself.

§. 545.*

The Geigenwerk, Geigeninstrument or Geigenclavicymbel is like any other ordinary harpsichord. It was conceived by a citizen of Nuremberg, Hans Hayde.† Galiläus‡ and others assert that it had already been invented.§ In place of jacks¶ it has 5 or 6 steel wheels covered with smooth parchment and coated with rosin or spike oil/lavender oil.‖ The wheels are turned by means of a large wheel and various rollers placed under the soundboard, operated either by both of the organist's feet** down below on the ground, or alternatively driven by hand by a pumper up top next to the strings, that keep the wheels turning at full speed. If one of the keys at the front end is depressed, then a string comes into contact with a wheel, and sounds as if it were being bowed with a violin bow. The large strings are of thick brass, almost as thick as the large ones on a bass viol.†† This [instrument] allows a composer to express all affects, piano or forte, at will, according to how firmly he depresses a key. This will not work with other harpsichords, and not even with organs. It is also possible to sustain a long note, just as on the organ. One can achieve an echo as if several different voices were present, and one can also use it for fun as a hurdy-gurdy or cittern. It also has drums built in, operated by a stop. But it requires diligent practice to become accustomed to pumping it and to achieve a light touch without fumbling about. All of the above comes from Praetorius.

* This paragraph is a free quote from Praetorius, *Syntagma musicum*, Vol. II, pp. 67–72.
† The name is actually Hans Haiden.
‡ Vicenzo Galilei.
§ i.e., before Hayde.
¶ or "keyshafts"; c.f. §.572 (note) and §.598.
‖ "oleum spicæ vel lavendulæ;" these are essentially the same substance: an oil used today in liniments and pharmaceutical preparations.
** i.e., pumping a treadle.
†† "auf dem Basse;" Praetorius writes "BaßGeigen."

§. 546.

It is not possible fully to conceive the instrument from this description; therefore it is necessary to take the trouble to travel there,‡‡ in order to compare this description with Mr. Gleichmann's work and see whether it is something new or merely something revived. If it is to be recognized as a true Violdigambenwerk or Clavier-

‡‡ i.e., to Ilmenau.

gamba heissen; so müssen die Seyten fleischern seyn, da sonst auch die metallenen Seyten durch Räder gerieben auch das piano und forte von sich hören liessen. Doch es ist genug, wenn ein Organist aus meiner Traktation von jeder Sache etwas weis, obschon zuweilen nur superficiellement. Es hat de Chales Tom. III. mundi mathemat. P. I. de Musica propos. 34. auch dergleichen Invention, die er von der Leyer genommen, und für etwas ganz neues ausgiebt. Vielleicht ist ihm Prätorii Beschreibung nicht bekannt gewesen. Denen zu Gefallen, die solches Werk nicht haben, will ich etwas aus dem Lateinischen ins Deutsche setzen und hier anführen, doch mehr auf den Verstand als auf die Worte sehen. Ich habe, sagt er, eine Leyer gehört, welche über die ordentlichen Palmulen noch andere hatte, die am meisten bey dem Schlusse gebraucht wurden, durch deren Hülfe etliche vorhin nicht klingende Seyten an das Rad getrieben und zum Klange gebracht wurden, so mir Gelegenheit gegeben, ein besonder Instrument zu ersinnen, welches in der Theorie sehr gut zu seyn scheint: weis aber nicht, ob es in der Praxis angehen möchte. Ich wollte nämlich ein ziemlich grosses Instrument, etwann ein Clavicymbel nehmen, und dieses nicht mit Drat, sondern mit Darmseyten beziehen, und anstatt der Docken wollte ich ein gross Rad oder 3 kleinere anbringen, welche mit einem Handgriffe gedrehet und mit Kolophonium bestrichen würden, daß sie die Seyten könnten zum Klange bringen. Die Seyten müßten so aufgezogen seyn, daß sie die Räder nicht berührten. Ueber den Seyten wären die Palmulen, wie sie auf Orgeln oder Claveßins zu seyn pflegen; und wenn die Palmulen angeschlagen würden: so brächten sie die Seyten an das Rad, daß sie klingen mußten. Es wär aber das Incommodum dabey, daß die Darmseyten ihren Ton nicht behielten, und kaum jemals zur vollkommenen Reinigkeit zu bringen wären: oder wenigstens bleiben sie nicht lange rein. Welchem Incommodo etliche durch elateria haben wollen entgegen gehen. Sollte das Incommodum gehoben werden; so würde es was recht schönes seyn um ein solch Instrument, und würde es unsern Claveßins weit vorzuziehen seyn. So weit de Chales. Was das Incommodum betrifft; so hat er sich dasselbe größer eingebildet, als es ist. Müssen doch die Seyten auf der Violine und dergleichen Instrumenten reine bleiben: und wenn sie sich verstimmen, macht man sie wieder reine, wie es auch mit unsern gemeinen Claveßins geschehen muß. Sonst habe noch gehört von Heydens Beschreibung des nürnbergischen Geigenwerks; vielleicht findet man auch daselbst etwas zur Nachricht. Ich habe sie aber niemals gesehen.

(**) Herrn Hohlefelds in Berlin Erfindung gehört auch hieher, s. Anl. 567. und anderwärts. Diese, wenn sie noch zur Vollkommenheit gebracht werden sollte, würde vielleicht die andern vorher beschriebenen Arten alle noch übertreffen.

§. 547.

Es folgt die Leyer. Man verwundere sich nicht, daß sich auch dieses verachtete Instrument unter den Organisten-Instrumenten präsentirt: denn wer weis nicht, daß es auch durch ein Clavier regieret werde? Prätorius Tom. I. P. II. Membr. II. c. XI.

Chap. XXIII. Concerning the Violdigambenwerk, etc.

gamba, then the strings must be gut, since metal strings rubbed by wheels will also produce a loud and soft sound. But it is sufficient if an organist gains some basic knowledge of each subject, although at times only superficial, from my treatise. In Vol. III of his [*Cursus seu*] *mundus mathematicus*, Part I, [Tract 22] "De Musica", proposition 34, de Chales records the same invention, which he derives from the hurdy-gurdy and represents as something entirely new. Perhaps Praetorius's description was not known to him. For the sake of those who do not possess this work, I will translate some of it from Latin into German and quote it here, paying more attention to the sense rather than a literal translation. He says: I have heard a hurdy-gurdy that in addition to the usual keys has other ones that are mostly used at cadences. By means of these [extra keys] several strings that have not previously been sounding are forced against the wheel and made to sound. This [invention] has provided me the occasion to conceive a special instrument that appears to be very good in theory, but I do not know whether it would work in practice. I would take a rather large [keyboard] instrument, let us say, a harpsichord, and string it not with wire strings, but with ones of gut. Instead of jacks I would install a large wheel or three smaller ones, turned by a handle and coated with rosin to make the strings sound. The strings must be mounted in such a way that they do not touch the wheels. Normal keys such as those on organs or harpsichords would be above the strings, and when the keys were depressed they would force the strings against the wheel, causing them to sound. This shortcoming it would have: gut strings do not hold pitch, and it is almost never possible to get them into perfect tune; or at least they do not stay in tune long. Some have tried to get around this defect by [using] *elateria*.* If this shortcoming could be overcome, then such an instrument would be truly beautiful, far preferable to our harpsichords. Here ends de Chales. As regards the shortcoming, he has pictured it as more major than it really is. The strings on a violin and other such instruments have to remain in tune, and if they go out of tune, one tunes them again, just as must also happen with our ordinary harpsichords. In addition, [I] have also heard of Heyden's description of the Nuremberg Geigenwerk.† Perhaps there is more information [about this instrument] to be found therein, but I have never seen it.(**)

(**) The invention‡ of Mr. Hohlefeld in Berlin also belongs here; see the *Anleitung* [§.252, p.] 567 and elsewhere.§ This [invention], if ever brought to perfection, would perhaps surpass all of the types previously described. [Agricola]

§. 547.

Next comes the hurdy-gurdy. It should come as no surprise that even this despised instrument appears among those with which organists should be familiar, for it is also operated by a keyboard, as everyone knows. Praetorius treats the hurdy-gurdy [in the *Syntagma musicum*], Vol. I, Part II, Membr. II, chap. XI [pp.361f.], as well as

---

* The reference is obscure. It may be referring to *elaterium*, a medicine (a strong purgative) prepared from the juice of *cucumis elaterium*, the wild or squirting cucumber, but its application and effect in this situation are unclear.

† Haiden wrote two pamphlets about the instrument, *Commentario de musicali instrumento* (Nürnberg: 1605) and *Musicale instrumentum reformatum* (Nürnberg, 1610); the latter was quoted in its entirety by Praetorius in his *Syntagma musicum*, Vol. II, pp. 68f.

‡ i.e., using horse hair to sound the strings instead of parchment.

§ *Anleitung*, §.262, p. 577.

c. XI. handelt von der Leyer; und Tom. II. P. II. c. XXIII. p. 49. handelt er ebenfalls davon; doch nicht von der kleinen Bettelmannsleyer, sondern von der italienischen. Diese italienische Leyer ist wieder bey ihm zweyerley, da er erst redet von der großen (Lirone perfetto, arciviolira, oder wie sie *Ludovico Zacconi* nennt arci viola di lira. Sie heißt auch Lira da gamba, λύρα ἐπιγνυδία,) die ist wie die Violdigamba; doch wegen der vielen Seyten ist das Corpus breiter. Man kann alle Compositiones darauf machen, weil sie oft 16 Seyten hat, deren 2. sich ausserhalb des Kragens befinden. Er hat auch ihren Accord, d. i. die Stimmung. Die kleine heißt Lira da braccio, hat 5 Seyten auf dem Kragen, und 2 ausserhalb. Er hat auch ihre Stimmung. Kircherus in *Musurgia* Tom. I. p. 487. Libri VI. hat die italienische im Riße, der er nur 12 Seyten zuschreibt: im Accorde aber kömmt er mit Prätorio nicht überein. Er lobt das Instrument, weil es nach Art der gemeinen Leyer mit seinem traurigen Gemurmel eine angenehme Musik mache und die Affekten errege. Er hat auch daselbst unsere sogenannte Bettelmannsleyer, davon wir reden. Er hat sie im Riße vorgestellt, und sagt, daß es zwar ein gemein Instrument sey, aber die Struktur und die Eintheilung der Seyten, deren sie 2 oder 4 habe, sey sehr ingeniös, und habe alle Veränderungen der Harmonie; es habe seine plectra und palmulas. (eben der Palmuln wegen ziehen wir es hierher) ꝛc. Weil es gar gemein ist, und von einem jeden bey den Bettlern kann gesehen werden; so halte ich mich dabey nicht auf, sondern sage nur noch dieses, daß das an den Leyern befindliche Clavier nur mit einer Hand gespielet werde: denn mit der andern wird das Rad gedrehet, wodurch die Seyten klingend gemacht werden.

Die gemeine Leyer nennet de Chales Basse de Viole Tom. III. pag. 2. und die Franzosen nennen es *Violon*, die große Leyer aber *Viole*. ibid. p. 17. propos. 12.

(**) Heut zu Tage heißt dies herrliche Instrument in Frankreich: *la Vielle*. Es giebt dort sogar Compositionen dafür.

Das XXIV. Kapitel.
Vom Organo Portaliti, Wasserorgel und Hänflings Claviatur; auch dem Xylorgano.

Inhalt:

§. 548. 549. Organon portatile. §. 550. 551 die Wasserorgel. §. 551. Hänflings Claviatur. §. 552. das Xylorganum. §. 553. Ein Anhang vom Katzenclavier.

§. 548.

Organon portatile ist eine solche Orgel, die man bequem mit sich herumtragen kann. Es wird dies Instrument zwar mit Pfeifen gemacht; daher es in dem Puncte, auch in der Windlade, und andern nöthigen Theilen mit dem Positiv überein-

Chap. XXIV. The *Organon Portatili*, Water Organ, 129

in Vol. II, Part II, chap. XXIII, p. 49. He does not, however, discuss the small beggar's hurdy-gurdy, but rather the Italian [Lira]. This [discussion of the] Italian Lira* is further subdivided into two parts, of which the first speaks of the large one (*Lirone perfetto, arciviolira*, or, as Ludovico Zacconi calls it, *arci viola di lira*. It is also called *Lira da gamba*, λυρα επιγονιδια), which is like a viol di gamba but wider due to its many strings. All sorts of pieces may be played on it, since it often has 16 strings, of which two are strung off the fingerboard. It has its own special tuning. The small one is called *Lira da braccio*, and has 5 strings on the fingerboard and two beside it. It also has its own [special] tuning. In his *Musurgia*, Vol. I, Book VI, p. 487,† Kircher has a sketch of the Italian [instrument], to which he ascribes only 12 strings; he also does not agree with Praetorius as to the tuning. He praises the instrument because it makes pleasant music, like the character of the ordinary hurdy-gurdy with its mournful murmuring, arousing the affections. He also discusses there our so-called "beggar's hurdy-gurdy", about which we will [now] speak. He depicts it in a sketch, saying that it is a common instrument, to be sure, but its structure and division of the strings (of which there are 2 or 4) is most ingenious, producing all variations of harmony. It has plectra[?] and keys (it is because of these latter that we include it here). Since it is so very common and can be seen with any beggar, I will not dwell on it. I will say only this, though, that the keyboard found on a hurdy-gurdy is played with only one hand, since the other one turns the wheel that makes the strings sound.

De Chales [in *Mundus mathematicus*,] Vol. III, p. 2, calls the common hurdy-gurdy *Basse de Viole*, and the French call it *Violon*, while they call the large hurdy-gurdy *Viole*; [see] ibid., p. 17, proposition 12.(**)

(**) Nowadays in France this splendid instrument is called *La Vielle*. Compositions are even [written] for it there. [Agricola]

* "Leyer;" The fact that the German names for the hurdy-gurdy and the Lyra are identical obscures the fact that they are entirely different instruments.

† *Iconismus* VIII, Fig. V.

Chapter XXIV.
Concerning the *Organon Portatili*, the Water Organ and Hänfling's Claviatur, as well as the Xylorganum

Contents:

§.548-549. *Organon portatile* . §.550-551. The Water Organ [Hydraulos]. §.551 [sic]. Hänfling's Claviatur. §.552 [sic]. The Xylorganum. §.553 [sic]. An appendix concerning the Katzenclavier [cat keyboard instrument].

§. 548.

The *Organon portatile* is a type of organ that a person can conveniently carry about. This instrument is made with pipes, to be sure, and therefore in this respect, as well as in its windchest and other necessary components it resembles the positiv. But it

einkömmt: allein es hat kein solches Clavier welches mit Händen gespielet wird, dahero es eigentlich nicht für die Organisten gehöret. Ich habe aber doch dessen allhier erwähnen wollen, weil der Name scheint etwas zu involviren, welches den Organisten die Präsumtion erwecken könnte als laufe es in ihre forum; doch wird es gar wenig werden.

§. 549.

Inwendig ist ein Clavier, wenigstens etwas, das demselben ähnlich stehet und dessen Stelle vertritt. Vor demselben liegt eine Welle, oder Cylinder, von Holz, in welchem hölzerne Arme eingesetzt sind, die die Palmulen drücken. Es sind aber diese Arme so ordiniret, daß sie durch das Drücken eine ordentliche Melodie zu wege bringen, etwan einen Choral, Diskant und Baß. Von aussen wird die Welle durch einen Griff, wie an der Leyer ist, gedrehet. Es können die Wellen so gemacht werden, daß eine einzige viele Chorale spielet. Wie aber die Welle oder Cylinder zu ordiniren, hat Kircherus in *Musurgia* Lib. IX. Tom. II. p. 312. seqq. mit mehreren ausgeführet, wovon ich aber nichts hierher setzen will, weil es, wie gemeldet, nicht eigentlich für den Organisten ist. Gedachter Kircherus nennet solche Instrumente Avtomata. Man kann auch besentete Instrument durch solche Cylindros klingend machen. Doch davon ist anjetzo nicht Zeit und Raum zu reden.

§. 550.

Die Wasserorgel heißt sonst auch Hydraulicum, von ὕδως, das Wasser, und ἀυλή eine Röhre. Dieß Instrument ist jenem ziemlich gleich, und bestehet es auch aus Pfeifen; aber der Wind wird nicht durch einen Blaßbalg, sondern durch das Wasser besorgt. Das Clavier wird gleichfalls durch einen Cylinder gedruckt, daher sich ein Organist, qua talis, darum nicht so sehr bekümmert. Doch weil die Benennung ziemlich organistisch scheint; so habe ich es des Nachschlagens wegen hierher gesetzt. Es ist diese Wasserorgel so alt, daß auch schon der alte Vitruuius Lib. X. c. 13. deren Struktur beschreibt, woraus es nach der Zeit die andern genommen, als Prätorius der Tom. I. P. II. M. II. cap. XX. p. 432. seqq. ex professo de *Organo hydraulico* gehandelt hat, auch von dessen Erfinder. Da sagt er: erat arae rotundae simile, & canales sive fistulas in aqua tenebat: qua per puerum mota, illae anima seu uita replebantur, nervulorum quorundam, seu lingularum inclusarum medio; atque ita suauissimum edebant sonum. Tom. I. P. I. M. IV. cap. XIV. zeigt er den Unterschied zwischen den Organis hydraulicis und unsern Orgeln, nam illius corpus una cum cicutis ex aere fusum unico cicutarum ordine constabat, & sonum per aquam infusam diversimode reddebat.

§. 551.

Kircherus in *Musurgia* Tom. I. Lib. IX. pag. 330. seqq. hat sich desfalls noch mehr bemühet, da er ex professo handelt de Organis hydraulicis. Er hat Vitruuii Text hingesetzt, der in vielen Stücken etwas obscur ist, und hat sich hernach, so viel ihm

Chap. XXIV. The *Organon Portatili*, Water Organ,

has no keyboard played with the hands, and thus does not actually concern organists. I am mentioning it here, however, since the name suggests that it involves matters organists might think pertinent to their profession; these [matters], though, will prove to be very few [in number].

§. 549.

Inside [the instrument] is a keyboard, or at least something that resembles one and takes one's place. In front of it stands a wooden roller or cylinder in which are inserted wooden tabs that depress the keys. These tabs are so arranged that when they depress [the keys] they create a regular melody, such as the treble and bass of a chorale. On the exterior there is a handle that turns the roller, like a hurdy-gurdy. The rollers can be made in such a way that a single one of them plays many chorales. In his *Musurgia*, Book IX, Vol. II, p.312f.,* Kircher has explained how to arrange the roller or cylinder, with several examples; I will not include any of them here, though, since, as I have said, it does not actually concern organists. The above-mentioned Kircher calls such instruments *Automata*.† It is also possible to make stringed instruments sound by means of such cylinders. But there is neither time nor space to discuss this here.

* Adlung's sketchy account of this instrument is based on Kircher's description, which is itself rather inaccurate.

† Vol. II, pp. 334f.

§. 550.

The water organ is also called *hydraulos*, from ὕδωρ, "water" and αὐλή, "a reed". This instrument is rather similar to the one just discussed; it also consists of pipes, but the wind is supplied not by a bellows, but by water. The keyboard is likewise played by a cylinder, and therefore an organist as such is not much concerned with it. But because the term appears rather organistic, I have included it here for the sake of reference. This water organ is so old that the ancient Vitruvius already describes its structure in [his *De architectura*,] Book X, chap. 13, from which others have subsequently drawn, such as Praetorius, who expressly treats the hydraulic organ as well as its inventor in [*Syntagma musicum*,] Vol. I, Part II, Membrum II, chap. XX, p. 432f.‡ There he writes: *erat arae rotundae simile, & canales sive fistulas in aqua tenebat: qua per puerum mota, illae anima seu vita replebantur, nervulorum quorundam, seu lingularum inclusarum medio; atque ita suavissimum edebant sonum* [it was similar [in shape] to a round altar, and it had tubes or pipes in water; when [the water] was set in motion by a boy, [the tubes or pipes] were filled with breath or life, by means of certain little sinews or little tongues that were inside; and so they produced the sweetest sound]. In Vol. I, Part I, Membrum IV, chap. XIV[, pp. 144-5], he demonstrates the difference between hydraulic organs and our organs, *nam illius corpus una cum cicutis ex aere fusum unico cicutarum ordine constabat, & sonum per aquam infusam diversimode reddebat* ... [For the body [of the hydraulic organ] together with its pipes was cast of brass, the pipes being arranged in a fixed order, and it gave forth sound of various sorts by means of the water poured into it ...].

‡ This should read "p. 430f." Both of the subsequent quotes are indeed from Praetorius, but neither is taken from Vitruvius.

§. 551.

In his *Musurgia*, Vol. I, Book IX, pp. 330f., Kircher has gone to even greater lengths in expressly discussing the hydraulic organ. He includes Vitruvius's text, which is rather obscure in many particulars, and then has endeavored to make it clearer, in-

ihm möglich gewesen, denselbigen deutlicher zu machen bemühet, auch zu besserm Verständnisse dieser dunklen und schweren Sache einen Abriß davon beygefüget. Ich verweise deswegen den Leser dahin, und sage nur dieß, daß Vitruvius keines Wassers gedenkt, dadurch das Werk seinen Wind empfangen hätte; doch hat es den Namen davon, weil in dem untersten Kasten das Wasser sich aufhält, um den motum tremulum zu produciren. Er weiset, wie man sie zu machen habe. s. Anleitung S. 344.

§. 552.

Die Claviatur des Herrn Hofrath Hänflings gehöret mit besserm Rechte hieher; nur Schade, das man nicht gar zu viel davon weis. Ich will unterdessen so viel hersetzen, als uns die Critica Musica Matthesonii Tom. I. p. 51. aus Onolzbach communiciret hat: die Claviatura (heißt es allda) des Hrn. Hofrath C. Hänflings hat wegen dessen Tode nicht publiciret werden können. Generaliter nota 1) daß man nur aus zweyen Tönen spielen lernen darf, da man sonst 12 oder 24 braucht. 2) kann man da eine Duodecima mit einer Hand erlangen. 3) kann man 1. 2. 3. 4. 5. ganze Töne höher und niedriger transponiren, ohne einen Fingersatz deswegen zu ändern, oder sich ein ander Zeichen einzubilden, nur daß man nicht auf das Clavier sehe, weil man sonst leicht confus werden könnte, wenn man sähe, daß man aus einen andern clave spiele, als auf dem Pappier stehet. 4) Wenn man auch die Fugen und Toccaten darauf spielen könnte, wär es ein schön Compendium; es käme auf die Probe an. Soweit die Critica. Sonst hat man die erste Nachricht von der Claviatura C. Henflingii aus einer Epistola eiusdem *de nouo suo systemate musico*, Onoldi d. 17. April 1708. data, welche zu lesen ist in Miscellaneis berolinensibus ad incrementum scientiarum, ex scriptis societatis regiae scientiarum exhibitis, editis, welche in lateinischer Sprache, mit verschiedenen Kupfern, zu Berlin 1710. in 4to heraus gekommen sind, und etwas über 2 Alphabet betragen. Sie befindet sich daselbst in Volumine I. Parte III. mathematica & mechanica continente, No. XXVIII. pag. 265—294. da er §. 43. u. f. unsere Claviere deswegen tadelt, daß durch die verschiedene Farben der Palmuln vox naturalis ab artificiali nicht allezeit unterschieden; it. daß Interualla von einer Größe doch nicht in einer Weite von einander liegen, (wie z. Ex. e f weiter von einander sind als c cis.) und man also die Finger weiter bey einem aussperren müßte, als bey dem andern, und daß man also bey jedem modo eine neue Application und Ordnung lernen müßte. Daher er sich Positive machen lassen, da er alles dieses verbessert, und könne man darauf vocem naturalem ab artificiali vollkommen unterscheiden, und die Intervalle hätten stets einerley Lage der Finger. Die Melodien durch 12 modos würden nur auf 2 verschiedene Arten zuwege gebracht, die doch einander so verwandt, daß man es für eine Art annehmen könnte. Mann könnte mit einer Hand eine 5te oder 6te über die Oktave greifen. Der Herausgeber der Miscellaneorum versprach, daß die Figur und Erklärung dieses Clauiarii im 2ten Bande folgen sollte: ich habe aber daselbst von dem Dinge nichts finden können.

sofar as he is able. In order to promote a better understanding of this obscure and difficult matter, he has included a sketch of it. I therefore refer the reader to his book, saying only that Vitruvius does not mean that the instrument uses water in place of wind; rather [the instrument] gets its name from the fact that the lowest reservoir is filled with water to produce the air pressure. He demonstrates how they are to be made. See [my] *Anleitung*, p. 344.

§. 552.

Privy Councillor Hänfling's Claviatur has a better right to be included here [than the instruments just discussed]; it is too bad that we know all too little about it. Until more is known, I will set down here that which Mattheson's *Critica musica* has imparted [in the report] from Onolzbach in Vol. I, p. 51. [A description of] the *Claviatura* (as it is called there) of Privy Councillor C. Hänfling could not be published due to his death. In summary, take note: 1) that it was necessary to learn to play in only two keys, while otherwise* 12 or 24 were needed; 2) it was possible to reach [the interval of] a twelfth with one hand; 3) it was possible to transpose up or down 1, 2, 3, 4, or 5 whole tones higher and lower without changing any fingering or imagining any other [clef] sign, except that one could not look at the keyboard, since it was easy to become confused when one realized that one was playing in another key than that notated; 4) if it were possible to play fugues and toccatas on it, it would have been a wonderful shortcut; this would need to be tested. Here ends [the material taken from] the *Critica*. In addition there is the first report about the *Claviatura* of C. Henfling from his letter *de novo suo systemate musico* [concerning his new system of music], from Onolzbach, dated April 17, 1708, which may be read in *Miscellaneis berolinensibus, ad incrementum scientiarum, ex scriptis societatis regiae scientiarum exhibiti, editis*, that was published in quarto with various plates in Berlin in 1710, amounting to somewhat more than two alphabets.† It is to be found in that publication in Volume I, Part III, *mathematica & mechanica continente*, No. XXVIII, p. 265–294, where in §.43f. he criticizes our [present] keyboard instruments for these reasons, that it is not always possible to distinguish a note that belongs to a key from one that does not‡ by different colors of keys, and also that intervals of the same size nevertheless do not lie the same distance from each other (e.g., e–f are further apart than c–c#), and thus it is necessary to extend the fingers further for one than another, and to learn a new fingering and arrangement for each key. Therefore he has had constructed a positive in which all these [shortcomings] are remedied. On it it is possible to distinguish perfectly a diatonic note§ from a chromatic,¶ and all intervals [of the same type] call for the same finger position. Melodies in all twelve keys are realized in only two different ways, so closely related that they could be perceived as one. It is possible to reach an octave and a fifth or sixth with one hand. The publisher of the *Miscellaneorum* promised that the configuration of this keyboard would follow in the second volume, together with an explanation, but I have been unable to find anything about the matter in it.

* i.e., on other keyboard instruments.

† for an explanation of this printer's terminology, see the translator's preface.

‡ or "a natural from an accidental"?

§ or "a natural"
¶ or "an accidental"

§. 553.

Es folgt das Xylorganum. Diese Art der Claviere beschreibt Kircherus in *Musurgia* Tom. I. Lib. VI. pag. 518. der es allezeit Zylorganon schreibt, da es doch von ξύλον ein Holz herkömmt. Es ist ein solch Instrument, da man anstatt der Pfeifen Hölzer in cylindrischer Figur, oder in figura parallelipipeda harmonisch also ordnet, daß wenn der Organist die Palmule drückt, dieselben mit ihren Hämmern an die Hölzer schlagen, und einen harmonischen Klang verursachen. Es müssen aus wohlklingenden Holze, das allerwegen glatt und gerade ist, Hölzer in cylindrischer Form, an der Zahl 26. gemacht werden, daß es eben 2 Oktaven austrägt. (Man könnte es auch wol größer oder kleiner machen.) Die Proportion der Hölzer wird seyn, wie die Proportion der Pfeifen in den Orgeln. Diese Hölzer legt man über ein hohl Gefäß, daß sie es nirgends berühren, ohne auf einer Linie. An die äusersten Theile der Palmule macht man die Hämmerchen. Er hat auch den Riß dabey. Sonst legt man die dazu geschickt gemachten Hölzer auf Stroh, und spielt mit hölzernen Klöppeln drauf, wie auf einem Hackebret. Man nenut dieß Instrument auf deutsch eine Strohfiedel. Anstatt der ausgedorrten Hölzer kann man auch Schmiede-Kohlen brauchen: noch besser aber sind wohlklingende Stahlstangen zu gebrauchen, welche sich mit vielem Vergnügen hören lassen.

§. 554.

Anhangsweise will ich aus dem Kirchero noch ein curiös Clavier hierher setzen, welches er l. c. pag. 519. beschreibt. Er sagt: Ohnlängst ist von einem berühmten und verschmizten Pickelhäringe ein solch Instrument, die Melancholie eines grossen Herrn zu vertreiben, gemacht worden. Er hat Katzen genommen, alle von verschiedener Größe, und hat sie in einen zu der Sache mit Fleiß gemachten Kasten also eingeschlossen, daß die Schwänze durch eine eingeschnittene Oeffnung giengen, und in gewissen Kanälen sich vest gemacht befanden. Die Katzen aber hat er nach ihrer verschiedenen Größe von Ton zu Ton also gesetzt, daß eine jede Palmula auf einen besondern Schwanz einer Katze passete; und hat das zur Belustigung des Fürsten verfertigte Instrument an einem bequemen Orte verborgen, welches aber hernach, da es gespielet worden, eine solche Harmonie von sich hören lassen, dergleichen die Stimmen der Katzen verursachen können. Denn die durch des Organisten Finger niedergedruckten Palmuln haben mit ihren Stacheln in der Katzen Schwänze gestochen, da dann diese darüber tolle geworden, und erbärmlich bald hoch, bald tief, geschryen, daß es die Leute hat können zum Lachen bewegen. Hæc ille. Hierbey erinnere ich, daß ich mir diese Mühe nicht geben möchte, weil eine Katze nicht einen Laut, sondern bald diesen bald jenen von sich hören lässet; daher es vergebens, wenn man sie so stellen wollte, jede nach ihren sono. Ich erinnere mich von einer gleichen Musik etwas in Prinzens Historie Kap. 17. §. 7. gelesen zu haben, und zwar durch Schweine anstatt der Katzen. Die muß auch sehr anmuthig (scilicet) geklungen haben. Doch genug hiervon. (**)   (**) Ach! ja wohl!

Hänfling's Claviatur and Xylorganum.

§. 553.

Next comes the Xylorganum. Kircher describes this sort of keyboard instrument in his *Musurgia*, Vol. I, Book VI, p. 518, always spelling it *Zylorganon*, even though it is derived from ξύλον* "wood." Instead of pipes, in this type of instrument bars of wood, either cylindrical or hexagonal, are arranged harmonically in such a way that when the keys are depressed their hammers strike the bars of wood and create a harmonious sound. Cylindrical wooden bars, 26 in number, must be made of resonant wood that is completely smooth and straight, so that there are exactly two octaves† (but it is also quite possible to make it larger or smaller). The proportions of the wooden bars are identical to the proportions of pipes in an organ. The bars are set above a hollow resonator without ever touching it except along a single line. Hammers are attached to the far end of the keys. [Kircher] has included a sketch with it. Alternately, the wooden bars, skillfully fashioned for this purpose, are laid on straw, and struck with wooden mallets, similar to a dulcimer. The German name for this instrument is "Strohfiedel." Instead of cured wood, charcoal‡ [rods] many be used. But it would be even better to use resonant steel bars, which are very pleasant to listen to.

* Adlung implies that, in light of the Greek word, the spelling ought to be Xylorganum.

† 26 bars would make two octaves plus an extra note.

‡ i.e., carbon.

§. 554.

As a postscript I will describe here yet another curious keyboard instrument that I have taken from Kircher, *l.c.*, p. 519. He writes: not long ago a famous and cunning buffoon fashioned an instrument of a sort intended to banish the melancholy of a great lord. He took cats of various sizes and shut them up in a chest, diligently made just for this purpose, in such a way that their tails protruded through openings cut through it and were secured in certain channels. Then he arranged the cats pitch by pitch, according to their size, assigning each key to a particular cat's tail. For the amusement of his prince he concealed the finished instrument in a convenient spot, and then when it was played, it produced harmony of the type created by the cat's cries; for when the organist's finger depressed the keys, the thorns on the end of them stuck into the cats' tails, driving the animals wild and making them yowl piteously both high and low, for the purpose of making people laugh. This is what [Kircher] says. In this regard let me mention that I would never have gone to this trouble, since a cat does not produce a single tone, but a variety of them; therefore it would be fruitless to try to arrange them pitch by pitch. I remember having read something about a similar [sort of] music in Printz's *Historie*,§ Chap. 17,¶ §. 7, but created by pigs instead of cats. It no doubt must have sounded quite charming as well. But enough of this. (**)   (**) Oh yes, indeed! [Agricola]

§ i.e., *Historische Beschreibung der edelen Sing- und Klingkunst.*

¶ This should read "Chap. 15."

Das XXV. Kapitel.
Von Lautenwerken und Glockenspielen.
Inhalt.

§. 555. Von der Laute und Theorbe. §. 556. ob sie dem Claviere vorzuziehen? §. 557. Mathesons und Barons Meynung. §. 558. das Corpus und die Seyten des Lautenwerks. §. 559. die Stege und der Klang. §. 560. Theorbenoktave. §. 561. Gleichmanns und anderer Lautenwerke. §. 562. zweychörichte. §. 563. Die Glockenspiele. §. 564. wie sie regieret werden? §. 565. durch Claviere. §. 566. 567. Beschreibung einer curiösen Uhr und eines Glockenspiels §. 568. Wiclefs Erfindung. 569. Etwas von Glockenspielen aus Francisci Sittenspiegel. §. 570. Eine die Automata betreffende Anmerkung.

§. 555.

Das Lautenwerk ist das schönste unter den Clavieren nach der Orgel, (**) und hat den Namen daher, weil es die Laute in dem Klange nachahmt, sowol was die Höhe und Tiefe, als auch die Delicatesse betrift. Die Laute selbst heißt Testudo, von der Figur der Schildkröte, die gleichen Namen führt, als welcher sie in sofern ähnlich ist, daß der Rücken oder hintere Theil wie ein Gewölbe krumm gemacht wird. Die Laute wird mit 10, 12 bis 14 Seyten bezogen, zuweilen auch mit 11; denn sie sind nicht alle gleich. Janowka in Claue p. 283. (oder vielmehr 183; denn das Buch ist von pag. 158. an bis zu Ende falsch paginirt) sagt, das Instrument sey bey ihnen so gemein, daß kaum soviel Ziegel auf den Dächern, als Lautenisten wären, und habe es 11. Chöre Seyten; (es sind aber fleischerne oder Darmseyten) die 2 obersten wären einfach, die übrigen doppelt, doch also, daß die 3 nächstfolgenden Chöre ihre Seyten überein klingend haben, oder in unisono, die andern 6 Chöre aber hätten sie in verschiedenen Oktaven. Er hat auch von deren Ambitu und Stimmung von C bis $\overline{\overline{d}}$, oder c bis $\overline{\overline{d}}$, gehandelt. Sie sollen von unten an zu rechnen so gestimmet werden C D E F G A d f a $\overline{d}$ $\overline{f}$. Die oberste Seyte heißt Cantarella, französisch Chanterelle. (welchen Namen auch die kleinsten Seyten auf der Chitarre, Geige, Mandora ꝛc. führen.) Er sagt weiter, daß die untersten 2 Chöre niemals mit den Fingern der linken Hand gegriffen werden, der 3te von unten sehr selten. Die Chöre würden nach der Natur des Modi, woraus man spielen wolle, bald so, bald anders, gestimmet, daß, wo der Modus cis, fis, gis, ꝛc. erfordere, man die Seyten darnach stimmen müsse. Die Laute heißt auch Chelys, bey den Italiänern Liuto; und hat von derselben Prätorius Tomo II. Parte II. cap. 24. pagina 49. mit Vorsatz gehandelt, wohin ich den Leser verweise, weil es dem Organisten eigentlich nichts angehet, als nur in sofern es dienet, die Natur und Struktur des Lautenclaviers zu verstehen. Es hat auch Kircherus in der Musurgia Tom. I. Lib. VI. c. II. p. 476. seqq. von der Laute gehandelt, da er sie auch im Risse hat mit 10. Chören Seyten, deren

---

(**) Nicht jedermann wird dieser Meynung seyn.

Chapter XXV.
Concerning Lute Harpsichords and Carillons

Contents:

§.555. Concerning the lute and theorbo. §.556. Whether they are to be preferred to keyboard instruments. §.557. Mattheson's and Barons's opinions. §.558. The case and strings of the lute harpsichord. §.559. The bridge and the tone. §.560. The theorbo octave. §.561. The lute harpsichords of Gleichmann and others. §.562. Two courses. §.563. Carillons. §.564. How they are operated. §.565. By keyboards. §.566-567. A description of a curious clock and a glockenspiel [connected with it]. §. 568. Wiclef's Invention. §.569. Something about carillons from Franciscus's [*Geschicht-Kunst u.*] *Sittenspiegel*. §.570. A note concerning automatic instruments.*

* See also §.549.

§. 555.

After the organ, the lute harpsichord is the most beautiful of the keyboard instruments,(**) and gets its name from the fact that it simulates the lute in its sound, both in range as well as in delicacy. The lute itself is called [by the Latin name] *Testudo*, because it is shaped like the turtle that bears the same name; it is similar to that animal in that its back or rear section has a bowed shape, like an arch. The lute is strung with 10, 12, or even 14 strings, or sometimes with 11; for not all lutes are identical. In his *Clavis*, p. 283 (or rather 183, since the book is incorrectly paginated from p. 158 to the end), Janowka writes that in his area the instrument is so common that there are hardly as many tiles on the roofs as there are lutenists. The instruments he is familiar with have 11 courses of strings (all of them being animal or gut strings); the two highest ones are single, the others doubled, but in such a way that the [doubled] strings of [each of] the next 3 courses sound at the same pitch, or in unison, while the remaining 6 courses are tuned in octaves at various pitches. He has also discussed its range, C - d'' or c - d''', and its tuning. Figuring from the bass, the strings should be tuned C, D, E, F, G, A, d, f, a, d', f'. The highest string is called the *canterella*, or *chanterelle* in French (the same name given to the highest string of the guitar, the violin and the mandolin). He further writes that the lowest two courses are never, and the third from the lowest very rarely, stopped with the fingers of the left hand. The courses are tuned sometimes this way, sometimes that, according to the make-up of the key in which one wishes to play; e.g., if the key requires c#, f#, g#, etc., then the strings must be tuned accordingly. The lute is also called *chelys*, and among the Italians it is named *liuto*. Praetorius has expressly discussed the lute in [his *Syntagma musicum*,] Vol. II., Part II, chap. 24, p. 49[f.], and I refer the reader there, since this is actually of no concern to an organist except insofar as it helps to clarify the character and structure of the lute harpsichord. In his *Musurgia*, Vol. I, Book VI, chap. II, p. 476f., Kircher also treats the lute, presenting a sketch of it with 10 courses of strings, whose tuning may be seen there as

(**) Not everyone would be of this opinion. [Agricola]

ren Accord dabey zu sehen. Er sagt, die Lauten und Theorben hätten gemeiniglich 10, 12 bis 14 Seytenchöre; und ist die Theorbe (etliche schreiben Thiorba, etliche Tiorba, wie denn Kircher aus Nachläßigkeit dreyerley Schreibarten in wenig Zeilen beysammen hat) von der Laute nur in soweit unterschieden, daß die Laute nur einen, die Theorbe aber einen doppelten Hals hat, welches er daselbst auch in Kupfer vorstellet. Die Franzosen sagen Tuorbe, Téorbe und Theorbe, und soll der Name von einem Neapolitaner seyn, der den Hals zuerst verdoppelt, wovon Kircher l. c. zu lesen. Diese Theorbe hat Hieronymus Capsperger, ein vornehmer Deutscher, so excolirt, und zur Vollkommenheit gebracht, daß es den Vorzug heut zu Tage den andern Instrumenten streitig macht. (**)

(**) Das ist viel gesagt. Es wird vielleicht heißen sollen: **Lauteninstrumenten:** und doch möchte noch nicht jedermann damit zufrieden seyn.

§. 556.

Es hat Kircher auch von den Seyten, von deren Länge und Eintheilung viel gehandelt. Er hat auch die Theorbe in doppelten Seyten vorgestellet, die Cantarella ausgenommen: Prätorius aber sagt, es sey die Theorbe mit der Laute eins, nur daß sie eine Oktave tiefer gehe, und lauter einzelne Seyten habe, wie er denn l. c. cap. 25. pag. 52. von der Theorbe mehr hat. Von deren Erfindung schreibet Prinz in der historischen Beschreibung der edlen Sing= und Kling=Kunst, Kap. 12. §. 20. daß sie von einem Marktschreyer erfunden worden, ohngefähr um das Jahr 1614. Die Laute und Theorbe werden von vielen sehr hoch gehalten, und wer dieselben recht spielen kann, (wozu aber viel gehört, und bey der Theorbe muß einer den Generalbaß von rechtswegen wissen) der wird viel Vergnügen davon haben. Aber daß ich sie von etlichen gar bis an den Himmel und bis über das Clavier habe erheben hören, ist zu viel. Das Clavier ist das vollkommenste und edelste Instrument, und wer demselben den Vorzug vor einer Laute, Harfe u. d. gl. wollte streitig machen, der gäbe zu verstehen, daß er im urtheilen etwas nach Affekten und aus Uebereilung verführe. Ich gestehe, daß man wegen der vielen Seyten viele Veränderungen darauf haben könne, das forte und piano kann man auch haben, indem man mit den Fingern der rechten Hand die Seyten anschlägt, mit der linken aber dazu greift; daher der musikalische Trichter Kap. 10. wohl gesagt, die Laute sey recht bezaubernd, wenn ein Meister drauf komme: Aber die Veränderungen sind lange nicht so, wie auf dem Claviere, da wol viermal soviel Seyten sind, und wo man die Veränderung der Modorum alle Augenblick haben kann, welche erst durch die Verstimmung bey der Laute zuwege gebracht wird: über dieß wird auch die Geschwindigkeit und Manieren keiner auf der Laute nachzumachen sich unterstehen, welche von einem rechten Meister auf dem Claviere angebracht wird. Ja, da man heut zu Tage durch die Wissenschaft des Claviers fast die meisten Instrumente nachmachen kann; so ist auch die Laute selbst darauf zu spielen, wie hernach zu sagen: auch hat man Lautenpedale dazu. (s. das 26. Kapitel.) Auf der Orgel können wir die

Laut=

Chap. XXV. Lute Harpsichords and Carillons

well. He states that lutes and theorbos normally have 10, 12, or 14 courses of strings, and the theorbo (some write *Thiorba*, some *Tiorba*, and out of carelessness Kircher has three spellings within a few lines) is distinct from the lute only in that the lute has only one neck while the Theorbo has two; this he also depicts in a plate.* The French call it *Tuorbe*, *Téorbe*, and *Theorbe*. The name is said to come from a Neapolitan who first constructed a lute with a neck twice as long; † read Kircher, l.c.‡ Hieronymus Capsperger, an eminent German, so refined the theorbo and brought it to perfection that today it contests other instruments for pre-eminence.(**)

* *Iconismus* VII, fig. III, following p. 476.
† i.e., as a normal lute.
‡ p. 476

(**)That is going too far. Perhaps this should read, "[other] lute instruments;" and even then not everyone would be satisfied with it. [Agricola].

§. 556.

Kircher§ also has a lengthy treatment of the strings, their length and arrangement. He depicts the theorbo with doubled strings, with the exception of the *Canterella*. But Praetorius says that the theorbo is the same as the lute, except that it extends an octave lower and has single strings exclusively; he discusses the theorbo further¶ in l.c., Chap. 25, p. 52. Concerning its invention, Prinz writes in his *Historische Beschreibung der edlen Sing-und Kling-Kunst*, Chap. 12, §. 20[, p. 135], that it was invented by a town crier, about the year 1614. Many people hold the lute and theorbo in very high regard, and anyone who can play them properly (which involves a great deal; and to play the theorbo requires by right a knowledge of figured bass) will derive much pleasure from them. But some exalt them to high heaven, even above keyboard instruments, and that is going too far. Keyboard instruments are the most perfect and noblest of all, and for anyone to contest their pre-eminence over the lute, harp, and the like, would suggest that his judgment has been led astray by emotion and rashness/undue haste. I will admit that their many strings permit much variety, and that one can also play loudly and softly on them, since the fingers of the right hand pluck the strings while the left stops the strings; thus [Fuhrmann in] the *Musikalischer Trichter*, Chap. 10, [p.90,] speaks well in saying that the lute is quite enchanting if played by a master. The variety [they can achieve], however, is far less than that on a keyboard instrument, where there are four times as many strings, and where variety in key is instantly available, something that can be achieved on the lute only by re-tuning. Furthermore no one would presume to match on the lute the rapidity [of execution] and the ornaments that a true master can achieve on a keyboard instrument. Indeed, since technology has made it possible today to imitate most instruments on the keyboard, the [sound of the] lute itself can also be had on one, as I will later explain. In addition there are also lute pedals (see Chap. 26‖). The organ can imitate the oboe, trumpet, vi-

§ Vol. I, p. 476.

¶ i.e., after his discussion of the lute in the preceding chapter.

‖ §.604.

Hautbois, Trompet, Violdigamba, Flôte douce ꝛc. nachahmen; außer der Orgel haben wir andere Veränderungen. Was brauchts aber viel Wesens? genung daß wir die Laute auf dem Claviere auch spielen können, und wenn man ja daraus so großen Staat macht; so geht sie doch quoad hoc momentum dem Claviere weit nach.

§. 557.

Es hat Herr Mattheson im Orcheſtre I. P. III. c. III. §. 14. von der Laute also geredet: „Die schmeichelnden Lauten (spricht er) haben mehr Partisans als sie „meritiren, und ihre Profeſſores sind so unglücklich, daß, wenn sie nur nach der „Wienerischen Art, oder nach der Parisischen Manier, ein Paar Alleman- „den daher kratzen können, sie nach der reellen muſikalischen Wissenschaft nicht ein „Härchen fragen, sondern sich mit ihrer Pauvreté recht viel wissen. It. wenn ein „Lautenist 80. Jahr alt wird, so hat er gewiß 60. Jahr gestimmet. Das ärgste „ist, daß unter 100. (insonderheit Liebhabern, die keine Profeßion davon machen) „kaum zwey capabel sind, recht rein zu stimmen, und dabey fehlet es noch über dem „bald an den Seyten, daß sie falsch oder angesponnen, absonderlich die Chanterelle; „bald an den Bünden, bald an den Wirbeln, so, daß ich mir habe sagen lassen, es „koste zu Paris einerley Geld, ein Pferd und Laute zu unterhalten." Diese und noch viel andere Ausdrücke wollten den Liebhabern der Laute gar nicht gefallen. Besonders war zu meiner Zeit in Jena ein Studiosus Juris, ein guter Lautenist, Ernſt Gottlieb Baron genauut, dem es durchaus nicht anstehen wollte, daß Herr Mattheson so spöttisch von der Laute geschrieben, deswegen er einen Traktat schrieb von der Historie der Laute, und darinn den Herrn Mattheson hart angriff. Der Traktat kam 1727. zu Nürnberg auf 14 Bogen in 8. mit Kupfern heraus unter dem Titul: Historisch-theoretische und praktische Untersuchung des Instruments der Laute. Aus diesem Buche ersieht man, daß der Herr Baron ein eben so eifriger Vertheidiger der Laute als ein starker Spieler derselben sey. Jetzo lebt er in Berlin als Königl. Theorbist, nachdem er vorher eine Zeitlang als Lautenist in Eisenach in Diensten gewesen. (**) Die Streitigkeit zwischen ihm und Mattheson mag ich hier nicht noch einmal erzählen, weil ich es schon in meiner Anleitung §. 265. S. 580. gethan habe; wiewol ich mich auch da der möglisten Kürze befliſſen.

(**) Er ist ungefähr im Jahr 1760 in Berlin gestorben.

§. 558.

Doch es möchte vielleicht bis dato einer mir nicht glauben, daß wir die Laute auf dem Claviere auch haben können, derowegen ich zur Sache selbst schreite. Ich habe bis itzt keine gesehen als die Herr J. N. Bach, in Jena verfertiget hat, welche aber gewiß recht schön gerathen. Einige sind fast in Form eines Clavicymbels, und die Seyten sind hinterwärts gelegt. Und weil die Lautenseyten wol in der Dicke,

Chap. XXV. Lute Harpsichords and Carillons 135

oldigamba, traverse flute, etc; and other varieties [in timbre] are available on other instruments as well. But what good is a lot of fuss about this? Suffice [it to say that] it is possible to play the lute from a keyboard. And no matter how big a thing anyone wants to make of it,* up to the present time they are still far inferior to keyboard instruments.

* i.e., the excellence of the lute and theorbo.

§. 557.

In his [*Neu-eröffnete*] *Orchestre* I, P. III, chap. III, §. 14[, pp. 274-6], Mr. Mattheson speaks thus of the lute:† "The cajoling lutes (says he) have more admirers than they deserve; their practitioners are so wretched that they don't give a fig for true musical understanding as long as they can scratch/plunk? out a few allemandes in the Viennese or Parisian fashion, but are confident in their pathetic bit of knowledge. Furthermore, if a lutenist attains the age of 80 years, he has assuredly spent 60 of them tuning. The most annoying thing of all is that out of any 100 of them (amateurs in particular, not professionals), there are hardly two who are capable of tuning precisely. Beyond that, there is always something wrong, either with the strings being faulty or becoming unwound[?] (especially the *chanterelle*), or with the frets, or the wrest pegs; indeed, I would go so far as to say that in Paris it costs as much money to maintain a horse as a lute." These and many other such statements were hardly calculated to please admirers of the lute. In particular, during my time in Jena there was a student of law, Ernst Gottlieb Baron, a good lutenist, who could not abide Mr. Mattheson's derisive remarks about the lute; therefore he wrote a tract on the history of the lute, sharply attacking Mr. Mattheson in it. The tract was published in 1727 at Nuremberg in 14 sheets in octavo, with copper plates, under the title *Historisch- theoretische und praktische Untersuchung des Instruments der Laute*. This book reveals that Mr. Baron is every bit as zealous a defender of the lute as a capable performer on it. He now lives in Berlin, being the Royal Theorbist, after previously having spent some time serving as a lutenist in Eisenach.(**) I will not recount here the dispute between him and Mr. Mattheson, since I have already done it in my Anleitung, §. 265, p. 580[-81], although availing myself there of all possible brevity.

† The following is indeed a quote, but a selective one; Adlung has omitted much of his source.

(**) He died in Berlin about the year 1760. [Agricola]

§. 558.

But up to this point perhaps there is someone who does not believe me [when I say] that it is possible to imitate the lute on the keyboard, and thus I will come right to the heart of the matter. Up until now I have never seen any except the ones built by Mr. J.N. Bach of Jena; those did indeed turn out very beautifully. Some are almost like a harpsichord in shape, with strings strung from front to back. Their strings are like those of the lute, being different from each other in thickness but not in length; or at

nicht aber in der Länge von einander unterschieden sind; so ist es auch allhier: wenigstens trägt der Unterschied der Länge soviel nicht aus, als bey dem Clavicymbel; folglich wird auch das corpus hinten nicht so schmahl und spitzig, als bey dem Clavicymbel. Das übrige an dem corpore ist einerley, wie auch die Decke oder Sangboden, das Clavier, die Docken oder Tangenten, der Anschlag durch Rabenfedern, die Wirbel ꝛc. Der Unterschied bestehet hauptsächlich in den Seyten und Stegen. Es müssen lauter Darmseyten seyn, sonst würde es keinen Lautenklang haben, und deren Länge muß die juste Proportion haben mit der Länge auf der Laute. Von rechtswegen sollte man zu jeder Palmula, in Ansehung der Dicke, eine besondere Seyte haben, wie man auf der Laute zu jedem Chore eine besondere Dicke hat: allein wo will man sie antreffen, da der clavium soviel sind von C bis $\bar{\bar{c}}$? Man muß also mit dem Zirkel die Seytenlänge von der Laute nehmen, und zwar von dem Stege an bis zu dem Finger wenn ich den Ton greife, und diese Länge trage ich auf das Lautenwerk. Nun sind die vordersten Wirbel in einer Weite zu setzen, wie bey dem Clavicymbel, daher folgt, daß man hinten keinen solchen Steg durfe anbringen wie bey einem Clavicymbel, sondern jede Seyte hat ihren besondern Steg, der auf den Sangboden aufgeleget wird, und über einen Zoll nicht groß ist, und wol nicht einmal so groß. Wenn man nun unten im C anhebt, wie sich die Laute anfängt; so nimmt man die Länge der Lautenseyte von dem Halse an bis zu dem Stege, und so lang macht man sie auf dem Lautenwerke vom vordersten Stege bis hinter, und wo die Länge zu Ende, da bringt man den kleinen Steg hin. Das Cis wird etwas kürzer, doch kann eben die Seyte bleiben; also kömmt der hintere Steg etwas weiter vor, soviel als nämlich ½ Ton auf der Laute austrägt. Das D hat auf der Laute seine besondere Seyte; folglich bekömmt das auch hier seine Länge völlig: Das Dis aber verliehrt etwas, soviel als der Seyte abgehet, wenn ich Dis auf der Laute greife. Und so gehts auch mit den folgenden. Wo eine Lautenseyte mehr Griffe hat, als einen, da behält man auch auf dem Lautenwerke eine Seyte etlichemal, und macht sie nur allezeit kürzer, soviel als nämlich durch das Greifen auf der Laut die Seyte kürzer wird. So geht es fort bis ins $\bar{\bar{c}}$. Das übrige mag einer selbst suppliren.

§. 559.

Es liegt aber auf der Laute die Seyte an keinem Drate, sondern oben und unten blos auf hölzernen Stegen: also muß man, wenn man den Klang nicht verfälschen will, auf dem hintersten Stege sowol als auf den vördersten keine Stifte von Drat appliciren, wie bey dem Clavicymbel, sondern die Seyten werden nur über den hölzernen Steg gelegt und an den Wirbeln angemacht, wobey man alle Winkel vermeidet, damit sie nicht zerreissen; auch kann kein Winkel werden, weil die Seyten auf den Stegen frey liegen: doch kann man subtile Kerben machen, und die darein legen. Damit aber die Gewalt der Federn die Seyte nicht hebe; so werden sie auf den Steg angeschraubt, je 2 und 2, unter ein schmales viereckigtes Blätlein. Wenn nun der Sangboden recht subtil gearbeitet wird, wie sonst bey den Lauten, und die Länge der Seyten ist

least the differences in their length are not as great as those of the harpsichord. Consequently the tail of the case is not so narrow and pointed as the harpsichord's. Everything else about the body is identical, as are the soundboard, the keyboard, the jacks, the pluck [accomplished] by raven quills, the wrest pins, etc. The difference consists chiefly in the strings and bridges. The strings must be exclusively of gut, else it would not have the sound of a lute, and their length must be precisely in proportion to those on the lute. By right each key should have its own separate string with its proper thickness, just as each choir on the lute has its own particular thickness; but where is one to find as many [sizes] as there are keys from C to c'''?* Thus the string lengths of the lute have to be measured with a compass, from the bridge to the point at which the finger stops the string to play the pitch, and this length must be transferred to the lute harpsichord. The nearest pins [i.e., the wrest pins] are placed [in a straight row] from side to side, as in a harpsichord, and consequently there can be no such bridge set at the back as there is in a harpsichord. Rather each string has its own separate bridge that is set on the soundboard, not over an inch long and sometimes not even as long as an inch. When beginning at low C (which is where the lute begins), one measures the length of the lute string from the neck down to the bridge, and then makes the string on the lute harpsichord that same length from the bridge nearest [the keyboard] backwards; where that length ends, there the small bridge is set. The C# needs to be a bit shorter, but the same]length of] string can be used for it, by placing the rear bridge somewhat further forward, i.e., the amount equal to a ½ step on the lute. The D on the lute is a separate string, and thus gets its full length on the lute harpsichord; but the D# is somewhat shorter, i.e., the amount the string is shortened when the lute string is stopped at D#. This is how it works with the rest of [the strings] as well. Where a string on the lute is stopped a number of times, strings [of the same length] are also used on the lute harpsichord [the same] number of times, [each successive] one being made shorter† by the same distance that the lute string is shortened when stopped. It continues like this up to c'''; the reader can furnish the rest.

* C - c''' is the range of the lute harpsichord, as Adlung tells us later in this paragraph.

† i.e., the small, separate bridge at the back of the string is moved forward.

§. 559.

The strings on a lute should not be resting on any wire, but exclusively on wooden bridges at both ends. Thus if the tone [of the lute harpsichord] is to be authentic, no wire [guide] pins can be driven into either the back or the front bridge, as in the harpsichord. The strings are merely strung over the wooden bridge and attached to the wrest pins, thereby preventing them from breaking by avoiding any angles. Another reason for avoiding angles is that the strings should lie unconstricted on the bridges; but it is permissible to make slight notches for them to lie in. To keep the force of the pluck from lifting the strings, they are screwed down in groups of two under a narrow rectangular little slip. Now if the soundboard has been planed good and thin (as is the case with lutes), and the length of the strings is in proper proportion

Kap. XXV. Von Lautenwerken u. Glockenspielen.

ist richtig neben ihrer Dicke, sie liegen auf Holz, der Anschlag geschiehet durch die Docken, gleich als wenn es Finger wären; so muß es nothwendig der Laute gleich klingen, und zwar im höchsten Grade und mit weit mehrerer Anmuth: denn das Nachsingen wird hier stärker seyn, weil der Sangboden größer ist, auch weil soviel Seyten da liegen, ganz frey, welche also zugleich ein Singen von sich hören lassen, wenn andere Seyten die mit ihnen harmoniren, angeschlagen werden. Daher Hr. J. N. Bach den besten Lautenisten betrogen hat, wenn er gespielet, und sein Lautenwerk nicht sehen lassen, daß man geschworen hätte, es sey eine ordentliche Laute. Man muß aber stets geschwinde und durch Brechungen spielen, wie man von geschickten Lautenisten zu hören gewohnt ist; auch muß man nicht aus dem Modo gehen: denn wo dieß geschiehet, wird es leicht gemerkt, weil auf der Laute ohne Verstimmung dergleichen Ausweichungen nicht zu haben sind. Z. E. Wenn ich eine Suite aus dem G gespielet, da Fis vorgekommen, und hernach wollte ich gleich aus dem a dur spielen, da cis, fis und gis vorkömmt; so würde ein verständiger Lautenist leicht merken, daß man keine Laute habe, weil man keines Verstimmens nöthig gehabt. Nur mangelt dieß dabey, daß man auf einer Laute das forte und piano haben kann, nachdem die Finger stark oder schwach anschlagen; allein auf dem Claviere kann man es nicht haben: Und wo man nur ein Clavier hat, da ist auch der Sache nicht zu helfen. Um diesen Umstand auch auf dem Lautenwerke nachzuahmen; so macht gedachter Herr Bach 2 oder 3 Claviere, eins forte, wie die Laute ordentlich geht (wiewol wenn sie am stärksten geht, ist doch der Klang noch ziemlich schwach) das andere piano, das dritte piu piano, und dadurch kann man dem Dinge auch etwas abhelfen. Nur fragt es sich: wo die Seyten hinkommen? Antwort: Es schickte sich sehr übel, wenn man wollte doppelte Seyten nehmen, wie auf dem Clavicymbel, oder gar dreyfach: sondern man läßt alle Claviere mit ihren Docken an eine Seyte schlagen. Die Docken stehen neben einander, 3 und 3, wie bey dem Claveßin; sie sind in einer Höhe. Die Federn sind von gleicher Stärke, und doch schlägt eine Reihe Döcken stärker als die andere. Woher kömmt das? Antw. die vörderste Reihe schlägt nicht weit vom Stege an, daher der Klang stark ist; die andere Reihe, oder das mittlere Clavier schlägt weiter vom Stege weg an, und dieß verursachet schon einen schwächern Klang; die hintere Reihe steht vom vördersten Stege am weitesten ab, und schlägt folglich am schwächsten an. Wollte einer von mir rationem physicam wissen, bey dem würde ich mich der hier nöthigen Kürze wegen deßfalls entschuldigen. Aber a posteriori kann es einer nur auf seiner Violine probiren, da er finden wird, je näher er nach dem Stege kömmt mit dem Bogen, desto stärker klingt die Seyte, denn da ist die Spannung der Seyte am größten und stärksten.

§. 560.

Wollte einer den hintern runden Theil der Laute auch mit einbringen unter den Sangboden über dem untersten Boden, der würde erfahren, daß der Klang noch besser

Chap. XXV. Lute Harpsichords and Carillons 137

to their thickness, if they lie across wood, and if the pluck is carried out by the jacks in the same way that fingers would do it, then [a lute harpsichord] of necessity will sound exactly like a lute, and indeed far more authentic and charming; for the resonance [in a lute harpsichord] will be more intense, since the soundboard is larger and since there are so many strings sitting there completely undampened, producing sympathetic vibrations when other strings that harmonize with them are plucked. Thus Mr. J.N. Bach, in playing this instrument out of sight, [was able to] deceive the finest lutenist; one would have sworn that it was a regular lute. But it is necessary to keep playing rapidly and in arpeggios, as skilled lutenists are accustomed to play. It is also necessary to stay in the same key; any modulation will immediately be noticeable, since one cannot depart from the key on a lute without retuning it. For example, if I have played a suite in G, in which f# appears, and thereafter I immediately begin to play in A major, in which c#, f# and g# appear, a competent lutenist would easily notice that it was not a lute, since no retuning was necessary. There is only this shortcoming, that the keyboard cannot produce a *forte* and *piano*, while a lute can do this according to the strength of the pluck by the finger. If there is only one keyboard, then this limitation is unavoidable. In order to imitate this characteristic on the lute harpsichord, the abovementioned Mr. Bach built two or three keyboards, one *forte*, the lute's normal dynamic level (though the tone is rather weak, even at its loudest), the second *piano*, and the third even more *piano*; by doing this he was able to improve the situation somewhat. But the question arises, "How do the strings all fit?"* The answer: It would not do at all to use two or even three choirs of strings, as on the harpsichord; rather the jacks of all the keyboards pluck the same set of strings. The jacks stand next to each other, three by three, as in a harpsichord; they are of the same height.† The quills are of equal stiffness, and yet one row of jacks plucks more loudly than another. How is this possible? Answer: the nearest row plucks not far from the bridge, and therefore the sound is loud; the second row, operated from the middle manual, plucks further back from the bridge, and this already causes a softer sound; the row furthest back stands the furthest from the nearer bridge, and consequently plucks the softest. I apologize that, for the sake of brevity, I cannot explain here the physical cause for this. But anyone who wants to experience this phenomenon can try it out on his violin. There he will find that the nearer he approaches the bridge with his bow, the louder the string sounds, for it is there that the string's tension is the greatest, the most intense.

* i.e., in a lute harpsichord with three keyboards.

† cf. §.518.

§. 560.

If anyone were to introduce the bowed back of a lute under the soundboard and above the bottom [of the instrument], that person would discover that the tone would be even more distinguished. Earlier we learned that the theorbo provides the bass for

sich ausnehme. Da wir nun vorhin gehöret, die Theorbe sey der Baß zur Laute; so hat Herr Bach, um sein Lautenwerk noch mehr zu perfectioniren, noch unten die fünfte Oktave dazu gethan, weil die Theorbe eine Oktave tiefer gehet, als die Laute. Und da nimmt man die Mensur mit dem Zirkel von der Theorbe. Es machte dieser Hr. N. J. Bach seine Lautenwerke gar accurat, daß sie der Laute vollkommen ähnlich klangen. Er machte auch alles sauber und fournirt; auch waren seine Lautenwerke so wie seine Clavicymbel ungemein leichte zu spielen. Und wenn man solche Werke in Acht nimmt, so halten die Seyten gut. Die Federn macht man durch Baumöhl, wie bey den Clavicymbeln, zähe. Er machte sie auch in anderer Figur, und habe ich welche in figura ouali bey ihm gesehen; ja man kann sie auch in Form eines Clavicytherii, oder einer andern Art der oben erzählten Claviere machen, wer sich die Mühe geben will. Es hat ein solch Lautenwerk unbeschreibliche Mühe und Accuratesse vonnöthen; hingegen wird auch ein gut Stück Geld dafür gezahlt, wie ich mich denn besinne, daß Herr Bach für eins mit 3. Clavieren (die aber nur von Buchsbaum und Ebenholz waren) 60. Reichsthaler bekommen. (**)

(**) Eine erschreckliche Summe, nach den heutigen Preißen!

§. 561.

Der Herr Joh. Georg Gleichmann, den wir oben wegen seiner Claviergamba gelobt, und der überhaupt ein guter Mechanikus ist, macht auch Lautenclaviere, welche forte, piano und pianissimo gespielt werden mögen, wie von ihm die Critica Musica To. I. pag. 254. anführt. Allein von dieser Arbeit habe ich nichts gesehen, weis also nicht, ob sie der Bachischen gleich kömmt. Sonst hat man auf Clavicymbeln, wie §. 514. angemerkt worden, auch einen Lautenzug; allein das klingt ganz anders, und hat nichts ähnliches in sich, als daß dadurch das helle Singen der Dratseyten gehemmet wird, als wären es Darmseyten. Die Proportion aber ist nicht wie auf der Laute. Sind doch die Davidsharfen auch mit Darmseyten bezogen, und doch ist der Harfenklang mit dem Lautenklange gar nicht einerley.

§. 562.

Die Lauten haben unten 2 Seyten zu jedem Chor, oben aber eine, und muß man auf dem Lautenwerke es auch so machen. Wie weit es 1 oder 2 Chöricht seyn müsse, ist von der Laute abzusehen; wie denn in etlichen doppelten Chören die Seyten in unisono sind, in andern nicht. Das observire man alles. Alsdann stehen auf jedem claue 2 Reihen Docken, deren eine zur rechten, die andere zur linken Seite anschlägt. Es bekommen die Lautenwerke keine Stimmen, wie die Claveßins, oder Stege, weil die Seyten hier keine Winkel aufwärts machen, wie bey den Claveßins, und folglich die Decke nicht unterwärts drücken können. Nur muß man sie an den Wirbeln nicht allzu

the lute. Thus in order to perfect his lute harpsichord even more, Mr. Bach added a fifth octave in the bass, since the theorbo extends an octave lower than the lute. In this case it is necessary to derive the scale from the theorbo with a compass. Mr. N. J.* Bach built his lute harpsichords very precisely, so that they sounded exactly like a lute. He also built everything neatly and veneered. Like his harpsichords, his lute harpsichords had an unusually light touch. If such instruments are taken care of, then the strings last a long time. As on the harpsichord, the quills are made tough by olive oil. I have seen [J. N. Bach] make lute harpsichords in another shape; I observed one the shape of an oval at his [home]. But anyone who wants to take the trouble can also make them in the form of a clavicytherium or any other type of keyboard instrument described above. An instrument such as the lute harpsichord requires indescribable labor and precision. On the other hand, it also commands a goodly price. I remember Mr. Bach getting 60 Reichsthaler for one with three manuals (it was, however, made entirely of boxwood and ebony). (**)

* sic; should be "J. N." (Johann Nicolaus).

(**) A frightful sum of money by today's prices! [Agricola]

§. 561.

Mr. Joh. Georg Gleichmann, who was commended above for his Claviergamba,† and who is indeed a good craftsman, also makes keyboard lutes that can be played forte, piano, and pianissimo, as is credited him in [Mattheson's] *Critica Musica*, Vol. I, p. 254. I have, however, not ever seen one of these instruments, and therefore do not know if they measure up to Mr. Bach's. To be sure, there is a buff stop on the harpsichord, as noted in §. 514, but it sounds completely different, the only similarity to gut strings being that it impedes the bright ring of the metal strings. But the proportion [of the strings] is not the same as on the lute. The harp of David‡ is likewise strung with gut strings, yet the sound of the harp is not at all like that of the lute.

† See §.543.

‡ i.e., the ordinary harp of Adlung's day.

§. 562.

Lutes have 2 strings for each course in the bass, but only one in the treble, and the lute harpsichord should follow this model. How much of it should be with single or double strings can be learned from the lute; in some of the double courses the strings are [tuned in] unison, but not in others§—heed all of this. Then on every key there are 2 jacks, one plucking on the right side [of the string] and one plucking on the left. Lute harpsichords do not have soundposts, as do harpsichords, nor do they have bridges,¶ since the strings do not rise up at [as sharp] an angle here as they do in a harpsichord, and consequently they cannot press the soundboard down. It is only necessary to be careful not to wind them down too far on the wrest pins. Violins

§ See §.555.

¶ Apparently this statement refers to the far bridge, the one that (in a harpsichord) rests on the sound board. The lute harpsichords that Adlung is describing do not have one long bridge in that location, but many small ones.

Kap. XXV. Von Lautenwerken u. Glockenspielen.   139

allzu tief winden. So müssen z. E. die Violinen und dergleichen, Stimmen (**) haben, weil sonst die Decke allzu sehr gedruckt würde, daß die durch die Bewegung der Seyten bewegte Luft die Decke nicht gehöriger maaßen in eine Bewegung setzen kann, welches doch allezeit geschehen muß.

(**) Eine Stimme in der Violine heißt eine kleine hölzerne Stütze, zwischen der Decke und dem untersten Boden, die aber an einem gewissen gar nicht willkührlichen Orte stehen muß. Das wissen zwar die Violinisten, aber nicht alle andere Leute.

Wollte man Clavierharfen oder Harfenwerke verfertigen; so nähme man die Proportion und die Struktur der Harfe vor sich, und machte dergleichen darnach, welches viel leichter werden würde, als bey den Lautenwerken. Ja man kann auch andere Werke auf das Clavier bringen. Doch dabey kann ich mich nicht aufhalten, weil mein Vorsatz nur dahin gehet, einem Organisten von solchen Dingen eine generale Erkänntniß beyzubringen. (**)

(**) Der Verfaßer dieser ** Anmerkungen erinnert sich, ungefähr im Jahre 1740. in Leipzig ein von dem Hrn. Johann Sebastian Bach angegebenes, und vom Hrn. Zacharias Hildebrand ausgearbeitetes Lautenclavicymbel gesehen und gehöret zu haben, welches zwar eine kürzere Mensur als die ordentlichen Clavicymbel hatte, in allem übrigen aber wie ein ander Clavicymbel beschaffen war. Es hatte zwey Chöre Darmseyten, und ein sogenanntes Octävchen von meßingenen Seyten. Es ist wahr, in seiner eigentlichen Einrichtung klang es, (wenn nämlich nur ein Zug gezogen war,) mehr der Theorbe, als der Laute ähnlich. Aber, wenn der bey den Clavicymbeln sogenannte, und auch hier §. 561. angeführte Lautenzug, (der eben so wie auf den Clavicymbeln war,) mit dem Cornetzuge gezogen wurde, so konnte man auch bey nahe Lautenisten von Profeßion damit betrügen. Herr Friderici hat auch dergleichen gemacht, doch mit einiger Veränderung.

§. 563.

Es folgen die gewaltigen Glockenspiele, wie sie das Orchestre I. nennet, dergleichen in Darmstadt, Stockholm, Hamburg, sonderlich in Nikolaithurme sind, da bey dem lezten auch ein Pedal ist, und worauf ein rechter Meister schöne gebrochne Sachen spielen kann. s. kaum angeführtes Orchestre I. P. III. §. 13. Im Anhange zum Niedt sagt Mattheson, daß dieses Glockenspiel 48. Glocken habe, deren Größte $\frac{1}{2}$ Ton sey, und mit dem Claviere des Hinterwerks regieret werde. Sonst sind dergleichen Glockenspiele auch zu sehen in Deventer, Schwoll, Amsterdam, Enkhüsen, Berlin, Potsdam und andern Oertern mehr, welche zum Theil mit einem Claviere regiert werden, nicht aber mit Fingern, sondern mit Fäusten, zum Theil aber durch Wellen und anhangendes Gewicht, deren Auflösung durch die Uhr verrichtet wird. Die Glocken werden von Meßing, auch von Erz, gegossen: (von Silber möchte es allzu kostbar werden;) doch müssen sie gar accurat gemacht werden, daß ihre Weite, Höhe und Stärke recht proportionirt ist, sonst wird der Klang confus werden, und nicht durchaus äqual oder proportionirt. Sie müssen auch vollkommen rein gestimmt werden: doch kann man durch das Abschleifen denen etwas helfen, die zu groß gerathen

S 3.   sind.

Chap. XXV. Lute Harpsichords and Carillons

and other like instruments, for example, must have soundposts,(**) since otherwise the soundboard receives so much pressure that the air set into motion by the vibration of the strings cannot adequately set the soundboard moving (yet it is essential that this happen).

> (**) A soundpost in a violin is a small wooden support between the soundboard and the back plate, that must be placed at a very specific spot, not just wherever one wishes. Violinists know this, of course, but many other people do not. [Agricola]

If anyone should wish to build a keyed harp or a Harfenwerk,* [here is how to do it]: first take note of the proportions and the structure of the harp, and then build the instrument according to these. This would be much easier that building a lute harpsichord. Indeed, a keyboard can be incorporated into other instruments as well. But I cannot dwell on this, because my intent extends only as far as imparting to an organist a general knowledge of such things.(**)

> (**) The author of these notes marked by ** remembers having seen and heard a lute harpsichord in Leipzig about the year 1740, designed by Mr. Johann Sebastian Bach and made by Mr. Zacharias Hildebrand. This instrument had a shorter scale than an ordinary harpsichord, to be sure, but in all other particulars it was constituted just like any other harpsichord. It had two choirs of gut strings, together with a so-called "little octave" of brass strings.† True, in its normal setting (when only one stop was drawn) it sounded more like the theorbo than the lute. But if the buff stop, as it is called in the harpsichord and also cited here in §. 561 (which operated just like the ones on harpsichords), were drawn with the *Cornetzug*,‡ one could almost deceive professional lutenists with it. Mr. Friderici§ has also made such an instrument, but with several differences. [Agricola]

§. 563.

Next come the mighty carillons (Glockenspiele), as [Mattheson's *Neu-eröffnete*] *Orchestre* [Vol.] I calls them, such as are found in Darmstadt, Stockholm, and Hamburg—in particular in the tower of the Nikolaikirche there. This last-named instrument has a pedal as well, and an accomplished master can play beautiful arpeggiated pieces on it; see Vol. I, Part III, [Chap. III,] §. 13¶ of the [*Neu-Eröffnete*] *Orchestre* just mentioned. In his appendix to Niedt's [*Musicalischer Handleitung anderer Teil*, p. 195], Mattheson says that this carillon has 48 bells, the largest of which weighs two tons,‖ and that it is operated by the Hinterwerk manual** [of the organ]. Such carillons are also to be found in Deventer, Zwolle, Amsterdam, Enkhuizen, Berlin, Potsdam and a number of other places. Some of these are played with a keyboard, though not with the fingers but with fists. Others are played by barrels [driven by] suspended weights, whose release is triggered by a clock. The bells are cast in brass or bronze (silver would be far too expensive), but they must be made very precisely so that their breadth, height and thickness are in correct proportion; otherwise their sound becomes muddled and not equal or balanced throughout [the entire compass]. They must also be tuned absolutely perfectly, which can be accomplished to some extent by grinding down the ones that have been cast too large. If a carillon is to be precisely [in tune],

---

* Also referred to today as a "harp-piano."

† at 4′ pitch?

‡ Neither Adlung nor Agricola explains this term. It may refer here to the 4′ stop with brass strings, but it more likely refers to a special set of jacks with brass plectra. Harpsichords built in Thuringia sometimes had such a set of jacks, as does the harpsichord by Christian Ernst Friederici of Gera that was owned by the Mozart family. For a description and photograph of this sort of jack, see: John Henry van der Meer, "A Little-Known German Harpsichord," in: Early Keyboard Studies Newsletter (a publication of the Westfield Center for Early Keyboard Studies), Vol. V, No. 3 (March 1991), p. 11.

§ probably Christian Ernst; he is mentioned in another note by Agricola elsewhere in this treatise, in connection with the Trost organ at Altenburg, in the *Zusatz zum Zehnten Kapitel*, Vol. I, p. 286.

¶ p. 273-4.

‖ The list of errata at the end of the book corrects the text, which reads here "a half a ton."

** cf. §.565. This sentence suggests that the carillon in question is at the Nikolaikirche in Hamburg, but Adlung is in fact referring to the one at the Nikolaikirche at Rostock.

sind. Soll ein Glockenspiel accurat werden; so muß man die Temperatur auch genau beobachten. Es werden diese Glocken in der Ordnung hingehänget, doch so, daß sie nicht wanken, und unter, zuweilen auch ausser der Glocke wird ein Hämmerchen angebracht, das darauf schlägt. Allein es würde der Klang bald unterdrückt werden, oder ein Rasseln entstehen, wo der Hammer auf der Glocke liegen bliebe; daher unter jedem Hammer eine Feder anzubringen, welche denselben gleich wieder zurücke stößt. Will man aber von der Proportion der Glocken weiter unterrichtet seyn; so schlage man Kircheri *Musurgiam* nach, L. VI. To. I. pag. 519. u. folg; Insbesondere aber von den Glocken bey den Glockenspielen To. II. Lib. VIIII. pag. 336. da er auch die Theile des Glockenspiels im Risse vorstellt.

§. 564.

Man sieht daselbst, daß die Bewegung solcher Hämmerchen, und die Bewegung des ganzen Werks entweder durch den Wind geschehe, daher die Camera æolica (Windkammer) gebauet werden muß, wozu er einigen Unterricht giebt, da er sie auf verschiedene Arten machen lehrt p. 308. u. f; Doch das geht den Organisten wenig an: Oder es wird das Werk regieret durch horizontal oder vertical angebrachte Cylinder oder Wellen, wie bey dem Organo portatili geschehen, als worauf die Melodien abgestochen werden durch eingeschlagene Stifte oder Arme. Wenn nun durch ein Gewicht dieser Cylinder gedrehet wird, wie bey einem Uhrwerke die Räder; so treffen diese Stifte oder Arme auf diejenigen, daran die Hämmerchen durch Abstrakten bevestiget sind, und regen dieselben, und verursachen den Anschlag. Zu der Abtheilung der Cylinder gehöret große Accuratesse, und geräth dieß selten recht.

§. 565.

Doch dieses itzt gesagte gienge den Organisten wenig an, wo man nicht die Glockenspiele auch durch Claviere regierte, wie §. 563. dergleichen aus einer Orgel angeführet ist. Man hat sie aber auch ausser der Orgel; doch kann man sich leicht einbilden, daß sie etwas schwer zu spielen sind, indem die Hämmerchen, zumal wo große Glocken sind, durch die Federn zurück getrieben werden. Bisweilen gehen sie durch das ganze Clavier, bisweilen hat man nur 2 oder 3 Oktaven. Ich habe vor etlichen Jahren ein schön Kunststück von einer Uhr gesehen, dabey ein Glockenspiel war, wovon ich doch curiositatis caussa etwas erzählen will, weil es sich der Mühe verlohnt.

§. 566.

Das Gehäuse war 9 Schuhe hoch und 2 Schuhe breit und dicke. Oben drauf präsentirte sich der Berg Golgatha mit der Gefangennehmung und Kreuzigung Christi, so alles durch die Uhr beweglich war. Unter denen, welche dem Herrn Christum gefangen nehmen wollten, war Judas, der sich im Vorbeygehen, anstatt des Kusses vor dem Herrn Christo bückete, worauf die Kriegsknechte den Herrn Christum umringeten, da denn Petrus mit dem Schwerte dem Hohenpriesters Knechte Malcho nach dem Ohr hieb,

the temperament must also be carefully attended to. These bells are suspended in order [of their size], but in such a way that they do not swing; and underneath each bell (or sometimes outside it) is mounted a mallet that strikes it. The sound would soon be suppressed, however, or a rattling would arise, if the mallet were allowed to remain resting on the bell. Thus under each mallet is mounted a spring that immediately thrusts it back away [from the bell]. If anyone would like further information about the proportions of the bells, consult Kircher's *Musurgia*, Book VI, Vol. I, p. 519f. For specific information about bells in carillons, see Vol. II, Book IX, p. 336,* where Kircher presents a sketch of the components of a carillon.

* *Iconismus* XIX.

§. 564.

There [i.e., in Kircher] it is evident that the movement of the mallets and the operation of the entire instrument may be effected by the wind. In that case a *camera æolica* or wind chamber must be constructed, and [Kircher] offers some information about how to do this by teaching various ways of making such a chamber (pp. 308f.). But this is of little concern to an organist. Alternatively [Kircher says] the instrument may be operated by means of barrels or rollers mounted either horizontally or vertically, as in an *Organon portatile*;† pins or pegs are driven into these to produce the melodies. When this barrel is driven by a weight, like the gears of a clock, then these pins or pegs come into contact with the [keys or levers] that are connected to the mallets by trackers, activating them [i.e., the mallets] and causing them to strike. Dividing off the barrel [to position the pins] requires great precision and seldom comes out correctly.

† cf. §.549.

§. 565.

But this last matter would be of little concern to an organist, if carillons could not also be operated from keyboards, just as §.563 has cited one operated from an organ [keyboard]. Carillons are also built apart from organs, but as you can well imagine, they are rather difficult to play (especially the ones with large bells), in that the mallets are forced back by springs. Sometimes their compass is as great as the entire keyboard,‡ but sometimes they extend only 2 or 3 octaves. Several years ago I saw a delightfully clever device. Within a clock there was a carillon, and I am going to tell about it for curiosity's sake, since it is worth the trouble to do so.

‡ i.e., 4 octaves.

§. 566.

The case was 9 feet high and 2 feet wide and deep. On top was depicted the mountain Golgotha with the arrest and crucifixion of Christ, and [the gears of] a clock caused the entire scene to move. Among those who were attempting to take the Lord Christ prisoner was Judas who, as he passed by, bowed down before the Lord Christ instead of kissing him, whereupon the soldiers surrounded the Lord Christ. Then Peter slashed with his sword at the ear of Malchus, the High Priest's servant, who made

Kap. XXV. Von Lautenwerken u. Glockenspielen.   141

hieb, der vor Schrecken und Schmerzen wunderliche Posituren machte. Es brachte auch einer den Herrn Christum mit dem Kreuze an einem Stricke geführet, und schlug im Fortgehen unterschiedlichemal auf ihn. Oben war die große Schlaguhr, um welche die 12 Apostel herumgiengen, welche mit ihren in Händen habenden Hämmern so vielmal an die Glocke schlugen, als es die Stunde erforderte. Auf der linken Seite stund ein Hahn, der, so oft es zwey Viertel schlug, mit beyden Flügeln, welche recht natürlich mit Federn gemacht waren, flatterte, den Hals zugleich in die Höhe streckte, den Schnabel aufsperrete, und einen ordentlichen Hahnenschrey that. Dieß hätte nicht natürlicher seyn können. Wenn es 3 Viertel schlug; so sang eine auf der rechten Seite stehende Amsel mit recht natürlicher Bewegung ein Präludium, etwan so, wo ich es nicht vergessen habe:

[Notenbeispiel]

Die Amsel war so natürlich gemacht, und mit Federn versehen, und die Stimme war ausnehmend schön. Beydes sowol der Amselgesang als auch der Hahnenschrey wurde durch einen inwendig liegenden Balg, und durch etliche angebrachte Pfeifchen (deren bey der Amsel 5. waren) verrichtet, die durch dratene Abstrakten geöfnet wurden; alles aber wurde durch Wellen und Räder verrichtet. (Sonst hat Kircher l. c. da er die automata machen lehrt, auch gezeigt, wie der Hahnen und anderer Thiere Geschrey durch Formirung hölzerner Körper und Glieder nachzumachen; doch dieß war anders.) Es präsentirte sich die Mutter Gottes den 25sten December mit unserm Heilande auf dem Arme. Denn es war inwendig ein großes Rad, welches in einem Jahre nur einmal herum kam, dieß brachte sie zu der Weinachtzeit sammt dem Christkindlein hervor. Sie war klein, etwann 1½ Finger lang, und stund in einem Behältnisse welches sich drehete. Wenn Maria die 3 Feyertage haussen gestanden, so drehete sich das Häuschen durch die Uhr wieder herum und verbarg sie wieder. Auf Heil. 3. Könige kam Herodes einen Taglang zum Vorschein. Die Uhr bestund im Zeiger der Minuten und Stunden, wobey des Mondes Ab- und Zunehmen durch das ganze Jahr, wie in der Luft, vollkommen schön observiret wurde; desgleichen auch der Sonnen Lauf, welcher zugleich des Tages und der Nächte Länge, nebst dem Auf- und Untergange, mit einem ordentlichen Stundenweiser accurat zeigete. Es war auch daran ein Zeiger, der die Monathe, Feste und Namenstage durchs ganze Jahr, wie auch die 12 himmlischen Zeichen, anzeigete, und also einen immerwährenden Kalender präsentirte. Noch war ein großer Zeiger, und mitten auf demselben noch ein kleiner, der link zeigete; beyde aber wiesen nur die Stunden.

§. 567.

Endlich, welches uns eben angehet, und weswegen wir es erzahlen, war ein **Glockenspiel** dabey, welches aus 29. meßingenen Glocken bestund, deren die Größte
wol

Chap. XXV. Lute Harpsichords and Carillons

strange contortions for fear and pain. Another led with a rope the Lord Christ bearing the cross, and struck him several times while they were passing by. On top was the large striking-clock, around which the 12 apostles revolved. They struck the chime the requisite number of times, according to the hour, with mallets that they held in their hands. On the left side there stood a cock that flapped both its wings (which were made quite naturally, with feathers) at the half hour, and at the same time stretched out his neck, opened his beak and let out a proper cocks-crow. This could not have been more realistic. At three quarters of the hour a blackbird standing on the right side sang with very natural motions a *praeludium*, something like this, if my memory serves me correctly:

The blackbird was very realistically made, even with feathers, and its voice was exceptionally beautiful. Both the blackbird's song and the cocks-crow were accomplished by means of a bellows lying inside [the case] together with a number of pipes that were mounted there (there were 5 of them for the blackbird). These pipes were operated by wire trackers, and the whole [operation] was accomplished by barrels and gears. (Kircher, l.c., in discussing the *automata** [i.e., mechanical instruments], also shows how to imitate the sounds of roosters and other animals by fashioning wooden bodies and limbs; but [this device] was different [than his].) On the 25th of December the Mother of God appeared with our Savior on her arm. On the inside there was a large wheel that rotated only once in a year, and this is what brought her forth together with the Christ child at Christmastime. She was small, about 1½ fingers long, and stood in a shrine that revolved.† After Mary had remained visible for the 3 festival days,‡ the clock caused the little shrine [containing her] to revolve and again hid her. On Epiphany Herod came into view for a day. The clock consisted of a minute hand and an hour hand, and the wax and wane of the moon throughout the entire year were also beautifully displayed, exactly as in the sky. The course of the sun was likewise displayed, this being indicated by an ordinary hour-hand, together with the lengths of days and nights and sun's rising and setting. There was also a hand that indicated the months, holidays and name-days throughout the whole year, as well as the 12 signs of the zodiac, thus presenting a perpetual calendar. In addition there was a large hand with a small one on top of it pointing backward[?]; both of them, however, only indicated the hour.

§. 567.

Finally—and this is what concerns us and why we are describing [this device]—there was a carillon [Glockenspiel] in it, consisting of 29 brass bells of which the

---

* *Musurgia*, Book IX, Vol. II, p. 343f.

† presumably on the wheel.

‡ The reference is unclear. The festival of Christmas traditionally lasts for 12 days. December 25 is Christmas Day, Dec. 26 is the Feast of St. Stephen, Dec. 27 is the Feast of St. John the Apostle, and Dec. 28 is the Feast of the Holy Innocents. It is possible that Adlung's statement should be interpreted in the sense of "...three of the festival days..."

wol keine 4tel Elle im Durchschnitte hatte. Dabey war ein Clavier, welches aus drey Oktaven bestund, darauf man spielen konnte, was man wollte; doch war es etwas zähe, wie ich, indem ich es selbst gespielt, anmerkte. Auf der andern Seite war aber auch eine Welle angebracht, die das Glockenspiel regierte, und die allezeit, wenn die Uhr schlug, von den Rädern regiert und gedrehet wurde, daß das Glockenspiel einen geistlichen Choral hören ließ, und zwar alle Stunden einen andern, bis es nach 12. Stunden wieder vornen anfing, weil der Chorale 12. waren, unter welchen sich nachfolgende hören ließen, als: Jesu, meines Lebens Leben; Freu dich sehr, o meine Seele; Nun bitten wir den heiligen Geist: O Gott du frommer Gott; und doch war es nur eine Welle, welche auch nicht anders durfte gestellet werden, als bis nach 12. Stunden. Sie stund perpendiculär, und hatte etwan im Durchschnitte $1\frac{1}{2}$ viertelellen, und die Länge mochte etwann $2\frac{1}{2}$ Ellen seyn. Die Stifte waren nur von Drat hinein geschlagen, gar klein, wie auf dem Clavichord, da man hinter dem Tuche die Seyten anhänget, dadurch regierte es die Hämmer. Soviel ich mich besinne, durfte die Welle nur einmal herumgehen, ehe ein Vers aus wurde, und unter dem Drehen senkte sich die Welle um etwas weniges, daß also, wenn sie über eine Stunde wieder in Bewegung gebracht wurde, andere Stifte die Hämmer regieren konnten, und zwar nicht nur den Diskant, sondern es gieng auch der Baß dazu und die Mittelstimmen, doch die leztern meistens gebrochen. Es hatte der damals lebende Gothaische Uhrmacher, der über die Uhren des Landes gesezt war, dieß künstliche Werk verfertiget, und wollte damit nach Wien reisen; um es zu verkaufen, wo mir recht ist, für 600. Reichsthaler. Er reisete damit durch Erfurt, bey welcher Gelegenheit man es im Gasthofe zum Propheten, wo er eingekehrt war, sehen konnte. Dieser Mann hatte die Kunst von sich selbst erlernet, d. i. er hatte in keiner ordentlichen Lehre gestanden, und sahe dabey simpel und gering aus, daß man solche Dinge in ihm nimmermehr gesucht hätte. An dem gedachten Werke sahe man viel curiöse Dinge, aber es gieng damit alles natürlich und begreiflich zu, ohne daß man nöthig gehabt hätte, es für Hexerey zu halten, wie es damals einige Leute ausschreyen, und den ehrlichen Mann eines commercii cum dæmonibus beschuldigen wollten.

§. 568.

Daß man auch ein Glockenspiel in einem Clavicymbel anbringen könne, lieset man in Mizlers musikalische Bibliothek, im 2ten Theile des ersten Bandes, S. 76. allwo er von Anspach meldet, daß der Orgelmacher Wiclef daselbst eine besondere Erfindung habe, ein Glockenspiel in einem Clavicymbel anzubringen, indem er nicht nur die Glocken aus selbst zusammengesezten Stoff so giesset, daß sie hell und rein klingen, sondern sie auch durch das Abdrehen aufs beste zu stimmen weis. Dieß muß allerdings was schönes seyn, und wünschte ich mir selbst ein solches Instrument zu besitzen. Da ich aber dergleichen nie habe zu sehen bekommen können; so wird der geneigte Leser mit der bloßen Anzeige vorlieb nehmen.

§. 569.

largest was not even a quarter of an ell in diameter. It had a keyboard consisting of three octaves, on which one could play anything one wished; its [action], though, was rather stiff, as I noted when playing it. On the other side there was also mounted a barrel that operated the glockenspiel. Every time the clock struck the hour, the barrel was turned by the gears, causing the glockenspiel to play a sacred chorale, a different one each hour for 12 hours, after which it began again. Thus there were 12 chorales, among which could be heard the following: *Jesu, meines Lebens Leben*; *Freu dich sehr, O meine Seele*; *Nun bitten wir den heiligen Geist*; *O Gott du frommer Gott*. Yet there was only one barrel, which could not be positioned differently until 12 hours were past. It stood upright, being about 3/8 of an ell in diameter and about 2½ ells long. The pins were just very small [pieces of] wire driven into [the barrel], like [the hitchpins] behind the cloth on a clavichord, on which the strings are hooked. It was by means of [these pins] that it operated the mallets. As best I remember, the barrel had to rotate only once before a verse was finished, and while it was rotating it sank ever so slightly. Thus when it was again set into motion an hour later, other pins were in a position to operate the mallets. It played not only the treble [i.e., the melody], but the bass and the inner voices as well; the latter, though, were mostly arpeggiated. The clockmaker living at that time in Gotha who was in charge of that principality's clocks built this skillful piece of work. He intended to travel with it to Vienna and sell it for 600 *Reichsthaler*, if I remember correctly. On the way he traveled through Erfurt with it, thus offering the opportunity for it to be seen at the *Gasthof zum Propheten*, where he was lodged. This man was self-taught, i.e., he had never served a normal apprenticeship; he seemed so naïve and humble that no one would ever have expected such a thing from him. There were many curious things to see in the piece of work described above, but everything worked realistically and comprehensibly, without having to attribute anything on it to witchcraft. Some people did indeed cry out at that time, trying to accuse that honest man of dealing with demons.

§. 568.

Mizler's *Musikalische Bibliothek*, Vol. I, Part II, p. 76, reveals that it is possible to install a glockenspiel in a harpsichord. [Mizler] reports that the organbuilder Wiclef in Ansbach has made an unusual invention by installing a glockenspiel in a harpsichord, in which he not only cast the bells out of a material he himself compounded, so that they sounded bright and clear, but also knew how to tune them expertly by filing them off. This must be something beautiful indeed; I wish I owned such an instrument myself. But since I have never had the chance to see an example of one, I beg the kind reader to be satisfied with the mere notice [about it].

§. 569.

Noch eins will ich dazu thun von Glockenspielen aus Erasmi Francisci Geschicht-Kunst-u. Sittenspiegel, S. 1316. u. folg. des 4ten Buchs, da er sagt: „Die „Sineser machen Werke von Erz, um einen Schall oder Klang damit zu geben: als „die Glocken, welche von unterschiedlicher Form und Klang fallen, nachdem sie kleiner „oder größer, und nicht unlieblich zusammen thönen; schier auf die Wiese, wie in Nie„derlande die auf den Thürmen oder Kirchen spielenden Glocken; wiewol diese recht „nach der Kunst geordnet sind, und wie ein Instrument oder Real Clavier gespielt wer„den. Mit welchen die Kirchthürme zu Deventer, Schwoll, Amsterdam, Enkhü„sen ꝛc. den durchreisenden Leuten eine besondere Anmuth machen, so oft die Uhren schla„gen. ∙ ∙ ∙ Die Claviere solches Werks müssen zwar mit den Fäusten nieder geschla„gen werden; weil die Finger zu schwach, doch kann man ein Clavicymbel von 49. „Glöcklein zurichten; daran die Claviere eben so leicht und wohl mit den Fingern be„griffen werden, als an den Spinetten und Orgeln. Wenn dann die Glocken mit höl„zernen Klöppeln gelinde geschlagen werden, indem ein jeder clavis seinen gewissen „Schwengel oder Knöpfel auf oder nieder ziehet; so übertrifft ein solch Glockenspiel al„le Süßigkeit der Seyten. Mersennus schreibt, das Glockenspiel in dem Thurm zu „St. Marien in Deventer bestehe aus 33. Glocken, auch gleich so viel Stricken und „Hammern oder Knöpfeln; unter welchen die größte einen groben Klang giebt. Der „Schwengel in der größten, wie die andern, ist am Stricke gebunden; doch gehen „die in Enkhüsen und Schwoll weit lieblicher, wenn sie noch so vollkommen sind, wie „zu meiner Zeit. Die Sineser hängen an die Absätze der Thürme Glöcklein, die der „Wind anbläst, und ein lieblich Getön macht." So weit Francisci. Er hat es auch in Kupfern vorgestellet.

§. 570.

Was sonst solche Automata betrifft, die durch Wellen oder Cylinder regiert werden; so ist zu wissen, daß man auch den Cylinder vor das Clavier machen könne, so, daß er durch Zacken die Palmuln niederdrücke, welcher Cylinder mit der Hand kann herum gedrehet werden, oder durch ein Wasserrad, oder Gewichte, oder elateria ꝛc. und kann man vielerley Wellen haben zur Abwechselung. (conf. de Chales l. c. prop. 39.)

Das XXVI. Kapitel.
Von dem Clavichord und Pedal.

Inhalt.

§. 571. Von dem Namen des Clavichords.   §. 572. 573. die Historie desselben.   §. 574. das Corpus. §. 575. die übrigen Haupttheile. §. 576. Wie sie stark und schwach klingen, und von den Registern

Chap. XXV. Lute Harpsichords and Carillons

§. 569.

I would like to add something else about carillons (Glockenspielen[*]) from Erasmus Franciscus's *Geschicht-Kunst-u. Sittenspiegel*, Book IV, p. 1316f.,[†] where he says: "The Chinese make instruments of bronze to give them a ringing sound like bells. They assume various shapes and sounds, according to whether they are smaller or larger, and sound quite lovely together, [wafting] clearly over the meadow like the bells that ring in the church towers in the Netherlands; although the latter are arranged quite artfully and played like an Instrument or a royal keyboard (Real Clavier[‡]). It is by these that the church towers at Deventer, Zwolle, Amsterdam, Enkhuizen, etc., greatly delight those who pass by, whenever the clocks strike... The keyboards of such instruments must be struck with the fists, to be sure, since fingers are too weak; but it is possible to construct a harpsichord with 49 little bells, on which the keys are just as light and easy for the fingers to play as those on spinets and organs. If the bells are struck gently with wooden mallets, by giving each key its own clapper or striker to raise or lower, then such a glockenspiel[§] greatly exceeds the sweetness of strings. Mersenne[¶] writes that the carillon in the tower of St. Mary's Church at Deventer[||] consists of 33 bells, with an equal number of ropes and mallets or strikers, the lowest [bell] of which produces a rough (groben) sound. The clapper in the largest [bell], like that of all the others, is also tied to a rope. The [carillons] at Enkhuizen and Zwolle, though, sound far lovelier, if they are still as perfect as [they were] in my day. The Chinese hang little bells on the offsets of towers, which are rung by the wind, making a sweet clangor." This is the end of the quote from Franciscus. He has also depicted it in an engraving.[**]

§. 570.

Concerning *automata*, [instruments] that are operated by rollers or barrels: one should realize that it is also possible to set the barrel in front of the keyboard in such a way that it depresses the keys by teeth. The barrel can be rotated by hand, by means of a water wheel, by weights, or by *elateria*,[††] etc. It is possible to have a number of rollers, for the sake of variety (cf. de Chales, l.c.,[‡‡] Prop. 39.)

---

[*] Adlung uses this word to denote a tuned set of bells, whatever their size; he does not distinguish between a glockenspiel and a carillon, as is done in English.

[†] The following quote from Franciscus, like other quotes in this treatise, is not exact. Adlung takes some liberties and also omits some sentences without indicating he has done so.

[‡] "Real" is "royal" in Spanish, and the Netherlands were Spanish territory until 1648; but the meaning is obscure.

[§] actually a variety of celesta.

[¶] Marin Mersenne, *Harmonie universelle*, Book VII, p. 42.

[||] Franciscus reads "Antwerp," as does Mersenne (*Harmonie universelle*, Book VII, p. 42).

[**] Plate no. XXIX, p. 1036, shows bells on the offsets of a tower. Plate no. XXXIV, p. 1317, shows the carillon at Antwerp.

[††] See §.546.

[‡‡] Vol. III, Tract 22.

Chapter XXVI.
Concerning the Clavichord and the Pedal-clavier.

Contents:

§.571. Concerning the name of the clavichord. §.572-573. Its history. §.574. Its body. §.575. The other main components. §.576. Some sound loud, others weak; and concerning stops.

Kap. XXVI. Von dem Clavichord u. Pedal.

gistern. §. 577 der Lautenzug. §. 578. Von deren Transposition. §. 579. Was bundfrey heisse. §. 580. zuweilen macht man dreyfache Seyten, auch wol gesponnene. §. 581. die Seyten sollen nicht zu schwach und nicht zu stark seyn. §. 582. und lieblich klingen. §. 583. Die Palmuln sollen tief fallen. §. 584. wie man dazu kommt. §. 585. besondere Art des Steges §. 586. Von den langen Decken. §. 587. die Fehler bey den Wirbeln; §. 588. bey den Stiften und Palmuln. §. 589. Wie das Stocken zu corrigiren. §. 590. die Vollkommenheiten des hypomochlii. §. 491 Was zu thun, wenn die Mensur nicht getroffen ist? §. 592. Vor Fett, Feuchtigkeit und Sonnenhitze nehme man die Clavichordien in Acht §. 593. Wie man 2 Claviere vorstellt §. 594. Clavicymbel Form & alia. §. 595. Man schlage modest drauf. §. 596 die untern Theile des Pedals. §. 597 der Kasten §. 598 Tangenten §. 599. Bindfaden oder Abstrakten. §. 600. Was von jenen zu halten? §. 601. Was von diesen zu sagen? §. 602. Von Erhaltung eines Pedals. §. 603. Clavicymbelpedal. §. 604 Anhänge-Pedal. §. 605. Ein paar Worte vom Pandoret und Orvals Claviere auf der Clarinette.

§. 571.

Beydes ist zwar sehr gemein und bekannt: jedoch damit in der Musica mechanica Organœdi nichts wegbleibe, was dazu gehört; so will ich von beyden etwas beybringen. Das Clauichordium hat den Namen von Chorda, eine Seyte, und Clauis, Schlüssel; oder von Cor das Herz, da man aber wol Clauicordium schreiben mußte, und würde die letzte Derivation daher seyn, weil das Clauicordium, wenn es rechter Art ist, und recht gespielet wird, so herzrührend und weit anmuthiger, als die meisten andern Instrumente, klinget. [85]) Denn man kann das forte und piano darauf einigermaaßen haben durch die Force des Spielers.

[85]) Von der Derivation dieses Worts s. Fuhrmanns musicalischen Trichter Kap. 10. S. 90. der Herr Verfasser hat auch oben §. 21. davon gehandelt.

§. 572.

Vom Clavicymbel und den bisher erzählten Instrumenten ist es sehr unterschieden, sonderlich darinnen, daß die Tangenten die Seyten nicht schnellen, wie bey jenen bisher geschehen, sondern nur unten anschlagen, wie die Struktur weiset. Aber deswegen hat es eben den Vortheil, daß man sich mit den Federn nicht placken darf, auch sind sie beständiger in der Stimmung, und, wenn die Mensur richtig, auch viel geschwinder und leichter zu stimmen, als jene, weil ordentlich 2, 3 bis 4 Claves auf eine Seyte schlagen, da dann, wenn die eine gestimmt, auch sogleich die andern reine sind. (s. Prätorius Synt. To. II. P. II. cap. 36 p. 60. seqq.) Deswegen braucht man sie auch bey der Information: denn wer darauf wohl gelernet, kann cæteris paribus auch auf Orgeln, Clavicymbeln, u. d. gl. fortkommen. Einige haben es zwar wegen der Heiserkeit verachtet; und ist es wohl wahr, daß viele allzu douce gerathen: aber man hat auch solche, die bey einer Musik von etlichen Violinen durchschlagen. Und gesetzt, sie gehen heiserer, als andere Instrumente; so bleibt die Delicatesse doch, und wird man die Manieren auf keinen andern so wohl exprimiren können als auf dem Clavichor-

Ch. XXVI. The Clavichord and Pedal-clavier.

§.577. The buff/lute stop. §.578. Transposing on them. §.579. What does "unfretted" mean? §.580. Sometimes the strings are tripled, and also even overspun. §.581. The strings should be neither too thin nor too thick, §.582. and sound sweet. §.583. The keyfall should be deep. §.584. How to achieve this. §.585. The proper form for the bridge. §.586. Concerning the long soundboard. §.587. Faults with the tuning pins. §.588. [Faults] with the [hitch]pins and keys. §.589. How to fix [keys that] stick. §.590. Merits of the balance rail. §.591. What to do if the scaling is not correct. §.592. The clavichord needs to be protected from grease, dampness and the heat of the sun. §.593. How to simulate two manuals. §.594. [Building it in] the shape of a harpsichord, and other matters. §.595. One should play moderately on it. §.596. The lower parts of the pedal. §.597. The [pedal] case. §.598. The [pedal] keylevers. §.599. [Should] twine or trackers [be used?] §.600. The case for the former. §.601. The case for the latter. §.602. Concerning the maintenance of a [clavichord] pedal. §.603. A pedal for a harpsichord. §.604. The pull-down pedal. §.605. A few words about the Pandoret and Orval's clarinet keyboard.

§. 571.

Both [the clavichord and its pedal] are very common and well-known. But in order to avoid omitting anything from the *Musica mechanica organœdi* that pertains to it, I will impart something about each of them. The clavichord gets its name from *chorda*, a string, and *clavis*, a key; or [alternatively] from *cor*, the heart, in which case the name must be spelled "clavicordium". The latter derivation would have come about because the "clavicordium", if it is of the proper sort and is well played, sounds so very touching, and far more charming that most other instruments.[85)] * For by means of the force [exerted] by the player it is possible in some measure to achieve *forte* and *piano* on it.

[85)] For the derivation of this word, see Fuhrmann's *Musicalischer Trichter*, Chap. 10, p. 90. The author [i.e., Adlung] has also dealt with it† above in §. 21. [Albrecht]

* N.B. Albrecht's footnote previous to this one, to §.507, was also numbered 85.

† i.e., the derivation of the word *clavis*.

§. 572.

It is far different from the harpsichord and the other instruments hitherto described, in that the tangents (Tangenten‡) do not pluck the strings, as in those previously described, but only strike them from beneath, as their structure shows. But for that reason they have the advantage that one need not bother with quills. Their tuning is also more stable and, if the scaling is correct, they are also far quicker and easier to tune than [harpsichords], since ordinarily 2, 3 or 4 keys strike one string, and thus when one [note] is tuned, the others are immediately in tune as well (see Praetorius, *Syntagma musicum*, Vol. II, Part II, Chap. 36, pp. 60f.). Anyone who has learned well on a clavichord can also handle an organ, harpsichord, or such, all things being equal; that is why these instruments are used for teaching. Some spurn them because they are so muted, and it is indeed true that many of them turn out too soft. But there are some that will hold their own in an ensemble of several violins.§ And even if they are more muted than other instruments, the fact remains that [their tone] is delicate; it is not possible to express the graces (*Manieren*) as well on any other [instrument] as on

‡ There is some inconsistency in the meaning of this word. In Vol. I, §.21, Adlung states that keys may also be called "Tangents". Here and in §.576 and §.589, however, he seems to use the word to signify the blades that strike the clavichord strings (this is consistent with the modern sense of the term). Elsewhere Adlung uses the term "Blechplatte" (§.575) or "Blatt" (e.g., §.584, §.589) for "blade". When he arrives at discussing the pedal clavichord (§.598), Adlung consistently uses "Tangent" to mean the key levers within the pedal case, and "Blatt" to mean the blade that strikes the string.

§ This statement is not as improbable as it might initially seem. For example, in the Smithsonian Museum in Washington, D.C. there is a painting by Januarius Zick (1732-97), entitled "Die Familie Remy in Bendorf bei Koblenz, 1776," that shows a clavichord being played in ensemble with several violins and a cello. C.P.E. Bach includes the clavichord among the instruments to be used for accompanying, and mentions that some singers prefer to be accompanied by the clavichord; see: Carl Philipp Emanuel Bach, *Versuch über die wahre Art das Clavier zu spielen*, Part II (Berlin: G.L. Winter, 1762), p. 2 (§.6); translated by William J. Mitchell as: *Essay on the True Art of Playing Keyboard Instruments* (N.Y.: W.W. Norton [c.1949]), p. 172 (§.6).

vichordio, daß also des Hn. Matthesons Ausspruch (Orch I. P. III. cap. III. §. 4.) doch richtig bleibt, wenn er sagt: die beliebten Clauicordia haben vor andern den Preiß. Es sind die Gemüther verschieden, und etlichen gefällt die douce Musik, andern die starke. So können etliche die kreischende Harfe nicht leiden; andere hören solche gerne. So geht es auch hier.

§. 573

Guido Aretinus soll die Clavichordien erfunden haben, wie Prinz in Historia Musices cap. X. §. 14. meldet; also wären sie viel 100. Jahre schon im Gebrauche gewesen. Wie aber alle Erfindungen anfänglich die Vollkommenheit nicht haben, die hernach durch fleißiges Nachsinnen erlanget wird: so kann man sich leicht die Rechnung machen, daß die alten Clavichordien so nicht gewesen, als die unsrigen heutiges Tages. Solches bezeuget auch Prätorius l. c. da er sagt, daß das Clavichordium aus dem Monochordo (nach Guidonis Scala, welche nur 20. Claves hatte) erfunden und eingetheilet worden. Anfangs, sagt er ferner, hatte man nur 20. Claves des generis diatonici, darunter nur 2. schwarze, (das sollen erhabene oder chromatische seyn) h und b̄: denn sie hatten nur dreyerley Semitonia, a b, h c, e f, wie noch in gar alten Orgeln zu sehen; hernach machte man aus dem chromatico mehr dazu, daß ein solches Clavier draus wurde: F G ᴳⁱˢ A ᴮ H c. ᶜⁱˢ &c. bis ins f̄ f̄is. Itzo (zu Prätorii Zeiten) fangen sie an von C bis f̄. Nach Prätorii Zeit hat sich das Clavier der Orgeln sehr geändert, und diese Veränderung hat sich auch mit andern Instrumenten, die Claviere haben, zugetragen, wie man denn schon längst die Clavichordien von C bis c̿ gemacht mit allen Semitoniis, oder besser zu reden, mit allen clauibus chromaticis. Nach und nach hat man das Clavier immer mehr erweitert, und oben zwar wenig, etwann das ā̄ (doch gar selten) unten aber noch viel claues eingerückt, und werden etliche gar bis ins 16füßige C gemacht, daß man also oft 5. ganze Oktaven drauf hat. Die Struktur der andern Theile ist auch nach und nach verbessert worden, so, daß man den Unterschied der alten und neuen wohl siehet; doch gerathen die neuen auch nicht alle gut, und manche machen sie gar elend.

§. 574.

Wir gehen zu der Hauptsache und beschauen die wesentlichen Theile des Clavichords. Das Corpus ist ordentlich länglich viereckicht, wenigstens pflegt es selten viel abzugehen. Die vier Seiten sind von weichem Holze, wie man denn gemeiniglich Tannenholz dazu zu nehmen pflegt; doch, wo sie von Nußbaum oder Birnbaum und d. gl. gemacht werden, so dauren sie länger und beständiger. Der Boden wird, wie bey dem Clavicymbel von weichem Holze gemacht. Die Länge des corporis wird in drey Theile getheilet, da unten ein Theil das Kästchen einnimmt, darinnen man die Seyten, Hammer,

Ch. XXVI. The Clavichord and Pedal-clavier.

the clavichord. Thus Mr. Mattheson's dictum ([*Neu-eröffnete*] *Orchestre* I, Part III, Chap. III., §.4[,p.262]) is correct when he says that the much-loved clavichords are to be praised above other [instruments].* [Human] temperaments vary; gentle music pleases some, while others like loud. Thus some cannot abide the rattling harp, while others like to listen to it. This is the way it is [with the clavichord], as well.

§. 573.

Guido d'Arezzo is said to have invented the clavichord, as Prinz reports in his *Historia musices*, Chap. X, §. 14.† Thus they would already have been in use for many centuries. But just as all inventions do not achieve perfection at the beginning, but later attain that state after diligent deliberation, so one can easily deduce that clavichords of old were not like those of today. Praetorius, *l.c.*,‡ testifies to this when he says that the clavichord was derived from dividing off the monochord (according to Guido's scale, which had only 20 notes (Claves)). In the beginning, he continues, there were only 20 diatonic notes, of which only two were black (that would be referring to the raised or chromatic ones), bb§ and bb'. There were only three types of semitones: a-bb, b-c, and e-f, as may still be seen in very old organs. Later more chromatic ones were added, resulting in the following keyboard: F G G# A B♭ B C C#, etc., up to f'' f#''. Now (i.e., in Praetorius's day) they extended from C to f''¶ [sic]. After Praetorius's time organ keyboards underwent a major transformation, and this change was also applied to other keyboard instruments. For a long time now clavichords have had all semitones, or more properly speaking, all chromatic notes from C to c'''.|| Their keyboards were gradually extended, and many notes were added, only a bit in the treble, to be sure, perhaps to d''' (but very seldom), but a good deal in the bass, some even extending down as far as the 16-foot C; thus there are 5 whole octaves on these instruments. The structure of the other parts has gradually been improved as well, so that the difference between old and new ones is quite evident. But the new ones do not always turn out well, and many [builders] make them very badly indeed.

§. 574.

Let us proceed to the point and examine the essential components of the clavichord. The case is ordinarily rectangular; at least, it is unusual to deviate much [from this shape]. The four sides are made of soft wood, normally of fir/spruce. But if they are made of walnut, pearwood or some such, they will be more durable and last longer. The bottom board is made of soft wood, as in a harpsichord. The case is divided into three sections along its length, the space beneath one of them being occupied by a compartment, several inches wide, in which are stored [extra] strings, the [tuning]

---

* Adlung is quoting freely; Mattheson's actual words are "... die vor andern beliebten Clavicordia, kleine und grosse, unter welchen allen die Flügel und Clavicordia den Preis behalten [... the keyboard instruments large and small, preferred to other [instruments], among all of which the harpsichord and clavichord take the prize]."

† p. 109. This assertion is doubtful. The clavichord seems to have developed during the later Middle Ages out of the monochord, whose origin is lost in antiquity.

‡ i.e., p. 60.

§ Adlung reads "h" (German "b natural"), but that is surely an error.

¶ Here Adlung finishes his free quote from Praetorius. The final statement embellishes upon Praetorius, who gives the upper limit of the compass as a'', c''' or d''', and occasionally f'''. (This should almost certainly read "a'', c''', d''' or f''';" Praetorius's plate XV, no. 2, has the compass C/E to f'''. Thus Adlung perpetuates Praetorius's confusion.)

|| While this statement is doubtless correct, it should not be construed to mean that *all* clavichords were built in this way. It is certain that fretted clavichords with short octaves in the bass continued in use well into the 18th century; thus various types of instruments existed simultaneously for quite some time.

Tuch und d. gl. aufbehält, etwan einige Zolle breit. Hierauf folgt das Clavier, in der Länge wie bey der Orgel; oder nachdem man es länger oder kürzer machen will, nämlich nach der Vielheit der Palmulen. Hernach folgt der dritte Absatz für die Decke oder Sangboden. Denn wo die Palmulen aufhören, da gehet die obere Decke an, und reichet bis zu Ende. Also wird sie unter den Seyten nicht continuirt, wie bey dem Clavicymbel. Sie muß übrigens gleicher Art seyn mit dem Sangboden des Clavicymbels, davon §. 523. geredet worden.

§. 575.

Auf dem Sangboden liegt ein Steg in die Breite, der entweder eine gerade Linie präsentirt, oder etwas krumm gebogen ist; dieser ist in forma prismatis, und oben mit soviel Stiften versehen, als das Clavichord Seyten haben soll. Unter der Decke oder Sangboden ist ein Steg aus einer Ecke in die andere. Die Wirbel werden auf dem Sangboden eingeschlagen, wie bey dem Clavicymbel. An der hintern Seite ist von der rechten zur linken eine eichene Leiste bevestiget, worauf die Mensur abgezeichnet, und die Stifte eingeschlagen sind, daran die Seyten hangen. Die Palmulen sind, wie bey dem Clavicymbel; nur daß anstatt der Docken meßingene Blechplatten eingeschlagen sind, damit sie an die Seyte schlagen. Damit sie aber auch nicht auf die Seite wanken; so werden in die Mitte des hintersten Endes Blechspitzen oder Fischbein eingeschlagen, daß sie in den eingeschnittenen Kerben laufen, und sich auf keine Seite legen können. Die Palmulen sind theils gerade, theils krumm, je nach dem es sich mit der Temperatur und Mensur thun läßt. Sie laufen vorn in Stiften, welche wie bey dem Clavicymbel und bey andern Clavieren über dem hymomochlio liegen, welches fast die Gestalt eines prismatis hat, doch oben etwas rund ist. Damit aber nichts heraus hüpfe; so ist über den Palmulen (nicht über den Stiften) ein Vorsetzbrett. Die Palmulen werden von außen so zugerichtet und geputzt, wie bey der Orgel. Die Seyten werden sodann aufgezogen wie bey dem Clavicymbel. Man nimmt meßingene Seyten dazu: und damit sie nach dem Anschlage ihren Klang bald verliehren; so windet man Tuch um die Seyten.

§. 576.

Dieß sind die Haupttheile. Nun sollen die Vollkommenheiten und Fehler folgen. Etliche Clavichordien klingen stark, etliche schwach. Jenes ist zu loben; dieß aber nicht. Doch was die Stärke anlanget, so möchte wol zuweilen Jemand wollen bey der Meditation, oder andern Umständen, piu piano spielen: nun darf man nur etwas auf den Steg legen, wie man bey den Violinen thut; so wird es gedämpft: allein man will sagen, daß es dem Singen solcher Instrumente schädlich sey, welches ich zwar noch nicht probirt; doch kann man es auch so machen: man deckt das ganze Clavichord zu, daß nur die Claviertasten frey bleiben, und so wird es weit

hammer, cloth* and such. Next† comes the keyboard, about the same size as on an organ, or longer or shorter as you wish, according to the number of keys. Thereafter comes the third section for the soundboard (Decke oder Sangboden). Where the keys end, there the soundboard begins across the top, and extends to the end [of the case]. Thus it does not extend under [the entire length of] the strings, as in a harpsichord. Furthermore, [the soundboard] must be of the same sort as that of a harpsichord, which was discussed in §. 523.

§. 575.

Across the breadth of the soundboard there lies a bridge, that either forms a straight line or is bowed into a curve. Its shape is that of a prism‡, provided on top with as many pins as the clavichord is to have strings. Beneath the soundboard is a rib [passing diagonally] from one corner to the other. The tuning pins are driven through the soundboard,§ as in a harpsichord. A plank of oak¶ is fastened on the back side, from right to left, on which the scaling‖ (Mensur) is marked off. Into this strip the pins are driven around which the strings are hooked. The keys are like those in a harpsichord, except that instead of jacks, brass blades (meßingene Blechplatten [i.e., tangents]) are driven into them, and these are what strike the strings. To keep [the keys] from shifting to the side, however, slips made of metal or fishbone** are driven into the middle of the back ends; these slips travel in slots cut into [the oak strip], preventing the keys from shifting to one side or the other. The key [levers] lie in part straight, in part at an angle, according to the requirements of temperament and scaling. [Further] forward they move on pins that lie atop the balance rail, as in harpsichords and other keyboard instruments. This balance rail is almost prismatic in shape, but slightly rounded off on top. To keep any [key] from popping out there is a nameboard above the keys (but not above the pins††). The part of the keys on the outside [of the case] are finished off and polished like those on an organ. Then the strings are put on as in a harpsichord. One uses brass strings for this. In order to dampen the sound right after the upwards pressure [of the tangent ceases], cloth [listing] is woven through the strings.

§. 576.

These are the principal components. Next follow the merits and shortcomings. Some clavichords have a bold sound, while others sound weak. The former is praiseworthy, but the latter is not. As concerns volume, though, someone might well want to play more softly at times, when in a meditative mood or for some other reason; then all that is necessary is to set something on the bridge, as is done to the violin,‡‡ and [the sound] will be muted. It is said, though, that this is harmful to the resonance of such instruments; this is something that I have never tested. But [the damping] could also be accomplished in this way: the entire clavichord could be covered,§§ with the exception of the keys, and then it would sound far softer than usual. The more of the sound-

---

* for damping.
† i.e., in the next section.

‡ i.e., a triangle, when viewed in cross section.

§ and into the wrest pin block, mounted below the sound board.
¶ i.e., the hitch pin block.
‖ here "Mensur" refers specifically to the proper length of the strings. In §.581 and §.588 Adlung calls the hitchpin block the "Mensur" as well, since the scalings are marked off on it, and in §. 578 he also uses the term for the keyboard back guide rack. The German term "Mensur" can also mean the relationship of string length to string thickness (as Adlung intimates in §.579). English has no exact equivalent for this variety of meanings; the usual translation, "scaling," refers only to the proper string length.
** i.e, whalebone (baleen).
†† i.e., further forward, toward the player.

‡‡ i.e., the mute.

§§ presumably by some sort of lid.

weit stiller klingen, als sonst. Je mehr von der Resonanzdecke oder Sangboden bedeckt ist, desto stiller wird der Klang seyn. Oder man lasse sich ein Clavichord mit Registern machen, welches so angehen möchte: Die Seyten werden paarweise etwas weit von einander gelegt: damit aber das corpus nicht allzubreit werden musse; so werden die 2 Seyten jedes Clavis so enge zusammen gebracht, als es das Vorhaben leiden will. Das Clavier wird vorwärts beweglich gemacht, wenn man nur das hypomochlium (das ist die Untere Leiste, darein die Stifte geschlagen werden) in eine horizontale Kerbe einschiebt zu beyden Seiten, daß man durch Handhaben dasselbe sammt dem ganzen Clavier auf beyden Seiten zugleich etwas weniges vorschieben könne, daß die Tangenten nur noch eine Seyte berühren. Man muß es aber just treffen, und nicht soweit ziehen, deswegen muß der terminus vor- und hinterwärts durch Stifte bemerkt seyn, daß das hypomochlium an sie stoße, und nicht weiter gerückt werden möge. Es gehört hierzu eine große Accuratesse, und dürfen die blechernen Tangenten nicht breit seyn, sonst würden sie die hintere Seyte nicht leicht verlassen, oder vorwärts an der benachbarten Seyte des andern Clavis naschen. Ob nun schon das Rücken wenig ist, und kaum soviel, als ein Messerrücken in der Breite austragt; so muß man doch um deßwillen die Kerben bey der Mensur etwas tiefer schneiden, als sonst, daß man in die Palmulen längere Stifte stecken könne, damit sie doch drinne bleiben, wenn schon das Clavier auswärts gerückt worden. Besser aber ists, wenn sich diese Kerbenleiste mit vorwärts zieht, welches auch leicht zu machen ist. Es könnte auch zuweilen die hintere Seyte dadurch alleine gebraucht werden; ja zuweilen hat man Clavichordien von 3 Chören, da könnte man durch etliche Rückungen des Claviers (wie bey dem Claveßin §. 516. gemeldet) bald die vorderste und mittelste, bald alle 3. Seyten anschlagen lassen. Sodann müßte das Clavier, wenn es alle 3. anschlägt, so stehen, daß es 2 mal hinterwärts, und 2 mal vorwärts geschoben würde. Ich habe aber noch nie gesehen, daß jemand einige Register sich hätte machen lassen; doch könnte es wol geschehen.

§. 577.

Man macht auch bisweilen den Lautenzug drauf, wie dergleichen ich öfters gesehen. Nahmlich die Blätter der Tagenten werden etwas breit, so, daß wenn die Breite in 2 Theile getheilet wird, jede Hälfte für sich breit genug sey, beyde Seyten anzuschlagen. Sodann legt man über die hintersten Hälften jedes Blats ein Leder oder Tuch, so subtil, als man es machen kann, leimet es zu beyden Seiten an, und macht sodann das Clavier auf die vorhin beschriebene Art beweglich, da es in dem ordentlichen situ durch die bloße Hälfte einen Klang verursachen wird, wie andere: bringt man durch das Rücken die belederte Hälfte unter die Seyten; so wird der Harfenklang weggenommen wie §. 514 bey den Claveßin geschehen. Diß will auch einen accuraten Meister haben.

§. 578.

Das Transponiren war §. 515. eine Vollkommenheit bey dem Claveßin; nun fragt es sich: ob auch auf dem Clavichordien dergleichen zu machen, wie etliche sich einbilden?

Ch. XXVI. The Clavichord and Pedal-clavier. 147

board that is covered, the quieter the sound will be. Or a clavichord could be constructed with stops. This is how that might work: the strings would be strung in pairs, somewhat separated from each other. To keep the case from being so wide, however, the two strings for each key would be set as close together as the design will permit. The keyboard could be shifted forward by inserting each side of the balance rail (the ridge beneath [the keys], into which the pins are driven) into a horizontal channel. By grasping it at both sides at the same time, the balance rail together with the keyboard could be shifted forward a bit, allowing the tangents (Tangenten) to contact only one string. The [mechanism] must be positioned exactly, though, and not shifted too far; therefore the nearer and further limits [of travel] have to be marked with pins, so that they block the balance rail, keeping it from being moved too far. Great precision is required for this. The metal tangents cannot be wide, otherwise they would not easily clear the string behind without nicking a neighboring string belonging to a key on the other side. Even though the shift is tiny, hardly amounting to the width of the back of a knife[blade], it is necessary for this reason to cut the slots [in the hitchpin block,] where the scaling is, a bit deeper [than usual]. Then longer slips can be set into the [back of] the keys, so that they remain in [the slots] when the keyboard is shifted outward. It would be better, though, if that [oak] strip shifted forward with the slots, and this is also easy to do. In this way the back string [of each pair] could at times be used alone. Indeed, clavichords sometimes have three courses, and in that case it would also be possible to play at times on only the nearest and middle strings, or at times on all three, by adjusting the keyboard in a certain way (as described in §.516 concerning the harpsichord). If [the tangents] are to strike [various combinations of] all three [strings], then the keyboard must be made so it can be adjusted to three positions. I have never seen any instrument furnished with stops, but it could surely be done.

§. 577.

I have occasionally seen clavichords that have buff/lute stops. In that case the tangent blades are made rather wide, so that if the width were divided into two halves, either one would be wide enough to strike both strings. A layer of leather or cloth, as thin as possible, is laid over the back half of each blade and glued to each side of it. Then the keyboard is made movable, according to the method described above. In its normal position the sound is created by the bare half [of the blade], just like other [clavichords]. When however the keyboard is shifted to bring the half covered with leather under the strings, then the [normal] harp-like sound will disappear, the same as happens in a harpsichord (see §. 514). It requires an exacting craftsman [to construct] this [mechanism], as well.

§. 578.

In §. 515 the transposing mechanism was [cited as] a virtue in the harpsichord. The question is, should this also be built into the clavichord, as some believe? In an-

bilden? Antw. Ich habe viel darüber gesonnen; aber bis dato noch nichts davon zu Markte bringen können. Erst dachte ich, daß Clavier könnte von der linken gegen die rechte Hand beweglich gemacht werden, welches geschehen könnte wie bey dem Clavicymbel: allein die Palmulen stecken hinten in den Kerben; oder man müßte das Brett, worauf die Seyten über der Mensur angeheftet sind, besonders machen, und unter dasselbe die Leiste mit den Kerben auch besonders, daß sie könnte unten mit fortgeschoben werden: allein daraus wird wieder nichts. Denn das Fundament sollte seyn, daß sodann die Tagenten zwar auf eben die Seyten schlügen, wie sonst, doch einmal weiter unten, als sonst, so viel nämlich das Spatium eines halben oder ganzen Tons austrägt: aber das ist nicht bey allen Seyten einerley. Denn ein halber Ton trägt in der untern Oktave wol ein und einen halben Zolle aus, daß also das Clavier $1\frac{1}{2}$ Zolle herabzuziehen wäre, wenn man ein Semitonium herabwärts transponiren wollte; oben aber wäre kaum $\frac{1}{2}$ Zoll nöthig: folglich, da das ganze Clavier gleichviel gerückt wird; so werden die obern Claves nie mit den untern reine, weil ein Semitonium viel weniger obenaus beträgt, wie der Augenschein lehrt. Von C bis $\overline{\overline{c}}$ verändern sich die Intervalle stets nach Proportion, und ist keins dem andern gleich. Wollte man das Clavier vorwärts schieben, wie bey den Registern §. 576; so achte ich es zwar nicht für unmöglich, doch wäre alsdann ein besonderer Fleiß nöthig in der Abtheilung, Lage des Steges und Aufziehung der Seyten, und doch wirds schwerlich angehen, wo die Tastatur nicht mehr als ein Chor hervorgezogen wird, daß ich andere Incommoda nicht erwähne. Es wäre wol möglich, einen Modum hiervon anzugeben; doch in der Praxi möchte es schwer fallen. Ich halte mich deswegen nicht dabey auf. Wir haben mehr zu betrachten.

§. 579.

Ferner ist als eine Vollkommenheit anzusehen, wenn ein Clavichord bundfrey ist. Viele sind so, daß 3 bis 4 Palmulen auf eine Seyte oder auf 1. Chor Seyten, schlagen: bundfrey aber heißt, wenn zum wenigsten bey jedem diatonischen Clave ein ander Chor System ist, daß die chromatischen mit eingehen. So würden z. E. $\overline{\overline{c}}$ und $\overline{\text{eis}}$, d und $\overline{\text{dis}}$ auf eine Seyte schlagen; e bliebe alleine, f und $\overline{\text{fis}}$ zusammen. ꝛc; oder man läßt $\overline{d}$ alleine, und $\overline{\text{dis}}$ und $\overline{e}$ schlagen zusammen u. s. w. Die unterste Palmulen von C an bis H haben alle ihre besondere Chöre; wenigstens bey denen die ich gesehen und gespielt, obschon in der mittlern und obern Oktaven 3 Palmulen zusammen schlagen. Fragt man: warum sie bundfrey seyn sollen? so gestehe ich zwar, daß wo die Mensur richtig ist, man es wohl könne reine stimmen, ob es schon nicht bundfrey ist, ja es ist bey der Stimmung ein großer Vortheil, weil, wo ein Clavis gestimmt, zugleich die andern reine sind, die auf eben die Seyten schlagen: Allein, wenn eine Seyte sich verstimmt; so sind gleich 3. Claves unrein, welches ein großes Incommodum ist. Und wenn man Bindungen macht, daß große oder kleine Sekunden neben einander angeschlagen werden; so hört man nur die obere der Gebundenen, wo sie an eine

swer: I have pondered this a great deal, but up to this point I have not yet discovered anything that is successful. At first I thought the keyboard could be made movable from left to right, as can be done in a harpsichord. But the keys are set into slots [in the hitchpin block] at the back . The board upon which the strings are attached above the keyboard back guide rack (Mensur*) could be made separate from the strip with the notches, so that the latter could be shifted back and forth underneath, with [the keyboard]. But that will not work, either, for the basic principle should be that the tangents should then strike the same strings as usual, yet at a distance equivalent to a half or a whole step higher or lower. This distance, however, is not the same for all the strings. In the lowest octave, a half step amounts to a good 1½ inches, so that the keyboard would have to shifted that far down in order to transpose a half step down. Barely a half inch is needed in the treble, though. Consequently, since the entire keyboard is shifted the same distance, the treble keys would never be in tune with the bass, because a half step amounts to much less in the treble, as can plainly be seen. The intervals vary proportionally from C to c′′′, and none of them is equal to any other. Someone might suggest drawing the keyboard forward [thus striking the next set of strings], as [happens] with the stops in §.576; this I do not consider impossible, but it would require particular pains in measuring it off, positioning the bridge and stringing [the instrument]. And it would likely create even more problems, if the keyboard were drawn any further forward than one set of strings, not to mention other inconveniences. It would indeed be possible to indicate a method for doing this, but in practice it is likely to turn out to be very difficult. Therefore I will not dwell on it any longer; we have other things to consider.

* see note accompanying §.575.

§. 579.

Furthermore, it should be considered a virtue if a clavichord is unfretted. Many [clavichords] are [built] so that 3 or 4 keys strike the same string or the same pair of strings. "Unfretted", in contrast, means that there is a separate set of strings for at least every diatonic key together with its chromatic [neighbor]. For example, c′′† and c#′ would strike the same string, as would d′ and d#′; e would stand alone; f′ and f#′ would be together, etc. Or the d′ could stand alone while d#′ and e′ strike the same string, etc. The lowest [octave of] strings from C to B-natural all have separate sets of strings; at least on those instruments that I have seen and played, even when three keys struck the same set of strings in the middle and upper octaves. Someone will ask, "Why should clavichords be unfretted?" I will admit that if the scaling is correct, [the instrument] can be tuned precisely, even when it is fretted. Indeed it is a great benefit in tuning, since when one note is in tune, the others that strike the same string are *ipso facto* in tune as well. However, if a [single] string goes out of tune, then three notes are right away out of tune, and this is a major inconvenience. And if suspensions/slurs are played in which major or minor seconds that are fretted together are struck, then only the upper [tone] on the fretted string is heard, since [both] are striking the same

† sic; should be c′.

ne Seyte schlagen. Diese Incommoditäten sind so beschaffen, daß sie die Harmonie verderben. Ich rathe dahero nie zu einem Clavichordio, welches nicht bundfrey ist. Wollte man aber das Wort bundfrey im engern Verstande nehmen, daß es soviel bedeuten sollte, als da man alle Bindungen frey machen könnte; so müßte man auch zu jedem chromatischen Clave einen besondern Chor Seyten haben: Und das ist gut; denn so wird die Harmonie auf keine Art gestört. Doch kostet dieß mehr Seyten; auch mehr Zeit zur Stimmung, und wegen der vielen Seyten muß das Corpus viel breiter werden. Doch macht man dergleichen Clavichordien heutiges Tages vielfältig, und man scheuet die Mühe und Unkosten nicht, die ein solches Clavichord erfordert, weil man längst eingesehen, daß diese Art für allen andern einen großen Vorzug hat. Man hat sich aber dabey in Acht zu nehmen, daß man die Seyten nicht gar zu enge zusammen bringe; denn sonst würde man mit dem Stimmhammer nicht bequem zwischen die Wirbel kommen können, und die Tangenten würden auch oft die benachbarten Seyten berühren: beydes aber würde dem Besitzer eines solchen Instruments verdrüßlich seyn.

Es fragt sich aber: warum die untern Palmulen allezeit bundfrey sind, da es sich doch der Harmonie wegen besser schickte, die obern bundfrey zu machen, wegen der Bindungen, Mordenten und andern Manieren, die untern aber nicht, weil man daselbst nicht leicht Bindungen und andern Spielmanieren macht? Antw. Das ist wahr, wenn es nur angienge. Allein, je größer die Distanz des Tangenten vom Stege ist, ein desto größer Stück der Seyte trägt ein Hemitonium, und noch mehr ein Ton aus. So müßten dann die Palmulen sehr weit von einander kommen, und würden sie endlich oben und unten sehr schief werden, daß sie fast nicht zu gebrauchen. Hebt man doch ißo im C die Palmulen gegen die linke Hand schief an, und läßt sie hart an einander liegen, so lange bis ein chromatischer Clavis mit dem diatonischen auf eine Seyte schlägt, welches gemeiniglich im e anhebt, da gehen die Palmulen von einander, und daselbst ist ein Semitonium schon so groß nicht, als unten; und doch kommen dadurch die obern Palmulen nach und nach gar schief gegen die linke Hand. Wo die Tangenten weit von einander gehen, da ist allezeit ein diatonischer und chromatischer Clavis auf einer Seyte. Je weniger es bundfrey ist, desto krummer werden die obern Palmulen. Wo aber jeder diatonischer und chromatischer Clavis seinen eigenen Chor Seyten besonders hat, da brauchen die Palmulen nicht von einander zu stehen; folglich werden sie auch nicht schief gelegt.

Die Abtheilung oder Mensur gehört für die Mechanicos Practicos. Wo diese nicht richtig ist, da ist sie entweder zu jung, und da halten die Seyten besser: oder sie ist zu lang, und da springen die Seyten, zumal wo der spitzige Winkel bey dem Stege dazu kömmt. Also muß alles nach dem Monochord und Zirkel; it. nach der Dicke der Seyte gemessen werden. Ist das Clavichord lang; so kann man den Steg, auch wol die Wirbel herab rücken. Sonderlich muß man die

Ch. XXVI. The Clavichord and Pedal-clavier. 149

string. These inconveniences are such that they spoil the harmony. For that reason I would never advise [getting] a clavichord unless it is unfretted. If one were to interpret the word "unfretted" in the narrower sense, however, meaning that each and every suspension could be played, then every chromatic note would also have to have a separate set of strings. That is a good thing, for then the harmony could never be disturbed in any way. But this would require more strings, as well as more time for tuning, and the case would have to be much wider, due to the great number of strings. But such clavichords are being made everywhere these days, and people are sparing neither the trouble nor the expense that such a clavichord requires, because they have finally perceived that this type [of instrument] is much to be preferred above all others. It is necessary to keep in mind, however, that the strings cannot be placed too close together, otherwise it would be difficult to get the tuning hammer [to fit] between the pins, and the tangents would often touch the neighboring strings—both of these [faults] would be annoying to the owner of such an instrument.

Then the question arises, "Why are the lower notes always unfretted? Would it not be more appropriate, for the sake of the harmony, to make the ones in the treble unfretted, for suspensions/slurs, mordents and other graces, but not the lower ones, since one does not readily perform slurs and other ornaments down there?" Here is the answer: this is true, if only it would work. The greater the distance the tangents are from the bridge, however, the larger the section of a string is required for a half step, to say nothing of a whole step. Thus the key [levers] would have to stand very far apart,[*] and they would finally get to be at an extreme angle at both ends, making them almost unusable. If the key [levers] on the left side beginning at [low] C are set at an angle and as close as possible to each other, up to the point where a chromatic and diatonic note are produced by the same string (this normally begins at e), then at that point the keys are spread apart and a half step is not as great as lower [in the bass]. Nevertheless by doing this the upper keys gradually come to be at a great angle to the left. Wherever the tangents lie far apart from each other, there a diatonic and chromatic note[†] are always produced from one string. The more fretted an instrument is, the more the treble keys will lie at an angle. But wherever each diatonic and chromatic note has its own separate set of strings, it is not necessary for the keys there to stand apart from each other; consequently they are not laid at an angle.

[*] i.e., at the back, where the tangents are located.

[†] i.e., adjoining pitches.

Marking out the length and thickness of the strings, or the scaling,[‡] is a matter for the craftsmen. If this is not correctly [done], then [the strings] are either too short, which preserves the strings better, or they are too long, and then the strings will break, especially when they also form a sharp angle at the bridge. Thus everything must be measured off with a compass, using the monochord as a model, and taking into account the thickness of the strings. If the clavichord is long, then the bridge or even the tuning pins may be shifted back. In particular the half steps must be measured off

[‡] See note accompanying §.575.

Semitonia recht theilen, und nach der besten Temperatur alles abzirkeln. Man bemerkt die Richtigkeit der Abtheilung an dem Clavichord und andern besayteten Instrumenten daran, wenn sie sich nicht, oder wenig, verstimmen. Allein es sollte hier nach Proportion geschehen, daß alle Seyten zugleich, und jede nach gehöriger Proportion änderten; denn so blieben sie unter sich rein, und spührte man den Mangel nicht eher, als wenn andere Instrumente mitgehen. Dabey wird aber erfordert, daß nicht nur die Proportion der Seyten in der Länge, sondern auch in der Dicke, richtig sey. Aber wer trifts? das Nachgeben der Wirbel ist zwar zuweilen Schuld am Verstimmen; aber nicht allezeit! sondern das meiste thut die Luft; eben so als oben bey den Blättern der Schnarrwerke gesagt worden.

§. 580.

Einchöricht habe ich noch kein Clavichord angetroffen: Denn sie gehen ohnedieß schwach genug. Ordentlich haben sie zwo Seyten zu einem jeden Chor. Diese Seyten sind entweder gelbe oder weiße. Diese sollen schöner klingen; jene aber rosten nicht: doch wenn die meßingenen Seyten recht gehärtet; so haben sie ebenfalls einen guten Klang, daher ich sie insgemein vorziehe. (s. §. 575.) Eine gelbe und eine weisse Seyte zusammen auf einem Chor taugen nicht viel; sie werden selten reine seyn, weil sie durch die Luft so wenig gleich verändert werden, als wo mann zweyerley Holz hat, da eins viel, das andere wenig, schwindet. Dieß ist auch bey den obigen Instrumenten zu merken gewesen. Auch darf nicht in einem Chor eine Seyte stärker seyn, als die andere, als welche unmöglich gleich klingen werden, weil die schwächere weniger gespannt wird, und daher ganz andere Vibrationen macht, als die stärkere. Die Proportion von oben bis unten muß just beobachtet werden. Wovon hernach zu reden. Zuweilen macht man die Clavichordien dreychöricht. Dieß ist sonderlich unten vom C bis c gebräuchlich: oder wo ein Clavichord tiefer anfängt, z. E. im Contra F; so wird es auch bis dahin dreychöricht gemacht. Die dritte Seyte ist zuweilen den übrigen gleich, und im C dem Tone nach achtfüßig, zuweilen aber zieht man solche eine Oktave höher; folglich muß man schwächere Seyten nehmen, nachdem das Clavichord lang ist. Die Mensur dieser Seyten anlangend; so giebt man ihnen die Länge, wie die Seyten haben, die von gleicher Dicke sind. So aber die Clavichordien lang sind, muß man ihnen einen besondern Steg geben. Aldann laufen sie über ihren Steg, nicht aber über den großen, sondern durch denselben, bis zu den Wirbeln. [86]) Z. E. wenn mein Clavichord kurz wäre, und ich wollte auf C, welches No. I. sonst hat, die Oktave ziehen; so sehe ich nach, was die Oktave c für eine Nr. hat. Das ist bey mir

---

[86]) Diesen Umstand pflegen die Claviermacher heutiges Tages wenig anzubringen, sondern anstatt daß sie den großen Steg sollten aushöhlen und die Seyten des Oktävchens durchziehen, bevestigen sie die Seyten gleich hinter dem kleinen Stege, und ziehen sie von der rechten Hand gegen die linke, und bringen die dazu benöthigten Wirbel in dem Mensurbalken an, so, daß man die Seyten des Oktävchens unten zur linken Hand stimmen muß.

exactly, and everything must be measured very precisely according to the best temperament. The correctness of the scaling on a clavichord or other stringed instruments will reveal itself by the instrument staying exactly, or at least mostly, in tune. But this should happen proportionately, so that all the strings drift out of tune at the same time and in proper proportion; in that way they stay in tune among themselves, and the shortcoming is not noticed until other instruments play with it. This requires that not only the length of the strings be in proper proportion, but their thickness as well. But how many [builders] get it right? True, tuning pins that slip are sometimes to blame for the out-of-tuneness, but not always! Rather the weather is the major factor, as has already been mentioned above in connection with the tongues of reed stops.[*]

§. 580.

I have never yet encountered a clavichord without doubled strings, since these [instruments] are feeble enough [in volume] to begin with. They normally have paired strings for each set. These strings are either brass or steel. The latter are said to sound more beautiful, but the former do not rust. And if brass strings have been properly hardened, they likewise produce a good tone; thus I prefer them, in general (see §.575). Pairing a brass and a steel string in the same choir is not a good idea; they will seldom be in tune, since [changes in] the weather affect them just as differently as two different kinds of wood, one of which shrinks more readily than the other. This [point] should also be noted with regard to the instruments already discussed. Furthermore, one string in a choir should not be thicker than the other, or they cannot possibly sound the same, since the thinner one is less tense than the thicker, and thus its vibrations are entirely different. The proportion must be adhered to exactly from top to bottom; this will be discussed further below. Sometimes clavichords are made with three strings per set. This is to be found particularly in the lowest octave, from C to c; or if the instrument extends lower, e.g., to contra F, then those additional notes are also given three strings. The third string is sometimes of the same pitch as the other [two], 8′ pitch at low C; but sometimes it is tuned an octave higher, and consequently thinner strings must be used, depending on the length of the clavichord. Concerning the scaling of these strings, they are given the same length as the other strings of that thickness. But if clavichords are long, they must have their own separate bridge. [These 4′ strings] pass over their own bridge, and then not over the large one, but through it, directly to the tuning pins.[86.)] For example, if my clavichord were short, and I wanted to string an octave [string] for [low] C, whose gauge is normally No. 1, then I would observe what gauge (N[umme]r) the octave, c, was. The way I build, it is

[*] There is no mention of weather in connection with reed tongues in the *Mmo*; in §.118 of the *Anleitung* (p. 373), however, Adlung does indeed treat this subject:
... reeds, however, are not stable [in tuning]. The colder the weather gets, the more the tongue bends toward the shallot, and the higher the pitch rises. The warmer the weather gets, the more the opposite happens. Therefore under the latter conditions the tuning wires must be driven downwards, forcing the tongue against the shallot; under the former conditions the tuning wire must be drawn upwards, allowing the tongue to bend away from the shallot. The smaller the stop is [i.e., the smaller the pipes], the more easily they go out of tune (y).
(y) a thin sheet is more easily warped by the sun than a thick board; therefore a thin tongue will be more affected by heat or cold than a thick one. A [reed] stop may well be in tune with itself, if built by a master, but not in relation to the flue stops ...

[86)] Keyboard builders of today are seldom accustomed to building this arrangement; instead of boring holes through the large bridge and drawing the octave strings through it, they fasten the strings right behind the small bridge and string them from right to left. They drive the necessary tuning pins into the hitchpin block (Mensurbalken[†]), and thus the octave strings must be tuned at the left side, at the bass end. [Albrecht]

[†] the oak strip described in §.575.

Kap. XXVI. Von dem Clavichord u. Pedal.

mit No. 4. Doch sehe ich wohl, daß bey c die Seyten nicht die ganze Länge haben: aber das C bekömmt die völlige Länge; also kann ich die No. 4. nicht schlechterdings hinziehen, sondern ich muß sie über einen besondern Steg laufen lassen, daß der klingende Theil kürzer werde, und so kurz als er bey c ist. (Der klingende Theil ist von der Tangente bis zum Stege.) Wenn ich aber No. 5. oder 6. genommen hätte; so würde ich fast des Steges nicht nöthig gehabt haben. ꝛc. Und wie man mit einem Clave verfährt, so macht man es auch mit den andern.

Zuweilen bespinnt man die untern Seyten mit Silberdrat. Nimmt man nun die ordentliche dahin gehörige Seyte, und bespinnt sie: so muß man solche eine Oktave tiefer stimmen, und wird sodann das C 16füßig. Nimmt man aber schwächere Seyten, und bespinnt sie; so können sie mit den andern unbesponnen in unisono seyn, nämlich 8' Ton. Denn man nimmt zu jedem Chor nur eine gesponnene Seyte, die andere bleibt ungesponnen. Wo man aber den Baß 3chöricht macht, da nimmt man zwo gesponnene und eine ungesponnene Seyte, und wird die letztere gemeiniglich eine Oktave höher gestimmt, wie bereits erwähnet worden. Das Spinnen selbst mag ich hier, um nicht weitläuftig zu seyn, nicht lehren. Die gesponnenen Seyten ziehet man gemeiniglich nur bis zum H, von unten an zu zählen, und so bekömmt der Baß eine besondere Gravität; doch bleiben sie bey veränderter Luft mit den andern Seyten nicht im Einklange stehen.

§. 581.

Was die Stärke der Seyten von oben bis unten anbetrifft: so ist es ein Fehler, wenn sie allzustark sind, sonderlich wenn der Steg zu weit oben stehet, und wenn die Seyten sehr krumm über demselben liegen, daß sie einen allzu merklichen Winkel machen. Denn alles dieses verursachet, daß die Seyten oft springen. Doch ist es auch ein Fehler, wenn die Seyten allzudünne genommen werden: denn so werden sie in der Stimmung nicht genug gespannt, daher, wenn man douce spielt, die Seyten ihren Klang sehr schwach geben: spielt man hingegen scharf, und greift das Clavichord an; so drücken sich die Seyten in die Höhe, und werden am Klange höher, da dann ein groß vitium ist, wo die Seyte in einer Stimmung bald hoch bald niedrig singet. Es kann aber nicht anders seyn: denn wird sie in die Höhe gedrückt; so formirt sie bey dem Tangenten einen Winkel, da die beyden extrema ruhen. Also wird die Seyte länger, und folglich schärfer gespannt, folglich auch etwas höher, welches zuweilen wol einen halben Ton austrägt. Diesem Fehler abzuhelfen, muß der Instrumentmacher bey Zeiten die Numern auf die Claves schreiben, daß man stets die rechten aufziehe. Oder wenn es schon verdorben; so muß man den Bezug wegthun, und es stärker beziehen. Oder zur Menage kann man nur die obern Seyten wegthun, die folgenden aber aufwärts fortrücken. Sind nur etliche zu schwach; so reißt man sie doch auch billig weg, sonst geschiehet auf demselben Clave, was sonst die andern alle thun. Doch müssen

number 4. But it is evident that at c the strings are not fully the length [of the instrument], while at C they are full-length. Thus I cannot simply use a number 4, rather I must have it pass over a separate bridge to make the sounding portion of it shorter, namely, as short as it is at c (the sounding portion extends from the tangent to the bridge). If I had used number 5 or 6, then I would scarcely have had any need for the bridge. This same treatment is applied to all the other notes, as well.

Sometimes the deeper strings are overspun with silver wire. If the string that normally belongs there were overspun, then it would have to be tuned an octave lower, making it a 16′. If thinner strings are overspun, however, then they can be [tuned] in unison with the other ones that are not overspun, namely at 8′ pitch. For each set of strings has only one string that is overspun, the others remaining not overspun. If the bass is to be given three strings per set, then there are two overspun strings and one that is not overspun, this last normally being tuned an octave higher, as has already been mentioned. I will refrain from describing the [process of] overspinning [the strings] here, for the sake of brevity. Ordinarily overspun strings are strung only up to b-natural (counting up from the bottom), and because of them the bass assumes a particular gravity. But when the weather changes they do not stay in tune with the other strings.

§. 581.

Concerning the thickness of the strings from the top [of the compass] to the bottom: it is a defect if they are too thick, and especially if the bridge rises too high, and the strings bend sharply as they pass over it, so that they make too noticeable an angle. It is often such conditions that cause the strings to break. But it is also a defect if the strings that are too thin are used, since then they will not be tense enough when tuned. Therefore if the instrument is played gently, the strings will produce a very weak tone, while on the other hand if the notes are attacked forcefully, then the strings are pushed upward and their pitch becomes sharper. For the strings of one pitch to sound at times sharp and at times flat is indeed a great defect. But this cannot be avoided, since if they are pushed upward, they form an angle at the tangents, since the two ends of the string are fixed. Thus the string is lengthened and stretched more tightly, and consequently gets somewhat sharper, sometimes as much as a half step. To prevent this fault,* the instrument maker must write the numbers [of the strings that have been used] on the keys in a timely manner when the instrument is built, so that the correct ones are always [used when] restringing. If the strings are already ruined, then they must be removed and [the instrument] restrung with thicker [strings]. Or to economize only the treble strings may be discarded and the lower ones may be moved upward [into their place]. If only certain [strings] are too thin, then these should simply be removed; otherwise the same thing will happen with this note (clave) as has happened with all the others.† But the strings must not be too thick, otherwise their tone will lack sweet-

* i.e., excessive sharping caused by the use of strings that are too thin.

† i.e., those whose strings are too thin.

die Seyten nicht zu ſtark ſeyn, ſonſt verliehrt ſich die Anmuth. So hält wol manches Clavichord oben in $\frac{z}{c}$ No. 7; allein es iſt beſſer, wenn man es ſchwächer beziehet, und hingegen etwas höher ſtimmt. Wenn aber der Steg weit oben liegt, und die ſtarken Seyten nicht halten; ſo muß man denſelben fortrücken, daß die Menſur kürzer wird; auch in der äuſſerſten Noth kann man die Stifte über der Menſur weiter herauf ſchlagen, wenn die Seyten nicht halten.

§. 582.

Ein Clavichord ſoll ſtark klingen, jedoch aber nicht ſo pochend, ſondern lieblich, auf Harfenart. Es ſoll auch lieblich und lange nachſingen. Dieſes iſt eben der Punkt, welcher den Inſtrumentmachern viel zu ſchaffen macht, und gerathen die Clavichordien ſelten nach ihrem Kopfe. Ja, ich habe geſehen, daß einer die Körper zweyer Clavichordien gleich machte, der Breite, Länge und Dicke nach; das Holz war zu allen Theilen in beyden auch gleich; die Decke war gut; die Seyten völlig überein: und doch war der Klang des einen gegen des andere doppelt ſo ſtark, auch weit anmuthiger, man mochte dieß oder jenes oben ſetzen. Nun fragt ſichs, wie das zugehe? Antw. Es könnten doch noch mehr Urſachen ſeyn, welche die Aenderung machen: und wenn mancher denkt, es ſey alles überein; ſo kann es unvermuthet an einem ſochen Theile, z. E. an dem Stege, Decke ꝛc. nicht eintreffen, ob es der Meiſter ſchon nicht merkt. Hierzu kömmt auch der Stand des Steges unter der Decke, da es nur auf ein Punkt ankömmt, ſo wird der Klang nicht, wie er ſeyn könnte, wie man ſolches aus der Stimme bey der Violine gar deutlich ſiehet. Etliche ſagen, wenn die Decke nicht in der Sonnenſtunde gelegt würde, nämlich wenn ſie aufgehet; ſo klängen ſie nicht ſo gut, als andere. Aber ſolche aſtrologiſche Anmerkungen gelten bey mir nicht viel.

§. 583.

Doch thut der Mechanikus ſoviel er kann, und ſiedet das Holz zur Decke aus, nimmt recht dürres Holz, arbeitet es dünne, ſetzt den Steg und die Stimme recht, ſonderlich hilft er auch der Stärke durch ſtarke Seyten; davon vorhin geredet worden; item durch einen richtigen Anſchlag der Tangenten. Ich will ſoviel ſagen, die Tangenten ſollen nicht ſo hoch liegen, daß die Blätter faſt an die Seyten reichen: denn ſolchergeſtalt darf man nur an die Palmulen rühren, ſo ſchlagen ſie gleich an. Es ſpielt ſich zwar fein; mir aber gefällt es nicht, weil 1) dadurch der Stärke viel abgehet. Will man daran zweifeln; ſo mache man die Probe, und laſſe die Palmulen vornen tiefer fallen, daß ſie alſo hinten höher ſteigen müſſen; ſo wird man davon überzeuget werden. 2) Sie heulen mehr, als andere. 3 Wenn man die Scholaren bey der Information daran gewöhnet, und ſie kommen hernach auf die Orgel, allwo die Palmulen ungleich tiefer fallen; ſo müſſen ſie von vorn anheben zu lernen: da hingegen, wenn ſie auf tieffallenden Clavichordien gewohnt ſind, es ihnen auf der Orgel gar nicht ſpaniſch vorkommen wird.

§. 584

ness. Thus many a clavichord contains a number 7 for c‴ in the treble;* but it is better to string this thinner and, to compensate, to tune it sharper.† If however the bridge at the top‡ lies too far [from the tangents] and the thick strings [therefore] do not hold, then one must move [the bridge] back [closer to the tangents], so that the scale§ becomes shorter.¶ In extreme situations where the strings do not hold, the pins on top of the hitchpin block (Mensur‖) can be driven in further up.

* i.e., the top string.
† i.e., the thinner strings have to be more tense to sound well.
‡ i.e., for the higher notes.
§ i.e., the length of the strings.
¶ See the note concerning the phenomenon of tensile pickup, accompanying §.510.
‖ See note accompanying §.575.

§. 582.

A clavichord must have a robust sound, but not percussive, rather, [the tone must be] lovely, in the manner of a harp. It must also continue to vibrate sweetly and at length. This is the very matter that causes the instrument maker much trouble; clavichords seldom turn out as they are envisioned. Indeed, I have seen a maker build two clavichords, both with cases of identical width, length and thickness, with identical woods throughout; the soundboard[s] were good, the strings absolutely identical—and yet the sound of one was twice as loud in comparison to the sound of the other. It was also far more pleasant—whichever you might consider more important. The question arises, "How did this happen?" Here is the answer: there could be several reasons that cause the difference. Even though many a person might think that everything was identical, there might be some unsuspected difference in one of the parts [named above], e.g., in the bridge or the soundboard, although the master craftsman did not notice it. The position of the rib** under the soundboard must also be taken into account; it need only be placed at a certain point, and the tone will not be what it [otherwise] might. This can be very clearly noted in [the positioning of] the soundpost in a violin. Some say that if a soundboard is not installed at dawn, when the sun rises, it will not sound as well as others. Such astrological observations, however, are not worth much, in my opinion.

** See §.575.

§. 583.

A craftsman, however, should do as much as he can.†† He should boil the wood for the soundboard, use completely cured wood, plane it thin, and position the bridge and the rib correctly. In particularly he should promote a robust tone by [using] thick strings, as has already been said, and by positioning the tangents to strike properly. Let me say this: the tangents ought not to sit so high that the blades almost reach up to the strings; if they do, then they strike if the player barely touches the keys. This feels good to play, but I am not in favor of it, because 1) the volume [of the instrument] is thereby greatly diminished.‡‡ If anyone doubts this, let him perform this test: adjust the keys so that their fronts fall lower, and thus that their back sections must rise higher—this will convince him. 2) they create more extraneous attack noise than other instruments. 3) If students become accustomed to it while they are being taught, and later transfer to the organ, where the key fall is of a different depth (ungleich tiefer), then they have to relearn everything from the beginning. If they become accustomed to clavichords with a deep keyfall, on the other hand, then the organ will not seem so foreign to them.

†† i.e., to make the instrument successful. This sentence serves to modify Adlung's statement in the previous paragraph that "clavichords seldom turn out as they are envisioned."

‡‡ because the tangents do not have enough travel to reach a velocity that allows them to strike the strings sharply.

§. 584.

Es fragt sich: wie hilft man, wenn man ein Clavichord hat, das allzuwenig fällt? Antw. das geht an, wenn sie nur hohe Blätter haben: denn da kann man sie nur tiefer einschlagen, oder abkneipen, so ist der Sache gerathen. Doch muß man sie von einerley Höhe machen; weil es ein Fehler ist, wenn eine Palmul tiefer fällt, als die andere. Die in der untersten Oktave kann man nach Proportion etwas länger lassen, weil die Bläter nicht so weit hinten stehen, als oben. Man muß sich aber hierbey hüten, daß man der Sache nicht zu viel thue. Denn dadurch geschiehet es zuweilen, daß die Stifte in den Kerben oben anschlagen, und ein Pochen verursachen. Dem geht man sodann damit entgegen, wenn man die Stifte tiefer bringt; Zuweilen schlagen auch die hintersten äusern Theile der Palmulen in der untern Oktave ans Tuch, welches auch ein Fehler ist, der daher entstehet, wenn man das Clavier allzutief will fallen lassen. Sollte hinten unter den Palmulen allzuhoch Tuch liegen, daß es unnöthig scheint; so nehme man es zum Theil weg, so werden sie auch besser anschlagen. Aber man muß auch kein Pochen oder Klappern verursachen, welches geschiehet, wenn die Hölzer auf das blosse Holz fallen, oder wenn das Tuch allzudünne ist.

§. 585.

Was den Klang betrift; so observirt man auf der Violine, daß je höher der Steg ist, desto stärker und pompichter klingen die Seyten: ist aber der Steg niedrig; so klingen sie etwas scharf und delicat nach Harfen Art. Da man nun auf Clavieren den Baß gerne pompicht und völlig hat, die obern Oktaven aber nach und nach delicater und harfenmäßig; so könnte man den Steg so machen, daß er oben im $\overline{\overline{c}}$ niedrig würde, hernach immer nach und nach höher, bis er im C um ein merkliches höher wäre, als oben. Was sonst die Figur des Steges anlangt; so liegt daran wenig. Doch gefallen mir die geraden am besten. Man richtet aber die Figur des Steges nach der Mensur. Der kleine Steg zum Oktävchen wovon §. 580. geredet worden) kann oben mit einem langen Drate belegt werden, wenn man die Seyten heller klingend haben will.

§. 586.

Um des Klanges willen machen andere die Resonanzdecken sehr lang: und da man bey den Alten sie kaum ¾ Elle lang gemacht; so werden sie ißo gemeiniglich noch mehr als noch einmal so lang verfertiget, damit sie besser nachsingen. Oben drauf macht man eine Oeffnung. Doch habe ich auch viel wohlklingende Clavichorde angetroffen, die dergleichen Oeffnung auf der Decke nicht hatten; hingegen muß auf der Seite eine Oeffnung seyn. Siehe was §. 524. gesagt ist. Andere machen die Decken wohl ¾ Ellen lang, und drüber; doch rücken sie den Steg darnach, wie auch die Wirbel, daß die Seyten nicht allzulang werden: Oder sie geben denselben etwas zu an der Länge und Dicke, stimmen sie aber um 2 oder 3 Töne tiefer. Dergleichen Arten klingen scharf und prächtig; doch sind sie in Musiken so wohl nicht zu gebrauchen, als andere, die höher

Ch. XXVI. The Clavichord and Pedal-clavier.

§. 584.

Now the question arises, "How do you adjust a clavichord with too shallow a key-fall?" The [remedy I will describe] will only work if their [tangent] blades lie [too] high. In that case, they need only be driven in further, or snipped off, and the matter is taken care of. But they have to be set at the same height, since it is a defect if one key falls deeper than the others. The [tangents] in the lowest octave can be left proportionately somewhat longer, since their [tangent] blades are not situated so far back [on the key levers] as in the treble. But be careful not to go too far,* because sometimes this lets the slips† strike the tops of their notches, causing a thumping. The remedy for this is to set the slips lower [in the key levers]. Sometimes the far ends of the key [levers] in the lowest octave strike the cloth;‡ this fault is the result of letting the keys fall too deep. If cloth§ should lie too high under far ends of the key [levers], then some of it should be removed; that will also help [the keys] to strike [properly]. But nothing should be allowed to create a thumping or rattling, which happens if wood strikes bare wood, or if the cloth is too thin.

* i.e., not to drive them in or snip them off too far.
† i.e., the guide pieces, driven into the backs of the keys, that move in the notches.
‡ i.e., the listing; see §.575.
§ there is a layer of felt on a ledge that protrudes from the bottom of the hitch pin block, which silences the far ends of the key levers as they fall (upon the release of notes); this is the first time that Adlung has mentioned this feature of the clavichord's construction.

§. 585.

Concerning the tone: observe that the higher the bridge is on a violin, the louder and fuller the strings sound. If the bridge is low, though, then they sound somewhat more brilliant and delicate, like a harp. Since the bass register of keyboard instruments is generally preferred to be rich and full, with the tone becoming gradually more delicate and harplike toward the upper octaves, the bridge can be made low in the treble at c''', gradually thereafter increasing in height until it is noticeably higher at low C than in the treble. As concerns the shape of the bridge, this does not much matter—though I am in favor of straight ones. The shape of the bridge, however, should be determined according to the scaling. The top of the little bridge for the 4' octave (discussed in §. 580) may be covered with a long [strip of] wire, if a brighter sound from the strings is desired.

§. 586.

For the sake of tone, some [builders] make the soundboard very long, so that, while earlier generations made them barely a ¼ of an ell long, now they are usually built more than twice that long, so that they resonate better. An opening is made on top;¶ but I have also encountered many sonorous clavichords that did not have such an opening in the soundboard. Then, however, there must be an opening in the belly rail. Note what has been said [about this matter] in §. 524. Others make soundboards as much as 1-¼ ells long or more, but then they adjust the bridge as well as the tuning pins accordingly, so that the strings do not become too long. Or they add a bit to the length and thickness [of the strings], but tune them 2 or 3 steps lower. Such instruments sound brilliant and majestic, but they are not as well suited for ensemble playing

¶ i.e., a rose.

höher gestimmt sind. Man macht auch um des Klanges willen die Körper viel höher, als sonst; ja man bringt alsdann zuweilen noch einen Sangboden unter den Palmulen an. Wo man den Steg darnach rückt, daß zwischen demselben und den Wirbeln ein merklicher Raum sey, daß die Seyten oben helle, und wie eine ordentliche kreischende Harfe klingen können, zwischen dem Stege und Wirbeln; so wird es das anmutige Singen eines Clavichords um ein merkliches vermehren, zumal wenn einer die rechte Proportion träfe, daß sie meistens mit den ordentlichen clauibus eingestimmt wären. Denn wie oben §. 536. gezeigt ist, so schlagen die Seyten cum Sympathia, und wenn eine Palmul anschlägt, so werden die Seyten über dem Stege auf Harfen Art dazu singen, soviel mit demselben Clave harmoniren. Jemehr nun solcher Harfenseyten mit einem Clave genau treffen, desto stärker wird das Nachsingen. Also kann man verstehen, wie es komme, daß einige Claves zuweilen vor andern nachsingen; nämlich, weil mehr Harfenseyten mit ihnen einstimmen. Daher darf man keine Stücke oben ansetzen: Denn solche Seyten, die geflickt sind, können nicht singen. Will man es nun in statu quo behalten; so darf nichts verrückt werden, weder vom Stege, noch von den Wirbeln. Wird der Steg verrückt; so gehet das Nachsingen weg, und kann etwann zu einem andern Clave kommen. Die Seyten unter dem Stege bis an das Tuch können wenig mitsingen, weil das Tuch sie dämpft.

§. 587.

Ein Hauptfehler ist auch, wenn die Wirbel allzu enge stehen, daß man mit dem Hammer und Zange nicht wohl dazwischen kommen kann (s. §. 579.) Ein Fehler ist auch, wenn sie nicht stark genug sind: denn sie werden durch die force der Seyten bald krumm gezogen. Sind sie aber einmal schwach, daß es nicht zu ändern; so muß man die Seyten, soviel möglich, weit unten anwinden, weil sodann ihre force weit geringer wird; doch müssen sie auch nicht ganz an die Decke rühren, weil dieß allzugroße Winkel bey den Seyten verursacht, auch weil sie leicht gar in die Decke rücken; und das taugt nicht. Bey solchen schwachen Wirbeln muß man sich auch in Acht nehmen, daß man sie nicht entzwey drehe. Ein Fehler ist auch bey den Wirbeln, wenn sie von Meßing sind. Dergleichen Wirbel rosten zwar nicht ein; aber sie sind zu glatt, und lassen sich durch die Gewalt der Seyten leicht herum drehen. Eisen ist besser; doch soll es kein Drat, sondern geschmiedet Eisen seyn: denn diese stehen vester. Wenn sie nicht tief genug eingehen, oder unten nicht spitzig genug sind; so muß man mit der Feile das letzte, und mit dem Bohrer das erste verbessern. Die Ordnung der Wirbel ist verschiedentlich. Man mache sie also, daß die Proportion der Seyten bleibt. Ein Hauptfehler ist auch, wenn die Wirbel keinen eichenen Grund haben, worinne sie vest stehen: denn das Fichten- oder Tannenholz, das einige dazu nehmen, schlägt sich bald weit, und sodann stehen die Wirbel nicht, und sie schlagen sich immer weiter hinein. Damit das lezte vermieden werde; so sollen auch die Wirbel nicht gar zu spitzig seyn.

§. 588.

as others that are tuned higher. There are those that make the cases much deeper than usual, for the sake of the tone; indeed, at times some install yet another soundboard underneath the keys. By positioning the bridge to allow a considerable space between it and the tuning pins, so that the treble strings are allowed to sound brightly (like the shrillness of an ordinary harp) between the bridge and the pins, the pleasant resonance of a clavichord is considerably increased, especially if the correct proportion is achieved so that their pitch is fairly close to the actual [sounding length of the] strings. For strings vibrate sympathetically, as has been demonstrated in §.536 above, and when a note sounds, then the strings on the other side of the bridge, as many of them as harmonize with that note, will resonate with it, in the manner of a harp. The more such sympathetic strings are in precise tune with a note, the more pronounced the resonance will be. Thus it is understandable how it happens that at times some notes resonate longer than others, since more of the sympathetic strings are in tune with them. Thus no pieces [of cloth] should be set on top of them [i.e., the sympathetic strings], since these strings will not resonate if they are interlaced [with cloth]. If one wishes to preserve this [sympathetic vibration] exactly as it is, then neither the bridge nor the tuning pins can be moved. Otherwise the resonance will disappear, and perhaps shift over to another note. The strings between the tangent and the cloth cannot resonate much, since the cloth dampens them.

§. 587.

It is a major fault for the tuning pins to stand so close to each other that it is difficult to get between them with a hammer and pliers (see §.579). It is also a fault for them not to be strong enough, since they are soon bent crooked by the pull of the strings. If they are already weak and cannot be changed, then the strings must be wound as close to the bottom as possible, because in that way they exert far less pressure. But they must not come into direct contact with the soundboard, since this causes too great an angle in the strings, and also because they can easily cut right into the soundboard—that is not good. With such weak pins one must also be careful not to twist them apart. It is also a fault for the pins to be made of brass. Such pins do not rust, it is true, but they are too smooth, and [thus] are too easily turned by the pull of the strings. Iron is better, but it must not be wire, but rather forged iron; pins of this type hold up better. If they are not sunk deeply enough, then the holes into which they are driven must be bored deeper; or if they are not tapered enough at the bottom end, then they must be filed more to a point. There are various arrangements for the tuning pins; but they should be laid out so that the proportion of the strings is maintained.* It is also a major fault for the pins not to have an oak foundation† that holds them tight; the spruce or fir wood that some use for this [purpose] soon lets [the pin holes] spread, and then the pins do not hold, and get driven further and further in. In order to avoid this latter problem, the pins should also not be too drastically tapered.

* See §.579 and §.586 above.
† i.e., wrest pin block.

Kap. XXVI. Von dem Clavichord u. Pedal.

§. 588.

Die Stifte, an welchen die Seyten über der Mensur hangen, sollen nicht gar zu kurz seyn, auch dabey etwas schief stehen, sonst hängen die Seyten nicht wohl. Bey dem Claveßin habe ich angerathen noch etliche Palmulen unter C anzubringen, welches auch hier gilt: und wenn es gleich bis ins C 16′ reichte; so könnte es nicht schaden. Die Ursach ist §. 25. zu lesen. Ein Fehler ists, wenn die Clavichordien zu schwer zu spielen sind. Der Mangel kömmt daher, daß der hintere Theil der Palmulen allzuschwer ist gegen den vordern Theil. Wenn der hintere allzuschwer und dicke gemacht ist, und ist noch dazu lang, wie bey breiten Clavichordien geschiehet, und der vordere Theil ist kurz; so muß es schwer zu drücken seyn: denn es fallen soviel momenta auf eine Seite, und die beyden Theile vor und hinter dem hypomochlio gehen allzuweit vom æquilibrio ab. Man soll also alles so zart arbeiten vorn und hinten, als es sich thun läßt, wenn es etwas soll ausstehen können. Dabey muß man aber, wenn die hintern Theile ja stark und lang werden müssen, auch die vordersten Theile länger und schwerer machen, daß die Gleichheit im Gewichte zwar nicht ist; doch daß die Ungleichheit nicht allzu groß sey. Das æquilibrium oder Gleichheit darf nicht seyn, sonst würde nach dem Anschlage die Palmula nicht wieder zurück fallen; deswegen ist es ein Fehler, wenn der Hintertheil nicht um etwas schwerer ist, als der Vordertheil. Daher kömmts, daß sie nicht so geschwind niederfallen. Wo dieser Fehler ist, da muß man in den Hintertheil der Palmul etwas Bley gießen, nur soviel als nöthig, daß er den Vordertheil merklich überwiege. Die Vordertheile der chromatischen Tasten sind kürzer, folglich haben sie auch viel weniger momenta gegen ihre Hintertheile, als die diatonischen. Daraus ist klar, daß der chromatischen Hintertheile dünner und leichter zu machen, als bey den diatonischen, wenn das Clavier durchaus soll gleich schwer zu spielen seyn. Zuweilen ist ein Clavier deswegen zähe zu spielen, weil die Löcher, worinnen die Stifte laufen, über dem hypomochlio etwas enge sind. Wenn man die weiter bohrt, und von der Unreinigkeit befreyet; so wird dem Mangel abgeholfen.

§. 589.

Ein Fehler ists, wenn die Claves stocken. Das kömmt zuweilen daher, daß sie zu enge liegen, und einander reiben. Da muß man etwas von der Seite abschaben. Oder, wenn sie sich verworfen haben; so muß man zuweilen ein gleiches thun, oder den Stift auf die Seite rücken, wonach die Spielung am stärksten ist. Zuweilen ist die Ursach, daß die hintern Stifte in den Kerben oder Ritzen Ungleichheiten antreffen; oder, wenn sie zumal von Fischbein sind, sich splittern; oder wenn sie zu kurz sind, und auf die Seite treten. ꝛc. Deswegen sie von Blech am besten zu machen. Auch müssen sie lang seyn, doch nicht gar zu lang, sonst geben sie gleichfall Anlaß zum Stocken. Es zeigt sich auch ein Stocken, wenn die Tangenten zwischen den Seyten geklemmt werden. Diesem hilft man ab, wenn man die Blätter anders rückt; auch wol durch das Tuch je-

Ch. XXVI. The Clavichord and Pedal-clavier.

§. 588.

The [hitch] pins driven into the top of the hitchpin block (über der Mensur*), around which the strings are looped, should not be too short, and should in addition stand at a bit of an angle; otherwise the strings are liable to slip off. In my discussion of the harpsichord† I suggested adding a few keys below C. This applies here, as well; in fact, it would do no harm if it extended all the way down to 16′ C. §.25 explains the origin of this [system of labeling pitches]. It is a defect if clavichords have too heavy an action. This shortcoming arises from the rear portion of the key being too heavy in relation to the forward portion. If the rear [portion] is made too heavy and thick, and is long in addition (as happens in wide clavichords), and the forward portion is short, then the action will inevitably be heavy, since a disproportionate amount of weight falls on one side [of the balance rail], and both sections—the one behind the balance rail and the one in front of it—are so far out of balance. Everything, both behind [the balance rail] and in front of it, needs to be fashioned as lightly as possible, consistent with the need for durability. In this regard, if the rear portion has to be long and heavy, then the forward portion must be made longer and heavier, not to the point that they are equal in weight, to be sure, but so that the imbalance is not too great. The two dare not be in perfect balance, otherwise the [rear portion of the] key would not fall back after being played. Thus it is a defect if the rear portion is not somewhat heavier than the forward one; this is why it will not drop down again very rapidly. If this fault exists, then some [molten] lead must be cast into the rear portion of the key, but only as much as is necessary to make it noticeably outweigh the forward portion. The forward portions of the chromatic keys are shorter; consequently they have far less weight in comparison to their rear portions than do the diatonic [keys]. This makes it clear that the rear portions of chromatic keys should be made thinner and lighter than those of the diatonic keys, if the keyboard is to have an even touch throughout [its compass]. Occasionally a keyboard is sluggish to play because the holes above the balance rail in which the [keys] pivot [on the] pins are somewhat [too] tight. If they are drilled a bit bigger and cleared of dirt, this shortcoming will be relieved.

* See §.575, note 16.

† i.e., §.507.

§. 589.

Sticking keys are also a fault. This is sometimes the result of their being too close to and rubbing against each other. Then a bit has to be shaved off their sides. Or they may have gotten warped; in that case sometimes the same remedy works, or the pin needs to be shifted toward the side that has the greatest amount of play. Sometimes the reason is that the rear slips in the slots or notches encounter unevenness; sometimes, if they are made of fishbone,‡ they splinter; or if they are too short, they [allow the keys to] shift to the side. That is why they are best made of metal. They must be long, but not too long, or they will again be the cause of sticking. Sticking also happens if the tangents (Tangenten) get caught between the strings. This can be remedied by re-adjusting the tangents (Blätter), or the cloth [listing] can pull each pair of

‡ i.e., whalebone (baleen).

des Paar Seyten enger zusammen zieht, doch nicht allzu enge, sonst schnarren sie. Sind sie noch zu breit, daß sie die Nachbaren berühren; so feile man die Ecken ab. Zuweilen stossen sie hinten an; und so bringe man die Stifte vorwärts, oder schneide etwas hinten ab. Fällt Staub zwischen die Palmulen; so muß man ihn fortschaffen. Zuweilen bleibt es vorn hangen: da muß man entweder an den äussersten Vordertheilen der Palmulen, oder besser an den Vorsetzbrette unter oder vor den Palmulen etwas abnehmen.

§. 590.

Die Stifte, worinnen die Palmulen laufen oder beweglich sind, werden in eine Leiste geschlagen, doch so, daß die chromatischen etwas weiter hinten stehen, um dem æquilibrio etwas näher zu kommen. Diese Leiste habe ich bisher hypomochlium, die Unterlage, genennet, und wird solche etwas stark gemacht, daß die Stifte stärker werden können, die man darein schlägt. Der obere Theil ist rund, und man überklebt ihn zuweilen mit Leder, Tuch oder Pergament; und über demselben wird zuweilen nichts, zuweilen aber eine sehr starke Dratseyte (zuweilen auch nur ein Bindfaden) recht straff ausgezogen, und oben und unten befestiget, daß sie auf dem hypomochlio aufliegt, um das Punctum besser zu determiniren, wo der vordere und hintere Theil sich berühren. Etliche machen den Faden in gerader Linie an; und das ist besser, als wenn er krumm ist; denn sonst wird ein Clavis schwerer werden, als der andere.

§. 591.

Es geschieht zuweilen, daß die Blätter der Tagenten oben scharf sind, und die Seyten desto eher durchschlagen; it. daß sie Kerbchen durch die Seyten bekommen: Dieß kann man mit der Feile wegschaffen. Es müssen diese Blätter stets gerade stehen: denn wo sie auf eine Seite stehen; so ist es ein Zeichen, daß die Mensur nicht getroffen. Wo sie vor- oder hinterwarts stehen, kann man sie leicht ausziehen und weiter vor- oder hinterwärts schlagen, daß sie gleich unter ihre Seyten zu stehen kommen: denn sonst schlagen solche nicht an beyde Seyten ihres Chors mit gleicher Stärke an. Doch wenn ich alles hier berühren wollte, müßte ich noch viel hersetzen. Ein jeder denke nun weiter nach. Was die Stimmung anlanget; so wird davon das folgende Kapitel etwas gedenken.

§. 592.

Bey Erhaltung der Clavichordien hat man wohl zu verhüten, daß man nicht Fett auf die Decke bringe: denn dadurch werden sie verdorben. Das Fett kreucht in die Poros, und wegen seiner Viscosität bleibt es drinnen, und geht auch wol weiter; daher die Luft nicht aller Orten durchkommen kann. Das Wasser ist zwar auch nichts nütze auf der Decke; doch wird dadurch nicht sowohl der Klang verdorben, als daß die Theile aus dem Leime gehen, und der Steg abspringt; übrigens geht es wieder heraus, und mischet sich unter die Luft, weil es nicht so zusammen hänget, wie das Fett oder Oel.

Ch. XXVI. The Clavichord and Pedal-clavier.

strings closer together—but not too close or they will rattle. If [the tangent blades] are still so broad that they touch the neighboring [strings], their corners should be filed off. Sometimes [the key levers] strike at the rear, and in that case the balance pins should be moved forward, or some of the back [of each key] should be cut off. If dust falls between the keys, it must be removed. Sometimes [a key] gets caught at the front, and then a bit has to be removed either from the front edge of the key, or better, from the board beneath or in front of the key.

§. 590.

The pins on which the keys pivot are driven into a board, with the chromatic ones placed a bit further back [than the diatonic ones], in order [for them] to come closer to being balanced. I have previously called this board the *hypomochlium*, the support*. It needs to be made quite sturdily, so that the pins that are driven into it can be all the stronger. Its upper surface is rounded, and at times a layer of leather, cloth or parchment is glued over it. Sometimes nothing rests on that layer, but at other times a length of very heavy wire (or sometimes just a piece of twine) is stretched very taut on it, and then fastened at both ends, so that it lies on the fulcrum, in order to mark the point more clearly where the forward and rear portions [of the key] meet. Some attach the twine in a straight line, which is better than making it crooked, since the latter will cause one key to have a heavier action than another.

* i.e., the balance rail.

§. 591.

Sometimes it happens that the blades of the tangents are sharp on top, and cut through the strings rather quickly. Sometimes the strings also make little notches in the blades; these can be removed with a file. The blades must always be straight; if they are bent to the side, it is a sign that the scaling is not right. If they stand [too far] forward or backward, they can easily be pulled out and driven in further forward or back, so that they come to stand directly under their strings. Otherwise they do not strike both strings of the set with equal force. But if I were to cover everything here, I would have to write down much more than this. Each [reader] can think [these matters] through for himself. As concerns tuning, the following chapter will mention something about it.

§. 592.

In maintaining a clavichord one must be careful not to get grease on the soundboard, for it will ruin the instrument. The grease soaks into the pores, and because it is viscous it stays there and even keeps penetrating further. Thus air cannot pass through at every point. Water on the soundboard is not any good, either; it does not so much harm the tone, though, as cause the sections to come unglued and the bridge to pop off. Otherwise it evaporates into the air and disappears, since it does not hang together like

Aus feuchten Oertern sind alle solche Instrumente wegzuschaffen, weil der Leim weich wird. Die Sonne darf auch nicht wohl drauf scheinen: denn die Theile dorren mit Gewalt, und die Decke springet gern, und dieses um so viel mehr, wenn das Holz nicht recht dürre gewesen. Durch die Ritzen aber, welche die Sonnenhitze bisweilen in der Decke verursacht, wird gleichfals der Klang verdorben, und kann man diesem Fehler nicht ganz abhelfen, ohne durch eine neue Decke; wol aber zum Theil, wenn man Späne in die Ritzen leimt, und es so gut, als möglich, wieder verwahrt. Der Klang selbst aber wird besser, wenn das Clavichord eine Zeitlang gespielt worden.

§. 593.

Daß die Unreinigkeiten und die Sonne nicht so frey darein agiren mögen; so kann man es in ein Futteral verstecken, oder wenigstens ein Lied oben drauf legen. Ueber die Stifte macht man ein Vorsetzbrett, welches auch durch Stifte kann veste gemacht werden, daß es die Claviere nicht vorwärts drucke. Man kann es fourniren, wie auch etliche übrige Theile des Clavifords mit Goldpapier bekleben, und nach Gefallen auszieren. Das Corpus selbst wird zuweilen ausgeeckt, in dieser Figur:

Wenn man auf solchen Clavichordien sich wie auf einer Orgel mit 2 oder mehrern Clavieren will lustig machen; so kann man entweder deren 2 über einander setzen: oder man kann 2 überein machen lassen von einerley Holz, Größe, Mensur rc. das letzte ziehe ich deswegen vor, weil, wenn sie sich verstimmen, sie zugleich auf oder abwärts sich ziehen, (wenn die Abtheilung richtig ist) und bleiben also unter sich reiner als wenn man 2 über einander setzt, die nicht zusammen gehören. Soll das Pedal auch dabey seyn; so wird es gemacht, wie hernach stehet.

§. 594.

Man könnte auch den Clavichordien eine Clavicymbel Figur, oder eine andere geben; doch dürfte das Clavier nicht zu tief zu liegen kommen. Wie den auch noch mehr dabey zu merken wäre, wenn ich mich wollte aufhalten; es wird dieß zu machen doch kein Mechanikus so leicht wagen. Was oben §. 524. vom Stege gesagt worden, trifft auch hier ein, und könnte man nach jener Vorschrift auch einen Steg auf den Clavichordien anbringen. Wie denn daraus leicht abzunehmen ist, daß der Klang durch das Drücken muß verändert werden, daß, wo nur etwas, (etwann ein Schlüssel) auf der Decke liegt, es gleich schnarrt. Legt man etwas auf den Steg; so wird es gedämpft. Sonst ist auch noch mehr von dem hierher zu ziehen, was oben vom Clavicymbel gesagt ist, welches man daselbst nachlesen mag; und verschiedenes, das daselbst nicht beygebracht ist, kann aus diesem Kapitel dorthin gezogen werden.

Was

grease or oil. All instruments of this sort should be kept away from damp places, since the dampness softens the glue. They should also be kept out of direct sunlight, since the parts dry out mightily, and the soundboard is likely to split; this is all the more true if the wood was not thoroughly cured [to begin with]. The cracks in the soundboard that are sometimes caused by the sun's heat will ruin the tone; this defect cannot be totally remedied without [installing] a new soundboard. But they may indeed be partially remedied by gluing shims into the cracks, sealing them up again as well as possible. The tone of the clavichord will improve after it has been played a while.

§. 593.

To prevent dirt and the sun from affecting it so much, [a clavichord] may be closed up in a case, or at least a lid may be placed over it. A nameboard is placed above the [balance rail] pins; it may be fastened by pins to keep it from pressing the keys forward. It may be veneered, just as other parts of the clavichord may be [decorated by] overlaying them with gold paper, and embellishing them according to one's fancy. Sometimes the corners of the case are left off, [resulting] in this shape:

If anyone wishes to take his ease on clavichords with 2 or more manuals as on an organ, then he may either set two of them together, one atop the other, or have 2 of them made identically, of the same wood, size, scale, etc. I favor the latter, because if they go out of tune, they go together, either sharp or flat (providing the design (Abtheilung*) is correct), and thus remain more in tune between themselves than when 2 are joined that do not belong together. If there is also to be a pedal, it should be built following the instructions below.†

* See §.579.

† §.596.

§. 594.

Clavichords may also be built in the shape of a harpsichord or some other shape; but the keyboard cannot be placed too low.‡ There is yet more that could be mentioned if I wished to dwell (on this topic); no craftsman would undertake building one of these lightly. What was said in §.524 above about the bridge also applies here. A bridge could also be installed in a clavichord following those instructions. It is easy to deduce from what has been said that the tone is unavoidably altered by [any kind of] pressure [on the soundboard], so that any little thing (say, a key) lying on the soundboard causes a rattle right away. If anything is set on the bridge, the [tone] will be dampened. There is yet more of what was said above about the harpsichord that could be applied here, which the reader may may consult for himself; and certain [information] that was not imparted there may be applied there from this chapter.

‡ i.e., too far beneath the level of the strings. The reason for this warning will become obvious when one compares the action of a harpsichord (relatively long jacks, resting on key levers) with that of a clavichord (relatively short tangents, driven into the key levers).

Was den Preiß der Clavichordien betrift; so ist derselbe, nach Beschaffenheit der Arbeit, sehr verschieden. Man kann zuweilen eins für 16. ggl. haben: aber die dienen gut zum Feuer, wenn man Fische kochen will; zumal wenn sie mit Sub-Semitonien versehen sind. Denn wir gewöhnen uns nicht dran, und gleichwol ist die Mensur bey solchen Dingern darnach eingerichtet. Man hat aber auch welche für 2, 4, 6, 10, 15, 20, 30, und mehrere Thaler.

§. 595.

Zu der Erhaltung der Clavichordien gehört auch, daß man sie zwar brauche, und im Spielen nicht allzufurchtsam sey; doch auch nicht so drauf schlage, als wolle man einen Ziehochsen todt machen. Die Seyten werden gar bald ruinirt, und wird man sie doch nicht zwingen, wenn sie von Anfang her schwach klingt. Von der Stimmung und Aufziehung der Seyten folgt Kap. 27. das nöthige.

§. 596.

Wir wandern endlich zum Pedale, als dem letzten Instrumente, welches uns aber nicht lange aufhalten wird, weil das meiste mit dem Clavichorde, oder auch mit dem Clavicymbel, überein kömmt. Man verfertiget nämlich die Pedalclaves, wie sie bey einer Orgel seyn müssen, nach ihrer Anzahl, Größe, Weite und Lage, versieht sie mit Federn, Stiften u. s. w. Besiehe was Kap. 2. §. 27. 28. 29. gesagt ist; das gehöret meistens auch hierher. Gut ists, wenn die Theile alle zusammen geschraubt werden, daß man sie von einander nehmen und forttragen kann. Hernach verfertiget man das Gestelle, welches einem Tischbocke nicht unähnlich ist, nur daß vornen die Scheiden eingeschnitten werden, wie §. 27. bey der Orgel geschahe. Hier ist dieß besonders, weil man sie höher aufschneiden müsse, weil man das punctum, wie tief sie im Spielen fallen sollen, nicht bestimmen kann, wie bey der Orgel; zumal wo man das Werk mit Bindfaden regiert. Daher auch nicht eben nöthig, sie mit Tuch auszufüttern. Das Gestelle wird so hoch, daß es mit dem darauf zu setzenden Kasten, und denen hernach darüber zu stehen kommenden Clavikordien der Höhe des Orgel-Claviers gleich wird, damit man stets einerley gewohnt sey.

§. 597.

Der Kasten kann gemacht werden, wie der Körper eines Clavichors; doch etwas länger, damit man 16 Fuß bequem darauf ziehen könne. Man macht auch das corpus tiefer, und den Steg hoch, damit es pompichter klinge, als das Clavichord. Man kann endlich wol zum Körper weich Holz nehmen, weil man die Veränderungen so nicht empfindet, als bey dem Manual. Die Decke, Steg, Seyten, Tuch und Wirbel werden wie bey dem Clavichord. Was nun dabey für Fehler oder Tugenden sind, das kann man beym Clavichord, oder auch bey dem Clavicymbel, lesen. Dieß ist hier zu merken, daß es nicht eben nöthig, das Pedal bundfrey zu machen: denn man macht

darauf

Ch. XXVI. The Clavichord and Pedal-clavier.

As concerns the price of a clavichord, it varies a great deal according to the quality of the work. Sometimes it is possible to get one for 16 *gute Groschen** (ggl.), but one like that is only good for firewood to cook fish, especially if it is provided with subsemitones. For we [today] are not accustomed to them [i.e., subsemitones], and the scaling is likewise arranged for such contraptions. But there are also instruments available for 2, 4, 6, 10, 15, 20, 30 thalers or more.

* 24 of these equal a Taler.

§. 595.

To maintain a clavichord it is also necessary to play it regularly, and not to be too timid in doing it. But on the other hand one should not beat on it as if killing a draft-ox; the strings will soon be ruined, and if they sound soft to begin with, one cannot force them. The necessary [steps] to string and tune them will follow in Chap. 27.

§. 596.

For our final instrument [to consider], let us turn to the pedal. It will not detain us long, since most [of its features] correspond to the clavichord, or to the harpsichord.† First the pedal keys are constructed, just like those of an organ in number, size, width and position, and they are provided with springs, pins, etc. Consult what is said in Chapter 2, §.27, 28 and 29; most of that applies here as well. It is good if the parts are all put together with screws, since then they can be disassembled and transported. The next thing to build is the stand, which looks rather like a trestle, except that sheaths [for the pedal keys] are cut into the front of it, just as in the organ (see §.27). The difference here is that‡ they must be cut deeper, since it is not possible to determine the lowest point to which they [the keys] will drop, as [one can] in the organ; this is especially true if the [pedal] instrument is operated by twine.§ Thus it is not necessary to line [the bottom of the sheaths] with cloth.¶ The stand should be high enough that with the box‖ sitting on it and the clavichords resting in turn on top of the box, [the entire assembly] is of the same height** as the manual[s] of an organ, so that the player becomes accustomed to the same [dimensions in both].

† depending on which of these instruments it is attached to.

‡ There is a correction to the printed text here that is noted in the *errata* at the end of Vol. II.

§ instead of trackers.

¶ i.e., to stop the fall of the pedal keys, since the action is stopped by the contact of the tangents with the strings.

‖ i.e., the pedal case.

** i.e., from the surface of the pedals to the manuals.

§. 597.

The case can be made like that of a clavichord, but somewhat longer, so that a 16′ can conveniently be strung in it. The case should also be deeper, and the bridge high, so that it sounds fuller and richer than a clavichord. Here, finally, soft wood may be used for the case, since changes†† in it are not as readily perceived as in the manual. The soundboard, bridge, strings, cloth [listing], and tuning pins are just like those in a clavichord. As far as its faults or virtues, they are those described in connection with the clavichord or with the harpsichord. Take note that it is not really necessary to make the pedal unfretted, since [notes] fretted [with each other] are seldom played together.‡‡ Thus one

†† i.e., arising from the weather.

‡‡ i.e., either simultaneously (as with suspensions) or slurred.

darauf selten Bindungen; also kann man sich des Vortheils bedienen, den man dadurch in der Stimmung, Aufziehung der Seyten u. s. w. haben kann. Hingegen scheinet hier nothwendiger, sie 3fach, oder dreychöricht, zu machen, damit es stärker klinge, und die Gewalt der Füsse aushalten könne. Und zwar geht dieß allhier durchaus also. Will man das eine Chor auf 16 Fuß spinnen; so wird es eine besondere Gravität geben. Sonst erinnere ich von den Seyten nichts, weil es bey dem Clavicymbel und Clavichorde geschehen.

§. 598.

Gut ists, wenn man das Pedal führt bis ins $\bar{d}$: denn zu Hause macht man solche Dinge öfterer, als auf der Orgel, welche bis ins $\bar{d}$ gesetzt sind. So ist auch gut, einen Deckel über das corpus zu legen: doch wenn die Decke offen bleibt, wenigstens an einem Theil; so gehet es stärker. Deswegen soll der Deckel über der Resonanzdecke a part können abgenommen werden. Die Seyten werden durch die Tangenten angeschlagen, die den Tangenten eines Clavichords gleich, mit Stiften in den Kerben, und mit Blättern (welche hier sonderlich stark und breit seyn müssen) versehen sind; nur daß der Anschlag oder vordere Theil nicht so ist. Denn sie werden durch die Füsse regieret. Sie können auch alle gerade liegen, weil mehr Raum da ist; denn hier hat man nur 2. Oktaven. Es werden diese Tangenten den Raum einnehmen, wie das Clavier von 4. Oktaven im Manuale, damit man einerley Mensur machen könne. Die Tangenten müssen auch etwas stärker werden, der Gewalt wegen. Wollte man das hypomochlium beweglich machen, und den Lautenzug hineinbringen, wie bey dem Clavichord; so gienge es auch an. Doch davon besehe man, was bey dem Clavichorde angemerkt worden.

§. 599.

Zwischen den Palmulen, darauf die Füsse stehen, und zwischen den Tangenten muß etwas seyn, dadurch eins das andere regiret. Die schlechteste, leichteste und wohlfeilste Art ist, daß man anstatt der Abstrakten bey der Orgel allhier guten Bindfaden nimmt, und selbigen hinter dem Scheidenbrette an die Palmulen anbindet. Man darf nur eine Kerbe in eine jede schneiden, und einen Knoten in den Bindfaden binden, und sodann in die Kerbe den Faden legen, daß der Knoten unten anliegt, und verhindert, daß der Faden nicht durchkreucht. Den Faden führt man sodann durch den Boden des Kastens, der deswegen eine Oeffnung haben muß. In das Vordertheil der Tangente, nicht weit vom Ende, bohret man ein Loch, steckt ein Zäpfchen durch, das oben breit ist, daß man wieder ein Loch durchbohren kann, und durch dieß Loch steckt man den Bindfaden, verwahrt das Ende auch mit einem Knoten, und drehet oder windet es durch den Pflock so lange um, bis der Faden straff angezogen ist. Doch daß auch die Tangente dadurch nicht in die Höhe gezogen werde. Man muß in das vordere Theil der Tangenten eine Kerbe schneiden, und den Faden dadurch führen, daß er nicht von der Seite ziehe, weil solches schädlich ist. So oft als der Faden sich dehnet und

schlot=

Ch. XXVI. The Clavichord and Pedal-clavier.

can take advantage of the benefits that [fretted construction] offers in tuning, stringing,* etc. On the other hand, it appears more necessary here to make the instrument with three sets of strings,† so that it sounds louder and can withstand the force of the feet;‡ this applies throughout the entire compass. If you wish to use overspun strings for the 16′ choir, this will produce an especially weighty [tone]. I have nothing else to say about the strings that has not already been discussed in connection with the harpsichord and clavichord.

§. 598.

It is good for the pedal to extend up to d′, since at home one plays things that go up to d′ more often than on the organ.§ It is also good to put a lid over the case; but if the lid remains open, at least one section of it, then the instrument will sound louder. For this reason the [section of the] lid over the soundboard should be removable separately. The strings are struck by keylevers¶ (Tangenten), like those of the clavichord, provided with [guide] pins in notches, and with tangents (Blättern‖) (which have to be especially strong and broad here). It is only the forward part [of the key],** where it is played, that is different, since it is operated by the feet. All [the keys] can lie straight, since there is more space available, [the compass] being only 2 octaves. The key levers here occupy the space that 4 octaves take up in the manual, and thus the scaling can be made uniform. The keys must also be somewhat sturdier due to the force [exerted on them]. If you wish, it is possible to make the balance rail movable in order to install a buff stop, as in a clavichord. Consult what has already been said about this in connection with the clavichord.††

§. 599.

There must be something between the part of the keys controlled by the feet and the key levers, so that the one can operate the other. The simplest, easiest and cheapest method is to use a good-quality twine here, instead of trackers as in an organ, tying the [key levers] to the pedals behind the sheath-board.‡‡ One need only cut a slot in each of them, tie a knot in the twine, and then insert the twine into the slot; the knot, being underneath, will prevent the twine from slipping through. The twine is then threaded through the bottom of the case, which must have an opening for this purpose. A hole is bored through the front of the key lever, not far from the end. Into this hole is inserted a peg that is somewhat wider on top, so that a hole can also be bored through it. The twine, this end of which is also secured with a knot, is threaded through this hole, and wound around the peg until the twine is drawn taut—but not so taut as to lift the [rear portion of the] key levers. A slot must be cut into the front end of the key lever and the twine guided through it, so that it does not pull from one side or the other, since that is harmful. Whenever the twine becomes stretched and slack, it should again be twisted

---

* i.e., fewer strings to install or tune; see §.608 below.

† i.e., three per note.

‡ i.e., the tangents propelled by the feet will strike much more forcefully than when propelled by the fingers.

§ it is not evident today why this would be the case.

¶ Here Adlung is envisioning key levers just below the strings in the pedal case, with tangents rising from them (just as in a normal clavichord), but instead of extending beyond the forward edge of the pedal case, they are connected (by means of twine or trackers) to the keys of a pedalboard that lies below the pedal case.

‖ See note, §.572.

** i.e., the pedals that lie on the floor and extend forward under the player's feet.

†† See §.577.

‡‡ See §.596.

schlotterich wird; so oft drehet man ihn wieder um den Pflock. Doch geschiehet es, daß durch die Gewalt der Pflock sich rückwärts drehet; daher man den Faden, wenn er einmal recht ist, lieber an denselben anbinde. Oder man mache den Knoten ganz knapp an, daß kein Drehen angehe, oder schade; wiewol man in diesem Falle nicht einmal eines Pflockes nöthig hat, und kann man den Faden nur an die Tangente binden.

§. 600.

Diese Art hat folgende Commoda. Es kostet nicht viel, und für 3 bis 4 Rthlr. kann man zuweilen ein solch Pedal haben.(**) Reisset ein Faden entzwey; so bindet man einen andern an. Auch erregt es kein Rasseln. Die Incommoda sind, daß sich die Faden nicht nur dehnen, sondern das Pflöckchen gehet auch herum. Doch allem kann man leicht entgegen gehen, und ist diese Incommodität so groß nicht, als die, daß, weil die Palmulen vielmehr Raum einnehmen, als die Tangenten, die Faden zuweilen nicht perpendicular herabhangen, sondern ganz schief. Daher es kömmt, daß die Palmulen sich auf die Seite ziehen lassen, und daß sich die Blätter und Stifte auf die Seite legen. Dem aber gehet man einigermaßen entgegen, wenn man die Blätter, sonderlich die Stifte in den Kerben brav stark macht, daß sie sich durch diese Gewalt nicht auf die Seite biegen lassen; und wird Fischbein zu solchen hintern Stiften nicht wohl dienen, auch das ordinäre Blech nicht, sondern ein stark breit geschlagener Drat oder Eisen. Wenn man das C unter die Tangente C fast perpendicular legt; so werden endlich die obern Palmulen allzuschiefe Faden bekommen. Daher ich rathen wollte, daß man es besser eintheilte, und das mittlere c unter seinen Tangenten legte, und sodann auf beyden Seiten continuirte; so würden sowol die untern, als auch die obern Claves etwas schiefe Faden bekommen; doch würde es auf solche Art nicht viel austragen: hingegen würde das Clavichord einen größern Theil von der Resonanzdecke des Pedals bedecken. Bey dieser Struktur ist nöthig, vorn eine Thür zu machen, daß man durchgreifen, und die Faden wieder an die Palmulen machen könne: It. oben im Kasten eine, daß man stets zu den Pflöckchen kommen könne, ohne das Clavichord abzuheben, oder das ganze Pedal fortzurücken. Wenn die Faden etwas von dem vordern Scheidenbrette entfernet sind, ists gut: damit man dasselbe nicht mit dem Knie an dieselben drucke, und sie spanne.

(**) Zu itzigen Zeiten gewiß nicht mehr.

§. 601.

Anstatt der Faden machen andere ordentliche Abstrakten, wie in der Orgel; daher sie Wellenbrettter, Stifte, Arme u. d. gl. anbringen müssen, wovon die Struktur oben Kap. 4. §. 48. — 51. zu lesen. Diese Abstrakten müssen, wie die Faden, hinter das Wellenbrett kommen, daß man sie auswendig mit den Füssen nicht beschädige. Das Incommodum hierbey ist, daß man das Rasseln so stark vernimmt, zumal da der Klang der Pedale schwächer ist, als bey der Orgel; auch kostet es viel, und wird

ein

around the peg. But it may happen that the peg rotates from the force [exerted on it]; thus it is better to tie the twine to it, once it is adjusted properly. Or the knots may be tied tight against [the top of the peg], to prevent any rotating from taking place and harming [the action]. In that case, though, the peg is not really necessary, either; the twine need only be tied to the key lever.

§. 600.

The method [described above] has a number of advantages. It does not cost much; at times such a pedal [instrument] may be had for [as little as] 3–4 Reichsthaler.(**) If a piece of twine breaks, then one need only tie another one on. It also does not give rise to any rattling. Its disadvantages are that the pieces of twine not only stretch, but also that the peg rotates. But all of these may easily be remedied. These disadvantages are not as significant as the fact that sometimes the pieces of twine do not drop perpendicularly, but at a considerable slant, since the keys take up much more space than the key levers. This causes the pedal keys to be pulled sidewards, and also the tangents and [guide] slips* to bend to the side. This can be prevented to some degree by making the tangents, and in particular the slips in their slots, good and strong, so that the force [exerted on them] does not bend them to the side. Fishbone† will not serve very well for these slips in the back [of the key levers], nor will ordinary sheet metal; rather [they call for] a strong [piece of] wire or iron, hammered flat. If low C is positioned almost directly under the key lever C, then the twine from the upper keys will end up having too great an angle. Therefore I would advise that it is better to distribute [the angle] by placing the middle [pedal] c under its key lever and then continuing [outward] on both sides. Thus both the lower as well as the upper keys will get twine at an angle, but by this method it would not amount to much. On the other hand, the clavichord would cover a considerable portion of the pedal's soundboard. The structure [of the pedal as described] makes a door in the front [of the pedal case] necessary, in order to be able to reach in and re-attach the twine to the key levers. There also needs to be one in the top of the case, so that the pegs are always accessible without needing to lift off the clavichord or to remove the entire pedal. It is good if the pieces of twine are at some distance from the forward sheath-board, so that no one's knee can press it against the [pieces of twine] and stretch them.

* See §.575.

† i.e., whalebone (baleen).

(**) This is certainly no longer true today. [Agricola]

§. 601.

Other [builders] make ordinary trackers, as in the organ, instead of [using] twine. That means that they must install roller boards, pins, arms and the like; these you may read about in Chap. 4, §.48–51 above. Like the pieces of twine, these trackers must be placed behind the roller board; if they were in front, the feet could harm them. The disadvantage of this arrangement is that they make such an audible clatter, especially since the sound of the pedal is more delicate than that of the organ. It also

ein solch Pedal nicht um einen so wohlfeilen Preiß verfertiget, als §. 600. gemeldet. Dieß hat es aber zum voraus, daß durch die Wellen die Abstrakten die Tangenten perpendicular abwärts ziehen.

§. 602.

Die Pedale werden gut erhalten, wenn man deren Theile nach der Vollkommenheit macht, die bey dem Orgelpedale vorgeschrieben worden §. 27. 28. 29. Sonderlich ist wohl zu beobachten, was §. 353. und 354. beygebracht worden. Hier ist noch anzumerken, daß man im Treten viel behutsamer seyn müsse, als bey der Orgel; sonst springen die Seyten: hingegen kann man bey der Orgel mit voller force treten, indem die Pedalclaves in den Scheiden nicht tiefer fallen können, als es nöthig; hier aber ist es anders. Die Stimmung kömmt im folgenden Kapitel vor. Wenn die Federn unter den Palmulen von Meßing sind; so werden sich wenig Veränderungen dabey zutragen: sind sie aber von Eisendrat; so rosten und zerbrechen sie bald; daher man zuweilen neue unterlegen muß, doch von gleich dickem Drate und Größe, damit sie gleich schwer zu treten sind. Es kann ein jeder dergleichen machen, wenn er nur eine Feile hat, um die Spitzen dran zu machen. Etliche lassen den Drat erst glüend werden: allein hierzu kann ich nicht rathen, indem mir der ungeglüete jederzeit nicht nur bessere Dienste gethan, sondern auch besser gedauert hat. Wenn die Federn zuweilen die Palmulen nicht hoch genug heben; so muß man sie frisch einrichten. Zuweilen ziehen sie sich aus ihren Löchern, welchen (wie auch allen übrigen Fehlern) man gar leicht abhelfen kann. Der Kasten soll nicht an dem Gestelle veste seyn, sondern nur angeschraubt, oder durch Stifte bevestiget, daß man alles auseinander nehmen könne.

§. 603.

Man kann die Kasten nicht nur wie die Clavichordien machen; sondern auch in Form eines Clavicymbels, daß die Seyten durch Federn angeschlagen werden: und das heißt ein Clavicymbelpedal. Wie nun das Clavicymbel schön lautet; so ist auch ein solch Pedal schön zu gebrauchen. Es braucht keiner besondern Beschreibung. Denn es ist wie ein Clavicymbel zu machen; doch nur mit 2. Oktaven: die Docken sind eben so; doch weiter aus einander gesetzt, weil 2. Oktaven den Raum einnehmen den sonst 4. Oktaven haben. Die Tangenten werden wie bey dem Clavichordienpedale, und das übrige unten wird wie ein ander Pedal. Auf gleiche Weise kann man sie in der Gestalt eines Clavicytherii, Instruments ꝛc. machen; auch kann man Glockenspiele also machen.

§. 604.

Eine compendiösere Art ist, wenn man zu dem Pedale keine besondere Körper oder Kasten verfertiget, sondern man läßt durch die Abstrakten oder Faden die Palmulen des Clavichords, Claveßins, Instruments, Lautenwerks ꝛc. selbst ziehen. Dieß geschiehet oft, und darf man weiter nichts dran thun, als Dratschlingen, oder auch Schrauben

costs a great deal—such a pedal cannot be built for so cheap a price as was reported in §.600. But it has this advantage: the rollers allow the trackers to pull the key levers straight down.

§. 602.

[Clavichord] pedals will hold up well if their parts are made according to the exacting standards that were prescribed for organ pedals in §.27, 28 and 29. In particular take note of the information imparted in §.353 and §.354. In addition it should be mentioned here that one must pedal much more cautiously than at the organ, or the strings will snap. In contrast, one can play the organ pedals with full force, since the sheaths prevent the pedal keys from falling any deeper than necessary; this is not the case [with the clavichord]. Tuning [the instrument] will be discussed in the following chapter. If the springs under the keys are of brass, they will be quite stable and dependable; if on the other hand they are of iron wire, they will soon rust and break. In that case it is necessary to replace them with new ones from time to time, being careful to use wire of the same size and thickness so that they continue to offer the same resistance to the feet. Anyone can make such springs if only he has a file to make points.*   *i.e., at the ends of the wire. Some anneal the wire first, but I cannot advise doing this, since the untreated wire has not only consistently given better service, but also has been more durable. If at some point the springs let the pedals sag, then they must be re-regulated. Sometimes they fall out of the holes [in which they are anchored], a fault that (just like all their other faults) is easily remedied. The [pedal clavichord's] case should not be affixed† to the   † i.e., glued. stand, but only screwed to it, or fastened with pins, so that the entire [assembly] may be taken apart.

§. 603.

The case need not always be constructed as a clavichord; it may also be made in the form of a harpsichord, with the strings being plucked by quills. This is called a harpsichord-pedal. Such a pedal produces a beautiful sound, just as a harpsichord does. It needs no special description, since it is made like a harpsichord, except with only a two-octave [compass]. The jacks are just the same, except that they are spaced further apart, since 2 octaves occupy the same same space [in the pedal] as do 4 octaves [in the manual]. The key levers are just the same as the clavichord-pedal's, and the [pedal board] beneath is like any other pedal. In the same way [such a pedal] may be built in the form of a clavicytherium, an "instrument",‡ etc., or even a Glockenspiel.   ‡ See §.540.

§. 604.

A more economical way is to build the pedal without a separate case, and to have trackers or twine pull down the actual [manual] keys of the clavichord, harpsichord, "instrument", lute harpsichord, etc. This is quite common; it requires nothing more than driving eyelets or screws into the [undersides of the] keys of such instruments, up

162 Kap. XXVII. Von andern Instrumenten, und

Schrauben in die Palmulen solcher Werke schlagen, so weit die zwo untern Oktaven reichen, wie bey den Orgeln zuweilen geschiehet (conf. Cap. VII. §. 127.) Doch scheinen hier die Wellenbretter, und Abstrakten nöthiger, als vorhin: denn die 2 Oktaven sind nicht so ausgedehnet, wie vorhin, daher die Faden gar zu schief zu stehen kommen würden, Sonst ist es freylich ein gut Compendium. (**) Will man endlich solche Körper von einander nehmen; so hänge man die Faden unten oder oben alle loß. ꝛc. Herr Bach in Jena machte ehedessen zu seinen Lautenwerken auch Pedale, welche eine ordentliche Theorbe im Klange präsentirten. (s. §. 560.)

(**) Es ist aber bisweilen sehr unbequem: zumal wenn man Sachen mit dem obligaten Pedale spielet, und zuweilen auf dem Claviere ein Ton anzuschlagen vorkömmt, der mit dem Pedale schon getreten ist; folglich nicht noch einmal, wie er doch sollte, anspricht. Es kann also dieses Compendium, so wie auch bey den Orgeln, durch nichts als eine dringend nöthige Ersparung entschuldiget werden.

§. 605.

Nun sollte ich auch wol noch etwas melden von dem Pandoret, und von Orvals Clavier auf der Clarinette: allein da ersteres heutiges Tages nicht leicht mehr gemacht wird, und letzteres von schlechtem Nutzen ist; so lasse ich es bey demjenigen bewenden, was ich davon in meiner Anleitung §. 259. und 60. beygebracht, und verweise den Leser dahin.

Das XXVII. Kapitel.
Von andern Instrumenten, und von der Stimmung besayeter Instrumente.

Inhalt:

§. 606. Ob ein Organist andere Instrumente kennen muß, die kein Clavier haben? §. 607. die Temperatur der Instrumente. §. 608. wenn sie bundfrey sind. §. 609. wie die Seyten bequem aufzuziehen. §. 610. noch einige Dinge beym Aufziehen. §. 611. Wie die Wirbel herauszuziehen. §. 612. der Anschlag muß stets gleich stark seyn. §. 613. Wie das Pedal nach dem Clavichord, und ein Clavichord nach dem andern zu stimmen.

§. 626.

Es fragt sich nun: ob ein Organist, als ein Liebhaber des Claviers, noch andere musikalische Instrumente zu wissen nöthig habe? Antwort: als ein Organist weis ich keine mehr. Die andern Instrumente, als: Hautbois, Flöten, Harfen, u. s. w. braucht er der Organistenkunst halber weiter nicht zu lernen, als wenn er etwan zur Composition eins oder das andere davon braucht, damit er die Höhe und Tiefe eines jeden Instruments wisse: item, was sie für Melodien lieben? ꝛc. Das gehet

as far as the two lowest octaves. This is sometimes done in organs as well (cf. Chap. VII, §. 127). But in this case rollerboards and trackers would seem even more necessary than previously, since the two octaves are not as spread out as before, and therefore the twine would end up being at far too acute an angle. Otherwise, of course, it is a good way to save money. (**) If anyone wants to disconnect the two units,* he need only disconnect the twine at the top or the bottom. Mr. [Johann Nicolaus] Bach in Jena also used to make pedals for his lute harpsichords, that sounded just like a real theorbo (see §.560).

* i.e., manual and pull-down pedal.

> (**) It is, however, sometimes quite inconvenient, especially if pieces with an obligato pedal part are being played. Then at times a note appears that needs to be played in the manual that is already being depressed by the pedal. Thus it does not sound again, although it surely ought to. Thus this economy [measure] can be excused, as in organs, by nothing other than an absolute necessity to save money. [Agricola]

§. 605.

I ought also to mention something about the pandoret, and about Orval's keyboard applied to a clarinet. But since the former is now seldom built these days, and the latter is of little use, I will let [these topics] rest with what I have imparted about them in my *Anleitung*, §. 259 and 260,† referring the reader to those sections.

† pp. 575–76.

Chapter XXVII.
Concerning other Instruments, and the Tuning of Stringed [Keyboard] Instruments.

Contents:

§.606. Should an organist be familiar with other instruments, ones that do not have a keyboard? §.607. Temperament for [stringed keyboard] instruments. §.608. if they are unfretted. §. 609. The most convenient way to string [these instruments]. §.610. A few additional points about stringing. §.611. How to extract tuning pins. §.612. The fingers must always exert an equal pressure [on each note when tuning a clavichord]. §.613. How to tune the pedal from the clavichord, and how to tune one clavichord from another.

§. 626. [i.e., §. 606.]

Now the question is, "Should it be necessary for an organist, as a lover of the keyboard, to know about other musical instruments?" The answer: being an organist, I am not conversant with others. The art of the organ does not require [an organist] to learn anything else about other instruments, such as oboes, flutes, harps, etc., other than their range, in case he uses one or the other of them in a composition, and what sort of melodies sound best on them. This [knowledge] has nothing to do with

het aber die Mechanik nichts an. Man kann von den meisten solche Nachrichten in Prätorii Synt. To. II. finden, und in andern hierzu dienenden Schriften. [87] Sollten aber mehr Clavierarten zum Vorschein kommen; so wird der Liebhaber der Musicae Mechanicae Organoedi solche am gehörigen Orte suppliren.

§. 607.

Ich will von der Temperatur und Stimmung der beseyteten Instrumente noch etwas gedenken: denn das Positiv und die Regale werden wie die Orgeln traktirt. Aber die beseyteten Instrumente haben etwas besonders. Wenn man dieselben will temperiren; so muß man sich zuvor um den ersten Ton bekümmern, und zwar so, daß man es stets so stimme, wie es einmal gestanden, im Chor- oder Kammertone, oder in einem andern. Weil nun durch das Wetter die Höhe sich ändert; so soll man eine Flöte, oder sonst beständiges Instrument (**) bey der Hand haben, daß man den rechten Ton wieder treffe. Sodann temperirt man, wie im 14ten Kapitel bey der Orgel gewiesen worden. Das Monochord könnte hier ziemlich gebraucht werden, weil Seyten gegen Seyten wohl zu stimmen sind. Allein man thut besser, wenn man nach der oben vorgetragenen Methode temperirt, und entweder durch Quinten, oder, welches ich fast vorziehe, durch Dissonanzen stimmt, wie es daselbst zu lesen im §. 411. Hernach stimmt man alles durch Oktaven. Wo man Register hat, als bey Claveßins ꝛc. oder wo man das Clavier vorwärts ziehen kann, da thut man am besten, man stimmt erst ein Register durch alle Claves rein; hernach das zweyte nach dem ersten; das dritte nach dem andern ꝛc. Bey Clavichordien geht das nicht an: denn da muß man jedes Chor nach allen Seyten rein stimmen.

(**) In Engelland macht man ziemlich große stählerne Gabeln zu diesem Gebrauche, welche den Ton am sichersten behalten, und auch sehr helle angeben.

§. 608.

Wann die Clavichordien ganz bundfrey sind; so hat man eben die Arbeit wie bey dem Claveßin; wenn sie aber nicht bundfrey sind; so kommt man kürzer davon, weil durch die Stimmung eines Chors 2 bis 3 Claves rein werden. Da darf man nur zum Exempel, f $\overline{c}$; $\overline{c}$ g; $\overline{g}$ $\overline{g}$; g d; $\overline{d}$ $\overline{a}$; $\overline{a}$ a; a e, und zum höchsten noch $\overline{e}$ $\overline{h}$ stimmen; so muß alles reine seyn. Mit $\overline{c}$ wird $\overline{cis}$, mit $\overline{d}$ dis, mit $\overline{e}$ f, (oder $\overline{d}$ ist allein, und $\overline{dis}$ ist bey $\overline{e}$) mit f $\overline{fis}$, mit g gis, mit $\overline{a}$ b gestimmt; oder $\overline{a}$ ist allein, und b bey $\overline{h}$. Wo drey Claves auf eine Seyte schlagen da darf man nur 1) $\overline{c}$ reine haben, so ist zugleich $\overline{cis}$ und $\overline{d}$ gut; 2) $\overline{e}$, so ist $\overline{dis}$ f gut; 3) g, so ist $\overline{fis}$ und gis gut; 4) $\overline{a}$, so ist b und $\overline{h}$ gut. Wird es aber nicht gut, und man hat in der Temperatur nicht gefehlet; so ist die Schuld an der falschen Mensur, welchem Uebel man nicht anders abhelfen kann, als durch Beugung der Tangenten auf die Seite, bis es reine wird.

[87] Die hierher gehörigen Schriften hat der Herr Verfasser in seiner Anleitung von S. 580. bis 585. in alphabetischer Ordnung nahmhaft gemacht; allwo sie der geneigte Leser selbst nachzuschlagen die Gütigkeit haben wird.

the mechanics [of the instruments]. Information about most of them may be found in Praetorius's *Syntagma musicum*, Vol. II,* as well as in other treatises pertinent to this topic.⁸⁷⁾ If other types of keyboard instruments should appear, however, then admirers of *Musica mechanica organoedi* should supply [information about] them at the appropriate point [in the text].

* In Parts I & II, pp. 1-79.

§. 607.

I would like to mention some other things about temperament and tuning for stringed instruments [in particular]. The positiv and the regals are treated like organs, but stringed instruments have special characteristics. Anyone who wants to temper them must first take the trouble to establish the first pitch, and indeed so that it is always tuned as it has previously been, either in choir pitch or chamber pitch, or at some other [pitch]. Since the weather causes the pitch level to change, one should have at hand a flute or some other stable instrument,(**) in order to establish again the correct pitch. Then tempering [the instrument] proceeds as has been shown in connection with the organ in Chap. 14. The monochord could very well be used for this, since strings tune well to other strings. But it would be better to temper according to the method presented above, either by tuning by fifths or (as I rather prefer) by dissonances, as described in §.411. Thereafter† everything is tuned by octaves. If there are stops, as on harpsichords, etc., or where the keyboard can be shifted forward,‡ then it is best to tune one stop completely, every note. Then the second choir is tuned to the first, the third to the second, etc. This does not work with clavichords; there all the strings of each note must be tuned pure together.

† i.e., after the first octave of pitches has been established.
‡ See §.516.

(**) In England rather large steel [pitch]forks are made for this purpose, that maintain their pitch most reliably and also produce it very clearly. [Agricola]

§. 608.

If a clavichord is completely unfretted, then the job is the same as with the harpsichord. If it is fretted, though, it saves some work, since 2 or 3 notes are in tune every time one set of strings is tuned. In that case one need only tune, for example, f–c′, c′–g′, g′–g, g–d′, d′–a′, a′–a, a–e′, and at the most e′–b-natural′ beyond that, and everything else is automatically in tune—with c′, c#′ is tuned, with d′, d#[′], with e′, f′ (or d′ is a single note, and d#′ is with e′), with f′, f#′, with g′, g#′, and with a′, b-flat′ (or a′ is a single note, and b-flat′ is with b-natural′). If [a set of] strings produces three notes, one need only tune 1) c′, and then c#′ and d′ are automatically in tune, 2) e′, and d#′ and f′ are in tune, 3) g[′], and f#′ and g#[′] are in tune, and 4) a′, and b-flat′ and b-natural′ are in tune. If [the tuning] does not sound well, and nothing is wrong with the temperament, then incorrect scaling is at fault. This is a defect that cannot be remedied in any other way than bending the tangents sideways until [the notes] are in tune.

⁸⁷⁾ The author has made the writings that are here pertinent available in alphabetical order in his *Anleitung*, from pp. 580–585. The gracious reader is kindly requested to consult them there for himself. [Albrecht]

§. 609.

Bey dem Ziehen der Seyten ist zu merken, daß man sie nicht allzugeschwind in die Höhe ziehe, sondern nach und nach: denn da dauern sie länger, wenn sie sich nach und nach ausdehnen können. Wenn unter dem Ziehen die Seyte nicht in die Höhe will, sondern unsers Drehens ungeachtet, in einerley Höhe bleibt, oder gar unterwärts gehet; so wird etwan die Seyte nicht derb genug um den Wirbel gewunden seyn, daher sie sich um ihn herum dreht, und die Seyte bleibet stets überein gespannet. Da muß man sie anders aufwinden. Zuweilen giebt es an dem andern Ende nach, wenn die Schlinge nicht recht gedrehet ist; da muß man eine andere daran machen. Ich wollte auch rathen, die Seyte nicht gleich an ihren Ort zu legen an ihren Stift, sondern sie in gerader Linie aufzuziehen, bis sie fast die rechte Linie hat: alsdann lege man sie an ihren Ort; so halten die Seyten besser. Wenn man die Schlinge drehet; so muß solches auch gemachsam geschehen. Man winde die Seyten an den Wirbeln nicht zu tief, sonst wird die Decke allzu sehr gedruckt; auch nicht zu hoch, sonst biegen sich die Wirbel, und die Seyte hebt sich; sondern in gerader Linie. Wenn man starke Seyten hat, daß man sie mit der Hend nicht halten kann, wenn man drehet; so kann man sie in Form einer Schlinge legen, und mit der Drathzange so lange halten, bis der Drehhammer das Seinige gethan.

§. 610.

Bey Clavichordien muß man die Seyten durch das Tuch stecken. Denn wo man sie wollte obenweg legen, würden sie hernach eine ungleiche Höhe und folglich einen ungleichen Anschlag haben. Man kann mit einer großen Hütersnadel gar bequem durchkommen mit sammt der Seyte; doch darf die Nadel keine Spitze haben, sonst hängt sie sich in das Tuch. Im Aufziehen muß man sich in Acht nehmen, daß man die Seyte um den Wirbel nicht link anbringe, oder die Seyten verwirre. Wo gesponnene Seyten mit den andern vermischt sind, und die Unreinigkeit ist von dem Wetter; so wird die eine Art mehr verstimmt seyn, als die andere. Die physikalischen Ursachen davon kann ich hier nicht anführen, weil ich mich der Kürze befleißigen muß.

§. 611.

Die Wirbel muß man mit einer besondern Zange herausziehen, und zwar fein gerade, damit die Löcher nicht ausgeweitet werden. Ehe man anfängt zu temperiren, so klopfe man die Wirbel etwas hinein, daß man nicht unter dem Stimmen hämmern müsse, als wodurch bey manchen Clavichordien und Claveßins eine neue Unreinigkeit verursacht wird.

§. 612.

Dieß ist nicht zu vergessen, daß, wenn man einen Clavem gegen den andern stimmt, man gleiche beständige Stärke bey beyden im Anschlage gebrauchen muß. Denn wenn ich z. E. $\bar{c}$ gegen f stimme, und das $\bar{c}$ etwas schwach anschlage, so werde ich die Seyten nothwendig müssen höher stimmen, weil, wenn ich schlage, dieselbe

tiefer

§. 609.

Note that in stringing [the instrument] the strings should not be tightened too quickly; they will last longer if they are stretched gradually. If a string does not rise [in pitch] when it is tightened, but stays at the same pitch no matter how much [the tuning pin] is turned, or even goes completely slack, then the string may not be wound tightly enough around the tuning pin. Thus it just keeps slipping around [the pin], remaining at the same level of tension. In that case it must be rewound. At times it comes loose at the other end,* if the loop is not twisted properly, and then another [loop] must be made in [the string]. I would also suggest that the string not be angled around its pin [on the bridge], but that it be tightened in a straight line until it is almost taut, and then angled over the bridge pin. In this way the string will hold better. Twisting the loop [in the string] must be done deliberately. The strings should not be wound too low on the tuning pins; this will cause too much pressure to be exerted on the soundboard.† They should also not be wound too high, or the tuning pins will bend or the strings will lift.‡ Rather the pins should be wound in a straight line.§ If the strings are so strong¶ that they cannot be held with the hand‖ while they are being tightened, then they can be bent in the shape of a loop and held with the pliers long enough for the tuning hammer to do its duty.

* i.e., at the hitch pin.

† i.e., because the strings will exert too much downward pressure on the bridge; see §.519.

‡ i.e., off the bridge.

§ i.e., at the height of the bridge.

¶ i.e., resilient.

‖ i.e., snug against the tuning pin, so they catch.

§. 610.

With clavichords, the strings must pass through [a latticework of] cloth [listing]. For if the cloth were simply threaded once [between the pairs of strings], they would thereafter have an unequal height, and as a result they would have an uneven touch.** With a large hatter's needle you can conveniently thread the entire string††; but the needle cannot have a point, otherwise it gets caught in the cloth. Be careful when stringing [an instrument] not to wind the string backward around the tuning pin, or to get the strings confused. If overspun strings are mixed in with the others, and the weather is causing [the instrument] to go out of tune, then one kind [of string] will be more out of tune than the other. I cannot cite the physical causes of this here, since I must endeavor to be brief.

** i.e., the key would have to travel further to contact one string of the pair than the other.

†† i.e., the one that is being replaced; this procedure allows the new string to pass through the latticework of the listing cloth, thus obviating the tedious work of removing and re-weaving the listing.

§. 611.

The tuning pins must be extracted with a special set of pliers, and must be drawn out absolutely straight, so that the holes are not widened. Before beginning to set a temperament, the tuning pins should be hammered in a bit, to keep from having to hammer [them in] in the middle of tuning; this causes many a clavichord and harpsichord to lose its tune again.

§. 612.

Do not forget that in tuning one note to another, the fingers must exert an equal pressure when playing both [notes].‡‡ If I tune, e.g., c′ to f, and strike the c′ somewhat weakly, then I must of necessity tune the strings sharper, since in striking it [weakly]

‡‡ Here Adlung is speaking specifically about the clavichord.

der Stimmung beseyteter Instrumente.

tiefer klingt, als sonst. Stimme ich weiter $\bar{g}$ gegen $\bar{c}$, und schlage schärfer an das $\bar{g}$ als das $\bar{c}$; so werde ich die Seyte tiefer ziehen müssen, wenn die Quinte soll rein werden; und das gehet so fort. Daher kann es gar leicht kommen, daß man alle Claves, je einen gegen den andern, hat reine gestimmt, und wenn man zusammen spielt, da man ordentlich allen Fingern einerley Stärke giebt; so ist alles unrein. Diese Anmerkung ist von Wichtigkeit, und wird man mit großem Verdruß bey deren Vernachläßigung das Stimmen etlichemal müssen von vorn anfangen; zumal wo die Seyten etwas schwach sind.

§. 613.

Das Pedal wird nach dem Clavichord eingestimmt; und vorige Anmerkung gilt auch hier, daß man im Treten immer einerley Stärke brauche, auch im Anschlage auf dem Manual, sonst wird es nicht reine. Man könnte nur einen Clavem nach dem Clavichord stimmen, oder wenigstens nur eine Oktave, etwan die mittelste von $\bar{c}$ bis $\bar{\bar{c}}$, oder von g nach $\bar{g}$: so auch wenn 2. Clavichordien überein werden sollen; das übrige aber könnte man oktavenweise stimmen, jedes für sich: und wenn die Stimmung des einen richtig ist, und man trift die andere Temperatur auch, und die Stimmung; so sollte hernach das Pedal und die Clavichordien vollkommen reine seyn. Aber zuweilen trift man es nicht. Daher auch nicht zu verachten, wenn man alle Claves des einen Claviers nach den Clavibus des andern stimmt; doch mit genauer Beobachtung der vorigen Anmerkung. Das übrige, was bey der Stimmung vorfallen möchte, mag ein jeder selbst observiren. Ich befleißige mich der Kürze.

Das XXVIII. Kapitel.
Ein Discurs von etlichen hierher gehörigen curiösen Materien.

Es ist zuweilen gemeldet worden, daß eine Kirche oder Ort nicht so einen guten Klang der Orgeln oder anderer Instrumente verursache, als die andere. Imgleichen, daß eine Orgelpfeife, oder Seyte, anders klinge, wenn man an diesem, anders aber wenn man an einem andern Orte steht. Es fragt sich: woher das komme? Darauf wird gezeiget werden: warum die Dicke oder subtile Luft den Klang verändere? Hierbey müssen wir vor allen Dingen die Natur der Luft und deren Bewegung zu Hülfe nehmen. Es ist die Luft ein subtiles flüßiges Wesen, etwas gröber als Aether, doch nicht so grob als das Wasser. [88] Wie sich aber die Proportion der Luft gegen das Wasser

---

[88] Man lese hierbey nach, was der Hr. M. Joh. Michael Schmidt in seiner vortreflichen Musico Theologia §. 30. u. folg. geschrieben.

it sounds lower than usual. If I go further and tune g′ against c′, striking the g′ more forcefully than the c, then I will have to tune the string lower in order to make the fifth perfect; and it continues in that way. Therefore it can very easily happen that someone tunes all the keys, each one after the other, and then in playing them (during which the fingers ordinarily employ an even touch) discovers that everything is out of tune. This remark is an important one; if it is neglected, one will have [to endure] the considerable annoyance of having to begin the tuning all over again from the beginning. This is especially true if the strings are somewhat thin.

§. 613.

The pedal is tuned from the clavichord, and the previous remark also holds true here: the feet must exert an equal force when playing each note, just as on the manual. Otherwise [the instrument] will not be in tune. It is possible to tune only one [pedal] note from the clavichord, or at the most only one octave (say, the middle one from c′ – c″, or from g – g′*). The same holds true if 2 clavichords are to be tuned together. Subsequent notes may be tuned in octaves, each instrument to itself. If one [of the instruments] is in good tune, and the temperament is correctly set and the tuning properly completed on the second, then the pedal and manual clavichords should be in perfect tune. Sometimes this is not successful, and therefore one ought not to disdain tuning all the notes of one keyboard from those of a second—but with precise attention to the remark above.† Since I am endeavoring to remain brief, each person may observe for himself anything else that might happen during tuning.

* These notes do not appear in the pedal. Adlung seems to be referring to the octave in the manuals from which the pedal temperament should be taken. The octaves that Adlung recommends tend to be the most stable and thus would recommend themselves as a reference for tuning over lower octaves that would sound in unison with the pedal, but might be less perfectly tempered.

† i.e., exerting equal force on the keys of both notes that are being tuned.

Chapter XVIII.
A Discourse on certain Curious Matters here pertinent.

It has sometimes been reported that a [given] church or place does not promote as good a tone from an organ or other instruments as other [places do]. Or that an organ pipe or a string sounds different when one is standing in one place than in another. The question is, "Why does this happen?" In this connection, [this chapter] will show why thick or thin air changes the sound. To do this, we must above all have recourse to the nature of air and its movement. Air is a thin, fluid entity, somewhat heavier/thicker than aether,‡ but not as heavy/thick as water.[88] Whether, however,

‡ Though Adlung is clearly predisposed to follow the research methods of empirical science, he reveals here, as elsewhere, the vestiges of pre-scientific beliefs. "Aether" is, in the pre-scientific worldview, the upper regions of space and the rarified element that is supposed to fill them.

[88] Consult in this regard what Mr. Joh. Michael Schmidt, M.A., has written in his excellent *Musico Theologia*, §. 30f.[, pp. 67f.] [Albrecht]

Wasser verhalte, ob es in Ansehung der Schwere wie 1 zu 800, oder 900 oder gar 1000, das lassen wir durch die Physicos untersuchen. Uns hilft es für diesesmal soviel nicht. Wer mit der Luftpumpe umzugehen weis, der kann nur eine hohle Kugel mit Luft in einer Wage wiegen. Man braucht sie nicht hinein zu thun; sie ist schon allerwegen. Die Schwere notirt man; hernach macht man eben die Kugel voll Wasser, und wiegt sie auch, und notirt das Gewicht. Auf solche Weise werden hernach die beyden Gravitäten können gegen einander gehalten, und erfahren werden, wie vielmal das Wasser schwerer sey, als die Luft. Man kann auch die Luft aus dem Gefäße ziehen, und das Gefäß alleine wiegen, und von beyden Schweren abziehen. Z. E. Ich hätte eine gläserne Kugel, die verwahrte ich wohl, und zöge durch die Luftpumpe die Luft heraus, und suchte durch die Wage ihr Gewicht ohne Luft, und es beträfe etwann 24 Loth. Hernach ließ ich wieder Luft hinein, und wägte es zusammen, daß etwann 25 Loth heraus kämen für das Glaß und die Luft. So thäte ich dann Wasser in die Kugel, (dadurch weicht die vorige Luft) soviel hinein gehen wollte, und wägte es auch, und befände die Schwere z. E. 972. Hernach zöge ich die 24. Loth, als die Schwere des Glases, davon ab: und so bliebe alsdann für das Wasser noch übrig 948 Loth. z. E. 972

$$\frac{972}{24}$$
$$\overline{948}$$

24 Loth von 25 Lothen abgezogen, bliebe für die Luft 1 Loth; folglich verhielte sich die Schwere der Luft zu dem Wasser wie 1 zu 948. d. i. wenn ich ein Stück Luft mir vorstelle, und ein Stück Wasser von gleicher Größe: so würde das Wasser 948mal schwerer seyn.

Diese Luft ist ganz um unsere Erdkugel herum, und wo sonst kein anderer Körper ist, wird jeder Raum dadurch angefüllet, ohne wenn durch Kunst die Luft weggebracht wird. Diese Luft ist in steter Bewegung; wird aber auch durch jeden Stoß noch mehr bewegt. Der Klang geschiehet aber also: wenn der Wind mit force in die Pfeifen bläset: so dringet er auch mit einer force durch die Ritze zwischen dem untern labio und dem Kern, von da in das corpus der Pfeifen, welches dadurch in eine zitternde Bewegung gesetzt wird, daraus ferner in die freye Luft, welche sie auf allen Theilen anstößt. Der Stoß gehet in der Luft motu tremulo fort, daß keine plaga ist, dahin diese zitternde Bewegung der Luft nicht sollte continuirt werden; folglich gehet sie auch in unser Ohr, und machet in uns eine Empfindung, die wir den Klang nennen. (conf. pluribus de *Chales* To. III. P. I. propos. 3. it. prop. 41. seqq.) Wenn die Luft, durch die Orgelpfeife modificirt, in einer solchen Bewegung ist, und sie stößt an harte Körper; so prallt sie wieder zurücke, eben als wenn man einen Ball vor eine Wand wirft, der auch zurücke springt. Hieraus folgt schon soviel, daß eine Orgel oder sonst ein Instrument müsse schärfer klingen, wenn es in einem eingeschlossenen Orte

air is related in weight to water in the proportion 1:800, 1:900, or even 1:1,000, we will leave for the physicists to investigate. It is not so helpful to us at this point. Anyone who knows how to operate an air pump need only weigh a hollow ball [filled] with air on a scale. There is no need to put air into [the ball]; it is already everywhere. The weight should be noted, and then the very same ball filled with water, weighed, and the weight noted. In such a way the weights of both may then be compared to each other, to discover how many times heavier water is than air. It is also possible to pump all the air out of a container and weigh the container alone, and then subtract [its weight] from both weights. For example, if I had a glass ball, I would make it airtight, and then draw the air out of it by means of an air pump. Then, using a scale, I would determine its weight without air; it would amount about 24 *Lot*.* Next I would again allow air into it and weigh [the two of] them together; it would turn about to be about 25 *Lot* for the glass and the air. Then I would fill the ball with water, as much as would go into it (thus displacing the air formerly in it), and weigh it as well. Let us say I found the weight to be 972 *Lot*. Next I would subtract 24 *Lot*, the weight of the glass, from that figure. Thus the weight remaining, 948 *Lot*, would be the weight of the water. For example:

* *Lot*: an old unit of weight that varied widely according to time and place; often 1/32 of a *Pfund*.

$$\begin{array}{r} 972 \\ -24 \\ \hline 948 \end{array}$$

By subtracting 24 *Lot* from 25 *Lot*, 1 *Lot* would remain as the [weight of the] air. Consequently the weight of the air is related to that of the water as 1:948. That is, if I imagine a unit of air, and then a unit of water of the same dimensions, the water would weigh 948 times more than the air.

This [element called] air entirely surrounds the earthly sphere on which we live. Any space that is not occupied by another object is filled with it, unless it is artificially removed. Air is in constant motion, but it is set into further motion by any thrust [against it]. This is how sound [from an organ pipe] is created: when wind surges into pipes under force, it forces its way through the slit between the lower lip [of the pipe] and the languid, and thence into the body of the pipe, setting it into vibration. Thence it proceeds into the open air, which is pressing against it on all sides. The thrust proceeds into the air in a vibrating motion, unless it encounters an obstacle (plaga†) that causes the vibrating motion to cease. Consequently it passes into our ears and creates in us a sensation that we call 'sound' (cf. many places in de Chales, *Mundum mathematicum*, Vol. III, Part I,‡ proposition 3, also prop. 41f). If the air as modified by the organ pipe assumes this sort of motion, and it strikes hard objects, then it rebounds, just as a ball will rebound when thrown against a wall. From this we can deduce this much, that an organ or any other instrument must sound more intense in an enclosed loca-

† See Chap. XII, footnote 1.

‡ i.e., Tract 22.

te stehet, als in einem offenen. Denn wenn ich eine Violine auf freyem Felde habe, wo keine Berge, Häuser ꝛc. sind, und ich streiche sie an; so vernehme ich zwar einen Klang, doch nur den, der von der ersten Bewegung der Luft und vom Zurückstoßen der flachen Erde herkömmt. Streiche ich die Violine in einem Zimmer oder Kirche; so macht nicht nur die erste Bewegung der Luft die Empfindung oder Stoß in meinem Ohre, sondern es stößt die Luft an allen Seiten an die Wände, Gewölbe ꝛc. an, und von dannen prallet sie zurücke, und giebt mir noch mehr Stöße an das tympanum in meinem Ohre, dadurch die Empfindung bey mir stärker wird. Je mehr also an einem Orte solche Theile sind, die den Stoß zurücke zu unsern Ohren schicken, desto stärker dünkt uns der Schall. Daher, weil nicht leicht ein Ort in allem also angelegt ist, wie der andere; so ist auch der Klang an einem nicht, wie an dem andern.

Wenn nun ferner die Luft ein solider Körper wäre; so würde der Stoß in gleicher Stärke continuiret. Wenn man z. E. einen Stab nimmt, denselben an dem einen Ende anstößt; so wird immer ein Theil des Stabes den andern treiben, bis ans Ende, und zwar mit gleicher force, weil kein Theil wegen der Festigkeit nachgiebt. Hingegen, wenn man einen Klumpen Wolle oder Pflaumfedern auf den Tisch legt, daß sie einander berühren, und man stößt sie an einem Ende stark an; so wird derselbe Stoß am andern Ende wenig, oder auch zuweilen gar nicht gemerkt werden: denn die Federn geben nach, und die erste, wenn man sie anstößt, biegt sich in ihren Theilen, propter porositatem, und stößt hernach die andere schon mit geringerer force, als sie von der Hand gestoßen worden; folglich, weil die andere Feder auch nachgiebt, so stößt sie die dritte mit noch weniger force, und diese die vierte u. s. f. bis endlich die letzten Stöße gar schwach werden: und wenn es in die Ferne vielmal continuirt wird; so merkt man gar keine Bewegung mehr. Eben so ists mit der Luft, die, wenn sie gestoßen wird, giebt auch nach, weil sie poros ist, und sich zusammen drücken läßt, auch als ein corpus elasticum hernach sich wieder ausdehnt: und hieraus folgen noch mehr Ursachen, warum es an einem Orte besser klingt, als am andern. Ist ein Ort größer, als der andere, so währt es lange, ehe der Stoß zu dem weit entfernten Orte kömmt: und da immer ein Theilchen Luft das benachbarte stößt, jedes aber nachgiebt; so wird der Stoß immer schwächer, und je weiter man von der Pfeife ist, desto schwächer wird die Empfindung oder der Klang. Folglich klingt es in engen und kleinen Orten schärfer, als in großen; cæteris paribus: denn man mag in dem kleinen Orte stehen, wo man will; so darf der Stoß nicht so lange continuiren bis ans Ohr, und verliert nicht allzuviel von seiner force. So wird man wohl leiden können, daß z. E. ein Gestück ¼ Meile von uns loßgebrannt wird: steht man aber gleich dabey; so ist man wol in Gefahr das Gehör zu verliehren, indem der Stoß von seiner force noch nicht viel verlohren, und also gar zu stark die das Gehör ausmachende Glieder bewegt, auch sie wol gar verletzt. Ein Paar Paucken in einer großen Kirche thun uns nichts: wenn sie aber in einer engen Stube mit gleicher force geschlagen werden; so thun uns die Ohren weh: und so ists mit allen Instrumenten.

tion than in an open one. For if I take a violin out into an open field where there are no mountains, houses, etc., and I draw a bow across it, then I do perceive a sound, to be sure, but only from the initial motion of the air and from its reflection by the flat earth [beneath]. If I draw the bow across a violin in a room or a church, though, it is not only the initial motion of the air that strikes my ear and makes a sensation in it, but also the air that has struck all about the room—the walls, the vault, etc.—and thence rebounds, striking my eardrum many times and causing a stronger sensation in it. Thus the more surfaces there are in a place that reflect the thrust back to our ears, the louder the sound seems to us. Therefore, since it is unlikely that one location is arranged in every respect just like another, the sound in one [location] is likewise not the same as in another.

Moreover, if air were a solid object, then the thrust would continue with the same [degree of] force. If, e.g., someone were to take a staff and strike it on one end, one section of the staff would drive the next, right to the [other] end, and with the same [degree of] force, since no section, being solid, would yield. On the other hand, if someone were to lay a wad of wool or down feathers* on a table in such a way that they were in contact with each other, and then struck them sharply at one end, very little or even none of that blow would be noticed at the other end. For the feathers yield. The first, when struck, bends at all points due to its porosity, and thus strikes the next with less force than the hand delivered to it. Consequently since the second feather also yields, it strikes the third with even less force. This continues to the fourth, etc., until the final blow becomes extremely weak. If this [action] is repeated many times over a distance, then no motion at all is perceived any more. This is just how it is with air; since it is porous, it yields when struck, allowing itself to be compressed and thereafter, being an elastic entity, to expand. From this may be deduced many reasons why the sound at one place is better than at another. If a [given] location is larger than another, then it takes a long time for the blow to arrive at its distant reaches; and since one air particle keeps on striking the next, which then yields, the blow gets weaker and weaker. Thus the further [the listener] is from a pipe, the weaker the sensation or sound. Thus sound in narrow, small places is more intense (schärfer) than in large ones, all things being equal, since no matter where [the listener] stands in a small place, the sound does not have very far to travel to reach his ear, and thus does not loose much of its force. Therefore, e.g., people can stand an cannon being fired a ¼ of a mile away, but anyone who is standing right beside it is in danger of losing his hearing, since its thrust has lost little of its force and moves the hearing apparatus far too violently, thus damaging it severely. A pair of kettledrums [being struck] in a large church does not affect us, but if they were to be struck with the same force in a small chamber, then our ears would hurt. The same holds true for all instruments.

* "Pflaumfedern" = "Flaumfedern."

Hieraus folgt auch dieß, daß eine Orgel schärfer klingen muß, wenn sie hinten an der Mauer anstehet, als wenn hinter ihr viel Platz gelassen wird. Denn im ersten Falle wird auch die hinten anstoßende Luft stark zurück prallen, und die Empfindung in uns vermehren: im andern Falle wird der Stoß etwas schwach, ehe er die Mauer oder Wand erreicht, und kömmt also gar schwach zu uns. Daher ist es gut, daß in solchen Falle sie wenigstens hinten, auf den Seiten und oben, wohl verschlagen werde.

Auch ist hieraus klar, daß eine Orgel stärker klingt, wenn zwischen ihr und dem Kirchenhimmel kein, oder wenigstens kein groß Spatium ist. Denn so schlägt die Luft mit der größten Gewalt oben an, und prallt wieder herab nach unsern Ohren, da sonst, wenn die Luft erst so weit in die Höhe zu stoßen ist, sie schwach wird, ehe sie hinauf kömmt. Ist aber gar kein sogenannter Himmel da; so wird der Klang viel geringer, weil das Zurückprallen von obenher mangelt, oder doch nicht so stark ist.

Auch pflegen eben deswegen die Orgeln schärfer zu klingen, wenn sie in der Kirche zur Seite gesetzt werden, als wenn sie gegen Abend oder Morgen stehen Denn im ersten Falle steht die Wand gegen über sehr nahe, von welcher der Schall mit der größten force zurück getrieben wird. Auch ist deswegen nicht wohl zu rathen, die Orgeln tief zu setzen, weil sie, anderer Incommoditäten zu geschweigen, nicht wohl gegen den Kirchenhimmel ihren Schall schicken können.

Ferner ist zu wissen nöthig, daß, je härter ein Körper ist, daran ein Ball oder anderer Körper stößt, desto stärker ist das Zurückprallen. Z. E. wirft man den Ball wider einen harten Stein, so prallet er mehr zurücke, als von einem Brette, weil das Brett etwas nachgiebt, es mag auch so wenig seyn, als es will; und alles was nachgiebt, das verursacht eine Schwächung des Stoßes. Wirft man den Ballen vor ein Tuch; so springt er noch weniger zurück, weil dasselbe noch mehr nachgiebt. Ergo, wenn die Flächen in einem Zimmer oder Kirche härter sind, als in einem andern; so wird die Luft daran frischer zurückprallen, folglich muß es in einer hölzern Kirche, oder wo der Himmel nur hölzern ist, so gut nicht klingen, als in einer gemauerten; it. in einer gemauerten kann es so gut nicht klingen, wenn hölzerne Emporkirchen drinnen gebauet sind, als wenn keine da sind. Daher es in den catholischen Kirchen ordinär schöner klingt, als in den unsrigen, weil wir mehr Holzwerk drinnen haben, als sie. Ferner muß es in einer gemauerten Kirche besser klingen, wenn harte Steine dazu genommen worden, als wo weiche sind. Besser muß es klingen, wo die Mauern von großen Quadratsteinen aufgeführet worden, als wo kleine Mauersteine dazu sind: denn zwischen diesen sind viele Ritzen und Kalk, welches so nicht zurücke schlagen kann, als die Steine selbst. Ist aber alles durchweißt; so ist es noch besser, weil dadurch auch die Pori der Steine verstopft werden. Eben hieraus ist offenbar, daß eine silberne Pfeife besser klingen müsse, als eine zinnerne, und diese besser, als eine von Bley: und je härter das Metall in der Vermischung genommen wird, desto besser wird der Klang. Man sieht auch, wie es möglich sey, die bleyernen Pfeifen im Klange zu verbessern,

It follows from this that an organ will inevitably sound more intense if there is a wall directly behind it than if a great deal of open space is left behind it.* For in the first instance the air that strikes the rear [wall] will rebound strongly, increasing our perception [of the sound]. In the second instance the thrust will be rather weak before it reaches the exterior or interior wall, and will be returned to us correspondingly weakly. Thus at least in such cases† it is a good thing to enclose organs completely at the back, at the sides and on top.

This also makes it clear that an organ sounds more intense if there is little or no space between it and the church ceiling.‡ For then the air strikes the ceiling with the greatest force and rebounds downward to our ears, while otherwise, if the air must first be thrust so far upward, it [i.e., the thrust] becomes weak before it reaches [the ceiling]. If there is no ceiling at all present,§ then the sound will be far less, since there will be very little, or at least less, rebound from above.

For the same reason, an organ usually sounds more intense if it is located on the side of a church than if it is at the west or the east end. For in the first instance the wall opposite stands very close, and reflects the [organ's] peal with the greatest force. It is also advisable not to place an organ too low, since then its sound cannot reach the church ceiling very well, to say nothing of other inconveniences.

Furthermore it must be understood that the harder the object against which a ball or some other object is thrown, the more forceful is the rebound. For example, if a ball is thrown against a hard stone, its rebound is greater than from a board, since the board yields a bit, no matter how little, and everything that yields results in a weakening of the thrust. If the ball is thrown against a cloth, then it rebounds even less, since [the cloth] yields even more. Therefore if the surfaces in one room or church are harder than in another, then they will reflect the air more sharply; consequently a wooden church, or even one in which only the ceiling is wood, cannot have as live acoustics as one build of masonry. Likewise in a masonry [church] the acoustics cannot be as live if wooden balconies are built around it as if they are not present. Thus Catholic churches are ordinarily more pleasingly resonant than ours, since ours have more wood in them than theirs.¶ Furthermore, a masonry church will have better acoustics if hard stone is used to [build it] than if soft stone is used. A building whose walls are built of large square stone building blocks will perforce have better acoustics than one built of small building stones; for between [the stones] there are many cracks filled with mortar, which is not as reflective as the stone itself. It is even better, though, if the entire [church] is whitewashed, since this seals the pores in the stone. From this [discussion] it is apparent that a silver pipe must sound better than a tin one, and tin pipe better than one of lead, for the harder the metal that is used in the alloy, the better the sound will be. It makes it clear how it is possible to improve the tone of lead pipes

---

* This is particularly true if the organ has no reflective case, as became more and more common during the 18th century in central Germany, and as Adlung seems to presume; see §.31 and §.346.

† i.e., if a great deal of open space is left behind the organ.

‡ "dem Kirchenhimmel"; the German word can signify either an (essentially) flat ceiling or vaulting.

§ Presumably this comment envisions a situation in which a church has no ceiling hung below the roof rafters, or perhaps it envisions a very high, vaulted church; in either instance, the organ will be far below any upper barrier that might reflect its sound.

¶ Already in the 16th century Lutheran church architecture had begun to evolve characteristics that distinguished it from Catholic church architecture. One of the most distinctive Lutheran characteristics was the presence of multiple balconies surrounding three sides of the church, the fourth side being reserved for the altar (on the floor), the pulpit (behind and above it) and the organ (often above the pulpit). This arrangement can already be seen in the chapel of the Wilhelmsburg Palace at Schmalkalden, dating from 1585-90. Although the balconies at Schmalkalden are of masonry, such balconies were ordinarily constructed of wood. They were not only a feature of new churches (e.g., the Frauenkirche at Dresden), but were installed in older gothic churches as well (e.g., the Marktkirche at Halle, or the Thomaskirche at Leipzig). Such balconies served not only to increase the occupancy, but also to allow the congregation to be gathered more closely around the pulpit, in order to hear more clearly the Word of God as it was being preached. They also tended to break up the space within the building, thus diminishing the reverberation (and perhaps as a result improving the clarity of sound).

Kap. XXVIII. Ein Discours von etlichen curiösen Materien. 169

bessern, wenn man nämlich dasselbe härtet, welches etliche durch Marcasit thun, etliche durch etwas anders. Item, wie hölzerne Pfeifen zu intoniren, wie metallene, wenn durch eine Masse deren Pori verstopft werden, und im Gegentheil das Holz dadurch hart gemacht wird. f. §. 92. Imgleichen, warum die Decken der Clavichordien und anderer Instrumente nicht wohl und scharf klingen, wenn sie naß oder grün sind, weil nämlich alsdann das Holz weicher ist, als sonst. Kommt Fett drauf; so bleibt es allezeit drinnen, und wird das Holz dadurch stets bey der Gelindigkeit erhalten, daher solches so schädlich ist: dahingegen das Wasser wieder ausdunstet; (f. §. 592.) und was mehr für consectaria aus dieser Lehre können gezogen werden. Eben also ist klar, daß einer Stube, worinnen man musiciren soll, sehr schädlich sey, wenn man sie täfeln läßt; it wenn man sie mit Tapeten beschlägt und f. w. Wenigstens muß man sie gipsen und weißen lassen: sonst klingen sie nicht.

Auch ist ferner zu untersuchen? warum bey kaltem oder feuchtem Wetter die Orgeln nicht so klingen, als bey trockenem und warmen Wetter? Aus der Naturlehre ist bekannt, daß, je wärmer es sey, desto mehr dehne sich die Luft, als ein elastischer Körper, aus: Hingegen je kälter es ist, desto mehr wird die Luft zusammen gedruckt. Wer es nicht weis oder begreifen kann, dem will ich jetzo, aus Liebe zur Kürze keine Beweisthümer a priori hersetzen, sondern nur durch täglich vorkommende Exempel es verständlich machen. Bekannt sind ja die Gläser an den Oellampen; wer solche führt, der wird ja wol gemerkt haben, daß, wenn ein solches Glaß nicht voll ist, und es wird in der Stube warm; oder man setzt es auf den Ofen, so tritt das Oel herunter in die Lampe, daß selbige zuweilen gar überläuft. Woher kömmt das? Antw. die Luft an dem leeren Orte wird durch die Wärme ausgedehnet wie ein Schwamm durch das Wasser, also hat sie hernach nicht mehr Raum, und drücket das Oel herab, daß sie Raum bekomme. Nun wird ja kein Mensch läugnen, daß die Luft, wenn sie dicke ist, nicht sollte anders beweget werden, als wenn sie ausgedehnt und subtil ist. Also wird in einer feuchten Luft der Stoß auch schwerlicher geschehen können, weil da die Luft schwerer ist, als sonst. Fragt man weiter, bey welcher Luft der Klang am besten; so antworte ich: bey der warmen und trockenen. Denn wo Wärme ist, da ist alles in besserer Activität und Motion, als wo es kalt ist; also kann die Luft viel leichter bewegt werden. Wo es trocken ist, da ist auch die Luft leichter zu bewegen, und sie continuirt auch ihre Bewegung besser. So wird man bey heiterm Himmel, sonderlich wo es warm ist, eine Uhr, Geschoß, Glocke u. d. gl. viel weiter und besser hören, als im feuchten oder kalten Wetter. Also ists wohl möglich, daß eine Orgel, oder ander Instrument zu dieser Zeit anders klinge, als zu einer andern. Hierzu kann noch kommen, daß in einer Kirche zu einer Zeit Leute sind, zur andern Zeit aber nicht; oder itzo mehr, ein andermal weniger. Nun erwäge man doch, was für Veränderungen der Luft dadurch vorgehen? Sie dunsten viel aus; ihr Athem ist feucht, und dadurch wird die Luft auch feucht. Will man es nicht glauben; so betrachte man nur

Ch. XVIII. A Discourse on certain Curious Matters 169

by hardening them, which some accomplish by using marcasite, others by some other [material]. It likewise [makes it clear] how wooden pipes may be voiced [to sound] like metal ones, by sealing their pores with a varnish. This makes the wood, ordinarily a soft material, hard; see §.92.* Finally, it makes it clear why soundboards of clavichords and other instruments do not sound good and bright if they are [made of] wet or green [wood], because then the wood is softer than [when it is dry]. If grease gets on [a soundboard], then it cannot be removed, and it will keep the wood soft; this is why it is so harmful. Water [on a soundboard], on the other hand, will evaporate (see §.592). Other conclusions could be drawn as well from the above precept. In the same way, it is apparent that it is very harmful to install panelling in a room for making music, or to cover it with wallpaper or some such. Such a room must at least be plastered and whitewashed; otherwise it will not be resonant.

* sic; should read "§.95."

Let us further examine why organs do not sound the same in cold or damp weather as they do when it is dry and warm. It is manifest from the laws of nature that the warmer it is, the more air expands, since it is an elastic substance. On the other hand, the colder it is, the more air becomes compressed. Out of respect for brevity I will not set forth any *a priori* proofs for those who do not understand or know about this; rather I will make it comprehensible by an example that happens every day. Everyone is familiar with the glass containers (die Gläser) on oil lamps. Anyone who has carried one will surely have noticed that if such a glass is not full, and the room is warm or it is set on a stove, the oil runs back down into the lamp, sometimes even causing it to overflow. What causes this? Answer: the warmth causes the air in the empty portion to expand, just as water does to a sponge. Consequently it does not have any more space, and pushes the oil downward to get it. No one will deny that air that is thick would have to behave differently than when it is expanded and thin. Thus in damp air the thrust will encounter more resistance, since the air is then heavier than otherwise. If anyone should further ask what type of air promotes the best tone, I would answer, "Warm and dry." For wherever warmth is, everything can move more actively and freely than where it is cold; thus air can much more easily be set into motion. Wherever it is dry the air is easier to move, and it also continues its motion more easily. When the sky is blue, and especially when it is warm, a clock [chime], a shot, a bell, etc., can be heard far further and more clearly than in damp or cold weather. Thus it is indeed possible that an organ or some other instrument might sound different at one time than at another. To this may be added that there may be people in a church at one time, but not at another; and there may be more or fewer [of them]. Now consider what sort of variations take place in the air because of this. They give off a great deal of vapor. Their breath is damp, and it causes the air to become damp. If anyone does not believe this, he need only observe the damp windows in a room in cold weather, where noth-

die feuchten Fenster in einer Stube bey kaltem Wetter, da keine Feuchtigkeit ist, ohne die Ausdünstungen der Menschen. Imgleichen, durch ihren Athem erwärmen sie einigermaßen die Luft, wozu auch die Dünste vom ganzen Leibe helfen. Denn wenn man Kleider an gehabt hat, und fühlt sie an; so sind sie warm. Wo ist die Wärme her, als aus dem Leibe? wären die Kleider nicht da; so gienge sie unmittelbar in die Luft, und modificirte sie. Ja das Zurückprallen der Luft wird durch das Tuchwerk, oder Kleidung, sehr geschwächt. Denn indem der Schall drauf fällt, giebt es nach, und schickt ihn nicht wieder zurück, oder doch sehr schwach: da sonst, wenn die Kirche leer von Leuten ist, die Luft wenigstens vor die hölzernen Stühle und den steinernen Boden stößt, und besser zurücke prallt, als vom Tuche. Es könnten noch andere Kleinigkeiten gemeldet werden, z. E. daß es gut sey, wenn eine Kirche gute Spiegelfenster habe, dadurch die Sonne dieselbe besser auswärmen könne, rc; aber es wird zu weitläuftig. Ein jeder denke selber weiter nach.

Nun müssen wir auch berühren, warum an einem Orte eine Pfeife besser klingt, als am andern, der doch ex hypothesi eben so nahe dabey ist: denn wäre er näher; so wäre es ohnedieß klar. Hier muß ich dieß voraussetzen, daß ein Körper, wenn er an einen andern Körper stößt und zurücke prallt, er entweder perpendicular oder gerade auffalle, oder schief. Das heißt aber perpendicular, wenn die Linie mit der Fläche des Körpers zu beyden Seiten gleiche Winkel macht. Z. E. es sey die Tab. III. fig 2. a b soll eine gleiche Wand seyn; von c kömmt ein Ball geflogen, und stößt in d an die Wand. Die Linie, worinnen der Ball läuft von c nach d ist perpendicular, weil die Ecken oder Winkel bey d auf beyden Seiten einander gleich sind, und die Linie c d sich weder mehr zu b neiget, als zu a, noch mehr zu a als zu b. So auch in concaven und convexen Körpern. Z E. Tab. III. fig. 3. da geht die Linie c d, wenn sie so fort continuirte, gerade nach und durch das Centrum der Kugel, also ist sie perpendicular. Wenn nun der Ball von c nach d, d. i perpendicular wiederfahret; so springt er auch perpendicular wieder zurück, und kömmt wieder an seinen vorigen Ort. Dergleichen thut auch die Luft, als darinn der Stoß perpendicular wieder zurücke kömmt, wenn er perpendicular hingegangen; und daraus ist das Echo entstanden, da ein Haus, Berg, rc. gerade mit seiner Fläche steht, daß der Stoß der Luft, der von uns kömmt, darauf perpendicular fällt, und auch wieder zu uns kömmt, ein- oder mehrmal. Solches Zurückprallen hilft uns wenig: es sey denn, daß wir bey der Orgelpfeife stehen, oder die Violin und dergleichen in Händen haben: denn wenn solche Oerter da sind, darauf die Luft perpendicular fallen kann; so kömmt der Stoß wieder zu uns zurück, vielmal oder einmal: und weil der Klang vom Zurückprallen langsamer zu unsern Ohren kömmt, als der, welcher vom ersten Aufschlage entstanden; so pflegen wir zu sagen: es schallt schön in der Kirche d. i. der Schall wird vielmal oder stark verdoppelt durch das Zurückprallen. Ist nun die Kirche lang; so kömmt der Schall oft gar spät zurück, daß wir auch im Musiciren schon einen andern haben verursacht; da giebts Confusion, und

ing is damp other than the vapor of human beings. By their breath they likewise warm the air to some degree, aided by the vapors [given off] by their entire body. If you are wearing clothes, touch them; [you will find that] they are warm. Where else does the warmth come except from the body? Were there no clothes present, then it would pass directly into the air, modifying it. Indeed, the rebounding of the air is greatly impeded by cloth or clothing. For cloth yields to whatever sound falls on it, reflecting it little or not at all, while otherwise, when the church is empty of people, the air at least strikes the wooden pews/choir stalls and the stone floor, and rebounds better than from cloth. Other trivia could also be mentioned— e.g., that it is a good thing for a church to have good clear-glass windows through which the sun can warm it up better—but these would make my remarks too lengthy. Each person may reflect on these things for himself.

Now we must also touch upon why a pipe sounds better [when it is placed] in one spot than in another that is nevertheless hypothetically just as nearby. If it [actually] were nearer, then this would be clear anyway. Here I am presupposing that when an object strikes another object and rebounds from it, it does so either perpendicularly (straight), or at an angle. By perpendicular, I mean that the line [of the object's travel] creates a right angle with the surface of the object [that is struck]. For example, in figure 2 of Table III,* a - b is supposed to represent a flat wall. A ball is thrown from c, striking the wall at d. The line in which the ball travels from c - d is perpendicular, since the angles on both sides of d are equal, and the line c - d leans no more or less toward b or a. The same holds true for concave and convex objects; e.g., in figure 3, Table III, the line c - d, were it to be extended, would pass directly to and through the center of the ball, and thus it is perpendicular. If the ball travels from c to d, i.e., perpendicular, then it will bounce back perpendicularly and return to it original location. The air does the same thing: its thrust returns perpendicularly if it has traveled hence perpendicularly. This is how an echo is created: a house, or a mountain, etc. presents a flat surface in such a way that the thrust of air coming from us falls upon it perpendicularly and returns to us by the same path, once or several times. This rebounding is not particularly helpful to us unless we are standing next to the organ pipe, or have a violin or some such [sound source] in our hands; for when surfaces are present upon which the air can fall perpendicularly, then the thrust returns to us, once or many times. And since the reflected sound reaches our ears later than that which arises from the primary attack, we are accustomed to say, "This church is beautifully reverberant," i.e., the reverberation greatly multiplies the sound and makes it strong. If the church is long, then we often perceive the sound's return quite late, so that in making music we have created a second [sound]. This causes confusion, to the point that [listeners] sometimes cannot

* In the *Musica mechanica organoedi*, Table III is found between p. 170 & 171 of vol. I.

und weis man zuweilen nicht, was gesungen wird. Doch wird den Musicis so die Arbeit leichter, wenn es viel zurücke prallt, weil sie nur etwas von Coloraturen wissen, das übrige, wie auch die Stärke der Instrumenten und Stimmen ersetzt die Repercußion.

Es fällt aber die Luft nicht allzeit perpendicular auf eine Fläche; folglich kann sie auch nicht wieder also zu unsern Ohren zurück kommen, sondern sie prallt ab, wo anders hin; doch unter gleichem Angulo inclinationis. Z. E. es sey eine Wand a b; (s. Tab. III. fig. 4.) ich stünde in c, und würfe den Ball nach e; so wäre das schief: denn e neigt sich mehr zu a, als zu b, also ist es nicht perpendicular, folglich kömmt der Ball nicht wieder zurück nach c, sondern er gehet von e nach d, daß der Winkel a e c so groß sey, als b e d. Auf ein ander Fleckchen kann der Ball nicht kommen. Nachdem nun eine Wand in der Kirche stehet, nach dem wird auch die Luft zurückprallen. Man hat aber soviel Wände, soviel Flächen von Stühlen, Pfeifen, ꝛc. daß dadurch der Stoß sehr motificirt wird. Nun kann es leicht seyn, daß die Theile des Gebäudes so disponirt sind, daß, wenn ich an einem gewissen Orte stehe, viel solche Stöße zu meinem Ohre kommen, da an dem andern solches nicht so seyn kann. Folglich klingts an einem Orte oft anders, als am andern. Man hat aber hierbey nicht nur auf die Flächen ganzer Wände, Gewölber, ꝛc. zu sehen, sondern auf solchen Flächen sind oft Ungleichheiten, die, so gering als sie auch immer seyn mögen, gleich den Stoß wo andershin continuiren.

Aus diesem allen sollten nun Bauherren schlüßen, wie die Orgeln anzulegen, imgleichen die Singchöre, die Kirchen, die Kanzeln darinne ꝛc. daß es keinem zu sauer anfäme. Von solchen Dingen könnte noch viel gesagt werden; allein es würde zu weitläuftig, und wer ein mehreres verlangt, der blättere die physikalischen mathematischen Bücher durch, die davon genug in sich fassen; daher ich auch keine allegire: es sind deren gar zu viel. Von dem perpendicularen und obliquen Zurückprallen der Luft, und wie man dadurch den Klang leiten kann wie die Sonnenstrahlen, kann man Kirchers Phonurgie, auch seine Musurgie nachschlagen; anderer z. E. de Chales l. c. nicht zu gedenken.

Es ist oben §. 332. gedacht worden, daß man ein schwaches Licht vor dem starken nicht sehe, und man deswegen hinter der Orgel kein Fenster zu dem Endzwecke machen solle, daß Licht durch die Orgel fallen möge. Wollte man den Grund dieser Wahrheit tiefer suchen; so könnte man sich auf die Analogie mit andern Sinnen berufen. Denn bey allen Sinnen, dem Gehör, Geruch, Geschmack, Fühlen, und also auch bey dem Gesichte finden wir, daß man vor einer starken Empfindung eine schwächere nicht vernimmt. Z. E. Wenn man bey den Glocken stehet, indem sie scharf in einander geläutet werden; so kann man des andern Rede nicht, oder sehr schwer, verstehen. Denn wenn wir etwas hören sollen; so muß durch die Luft das tympanum im Ohre in

tell what is being sung. But a pronounced reverberation makes work easier for the musicians, since they need only be able to perform a few embellishments; the rest, including weakness in the instruments and voices, is compensated for by the reverberation.

Air, however, does not always strike a surface perpendicularly, and consequently it cannot [always] return to our ears. Rather it rebounds somewhere else, but of course at the same angle of incline. For example, if there were a wall a - b (see Table III, fig. 4),* and I were to stand at c and throw the ball toward e, that would be at an angle, since c leans more toward a than b (thus it is not perpendicular). Consequently the ball would not return to c, but would travel from e toward d, creating an angle a-e-c that is the same size as b-e-d. The ball cannot end up at any other spot. The position of a wall in a church will determine the angle of the air's rebound. But there are so many walls and so many surfaces—pews, pipes, etc.—that they greatly modify the [air's] thrust. It may well be that the parts of a building are so laid out that if I am standing at a given spot many such thrusts reach my ears, while at another spot this is impossible. Consequently the sound will often be different at one spot than at another. In this regard it is not only the surfaces of all the walls, vaults, etc., that have to be taken into account, but also the unevennesses that are often found in such surfaces that, no matter how minor they might be, immediately direct the thrust somewhere else.

* between p. 170 & 171 of vol. I.

Taking all of this into account, architects/master builders ought to decide how to design the layout of organs as well as choirs, churches and the pulpits in them, etc., so that no one is vexed [by an inability to hear]. A great deal more could be said about such things, but it would get too long-winded. Anyone who requires more [information] can leaf through books on the mathematics of physics that contain plenty of this sort of thing. I will not cite any of them, since there are more than enough of them. Concerning the perpendicular and oblique rebounding of air, and how it may be used to direct the sound like the sun's rays, consult Kircher's *Phonurgia*† as well as his *Musurgia*,‡ not to mention other such as de Chales, l.c.§

† Book I, pp. 6f.
‡ Vol. II, Book IX, pp. 239f.
§ Vol. III, Tract 22.

§.332 above mentions that a feeble light is not visible against a bright one, and for that reason no window should be placed behind the organ for the purpose of letting light pass through the organ. If anyone wishes to investigate the reason for this truth more thoroughly, he may refer to analogies in the other senses. For with all the senses—hearing, smell, taste, feeling and also with sight—we find that a weak sensation is not perceived above a strong one. For example, if someone stands beside bells while they are being rung briskly altogether, that person can understand it only barely or not at all when another person is talking to him. For in order for us to hear anything, the air must set the eardrum in motion. But the pealing of the bells has already

eine Bewegung gebracht werden; allein durch den Schall der Glocken ist es schon in der stärksten Bewegung, und kann einen so geringen Anstoß der Luft, den wir mit unserer Rede machen, nicht besonders empfinden. So würde ein Musikdirektor ungereimt handeln, wenn er zu einer Laute wollte die lärmenden Pauken mit Force hören lassen. ꝛc. Was den Geruch betrift; so ist bekannt, daß man, wenn die Luft verfälscht ist, Schnupftabak dawider gebrauche. Wozu soll er? wird denn deswegen die Luft nicht mehr stinkend seyn? Antw. Ja; allein wir empfinden vor dem Schnupftabak das üble Riechen der Luft nicht, weil jener die Nerven so stark afficirt, und den Saft darinnen so stark bewegt, daß das andere nicht empfunden wird. Den Geschmack anlangend; so wird man bey scharf gesalzenen Speisen den andern Geschmack wenig vor dem Salze empfinden. Bey dem Fühlen ist auch so: z. E. wenn es einen juckt, s. v. so hilft man sich durch das Kratzen, da durch dessen starke Empfindung jenes nicht empfunden wird, nicht als wenn jenes dadurch allezeit gehindert würde. Also, wenn einer einen braven Buckel voll Schläge bekömmt, fühlt er es in dem Moment, da er die Schmerzen fühlt, nicht, wenn ihn einer angreift. Eben also ist es auch mit dem Gesichte, z. E. wer am Tage wollte nach den Sternen sehen, der würde sich vergeblich bemühen, ob schon der Himmel so voll Sterne ist, als des Nachts: denn das starke Sonnenlicht afficirt ihn so sehr, daß er das schwache Sternenlicht nicht empfindet. Auch sogar ein wirklich Licht wird vor einem reflectirten und refringirten Lichte nicht gesehen, wenn jenes allzu geringe ist. Z. E. Bey der Dämmerung, da die Sonne wirklich untergegangen, sehen wir nicht gleich alle Sterne, sondern erst die großen. ꝛc. Kömmt einer aus dem Hellen in einem Ort, der nicht gar finster ist; so wird er das darinnen sich wirklich findende Licht nicht sehen, sondern alles wird ihm schwarz seyn, bis der motus, welcher in den Nerven vom starken Licht entstanden, vergangen, alsdann wird er sehen. Zündet einer bey Tage ein Licht an; so wirft es keinen besondern Schein von sich. Eben als wenn man in einen Galanteriekram kömmt, und viel sehenswürdige Sachen antrift; so sind unsere Augen gleichsam an die Raritäten so angeheftet, daß wir geringe Dinge darinnen nicht wahrnehmen. So sagt man: **Kleider machen Menschen;** d. i. in einem saubern Kleide gefällt ein Mensch dem andern besser, als in einem geringen. Was ist die Ursach? Antw. weil uns das Kleid in die Sinne fällt, und eine Empfindung bey uns macht; so kann uns die Larve so eine starke Empfindung nicht machen, und die Narben, üble Proportion der Glieder, die Farbe u. s. w. werden von uns gar nicht, oder doch nicht sattsam empfunden und betrachtet. Denn die Sinnen beziehen sich auf das, was am stärksten afficirt. Daher sagt man auch daß die Liebe blind sey, und, wie Lutherus sagt in der Glosse Syrach am 25, denkt mancher, er habe was schönes, und ist hernach doch wol ein garstiger Balg. Denn die Heftigkeit des Affekts verdirbt die Sinnen, daß wir mehr regardiren auf das, was mit der Wollust sich reimt, als auf andere Dinge, welche erst hernach beobachtet werden, wenn sich die Heftigkeit des Affekts geleget. So ist mancher mit seinen Leibes- und Gemüthsaugen so erpicht auf das Geld, Hoheit, und Schönheit einer Wei-

set it into the most violent motion, and thus it cannot perceive such a minor thrust of air as is created by our speech. Thus a director of music would be acting absurdly if he were to combine a thundering kettledrum with a lute. As regards [the sense of] smell, it is well known that one should take snuff to combat polluted air. Why is this? Will it not make the air stink even more? The answer is, "Yes; but the [smell of the] snuff masks the vile smell of the air, since the former so strongly affects the nerves, and agitates the juices in them so much, that the latter is not perceived. With regard to taste: if one is eating heavily salted foods, the taste of other [foods] is very little perceived above the salt. The same holds true with [the sense of] feeling. For example, if someone has an itch, he immediately (s.v.*) tries to alleviate it by scratching, so that [the itch] might not be felt above the stronger sensation [of the scratching]—not that the itch is always stopped by doing this. If someone gets a sound thrashing, he feels nothing at the moment in which he is attacked. It is the same with [the sense of] sight. For example, anybody who tries to see the stars during the day will trouble himself in vain, even though the sky is just as full of stars [then] as at night. For the strong sunlight makes such an impression on him that he cannot perceive the feeble light of the stars. Even an actual light, if it is too weak, will not be seen above a reflected or refracted light. At dusk, after the sun has fully set, we do not see all the stars at once, but only the major ones at first. If anyone come inside out of bright daylight, even though the place is not entirely dark, he will not see the light that is actually present in the room. Rather, everything will be black to him until the activity caused in his nerves by the bright light has past, and then he will see. If someone kindles a light by day, it will not throw off any noticeable glow. Likewise, if someone enters a fashion accessories shop (Galanteriekram) and encounters many interesting things, his eyes will be so focused on what is unusual that he does not perceive the ordinary things that are there. There is a saying, "Clothes make the man;" i.e., a man in fine clothing makes a better impression than one in inferior clothing. Why is this? Because the clothing strikes our senses, making an impression on us. Thus his face cannot make as strong an impression on us, and we notice his scars, his poorly proportioned limbs, his color, etc, very little, if at all. For the senses focus on that which affects them the most strongly. Thus it is said that love is blind, and as Luther says in his Commentary on Sirach 25, many a fellow thinks he has a beautiful [woman], who later turns out to be a nasty old bag.† For the intensity of the emotions corrupts the senses, so that we take more regard of that which tallies with sensual pleasure than of other things; these we notice only later, when the intensity of the emotions has settled. Thus many a man is so intent with all of his bodily and spiritual desire upon a woman's money, high standing and beauty, that

* This is not a standard abbreviation, either in German or Latin. Its sense seems to be "immediately" (or perhaps "instinctively"?).

† Adlung is referring to one of Luther's marginal commentaries on the book of Jesus Sirach (in the Old Testament Apocrypha), in Chap. 23 (not 25, as Adlung has it), vs. 24 of his German translation of the Bible. See: *D. Martin Luthers Werke... Die Deutsche Bibel*, Vol. 12. Weimar: Hermann Böhlaus Nachfolger, [1883] 1961, p. 211.

besperson, daß er nicht im Stande ist, von ihrem übrigen Qualitäten zu urtheilen, daß auch die Politici eine Regel machen müssen, daß man im Heyrathen es nie zu einem großen Affekte sollte kommen lassen; it. man solle anderer Leute Rath und Einschläge dabey brauchen ꝛc. Doch zur Sache. Das Licht der Sonnen ist um soviel stärker, als weniger es reflektirt wird: und wo es gar nicht reflektirt wird, sondern in gerader Linie von der Sonne herkömmt, da ist es am allerstärksten. (Was Brenngläser und Brennspiegel dabey thun, das gehet uns jetzo nichts an.) Wenn nun hinter der Orgel eine Oefnung ist, dadurch das Licht durch die Orgel herab fällt in die Kirche; so wird es Vormittags, (wenn die Orgel gegen Morgen stehet) oder Nachmittags (wenn sie gegen Abend stehet) unmittelbar von der Sonne herkommen, die Sonnenstrahlen aber, die von der Seite durch die Fenster alsdann auf die Pfeifen und Orgel fallen, sind schon vielmal gebrochen, und werden von der Orgel reflektirt, folglich viel schwächer als jenes Licht; also werden die Strahlen, die von der Orgel abprallen, zu uns zwar kommen: allein wir werden sie vor jenem Lichte nicht sehen, oder doch nicht recht. Ist die Sonne nicht gerade hinter der Orgel; so wird man dieselbe wol sehen, aber doch nicht so gut, als wenn gar kein Licht durch die Orgel fällt. Denn je dunkler der Ort ist, wo ein Licht stehet, desto heller scheint das Licht. Diese Betrachtung dient auch dazu, daß wir die Ursach sehen von dem, was Kap. 8. gesagt worden, warum die Quinten- und Terzenregister nicht eher zu ziehen, bis andere Oktavstimmen, in gehöriger Menge, dabey sind, daß sie von denselben überschrieen werden, d. i. daß sie keine besondere und starke Empfindung bey uns machen. Denn ‚emehr die andern Stimmen schreyen, desto mehr wird die facultas percipiendi dorthin gelenket, und sie merkt auf das andere nicht so stark.

Ferner möchte einer zu wissen verlangen, warum die Mäuse die metallenen Pfeifen angehen, da wir sonst nicht finden, daß in Häusern ein Gleiches geschehe. Die Ursache kann diese seyn: Es findet sich an den metallenen Pfeifen der Salpeter, zuweilen viel, zuweilen weniger, der ist süße, und schmeckt den Mäusen wohl, weswegen sie solchen fleißig aufsuchen, und bey aller Gelegenheit das Pfeifwerk zugleich beschaben. Doch fragt sichs weiter: woher der Salpeter bey den Pfeifen komme? Hierauf dient zur Antwort, daß aus der Erde beständig allerhand wässerige, schwefelichte, metallene, salpetrichte ꝛc. Dünste oder Partickelchen aufsteigen, womit also die Luft beständig angefüllet ist, und zwar nach Beschaffenheit des Erdreichs, je an einem Ort in größerer Menge, als an einem andern. Ob nun wol an manchen Orten nicht so viel Salpeter in der Luft wäre; so kann doch derselbe durch die Bewegung der Luft, welche nie aufhöret, von andern Orten hergebracht werden. Diese, wie andere Dünste der Luft, hängen sich an die Körper, sonderlich an die feuchten und kalten, dergleichen die Metalle sind. Je geringer nun und unreiner das Metall ist, desto geschwinder hängt sich der Salpeter an; folglich spührt man solches mehr bey geringerm Metalle, wo viel Bley darunter ist, als bey zinnern Pfeifen, weil das Bley unreiner, feuchter, und die Dünste

ste

Ch. XVIII. A Discourse on certain Curious Matters 173

he is in no condition to evaluate the rest of her qualities. This is why the authorities have had to make a rule that, when a man is intent upon marriage, he must never allow himself to get worked up emotionally, and must likewise avail himself of the advice and suggestions of other people. But to the point: the less the light of the sun is reflected [before we perceive it], the stronger it is, and it is at its strongest if it is not reflected at all, but reaches us in a direct line from the sun (how burning glasses and concave mirrors affect it does not concern us here). If there is a window behind the organ through which light shines into the church, passing through the organ, then in the morning (if the organ is at the east end) or in the evening (if it is at the west end) the light will proceed directly from the sun. The rays of the sun that fall through the side windows upon the [façade] pipes and the organ [case], however, have already been deflected many times and are reflected off the organ. Consequently they are much feebler than the light [that proceeds directly through the organ]. Thus the rays that are reflected by the organ do indeed reach us, but the direct light prevents us from perceiving them, or at least from perceiving them properly. If the sun is not directly behind the organ, then [the reflected rays] can indeed be seen, but still not as well as if no light at all were passing through the organ. For the darker the place from which a light shines, the more brilliant the light will appear. This observation also serves to clarify for us the reason behind what was said in Chap. 8* about not drawing fifth- and third-sounding stops before an ample number of unison-sounding stops, so that the latter do not outweigh the former, i.e., so that we do not perceive them especially intensely. For the more sound the other stops† make, the more our faculty of perception will be drawn to them, and the less strongly it will notice the others.‡

* §.215f.

† i.e., the unison-sounding stops.
‡ i.e., the mutations.

Moreover, there might be someone who would like to know why mice attack metal pipes, since we do not find anything similar happening in homes. It may be for this reason: saltpeter is found on metal pipes,§ sometimes more, sometimes less. It is sweet and the mice like its taste, and this is why they diligently seek it out, immediately gnawing on the pipes at every opportunity. This gives rise to another question: where does saltpeter on the pipes come from? The answer to this is that all sorts of vapors or tiny particles—aqueous, sulfurous, metallic, saltpetric, etc.—are constantly rising up out of the earth. The atmosphere is thus constantly filled with these, according to the characteristics of the [particular] region of the earth, in greater quantity in some places than in others. Even though there is not all that much saltpeter in the air in many places, the ceaseless movement of the air can bear it in from other places. This, just as other airborne vapors, clings to objects, especially to damp and cold ones such as those of metal. The more inferior and impure the metal is, the more readily the saltpeter clings to it. Consequently its effects are noticed more in inferior metal that has a large lead content¶ than in tin pipes, since lead is more impure and damp, and is more liable to attract

§ cf. Chap. 12, §.383 & §.384

¶ cf. §.87 & §.383.

ste in der Luft, folglich auch den Salpeter an sich zu ziehen fähiger ist, als Zinn. Deswegen ist auch oben gerathen worden, daß man nicht allzuviel Bley zum Pfeifwerke nehmen solle, nicht nur des Klanges wegen, sondern auch des Salpeters wegen. Es hängen sich zwar auch andere Dünste an; allein nach denselben gehen die Mäuse nicht: auch durchdringen und zerbeissen sie das Metall nicht, wie der Salpeter, als welcher in 30 und weniger Jahren die Füße der Pfeifen durchfressen kann, daß sie sich setzen, und endlich gar verderben. Es findet sich aber der Salpeter meistens inwendig in den Spitzen der Füsse, so, daß, wenn man die Pfeife in den Mund nimmt, das Maul voller Süßigkeit und Salpeters wird, weil der Wind aus dem Balge hier anstößt, und solche Partickelchen mit dahin führt. Deswegen habe ich oben gerathen, die Füße lieber von Zinn zu machen: denn gesetzt, es hängt sich der Salpeter auch an die zinnernen Füße; so kann er doch dieselben wegen der Härte so leicht nicht durchfressen. Je weniger Bley unter die Pfeifen kömmt, desto länger werden die Pfeifen vor dem Salpeter dauren.

Ferner ist zu untersuchen, warum eine kurze Seyte höher klingt, als eine lange, und eine starkgespannte höher, als eine, die nicht so stark gespannet ist? Woraus hernach leicht abzunehmen, daß kleine und enge Pfeifen höher, als größere klingen müssen: wie auch, daß die gedeckten Pfeifen beynahe einen noch einmal so tiefen Klang von sich hören lassen.

Es ist voraus zu setzen, daß der Klang um soviel höher werde, als viel stärker die Luft beweget wird nach unserm Ohre zu. Z. E. Wenn man eine Flöte stark anbläset; so giebt sie einen höhern Sonum von sich, als sonst, welches zuweilen $\frac{1}{4}$ oder $\frac{1}{2}$ Ton austrägt: zuweilen aber, wenn die force groß ist, gehet sie wohl eine Oktave und mehr, höher, ob man schon immer einerley Löcher offen hält. (**) Nimmt man eine schlanke Weidenruthe, und schlägt damit in die Luft; so wird man den Sonum um so viel erhöhen, als man stark schlägt.

(**) Daß dieses nicht von der vermehrten Stärke der Luft herkomme, hat Hr. Quanz in seiner Anw. erwiesen. Siehe das. S. 45 u. f.

Weiter ist voraus zu setzen, daß die Stärke oder force der Bewegung der Luft mit ihrer Geschwindigkeit einerley sey. Denn wie macht man es, wenn man die Flöte stark anblasen will? Antw. man stößt die Luft mit der größten Geschwindigkeit hinein, daß sie ihre tremores geschwinde thun muß. Will man die Luft stark mit der Ruthe schlagen; so beweget man diese geschwinder.

Eine jede Seyte, wenn sie gerühret wird, wird in eine Bewegung gebracht, daß sie zittert, und hin und wieder schlägt. So lange nun das Zittern dauret, so lange klingt sie auch. Diese Schläge hin und her nennet man Vibrationes oder Diadromos. Je schneller diese Bewegung ist, desto stärker schlägt die Seyte die Luft, weil die Geschwindigkeit und Stärke eins ist. Nun fällt es auch in die Sinnen, daß eine stark ge-

Ch. XVIII. A Discourse on certain Curious Matters

the vapors in the air, such as saltpeter, than tin is. This is the reason for the advice given above* not to use too much lead in pipes, not merely for the sake of tone, but also because of saltpeter. True, other vapors will also cling [to pipes], but the mice are not attracted by these. They also do not penetrate and corrode the metal as saltpeter does; it can eat through the feet of pipes in 30 years or less, causing them to settle and finally ruining them entirely. Saltpeter is found mostly on the insides of the toes of [pipe] feet, so that anyone who puts a pipe [foot] to his mouth gets a mouthful of sweet taste and saltpeter. [The reason for this is] that the wind [traveling] from the bellows strikes here [first], bearing such tiny particles with it. This is why I have advised above† that it is better to make the feet of tin. For granted that saltpeter also clings to tin feet, nevertheless it cannot so easily corrode them, since [tin] is so hard. The less lead that goes into pipes, the longer the pipes will resist [the growth of] saltpeter.

 Next we should investigate why a short string sounds higher than a long one, and why one that is tightly strung sounds higher than one that is not as tight. It is easy to deduce from this that small, narrow pipes must sound higher than large ones, and also that stopped pipes produce a sound almost twice as low [as their lengths would indicate].

 It is to be presupposed that the sound will be higher in proportion to the increased energy with which the air is propelled toward our ears. For example, if a flute is blown forcefully, it produces a higher pitch than it otherwise would, sometimes amounting to as much as a ¼ or a ½ step. Sometimes, though, if the force [of the wind] is great, it overblows by an octave or more, even though the same [finger]holes are left unstopped. (**) If you take a slender willow switch and strike the air with it, the more forceful the motion, the higher the pitch will rise.

 (**) Mr. Quantz has demonstrated in his *Anw.*,‡ p. 45f.,§ that this is not caused by the increased force of the air. [Agricola]

 Moreover, it is to be presupposed that the strength or force of the air's motion is the same as its speed. For what does a person do if he wants to play a flute forcefully? He forces the air into it with the greatest rapidity, causing it to make its vibrations quickly. If someone wants to strike the air [more] forcefully with the switch, he will move it more quickly.

 Any string, when it is touched, is set into motion, making it vibrate or beat back and forth. The sound will last as long as the vibration. These beatings back and forth are called *vibrations* or *diadromos*. The faster this motion is, the more forcefully the string strikes the air, since speed and force are the same. The senses perceive that a

* Chap. 6, §.87.

† §.383.

‡ Johann Joachim Quantz, *Versuch einer Anweisung die Flöte traversiere zu spielen...*

§ actually p. 46.

gespannte Seyte viel geschwinder schlägt, und in einem Moment mehr Vibrationes macht, als eine andere, die nicht so stark gespannt ist: ergo wird davon eine schärfere Empfindung bey uns erweckt, welche wir höher nennen; auch wird die Seyte wirklich kürzer, wenn man sie stärker spannt: denn man windet ja einen Theil auf den Wirbel. Es kann aber das starke und schwache Spannen oder Ausdehnen der Seyte auf unzähliche Arten variiren, daher so unzähliche Arten des Stoßes der Luft, und folglich auch des Klanges, sind, der deswegen bald so hoch, bald so hoch wird. Aus eben dem Grunde nennen wir auch den hohen Klang sonum acutum, weil er eine schärfere Empfindung bey uns macht, auch deshalben durchdringender ist. Wie die Bewegungen eines Penduli variiren in der Geschwindigkeit, nachdem der Faden stark oder schwach angezogen ist, durch ein geringes oder groß Gewicht; so ists auch hier. Ich könnte von dem ungleichen Zittern viel sinnliche Exempel anführen; allein es würde zu weitläuftig.

Was ferner betrift die kurze und lange Seyte; so wird jene um soviel geschwinder ihre Vibrationes verrichten, als wieviel sie kürzer ist, als die längere. Sind die Vibrationes geschwinder; so ist das Stoßen stärker in der Luft: ergo der Klang höher. Eben wie bey dem Pendulo die Geschwindigkeit der Diadromorum variirt nach der Länge des Penduli, und je länger es ist, desto langsamer schlägt es von einer Seite zur andern. Etliche haben daher die Proportion der Vibrationen ausrechnen wollen, daß sie gesetzt: wenn z. E. von der und der Seyte, die diese oder jene Länge hat, soviel Vibrationes gemacht werden, daß wir den daher entstehenden Klang c nennen, wie viel Vibrationes werden gemacht werden müssen, wenn es eine Quinte höher klingen soll, und wie viel wird die Seyte an der Länge verliehren, oder stärker angezogen werden müssen, damit die Geschwindigkeit um so viel wachse. Solche Rechnungen gehen schon an; allein, wer in der Mathematik nichts gethan, der wird doch davon nichts fassen. Mathematici aber können es selbst nachrechnen, daß ich also nicht nöthig habe, es hier zu thun. Es wird wie bey den Pendulen seyn. Der Herr Sauveur in Frankreich hat sich die Mühe gegeben, auszurechnen, wie viel Schläge, Diadromos oder Vibrationes jeder Ton in Zeit einer Secunde mache. Wie solches zu lesen in Histoire de l'Academ. Roy. des Sciences von Anno 1700 und 1713. Conf **Matthesons forschendes** Orchestre P. I. C. I. p. 79. not. 5. ad §. 54. Eine Stunde wird in 60 Minuten getheilt, da die Secunde der 60ste Theil von einer Minute ist. Es ist subtil, doch nicht gar zu verachten. Aus Sauveur hat es die **Organisten-Probe** §. 152. der Vorbereitung. Doch ist eben nicht nöthig, die Vibrationen zu zählen; genug daß man eine Proportion hat, daß, wenn z. E. C 8 Vibrationen macht, D derselben 9 hervorbringt, s. auch **Organisten-Probe** §. 154. ibid.

Hieraus ist auch leichtlich abzunehmen, warum eine enge Pfeife höher, als eine weite, und eine kurze höher, als eine lange klinge. Weil das große corpus langsamer

Ch. XVIII. A Discourse on certain Curious Matters 175

tightly stretched string beats much faster, making more vibrations per second than another that is not as tightly stretched. Therefore [such a string] awakens in us a more intense sensation, which we call "higher." The string actually does become shorter when it is stretched more tightly, since part of it is wound around the tuning pin. The greater or lesser tightening or loosening of a string can vary infinitely; thus there are countless levels of thrust [of which the air is capable], and consequently the pitch may vary infinitely. For the same reason we call high pitch *sonum acutum*, since it makes a more intense sensation in us, and since it is more penetrating. Just as the motions of a pendulum vary in speed according to whether its cord is made tighter or looser by a greater or lesser weight, so it is [with pitch]. I could cite many [other] perceptible examples of unequal vibration, but they would become too lengthy.

Furthermore, as concerns a short or a long string: a short string will vibrate faster in proportion to how much shorter it is than the longer string. If the vibrations are more rapid, then it strikes the air more sharply, and therefore the sound is higher. The speed of the vibrations are just like a pendulum; the longer the pendulum is, the slower it swings from one side to another. Therefore some have attempted to calculate the proportion of the vibrations by positing that if, e.g., such and such a string of this or that length vibrates at a certain rate, creating a pitch that we call "c", then how many vibrations would there have to be to make it sound a fifth higher, and how much shorter would the string have to be, or how much more tightly stretched, to increase its speed by so much. Such calculations are indeed possible, but anyone who is not conversant with mathematics will not comprehend any of it. Mathematicians can figure it out for themselves, though, and thus I do not feel constrained to do it here. It works the same as with a pendulum. Mr. Sauveur in France has taken the trouble to calculate how many beats or vibrations each pitch makes in the course of a second. This may be read in the *Histoire de l'Academ. Roy. des Sciences*, 1700 and 1713;* cf. Mattheson's *Forschende Orchestre*, Part I, Chap. I, p. 79, note "s" to §.54. An hour is divided into 60 minutes, while a second is a 60th part of a minute. [His argument] is subtle, but not to be disdained. §.152 of the *Organisten-Probe*† has its genesis in Sauveur's work. But it is not really necessary to count the vibrations. It is enough that a proportion is established, so that if, e.g., "C" makes 8 vibrations, "D" will produce 9 of them; see also the *Organisten-Probe*, §.154.‡

* Joseph Sauveur's papers were published in the *Histoire de l'Académie royale des sciences* [1701-13], published in Paris, 1704-16.

† Johann Mattheson, *Exemplarische organisten-probe...*, pp. 104-5.

‡ p. 106.

From this it is easily deduced why a narrow pipe is taller that a wide one, and why a short one produces a higher pitch than a long one. Since a larger object vibrates more

tremulirt, als ein kleines; so wird auch die Luft, von dem Körper angestoßen, langsame tremores machen, und das Ohr nicht so stark afficiren. Auch kann etwas thun, daß in kurzen Pfeifen die Luft nicht so lange herumgedrehet wird, sondern bald oben hinaus marschirt nach unserm Ohre, ehe sie viel von ihrer Kraft verliert: da hingegen bey einer langen Pfeife die Luft sehr geschwächt wird, ehe sie zu dem Ohre kömmt. Man siehet auch solches daraus, weil, wenn die Bälge schärfer in das Pfeifwerk blasen, es auch höher klingt, als bey schwachem Winde, weil alsdann die Luft darinnen in stärkerer Bewegung ist, als sonst, und uns mehr afficirt. Wollte jemand zweifeln, daß diese Bewegung verschiedentlich sey; so wird er doch erstlich überhaupt zugestehen müssen, daß der motus tremulus in sono sey, oder daß kein Sonus sey absque motu tremulo. Es hat dieses schön ausgeführt de Chales in Mundo Mathem. To. III. P. I. prop. 3. it. 41 & 42. Auch ist dieses in großen Pfeifen empfindlich. z. E. wenn eine 16füßige Pfeife klingt, so schwach sie auch gehöret wird, so wird doch gar oft das ganze Chor zittern, daß man es fühlen kann; wenn nämlich solche Körper mit dem sono eine Proportion haben. Auch darf man nur die Pfeife anfühlen; so wird man von dem Zittern genug überzeuget werden. Bey kleinen Pfeifen werden endlich die tremores so geschwind gehen, daß man sie nicht merkt, sondern denkt, es geschähe der Sonus immer fort. Bey großen Pfeifen in den Schnarrwerken hört man das Zittern; bey kleinen schon nicht so wohl; ja man fühlt es auch. Denn man blase mit dem Munde eine Schnarrstimme an; so wird das Blat stark genug tremuliren. Daß man aber in sonis acutis die Vibrationes nicht vernimmt, das hat das Gehör mit andern Sinnen gemein. Können doch die Augen die, aus der Canone geschossene, Kugel auch nicht sehen; gleichwol ist sie vor dem Gesicht vorbey marschirt. Was ist die Ursach? Antw. die Geschwindigkeit. Denken wir doch auch, wenn die Feuerwerker ein umlaufend Rad präsentiren, es sey ein feuriger Zirkel, oder runde Scheibe, da es doch nur eine Linie ist. Diese tremores der Pfeifen bleiben ordentlich einmal so geschwind, als das anderemal; daher was heute diese Pfeife für einen Ton von sich hören lassen, den läßt sie auch morgen hören; doch durch die force des Anblasens wird eine wiewol geringe Veränderung gespührt, weil durch eine große Gewalt des Windes das corpus der Pfeife in eine schnellere Bewegung gesetzt werden kann, wie man sieht, wenn man den Bälgen mehr Wind giebt, oder wenn man eine Pfeife mit dem Munde stark anbläset, daß die Pfeifen höher gehen. Ich weis also nicht, wie de Chales l. c pag. 4. meynen kann, daß durch die Gewalt gar keine Aenderung geschehen könne. Er beruft sich zwar auf das Pendulum, als wodurch er die ganze Lehre erkläret; allein, es ist doch bekannt, daß, wenn mit der Hand scharf wider das Pendulum gestoßen wird, solches in dem Moment, da der Stoß geschiehet, geschwinder fortlaufe, als es seiner Schwere und Länge nach thun würde.

Die gedeckten Pfeifen gehen ordentlich noch eins so tief, als die offenen. Es fragt sich: warum? Antw. der Wind gehet durch die Oeffnung in das corpus und

slowly than a small one, the air that is struck by that object makes slower vibrations, affecting the ear less intensely. Another contributing factor may be that the air does not get tossed about as long in short pipes, but proceeds sooner out of the top [of the pipe], reaching our ears before losing very much of its force, while on the other hand the air is greatly weakened in a long pipe before it reaches our ears. This may be seen by the fact that if the wind blows more forcefully into the pipes, they then sound higher than they do with a gentler wind, since then the air in them is in more intense motion, and affects us more. If anyone doubts that this motion varies, he will at least have to admit that vibration is in the sound [itself], that there is no sound without vibration. De Chales has already dealt with this at length in his *Mundum mathematicum*, Vol. III, Part I,* prop. 3, it. 41 & 42. This [vibration] is even perceptible in large pipes; e.g., when a 16-foot pipe is sounding, then the entire choir area will very often vibrate perceptibly, no matter how soft the sound may be—providing that such bodies† are in [proper] proportion to the pitch [being sounded]. Also, one need only touch the pipe to be sufficiently convinced of its vibration. As the pipes become smaller the vibrations finally become so rapid that one does not perceive them, but thinks that the sound is continuous. The vibration is heard in the large reed pipes—indeed, it is also felt—but not so readily in the smaller ones. Simply place your mouth on a reed pipe and blow; the tongue will vibrate readily enough. Hearing has this in common with the other senses, that the vibrations are not perceived in high sounds. Your eyes also cannot see a ball shot out of a cannon, even though it passes right in front of your face. Why is this? Because it is moving so rapidly. Think about this as well: if fireworks are presenting a revolving wheel, it looks like a fiery circle or a round disc, yet [in reality] it is merely a [revolving] line [of light]. These vibrations in a pipe ordinarily remain constant from one time to the next, so that a pipe will produce the same pitch tomorrow that it produces today. The force of the wind's attack, though, will cause a noticeable change, no matter how slight, since the great force of the wind sets the body of the pipe into more rapid motion, as is evident by the rise in the pipes' pitch if the bellows are pumped harder, or if a pipe is blown forcefully with the mouth. Thus I do not know how De Chales, *l.c.*,‡ p. 4, can assert that force cannot bring about any variation. He is referring to the pendulum, to be sure, explaining the entire theory by means of it. But it is well-known that if a pendulum is struck sharply with the hand, it will travel more rapidly at the moment the blow occurs than its weight and length would call for.

Stopped pipes ordinarily sound an octave lower [according to their length] than open ones. Why is this so? The answer: the wind passes through the opening [i.e., the flue] into the body [of the pipe], setting up its vibrations and movements right up to

* i.e., Tract 22.

† i.e., the dimensions of the choir area.

‡ Vol. III, Tract 22.

verrichtet seine Vibrationes und Bewegungen bis hinauf an den Deckel: weil er aber da keinen Ausgang findet; so kehrt er wieder zurück, und geht durch den Aufschnitt heraus, und hat also just einen noch eins so langen Weg zu wandern, wird demnach auch noch eins so schwach werden, und folglich keinen andern Stoß im Ohre machen können, als noch eins so tief, und viel schwacher, als andere.

Eben hieraus ist abzunehmen, warum ein Instrument, welches schwach bezogen, nicht so scharf klingt, als ein anders. Nämlich, weil die Seyte schlotternd wird, und keinen scharfen Stoß der Luft geben kann. Wenn man hingegen die Seyte allzu dicke nimmt; so wird sie straff angezogen: und wenn sie in Bewegung gesetzt wird; so stößt sie die Luft stark an. Doch ist auch sie selber schwer anzuschlagen, wie auch die Pfeifen schwer anzublasen sind, wenn sie allzuweit sind, daher der Klang sehr wild wird.

Ferner wollen wir allhier die Frage aufwerfen: warum zwey Soni gegeneinander wohl lauten, oder consoniren, andere aber nicht? Antw. Dieß ist aus der Lehre von den Vibrationen zu erklären, davon in diesem Kapitel schon etlichemal geredet worden. Auch kann man nachschlagen, was §. 536. bey der Sympathie gesagt worden. Wenn die Vibrationen, die von zweyerley Körpern entstehen, wie es allezeit ist, wenn zwey Soni, oder mehrere, da sind, oft zusammen treffen, daß sie motu recto, und zwar vollkommen in einem Punkte miteinander treffen; so gefällt das den Ohren, widrigenfalls dissoniren sie. Je öfter nun die Vibrationes zugleich eintreten, desto vollkommener ist die Consonanz. Also wenn zwene Körper, zwo Seyten oder Pfeifen, ihre Vibrationes vermöge ihrer Länge und Dicke so haben, daß sie alle Schläge mit einander zugleich absolviren; so sind sie in unisono: wo der eine zweymal schlägt in der Zeit da der andere einmal fertig wird; so ists die Oktave: schlägt der eine viermal, da in eben der Zeit der andere einmal schlägt; so ists die Superoktave ꝛc. Schlagen sie so, daß sie auf den dritten Schlag eintreffen, oder daß einer zwey Schläge thut in der Zeit, da der andere 3 verrichtet: so ists die Quinte. ꝛc. Je weiter die Proportionen von der Simplicität abgehen, desto größer ist die Zahl der Zeit, in welcher sie zusammen treffen, und bey den Dissonanzen ists so, daß sie sehr spät zusammen treffen.

Ferner möchte jemand wissen wollen: warum die Oktaven und Quinten in die Orgeln mit Fleiß gesetzt würden, da man sie doch im Spielen und in der Composition so ernstlich verbietet? Antwort: Es ist ein Unterschied unter den Oktaven und Quinten in den Registern, und unter ihnen, wenn man sie im Greifen zwey- oder mehrmal hintereinander in einerley Stimmen anbringt. Wenn sie in die Orgel gebracht werden; so sind sie vollkommen eingestimmt ohne Temperatur, und alsdann klingen solche Quinten und Oktaven zusammen als eine Pfeife, und werden so sehr nicht gemerkt, als wenn wir Quinten greifen, weil wir sie alsdann nicht rein, sondern temperirt, hören, welcher unreine Klang penetranter ist. Diese Raison könnte doch obiectiones veranlassen,

the cap. But because it finds no exit there, it returns and passes out through the cut-up. Thus it has exactly twice the distance to travel, and accordingly becomes twice as feeble. Consequently the only impact it can make on our ears is one that is twice as deep and much weaker than other [open pipes].

It can likewise be deduced from this why an instrument that is lightly strung does not sound as brilliant as another: namely, because the strings become wobbly and cannot give a sharp thrust to the air. If on the other hand strings that are too thick are used, when they are drawn taut and are set into motion, they strike the air forcefully. But such strings are difficult to pluck, just as pipes are difficult to wind if they are very wide, making the sound very wild.

Furthermore, this question should be raised here: why do certain intervals sound good? Why are they consonant, when other intervals are not? The answer: this is explained by the theory of vibrations, of which we have already spoken several times in this chapter. You may also consult what was said in §. 536 about sympathetic vibration. If the vibrations that arise from two objects (which is always the case if there are two or more sounds present) repeatedly encounter each other at compatible speeds, so that at one point they coincide perfectly, then [the resulting interval] is pleasing to the ear, failing which they are dissonant. The more often the vibrations coincide, the more perfect the consonance. Thus if two objects—two strings or pipes—are by virtue of their length and thickness possessed of such vibrations that all their beats exactly coincide, then they are in unison. If one beats twice in the time that it takes the other to beat once, then they form an octave. If one beats four times in the time it takes the other to beat once, then they form two octaves (die Superoctave), etc. If they beat so as to coincide at every third beat, or so that one beats twice in the time it takes the other to beat three times, then they form a fifth, etc. The further the deviation is from a simple [ratio], the greater the amount of time it takes for them to coincide. That is how it is with dissonances; they coincide very seldom.

Next, someone might want to know why octaves and fifths have deliberately been placed in organs, since they are so completely forbidden in performance and in composition. The answer: there is a distinction between the octaves and fifths found among the stops and those that are created by playing two or more of them in succession in the same voices. When they are brought into the organ they are not tempered, but are perfectly in tune, and fifths and octaves such as these then sound together as one pipe. Thus they are not as conspicuous as fifths that are played with the fingers, which are not pure, but tempered, since the impure sound is more penetrating. This explanation could give rise to objections, however, since some [authors], such as Werkmeis-

indem etliche, als Werkmeister in Hodego, sagen, es wäre der Progreß in zwoen Quinten verboten, wegen der Vollkommenheit, weil die Natur die Veränderung liebte, dergleichen man hier nicht hätte: denn wenn dieß wahr wäre; so wären die Registerquinten noch vollkommener, als die gegriffenen, folglich noch mehr zu vermeiden. Antw. Weil man sie nicht viel hört, wegen der vielen dazu gezogenen Stimmen; so können sich paßiren, da sie uns in der Schärfe gute Dienste thun. Wer mit dieser Solution nicht zufrieden, dem kann ich nicht helfen; ich weis für diesesmal keine bessere, wobey sie nicht eben soviel, und wol noch mehr ercipiren ließe. (**) Die Oktaven anlangend; so möchte man es wol ex collisione regularum erklären. Wir möchten gerne Oktaven vermeiden; gleichwol wollen wir die Harmonie gerne verstärken, welches ohne Oktaven nicht wohl zu haben; Es soll nicht so sehr brummen; so muß man klare Stimmen haben: es soll nicht so sehr quiksen, sondern auch eine männliche Gravität haben; so muß man tiefe Stimmen nehmen. Keine aber unter allen Intervallen schicken sich dazu, als Oktaven und Quinten; folglich müssen wir sie mit hineinbringen, weil doch an der Vermeidung der Oktaven soviel nicht gelegen, als hieran, und sonst die leges minus necessariæ allezeit den magis necessariis nachstehen müssen. Stellen doch die Musikdirektores auch wol ein Violoncello zu einem großen Violon, und lassen sie in Oktaven miteinander einher gehen; singt doch der Cantor mit seinen Jungen auch die Chorale in Oktaven; setzen doch die Componisten mit Fleiß viel Oktaven hintereinander: Also müssen sie ja für keine Todsünde, und absolut böse Sache achten, Oktaven zu spielen. Also ist das Verbot von Vermeidung der Quinten und Oktaven so beschaffen, daß wo ein ander Gesez entgegen stehet, jenes Verbot weichen muß. Unterdessen will ich keinen Patron oder Advokaten solcher Progressen abgeben, es möchte mir es sonst jemand für einen Eigensinn auslegen; sondern ich bleibe dabey, daß der Veränderung wegen man sie im Spielen, soviel möglich, meide. Wollte sonst jemand einen Appetit bekommen, dieser Roßquinten und Pferdeoktaven Vertheidigung anzuhören, der wandere bey die Juristen, die sich besser zu Advokaten schicken, als ich. Z. E. zu D. Treibern in Erfurt, der in seiner sonderbaren Invention eine Arie aus allen Tönen

zu

(**) Warum hat doch Hr. Adlung hier nicht angeführet, daß, bey jeder etwas tiefen Seyte, die gelinde mit tönende gedoppelte Quinte oder Duodecima, und die dreyfache Terze oder Septendecima von feinen Ohren vernommen werden kann? Dies allein würde, deucht mir, erklären, warum hinlänglich durch Octavenstimmen bedeckte Quinten- und Terzen-Stimmen, in der Orgel, dem Gehör nicht allein nicht widrig, sondern so gar zur Ausfüllung nothwendig sind. Man verzeyhe dem Anmerker diese Frage Ueberdieß ist ja noch ein sehr großer Unterschied, unter gelinde mitlautenden, und unter nach einander angeschlagenen Quinten, welche mit den andern Tönen gleich stark klingen, und von allen Registern gleich stark angegeben werden, welche Register noch überdieß ihre gelinden wesentlich mittönenden Quinten und Terzen auch bey sich haben. Aber, ist nicht etwan das gelinde Mittönen der Quinte und Terze bey jedem Tone selbst vielleicht noch Zweifeln unterworfen? Wer kann, beliebe das musikalische Publicum hierüber, wo möglich noch deutlicher und gewisser, als bisher geschehen, zu belehren.

ter in his *Hodegus*,* say that movement by two [consecutive] fifths is forbidden because of their perfection, since nature prefers variety, a thing they do not have. But if this were true, then the fifths created by the stops, being even more perfect than those played by the fingers, ought all the more to be avoided. The reply to this is that they are little perceived, due to the many stops drawn with them. This is why it is possible for them to give good service in providing intensity. At this point I cannot offer any better [explanation] to anyone who is not satisfied with this solution, since I know of none better that does not give rise to at least as many objections, and perhaps even more.(**) Concerning [consecutive] octaves, they might well be explained by the conflict of rules.† We should surely avoid octaves, although it is desirable to intensify the harmony, something that cannot be accomplished without octaves. [The sound] must not growl so much, and thus clear stops are necessary; it should not squeak so much, but have a masculine gravity, and thus one must have low stops. But there are not any other intervals better suited for these purposes than octaves and fifths. Consequently they must be included, since avoiding octaves is not as important as achieving a good harmony, and furthermore less necessary precepts must always yield to more necessary ones. After all, music directors combine a violoncello with a large bass viol, letting them proceed in parallel octaves [in playing the continuo]; a cantor sings chorales in octaves with his boys; composers deliberately set many consecutive octaves. Therefore it must not be considered a deadly sin and an absolutely evil thing to play [consecutive] octaves. Thus the prohibition of [consecutive] fifths and octaves is so constituted that if another precept stands opposed to it, that prohibition must yield. Meanwhile I will not yield to any patron or advocate of such progressions, even though someone might construe it as obstinacy on my part. I maintain that for the sake of variety they ought to be avoided as much as possible in performance. If anyone develops an appetite for hearing a defense of these horse-fifths and horse-octaves, he should betake himself to the lawyers, who are better suited as advocates than I am. For example, [they could turn] to Dr. Treiber in Erfurt, who in his odd inventive urge has used these miserable

* Chap. 34, pp. 106f.

† Adlung explains this statement in the sentences following it, coming to the conclusion that "avoiding octaves is not as important as achieving a good harmony."

(**) Why has Mr. Adlung not mentioned here that whenever any rather low string [is sounded], a octave fifth or duodecima and a seventeenth or septendecima can be perceived by acute ears, gently sounding along with [the fundamental]? It seems to me that this [fact] alone would explain why organ stops sounding fifths and thirds, if they are sufficiently covered by octave-sounding stops, not only sound unobjectionable, but are actually necessary for filling out [the sound]. The editor begs the reader's pardon for [his impudence in asking] this question. Furthermore, there is a very big difference between fifths that gently sound simultaneously and those played successively that sound equally prominent with the other pitches, being sounded equally loudly by all the stops, stops that have in addition their innately-sounding gentle fifths and thirds. But are not perhaps these fifths and thirds that gently sound along with each pitch themselves subject to doubt? Let anyone who is able [to do so] explain this, if possible even more clearly and convincingly than before, for the benefit of the musical public. [Agricola]

zu componiren ꝛc. sich der armen Oktaven und Quinten mit ziemlichem Ernste angenommen. Ein mehreres hiervon zu sagen, ist hier der Ort nicht, weil es mit größerm Rechte in den Anweisungen zum Generalbasse vorgetragen wird. ꝛc.

Ferner wollen wir etwas reden, woher es komme, daß eine Pfeife sich überbläßt; z. E. daß die Querpfeife in der Orgel eine Oktave, auch wol mehr, sich überblasen muß; imgleichen, daß z. E. die Violdigamba, Violon, ꝛc. wenn sie nicht accurat gemacht sind, sich überschreyen in die Quinte, zuweilen auch in die Oktave. Auch was das Jilpen in den Pfeifen verursache; it. wie es möglich, daß die Quintatön 2 sonos zugleich hören lasse? Es ist dieß eine desperate Materie; doch wollen wir etwas davon lallen: gleichwol aber dasselbige nur für probabel ausgeben; dem aber es auch nicht wehren, der es für etwas mehreres annimmt. Die Luft in den Pfeifen von deren einem Ende bis zum andern können wir uns vorstellen als eine lange Seyte, die ihre Vibrationes ihrer (folglich auch der Pfeifen) Länge nach, in einer gewissen Zeit absolvirt: und zwar geschieht solches desto geschwinder, je kürzer eine Seyte oder Pfeife, folglich auch je kürzer die columna oder linea aeris in der Pfeife ist. Wenn das Anblasen etwas verstärkt wird; so wird solcher sonus etwas weniges höher, wie zuvor gedacht worden: doch trägt dieß kaum den 10ten Theil eines Tons, ja wol noch weniger aus, weil durch die force des Windes diese Luft in der Pfeife um etwas geschwinder bewegt wird, daß die tremores eher von einem Ende zum andern kommen, als vorhin. Allein wenn das Anstoßen des Windes allzustark geschieht in die Peife; so kann die Luft darinne, wegen ihrer Länge, den tremorem ohnmöglich so geschwind bis an das andere Ende fortpflanzen, weil sie doch ein Körper ist, und solche tremores doch eine, obwol gar kleine, Zeit erfordern. Auch kann das corpus der Pfeifen wegen seiner Länge so geschwind nicht tremuliren, als es wol die force des sie anblasenden Windes erforderte. Also muß etwas anders geschehen. Es fragt sich aber: Was? Antwort: nothwendig eine Theilung der Pfeife und der columnæ aeris. Denn ein sonus muß folgen, weil der motus aeris und der Pfeife tremulus ist, welches durch die Geschwindigkeit, nicht geändert wird: aber die ganze Pfeife und die Luft können, wie gesagt, so geschwinde nicht tremuliren; ergo geschieht die Theilung. Es läßt sich aber eine Theilung in allen besser machen, wenn man Etwas in 2 gleiche Theile theilt. Dieß begreifen unsere Sinne am leichtesten. Auch in 4 gleiche Theile, oder Viertel; doch ist es so deutlich nicht als die Mediation. Auch in 8 Theilen ist es noch ziemlich leicht zu verstehen. Imgleichen, wenn ein Ding in 3 Theile getheilet wird, und solcher Theile 2 sollen genommen werden. Dieß ist auch gar natürlich. Oder wenn man ¾ haben will. Dieß sind Proportiones consonantiarum 1—2. 1—4. 1—8. 2—3. 3—4. Und diese Arten der Theilung treffen wir auch bey dem Klange der Pfeifen an, und zwar, je größer die Pfeifen angenommen werden, desto mehrmal geschieht eine solche Theilung durch diese Sprünge: Oktave, Quint, Superoktave, Terz über derselben, und Quinte über der Superoktave. ꝛc. Denn bey großen Pfeifen muß die Theilung

octaves and fifths in all seriousness in composing an aria in all keys.* This is not the place to say more about this, since it is more properly introduced as part of instructions for playing figured bass.

    Next we should discuss a bit why it is that a pipe overblows; e.g., the organ stop Querpfeife overblows an octave or even more, and the Violdigamba, Violon, etc., overblow a fifth or at times even an octave if they are not accurately made. [We should] also [discuss] what causes pipes to overblow, as well as how it is possible for a Quintatön to produce two tones at once. These are unrelated matters, yet we ought to speak a bit about them, representing the [proposed theories], though, as only probable [causes]. We do not want to prevent anyone from holding that there is more to it. We may imagine the [column of] air within a pipe from one end to the other as a long string, that completes its vibrations according to its length (which is the same as the pipe's) within a given time. The shorter the string or pipe is, and consequently the shorter the column or line of air in the pipe is, the faster [the vibrations] occur. If the winding is somewhat increased, such a tone† will become ever so slightly sharper than it previously was (this will amount, though, to barely a tenth of a step or even less), because the force of the wind sets the air in the pipe into somewhat faster motion, causing its vibrations to pass from one end to the other more quickly than previously. If the rush of the wind into the pipe is too strong, though, then the air inside it, due to its length, finds it impossible to transmit the vibration to the other end, since it is after all an object, and such vibrations require time, albeit very little. Due to its length, the body of the pipe also cannot vibrate as quickly as the force of the wind blowing into it requires. Therefore something else has to happen. The question is, what? Here is the answer: a division of the pipe and the column of air becomes inevitable. For of necessity a sound must occur, since the motion of the air and of the pipe is a vibration, and this cannot be altered by the speed [of the wind]. The whole pipe and the air, however, cannot vibrate that quickly, as has already been said. Therefore the result is a division. A division is most easily accomplished if something is divided into two equal parts; this is quite obvious to our senses. [The division may] also be into 4 equal parts, or quarters, though this is not as obvious as two halves. It is still relatively easy to conceive of 8 parts, and likewise quite natural for a thing to be divided into 3 parts in a ratio of 2:1. This also holds true for the ratio 3:4. These are the ratios of the consonances: 1:2, 1:4, 1:8, 2:3, 3:4. We also encounter these sorts of divisions in the sounds of pipes; indeed, the larger the pipe, the more often such a division takes place, by these leaps: octave, fifth, fifteenth, seventeenth, nineteenth, etc.‡ For in large pipes the division must be

---

* Dr. Johann Philipp Treiber, *Sonderbare Invention: Eine Aria in einer eintzigen Melodey aus allen Tonen u. Accorden, auch iederley Tackten, zu componiren.* Jena: C. Junghans, 1702.

† i.e., the one created by the vibrations.

‡ Here Adlung is speaking about the overtone series.

lung gar vielmal wiederholet werden, daß sie solche geschwinde Vibrationes machen, und folglich einen so hohen sonum von sich geben können. Bey kleinern Pfeifen ist es nicht so vielmal nöthig; doch geschieht es auch etlichemal. Daher wenn die Pfeife allzugroß, und das Anstoßen der Luft allzustark ist; so giebt sie eine Oktave höher an, und das nennen wir: sie überbläset oder überschreyet sich. Und dieß thut z. E. die Querpfeife in der Orgel, welche sehr enge, doch auch sehr lang gemacht wird, eben deswegen, damit sie so geschwinde Vibrationes nicht machen, sondern dieselben verdoppeln, und also die Oktave angeben möge. Bey andern Pfeifen geschiehet es wider unsern Willen, z. E. bey der Violdigamba, Violon, ꝛc. zumal wenn die Materie dazu weich, und die Blätter sehr schwach gemacht sind. Denn ein dünnes und schwankendes corpus läßt sich so geschwinde nicht hin und her bewegen, als ein starkes. Z. E. wenn man eine Peitsche mit einer solchen Geschwindigkeit wollte hin und wieder schlagen, als einen Stecken der steif ist, das würde nicht angehen. Folglich ist solchen Pfeifen nicht leicht zu helfen. Es finden sich zwar dabey noch mehrere Phænomena, z. E. der Violon und die Violdigamba geben zuweilen ihren richtigen Ton an im ersten Anstoße; allein wenn man lange anhält, so überblasen sie sich. Aber man sieht leicht, daß, wenn ich alles berühren wollte, aus diesem letzten Kapitel ein besonderer Traktat werden würde, welches aber meiner Absicht nicht gemäß wäre.

Wenn nach der ersten Theilung die Stücke der Luft, Seyte und Pfeife, noch zu groß sind; so geschieht die Theilung in allzugroßen Pfeifen wieder durch die Hälfte, und dieß giebt die Superoktave, hernach (und in kleinern Pfeifen zum andernmal) geschieht es durch die Quinte. Und dieß thun etliche Querpfeifen, und besonders die gedeckte Art, s. §. 178. Würde man die force noch mehr verstärken; so würde wieder eine Oktave gehöret werden, hernach die Terz höher u. s. w. Es kann dieses ein jeder an den gemeinen Flöten probiren, da ohne Aenderung der Löcher blos durch die force eine Oktave, zuweilen die Superoktave, Quinte ꝛc. zuwege gebracht wird.

Das Filpen der Pfeife ist nichts anders, als ein solches Ueberblasen oder Uebergallen, da durch eine falsche Situation des Kerns und der Labien die Luft der Pfeife durch die äusere Luft allzustark angetrieben wird. Wenn solche Fehler corrigirt werden; so läßt das Filpen nach. Wollte ich es augenscheinlich machen; so würde dieser Discours zu weitläuftig werden.

Zuweilen geschiehet solche Theilung auch in der Kehle des Menschen, daß dadurch ein höherer Sonus produciret wird, als deren Länge und Weite sonst produciren können; da man abermal eine reine Oktave vernimmt: daher sodann ein Tenorist den Diskant und ein Baßist den Alt, oder auch den Diskant singen kann. Dieß heißt man deswegen mit halber Stimme singen, wegen solcher Theilung; auch nennt man es ein Falset, und diejenigen, welche auf sothane Art singen, heißen Falsetisten. (Von
falsus

repeated many times in order for them to make such rapid vibrations and thus produce such high pitches. So many divisions are not necessary in small pipes, but several of them do indeed occur. Therefore if a pipe is very large and the attack of the wind is very strong, it sounds an octave higher; then we say "it is overblowing." This is what happens, e.g., with the organ stop Querpfeife, which is [purposely] made very narrow but also very long, in order for it not to make such rapid vibrations, but to double them, thus producing an octave. In other pipes this [overblowing] happens against our wishes, as e.g. in the Violdigamba, Violon, etc., especially when they are made of soft material* and their pipe walls are very weak. For a thin, wobbly object cannot be moved back and forth as rapidly as a solid one. For example, it would not be possible for someone to swing a whip back and forth at the same rate of speed as a rod that is rigid. Consequently there is not much that can be done with such pipes. There are several [other] phenomena connected with this. For example, the Violon and the Violdigamba sometimes sound their proper pitch at the moment of attack, but overblow if [the tone] is held longer. But it is obvious that if I were to touch upon everything [concerning this topic], this final chapter would become a separate treatise, which would not be consistent with my purpose.

* i.e., a soft metal, such as lead.

If the sections of air, string or pipe are still too large after the first division, then in very large pipes there is a second division into halves, producing the fifteenth. Next it happens at the fifth (in smaller pipes this occurs at the second division). Some Querpfeifen behave this way, especially stopped ones; see §. 178. If one were to increase the force [of the wind] even more, it would produce the octave above, and then a third above that, etc. Anyone can try this out on an ordinary flute, creating an octave [above the basic pitch] and sometimes the superoctave, the fifth, etc., without changing [fingers on] the holes, merely by the force [of the breath].

Poor speech (das Filpen†) in a pipe is nothing other than a type of overblowing in which the air from a pipe is propelled too forcefully through the outside air, due to the incorrect placement of the languid and the lips. If faults such as these are corrected, then the poor speech ceases. If I were to explain/illustrate this in greater detail, this discourse would become too lengthy.

† See also §.84 and §.386.

Sometimes such a division also occurs within the human throat, producing a higher pitch than its length and width could otherwise produce. Once again the pitch that results is just an octave [higher]. Thus a tenor can sing in the treble range, and a bass can sing alto or even treble. Because of this division, this is called "singing in half voice." It is also called "falsetto," and those who sing in this manner are called "fal-

falsus falsch, weil sie nicht den wahren Ton, sondern einen gezwungenen von sich hören lassen.)

Wenn man auch mit andern Sachen ein Experiment machen will; so nehme man z. E. ein groß Blech und schlage es sachte an; so wird man dessen tremores mit Augen sehen, und den tiefen Sonum hören: hernach schlage man stärker; so wird man observiren, daß nicht das ganze Blech tremulirt und klingt, sondern nur die Hälfte. Dieß Experiment hat schon Galiläus gemacht. Nimmt man Gläser, und füllet sie mit Wasser, und reibt mit dem Finger deren Rand; so wird man die Oktave drüber vernehmen, wenn das Reiben mit großer force geschiehet. Eine Glocke, wenn sie sehr dicke ist, klingt oft höher, als eine andere dünnere, ob diese schon eben nicht länger, auch zuweilen nicht einmal so groß, als jene ist; weil die Dicke sich überschreyet, da sie so geschwinde nicht tremuliren kann. Bey den Glocken (aber auch bey den andern Dingen) findet sich noch dieses, daß sie oft nicht nur einen Sonum von sich hören lassen, so, daß man oft nicht weis, was man der Glocke für einen Sonum zueignen soll. Es klingen die Oktaven, Quinten ꝛc. mit. Nun fragt sichs: wie geht das zu? Antw. die Theile klingen zugleich, da sonst bey mancher Theilung nur der eine Theil gehöret wird, nicht aber die andern. Es geschiehet dieses bey dicken Glocken, und wenn der Anschlag allzuscharf geschiehet; da man, wenn mit dem Finger an die Glocken gerühret wird, nur einen Sonum vernimmt. Dieses observiren wir auch bey den Flöten, welche, wenn man sie scharf anbläset, auch etliche Sonos zugleich hören lassen. In der Orgel finden wir dieß bey der Quintatön, als welche die Quinte zugleich mit hören läßt. Das übrige überlasse ich dem Leser zu selbstbeliebiger Untersuchung. Man kann aber von solcher Materie nachlesen, was de Chales hat l. c. prop. 16. da er die Saltus Tubæ auf solche Weise erkläret; auch prop. 17 und 18, anderer Pfeifen.

Es ist bekannt, daß die Phænomena bey der Trompete, den Waldhörnern, Posaunen ꝛc. die Ingenia der Physicorum ziemlich exercirt haben, als welche auch nicht stuffenweise in der Tiefe fertgehen, sondern durch lauter Sprünge, und zwar so, daß man erst durch die Verstärkung des Windes die Oktave vernimmt; hernach die Decime, oder Quinte über der Oktave; hernach die erhöhete Oktave; alsdann die große Terz: hernach die kleine Terz, oder Quinte über der Oktave; hernach springt sie wieder eine Quarte höher in eine Oktave; von da steigt sie erst per tonos, (wiewol man heutiges Tages auch das b auf der Trompete gut haben kann, nämlich unter dem c, darein sie per saltum Quartæ zuletzt kam. 1) Diese Saltus Tubæ erklärt de Chales l. c. pag. 23. u. f. durch die Tubam marinam oder Marintrompete, welche gleiche Phænomena macht, die er gar artig vorstellt, und die ganze Seyte der Marintrompete mittheilt durch solche saltus. Hernach sagt er, daß bey einer gemeinen Trompete, wenn man sie gelinde anbläßt, die ganze Luft darinnen, als eine Seyte, ihre Vibrationes macht, nach ihrer Länge. Wenn aber die Trompete schärfer angeblasen wird; so wird die Luft forciret

Ch. XVIII. A Discourse on certain Curious Matters

settists," from *falsus*, "false," since they do not produce their natural pitch, but one that is forced.

Here are some experiments regarding other matters. Take a large sheet of metal and tap it softly; then you will be able to see it vibrate with your eyes, and hear the low pitch. Then hit it harder, and you will observe that the whole sheet does not vibrate and sound, but only half of it. Galileo already carried out this experiment [many years ago]. If you fill a glass with water and rub its rim with your finger, you will hear a pitch; rub it harder, and you will perceive the octave above it. A bell that is very thick often sounds higher than another that is thin, even though the latter is no longer, and sometimes not even as large, as the former; the thickness causes it to sound its octave, since it cannot vibrate as rapidly. With bells, as well as with other objects [that are struck], it is frequently the case that they produce more than one pitch, so that it is not clear what pitch to assign to a bell—the octaves, fifths, etc., sound as well [as the fundamental]. The question arises, "What causes this?" The answer: with many divisions only one section [of the division] is heard, but [in a bell] all the sections sound simultaneously. This happens if thick bells are struck too sharply, for if you tap a bell with your finger, you will perceive only one sound. This [phenomenon] may also be observed in flutes; if they are blown forcefully, they also produce several pitches at once. You will also find this to be the case with the organ stop, the Quintatön, in which the fifth sounds simultaneously with [the fundamental]. I will leave other matters for the reader to investigate at will. Regarding such matters, though, you may consult what De Chales says, *l.c.*,* prop. 16, where he explains the leaps† of a trumpet in the same way; he does the same for other wind instruments in prop. 17 and 18.

* Vol. III, Tract 22.

† i.e., in the overtone series.

It is well-known that [the following] phenomena connected with the trumpet, the hunting horn, the trombone, etc., have exercised the ingenuity of physicists to a considerable degree. Such instruments do not ascend stepwise in the bass, but only by leaps, in such a way that only when they are blown harder do they produce an octave, then a twelfth (Decime‡) or fifth above that octave, then a fifteenth, then a major third [above it], then a minor third [above that] (or a fifth above the [super]octave). Next they leap upward a fourth to an octave,§ and only then do they ascend by step (although these days is is also possible to produce the b below c on the trumpet dependably—the c last mentioned above, that was arrived at by the leap of a fourth.¶ De Chales explains this leap in a trumpet in *l.c.*,‖ p. 23f. by means of a tromba marina, which exhibits the same phenomena. He demonstrates it very nicely, dividing up the entire [length of] the tromba marina's string into such leaps. Then he says that if an ordinary trumpet is blown gently, all of the air in it vibrates, just like a string, according to how long it is. If however the trumpet is blown more forcefully, the air is forced

‡ sic; this should read "Duodecima," i.e., twelfth.

§ i.e. a twenty second.

¶ Adlung seems to presume that the overtone series he is describing above is being performed on a trumpet whose fundamental tone is CC, although he does not expressly state this.

‖ Vol. III, Tract 22.

182 Kap. XXVIII. Ein Discours von etlichen curiösen Materien.

ciret zu einem geschwindern tremore, als sie ihrer Länge nach auszuüben fähig ist, eben wie ein langes Pendulum so geschwinde sich nicht bewegen kann. Hernach sagt er weiter: die ganze Seyte wird demnach in 2. Theile getheilet, daß jeder Theil seine Vibrationes für sich mache. Sie wird aber mehr in 2. Theile getheilet, als in andere, weil die Seyte dieser Theilung am wenigsten entgegen ist. Auch muß sie in consonirende Theile getheilet werden, weil die ganze Seyte zur Bewegung angetrieben wird, doch aber nicht also kann getheilet werden, daß die Bewegungen einander zuwider wären, und daß eine Bewegung die Bewegung des andern Theils hinderte.

Endlich möchte jemand noch gerne wissen wollen, wie man das äußere Pfeifwerk einer Orgel poliren, und demselben eine Silberfarbe geben könne. Die wohlfeilste Art ist diese: Man nimmt weiße Marmorsteine, (dergleichen genug auf dem Felde zu finden,) so weiß als man sie finden kann, und brennet sie in dem Töpferofen zu Pulver; doch muß man sie nicht lassen schwarz werden. Hernach vermischt man dieses Pulver mit Wasser, und scheuret die Pfeifen wohl ab. Sonst gehet auch folgende Manier wohl an: Man nimmt Saturnum oder Bley, schmelzt dasselbe, und thut Mercurium darunter, und bestreicht damit die Pfeifen. NB. Man muß den Saturnum zuvor etwas lassen abkühlen, sonst gehet der Mercurius in die Luft.

Hiermit beschließe ich meine Musicam Mechanicam Organœdi, und nehme mit folgenden Worten des Horaz von einem jeden meiner geehrtesten Leser Abschied.

Viue: Vale. Si quid nouisti rectius istis;
Candidus imperti: si non, his vtere mecum.

(**) Noch

to vibrate more rapidly than it is capable of doing, considering its length, just as a long pendulum cannot move very rapidly. He continues by saying that the entire string* is accordingly divided into two sections, so that each part makes its own vibrations. It is more likely to divide into two sections than in any other way, because the string offers the least resistance to this division. Furthermore it has to divide into sections that are consonant, since the whole string is set into motion, and cannot then divide itself into sections that are mutually opposed to each other, causing the motion of one to hinder that of the other.

* i.e., of the tromba marina.

In closing, there might be someone who would like to know how to polish the façade pipes of an organ to give them a silvery sheen. The cheapest way is this: take a piece of marble (plenty of them may be found out in the fields), as white a one as you can find, and bake it in a potter's kiln [until it turns] to powder. Do not, however, let it get black. Then mix this powder with water and scour the pipes thoroughly. Another way that works is this: take some *saturvum* [sic] or lead and melt it, mixing mercury with it, and brush it onto the pipes. But note: the *saturnum*† must be allowed to cool a bit before doing this, or the mercury will evaporate.

† If the correct spelling of the word is *saturnum*, then perhaps Adlung means "red lead," Pb_3O_4, sometimes used to protect metals from corrosion.

With this I will bring my *Musica mechanica organœdi* to a close, taking leave of each of my honored readers with the following words from Horace:

> Vive: Vale. Si quid novisti rectius istis;
> Candidus imperti: si non, his utere mecum.‡
>
> [Farewell! and if my doctrine seem amiss,
> With candor set me right:—if not, take this!§]

‡ Horace (Quintus Horatius Flaccus), *Epistles* I.6 (To Numicius, on How to Be Happy), "nil admirari" (final lines).

§ Translation: *The Complete Works of Horace*, ed. Casper J. Kraemer, Jr. New York: Modern Library (Random House, Inc.), 1936, p. 324.

[Pages 183–185 of Volume II of the Mmo contained "Yet another supplement to Chapter 10." These pages have been transferred to follow the stoplists of Chapter 10 and the first supplement to Chapter 10, following page 291 of Volume I.]

www.ingramcontent.com/pod-product-compliance
Lightning Source LLC
Chambersburg PA
CBHW081414230426

43668CB00016B/2234